Alfred the Great

Alfred the Great

Papers from the Eleventh-Centenary Conferences

Edited by the late
TIMOTHY REUTER

ASHGATE

Published by
Ashgate Publishing Limited
Gower House, Croft Road
Aldershot, Hants
GU11 3HR
England

Ashgate Publishing Company
Suite 420
101 Cherry Street
Burlington, VT 05401-4405 USA

Ashgate website: http://www.ashgate.com

British Library Cataloguing in Publication Data
Alfred the Great. - (Studies in early medieval Britain)
    1.Alfred, King of England 2.Great Britain - Kings and
    rulers - Biography 3.Great Britain - History - Alfred,
    871-899
    I.Reuter, Timothy
    942' .0164'092

Library of Congress Cataloging-in-Publication Data
Alfred the Great / edited by Timothy Reuter.
        p. cm. -- (Studies in early medieval Britain)
    Papers originally delivered at a conference at the Wessex Medieval Centre, University of Southampton, Sept. 1999 and in London in Oct. 1999.
    Includes bibliographical references.
    ISBN 0-7546-0957-X (alk. paper)
        1. Alfred, King of England, 849-899--Congresses. 2. Great Britain--History--Alfred, 871-899--Congresses. 3. Anglo-Saxons--Kings and rulers--Biography--Congresses. 4. Great Britain--Kings and rulers--Biography--Congresses. 5. Wessex (England)--Kings and rulers--Biography--Congresses. I. Reuter, Timothy. II. Series.

DA153 .A39 2003
942.01'64'092--dc21
[B]

2002071148

ISBN 0 7546 0957 X

Typeset by Manton Typesetters, Louth, Lincolnshire, UK.
Printed by MPG Books Ltd, Bodmin, Cornwall.

STUDIES IN EARLY MEDIEVAL BRITAIN – 3

Contents

ALFREDIAN GOVERNMENT AND SOCIETY

ALFRED AND CONTEMPORARY RULERSHIP

ALFRED AS ICON

Foreword

The *Studies in Early Medieval Britain* are intended to illuminate the history and society of the island of Britain and of its various regions between the fifth and the twelfth centuries. The series will include volumes devoted to different aspects and phases of that long period, between the collapse of Roman imperial authority and the establishment of French-speaking aristocracies in different areas in the eleventh and twelfth centuries. It is planned to be a focus for interdisciplinary collaboration between historians, archaeologists, philologists and literary and cultural scholars. It will respect the differences between their disciplines, but facilitate communication between them. A very substantial body of evidence survives from the early Middle Ages, but much of it is fragmentary and difficult to understand. The task of early medievalists is to master the necessary technical skills without weakening the fascination of their subject. There is a large public, lay and academic, whose interest in the origins of our society, culture, and institutions has been whetted at school, college or university, by local studies in adult education or by popular television programmes. The *Studies in Early Medieval Britain* will therefore seek to reach this public by eschewing inaccessible jargon, and by explaining the early medieval past with the help of good illustrations and diagrams. The objective is to maintain the highest standards of scholarship, but also of exposition. It will therefore be open both to works of general synthesis and to monographs by specialists in particular disciplines attempting to reach a wider readership. It will also include collaborative studies by groups of scholars.

It is a great pleasure to welcome to the series a volume devoted to the reign, times and reputation of King Alfred of Wessex. King Alfred was one of the giants of the early Middle Ages, who played a key role in the development of an English kingdom and of an English culture. The contributors to this volume have not been able to do justice to all his multi-faceted talents and achievements, but they have pointed the way towards a reassessment of his roles. Behind this volume lies a memorable conference held in the University of Southampton in September 1999 in celebration of the 1100th anniversary of the king's death. That gathering owed much to the drive and enthusiasm of the late and much lamented Professor Timothy Reuter, who had selected the speakers and chaired the organizing committee and who then undertook the key editorial work of forging a balanced volume from the proceedings to fit this series. It is therefore a great sadness that Timothy's premature demise prevented him from seeing the published form of a volume that he had done so much to create. Professor David Hinton has very kindly stepped into the breach and has steered the volume through its final stages at press, thus enabling it to remain very much a South-ampton product. It is my hope that this volume will serve as a bright memorial to the contribution that Tim Reuter made to the development of early medieval studies in Britain. It should also redound to the continued credit of the University of Southampton's wisdom in establishing its Wessex Medieval Centre, in which he was so much involved.

NICHOLAS BROOKS

University of Birmingham
October 2002

Timothy Reuter died on 14 October 2002, not long after he had sent the text of *Alfred the Great* to the publisher. A fuller tribute to him will appear with a collection of his essays being prepared by Professor Janet Nelson; meanwhile, this book will be a memorial to the work that he so often did so unstintingly for others.

DAVID A. HINTON

University of Southampton
April 2003

Preface

Alfred has had an iconic resonance for modern English (conceivably even 'British') history and consciousness since Ruskin's time at the latest, as Barbara Yorke shows in her contribution below (Chapter 21). Given that fact, but far more importantly the shifts in our approach to our more recent past, it seemed both inevitable and necessary that we should commemorate the eleven-hundredth anniversary of Alfred's death with an international conference. This was held under the auspices of the Wessex Medieval Centre at the University of Southampton in September 1999; another, smaller but also illustrious group of lectures was delivered a month later in London in association with a small exhibition held there to commemorate the centenary. Almost all of the papers given at the two events are gathered in this present volume, though three contributors either could not deliver in time or else have planned to publish elsewhere. Fortunately, Michael Lapidge has been able to contribute the paper which he was prevented by other commitments from delivering in person at the Southampton conference, so this volume will substantially advance our study and understanding of a significant period in English (and indeed Archipelagic) history, and in particular it will provide, for the first time on this scale, a full contextualization of Alfred by setting him against contemporary rulers right across Europe, even examining the striking parallels with contemporary Bulgarian and Byzantine rulers. It also allows Alfred the writer and literary patron to meet Alfred the ruler and warrior.

The volume has gone to press as quickly as was practicable, given the editor's other commitments and the difficulties of getting copy and responses to queries from nearly two dozen separate contributors. Editors of volumes like this should keep their curses (few, in my case) to themselves, but should ensure that they do not leave anyone unthanked who should be thanked. I am grateful to Professor Nicholas Brooks for taking this volume on for the distinguished series he edits, and to Ashgate for being supportive and understanding as I worked my way through editing the volume. I am also grateful to my contributors, most of whom answered my pedantic queries promptly and put up with my editorial delays with very good grace. And I am deeply grateful to my family for tolerating my absences 'editing Alfred' along with all the other similar absences. Although references to the debts academics owe to their families are in danger of becoming even more of a mere literary commonplace than some of the topoi we as historians expect to find in writers like Asser, they illustrate a profound truth about topoi: these are indeed often conventional, but the conventions exist because they meet a real and often-felt need.

Southampton
January 2002

Abbreviations

Old English works associated with Alfred (these are cited by edition where the text of a specific edition is significant in context, otherwise by canonical reference alone)

ASC
: *Anglo-Saxon Chronicle*, cited by year and version ('*A*', etc.). Editions: *Two of the Saxon Chronicles Parallel*, ed. C. Plummer (2 vols, 1892–9); *The Anglo-Saxon Chronicle: A Collaborative Edition, 3, MS A*, ed. J. Bately (1986); *The Anglo-Saxon Chronicle: A Collaborative Edition, 4, MS B*, ed. S. Taylor (1983); *The Anglo-Saxon Chronicle: A Collaborative Edition, 5, MS C: A Semi-Diplomatic Edition with Introduction and Indices*, ed. K. O'Brien O'Keefe (2001); *The Anglo-Saxon Chronicle: A Collaborative Edition, 6, MS D*, ed. G. P. Cubbin (1996). Translations: *The Anglo-Saxon Chronicle: A Revised Translation*, eds D. C. Douglas, S. I. Tucker and D. Whitelock (1961; reprinted in *EHD*, pp. 145–245); *The Anglo-Saxon Chronicle*, trans. M. Swanton (1998)

Bede
: *König Alfreds Übersetzung von Bedas Kirchengeschichte*, ed. J. Schipper, Bibliothek der angelsächsischen Prosa 4 (Leipzig, 1897–99); *The Old English Version of Bede's Ecclesiastical History of the English People*, ed. T. Miller, EETS OS, 95, 96, 110, 111 (1890–98)

Boethius
: *King Alfred's Old English Version of Boethius De Consolatione Philosophiae*, ed. W. J. Sedgefield (1899); *Alfred's Metres of Boethius*, ed. W. Griffiths (1991)

Dialogues
: *Bischofs Wærferth von Worcester Ubersetzung der Dialoge Gregors des Grossen über das Leben und die Wunderthaten italienischer Väter und über die Unsterblichkeit der Seelen*, ed. H. Hecht, 2 vols (Leipzig, 1900–1907)

Martyrology
: *The Old English Martyrology*; editions: *Das altenglische Martyrologium*, ed. G. Kotzor, Abhandlungen der bayerische Akademie der Wissenschaften, phil.-hist. Klasse 88. 2 vols (Munich, 1981); *An Old English Martyrology*, ed. G. Herzfeld, EETS OS 116 (1900)

Orosius	*King Alfred's Anglo-Saxon Version of the Compendious History of the World by Orosius*, ed. J. Bosworth (1859); *The Old English Orosius*, ed. J. M. Bately, EETS ES 6 (1980)
Pastoral Care	*King Alfred's West-Saxon Version of Gregory's Pastoral Care*, ed. H. Sweet, EETS OS 45, 50 (2 vols, 1871–2; repr. 1958, with corrections by N. R. Ker)
Psalms	*Liber Psalmorum: the West-Saxon Psalms*, ed. J. W. Bright and R. L. Ramsay (Boston and London, 1907)
Soliloquies	*King Alfred's Version of St. Augustine's "Soliloquies"*, ed. T. A. Carnicelli (Cambridge, MA, 1969)

Other primary and secondary sources

AB	*Annales Bertiniani*: editions: *Annales de Saint-Bertin*, eds F. Grat, J. Vielliard and S. Clémencet (Paris, 1964); *Quellen zur karolingischen Reichsgeschichte II*, ed. R. Rau (Darmstadt, 1958), pp. 11–287; translation: J. L. Nelson, *The Annals of Saint-Bertin* (1991)
Abels, *Alfred*	R. Abels, *Alfred the Great: War, Kingship and Culture in Anglo-Saxon England* (1998)
AC	E. Phillimore, 'The *Annales Cambriae* and Old Welsh Genealogies', *Y Cymmrodor*, 9 (1888), 152–69
AF	*Annales Fuldenses*: editions: *Annales Fuldenses*, ed. F. Kurze, MGH SRG, Hanover, 1891; *Quellen zur karolingischen Reichsgeschichte III*, ed. R. Rau (Darmstadt, 1960), pp. 19–177; translation: T. Reuter, *The Annals of Fulda* (1992)
AI	S. Mac Airt (ed. and trans.), *The Annals of Inisfallen (MS. Rawlinson B.503)* (Dublin, 1951)
ASE	*Anglo-Saxon England*
Asser	Asser, *Vita Aelfredi regis*, ed. W. H. Stevenson, *Asser's Life of Alfred together with the Annals of St Neots erroneously ascribed to Asser* (1904)
Attenborough, *Laws*	*The Laws of the Earliest English Kings*, ed. and trans. F. L. Attenborough (1922)
AU	S. Mac Airt and G. Mac Niocaill (eds), *The Annals of Ulster (to A.D. 1131)* (Dublin, 1983)
AV	*Annales Vedastini*: editions: *Annales Xantenses et Annales Vedastini*, ed. B. von Simson, MGH SRG (Hanover, 1909); *Quellen zur karolingischen Reichsgeschichte II*, ed. R. Rau (Darmstadt, 1958), pp. 289–337
AX	*Annales Xantenses*: editions: *Annales Xantenses et Annales Vedastini*, ed. B. von Simson, MGH SRG

	(Hanover, 1909); *Quellen zur karolingischen Reichsgeschichte II*, ed. R. Rau (Darmstadt, 1958), pp. 339–75
Æthelweard	*The Chronicle of Æthelweard*, ed. A. Campbell (1962)
BCS (with no.)	W. de Gray Birch, *Cartularium Saxonicum* (3 vols, 1885–99)
Bede, *HE*	Bede, *Historia Ecclesiastica*, cited by book and chapter; editions: C. Plummer, *Venerabilis Baedae Opera Historica* (2 vols, 1896–1902), I.1–362; B. Colgrave and R. A. B. Mynors, *Bede's Ecclesiastical History of the English People* (1969, revised 1991)
CCCM	Corpus Christianorum Continuatio Mediaevalis
CCSL	Corpus Christianorum Scriptorum Latinorum
CR	Aurélien de Courson (ed.), *Le cartulaire de Redon* (Paris, 1863) (cited by charter no.); facsimile: *Cartulaire de l'abbaye Saint-Sauveur de Redon* (Rennes, 1998)
CSEL	Corpus Scriptorum Ecclesiasticorum Latinorum
EETS ES	Early English Text Society, Extra Series
EETS OS	Early English Text Society, Original Series
EHD	*English Historical Documents*, 1: *c. 500–1042*, ed. D. Whitelock (2nd edn, 1979)
EHR	*The English Historical Review*
Harmer, *Documents*	*Select English Historical Documents of the Ninth and Tenth Centuries*, ed. F. E. Harmer (1914)
JEccH	*Journal of Ecclesiastical History*
Keynes and Lapidge, *Alfred*	*Alfred the Great: Asser's* Life of King Alfred *and Other Contemporary Sources*, trans. S. D. Keynes and M. Lapidge (1983)
Liebermann, *Gesetze*	*Die Gesetze der Angelsachsen*, ed. F. Liebermann (3 vols in 4, Halle, 1903–16)
MGH	Monumenta Germaniae Historica, with subseries:

	AA	Auctores Antiquissimi
	D, DD	Diplomata Karolinorum (4 vols, Berlin, 1906–94) and Diplomata regum Germaniae ex stirpe Karolinorum (4 vols, Berlin 1932–60), cited as D with abbreviated ruler name (A for Arnulf, LtG for Louis the German) and diploma number
	Poetae	Poetae Latini, Berlin, 1881–
	SS	Scriptores in Folio, Hanover, 1829–
	SRG	Scriptores rerum Germanicarum in usum scholarum, Hanover, 1868–
	SRG NS	Scriptores rerum Germanicarum in usum scholarum, nova series, Berlin and Hanover, 1922–

Migne, *PL*	*Patrologiae Latinae cursus completus*, ed. J.-P. Migne, 221 vols, Paris, 1847–64
PBA	*Proceedings of the British Academy*
PMLA	*Proceedings of the Modern Language Association*
Regino	Regino of Prüm, *Chronicon*; editions: *Reginonis Prumiensis Chronicon*, ed. F. Kurze, MGH SRG (Hanover, 1895); *Quellen zur karolingischen Reichsgeschichte III*, ed. R. Rau (Darmstadt, 1960), pp. 179–319
S (with no.)	P. H. Sawyer, *A Hand-List of Anglo-Saxon Charters*, Royal Historical Society Guides and Handbooks 8 (1968); a revised edition [S 1–1602], ed. S. E. Kelly, is available online at http://www.trin.cam.ac.uk/chartwww/
SC	Sources Chrétiennes, Paris, 1952–
s.a.	*sub anno* (without date)
Smyth, *Alfred*	A. Smyth, *Alfred the Great* (1995)
s.v.	*sub verbo* (under the specified word)
TLMAS	*Transactions of the London and Middlesex Archaeological Society*
TLS	*Times Literary Supplement*
TRHS	*Transactions of the Royal Historical Society*

List of Illustrations

INTRODUCTION

Chapter 1

Placing King Alfred

James Campbell

Placing King Alfred is, in some ways, easy. There is no difficulty in seeing him as a key member of the family which, in four generations, transformed England. Yet the historian of Alfred must be tormented by the wealth, poverty and imbalance of the sources. It is above all the translations which give historical weight and depth to Alfred and his enterprises. Their autobiographical elements may afford unique insight into the mind of a Dark Age king, even if the arrows of insight have to be winged by the feathers of speculation. It is hard to dissociate the *Chronicle*, our main narrative source, from the court, not least because of the strong evidence for a fair number of early or very early manuscripts. But the *Chronicle* is a peculiar production. It is odd that a very high proportion of its Alfredian annals are devoted to continental events (including some unconnected to Viking movements); odd that the annal for 757 (which has made Cynewulf and Cyneheard famous in some circles) should be so disproportionately long; odd that pretty important events, which one might expect to be noted, are not and that surprisingly little is said about the destruction of monasteries.[1] Much fruitful analysis has been devoted to the *Chronicle*, not least by Dr David Howlett, who has argued powerfully that elements which can appear rough or hasty are, in truth, the result of a careful contrivance in 'biblical style' with a strong numerological element.[2] The striking continental emphasis could be accounted for by a major input from Athelney, with its Old Saxon abbot and Frankish monks.[3] The *Chronicle*'s 'local' Somerset information could derive from Athelney rather than from Stenton's West Country noblemen, with his 'personal reasons, not now to be discovered'.[4]

Consider something Mr Wormald shows us about the laws of Alfred. Modern editions do not bring out that in the earliest manuscript Alfred's laws and Ine's appear together in sequence, Ine following Alfred, in continuous numeration. In their numbered clauses the compilers occasionally push together items which have no essential connection. Thus chapter 9 of the joint code contained a law on the killing of pregnant women, went on to the ratio between

---

[1] D. Whitelock, *From Bede to Alfred: Studies in Early Anglo-Saxon Literature and History* (1980) XIII, 8; D. N. Dumville, *Wessex and England from Alfred to Edgar* (1992), 31.

[2] D. R. Howlett, *British Books in Biblical Style* (Dublin, 1997), 337–44.

[3] Asser, c. 94, p. 81.

[4] F. M. Stenton, *Preparatory to Anglo-Saxon England* (1970), 106–15, esp. 114.

fine and restitution, and to change in the fines for the theft of gold, horses and bees.[5] Alfred's laws (including Ine's) number one hundred and twenty items: a sacred number, that of the years in the life of Moses, the great biblical lawgiver. The merging of disparate provisions in single numbered clauses relates to the need to meet a target of one hundred and twenty. Apparent bodge may really be numerical contrivance, certainly in relation to such a chapter as no. 9 of the laws, very plausibly in relation to the annal for 757. (It is worth emphasis that the *Chronicle* and the *Laws* both appear for the first time in a surviving manuscript in Corpus Christi College Cambridge, Ms. 173, as part of the same package.) The *Chronicle* expresses not only contrivance possibly compounded by haste, but also deception, demonstrably. A crucial instance is the annal for 874. This represents Ceolwulf II of Mercia as 'a foolish king's thegn' who became (we are given details) a puppet of the Vikings. Study of charters, and above all of coins, brings this slighting observation into question, suggesting that Ceolwulf had significant power, and proving that he was associated with Alfred, not least in the issue of a reformed coinage.[6] In such ways as this the intricate work of numismatists has established or suggested something of the realities which may lie behind such bleak bulletins as the *Chronicle* provides for the 870s: not least on the relations between Mercia and Wessex, Ceolwulf and Alfred, and between both and London. Such work shows that the *Chronicle* is by no means always a summary of the truth, but sometimes a façade hiding the truth. Professor Smyth has reasonably suggested that, once the lid is off the range of possibilities, we could regard Alfred as a candidate for having been a Viking 'puppet' in the period concerned.[7] The annals of the *Chronicle* from 899 to 902 or 903 demonstrate how impoverished and secretive may be its earlier account of Alfred's reign, how silent on dissidence and on tensions in the royal family. By contrast, revealing indeed is its account of the 'rebellion' of Æthelwold upon his uncle Alfred's death. He was accepted as king by the Northumbrian Danes and won support in Essex and East Anglia. When he met his death in battle he was accompanied by a king who may have been king of East Anglia and also by a possible claimant to Mercia.[8] The English political scene is revealed as by a lightning-flash. It is by no means that which the annals for Alfred's reign lead one to suppose. Had Æthelwold won what proved to be his last battle he would be famous as the founder of united England; and Alfred's reign would be seen far otherwise than is usual.

---

[5] P. Wormald, *The Making of English Law, King Alfred to the Twelfth Century* (1999), 267–70.

[6] Keynes, 'King Alfred and the Mercians', in *Kings, Currency and Alliances. Southern England in the Ninth Century*, eds M. A. S. Blackburn, D. N. Dumville and S. D. Keynes (1998); S. D. Keynes and M. A. S. Blackburn, 'A corpus of the *Cross and Lozenge* and related coinages of Alfred, Ceolwulf II and Archbishop Æthelred', ibid., 125–50.

[7] Smyth, *Alfred*, 47–50.

[8] J. Campbell, 'What is not known about the reign of Edward the Elder', in *Edward the Elder*, eds N. J. Higham and D. Hill (2001), 12–24, at 20–21.

If the *Chronicle* is something of an entrancing fraud, at least it is a source we have. What of sources which we may have lost? This is a very large subject. It can be summed up thus. So far as surviving documents take us, ninth-century England was notably, strikingly, less well documented than were lands across the Channel. How far is this contrast one of the reality of the past, how far one of the survival of sources? Or, to put it another way, how far was Alfred's government as nearly dependent on the written word as was that of his Carolingian contemporaries? It is possible that whole classes of document have been lost. Two instances suggest how near this possibility may come to likelihood. One is the passage in which Asser describes how Alfred gave him the monasteries of Congresbury and Banwell, accompanying the gift by a *multiplex supputatio* listing everything 'in' these monasteries.[9] *Multiplex supputatio* sounds as if it may denote a polyptych or *brevis* such as were used in Carolingian estate surveys. The presence of such documents in Alfred's England is not otherwise demonstrable. If two royal monastic properties were thus described, others probably were too. A second straw in the wind is the seal-die of Æthelwold, the last known bishop of *Dommoc*. Æthelwold is otherwise known only from his profession of obedience to the archbishop of Canterbury. His accession can be placed in some year between 845 and 870. No one knows when he died. So far as written sources go he is an episcopal will o' the wisp; but he had a bronze seal matrix, nearly three inches high.[10] What did Æthelwold authenticate with this fine object? It need not have been documents: it could have been relics; or the seal could have been used in connection with ordeal, if ordeal exists in England in this bishop's time. But it *could* have been documents, perhaps such a certificate (*insigle*) as, in the next reign, a man in pressing difficulties obtained to attest a visit to Alfred's tomb.[11] In any case this matrix (lost in the course of a Danish attack on East Anglia?) *could* stand for the multiplication of various kinds of document, none now surviving.

A great handicap in trying to understand Alfred is that other sources are too thin to provide any density of context. What little we do know floats very loosely, certainly so far as sources from England are concerned. But continental information can provide helpful context. Two examples, among the very many possible, of how they can make insular information fit into convincing place are these. Asser tells us how the young Alfred was instructed by his mother. His account fits with what we learn from continental sources about the

---

[9] Asser, c. 81, pp. 67–8; Campbell, 'Edward the Elder', 12–14.

[10] T. A. Heslop, 'English seals from the mid-ninth century to 1100', *Journal of the British Archaeological Association*, 133 (1980), 2–3. The suggestion by S. Rigold in P. Wade-Martins, *Excavations in North Elmham Park, 1967–72*, East Anglian Archaeology 9 (2 vols, 1980), I 10, that the matrix is that of a tenth-century bishop is much weakened by Heslop's demonstration of the closeness of its design to that of ninth-century coins.

[11] BCS 591 (S 1445).

part mothers could play in the education of their sons: Dhuoda's *Liber Manualis* is by no means the only evidence.[12] Second: Alfred, Asser says, twice visited Rome, at the ages of about four and six, accompanied by his father on the second occasion but not the first. The *Chronicle* tells of the first visit, but not the second. Arguments, no less extensive than inconclusive, can be conducted on these episodes. Did Asser, using an early version of the *Chronicle*, just guess that Alfred accompanied his father Æthelwulf on the alleged second visit? Or did the compilers of the *Chronicle*, dashing to meet a hypothetical deadline, forget to mention that when Æthelwulf went to Rome he took toddler Alfred with him? What seems particularly strange about these episodes is the deployment of an infant in this way. Our capacity to accept its plausibility is helped by observing that in the next century the Ottonians did much the same thing. Otto III was made to take the field against the Slavs at the age of six. His uncle Bruno was sent to Utrecht at the age of four and miraculous events were said to have attended his coming.[13] It was not, of course it was not, a world in which things were seen as now we see them. Consider, for example, Professor Stanley's interpretation of the passage in the 'Fonthill letter' in which is described an occasion when Alfred did justice, standing, while he washed his hands in the bower at Wardour.[14] Stanley argues powerfully that the king's remaining standing indicates that he was giving an arbitration rather than a formal judgement and that his washing his hands was a reminiscence of Pontius Pilate. The conventions and attitudes which lie behind parts of such texts could be as alien to modern westerners as those of a Japanese painting. It is failure to enter into a world of sometimes alien thought which has helped largely to produce what one might term 'the Curse of King Alfred': a tendency for learned scholars of good judgement to lurch occasionally into nonsense when they come to write about that king. An example is V. H. Galbraith's belief that Asser's account of Alfred's illness was a guarantee of inauthenticity, inconsistent with Alfred's having been the 'simple, great-hearted warrior' whom Galbraith somehow knew him to have been.[15] There are other instances of the Curse at work.

Modern scholarship has illuminated great changes in the ninth-century relations between English rulers and the Church. The sources raise difficulties but one need hardly doubt that the reign of Alfred should be put into a context of major ecclesiastical change. Our knowledge of what happened is largely due to

[12] J. J. Contreni, 'The Carolingian renaissance: education and literary culture', in *The New Cambridge Medieval History, II: 700–900*, ed. R. McKitterick (1995), 709–57, at 718–19.

[13] K. J. Leyser, *Rule and Conflict in an Early Medieval Society* (1979), 86–7.

[14] E. G. Stanley, *Die angelsächsische Rechtspflege und wie man sie später angefasst hat*, Bayerische Akademie der Wissenschaften, philosophisch- historische Klasse Sitzungsberichte Jahrgang 1999, Heft 2 (Munich, 1999), 165–70.

[15] V. H. Galbraith, *An Introduction to the Study of History* (1964), 128. See now P. Kershaw, 'Illness, power and prayer in Asser's *Life of King Alfred*', *Early Medieval Europe*, 10 (2001), 201–24.

the work of Professor Brooks[16] and Dr Cubitt.[17] They show that the Church in the period before the Viking assault was more complex, and more sophisticated, than has commonly been supposed. Salient features in the pre-Viking period were as follows. First, the Church was rich indeed. Monasteries became very numerous. By 800 there were approaching thirty in the diocese of Worcester alone.[18] The proportion of landed wealth involved was enormous. Professor Brooks shows that the ecclesiastical share of Kent was of the order of a third, or more.[19] Generously pious kings may have been, as Bede indicated in his *Letter to Egbert*, sore saints for the Crown; contemporaries might have agreed with Chilperic, as reported by Gregory of Tours long before: 'see how our wealth has gone to the churches! Only bishops rule nowadays.'[20] Not only the wealth but the power of the Church was great indeed. This can be variously shown, not least by the authority of the provincial synods which, Dr Cubitt demonstrates, met regularly for seven or so generations from the time of the archbishop Theodore. It is important that these synods exercised jurisdiction in disputes over ecclesiastical lands.[21] Although kings played a part in this, it was by no means necessarily a determinative part and kings were not always present for ecclesiastical cases. In the eighth century, Dr Cubitt argues, archbishops rather than kings were the pivotal figures in the synods.[22] The wealth of archbishops' churches must have reinforced their power; and in addition such a prelate as Archbishop Wulfred (805–32) could be rich in his own right.[23] Archbishops were given very high precedence. In the best text of the proceedings of the legatine council of 786, they witness before the kings, who in turn precede the other bishops (although in charters of Offa and Coenwulf recording embodying synodal decisions the king comes first).[24] Archbishops' status was further shown by their enjoying the rare privilege of striking coin.[25] The first identifiable coins struck by an archbishop of Canterbury bear, remarkably, the name of Archbishop Jænberht, with on their other side that of Offa. (This is one of the various indications that the relations between the two are not to be summed up in terms of simple or constant enmity.) Archbishop Wulfred's coins bear his name alone, without the king's, and display

---

[16] N. P. Brooks, *The Early History of the Church of Canterbury Christ Church from 597 to 1066* (1984).

[17] C. Cubitt, *Anglo-Saxon Church Councils c. 650–c. 850* (1995).

[18] W. Stubbs, 'The cathedral, diocese and monasteries of Worcester in the eighth century', *Archaeological Journal*, 19 (1862), 236–52.

[19] Brooks, *Canterbury*, 105–7, 206.

[20] J.-M. Wallace-Hadrill, *The Frankish Church* (1983), 124.

[21] Cubitt, *Councils*, 21, 24–25, 65–76.

[22] Cubitt, *Councils*, 48–9, 53–5, 57, 217, 222–3.

[23] Brooks, *Canterbury*, 132, 140–41.

[24] *Epistola Karolini Aevi II*, ed. E. Dümmler, MGH Epistolae 4 (Berlin, 1895), no. 3.

[25] C. E. Blunt, 'Ecclesiastical coinage in England', *Numismatic Chronicle*, 6th series 20 (1960), ii–x; C. E. Blunt, C. S. S. Lyon and B. H. Stewart, 'Coinage of southern England 796–840', *British Numismatic Journal*, 32 (1963), 9–10, 19–22, 40–41, 69–71; cf. Brooks, *Canterbury*, 132–3.

a tonsured bust of the archbishop; it is suggested that this grand issue may be associated with Ecgberht's gaining control of the Canterbury mint in 825 and, if so, could indicate the power of the archbishop in relation to the king. The later coins of Archbishop Ceolworth (833–70) replace the bust of the archbishop by the bust of the king. The issue of coins in the name of the archbishop continued into the pontificate of Plegmund (890–923); several types are known, including one in which the name of the king again joins that of the archbishop. Thereafter, although the archbishops retained minting rights, coins were no longer struck in their name. Here, and not only here, Plegmund appears as the last representation of an *ancien régime*. The position of York was equally interesting, if not more so. The first English coins struck by an identifiable ecclesiastical authority are silver, bearing the name of Ecgberht, bishop, then archbishop of York, with the king's name on the reverse. Eanbald II (796–808 or later) issued base metal coins in his name alone. The last known coins in the name of an archbishop of York were those of Wulfhere 854–92 or 900. As often in the deep waters of the Dark Ages, the coins intimate as much (sometimes more) than do the documents.[26]

Liebermann made a most interesting, indeed imaginative, suggestion about the origins of the authority of the archbishops of York, namely that it might in part have derived from that of such pagan high priests as Coifi, whose high status is shown by Bede's having him speak first in the Northumbrian debate on the acceptance of Christianity.[27] If the idea seems wild it is only because almost total ignorance of the institutions of Anglo-Saxon paganism stands in the way of any serious judgement on what it may have contributed to the Anglo-Saxon Church, for example to the power to tax, which appears at a remarkably early date and may have formed a significant element in episcopal power; Bede says that not a single village was exempt from *tributis antistiti reddendis*.[28]

The wealth of the Church, the power of archbishops and bishops and of synods, and the needs and ambitions of kings and nobles met in many-sided tensions and conflicts. Kings wished to own and control monasteries, sometimes as an element in the subjugation of other kingdoms.[29] Sometimes bishops, in England as on the Continent, claimed to own and control monasteries in their dioceses. Noble families wished to own monasteries, sometimes in defiance of kings and bishops. Kings could resent episcopal power and synodical authority. Papal power could occasionally be invoked and deployed in defence or defiance of one or more of these interests.

Expressive and characteristic of these tensions were three related phenomena: first, grants or agreements (almost concordats) seeking to regulate relations

---

[26] Cubitt, *Councils*, 207, for the numismatic evidence for the bishop of London having coinage rights for a period in Offa's reign.

[27] F. Liebermann, *The National Assembly in the Anglo-Saxon Period* (Halle, 1913), 3.

[28] *Venerabilis Baedae Opera Historica*, ed. A. Plummer, 2 vols (1896), i, 410.

[29] Cubitt, *Councils*, 226–7.

between two or more of the conflicting powers; second, major conflicts between kings and archbishops; and third, papal intervention, repeated and sometimes effective. The complexities of king–church relations are reflected in general grants or agreements, in particular Wihtred's grant of tax exemptions to the Kentish churches in 699,[30] and indeed in forgeries of such agreements made at Christ Church Canterbury in the ninth century.[31] The great quarrels between kings and archbishops are, of course, those in the late eighth and early ninth centuries, between Offa and Ceolwulf, kings of the Mercians, and Jænberht and Wulfred, archbishops of Canterbury.[32] The importance of Roman authority can be seen in the number of papal grants to monasteries of exemption from episcopal and other authority in the late seventh and the eighth centuries.[33] The relative weakness of kings is revealed, almost paradoxically, in the conflict between Offa and his archbishop. That the upshot of the conflict was not the removal of Jænberht but the division of the archdiocese and the elevation of Lichfield to archiepiscopal status indicates that the best Offa could achieve was compromise, and that only with papal help. Contrast what happened in 956. When King Edgar found the new archbishop of Canterbury, Byrthelm, too soft, or politically unacceptable, he sent him back to Wells and replaced him by Dunstan *ex divino respectu et sapientum consilio.*[34]

It is not easy to come to terms with, or to establish a plausible context for, the power of bishops, monasteries and synods in early England. Two observations may be hazarded: first, that ecclesiastical circumstances in Gaul, both in the Merovingian period and later, bore resemblances to those of pre-Viking England, particularly in relation to episcopal power; and second, that the very long-lasting powers of one English see may have derived from such an early period. The community of St Cuthbert later believed that its powers related to a grant made by the Danish Guthred in 882 or 883 in return for their help in making him king in Northumbria.[35] The story, if true, implies how powerful they already were. If so, the origins of the great franchise of the bishops of Durham, enduring until 1836, survived from a period when extensive episcopal authority was more commonly found.

South of the Humber the ninth century saw a change in church–king relations. The last known 'concordat' was the agreement of 838. By this, King Ecgberht promised patronage and protection to the church of Canterbury while

---

[30] Brooks, *Canterbury*, 78, 183.

[31] Ibid., 191–7.

[32] Ibid., 118–27, 180–86.

[33] W. Levison, *England and the Continent in the the Eighth Century* (1946), 22–33.

[34] *Memorials of Saint Dunstan*, ed. W. Stubbs, Rolls Series (1874), 38; Brooks, *Canterbury*, 238–9.

[35] D. J. Hall, 'The community of St Cuthbert: its properties, claims and rights from the ninth century to the twelfth', University of Oxford D. Phil. thesis (1983), 72–8, 198–211; D. P. Kirby, 'Northumbria in the reign of Alfred the Great', *Transactions of the Architectural and Archaeological Society of Durham and Northumberland*, 11 (1965), 335–8.

the archbishop, Ceolnoth, promised firm and unbroken friendship to the king. A sophisticated compromise was reached on lordship over the monasteries of Kent. The 838 agreement was confirmed in the following year both by a West Saxon council and by a Southumbrian synod.[36] The elaboration of the agreement and of the accompanying proceedings is strongly suggestive of their importance in the establishment of West Saxon hegemony. They seem to speak of a kind of constitutionalism associated with balances of power. Soon after 838 evidence for Southumbrian synods dies away; so too, and significantly, does the charter evidence suggesting synodical jurisdiction over bookland.[37] It is also noteworthy that the last grant for several generations by a king to Christ Church Canterbury was made by Ecgberht at about this time.[38]

Here care is needed. Much evidence may have been lost; this is indicated by the importance of the documents which survive in single copies only. This is true for example of the text of the proceedings of the fundamentally important synod of Chelsea, 816.[39] A letter from Bishop Wealdhere to Archbishop Berhtwald (*c.* 704–5) provides almost the best evidence for the wide authority of a synod and the extent to which a bishop need not have been in the pocket of his king. It has survived only by the skin of its teeth. Some tidy twelfth-century person had endorsed it for the waste-parchment basket: *inutilis*.[40] The essence of the problem of the sources is summed up by Dr Cubitt: 'Any assessment of the Anglo-Saxon church is rendered intensely problematic by ... disparity between the sophistication of the evidence and its paucity.'

All the same, it must be that the period from Ecgberht's reign to that of Edward the Elder saw major changes in the relationships between kings and Church. Thus a transformation appears in the way in which archbishops of Canterbury were appointed. Between 631 and 923 only one, Cuthbert, 740–60, was appointed by translation, technically uncanonical (and it is not quite certain that he was actually translated). After the death of Alfred's archbishop Plegmund (who, it is worth noting, was a Mercian, not a West Saxon) in 923 every archbishop until 1020 came to Canterbury by translation. It is not improbable that Alfred had at one stage intended a major change in archiepiscopal appointment: he may have had it in mind that the Frank Grimbald should become archbishop.[41] If this had come about Grimbald would have been the first known non-Anglo-Saxon bishop appointed to an English see since 670. In point of fact that distinction was held by Asser. Asser was given the very important see of Sherborne. Why should Alfred have appointed a loyal and well-rewarded courtier–

---

[36] Brooks, *Canterbury*, 143–7, 197–203; Cubitt, *Councils*, 237–8.

[37] Cubitt, *Councils*, 238–9.

[38] Brooks, *Canterbury*, 145–7.

[39] Cubitt, *Councils*, 2, 62–3 (though Dr Cubitt inclines to the view that the canons of major councils have not been lost).

[40] *EHD*, no. 164.

[41] Brooks, *Canterbury*, 152–3.

scholar to this great see? Perhaps it was too important to entrust to a West Saxon or even to an Englishman. Earlier ninth-century bishops of Sherborne appear as men of power. Heahmund (867 × 868–71) died in battle against the Danes.[42] His predecessor Eahlstan (816 × 825–67) is mentioned not only in contexts suggesting military authority (twice) but also as a leading rebel against Æthelwulf.[43] When Asser died Edward the Elder divided the see into three – not with simply pastoral efficiency in mind, perhaps?

Questions arise as to the attitudes of Alfred towards ecclesiastical property. Professor Brooks pointed out how much ecclesiastical property in Kent and elsewhere passed into royal and other secular hands, as appears largely at about this time.[44] Professor Fleming developed the argument with further examples.[45] Professor Dumville argues that she has put too much faith in doubtful evidence, and is uneasy about some of her general conclusions. Nevertheless he accepts the broad case that the Viking invasions very probably led to considerable ecclesiastical lands passing into secular, including royal, hands.[46] While there was nothing necessarily new about kings and other laymen plundering churches as opportunities served, the scale of the plunder in this period seems extraordinary. Asser, as usual, sheds some useful light. While, on the one hand, he shows Alfred as a monastic founder, on the other his account of how the king gave him the monasteries of Congresbury and Banwell shows him regarding these establishments as property to be given as reward, admittedly to an ecclesiastic. Thus, in seeking to place Alfred's regime in relation to the Church, he can be seen as profiting from a series of changes, beginning, it seems, in the reign of his grandfather. These reduced the power of the bishops and councils and gave the king more power over ecclesiastical property than that for which his great Mercian predecessors had struggled so hard.

To approach the history of Alfred and the Church from another angle, that of the laws, the translations and Asser is to read another story, an almost Carolingian one: the attempt to discipline a whole society in the paths of righteousness. The legislative part of the story begins with the laws of Wihtred and of Ine. These laws tell one at least of the aspiration towards a quasi-theocratic state, for example their attempts to enforce infant baptism and sabbath observance. In the early history of English law the major divide, *prima facie*, comes not between the earliest codes and that of Alfred, as one might have suspected. Rather does it come between the earliest Kentish laws and those of Ine and Wihtred. In the 'codes' of Ethelbert and of Hlothere and Eadric the only provisions having anything visibly to do with Christianity and the Church are the earliest provisions

---

[42] *ASC*, *s.a.* 871.

[43] *ASC*, *s.a.* 823, 845, 867; Asser, c. 12, p. 9.

[44] Brooks, *Canterbury*, 205–6.

[45] R. Fleming, 'Monastic lands and England's defence in the Viking Age', *EHR*, 100 (1985), 247–65.

[46] Dumville, *Wessex and England*, 29–54, esp. 33, 36, 40, 52–3.

of Ethelbert's code, dealing with the theft of ecclesiastical property.[47] By contrast those of Ine and Wihtred abound in godly purpose. Another, and it may be
related, contrast is that while the later laws not infrequently invoke physical
penalties, the two earliest sets do not. An example of the contrast is that between
Ethelbert 5 laying down a penalty of fifty shillings for 'slaying a man on the
king's premises' and Ine 6 and Alfred 7, which envisage the possibility of the
death penalty for fighting in the king's hall (or in the case of Alfred 7 even for
drawing a weapon there).[48] There are major developments between the laws of
Ine and of Wihtred, and those of Alfred, nearly two hundred years later, above all
in relation to lordship. Nevertheless when Alfred jammed his laws and those of
Ine together, this can be seen as a recognition that they were very largely of the
same kind, the regulations aimed towards a strictly run and religiously inspired
state.

It is in a context of power used with such intentions that we should put
Alfred's educational campaign. That this campaign really existed is corroborated
above all by the Alfredian translations; but there is an understandable tendency to
boggle at some of what Asser tells about it. In this context it is important, and
should be commonplace, that the Alfredian campaign had been preceded by others
intended to change society. The first was the initial conversion. Obedience to
secular authority was important in this. What else are we to deduce from Bede's
account of Paulinus's baptizing in the river Glen – for thirty-six days, all day long
from morn till eve?[49] These catechumens do not sound like volunteers. If the
Alfredian campaign was an effort to initiate something like a revolution among the
possessing classes, it is worth bearing in mind that something of the kind had
happened before, at the conversion and also as an antecedent to, or part of, the
great wave of monastic foundation at the time of Bede. Not only was vernacular
learning of fundamental importance for Alfred, it must have been crucial to the
English Church from the beginning. While one cannot be altogether certain, it is a
reasonable guess that the art of writing in Old English was invented by an Italian
cleric very early in the seventh century. Any alternative hypothesis introduces
major complications. There is a little additional evidence for early interest in the
vernacular at Canterbury[50] (though it has to be said that Richardson and Sayles's
alternative theory of a largely pagan origin for the laws and for English literacy is
beyond disproof, or proof).[51] Cuthbert describes how in his last hours Bede
translated the Gospel of John. This is suggestive of the importance of the vernacular in the eighth-century Church, as is the eighth-century date of at least some of
the vernacular poetry. That Bede's translation is lost and that so much of the poetry

---

[47] H. G. Richardson and G. O. Sayles, *Law and Legislation from Æthelberht to Magna Carta*
(1966), 3–4.
[48] Liebermann, *Gesetze*, I, 3, 91, 53.
[49] Bede, *HE*, II 15.
[50] Brooks, *Canterbury*, 95–6.
[51] Richardson and Sayles, *Law and Legislation*, 6–10.

is undatable is a reminder that there may have been far more vernacular religious writing before Alfred's time than can be proved.

Some odd things emerge about the modalities of the learning and literacy campaign. First, among those of Asser's statements which can seem superficially bizarre is one in his chapter 106: Alfred laid down that those important people who were too old to learn to read should get their children or their *servi* to read to them. Children one can understand, but *servi*, how could that be? The will of the great tenth-century lady, Æthelgifu, gives a clue, for in it she frees a priest, Edwin.[52] Canon law said that all priests should be free: Edwin had, plainly, been unfree. More remarkable is the statement by Gaimar, writing in about 1140, that the *Anglo-Saxon Chronicle* was, or had been, publicly available in Winchester Cathedral, bound with a chain, so that anyone might read it, but not remove it.[53] Two things lend plausibility to Gaimar's account: his known connections with Hampshire, and the possible implications of the relationship between what he says and what Alfred suggests about public availability in his introduction to the translation of the *Pastoral Care* of Gregory the Great.[54] The background to the extensive lay literacy in the tenth century (well brought out by Professor Keynes) could well be the success of the Alfredian campaign.[55]

The key question in relation to Alfred's laws and schemes is: how real was his power to command? Much can be understood on the hypothesis that his achievements reflect rather elaborate organization, very effective, at least intermittently. Another way of putting this is to say that Alfred should be understood in the context in which Offa's Dyke is important. Mercia was not Wessex; and Mercia fell. This does not alter the Dyke's demonstration of the administrative capability of early England. It is not so very easy to deny that ninth-century Wessex, like eighth-century Mercia, had very considerable administrative capacity integrated into social organization. A sufficient demonstration is the burghal system, so well examined in the volume by Drs Hill and Rumble.[56] Their evidence is inescapably of a great feat of government.

One may wonder about the nature of the learning which lay behind such accomplishments. Assessment operations of the kind summarized in the Burghal Hidage required, or would be facilitated by, an arithmetical facility not easily come by in the world of Roman numerals. Arithmetic was a subject for ecclesiastical study, not least because it was required in chronological computation.[57]

---

[52] *The Will of Æthelgifu: A Tenth-Century Anglo-Saxon Manuscript*, ed. D. Whitelock (1968), 8–9, 32–3.

[53] *L'Estoire des Engleis by Geffrei Gaimar*, ed. A. Bell, Anglo-Norman Text Society 14–16 (1960).

[54] I have discussed this at greater length in 'Edward the Elder' (cf. n. 8 above).

[55] S. Keynes, 'Royal government and the written word in late Anglo-Saxon England', in *The Uses of Literacy in Early Medieval Europe*, ed. R. McKitterick (1990), 226–57.

[56] *The Defence of Wessex: the Burghal Hidage and Anglo-Saxon Fortifications*, eds D. Hill and A. R. Rumble (1996).

[57] Contreni, 'Carolingian renaissance', 739–41.

Did biblical studies help the administrator in the sense that they might have inspired him in ways more practical than general? It is interesting that the books of Kings and Chronicles have many references to lists and surveys and indeed to service by rota, most in connection with David and Solomon,[58] who were undoubtedly associated with Alfred. The basic units of biblical armies were hundreds, as they may have been of Alfred's.[59] Hebrew rulers had a system of fortified cities just as did the kings of Wessex.[60]

A further indication of the power of the West Saxon state comes from the annals of the *Chronicle*, in their repeated references, from 802 onwards, to the armed forces of shires, each led by its ealdorman. It looks as if the historic shires of Wessex were there by the early ninth century, if not by the late seventh.[61] An important, if largely unanswered, question arises about the nature of the military service which produced the shire armies. We know that in some, maybe much, of England in the eleventh century, a system prevailed by which each five hides provided pay for a soldier for two months. Could such a system have prevailed much earlier? There is one reference of *c.* 800 in a Mercian charter to an estate of thirty hides providing five men, but this appears rather as a concession.[62] An entry in the *Chronicle* for 893 may illustrate the problems a little. It mentions an English force abandoning their siege of the Danes on an island in the Colne because 'they had completed their term of service and their provisions (*mete*) were exhausted'. This could suggest an ordered system at least comparable to that of the eleventh century (and indeed one recalls the C version of the *Chronicle* where it describes Harold II's troops returning home because their provisions were exhausted).[63]

Frankish annals provide more administrative details than do their English counterparts. It is probable that this reflects not so much the superiority of Frankish administration as that of Frankish annalists. Such a passage as that which appears in the annals of Saint-Bertin for 869 probably gives a better indication of how Alfred organized things, *mutatis mutandis*, than does anything in the *Anglo-Saxon Chronicle*. 'Charles gave orders that there should be sent to Pîtres one young warrior for every hundred *manses* and a cart with two oxen for every thousand *manses* … to complete and then guard the fort which the king had ordered to be built out of wood and stone.'[64] Frankish annals provide an interesting insight into the arrangements of another Dark Age state, Denmark. This is in a passage relating to the construction of the *Danevirke*, describing how

---

[58] For Asser's putting Alfred into a context influentially derived from the Book of Kings, Wormald, *Making of English Law*, 122.

[59] 2 Kings 11: 4–9; 1 Chronicles 13: 1; 2 Chronicles 1: 2.

[60] 2 Chronicles 11: 5; 14: 7; 17: 12.

[61] H. M. Chadwick, *Studies on Anglo-Saxon Institutions* (1905), 191–4, 282–90.

[62] Stenton, *Anglo-Saxon England*, 291.

[63] *ASC, s.a.* 893; *ASC* 'C', *s.a.* 1066.

[64] *AB*, ed. Rau, 186, 188 (trans. Nelson, 153–4).

King Godfred built a *vallum* from the Baltic to the North Sea in 808.[65] This account exaggerates somewhat; at least part of the fortification was already in existence.[66] But this does not diminish the interest of what the annalist says about the building of the fortification. Godfred was on his way back from a campaign and: 'diviso itaque opere inter duces copiarum domum reversus est'. 'Having divided the work among the leaders of the forces he returned home.' It sounds as if the army built the fortification. This reminds one of how fortification work and military service are bracketed together in English charters.

One of the most difficult areas of Alfred's activity to place is his relationship to the Scandinavians. In our principal narrative sources the story is plain and straightforward: that of his heroic leadership of the united Christian English against the Danes. But the mere fact that Asser mentions a monk of Viking origin (*paganicae gentis*) among the community at Athelney is by itself enough to complicate the picture.[67] The use of *paganus* to indicate ethnicity rather than belief indicates an evolution both in meaning and in attitude.[68] It is important that the relationships between Scandinavia and the rest of north-western Europe were long-standing. Intercourse between Gaul and Scandinavia was a long story.[69] By the ninth century it was on the highest level: the leading instance is that of Harold, king of Denmark, helped back to his throne in 819 by Louis the Pious, to whose court he paid a famous and glorious visit in 826.[70] Indications of high-level contacts at Alfred's court are the presence of Ohthere and the detailed knowledge of Viking enemies which the *Chronicle* can show. The Scandinavian relationship is crucial for understanding one of the possible contexts for a text for which an Alfredian context is possible, though controversial: *Beowulf*. The principal argument for a pre-Viking invasion date for the poem rests on a conviction that its speaking of Danes with praise and respect excluded the possibility of its having been written once the invasions had begun. To quote Professor Whitelock, this is not 'how men like to hear the people described who are burning their homes, pillaging their churches, ravaging their cattle and crops, killing their countrymen or carrying them off into slavery'.[71] With all respect to Professor Whitelock's great services to learning, it has to be said that this is another example of the working of the Curse of King Alfred. There is little difficulty in imagining a plausible

---

[65] *Annales regni Francorum*, ed. R. Rau, Quellen zur karolingischen Reichsgeschichte I (Darmstadt, 1957), pp. 88–9.

[66] H. Hellmuth Andersen, H. J. Madsen and O. Voss, *Danevirke*, Jysk Arkaeologisk Selskabs-Skrifter, 13, 2 vols (Copenhagen, 1976), i, 102.

[67] Asser, c. 94, p. 81.

[68] Cf. Asser, c. 76, p. 60.

[69] For example the contributions to *Sveagold und Wikingerschmuck aus Statens Historista Museum Stockholm* (Cologne, 1968) by K. Böhner, 168–98 and T. Capelle, 199–208.

[70] *Ermold le noir. Poème sur Louis le Pieux et épitres au roi Pépin*, ed. E. Faral (Paris, 1932), 155–91.

[71] D. Whitelock, *The Audience of Beowulf* (corrected edn, 1958), 25.

ninth- or tenth-century context for *Beowulf.* Professor Lapidge has found evidence suggesting a special connection with Wessex. It is most interesting, but not fully conclusive.[72] One might for example put the poem into a northern context, such as that in which Archbishop Wulfhere (852–92 or 900) pursued his long and doubtless interesting career (though important work by Dr Newton has reminded us not to be over-dogmatic in assigning a late date to the poem).[73]

Aspects of the Anglo-Scandinavian relationship, friendly or the reverse, are partly illuminated by considering the Frisian involvement. The *Chronicle* says that in a naval encounter in 896 there were Frisians with the English forces. That three of these are named indicates that they were men of some importance. Their presence is indicative of the importance for England of the Low Countries; and of the extent to which the areas round the southern narrows of the North Sea were involved together. Scandinavia had a long connection with Frisia. For example it is said that Old Norse is indebted to Frisian for major maritime words: among them those for 'sail', 'boat' and 'anchor'.[74] Some Frisians had for long lived under Danish rule.[75] Viking armed involvement in Frisia was on a very serious scale through much of the ninth century.[76] The complexity of the long-standing Anglo-Frisian as well as Frisian–Scandinavian relations is a reminder of both how important and how ambiguous Alfred's involvement with Frisia may have been. The marriage of his daughter, Ælfthryth, to Baldwin II of Flanders presumably marks an important element in his policy towards the Low Countries. It is, however, characteristic of the difficulties of the *Chronicle* that it says nothing about this marriage though Æthelweard, later, mentions it. There is no reason to suppose that ninth-century politics or foreign policies were any less complicated than those of later centuries. But we know much less about them. How did Alfred secure the services of Frisians, as indeed of other foreigners? He must have paid them; presumably they were among those foreigners to whom he gave *pecunia* and *potestas*. They may well have been among his *bellatores*, whom he paid annually.[77]

This is a reminder of the extent to which Alfred's power and successes had economic bases. It is only in fairly recent years that any attention has been paid to this: the magnetic draw of the Alfredian sources towards explanation in terms more moral than financial has limited historians' imagination. Dr Maddicott, in

---

[72] M. Lapidge, '*Beowulf,* Aldhelm, the *Liber Monstrorum* and Wessex', *Studi Medievali,* 3rd ser. 23 (1982), 151–91 (reprinted in his *Anglo-Latin Literature 600–899* (1996), 271–312); cf. A. C. Murray, 'Beowulf, the Danish invasions and the royal genealogy', *The Dating of Beowulf,* ed. C. Chase (Toronto, 1981), 101–12.

[73] S. Newton, *The Origins of Beowulf and the pre-Viking Kingdom of East Anglia* (1993).

[74] H. Sketelig and H. Folk, *Scandinavian Archaeology* (1937), 346, cf. 193, 336, 420.

[75] L. Musset, *Les Pays scandinaves au moyen âge* (Paris, 1951), 26.

[76] S. Coupland, 'The Vikings in Francia and Anglo-Saxon England to 911', *Cambridge Medieval History II,* ed. McKitterick, 190–201, at 192, 197, 199.

[77] Asser, cc. 100 and 76, pp. 86, 60.

1989, first drew attention to the likely wealth of Wessex.[78] Professor Nelson, in 1986, suggested that the king may have gained by control, indeed manipulation, of the currency; although later research has extended knowledge beyond what was available to her, the strength of her general case remains.[79] It is reasonable to suppose that Alfred had an economic policy integrated with his military policy, not least in the founding and rebuilding of towns and the association of some of them with inland mints, a new departure – and, more crudely, in plundering (not least, it may well be in plundering from the Danes what they had plundered from others).[80]

So deficient are the sources that, however one manoeuvres to fill gaps, or to change angles of vision, much remains, most inconveniently, hidden. The best examples of this are the dates of the introduction into England of ordeal as a normal part of the judicial system and of tithe as a due levied under the sanction of royal power.[81] Both institutions formed part of the Carolingian system. Both institutions were important in England. Ordeal, for something like three centuries until the fourth Lateran Council (1215) forbade the clergy to play a part in it, provided a means whereby a society which was poorly policed, and which lacked adequate means of proof, could deploy divine authority to appear to detect, sometimes actually to identify, evil-doers, and so to punish them. It was established in England well before the year 1000. Tithe was the foundation of the English parochial system. As an instrument of ecclesiastical taxation it retained a certain force, and provoked a certain indignation well into the twentieth century. It was known in some form in England from the seventh century. The duty of paying it is emphasized in the legatine decrees of 786. It is not, however, mentioned in any royal laws until it appears in those of Athelstan. His ordinance on tithe says it is to be paid from his lands and those of his bishops, ealdormen and reeves, and it may be this decree which is referred to in the Kentish document known as Athelstan III.[82] Before the end of the tenth century it was a universal obligation. Ordeal may be mentioned in the laws of Ine; but

---

[78] J. R. Maddicott, 'Trade, industry and the wealth of King Alfred', *Past and Present*, 123 (1989), 3–51.

[79] J. Nelson, 'Wealth and wisdom: the politics of Alfred the Great', *Kings and Kingship*, ed. J. Rosenthal, Acta 11 (1986 for 1984), 39–43. Cf. the contributions by Blackburn and by Blackburn and Keynes to *Kings, Currency and Alliances* (above, n. 6), 105–24, 125–50.

[80] Asser's version of the annal for 885 'classem suam ... plenam bellatoribus, in orientales Anglos dirigens, praedandi causa, transmisit' (c. 67, p. 50) makes explicit what the *Chronicle* cloaks under the evasive *sænde*, 'sent', *Two of the Saxon Chronicles Parallel*, i, 78; cf. Asser, c. 53, p. 41.

[81] For ordeal in general R. Bartlett, *Trial by Fire and Water* (1986) esp. 24–32, 62–9, and for tithe P. Viard, *Histoire de la dîme ecclésiastique principalement en France jusqu'au décret de Gratian* (Paris, 1909) and G. Constable, *Monastic Tithes from their Origins to the Twelfth Century* (1964). The still not entirely solved problems of the 'decimations' of Æthelwulf of Wessex are set out by H. P. R. Finberg, *The Early Charters of Wessex* (1964), 187–213; cf. Keynes and Lapidge, *Alfred*, 69–70, 232–4.

[82] Liebermann, *Gesetze*, I, 146–9, 170. I have used the translations by Attenborough, *Laws*.

the text is questionable. Otherwise it does not appear until the 'first code' of Edward the Elder, then frequently in (and after) the 'second code' of Athelstan.[83] One could fancy the possibility of these laws showing a rationale for the introduction of ordeal. Its first mention, in I Edward clause 3, relates entirely to men whose oaths have proved inadequate. They are such as have had a charge proved against them contrary to their oath, or the oath on their behalf has collapsed, or has been overborne by stronger testimony. Such people are no longer to be allowed to clear themselves by oath, but only by ordeal. The weakest point of a legal system largely cemented by trust in oaths is of course perjury. In this legislation we may (possibly) see the introduction of ordeal as a recourse for dealing with proved or likely perjurers. Then under Athelstan would come its more widespread use. The spelling out of procedure for ordeal in Athelstan's 'second code' could possibly indicate its being something relatively new. (In any case, whenever ordeal was introduced, the diffusion of knowledge of reasonably uniform procedures is likely to have been a major administrative challenge.) Arguments from silence are especially dangerous in a Dark Age context; but ordeal and royally enforced tithe are so much in accord with the general tenor of Alfred's programmes that it is tempting to suppose that their absence from his laws does not prove their absence in reality (two-edged though this argument is). If this was not so, then his immediate successors were mighty innovators. The difficulties here are such as to discredit any attempt to claim a knowledge of the Alfredian regime that is more than threadbare and ragged.

Where then do we place Alfred? In an English context generalizations offer themselves, none the less true for their millennial banality. He was the victor in a long and determined war. He certainly led a cultural and religious effort, encapsulated in an unparalleled series of translations. How much further can one go with security? Some of Alfred's success depended upon the deployment and manipulation of systems of order, exploitation and control which had a long past in the Anglo-Saxon lands. Offa's Dyke is inevitably part of the background to the Burghal Hidage, and the system which it outlines and reveals. At the same time Alfred's reign, as is suggested above, is at an important, it may well be a determinative, stage in the relationships between Church and kings. There had been an age of archiepiscopal and episcopal power, of numerous, and often wealthy monasteries, one which saw struggles for power between kings, bishops, abbeys and magnates. Most of the episodes and details of this struggle are lost but we know just enough to see, for example, that papal power could sometimes count. In the ninth century much changed. By the tenth kings were more firmly in control of the Church, of churches. This was true of the South; but not necessarily in the North.

The pre-Viking era in England is sometimes called the 'age of the minsters'. It was also the age of major coastal trading sites, *emporia*. It is hard not to

---

[83] Liebermann, *Gesetze*, I, 140, 152–7, 162.

imagine connection between the minsters and the *emporia*. The ecclesiastical wealth which Alfred emphasized surely in large part derived from that of a society provided with trading centres so extensive that it is timid not to call them towns. (And, as is becoming apparent, this society was provided, at least in some areas, with lesser trading places, the 'productive sites' which maybe were satellites of the *emporia*.[84]) The *emporia* and very many of the minsters disappeared or diminished in the earlier ninth century. It seems perverse to deny the likely association of both catastrophes with Viking invasion. The Viking danger is obviously reflected in a contrast between the *emporia* and the new or renewed towns of about Alfred's time, for the latter were fortified as the former were not. Similarly, a characteristic of Alfred's two monastic foundations, Shaftesbury and Athelney, is that both were fortified. No doubt we should, with King Alfred, consider, though we can hardly hope to measure, the extent to which monastic decline or transmogrification was due to 'non-Viking' causes. It would, indeed, be wrong to disregard the royal diagnosis of excessive prosperity. In his famous introduction to the *Pastoral Care* of Gregory the Great, Alfred explicitly put the decay of learning in a period before the Viking assault. It is as if clerics had said: 'Our ancestors, who formerly maintained these places, loved wisdom, and through it they obtained wealth and passed it on to us ... We have now lost the wealth as well as the wisdom!'[85] That self-indulgence came to succeed study is by no means the only possible explanation for Bede's having no known ninth-century English theologians as his heirs; but it is serviceable. Whatever the causes, one can hardly doubt that when Alfred lamented the decay of learning in England he was referring to a process of destruction and decay comparable in its impact at least to the Dissolution of the Monasteries. The evidence is everywhere. Perhaps most striking is the dependence of the transmission of Bede's *Ecclesiastical History* (not to speak of his other works) on manuscripts preserved on the Continent.[86] Important though the school of Theodore at Canterbury was, no trace of his Antiochene theology remained in England, and non-English centres seem to have been wholly responsible for the transmission of his penitential and legal learning.[87] Similarly indicative of great loss is the known existence of such a monastic leader as Botulf, of whom we have little more than general indications, which, however, are enough strongly to suggest that he was eminent in monastic learning.[88] Beside this can be set the discovery of a probable monastic

---

[84] P. Sawyer, *Anglo-Saxon Lincolnshire* (1998), 171–8; K. Ulmschneider, 'Archaeology, history and the Isle of Wight in the Middle Saxon period', *Medieval Archaeology*, 43 (1999), 19–44.

[85] The translation is that of Keynes and Lapidge, *Alfred*, 125.

[86] *Bede's Ecclesiastical History of the English People* (1991), eds B. Colgrave and R. A. B. Mynors (rev. edn, 1991), xxxix–lxxiii.

[87] T. Charles-Edwards, 'The Penitential of Theodore and the *Iudica Theodori*', in M. Lapidge (ed.), *Archbishop Theodore* (1995), 141–74.

[88] J. Campbell, 'East Anglian sees before the Conquest', *Norwich Cathedral, Church, City and Diocese 1096–1996*, eds I. Atherton and others (1996), 12; *The Blackwell Encyclopedia of Anglo-Saxon England*, eds M. Lapidge and others (1999), s.v. Botwulf.

site such as that at Brandon, totally unknown to written sources, but providing
not only styluses, but a most impressive fragment of niello-inlaid gold, as if
from a book-cover.[89] Anyone who doubts Viking destruction should produce
another explanation for the almost complete absence of pre-Scandinavian invasion charters from the area of the Danelaw. One of the most impressive of
recorded early English church councils must have been that held at *Clovesho* in
803 by thirteen bishops from the province of Canterbury accompanied by sev-
enty-nine abbots, priests and other clerics. No such extensive an assembly could
have been held in England a hundred years later; and the learning and assumptions of the English clergy when Alfred died were a long way from those of the
clerics who had made their way to *Clovesho* in 803.[90] Alfred's, and succeeding,
generations had to make new worlds.

In all questions of intellectual life or administrative organization Carolingian
comparison matters a lot. It is a truism to say that cross-channel connections and
parallels were hardly less determinative than numerous. It is in the nature of
comparison to raise questions at least as readily as to provide answers. In
particular, contrasts raise questions. It is not difficult to fit Asser's *Life* into a
Carolingian context which includes the biographies of Louis the Pious and
Einhard. But why were manuscripts of Einhard almost certainly very much more
numerous than those of Asser?[91] The problem is part of a larger one. Carolingian
writers were numerous. Carolingian manuscript production was very extensive:
over sixty male authors within the empire between the last generation of the
ninth century and the first decade of the tenth are known by name.[92] According
to one estimate, the Carolingian scriptoria may have produced as many as
50,000 texts in the ninth century.[93] In a modern edition Carolingian poetry
amounts to some 3200 pages.[94] Ninth-century English performance in such
regards was meagre to the point of being contemptible. A likely demonstration
of English intellectual decay, or idleness, in the ninth century is the absence of
any known *vita* of Swithin until Lantfred's of *c.* 975. And Lantfred was not
English, in this resembling many of the authors whose Latin works survive from
late Anglo-Saxon England.[95] There are some grounds for believing his cult to
have originated not too long after his death, between 862 and 865, in particular

---

[89] L. Webster and J. Backhouse, *The Making of England: Anglo-Saxon Art and Culture. A.D.
600–900* (1991), 81–8.

[90] A. W. Haddan and W. Stubbs, *Councils and Ecclesiastical Documents Relating to Great
Britain and Ireland*, 3 vols (1869–78), iii, 545–8.

[91] It would not be easy to demonstrate that there were ever more than two manuscripts of
Asser's work. The five manuscripts of Einhard's work surviving from before AD 1000 show that
there must have been others: *Eginhaud. Vie de Charlemagne*, ed. L. Halphen (Paris, 1947), xiii–xx.

[92] Contreni, 'Carolingian renaissance', 719.

[93] Ibid., 711.

[94] Ibid., 753.

[95] M. Lapidge, *Blackwell Encyclopedia,* s.v. provides a succinct survey of the evidence for
the cult of Swithin.

the situation of his tomb. One might have supposed that the *Anglo-Saxon Chronicle* would have mentioned such a prelate. But he does not appear in any version of the *Chronicle* earlier than 'F' of *c.* 1100. The *Chronicle* is such that it can be shown that various hands took a certain amount of trouble over it; it has been powerfully argued that this trouble involved composition in a 'biblical' style such as to convey messages decodable only by the practised.[96] So much said, it should be admitted that as an exercise in the provision of ordered information the *Chronicle* compares dismally with the 'Royal Frankish Annals' and those of 'Saint-Bertin'. And the efforts of English annalists soon peter out into the thin and unorganized. To compare writings in England and in the Carolingian, and former Carolingian, world over approaching three centuries is to find, in broad but not meaningless, terms a contrast, which poses another problem in 'placing' Alfred. Consider for example the continental achievement in the various genres which can be loosely summed up as 'historiography' before the eighth century and after the eleventh. Whom has England to put beside Nithard, Floduard, Richer, Liudprand and Widukind? True, the very extent of the Carolingian lands helped to ensure that there were more possible centres of production there than in England, but that can by no means be the whole explanation, for the English/ continental contrast had not applied in the eighth century, and ceases to apply in the twelfth. The drought in serious English writing begins before Alfred, and continues long after his day. Both before and after him isolated works were produced which showed, surprisingly showed, that there was more competence and learning about than might otherwise have been supposed in this regard: Æthelwulf's *De Abbatibus* can stand for monastic learning *c.* 800 and Æthelweard's *Chronicle* for learning among the secular great nearly two centuries later. Thus, although the Alfredian translations do show a certain amount of learning, sparsely evidenced among Englishmen at this time, the context in which these works belong is one in which very little had been composed in the generations before and little was to be composed in the generations after. The strength of the vernacular tradition in England is in part a tribute to the weakness of Englishmen's Latin.

To place Alfred in a context which takes account of the non-Carolingian as well as the Carolingian realms is again to be reminded of the deficiency of our sources. In parts of the British Isles other than England, Viking assault helped to transform political organization, though not necessarily in the same ways. In Scotland the Viking onslaught may have contributed to changes in royal succession systems and so to the ultimate union of the kingdom.[97] It has been argued that the Vikings had somewhat comparable results in Ireland, that their assaults jolted the country out of the old tribal framework.[98] But the extent to which the political organization of pre-invasion Ireland was in a sense archaic is now

---

[96] Cf. above, p. 3.

[97] B. Hudson, *Kings of Celtic Scotland* (Westport, 1997), 151–2.

[98] D. A. Binchy, 'The passing of the old order', in *The Impact of the Scandinavian Invasions*, ed. B. O'Cuiv (Dublin, 1975), 119–32, esp. 130–31.

seriously questioned; and it is suggested that Irish resistance having been more effective than English reveals something important about Irish organization.[99] In Wales the sources are inferior to those from Ireland; but enough to show that moves towards union there were always fleeting; it does indeed seem that, as Professor Ó Corráin puts it, Wales under Viking and English pressures became 'an unstable land of unresolved segmentary struggles and quick-moving dynastic warfare'.[100] What comparison with other parts of the archipelago brings out, in particular, is the importance both of succession-systems (and changes in them) and also of access to urban and commercial resources.

It is in regard to relations to the Scandinavians and their world that the greatest difficulties and the widest possibilities arise. One can be sure that the principal sources from England misrepresent to us the balance between antagonism and assimilation; but how far this is so one can hardly tell. This particular problem is a characteristic one. The unique nature of the Alfredian translations, and the extent to which the narrative sources are concentrated on the king, combine to fox our capacity to place King Alfred at least as much as they do to further it. The most important developments in England were administrative and economic. They are also the worst documented. The Church in England was a mighty force; and one which very probably came much more under royal control between the early ninth century and the early tenth. We seem to move from the late seventh- and eighth-century circumstances in which some ecclesiastics enjoyed powers not too dissimilar from those which some of their continental contemporaries enjoyed to one in which the royal power over the Church or churches was greater (south of the Tees). Alfred's reign was an important part of a major transition in royal–church relationships in England. An indication of how far England came to diverge from France and Germany in this regard is to pose a question 'Why were there no episcopally controlled towns in England?' During the tenth century power and growth, above all at parish level, were financed by tithe enforced by royal power. The strongest indication of how far England was a theocratic state was the role of ordeal in the judicial system. That we cannot be sure when either tithe or ordeal were introduced indicates a peculiar paradox. Increasingly united England was a polity of Carolingian type, but it has not left records or writings on anything like a Carolingian scale. It replaced a very different and much less united land, that of the *emporia* and the minsters, one in which for several generations coins did not bear the names of kings, and in which bishops, especially archbishops, enjoyed an authority not easily paralleled later. Alfred's world was a new one: illuminated for us by shafts

---

[99] D. Ó Corráin, 'Viking Ireland. Afterthoughts', in *Ireland and Scandinavia in the Early Viking Age*, eds H. B. Clarke, M. Ni Mhaonaigh and R. O'Floinn (Dublin, 1998), 412–52. Cf. however C. O'Doherty, 'The Vikings in Ireland, a review', in the same volume, 288–330, emphasizing, *inter alia*, the 'militarization' of Irish society.

[100] D. Ó Corráin, 'Ireland, Scotland and Wales to the early eleventh century', *Cambridge Medieval History II*, ed. McKitterick, 43–63, at 63.

of knowledge, but at best dimly visible. The field is a wide one for guesswork, which may be glorified as quasi-informed speculation. For example, may there have been connections between the Alfredian emphasis on vernacular learning, increased royal control over the Church, the paucity of signs of deep ecclesiastical learning, and the organization of a formidable state apparatus? Could Alfred have helped to inaugurate a regime in which ability and ambition were more narrowly focused than previously, focused on royal service, and, when they expressed themselves in writing, doing so in English and largely for the purposes of a quasi-theocratic state?

THE SOURCES

Chapter 2

Asser's reading

Michael Lapidge

According to c. 79 of his *Vita Ælfredi*, Asser, sometime bishop of St David's in Wales, first met King Alfred at Dean in Sussex, probably in 885, and was invited by the king to become a member of the royal household. Asser's presence at Alfred's court will have afforded the king the immense benefit of insight into Welsh politics, but the English realm will also have derived 'benefit in every respect from the learning of St David' (*illa adiuvaretur per rudimenta Sancti Degui in omni causa*), at least to the best of Asser's abilities, as he modestly observes.[1] There is no doubt that, once arrived in England (probably in 886), Asser became involved in the various scholarly projects which Alfred was sponsoring. Thus Alfred explicitly acknowledges help received *æt Assere minum biscepe* ('from Asser my bishop') in the preface to his translation of Gregory's *Regula pastoralis*.[2] Several centuries later William of Malmesbury recorded in his *Gesta pontificum Anglorum* (*c.* 1125) that Asser expounded the text of Boethius, *De Consolatione Philosophiae*, for the king:

> Asserus, ex Sancto Dewi evocatus, non usquequaque contempnendae scientiae fuit, qui librum Boetii de Consolatione Philosophiae planioribus verbis elucidavit, labore illis diebus necessario, nostris ridiculo. Sed etiam iussu regis factum est, ut levius ab eodem in Anglicum transferretur sermonem.[3]

As an intimate of the king, Asser may also have participated in other translations, but the extent of this involvement cannot be defined.

---

[1] Ed. Stevenson, p. 65; trans. Keynes and Lapidge, *Alfred*, 94.

[2] *Pastoral Care*, ed. Sweet, 1, 7.

[3] *Willelmi Malmesbiriensis monachi de gestis pontificum Anglorum*, c. 80, ed. N. E. S. A. Hamilton, Rolls Series (1870), 177: 'Asser, summoned from St David's, was a man of not despicable learning in many respects; he expounded the book of Boethius *De Consolatione Philosophiae* in plain language, a task which in those days was a necessity, but in our days an absurdity. But at the king's command it also came about that it could easily be translated by him [the king] into English.' William makes a similar observation in his *Gesta regum Anglorum,* c. 122.4, eds R. A. B. Mynors, R. M. Thomson and M. Winterbottom, *William of Malmesbury: Gesta Regum Anglorum* I (1998), 190: 'Hic [Asser] sensum librorum Boetii De Consolatione planioribus uerbis enodauit, quos rex ipse in Anglicam linguam uertit'. See also D. Whitelock, 'William of Malmesbury on the works of King Alfred', in *Medieval Literature and Civilization: Studies in Memory of G.N. Garmonsway*, eds D. A. Pearsall and R. A. Waldron (1969), 78–93, at 89–90. The source of William's information is unknown; Æthelweard, who in his *Chronicon* mentions the king's translation of Boethius, makes no mention of Asser.

By the same token it is difficult to estimate the nature of the *rudimenta Sancti Degui*, the extent of the Latin training which Asser received at St David's and brought with him to England. Very little is known about Latin learning in Dark Age Wales;[4] and in any case we should be obliged to distinguish between works which Asser may have studied in Wales and others which he may have encountered for the first time in England. The only reliable evidence can be the identifiable sources quoted by Asser in the *Vita Ælfredi*. In his edition of 1904, Stevenson carefully identified most of Asser's explicit quotations (those intro-duced by phrases such as *sicut scriptura dicit*), and these included nine quotations from the Bible, and one each from Caelius Sedulius, *Carmen paschale* (c. 1), Gregory, *Regula pastoralis* (c. 102), and Augustine, *Enchiridion* (c. 103). (A few explicit quotations went unidentified,[5] and Asser's knowledge of other works, such as Einhard's *Vita Karoli*, is evident from context if not from verbal debt.) Of these texts, Caelius Sedulius was read as a school text throughout Europe in the early Middle Ages;[6] the *Regula pastoralis* was translated by Alfred and his advisers (including Asser) and could have been read by Asser for the first time at Alfred's court; and Augustine's *Enchiridion* could have been read there along with other Augustinian works while Alfred was translating Augustine's *Soliloquia*.[7] More recent scholarship has added a few titles to this meagre list: Vergil's *Aeneid*, Aldhelm's prose *De virginitate*, Bede's *Historia ecclesiastica*, and the Cambro-Latin *Historia Brittonum*.[8] In sum, this modest list would seem to lend support to William of Malmesbury's impression that Asser was in no sense a scholar of vast learning.

It is nevertheless possible to qualify this impression somewhat by the use of modern scholarly resources. The past decade has seen the publication of various electronic databases of classical and Christian Latin authors,[9] and these

---

[4] See M. Lapidge, 'Latin learning in Dark Age Wales: some prolegomena', in *Proceedings of the Seventh International Congress of Celtic Studies*, eds D. E. Evans, J. G. Griffith and E. M. Jope (1986), 91–107.

[5] One of these, that in c. 88 ('super modicum fundamentum aedificat iustus et paulatim ad maiora defluit') was recently identified as a quotation from the (probably Hiberno-Latin) *Proverbia grecorum*: see A. Scharer, 'The writing of history at King Alfred's court', *Early Medieval Europe*, 5 (1996), 177–206, at 198. See also below, p. 42. The hexameter in c. 90 ('invigilant animi, quibus est pia cura regendi') is from Corippus, *In laudem Iustini*, iii. 139.

[6] See M. Lapidge, 'The study of Latin texts in late Anglo-Saxon England, I. The evidence of Latin glosses', in *Latin and the Vernacular Languages in Early Medieval Britain*, ed. N. Brooks (1982), 99–140, at 113–16.

[7] It is interesting to note that a copy of the *Enchiridion* is found in London, Lambeth Palace Library, 237, fols 146–208, a manuscript written probably at Arras in the second quarter of the ninth century which was in England by the early tenth. Could this manuscript have been brought to England by Grimbald? And read at Alfred's court by Asser?

[8] Keynes and Lapidge, *Alfred*, 54. The evidence there adduced for Asser's knowledge of Vergil points instead to Orosius (see below, p. 34, n. 31); but there may be other evidence for familiarity with Vergil.

[9] In what follows I draw on three such databases: CLCLT4 = the CETEDOC Library of

tools allow the possibility of identifying the sources of a medieval Latin author's diction with a precision that would have been unimaginable a generation ago. Of course it needs to be stressed that the evidence thrown up by word searches in a computer database needs to be carefully weighed: if a particular combination of words in Asser is found to occur in (say) fifty patristic authors, there is no chance of identifying Asser's source; if it occurs in only a few authors, one is obliged to decide which of these authors is most likely to have been known to Asser (often this matter can be decided by the recurrence of a particular author in repeated word searches). Even if a distinctive phrase is found to occur only in Asser and in one antecedent author, one must still ask whether that author is likely to have been known to Asser, and whether the phrase is distinctive enough to rule out the possibility of independent formulation. With these considerations in mind, therefore, the databases suggest that Asser's reading included the following texts.

Classical Latin poets

Asser has an excellent command of the technical Latin terminology for war and battle: troop deployment and manoeuvre, encampment, attack and defence, and so on. He no doubt learned some of this military vocabulary from his reading of the classical poets, some from late Roman historians, and some from Orosius (who himself drew on earlier Roman historians). Two phrases appear to be poetic in origin:

castris erumpent (c. 20): Lucan, *De bello ciuili* iv. 732: 'Curio nocturnum **castris erumpe**re cogit'.

densa testudine (c. 56): Vergil, *Aen.* ix. 514: 'cum tamen omnis / fere iuuet subter **densa testudine** casus'; but cf. Lucan, *De bello ciuili* iii. 474 (imitating Vergil): 'ut tamen hostiles **densa testudine** muros'.

Roman historians

It is a curious aspect of Roman historiography that the principal sources of Roman history – Livy and Tacitus – were virtually unknown during the early Middle Ages. Even such important historians as Sallust and Caesar were seldom read before the eleventh century. In their stead circulated a number of epitomes and compendia of Roman history, of which the most widely read were the

Christian Latin Texts, ed. Paul Tombeur (Turnhout, 2000); BTL = the Bibliotheca Teubneriana Latina, ed. CETEDOC (Turnhout, 1999); and PLD = the Chadwyck-Healey Patrologia Latina Database (1995).

Breviarium of Eutropius (completed in 369), which covers the history of Rome from its foundation until the reign of Valens (to whom Eutropius dedicated the work),[10] and the *Epitome* of Justinus (3rd century AD?), which presents a concise digest of the massive (but lost) *Historiae Philippicae* of Pompeius Trogus.[11] Because both these works circulated in early Anglo-Saxon England,[12] they may both have been known to Asser, and may have left their mark on his language, particularly his impressive command of military vocabulary. The difficulty is that the *Breviarium* of Eutropius was almost wholly incorporated into the later *Historia Romana* of Paulus Diaconus,[13] and much of Justinus was taken over by Orosius in his *Historiae adversus paganos* (see below), so it is not always easy to distinguish a phrase taken directly from Eutropius or Justinus from one taken from a later epitomator, such as Orosius or Paulus Diaconus. In the few examples which follow, I cite phrases which occur only in one or other of the Roman historians.

pugnatum esset (c. 5): Eutropius, *Breviarium* iii. 10. 2.[14]

Romam perrexit (c. 11): Eutropius, *Breviarium* ii. 12. 1.[15]

in bellum prorumperet (c. 38): Justinus, *Epitoma* xxiv. 1. 1: '**in bellum prorump**unt'.

sequentis temporis successu (c. 81): Justinus, *Epitoma* i. 8. 14: 'sed continuo totius **temporis successu**'.[16]

---

[10] Ed. H. Droysen, MGH AA 2 (Berlin, 1878). See the valuable introduction in *Eutropius: Breviarium*, trans. H. W. Bird, Translated Texts for Historians, 14 (1993), vii–lvii.

[11] Ed. O. Seel (Leipzig, 1972). For the transmission, see O. Seel, 'Die justinischen Handschriftenklassen und ihr Verhältnis zu Orosius', *Studi italiani di filologia classica*, 11 (1934), 255–88, and 12 (1935), 5–40.

[12] Eutropius is quoted by Bede, *HE* i. 3, and Alcuin's reference in his poem on York to 'Pompeius' among the *historici veteres* almost certainly refers to the *Epitome* of one Pompeius Trogus made by Justinus, of which there is a surviving fragment of possible eighth-century York origin: see J. Crick, 'An Anglo-Saxon fragment of Justinus's *Epitome*', *ASE*, 16 (1987), 181–96.

[13] See L. B. Mortensen, 'The diffusion of Roman histories in the middle ages. A list of Orosius, Eutropius, Paulus Diaconus and Landolfus Sagax manuscripts', *Filologia Mediolatina*, 6–7 (1999–2000), 101–200. There is no early Anglo-Saxon manuscript of the *Breviarium*. Two manuscripts of the *Historia Romana* survive from the very end of the Anglo-Saxon period: Cambridge, Corpus Christi College 276, fos 1–54 (s. xi^ex; listed Mortensen, no. 23) and Cambridge, Trinity College O. 10. 28 (s. xi/xii; listed Mortensen, no. 24).

[14] Ed. Droysen, 52.

[15] Ibid., 32.

[16] These words of Justinus refer to the Persian king Cyrus; Orosius takes them over in his discussion of Cyrus: 'igitur idem Cyrus proximi temporis successu Scythis bellum intulit', *Historiae* ii. 7. 1, ed. K. Zangemeister, CSEL 5 (Vienna, 1882), 98. The phrase is otherwise unattested in the electronic databases, but it is impossible to determine which of the two may have been Asser's source.

The Bible

Stevenson carefully identified those biblical quotations which Asser specified as such (by introducing them with wording such as 'sicut scriptum est', and so on), and was able to show, interestingly, that Asser quoted both from the Vetus Latina and from Jerome's Vulgate translation. In addition to the specific quotations, there are various places in the text where Asser's wording is apparently based on reminiscence of the Bible (in such cases it is not possible to determine whether the reminiscence is based on the Vetus Latina or the Vulgate).

firmum foedus cum Cantuariis pepigerunt (c. 20): Gen. 14: 13 ('hi enim **pepiger**ant **foedus cum** Abram'); Exod. 6: 4 ('**pepigi**que **foedus cum** eis'); 34: 27 ('**cum** Israel **pepigi foedus**'); Deut. 29: 1 ('illud **foedus** quod **cum** eis **pepigi**t'); Judges 9: 46 ('ubi **foedus cum** eo **pepigerant**'); and so on.

laborat non in vanum (c. 22): Ps. 126: 1 ('nisi Dominus aedificaverit domum, **in vanum labora**verunt qui aedificant eam').

congregatoque exercitu (cc. 27, 36): Num. 21: 23 ('quin potius **exercitu congregato** egressus est').[17]

ad locum certaminis citius advenissent (c. 38): 1 Kgs 14: 20 ('et **ven**erunt usque **ad locum certaminis**').

Christiani ab inferiori loco aciem dirigebant (c. 39): Gen. 14: 8 ('et **dir**exerunt **aciem** contra eos'); Josh. 8: 13 ('omnis vero reliquus exercitus ad aquilonem **aciem dirigebat**'); 8: 14 ('**dir**exitque **aciem** contra desertum').

exercitus in duas se turmas divisit (c. 66): Num. 2: 32 ('per domos et **turmas divisi exercitus**'); Judg. 9: 43 ('et **divisit in** tres **turmas**').

oblivioni <non> traderem (c. 95): Gen. 41: 30 ('ut **oblivioni trad**atur cuncta retro abundantia'); Ecclus. 9: 5 ('**oblivioni trad**ita est memoria eorum'); Ezek. 33: 13 ('omnes iustitiae eius **oblivioni trade**ntur').

morte turpissima (c. 97): Wisd. 2: 20 ('**morte turpissima** condemnemus illum').

ad denarios pensari in bilibri (c. 104): Rev. 6: 6 ('**bilibri**s tritici **denario**, tres **bilibr**es hordei **denario**').

---

17 Asser could equally have taken the expression from either Orosius, *Historiae* vi. 2. 13: 'magno exercitu breui congregato' (ed. Zangemeister, 359) or Bede, *HE* iii. 14: 'siquidem congregato inuicem exercitu', both of whom were drawing on the biblical passage.

Athanasius, *Vita S. Antonii*, trans. Evagrius

The *vita* of St Antony (d. 356) was first composed in Greek by Athanasius, bishop of Alexandria (d. 373), but was translated twice into Latin. The second of these translations, by Evagrius of Antioch, was made at some point in the early 380s, and became one of the foundational texts of western hagiography. It was studied in early Anglo-Saxon England at the school of Theodore and Hadrian at Canterbury, and served as a model for Anglo-Latin hagiographers such as the anonymous Lindisfarne author of the *Vita S. Cuthberti* and Felix in his *Vita S. Guthlaci*. There is no difficulty in assuming that the text was known to Asser, and two particular phrases may represent reminiscences of his reading of it.

velut apis prudentissima (c. 76): *Vita S. Antonii*, c. 3: 'si quem vigilantem in hoc studio compererat, procedens, quaerebat **ut apis prudentissima**; nec ad habitaculum suum ante remeabat, nisi eius quem cupiebat frueretur aspectibus; et sic, tanquam munere mellis accepto, abibat ad sua'.[18]

semper inter prospera et adversa (c. 92): *Vita S. Antonii*, c. 40: 'similiter agnosce-batur Antonius, quia **semper** eamdem faciem **inter prospera et adversa** retinens'.[19]

Cassian

The *Conlationes* of Cassian (d. *c.* 435) were written between 420 and 429 and record twenty-four conversations between either Cassian or his colleague Germanus and a number of desert anchorites whom Cassian visited in Egypt in 382; they became one of the fundamental sources of western monastic spiritual-ity. The *Conlationes* circulated widely in manuscript, and were well known to early Insular authors such as Aldhelm and Bede.[20]

ineffabili patris clementia (c. 12): *Conlat.* ix. 22: 'o **ineffabili**s Dei **clementia**'.[21]

in paupertate et miseria leto tenus vituperabiliter vitam duxit (c. 15): *Conlat.* iii. 9: 'qui eas non habens **uituperabiliter pauper** et nudus est'.[22]

---

[18] Migne, *PL* 73, 128. Although the phrase *apis prudentissima* clearly derives from the *Vita S. Antonii*, Asser's subsequent elaboration of the simile derives from Aldhelm's prose *De virginitate*, c. 6 (see below).

[19] Migne, *PL* 73, 156. Note that the phrase also occurs in Gregory, *Homiliae in Hiezechielem* ii. 2, ed. M. Adriaen, CCSL 142 (Turnhout, 1971), 226, and in Bede, *In primam partem Samuhelis libri IIII* i. 6, ed. D. Hurst, CCSL 119 (Turnhout, 1962), 50.

[20] There is, however, no early manuscript of the work from Anglo-Saxon England, the earliest being Oxford, Bodleian Library, Hatton 23 (Worcester, s. xi[2]) and Salisbury, Cathedral Library (s. xi[ex]), from the very end of the Anglo-Saxon period.

[21] Ed. J. Petschenig, CSEL 13 (Vienna, 1886), 270.

[22] Ibid., 80.

aetate erat provectior (c. 25): *Conlat.* xi. 4: 'et duobus aliis **prouectior** esset **aetate**'.[23]

portum optatae quietis (c. 73): *Conlat.* x. 8: 'et post longa naufragia uelut **portum quietis** intrare'.[24]

non sine labore (c. 84): *Conlat.* ii. 24: 'et in tantum hoc **non sine labore** perficitur'; vi. 15: 'recuperare rursus **non sine labore** poterit'.[25]

divino instinctu (c. 87): *Conlat.* ii. 6: 'nequaquam credens **instinctu** factum **diuino**'.[26]

fidei rudimenta (c. 81): *Conlat.* xi. 1: 'post prima **fidei rudimenta**'.[27]

Orosius

The *Historiae adversum paganos* by the priest Orosius, from Braga in Spain, was throughout the Middle Ages one of the most widely circulated sources of early Roman history (it survives in more than 200 manuscripts). The work, which treats world history up to AD 416, was completed at Rome in 417 at the suggestion of Augustine, who intended that the *Historiae* form a sort of complement to his own treatise *De ciuitate Dei*; its central argument is that, even during times of pagan barbarity, humanity was guided by divine providence. The work survives in a number of Anglo-Saxon manuscripts, and was translated into Old English in King Alfred's day (see below).

inter tantas bellorum clades (c. 21): *Hist.* ii. 5. 6: 'urguet se atque inminet sibi extra illas apertas **bellorum clades**'; v. 1. 5: 'quibus modo **bellorum clades** modo pacis condiciones perhorrescens'.[28]

maxima suarum copiarum parte occisa (c. 39): *Hist.* ii. 7. 2: 'regina tertiam **partem copiarum** ... mittit'; iv. 6. 24: 'se neque bello **partem** instructu **copiarum**'; v. 19. 9: '**parti copiarum**'; vi. 2. 15: '**partem copiarum** instructam

---

[23] Ibid., 316.

[24] Ibid., 296.

[25] Ibid., 62, 316.

[26] Ibid., 46.

[27] Ibid., 314. The phrase *fidei rudimenta* was picked up from Cassian by later authors, notably Cassiodorus, *Expositio psalmorum I–LXX*, ed. M. Adriaen, CCSL 97 (Turnhout, 1958), 298, 303 and Aldhelm, who uses it in the prose *De virginitate* cc. 13, 25, 35, ed. R. Ehwald, MGH AA 15 (Berlin, 1913–19), 242, 257, 277, and Bede, *In Genesim* iv. 21, in *Libri Quatuor in Principium Genesis usque ad Nativitatem Isaac et Eiectionem Ismahelis*, ed. C. W. Jones, CCSL 118A (Turnhout 1967), 238; it could have been taken by Asser from any one of these sources.

[28] Ed. Zangemeister, 93, 277. The phrase *bellorum clades* is fairly clearly an Orosian formulation; no occurrence of the phrase is found outside Orosius in PLD, CLCLT4 or BTL.

armis domum abire praecepit'; vi. 11. 22: 'ambos duces cum **parte copiarum** plurima in campum euocatos'.[29]

navali proelio contra paganicas naves in mare congressus est (c. 64; cf. c. 48): *Hist.* iv. 8. 4: 'Hannibal ... infeliciter cum Romanis **nauali proelio congressus** et uictus'.[30]

consertoque navali proelio (c. 67): *Hist.* iv. 8. 6: '**conserto nauali proelio** Carthaginenses in fugam uersi'.[31]

temporis successu (c. 81): *Hist.* ii. 7. 1: 'idem Cyrus proximi **temporis successu**'.[32]

multis opibus refertam (c. 91): *Hist.* ii. 11. 3: 'regiis **opibus referta**'.[33]

Cassiodorus

Of the various patristic commentaries which framed the exegetical thought of the early Middle Ages, the *Expositio psalmorum* by Cassiodorus (d. *c.* 580) was probably the most important text for aiding understanding of the Psalms. It survives in hundreds of manuscripts, and was studied in Anglo-Saxon England from the time of Archbishop Theodore onwards.

omnia praesentis vitae suae impedimenta et dispendia (c. 25): *Expositio psalmorum* [Ps. cii]: '**impedimenta** aeternae **uitae**'.[34]

---

[29] Ed. Zangemeister, 98–9, 222, 329, 360, 387. The word *copiae* (and hence phrases like *pars copiarum*, etc.) was frequently used by Roman historians to describe a military force (or part of it), and hence is frequently attested in, for example, Livy (30×), Sallust, Caesar, Curtius Rufus and Justinus. But since there is conclusive evidence that Asser had read Orosius, he is the most likely source for Asser's use of the phrase (though Justinus cannot be ruled out). Cf. also Bede, *HE* IV 26: 'fugam hostibus, in angustias inaccessorum montium, et cum maxima parte copiarum quas secum adduxerat extinctus' (eds Colgrave and Mynors, p. 428). On Asser's probable knowledge of the *Historia ecclesiastica*, see below.

[30] Ed. Zangemeister, 227.

[31] Ibid., 228. The ultimate source for the formulation is probably Vergil, *Aen.* ii. 397–8 ('per caecam congressi proelia noctem/conserimus'); but the configuration of the three words shows unambiguously that Orosius was Asser's source for this phrase (the statement about Asser's knowledge of Vergil in Keynes and Lapidge, *Alfred*, 221, n. 104 thus needs to be corrected).

[32] Ed. Zangemeister, 98. The phrase also occurs in Justinus, *Epitome* i. 8 (see above), a source which Asser may also have known.

[33] Ed. Zangemeister, 108.

[34] *Expositio psalmorum LXXI–CXL*, ed. M. Adriaen, CCSL 98 (Turnhout, 1958), 915. The phrase *vitae ... dispendia* may derive from Christian–Latin poetry: cf. Paulinus of Nola, *Carm.* xxi. 510 ('construis in pretium vitae dispendia terrae') and Dracontius, *De laudibus Dei* iii. 141 ('temporis exigui si sint dispendia vitae').

adunatis viribus (cc. 27, 36, 69): ibid. [Ps. cii]: 'ut harmonia fideli laus Domini **adunatis uiribus** assonaret'.[35]

toto cordis affectu (c. 99): ibid. [Ps. lxi]: 'ut **toto cordis affectu** sperare debeat semper in Domino'; [Ps. lxxiii]: '**toto cordis affectu** clamare noscuntur'.[36]

mirabili dispensatione (c. 101): ibid. [Ps. xxx]: 'hominumque corda pro sua **mirabili dispensatione** conuertere'; [Ps. lvi]: 'ut **dispensatione mirabili** faceret eximium'.[37]

Dei fretus misericordia (c. 103): ibid. [Ps. xxii]: 'diuina **misericordia fretus**'.[38]

Gregory the Great

Gregory the Great, who was pope from 590 to 604, was regarded from the time of Bede onwards (if not before) as the progenitor of the English Church, and his writings were studied devotedly throughout the Anglo-Saxon period. Asser, for example, quotes verbatim from Gregory's *Regula pastoralis* in c. 102 of his *Vita Ælfredi* (a work which he helped King Alfred to translate). But he no doubt knew other writings by Gregory. Two striking verbal parallels indicate that he was familiar with Gregory's *Dialogi*, a work which was translated at Alfred's request by the Mercian bishop Wærferth.[39]

a primaevo iuventutis suae flore (c. 16; cf. c. 74): *Dialogi* i, prol. 2: 'mihi **a primaeuo iuuentutis flore** amicitiis familiariter obstrictus'.[40]

pro utilitate animae suae (c. 16): *Dialogi* iv. 31: 'et mecum colloqui de **animae utilitate** consueverat'.[41]

By the same token, various verbal parallels indicate that Asser was familiar with Gregory's longest work, the *Moralia in Iob*.[42]

---

[35] CCSL 98, 914.

[36] *Expositio psalmorum I–LXX*, ed. M. Adriaen, CCSL 97 (Turnhout, 1958), 542; CCSL 98, 684.

[37] CCSL 97, 268, 512.

[38] Ibid., 97, 212.

[39] Asser refers explicitly to the translation by Wærferth in his *Vita Ælfredi*, c. 77 (trans. Keynes and Lapidge, *Alfred*, 92); the OE text itself bears no indication of authorship. For helpful discussion, see M. Godden, 'Wærferth and King Alfred: the fate of the Old English *Dialogues*', in *Alfred the Wise*, eds J. Roberts, J. L. Nelson and M. Godden (1997), 35–51.

[40] Ed. A. de Vogüé, SC 260 (Paris 1979), 10; the phrase is ultimately from Vergil, *Aen*. vii. 162 ('et primaevo flore iuventus').

[41] Ed. A. de Vogüé, SC 265 (Paris 1980), 104.

[42] Ed. M. Adriaen, books 1–10, CCSL 143 (Turnhout, 1979); books 11–22, CCSL 143A

eandem pestiferam tabem post se submitteret (c. 13): *Moralia in Iob* v. 7. 12: 'ne **pestifera tabe**s putredinis sub boni specie lateat coloris'.[43]

in magna tribulatione (c. 53): *Moralia in Iob* xxvi. 45. 82: 'sed tamen sine **magna tribulatione** non agitur'.[44]

viriliter pugnavere (c. 69): *Moralia in Iob* xvii. 16. 22: 'qui contra hanc **uiriliter pugna**nt'.[45]

arx munitissima (c. 92): *Moralia in Iob* xvii. 16. 22: 'simplicitas cordis **arx munitissima**'.[46]

divitiarum abundantia (c. 93): *Moralia in Iob* xxxi. 47. 96: 'altitudines autem terrae sunt, lucra rerum, blandimenta subditorum, **diuitiarum abundantia**'.[47]

Miscellaneous patristic sources

There are various phrases and formulations in Asser which occur uniquely in one of the following patristic sources. In all these cases one would need corroborating evidence of some kind to be certain that the work was known, or could have been known, to Asser. What has to be weighed in each case is the fact that the particular phrase occurs only in Asser and in the individual patristic text. The texts in question are: Augustine, *De quantitate animae*; Quodvultdeus, *Sermo .ii. de symbolo*; Arnobius Iunior, *Commentarius in psalmos*; and Julianus Pomerius, *De vita contemplativa*.

(Turnhout, 1979); books 23–35, CCSL 143B (Turnhout, 1985). Scharer ('The writing of history', pp. 188–9) adduces suggestive evidence for thinking that Asser may have known the *Moralia*; the parallels cited here help to strengthen his case. It is interesting to note, therefore, that a surviving copy of the *Moralia*, now Oxford, Bodleian Library, Bodley 310, fols 1–154, was written in eastern France in the second half of the ninth century, and was very possibly in England before 1100; this information opens the possibility that Bodley 310 was a manuscript brought to England by either Grimbald or John the Old Saxon, and it therefore deserves investigation for signs of Anglo-Saxon use.

[43] CCSL 143, 226.

[44] Ibid., 143B, 1328.

[45] Ibid., 143A, 865. Cf., however, Paulus Diaconus, *Historia Langobardorum* vi. 54, ed. G. Waitz, MGH Scriptores Rerum Langobardicarum 1 (Hanover 1878), 184: 'Peredeo viriliter pugnans occubuit'. Paulus Diaconus presumably took the formulation from Gregory; for evidence that Asser had read the *Historia Langobardorum*, see below.

[46] The phrase occurs as a rubric in some manuscripts of the *Moralia* (see Migne, *PL* 75, 1007), but not those which serve as the basis for the edition printed in CCSL.

[47] CCSL 143B, 1617.

tantillo tempore (c. 12): cf. Augustine, *De quantitate animae*, c. 22 [39]: 'creuisse illum **tantillo tempore**'.[48]

ad desideratum ac tutum patriae suae portum … perducere contendit (c. 91): cf. Quodvultdeus, *Sermo .ii. de symbolo*, c. 2: 'peruium iter carinae suscipiens, motu congruo, flatu uentorum, dirigens gressus, ut ad **portum desideratum … perducam**'.[49]

ut Iudaico more dominum suum dolo circumvenirent (c. 96): cf. Arnobius Iunior, *Commentarius in psalmos* [Ps. cxlviii]: 'denique dum constat, quod filii Abrahae essent hi qui **Dominum** nostrum Iesum arte se putabant et **dolo circumuenire**'.[50]

pulchritudine principalis litterae illius libri illectus (c. 23): cf. Julianus Pomerius, *De vita contemplativa* iii. 17: 'ac **pulchritudine** virtutis **illectus**'.[51]

Aldhelm

Asser's knowledge of Aldhelm's writings, at least of the massive prose *De virginitate*, is certain from the manner in which he amplified the mention of the *apis prudentissima* (c. 76) – a phrase and topos which he took from the *Vita S.*

---

[48] Ed. W. Hörmann, CSEL 89 (Vienna, 1986), 180. It should be noted that this work was *not* known to Bede, according to the estimate of M. L. W. Laistner, 'The library of the Venerable Bede', in *Bede, his Life, Times and Writings*, ed. A. H. Thompson (1935), 237–66, and no other Anglo-Saxon author appears to have known it: there is no surviving Anglo-Saxon manuscript of the work, and it is not mentioned in any surviving Anglo-Saxon booklist. Indeed Alcuin at one point states specifically in his treatise *De animae ratione*, c. 13, that he has never seen the work (PL ci. 645). This negative evidence has to be weighed against the one striking phrase in Asser which apparently occurs nowhere else but Augustine *De quantitate animae*.

[49] *Opera*, ed. R. Braun, CCSL 60 (Turnhout, 1976), 337. As far as I am aware, there is no evidence that the sermons of Quodvultdeus were ever known in Anglo-Saxon England.

[50] Ed. K.-D. Daur, CCSL 25 (Turnhout, 1990), 255. This psalm-commentary of Arnobius Iunior (fl. s. v) is not mentioned in any surviving Anglo-Saxon booklist, and no Anglo-Saxon manuscript survives (a fact which is not, perhaps, surprising, given that only three manuscripts of the work survive, all of them continental, two of the tenth century, one of the fifteenth: see Daur's edition, xviii). However, the work was certainly known to Bede, who quotes verbatim from it in *De temporum ratione*, c. 56, ed. C. W. Jones, CCSL 123B (Turnhout, 1977), 468; and see Laistner, 'The library of the Venerable Bede', 254, 263.

[51] Migne, *PL* 59, 500. On the early medieval circulation of this work, see M. L. W. Laistner, 'The influence during the middle ages of the treatise *De vita contemplativa* and its surviving manuscripts', in his *The Intellectual Heritage of the Early Middle Ages*, ed. C. G. Starr (New York, 1972), 40–56, at 53: 'In view of the popularity enjoyed by Pomerius' book on the continent during the ninth century, it is hard to believe that a copy did not reach England at that time; but, in the absence of definite evidence, it must remain an open question whether the book was available in any English library before the Norman Conquest.'

Antonii (see above) – in the florid manner of Aldhelm's prose *De virginitate* (c. 4):[52]

Asser: 'atque etiam tam devotam erga studium divinae sapientiae voluntatem eius cognoscens, **immensas** omnipotenti Deo **grates**, extensis **ad aethera** volis, tacitus quamvis, persolvi' (c. 88).

Aldhelm: 'scripta … suscipiens erectis **ad aethera** palmis **immensas** Christo pro sospitate vestra gratulabundus impendere **grates** curavi' (c. 1).[53]

This parallel is supported by the fact that at various points in his *Vita Ælfredi* Asser uses phrases which, to judge from the electronic databases, are unmistakably Aldhelmian:

mentis ingenium (c. 22): prose *De virginitate*, c. 4: 'vestrum, ni fallor, memoriale **mentis ingenium**'.[54]

sospite vita (c. 79): *Carmen de virginitate* 603 and 2337; cf. 1114, 1563 and 1974.

subnixis precibus (c. 89): prose *De virginitate* cc. 37 and 47;[55] *Carmen de virginitate* 1272, 1933 and 2031.

Bede

Because of their accessible style and clear exposition, the corpus of Bede's writings, including his great *Historia ecclesiastica gentis Anglorum*, was studied through England and continental Europe almost from the moment of their completion. Knowledge of the works of Bede would not be unusual in any Insular Latin author; Asser reveals familiarity with two Bedan works, the *Historia ecclesiastica* and the treatise *De temporum ratione*. Of these, the *Historia ecclesiastica* was translated into Old English in King Alfred's day,[56] and on historical grounds was very probably known to Asser;[57] several verbal parallels reinforce this probability.

docibilis memoriter retinebat (c. 22): *HE* IV 24: 'cuncta quae dormiens cantauerat, **memoriter retin**uit'.[58]

---

[52] As suggested in Keynes and Lapidge, *Alfred*, 53–4.

[53] MGH AA xv. 229.

[54] Ed. Ehwald, 232.

[55] Ibid., 281, 300.

[56] For an overview of the evidence for date and attribution of the OE Bede, see D. Whitelock, 'The Old English Bede', *PBA*, 48 (1962), 57–90.

[57] For the suggestion that Asser derived his knowledge of the site of London from Bede, *HE* ii. 3, see Keynes and Lapidge, *Alfred*, 231, n. 16.

[58] Eds Colgrave and Mynors, 416. Asser's words refer to the young Alfred's feats of memoriz-

bonis moribus instituere et literis imbuere (c. 76): *HE* IV 1: 'sacris **literis** diligenter **imbu**tus monasterialibus simul et ecclesiasicis disciplinis **institu**tus'.[59]

divino fultus adminiculo (c. 91): *HE* I 33: 'regio **fultus adminiculo**'.[60]

Bede's *De temporum ratione* was the most widely studied computistical manual of the early Middle Ages (it survives in some 250 manuscripts).[61] It is not surprising that Asser should have known it, as two striking parallels suggest:

omnia praesentis vitae curricula (c. 24): *De temporum ratione*, c. 2, '**omnia** mortalis **vitae curricula**'.[62]

aequali lance (c. 99): *De temporum ratione*, c. 6, '**aequali lance** lumen tenebrasque pendebat'.[63]

Paulus Diaconus

Paulus Diaconus, grammarian and historian and sometime member of Charlemagne's entourage, was a monk of Monte Cassino who was at work on his *Historia Langobardorum* at the time of his death in the 790s. Although unfinished, the *Historia Langobardorum* accomplished for the Langobards what Bede's *Historia ecclesiastica* had done for the English, by giving literary expression to a sense of national identity.[64] The work was widely popular and is preserved in nearly two hundred manuscripts. There is, however, no surviving manuscript of the work from Anglo-Saxon England, and no evidence to suggest that it was ever read in England before the Conquest.[65] Nevertheless, various phrases used by Asser are anticipated in Paulus Diaconus (esp. military terminology), and it is

---

ing Old English verse; Bede's refer to the story of Caedmon. Asser's verbal reminiscence is therefore probably intentional.

[59] Eds Colgrave and Mynors, 328.

[60] Ibid., 114.

[61] Interestingly, there are three manuscripts of the *De temporum ratione* written in ninth-century France which subsequently were owned in Anglo-Saxon England: London, British Library, Cotton Vespasian B. vi (Saint-Denis, s. ix$^{2/4}$); Royal 15. B. XIX, fols 36–78 (Rheims, s. ix$^{4/4}$); and Salisbury, Cathedral Library, 158 (France, s. ix^2 or ix/x). One or more of these manuscripts could have been brought to England by Grimbald or John the Old Saxon, and consulted by Asser at Alfred's court.

[62] CCSL 123B, 274.

[63] Ibid., 291.

[64] See discussion by W. Goffart, *The Narrators of Barbarian History (A.D. 550–800)* (Princeton, NJ, 1988), 329–431.

[65] There is a single manuscript dating from the second half of the eleventh century which was written at Mont Saint-Michel and subsequently owned by St Augustine's, Canterbury: London, British Library, Royal 13.A.XXII.

worth at least raising the question of whether Asser had knowledge of the *Historia Langobardorum*.

per fugam elapsi (c. 6): *Historia Langobardorum* iii. 29: 'Galli autem vehementer afflicti, etsi multi capti, plurimi tamen **per fugam elapsi**'.[66]

fugam arripiunt (c. 18): *Historia Langobardorum* iv. 37: 'statim ascensis equis, **fugam arripiunt**'.[67]

paratae ad bellum (c. 67): *Historia Langobardorum* i. 24: 'Langobardi econtra **parati ad bellum**'.[68]

stragesque populorum (c. 83): *Historia Langobardorum* v. 36: 'maximae **populorum** factae sunt **strages**'; v. 41: 'maxima **populorum** facta est **strages**'; vi. 35: 'multa **strages populorum**'.[69]

Conclusions

The above evidence suggests that Asser's reading was somewhat more extensive than has previously been suspected, although by comparison with Insular authors such as Aldhelm and Bede it could scarcely be described as vast. It is interesting to attempt to correlate this information with other evidence of scholarly activity at King Alfred's court. For example, Asser's knowledge of Gregory's *Dialogi* squares with the fact that this work was translated into English for King Alfred by Wærferth, and his knowledge of Bede's *Historia ecclesiastica* might also be relevant to the origin of the Old English Bede. The fact that Asser was familiar with the *Expositio psalmorum* of Cassiodorus, in combination with his arguable knowledge of the psalm-commentary of Arnobius Iunior, may be a reflection of the king's interest in the psalter and his work in translating the first fifty psalms; one can imagine Asser consulting both Cassiodorus and Arnobius in order to explain to the king interesting doctrinal points as the translation proceeded. On the other hand, although William of Malmesbury believed that Asser had assisted the king in translating Boethius' *De Consolatione Philosophiae*, the fact that no identifiable quotation or phrase from the work has been identified in the *Vita Ælfredi* may cast doubt on the reliability of William's statement.[70]

---

[66] Ed. Waitz, 108.

[67] Ibid., 129.

[68] Ibid., 62.

[69] Ibid., 156, 161, 176.

[70] It also weighs against the possibility that annotations in a tenth-century manuscript of the *De Consolatione Philosophiae* (now Vatican City, Biblioteca Apostolica Vaticana, lat. 3363) are in Asser's hand: see M. B. Parkes, 'A note on MS Vatican, Bibl. Apost., lat. 3363', in *Boethius: his Life, Thought and Influence*, ed. M. Gibson (1981), 425–7.

More interesting is the case of Orosius. The evidence presented above indicates unequivocally that Asser had studied Orosius. Janet Bately, in her masterly edition of the Old English Orosius, has suggested, on the basis of recurrent patterns of (mis)spelling of Latin proper names in the Old English text, that such spelling probably derives from dictation by a native Welsh speaker.[71] The production of the Old English Orosius is unambiguously associated with King Alfred, even though (on stylistic grounds) he is unlikely to be its author. Asser's familiarity with the Latin text, as witnessed in his *Vita Ælfredi*, helps to confirm the linguistic evidence adduced by Bately, namely that it was Asser who dictated the Old English translation of the Latin Orosius.[72]

Asser's familiarity with the Latin Orosius, and his involvement in its translation, raises a more difficult question: whether Asser was familiar with Orosius from his training in Wales – in which case the Orosius would constitute an illustration of the *rudimenta Sancti Degui* which Asser brought with him from Wales – or whether he first encountered the text at Alfred's court. Various evidence bears on this question. The text of Orosius was certainly available in late Roman Britain, since it was laid heavily under contribution by Gildas.[73] It subsequently entered Welsh scholarly tradition, to judge from the text of the scholastic colloquy known as *De raris fabulis*, a work which was evidently redacted in ninth-century Wales;[74] the author is describing a battle between the Welsh (*Britones*) and English (*Saxones*) in which God gave victory to the Welsh:

> et dedit Deus uictoriam Britonibus ideo quia humiles sunt necnon et
> pauperes et in Deo confiderunt et confessi sunt et corpus Christi
> acceperunt antequam metredaticum uel duellum inierant.[75]

The exceedingly rare noun *metredaticum*, glossed as *duellum* (an archaic spelling of *bellum*), derives from an adjectival form of the name Mithridates, the Pontic general who was finally destroyed by Pompey; it results from a misunderstanding of a lemma in Orosius: 'Sulla cui post consulatum Mithridaticum

---

[71] *Orosius*, ed. Bately, cxiv: 'It seems likely, therefore, that a large number of the variant spellings of proper names in Or. [the Old English Orosius] are the result of dictation, and that quite possibly dictation by either a Welshman or an Englishman trained in Latin pronunciation by a Welshman' (in her n. 5, however, she presents additional evidence for rejecting the latter possibility).

[72] It should also be recalled that there are close verbal parallels between the OE Orosius and a version of the *Anglo-Saxon Chronicle* (see *Orosius*, ed. Bately, lxxxiii–lxxxvi); that Asser based the earlier part of his *Vita Ælfredi* (up to c. 86) on the Anglo-Saxon Chronicle; and that the earliest recension of the Anglo-Saxon Chronicle was almost certainly produced under Alfred's patronage.

[73] N. Wright, 'Did Gildas read Orosius?', *Cambridge Medieval Celtic Studies*, 9 (Summer 1985), 31–42.

[74] *Early Scholastic Colloquies*, ed. W. H. Stevenson (1929), 1–11. For the various phases of redaction of *De raris fabulis*, see Lapidge, 'Latin learning in Dark Age Wales', 94–7.

[75] *Early Scholastic Colloquies*, 9; cf. 10: 'Et iterum audiuimus uastationes magnas et metridatica uel duellia.'

bellum obuenerat.'[76] If Orosius was studied in Welsh schools (as the misunderstood lemma embedded in *De raris fabulis* seems to imply), then Asser may well
have known the text before he came to England.

How many other such texts had Asser studied in Wales? Because our
knowledge of Dark Age Welsh schools is so severely limited, it is not possible to
answer this question satisfactorily, but one text deserves mention. In c. 88 of his
Vita Ælfredi, Asser includes the following quotation: 'sicut scriptum est, "super
modicum fundamentum aedificat iustus et paulatim ad maiora defluit"'.[77] Anton
Scharer[78] was the first to identify the source of this quotation in the anonymous
Proverbia grecorum, a set of maxims (having no Greek source, in spite of the
title) of probable seventh-century Irish origin.[79] Because many of the *Proverbia
grecorum* were incorporated by Sedulius Scottus into his *Collectaneum
miscellaneum*, and because there are structural similarities between Asser's *Vita
Ælfredi* and another work of Sedulius which draws on the *Proverbia grecorum*
(namely the *Liber de rectoribus Christianis*), Scharer supposed, reasonably
enough, that Asser knew the *Proverbia grecorum* by way of Sedulius Scottus.[80]
However, it is equally possible that Asser knew the text from his schooling in
Wales, because there is independent evidence that the *Proverbia grecorum* were
available in ninth-century Wales. In the aforementioned colloquy *De raris fabulis*,
the master at one point assures the student that he will be able to explain any
difficulties in the book which they are to study together:

> Deduc mihi huc, ut ostendam tibi diligenter, quia nil obscurum erit in
> illo libro, Deo adiuuante, si ante faciem meam peruenerit, quia,
> 'Facies sapientis manifestat ignota uel obscura'.[81]

The quotation here is from the *Proverbia grecorum*.[82] Accordingly, if the
Proverbia grecorum were known to the ninth-century Welsh redactor of *De raris
fabulis*, they might equally have been known to Asser from his schooling at St
David's, in which case there is no need to hypothesize Sedulius Scottus as an
intermediary.

It is unfortunate that so little is known of Latin learning in Dark Age
Wales: given the paucity of surviving manuscripts from Welsh scriptoria and of
Latin writings by Welsh scholars, it is not possible to explore Asser's intellectual

---

[76] *Hist.* vi. 2. 5 (CSEL v. 357). The lemma *Mithridaticum bellum* was excerpted from the text
by a glossator, and subsequently misunderstood as lemma + gloss, in other words that *bellum* was
an explanation of the enticing 'noun' *mithridaticum*, spelt *metredaticum*.

[77] Ed. Stevenson, 74; trans. Keynes and Lapidge, *Alfred*, 100.

[78] 'The writing of history', 198.

[79] D. Simpson, 'The "Proverbia Grecorum"', *Traditio*, 43 (1987), 1–22; the maxim quoted by
Asser is at 11.

[80] 'The writing of history', 197.

[81] *Early Scholastic Colloquies*, 3.

[82] Simpson, 'The "Proverbia Grecorum"', 11: 'Facies sapientis manifestat ignota; facies stulti
caliginem super scientiam inducit.'

background, save to say that he may have owed his knowledge of two texts –
Orosius and the *Proverbia grecorum* – to his training in Wales, and that these
texts formed part of the *rudimenta Sancti Degui* which he brought to Alfred's
court. How many other texts were involved cannot be determined. What is
important to stress, however, is that the range of Asser's reading was much
greater than has previously been suspected.

Appendix: The Authenticity of Asser

It will be clear from the foregoing discussion that the range of reading which may be attributed to Asser is entirely consonant with the picture of a bishop trained at St David's who subsequently had access to books at the palace school of King Alfred. The point deserves to be stressed in light of the recent contention by A. P. Smyth[83] that the *Vita Ælfredi* is not an authentic work by the ninth-century Welsh bishop, but rather a forgery perpetrated by a late tenth-/early eleventh-century monk at Ramsey, presumptively Byrhtferth, the corpus of whose Latin writings were produced at Ramsey between *c*. 990 and *c*. 1016.[84] Like many other scholars, I regard Smyth's case for forgery as preposterous,[85] and adduced arguments to that effect in a newspaper review published very soon after the book's appearance;[86] however, because of the ephemeral nature of newspapers, I have thought it appropriate to restate the arguments here in a more permanent form.

Smyth's argument is two-pronged. He alleges, first, that the *Vita Ælfredi* betrays 'heavy indebtedness' (p. 302) to a *vita* of the layman Gerald of Aurillac, written *c*. 940 by Odo of Cluny, and hence must, on these grounds alone, have been composed after the death of Asser in 909; and, second, the many stylistic similarities which the *Vita Ælfredi* shares with Byrhtferth's other Latin writings imply that he must be its author–forger. Neither of these arguments is deployed rigorously and neither can be sustained. On the question of whether the *Vita Ælfredi* is indebted to the work of Odo, Smyth advances a list of the most general similarities: Odo's *Vita Geraldi* treats the life of a layman, Asser's King Alfred was a layman; Gerald had an illness (leprosy), so did Asser's King Alfred (piles); Gerald spent much time in prayer, so did Asser's King Alfred; Gerald made wax candles for votive purposes, Asser's King Alfred made a large wax candle in order to measure time; and so on. At no point does Smyth quote so much as a single Latin phrase or sentence to illustrate a verbal link between Odo and Asser. And how was Byrhtferth the forger supposed to have known Odo's *Vita Geraldi*? Smyth makes no mention of the manuscript transmission of the work (in fact it is preserved solely in four French manuscripts; there is no English manuscript, and no evidence that it was ever known in England); in-

---

[83] Smyth, *Alfred.*

[84] For the corpus of Byrhtferth's writings, as it is now known, see *Byrhtferth's Enchiridion*, eds P. S. Baker and M. Lapidge, EETS SS. 15 (1995), xxv–xxxiv. Note that, among these writings, is a historical miscellany which Byrhtferth probably entitled *Historia regum*, Part IV of which contains extensive extracts from Asser's *Vita Ælfredi*. So there is no doubt that Byrhtferth was familiar with Asser's work; the question is whether he forged it.

[85] Smyth's historical arguments were demolished comprehensively by S. Keynes, 'On the authenticity of Asser's *Life of King Alfred*', *JEccH*, 47 (1996), 529–51; for further demolition, see the review of Smyth's book by D. N. Dumville in *Cambrian Medieval Celtic Studies*, 31 (Summer 1996), 90–93. There is a balanced assessment of the question in Abels, *Alfred*, 318–26.

[86] *The Times Higher Education Supplement*, 8 March 1996, 20.

stead, he hypothesizes that Odo *could* have deposited a copy of the *Vita Geraldi* at Fleury, and that Abbo of Fleury, Byrhtferth's teacher, *could* have brought it to England with him in 985. If so, the manuscript has left no trace either at Fleury or in England (whereas there are abundant traces in later English manuscripts of works demonstrably brought by Abbo from Fleury, such as Helperic's *De computo*[87]). In the absence of a demonstrable verbal link between Odo and Asser, such hypotheses are otiose, and the argument that the *Vita Ælfredi* depends on Odo's work remains unproven.

Smyth's second line of argument is equally poorly handled. He argues that the Latin style of the *Vita Ælfredi* is indistinguishable from that of Byrhtferth: therefore Byrhtferth was its author. Smyth points, for example, to the large number of polysyllabic adverbs ending in *-iter* which are found in Byrhtferth and the *Vita Ælfredi*, and duly lists these in an appendix (pp. 699–702). The difficulty with Smyth's list, however, is that it is not sufficiently discriminating; thus, for example, he includes conjunctions such as *qualiter* and the noun *arbiter* (!). It is true that the words *inedicibiliter* or *immarcescibiliter* found in Byrhtferth – but not in the *Vita Ælfredi* – are rare; whereas the words which make up the bulk of Smyth's list, such as *aequaliter*, *breuiter*, *feliciter* and *pariter*, are common coin, and their occurrence in any Latin work cannot be used as a criterion of authorship. The same may be said of Smyth's other vocabulary tests. He points to various vocabulary which he regards as rare, including agentive nouns in *-or* such as *rector*, superlative adjectives such as *piissimus*, diminutives such as *seruulus*, and the negative *immo*. But none of these words is unusual or distinctive. Worse yet, apparent ignorance of Latin leads him to regard as similarities features that are manifest differences. He points to the repeated use of the phrase *die noctuque* in the *Vita Ælfredi*, and compares it to phrases such as *diebus et noctibus* in Byrhtferth. The form *noctu* is an archaic ablative of *noctus* (contrast *nox* and *nocte*), and the author of the *Vita Ælfredi* was evidently so pleased with this archaism that he repeated it eleven times. Byrhtferth never once uses *noctu*, always *nocte* or *noctibus*.

But the argument against Byrhtferth's alleged authorship of the *Vita Ælfredi* is not that Smyth has handled the putative stylistic similarities carelessly and inconclusively, but rather that he has not attended sufficiently to palpable differences between the works, as the example *noctu/nocte* illustrates. In his genuine writings, Byrhtferth used a large number of personalized clichés: *luce clarius*, *mente sagaci*, *aureus sol*, *uaga Lucina*, *Romuleae sedes* for Rome, and so on. None of these is found in the *Vita Ælfredi*. On the other hand, the author of the *Vita Ælfredi* used a number of his own clichés: *die noctuque*, *adunatis uiribus*, *suatim utens*, *uiam uniuersitatis adiens*. None of these is used by Byrhtferth. Throughout his writings Byrhtferth shows an inability to master the use of the

---

[87] See P. McGurk, '*Computus Helperici*: its transmission in England in the eleventh and twelfth centuries', *Medium Aevum*, 43 (1974), 1–5.

passive infinitive (a situation compounded by the nature of deponent verbs), so that he normally writes *legi* where *legere* is required, and vice versa. No such confusion is found in the *Vita Ælfredi*, whose author competently distinguishes active from passive infinitives throughout. The author of the *Vita Ælfredi* had a penchant for stringing together ablative absolute phrases, whereas Byrhtferth avoids such usage. In fact the difference between the styles can clearly be seen in those passages of Asser which (on my view of the evidence) Byrhtferth copied into his historical miscellany, where Asser's phrase *Romam perrexit* is characteristically recast by Byrhtferth as *Romuleas adire sedes coepit*. The distinction between the two styles could scarcely be clearer.

Evidence against Smyth's case is also provided by the sources drawn on by the two authors. It is true that there is some inevitable overlap: both authors quote from the *Carmen paschale* of Caelius Sedulius, and both knew Aldhelm's prose *De virginitate* and Bede's *Historia ecclesiastica* and *De temporum ratione*, as well as Cassiodorus, *Expositio psalmorum* and Gregory's *Dialogi* and *Moralia in Iob*. But these texts were staple reading in Insular schools, and no argument can be based on such knowledge. More striking is the fact that Byrhtferth quotes from a large number of school texts – the *Disticha Catonis*, the *Epigrammata* of Prosper of Aquitaine, the *Historia apostolica* of Arator, Macrobius's Commentary on the Dream of Scipio – which are unknown to Asser. On the other hand, Asser quotes (as we have seen) from the *Proverbia grecorum*, a text which was known in ninth-century Wales but which, to the best of my knowledge, was unknown in Anglo-Saxon England. On two occasions in the *Vita Ælfredi* the Bible is cited in the pre-Jerome version known as *Vetus Latina* or 'Old Latin', a version which had, in England at least, been replaced by Jerome's Vulgate no later than the eighth century. In Wales, however, the Old Latin Bible was used down to the end of the eleventh century.[88] The Old Latin citations in the *Vita Ælfredi* are wholly consonant with what we know of ninth-century Cambro-Latin culture, and wholly in contradiction to the (thoroughly well-attested) use of Jerome's Vulgate in tenth-century England. Byrhtferth, for example, quotes the Bible some 250 times, always in the Vulgate version. Again, the contrast between Asser and Byrhtferth could not be more stark.

Smyth's argument fails because he does not have sufficient command of Latin grammar, or sufficient knowledge of Latin style, to conduct it properly. I have recently had occasion to comment on the dangers which lie in store for medieval historians who do not have sufficient knowledge of Latin to deal competently with primary sources.[89] Smyth's book on Alfred presents a terrifying demonstration of these dangers. It is not simply that he is unable to handle stylistic evidence competently, as I have already indicated. On many occasions when he quotes Latin *in extenso*, his quotations contain error, often of a serious

---

[88] See Lapidge, 'Latin learning in Dark Age Wales', 92–4.

[89] M. Lapidge, 'The edition of medieval Latin texts in the English-speaking world', *Sacris Erudiri*, 38 (1998–9), 199–220, at 213–15.

nature: *iterpretatur* (p. 162), *glaucomate caecicatis* (p. 205), *lepprum aut caccitatem* (p. 209), *utriusque linguae libri Latini scilicet et Saxonicae* (p. 220), *ad monachium habitum* (p. 261), *nec non et nonagesimo supsedimus* (p. 292), *gentem illam devantans dominio Burgredi subdit* (p. 363), and so on. Errors such as these undermine any confidence in his ability to read and interpret primary Latin sources, and indeed Smyth's comments often lead one to suspect that he has never so much as glanced at the primary sources on which he bases his argument: he twice, for example, refers to the *Encomium Emmae reginae* as 'a praise poem on Emma' (pp. 162, 164). It is for reasons such as these that Smyth's case against the authenticity of Asser's *Vita Ælfredi* cannot be sustained.

Chapter 3

Alfredian arithmetic –
Asserian architectonics

David Howlett

In two earlier books I tried to demonstrate from internal evidence alone that the *Vita Ælfredi Regis* is an integrated authentic work of architectonic genius, published by Asser of Saint David's in AD 893.[1] Here I present from earlier books an outline that illustrates the structure of the complete work.

Part I

3	A	I	(1)	Genealogy
	B	II	(2)	Mother's ancestry
	C	III	(3.1–10.9)	Chiastic annals 851–55, Alfred's royal anointing by the pope at the crux
6	D1	IV	(11.1–6)	Donation of Æthelwulf
	2	V	(11.6–10)	Alfred's journey to Rome
	3	VI	(11.10–13.8)	Æthelwulf's marriage to Judith and Æthelbald's usurpation
	3′	VII	(13.8–15.26)	Æthelwulf's policy toward Judith and Eadburh's scandal
	2′	VIII	(16.1–12)	Æthelwulf's will after returning from Rome
	1′	IX	(16.12–38)	Æthelwulf's benefaction
9	E	X	(17)	Æthelbald's uncanonical marriage to Judith
	F	XI	(18.1–19.5)	Æthelbald's and Æthelbryht's burials at Sherborne
	G	XII	(20)	The Danes in Kent (a chiasmus)
	H	XIII	(21.1–9)	The Danes' arrival in East Anglia
	I	XIV	(21.9–25.17)	Echo of Einhard, naval imagery, Alfred and the poetry manuscript

---

[1] D. Howlett, *The Celtic Latin Tradition of Biblical Style* (Dublin, 1995), 273–333; *British Books in Biblical Style* (Dublin, 1997), 365–445.

	H′	XV	(26)	The Danes' departure from East Anglia
	G′	XVI	(27)	The Danes in Northumbria (chiasmus and parallelism)
	F′	XVII	(28)	Ealhstan's burial at Sherborne
	E′	XVIII	(29.1–6)	Alfred's canonical marriage to Ealhswith
6	D′1	XIX	(29.6–12)	Alfred's mother-in-law Eadburh
	2	XX	(30.1–46.12)	Victory at Ashdown
	3	XXI	(46.12–51.4)	Naval victory of 875
	2′	XXII	(52.1–58.5)	Victory at Countisbury
	3′	XXIII	(59.1–68.9)	Naval victory of 882
	1′	XXIV	(68.9–70.11)	Alfred's stepmother Judith
3	C′	XXV	(71)	Alfred's relationship with the pope
	B′	XXVI	(72)	The Danes in East Anglia, echo of Einhard, naval imagery, Alfred's wife
	A′	XXVII	(75.1–15)	Alfred's descendants

Part II

	A	XXVIII	(75.16–31)	Education of children at the court school
9	B1	XXIX	(76.1–9)	Alfred's construction amidst difficulties
	2	XXX	(76.9–77.24)	Love of wisdom, summoning of scholars to the court, translation into Old English, comparison of Alfred with Solomon and the most prudent bee
	3	XXXI	(77.22–26)	Alfred's inability to read Latin
	4	XXXII	(78)	Summoning of continental scholars Grimbald and John
	5	XXXIII	(79–81)	Summoning of Asser
	4′	XXXIV	(82–86)	Continental history, annals 886–7
	3′	XXXV	(87)	Alfred's ability to read and translate Latin
	2′	XXXVI	(88.1–90.12)	Love of wisdom, learning with the king's scholar, translation into Old English, comparison of Alfred with the Repentant Thief and the most fertile bee
	1′	XXXVII	(91.1–28)	Alfred's construction amidst difficulties

	C	XXXVIII	(91.28–35)	Naval imagery
6	B'1	XXXIX	(91.36–72)	Alfred's dealings with his civil servants
	2	XL	(92–98)	Alfred's monastic foundations
	3	XLI	(99.4–104.13)	Alfred as administrator
	3'	XLII	(104.13–36)	Alfred as inventor
	2'	XLIII	(105.1–10)	Alfred as defender of the poor
	1'	XLIV	(105.10–106.46)	Alfred's dealings with his civil servants
	A'	XLV	(106.46–63)	Education of older men in Alfred's service

Having paid insufficient attention to the autobiographical narrative that relates Alfred's summoning of Asser to his service, I analysed that passage in a third book as a composition of thirty-three sentences, coincident with its position as chapter XXXIII, and 885 words, coincident with the year of the events recorded, AD 885.[2]

Here I consider the sections of the *Life* labelled B'3–3', chapters XLI–XLII (99.1–104.36) on Alfred as administrator and inventor. Divisions of the account into parts and sentences numbered on the left are mine, putatively Asser's. I have marked the rhythms of the cursus.

Pars I

1 His ita definitis solito suo more intra semet ipsum cogitabat quid adhuc addere potuisset quod plus placeret ad piam méditatiónem:

non inaniter incepta utiliter inuenta utílius seruáta est.

Pars II

2 Nam iam dudum in lege scriptum audierat Dominum decimam sibi multipliciter redditurum promisisse atque fideliter seruasse decimamque sibi multipliciter redditúrum fuísse.

3 Hoc exemplo instigatus et antecessorum morem uolens transcendere dimidiam seruitii sui partem diurni scilicet et nocturni temporis nec non etiam dimidiam partem omnium diuitiarum quae annualiter ad eum cum iustitia

Part I

1 With these things so defined, in his own habitual custom he used to think within himself what further he could add that would conduce more to holy meditation:
not emptily conceived, it was usefully come upon, more usefully observed.

Part II

2 For long ago he had heard written in the Law that the Lord had promised Himself bound to give back multiply a tenth [given] to Himself, and faithfully observed that He would be bound to give back multiply a tenth [given] to Himself.

3 Driven on by this example and wishing to ascend beyond the custom of [his] ancestors, a half part of his own service, understand of diurnal and nocturnal time, and also a half part of all the riches which had been accustomed to come through to him,

---

[2] D. Howlett, *Cambro-Latin Compositions: Their Competence and Craftsmanship* (Dublin, 1998), 84–94.

moderanter acquisitae peruenire consueuerant Deo deuote et fideliter toto cordis affectu pius meditator se datúrum spopóndit.

acquired annually by measure with justice, the pious meditator promised himself bound to give devotedly and faithfully with the whole affection of [his] heart.

4 Quod et quantum potest humana discretio discernere et seruare subtiliter ac sapienter adimplére stúduit.

4 Which also as far as human discretion can discern and observe he was attentive subtly and wisely to fulfil.

5 Sed ut solito suo more cautus euitaret quod in alio diuinae scripturae lóco caútum est,

5 But that in his own habitual custom he, cautious, might avoid what in another place of divine scripture has been cautioned against,

Si recte offeras recte autem non diuidas peccas,

If you offer rightly, but you do not divide rightly, you sin,

quod Deo libenter deuouerat quo modo recte diuidere pósset cogitáuit,

he thought in what manner he could rightly divide what he had freely vowed to God,

et ut dixit Salomon, Cor regis in manu Domini, íd est consílium.

and as Solomon said, The heart of the king, that is counsel, [is] in the hand of the Lord.

6 Consilio diuinitus inuento omnium uniuscuiusque anni censuum successum bifarie primitus ministros suos diuidere aequali lánce imperáuit.

6 With counsel divinely come upon he commanded his own ministers first to divide in two parts with equal balance the revenue of all taxes of each year.

Pars III

Part III

7 His ita diuisis partem primam saecularibus negotiis pertinere addixit quam etiam in tribus partibus sequestrari praecepit cuius primam diuisionis partem suis bellatoribus annualiter largiebatur item suis ministris nobilibus qui in curto regio uicissim commorabantur in pluribus ministrantes mínistériis.

7 With these things so divided, he assigned to pertain to secular business the first part, which he also ordered to be sequestrated in three parts, the first part of which division he generously bestowed annually on his own warriors, in the same way to his own noble ministers, who used to dwell together by turns in the royal court ministering in many ministries.

8 Ita enim ordinabiliter agebatur regalis

8 For the royal household was so arranged by order

familiaritas tribus omni tempore uicíssitudínibus in tribus namque cohortibus praefati regis satellites prudentissime díuidebántur ita ut prima cohors uno mense in curto regio die noctuque administrans cómmorarétur

menseque finito et adueniente alia cohorte prima dómum redíbat

et ibi duobus propriis quiuis necessitatibus studens commorabátur ménsibus.

9 Secunda itaque cohors mense peracto adueniente tertia domum redibat ut ibi duobus commorarétur ménsibus.

10 Sed et illa finito unius mensis ministerio et adueniente prima cohorte domum redibat ibidem commoratura duóbus ménsibus.

11 Et hoc ordine omnibus uitae praesentis temporibus talium uicissitudinum in regali curto rotatur ádministrátio.

Pars IIII

12 Talibus itaque primam de tribus praedictis partibus partem unicuique tamen secundum propriam dignitatem et etiam secundum proprium ministerium lárgiebátur.

13 Secundam autem operatoribus quos ex multis gentibus collectos et comparatos propemodum innumerabiles habebat in omni terreno aedifício edóctos.

at every time in three successions,
for the adherents of the aforesaid king were divided most prudently in three cohorts
so that the first cohort would dwell together for one month ministering in the royal court by day and by night,
and with the month finished and another cohort coming, the first used to go back home
so that it would dwell together there for two months being attentive to their own proper needs.

9 And so the second cohort, with a month run through, a third coming, used to go back home and it would dwell together there for two months.

10 But that one also, with the ministry of one month finished and the first cohort coming, used to go back home bound to dwell together at the very place for two months.

11 And in this order in all times of the present life the administration of such successions is rotated in the royal court.

Part IIII

12 And so to such men the first part from the three aforesaid parts he generously bestowed on each, but according to his proper dignity and also according to his proper ministry.

13 The second, however, on the workers, almost innumerable, whom he had collected and got together from many peoples, instructed in every earthly art of building.

14 Tertiam autem eiusdem partem aduenis ex omni gente ad eum aduenientibus longe propeque positis et pecuniam ab illo exigentibus etiam et non exigentibus unicuique secundum propriam dignitatem mirabili dispensatione laudabiliter et sicut scriptum est, 'Hilarem datorem diligit Deus', hiláriter impendébat.

14 The third part of this, however, to the comers from every people coming to him, placed from far away and near, both asking from him and also not asking, to each according to his proper dignity with wondrous dispensation in praiseworthy manner and as it is written, 'God loves a cheerful giver', cheerfully he weighed out money.

15 Secundam uero partem omnium diuitiarum suarum quae annualiter ad eum ex omni censu perueniebant et in fisco reputabantur sicut iam paulo ante commemorauimus plena uoluntate Déo deuóuit et in quatuor partibus aequis etiam curiose suos ministros illam diuidere imperauit ea conditione ut prima pars illius diuisionis pauperibus uniuscuiusque gentis qui ad eum ueniebant discretissime érogarétur.

15 The second part of all his own riches, in truth, which used to come through to him from every tax and were reckoned in the treasury, just as a little before now we have called to mind, with a full will he vowed to God, and in four equal parts he commanded his own ministers carefully to divide that on that condition that the first part of that division should be disbursed most discreetly to the poor men of every people who came to him.

16 Memorabat etiam in hoc quantum humana discretio custodire poterat illius sancti papae Gregorii obseruandam esse sententiam qua discretam mentionem diuidendae elemosinae ita dícens agébat, Nec paruum cui multum nec multum cui paruum nec nihil cui aliquid nec aliquid cui nihil.

16 He used to call to mind also as far in this respect as human discretion could guard the sentence of that holy pope Gregory bound to be observed, in which he made discreet mention of alms to be divided, saying thus, Neither little to whom much nor much to whom little nor nothing to whom something nor something to whom nothing.

17 Secundam autem duobus monasteriis quae ipse fieri imperauerat et seruientibus in his Deo de quibus paulo ante latius dísserúimus.

17 The second, however, to two monasteries which he himself had commanded to be made and to those serving God in them, about whom we have discoursed

18 Tertiam scholae quam ex multis suae propriae gentis nobilibus et etiam pueris ignobilibus studiosissime cóngregáuerat.

19 Quartam circum finitimis in omni Saxonia et Mercia monasteriis et etiam quibusdam annis per uices in Brittannia et Cornubia, Gallia, Armorica, Northanhymbris, et aliquando etiam in Hibernia ecclesiis et seruis Dei inhabitantibus secundum possibilitatem suam aut ante distribuit aut sequenti tempore erogare proposuit uita sibi et prósperitàte sálua.

Pars V
20 His ita ordinabiliter ab eodem rege dispositis memor illius diuinae scripturae senténtiae qua dícitur, Qui uult elemosinam dare a semet ipso debet incipere, etiam quid a proprio corporis sui et mentis seruitio Deo offerret prudenter éxcogitáuit.

21 Nam non minus de hac re quam de externis diuitiis Deo offerre proposuit quin etiam dimidiam partem seruitii mentis et corporis in quantum infirmitas et possibilitas atque suppetentia permitteret diurno scilicet ac nocturno tempore suapte totisque uiribus se redditurum Déo spopóndit.

more widely a little while before.

18 The third to the school which he had most attentively gathered from many noble and also not noble boys of his own proper people.

19 Fourth, to the neighbouring monasteries in all Wessex [lit. Saxony] and Mercia and also in certain years by turns in Wales [lit. Britain] and Cornwall, Gaul, Brittany [lit. Armorica], the land of the Northumbrians, and sometimes also in Ireland, to the churches and the inhabiting servants of God, according to his own possibility he either distributed before or proposed to distribute in a succeeding time, if life and prosperity were secure for him.

Part V
20 With these things so disposed in order by the same king, mindful of that sentence of divine scripture in which it is said, He who wishes to give alms ought to begin from himself, he thought out prudently also what from the proper service of his own body and mind he might offer to God.

21 For he proposed to offer to God not less from this matter than from external riches, moreover a half part of the service of mind and body as far as infirmity and possibility and opportunity would permit, understand by diurnal and nocturnal time, in his own fashion and with his whole abilities he promised to give himself to God.

22 Sed quia distantiam nocturnarum horarum omnino propter tenebras et diurnarum propter densitatem saepissime pluuiarum et nubium aequaliter dignoscere non poterat excogitare coepit qua ratione fixa et sine ulla haesitatione hunc promissum uoti sui tenorem leto tenus incommutabiliter Dei fretus misericordia cónseruare pósset.

22 But as he could not altogether understand the extent of the nocturnal hours on account of shadows and equally of the diurnal very often on account of the density of the rains and clouds, he began to think out by what reasoning fixed and without any hesitation, relying on the mercy of God, he could keep incommutably this promised tenor of his own vow to the point of death.

Pars VI

Part VI

23 His aliquandiu excogitatis tandem inuento utili et discreto consilio suos capellanos ceram offerre sufficienter imperauit quam adductam ad denarios pensari in bilíbri praecépit.

23 With these things thought out for a long time, finally with useful and discreet counsel come upon, he commanded his own chaplains to offer wax sufficiently, which brought forth he ordered to be weighed against pennies in a scale.

24 Cumque tanta cera mensurata fuisset quae septuaginta duos denarios pensaret sex candelas unamquamque aequa lance inde capellanos facere iussit ut unaquaeque candela duodecim uncias pollicis in se signatas in longitúdine habéret.

24 And when as much wax had been measured as would weigh seventy-two pence, he ordered the chaplains to make therefrom six candles, each in equal balance, so that each candle would have twelve inches by the length of a thumb marked on it.

25 Itaque hac reperta ratione sex illae candelae per uiginti quatuor horas die nocteque sine defectu coram sanctis multorum electorum Dei reliquiis quae semper eum ubique comitabantur ardéntes lucescébant.

25 And so with this reasoning discovered, those six candles through twenty-four hours by day and by night without defect before the holy relics of many of the elect of God which used to accompany him everywhere, burning, used to shed light.

26 Sed cum aliquando per diem integrum et noctem ad eandem illam horam qua anteriori uespera accensae fuerant candelae ardendo lucescere non

26 But since sometimes through an entire day and night to that same hour in which on the previous evening they had been lighted the candles could

poterant nimirum uentorum uiolentia inflante, quae aliquando per ecclesiarum ostia et fenestrarum, maceriarum quoque atque tabularum, uel frequentes parietum rimulas nec non et tentoriorum tenuitates die noctuque sine intermissione flabat, exardescere citius plus debito ante eandem horam finiendo cursum suum cogebantur, excogitauit unde talem uentorum sufflationem prohibére potuísset,

not by burning shed light, because, of course, of the inblowing violence of the winds, which used to blow sometimes through the doors and windows of the churches, or also the frequent little cracks of the stone walls and the panels of the walls, and also the thinnesses of the tents by day and by night without intermission, they were compelled to burn out more quickly than they ought, finishing their own course before the same hour, he thought out how he might be able to prohibit such blowing of the winds,

consilioque artificiose atque sapienter inuento laternam ex lignis et bouinis cornibus pulcherrime constrúere imperáuit.

and by counsel artfully and wisely come upon he commanded to construct most beautifully a lantern from woods and bovine horns.

27 Bouina namque cornua alba ac in una tenuiter dolabris erasa non minus uitreo uásculo elúcent quae itaque laterna mirabiliter ex lignis et cornibus ut ante díximus fácta, noctuque candela in eam missa exterius ut interius tam lucida ardebat nullis uentorum flamínibus impedíta, quia ualuam ad ostium illius laternae ex cornibus idem fieri imperáuerat.

27 For bovine horns, white and shaved by axes thinly in one [layer], emit light not less than a glass vessel, and so the lantern [was] made wondrously from woods and horns, as we said before, and by night the candle put into it burned as lucid without as within, impeded by no blowings of the winds, because he had commanded a hinge to be made for a door of that lantern in the same way, from horns.

28 Hoc itaque machinamento ita facto sex candelae unaquaeque post alteram per uiginti quatuor horas sine intermissione nihil citius nihil tárdius lùcescébant, quibus extinctis aliae íncendebántur.

28 And so, with this machine so made, six candles, each after the other through twenty-four hours without intermission used to shed light, nothing more quickly, nothing more slowly, which extinguished, others were ignited.

Here follows the text arranged to illustrate the chiastic and parallel statement and restatement of words and ideas.

A1   Nam iam dudum in lege scriptum audierat

A2   Dominum decimam sibi multipliciter redditurum promisisse atque fideliter seruasse

decimamque sibi multipliciter redditurum fuisse.

A3   Hoc exemplo instigatus et antecessorum morem uolens transcendere

A4   dimidiam seruitii sui partem

A5   diurni scilicet et nocturni temporis ...

A6   Deo deuote et fideliter toto cordis affectu pius meditator se daturum spopondit ...

A7   Sed ut solito suo more cautus euitaret quod in alio diuinae scripturae loco cautum est,

Si recte offeras recte autem non diuidas peccas, quod Deo libenter deuouerat quo modo recte diuidere posset cogitauit,

A8   et ut dixit Salomon, Cor regis in manu Domini id est consilium.

Consilio diuinitus inuento

A9   omnium uniuscuiusque anni censuum successum bifarie primitus ministros suos diuidere aequali lance imperauit.

B   His ita diuisis

C1   partem primam saecularibus negotiis pertinere addixit

quam etiam in tribus partibus sequestrari praecepit

C2a   cuius primam diuisionis partem suis bellatoribus annualiter largiebatur ...

C2b   Secundam autem operatoribus ...

C2c   Tertiam autem eiusdem partem aduenis ex omni gente ad eum aduenientibus ...

D   sicut scriptum est, Hilarem datorem diligit Deus, hilariter impendebat.

C'1   Secundam uero partem omnium diuitiarum suarum ... in quatuor partibus aequis etiam curiose suos ministros illam diuidere imperauit, ea condi-tione

C'2a   ut prima pars illius diuisionis pauperibus uniuscuiusque gentis qui ad eum ueniebant discretissime erogaretur ...

C'2b   Secundam autem duobus monasteriis ...

C'2c   Tertiam scholae ...

C'2d   Quartum circum finitimis in omni Saxonia et Mercia monasteriis ... ecclesiis et seruis Dei inhabitantibus ...

B'   His ita ordinabiliter ab eodem rege dispositis

A'1   memor illius diuinae scripturae sententiae qua dicitur,

A'2   Qui uult elemosinam dare a semet ipso debet incipere,

A'3   etiam quid a proprio corporis sui et mentis seruitio Deo offerret prudenter excogitauit ...

A'4   dimidiam partem seruitii mentis et corporis ...

A'5   diurno scilicet ac nocturno tempore

A'6   suapte totisque uiribus se redditurum Deo spopondit.

A'7   Sed quia distantiam nocturnarum horarum omnino propter tenebras et diurnarum propter densitatem saepissime pluuiarum et nubium aequaliter dignoscere non poterat, excogitare coepit qua ratione fixa et sine ulla haesitatione hunc promissum uoti sui tenorem leto tenus incommutabiliter Dei fretus misericordia conseruare posset.

A'8   His aliquandiu excogitatis tandem inuento utili et discreto consilio

A'9   suos capellanos ceram offerre sufficienter imperauit, quam adductam ad denarios pensari in bilibri praecepit.

Cumque tanta cera mensurata fuisset quae septuaginta duos denarios pensaret, sex candelas, unamquamque aequa lance, inde capellanos facere iussit … .

Let us first consider features that Asser infixed to guarantee the integrity of discrete sentences:

- In sentence 3 Asser marked half in the ninth of seventeen words, *dimidiam*. The central twenty-fourth of forty-seven syllables is *-mid-*. From | *Hoc* to the space after *transcendere* | there are sixty-five letters and spaces between words, and from | *dimidiam* to *temporis* | inclusive there are sixty-five letters and spaces between words. He marked half of *nec non etiam dimidiam partem omnium diuitiarum*, in the fourth of seven words, *dimidiam*. He marked the half part of the syllables at *dimidiam par* | *tem*. The twenty-fourth letter from the beginning and from the end of the clause is the *p* of *partem*.
- Sentence 5 divides symmetrically at the twenty-third of forty-five words, *Si recte offeras recte autem non diuidas* | *peccas* |. The clause *quo modo recte diuidere posset cogitauit* divides symmetrically at | *diuidere*.
- Sentence 6 divides into two parts at | *bifarie*. The second half divides into two parts at | *diuidere*.
- In sentence 7 the seven words *quam etiam in tribus partibus sequestrari praecepit* divide by sesquitertian ratio 4:3 at *tribus* |.
- In sentence 8 the nineteen words from | *Ita enim* to *diuidebantur* | divide into thirds at | *tribus* and *tribus* |. The words *prima cohors uno mense in curto regio* contain thirty-one letters, one for each day of a month. The words *uno mense in curto regio die noctuque administrans commoraretur menseque finito* contain thirty syllables, one for each day of a month.
- In sentence 9 the words *secunda itaque cohors mense peracto* contain thirty-one letters. The fourteen words of the sentence divide by sesquitertian ratio 4:3 at | *tertia*.
- The fifty-five words of sentence 15 divide by sesquitertian ratio 4:3 at *quatuor partibus* |.
- In sentence 24 there are sixty-six letters before | *sex*.

- There are twenty-four sentences before sentence 25, in which the twenty-fourth syllable from the beginning is the last of *uiginti quatuor* |, and the twentieth word from the end is *uiginti*.
- In sentence 28 the sixth word is *sex* |, and after *uiginti quatuor* | there are twenty-four syllables to the end of the clause.

We may next consider features that Asser infixed to link adjacent sentences. In sentences 2–3 there are from | *Nam iam dudum* to the space after *annualiter* | inclusive 365 letters and spaces between words, one for each day of a year, *annualiter*. In sentences 8–10 there are between the phrases *et adueniente alia cohorte prima domum redibat* | and | *et adueniente prima cohorte domum redibat* thirty words.

We may proceed to examine features Asser infixed to guarantee the integrity of larger units of the passage. The twenty-eight words of Part I and the 142 words of Part II together comprise 170 words, of which one-tenth is 17. The seventeenth word of Part II sentence 2 is *decimamque*. The seventeenth syllable of sentence 2 is the first of *decimam*. Together *decimam* and *decimamque* contain seventeen letters.

Finally, we may consider features that Asser infixed to guarantee the integrity of the entire passage. Part I sentence 1 contains twenty-eight words, the key to the twenty-eight sentences of the entire passage. Part II sentences 2–6 imply division into two parts. Part III sentences 7–11 imply division into three parts, dividing into thirds at the word *tribus* in sentence 8. Part IIII sentences 12–19 imply division into four parts. The crux of the chiasmus is the fourteenth of twenty-eight sentences.

The literal translation offered above allows one to make sense of details explained in a recent popular book as errors.[3] One need not suppose that in sentence 1 'a feminine singular relative pronoun, *quae*, modifying *meditationem* and serving as the subject of the past participle *incepta … inventa … servata*, has apparently fallen out after *meditationem* and before *inaniter*'. The coincidence of twenty-eight words here with twenty-eight sentences in the entire passage suggests that nothing is missing from the first sentence. Nor need one suppose that in sentence 2 'The passage is probably corrupt through dittography.'

Charles Plummer 'wholly and entirely' distrusted Asser's account of Alfred's sevenfold division of revenues, affirming that 'at this point of his work Asser was attacked by an acute fit of imagination'.[4] Here, as elsewhere, Alfred adapted his policy and Asser his narrative to a biblical model, as comparison with 1 Kings 5: 13–14 shows clearly:

> legitque rex Salomon operas de omni Israhel et erat indictio triginta
> milia uirorum mittebatque eos in Libanum, decem milia per menses

---

[3] Keynes and Lapidge, *Alfred*, 272–4.

[4] C. Plummer, *The Life and Times of Alfred the Great, Being the Ford Lectures for 1901* (1902), 130.

singulos uicissim, ita ut duobus mensibus essent in domibus suis; in tribus namque cohortibus praefati regis satellites prudentissime diuidebantur, ita ut prima cohors uno mense in curto regio die noctuque administrans commoraretur menseque finito et adueniente alia cohorte prima domum redibat et ibi duobus propriis quiuis necessitatibus studens commorabatur mensibus.

With Asser's account of Alfred's invention of the horn lantern one may compare Solomon's construction of lamps and lampstands in 1 Kings 7: 49. In this entire passage there are many indications of imagination, but imagination in a different sense, and imagination of a much higher order than Plummer meant. The coherence of the passage is like that of the whole book in which it is embedded. Both arithmetic detail and comprehensive architectonic structure bear eloquent witness to the systematic thought and administrative genius of both the English king and his Welsh tutor and biographer.

Chapter 4

The *Anglo-Saxon Chronicle* and the idea of Rome in Alfredian literature

Susan Irvine

The various versions of the *Anglo-Saxon Chronicle* offer a curious set of entries for the four successive years 887–90, exemplified here by *MS A*:

> [887] ... 7 þy ilcan geare þe se here for forþ up ofer þa brycge æt Paris, (7) Eþelhelm aldormon lędde Wesseaxna ęlmessan 7 Ęlfredes cyninges to Rome.
> [888] AN. .dccclxxxviii. Her lędde Beocca aldormon Wesseaxna ęlmessan 7 Ęlfredes cyninges to Rome, 7 Eþelswiþ cuen, sio wæs Ęlfredes sweostor cyninges, forþferde, 7 hire lic liþ æt Pafian. 7 þy ilcan geare Eþered ercebiscep 7 Eþelwold aldormon forþferdon on anum monþe.
> [889] AN. .dccclxxxviiii. On þissum geare næs nan fęreld to Rome, buton tuegen hleaperas Ęlfred cyning sende mid gewritum.
> [890] AN. .dcccxc. Her lędde Beornhelm abbud Westseaxna ęlmessan to Rome 7 Ęlfredes cyninges ...[1]

The material stands out from its context because of its insistent focus on journeys to Rome undertaken by Alfred's representatives. In a sense there is nothing extraordinary about this; why should a chronicler not choose to report missions to Rome amongst other memorable events for a particular year? But one entry in particular, that for 889, seems to lend an undue prominence to the Roman missions. The Roman mission is the only subject covered in 889, and yet no mission took place in that year. The annal for 889 is taken up with reporting that an event did not happen.

We expect chroniclers, and historians for that matter, to omit or alter material that seems irrelevant or indeed inconvenient for their immediate purposes. Several scholars, such as Walter Goffart, Ruth Morse, Patrick Geary and Elisabeth

---

[1] *ASC 'A'*, ed. Bately, 53–4; trans. *EHD*, 200: '[887] ... And the same year in which the army went up beyond the bridge at Paris, Ealdorman Æthelhelm took to Rome the alms of King Alfred and the West Saxons. [888] In this year Ealdorman Beocca took to Rome the alms of the West Saxons and of King Alfred. And Queen Æthelswith, who was King Alfred's sister, died, and her body is buried in Pavia. And the same year Archbishop Ethelred and Ealdorman Æthelwold died in the same month. [889] There was no expedition to Rome in this year, but King Alfred sent two couriers with letters. [890] In this year Abbot Beornhelm took to Rome the alms of the West Saxons and of King Alfred. ... '

van Houts, have recently shown how commonplace it was for medieval historians to tinker with the course of events to influence the response of their contemporary audiences.[2] For a chronicler, omitting the irrelevant was part of the job: only the most significant events of any one year could be selected. But for the Anglo-Saxon chronicler, the failure to send an expedition to Rome was apparently serious enough to stand alone as the matter for report in 889; the chronicler goes on to observe – 'almost apologetically', notes Richard Abels – that Alfred did at least send two couriers with letters.[3] Given that expeditions to and from Rome are mentioned only sporadically in the *Anglo-Saxon Chronicle*, why should this lack of an expedition to Rome in 889 be considered newsworthy, and why should the chronicler have been moved to excuse it? I will attempt to answer these questions by looking first at the wider context of this entry in the *Chronicle*, and then by looking at perspectives on Rome in other literature composed in Alfred's lifetime.

Two earlier annals in the *Chronicle* offer some background to the series of payments reported for 887–90. The annal for 885, which focuses mainly on Alfred's military activities in East Anglia and the succession of kings amongst the Franks, includes a report of the death of Pope Marinus: '7 þy ilcan geare forþferde se goda papa Marinus, se gefreode Ongelcynnes scole be Ęlfredes bene Westseaxna cyninges, 7 he sende him micla gifa 7 þære rode dęl þe Crist on þrowude'.[4] Evidence from the vocabulary of the *Chronicle* up to 890 ana- lysed by Janet Bately suggests that the annal for 885 is probably by the same chronicler as the four for 887–90.[5] This annalist, it would seem, was particularly interested in recording how seriously Alfred and the West Saxons took their obligations to Rome.

The second reference to England's dealing with Rome is more problem- atic. It appears in the annal for 883 or 884 in every manuscript of the *Chronicle* except for the earliest one, *MS A*. I cite here *MS B*'s version:[6]

> 7 Marinus se papa sende lignum Domini Ælfrede cinge. 7 þy ilcan geare lædde Sighelm 7 Æþelstan þa ælmessan to Rome [þe Ælfred cyning gehet þyder], 7 eac on Iudea to Sancte Thome 7 to Sancte Bartholomeæ, þa hie sæton wiþ þone here æt Lundenne, 7 hie þær Godes þances swiþe bentiþige wurdan æfter þam gehate.[7]

---

[2] W. Goffart, *The Narrators of Barbarian History (A.D. 550–800)* (Princeton, NJ, 1988); R. Morse, *Truth and Convention in the Middle Ages: Rhetoric, Representation, and Reality* (1991); P. J. Geary, *Phantoms of Remembrance: Memory and Oblivion at the End of the First Millennium* (Princeton, NJ, 1994); E. van Houts, *Memory and Gender in Medieval Europe, 900–1200* (1999).

[3] Abels, *Alfred*, 190.

[4] *ASC 'A'*, ed. Bately, 52–3; trans. *EHD*, 198–9: 'That same year there died the good pope, Marinus, who had freed from taxation the English quarter at the request of Alfred, king [of the West Saxons]. And he had sent him great gifts, including part of the Cross on which Christ suffered.'

[5] J. Bately, 'The compilation of the Anglo-Saxon Chronicle, 60 BC to AD 890: vocabulary as evidence', *PBA*, 64 (1978), 93–129, at 109.

[6] See *ASC 'A'*, ed. Bately, cvii.

[7] *ASC 'B'*, ed. Taylor, 38, with additions in square brackets from *ASC 'D'*, ed. Cubbin, 28; trans. *EHD*, 197: 'And Pope Marinus sent some wood of the Cross to King Alfred. And that same

Given its omission from *MS A*, this material is unlikely to have been in a lost original, but on the other hand it must have been added at an early stage to have been included in all the other manuscripts. The use of the Latin 'lignum Domini' here for the wood of the Cross in contrast to the Old English 'þære rode dęl þe Crist on þrowude' of the 885 entry may suggest that this addition was made by a redactor who independently introduced this material into the 883 entry unaware of the 885 reference. In any case a separate annalist or scribe from the one who wrote the 885–90 entries has been prompted to mention the gift from Pope Marinus to Alfred and Alfred's almsgiving to Rome.

The entry's reference to a siege of London meant that historians tended until recently to treat it as a misplaced addition, designed originally to slot into the entry for 886.[8] Even if the death of Pope Marinus in 884 did not make this extremely unlikely, it has been argued recently by Simon Keynes that a siege of London did take place in 883, although Alfred did not actually occupy the city until 886.[9] Janet Nelson has further suggested that Alfred's gaining control of London and his sending of an embassy to Pope Marinus in Rome in 883 may indicate that Alfred had in mind a plan, later abandoned, to shift the metropolitan see to London.[10] But, given that the plan was abandoned by 890, the question of why an annalist or scribe, presumably after 890 since the passage is not in the earliest *MS A*, was moved to add material on Marinus, almsgiving, and London to the 883 annal remains unanswered.

The information offered by the annals for 883 and 885 that Pope Marinus freed the English quarter in Rome from taxation and sent great gifts to King Alfred can be assumed to explain why the almsgiving expeditions took place: as Keynes notes,

> it is not so surprising, under these circumstances, that Alfred responded by instituting a series of seemingly regular payments of alms to Rome, despatching his representatives with such ceremony, and evidently attaching so much importance to their comings and goings, that the expeditions were duly recorded in the Anglo-Saxon Chronicle.[11]

---

year Sigelm and Athelstan took to Rome the alms [which King Alfred had promised thither], and also to India [Iudea in B and C] to St. Thomas and St. Bartholomew, when the English were encamped against the enemy army at London; and there, by the grace of God, their prayers were well answered after that promise.'

[8] See F. M. Stenton, *Anglo-Saxon England* (3rd edn, 1971), 258, n. 3; *EHD*, 197, n. 6; Keynes and Lapidge, *Alfred*, 266, n. 198; Smyth, *Alfred,* 101.

[9] S. Keynes, 'King Alfred and the Mercians', in *Kings, Currency and Alliances: History and Coinage of Southern England in the Ninth Century*, eds M. A. S. Blackburn and D. N. Dumville (1998), 1–45, at 21–3.

[10] J. L. Nelson, 'The political ideas of Alfred of Wessex', in *Kings and Kingship in Medieval Europe*, ed. A. J. Duggan (1993), 125–58, at 154–7.

[11] S. Keynes, 'Anglo-Saxon entries in the *Liber Vitae* of Brescia', in *Alfred the Wise: Studies in Honour of Janet Bately on the Occasion of her Sixty-fifth Birthday*, eds J. Roberts and J. L. Nelson with M. Godden (1997), 99–119, at 117.

It is worth noting, however, that gifts and payments to Rome such as those offered by Alfred were not by any means unprecedented in Anglo-Saxon England. A letter written in 798 by Pope Leo III to Cenwulf of Mercia acknowledges King Offa's promise to send 365 mancuses each year to Rome for the support of the poor and the provision of lights.[12] Neither the promise nor any payment is recorded in the *Chronicle*. King Æthelwulf, in his will, ordered that every year 300 mancuses should be given to Rome, to be divided between the purchase of oil for lamps in churches and the pope.[13] Again no payments are recorded in the *Chronicle*. Perhaps they were never made or perhaps they were not sufficiently significant to be recorded. Again the entries for 887–90 stand out in contrast: not only are the payments important enough to be recorded, but even when payment is not made it is treated as a matter worthy of record.

None of the alms payments of the late 880s entailed Alfred himself visiting Rome. But in his childhood Alfred had visited Rome at least once and probably twice.[14] His first visit to Rome is recorded in the *Chronicle*, and vested with a significance which, as historians have shown, is anachronistic and misleading: '[853] … 7 þy ilcan geare sende Eþelwulf cyning Ælfred his sunu to Rome. Þa was domne Leo papa on Rome 7 he hine to cyninge gehalgode 7 hiene him to biscepsuna nam'.[15] The same misunderstanding of the nature of the ceremony is shown by Asser in his account of Alfred's anointing as king by Pope Leo.[16] A letter from Pope Leo IV to Æthelwulf, however, originally thought to be an eleventh-century forgery but now accepted as genuine,[17] describes the ceremony more objectively as a consular investiture.[18] In the 853 annal of the *Chronicle*, which as Janet Bately notes 'has more the ring of a remark made by a chronicler writing in Alfred's reign than that of someone writing under Æthelwulf or indeed under Alfred's rebel-

---

[12] See *EHD*, 862, no. 205; see also Stenton, *Anglo-Saxon England*, 217, n. 1.

[13] Asser, c. 16, 15–16.

[14] Although the *ASC* reports only one visit by Alfred, Asser mentions that Alfred also accompanied his father on his journey to Rome two years later: Asser, c. 11, p. 9. At the end of his translation of Augustine's *Soliloquies*, Alfred may be recalling his own view of Rome: 'me þincð nu þæt ic wite hwa Romeburh timbrode … nat ic no ði hwa (Rome)burh timbrede þe ic self hyt gesawe' (*Soliloquies*, ed. Carnicelli, 97; trans. Keynes and Lapidge, *Alfred*, 152): 'I suppose that I know who built Rome … Yet I do not *know* who built Rome because I saw it myself.' See also J. L. Nelson, 'The Franks and the English in the ninth century reconsidered', in *The Preservation and Transmission of Anglo-Saxon Culture*, eds P. E. Szarmach and J. T. Rosenthal (Kalamazoo, 1997), 141–58, at 145–6 and 148.

[15] *ASC 'A'*, ed. Bately, 45; trans. *EHD*, 189: 'And that same year King Æthelwulf sent his son Alfred to Rome. The lord Leo was then pope in Rome, and he consecrated him king and stood sponsor to him at confirmation.'

[16] Asser, c. 8, 7.

[17] For the argument that the document was a forgery, see J. L. Nelson, 'The problem of King Alfred's royal anointing', *JEccH*, 18 (1967), 145–63, but see now her 'The Franks and the English', 145 and n. 30.

[18] See *EHD*, 880 (no. 219).

lious eldest brother Æthelbald', the conferment of consulship becomes papal consecration of a king.[19] Whether as a result of misinterpretation or for purposes of propaganda, it is likely that this reinterpretation stems from Carolingian precedent. A series of imperial coronations by the pope, most momentously that of Charlemagne in 800, took place throughout the ninth century among the Carolingians. Historians have noted particularly the parallels between the *Chronicle*'s 853 entry and Frankish annals describing the Roman anointing of Charlemagne's sons in 781.[20] It might also be noted that in 850, when Louis II was crowned emperor, the *Annals of Saint-Bertin* inform us Louis was sent to Rome by his father Lothar I.[21] Moreover, given that the 853 annal was probably written in Alfred's reign, the imperial coronation of Charles the Bald in 875 may also have been in the chonicler's mind.[22] Links between Charles the Bald's Francia and England, confirmed by the marriage between Charles's daughter Judith and King Æthelwulf, have been well documented.[23] Whatever prompted the reinterpretation of events, it is clear from the *Chronicle* entry for 853 that the perception of Alfred as having been consecrated king by the pope in Rome was one the chronicler wished retrospectively to instill.

The entries for 853, 883, and 885 to 890 provide important evidence that chroniclers writing in Alfred's reign viewed links between England and Rome as particularly worthy of report. This curious emphasis, given that, in Peter Sawyer's words, the *Chronicle* from 865 to 920 'is little more than the record of the struggle of the West Saxon rulers against the Scandinavians', merits further exploration.[24] I propose to look first at other works written in the vernacular in the period of Alfred's reign, in particular Alfred's own translation of Boethius's *De Consolatione Philosophiae*, and then consider the implications of other documentary evidence.

Boethius's *De Consolatione Philosophiae* is self-evidently philosophical rather than historical in its primary interests. Boethius himself, however, included a considerable number of allusions to Roman history, and Alfred, where he chooses to incorporate these into his translation, adapts and embellishes them independently of his source. Alfred also adds some historical references where his source has none. The opening section of translation is one such independent addition. It offers a historical summary of the events which led up to Boethius's imprisonment, beginning as follows:

---

[19] See Bately, 'The compilation', 112–13, n. 4. Bately (113, n. 2) also compares the annal for 853 with the use of 'gehwæþere hond' in the annal for 871.

[20] See, for example, Nelson, 'The problem of King Alfred's royal anointing', 162, and J. M. Wallace-Hadrill, 'The Franks and the English in the ninth century: some common historical interests', in *idem, Early Medieval History* (1975), 201–16, at 212.

[21] *AB*, trans. Nelson, 69.

[22] Ibid., 189.

[23] See, for example, P. Stafford, 'Charles the Bald, Judith and England', in *Charles the Bald. Court and Kingdom*, eds M. T. Gibson and J. L. Nelson (2nd edn, 1990), 139–53.

[24] P. H. Sawyer, *The Age of the Vikings* (2nd edn, 1971), at 14.

On ðære tide ðe Gotan of Sciððiu mægðe wið Romana rice gewin up
ahofon, 7 mid heora cyningum, Rædgota 7 Eallerica wæron hatne,
Romane burig abræcon, 7 eall Italia rice þæt is betwux þam muntum
7 Sicilia þam ealonde in anwald gerehton, 7 þa æfter þam
foresprecenan cyningum þeodric feng to þam ilcan rice. Se Ðeodric
wæs Amulinga; he was cristen, þeah he on þam arrianiscan gedwolan
þurhwunode. He gehet Romanum his freondscipe, swa þæt hi mostan
heora ealdrihta wyrðe beon. Ac he þa gehat swiðe yfele gelæste, 7
swiðe wraðe geendode mid manegum mane. Þæt wæs to eacan oðrum
unarimedum yflum þæt he Iohannes þone papan het ofslean. Þa wæs
sum consul, þæt we heretoha hatað, Boetius wæs gehaten; se wæs in
boccræftum 7 on woruldþeawum se rihtwisesta.[25]

Alfred has conflated a series of events which took place over more than a
century. The source for the first part of the passage has been identified as the
anonymous Old English translation of Orosius's *Historiarum adversum paganos*,
where Alaric and Radagaisus are also presented as if they invaded and ruled
Italy together.[26] The OE *Orosius* ends at this point, and it looks as though Alfred
has carried on where the *Orosius* translator left off. Each of the two authors,
however, offers a quite different perspective. For the translator of the OE *Orosius*,
the sacking of Rome by Alaric is a sign of God's mercy because the Romans'
misdeeds are so lightly avenged.[27] For Alfred, the sacking of Rome by Alaric
and Radagaisus is the first of a series of violent deeds which culminate in the
unjustified imprisonment of Boethius by Theodoric.[28] Alfred, unlike the *Orosius*

---

[25] *Boethius*, 7; trans.: 'In the time when the Goths from the nation of Scythia waged war
against the Roman empire, and with their kings named Radagaisus and Alaric stormed the city of
Rome, [they] subjugated the whole of the kingdom of Italy between the mountains and the island of
Sicily; and then after those aforesaid kings Theodoric succeeded to the same kingdom. Theodoric
was an Amuling; he was a Christian but he continued in the Arian heresy. He promised the Romans
his friendship, allowing them to be in possession of their ancient rights. But he carried out that
promise very badly, and he ended very cruelly with many a crime. It was in addition to countless
other evils that he ordered Pope John to be killed. There was at that time a consul (which we call a
chief) called Boethius, who was extremely wise in book learning and worldly customs.' Translations are my own unless otherwise stated.

[26] See D. Whitelock, 'The prose of Alfred's reign', in *Continuations and Beginnings: Studies
in Old English Literature* (1966), 67–103, at 82, n. 3, and *Orosius*, ed. Bately, xcii.

[27] In his final chapter (entitled 'Hu God gedyde Romanum his mildsunge' ['How God showed
his mercy to the Romans']), he explains: 'God gedyde his miltsunge on Romanum, þa þa he hiora
misdæda wrecan let, þæt hit þeh dyde Alrica se cristena cyning 7 se mildesta, 7 he mid swa lytle
niþe abræc Romeburg þæt he bebead þæt mon nænne mon ne sloge' ['God showed his mercy to the
Romans when he had their wrongful deeds avenged, in that the most merciful Christian king Alaric
performed it, and he conquered Rome with so little harm that he commanded that no man should be
slain']; see *Orosius*, ed. Bately, 8 and 156.

[28] Alfred's attitude is more clearly conveyed in the verse rendering of his original prose
version: the advancing Goths he describes as 'monig ... Gota gylpes full, guðe gelysted' ['many a
Goth full of boasting, desiring battle']; the defeated Romans are 'seo wealaf' ['the woeful remnant'], and 'giomonna gestrion sealdon unwillum eþelweardas, halige aðas; wæs gehwæðeres waa'
['defenders of the homeland unwillingly gave up ancestors' treasure [and] holy oaths; there was
affliction on every side']; see *King Alfred's Boethius*, ed. Sedgefield, 151–2.

translator, discerned no justification for the presence of the Goths in Rome; instead he chose to depict Boethius as an exemplary upholder of Christianity confronting an unrighteous usurper.

Alfred's approval for Boethius may stem from his recognition of the similarity of their two situations.[29] A comparison of the opening of Alfred's *Boethius* with the *Chronicle* suggests how, to Alfred, the plight of Boethius and the Romans in the face of the barbarian invasion must have appeared analogous to the situation he and his countrymen faced. The annal for 878, for example, describes an invasion which resembles that outlined by Alfred at the opening of his *Boethius*:

> Her hiene bestęl se here on midne winter ofer tuelftan niht to Cippanhamme 7 geridon Wesseaxna lond 7 gesæton 7 micel þæs folces (7) ofer sę adræfdon, 7 þæs oþres þone mæstan dęl hie geridon 7 him to gecirdon buton þam cyninge Ęlfrede.[30]

The annalists also allude frequently in the *Chronicle* to the breaking of promises by the Danes. The annal for 876 offers one example:

> Her hiene bestęl se here into Werham Wesseaxna fierde, 7 wiþ þone here se cyning friþ nam, 7 him þa aþas sworon on þam halgan beage, þe hie ær nanre þeode noldon, þæt hie hrędlice of his rice foren, 7 hie þa under þam hie nihtes bestęlon þære fierde se gehorsoda here into Escanceaster.[31]

Between them, these two passages contain all the elements that Alfred incorporates into the opening of his *Boethius*: violent occupation of a country by barbarians, submission of the people, swearing of oaths by the enemy, breaking of those oaths, and the stand of one man (Alfred in one, Boethius in the other) against the enemy. The similarities between Roman history and contemporary Anglo-Saxon England must have struck more than the king himself in the late ninth century.

Prominent in Alfred's summary in his *Boethius* is the figure of Theodoric, who acts as a foil to 'se rihtwisesta' Boethius. Theodoric is a king whose abuse of his royal status earns him unremitting condemnation by Alfred: 'þam unrihtwisan cyninge' ('the unrighteous king'), 'se wælhreowa cyning Ðeodric'

---

[29] See M. Godden, 'King Alfred's Boethius', in *Boethius: His Life, Thought and Influence*, ed. M. Gibson (1981), 419–24, at 419.

[30] *ASC 'A'*, ed. Bately, 50; trans. *EHD*, 195: 'In this year in midwinter after twelfth night the enemy army came stealthily to Chippenham, and occupied the land of the West Saxons and settled there, and drove a great part of the people across the sea, and conquered most of the others; and the people submitted to them, except King Alfred.'

[31] *ASC 'A'*, ed. Bately, 50; trans. *EHD*, 194–5: 'In this year the enemy army slipped past the army of the West Saxons into Wareham; and then the king made peace with the enemy and they gave him hostages, who were the most important men next to their king in the army, and swore oaths to him on the holy ring – a thing which they would not do before for any nation – that they would speedily leave his kingdom. And then under cover of that, they – the mounted army – stole by night away from the English army to Exeter.'

('the cruel king Theodoric') . Elsewhere in his translation, Alfred, independently of his source, cites Theodoric as an example of the abuse of royal power. In Book II pr. 6 of his source, Lady Philosophy asks with rhetorical flourish: 'Quid autem de dignitatibus potentiaque disseram, qua uos uerae dignitatis ac potestatis inscii caelo exaequatis? Quae si in improbissimum quemque ceciderunt, quae flammis Aetnae eructantibus, quod diluuium tantas strages dederint?'[32] Alfred reproduces the sense of the original but inserts specific examples of his own:

> Hwæt, se eower wela þonne 7 se eower anweald, þe ge nu weorðscipe
> hatað, gif he becymð to þam eallra wyrrestan men, 7 to þam þe his
> eallra unweorðost bið, swa he nu dyde to þis ilcan Þeodrice, 7 iu ær
> to Nerone þæm casere, 7 oft eac to mænegum hiora gelicum, hu ne
> wile he ðonne don swa hi dydon 7 get doð, ealle ða ricu þe him under
> bioð oðð awer on neaweste, forslean 7 forheregian, swæ swa fyres
> leg deð drigne hæðfeld, oððe eft se byrnenda swefel ðone munt
> bærnð þe we hatað Etne, se is on Sicilia ðæm ealonde; swiðe onlic
> ðæm miclan flode ðe giu on Noes dagum wæs.[33]

The names Theodoric and Nero may be from Roman history, but the vocabulary suggests that Alfred once again has in mind its application to his own situation. The description of these tyrants 'forslean 7 forheregian' ('destroying and ravaging') the kingdoms subject to them or near them recalls the behaviour of the invading Danes whose leaders must have epitomized for Alfred the abuse of power. The wide geographical and historical range of the allusions here only serves to emphasize the implied significance of the past in interpreting the present.

The reference in this passage to the earlier Roman emperor Nero was presumably prompted by the subsequent metre in the Boethian source, which recounts Nero's violent deeds (Book II, m. 6). In his rendering of this metre Alfred characteristically casts into discursive form the static poetic images of his source. Hence 'urbe flammata' ('the city blazing') becomes 'Se het æt sumum cyrre forbærnan æalle Romeburg on anne sið æfter þære bisene þe gio Trogiaburg barn. Hine lyste eac geseon hu seo burne, hu lange, 7 hu leohte be þære

---

[32] *Anicii Manlii Severini Boethii Philosophiae Consolatio*, ed. L. Bieler, Corpus Christianorum, Series Latina, 94 (Turnhout, 1957), 29. Trans. *Boethius, The Theological Tractates and the Consolation of Philosophy*, eds H. F. Stewart, E. K. Rand and S. J. Tester, Loeb Classical Library (Cambridge, MA, 1978), 209: 'But what shall I say of your worthy offices and power, which you praise to high heaven, being ignorant of true worth and real power? When such things have fallen into the hands of the worst of men, what Etnas with belching flames or what floods have caused greater destruction?'

[33] *Boethius*, 34; trans.: 'Indeed if your wealth and power, which you now call honours, fall into the hands of the worst man of all, and the one most unworthy of all to have them, as now they did to this very Theodoric, and long ago to the emperor Nero, and often also to many like them, surely he will act as they did, and still do, destroying and ravaging all the kingdoms subject to them or anywhere near them, just as fire destroys the dry heath, or as the burning sulphur burns the mountain we call Etna which is in the island of Sicily; also like the great flood which happened long ago in the days of Noah.'

oðerre'.[34] Alfred's expansion here, as Brian Donaghey noted, was probably prompted by the commentary of Remigius of Auxerre: Remigius's note 'uolens uidere quantum fuerit troie incendium' similarly ascribes to Nero the motive of wishing to compare the burning of Troy.[35] But the image of burning recalls the simile of fire consuming the heath in the passage which was previously applied to Nero and Theodoric, and it seems plausible that in Nero's pyromania Alfred sees reflected the destructive tendencies of the invading Danes.

Nero and Theodoric, former kings of Rome, apparently represent for Alfred the archetypal 'unrighteous kings'.[36] The reign of Tarquin Superbus and then the leadership of the consuls who overthrew him are also cited by Alfred as examples of the abuse of power.[37] Rome offered for Alfred a wealth of *exempla* depicting poor rulers. But Rome also boasted its share of wise and righteous leaders, as Alfred is at pains to show: not just Boethius himself, but also Cicero is a 'Romana heretoga' ('Roman consul') and an 'uðwita' ('philosopher'), Brutus Cassius is 'se foremæra 7 se aræda Romwara heretoga' ('the famous and bold Roman consul'), Cato is 'se wisa 7 fæstræda ... Romana heretoga; se wæs openlice uðwita' ('the wise and steadfast Roman consul who was clearly a thinker'), and the poet Catullus is described as a 'heretoga on Rome, swiðe gesceadwis mon' ('a consul in Rome, a very intelligent man'; Alfred was correct about the intelligence but not about the rank of consul).[38] Alfred even invents a Roman prince Liberius (his name is the result of a misreading, admittedly) whose wisdom brings him praise and honour,[39] and Hercules, according to euhemeristic tradition a king before he became a Roman god, is, as I have shown elsewhere, presented by Alfred as the epitome of skill and intellect.[40]

---

[34] *Boethius*, 39; trans.: 'Once he ordered the whole city of Rome to be set on fire simultaneously, following the precedent of the burning long ago of Troy. He desired to see how long and brightly it would burn compared with the latter.'

[35] B. S. Donaghey, 'The sources of King Alfred's translation of Boethius's *De Consolatione Philosophiae*', *Anglia*, 82 (1964), 23–57, at 55. For further discussion of the sources of this passage, see J. Bately, 'Those books that are most necessary for all men to know: the classics and late ninth-century England, a reappraisal', in *The Classics in the Middle Ages*, eds A. S. Bernardo and S. Levin, Medieval and Renaissance Texts and Studies, 69 (Binghampton, NY, 1990), 45–78, at 61–2 and 77, n. 123.

[36] In rendering two allusions to 'Nero' later in his source, Alfred independently refers to him as 'se unrihtwisa cyning Neron'; see *Boethius*, 64 and 66. He independently introduces Theodoric as an example of an 'unrihtwisan cyninges' who stands out for 'his dysig 7 his unrihtwisnes'; *Boethius*, 62.

[37] *Boethius*, 34–5. For his rendering of this passage from Boethius Book II, pr. 6, Alfred also draws probably on either Orosius's *History* or the Remigian commentary; see Bately, 'Those books', 61.

[38] *Boethius*, 143, 46, and 61. See also Bately, 'Those books', 53.

[39] *Boethius*, 36; see also Bately, 'Those books', 50.

[40] S. Irvine, 'Wrestling with Hercules: King Alfred and the classical past', in *Court Culture in the Early Middle Ages: The Proceedings of the First Alcuin Conference*, ed. C. E. Cubitt (Turnhout, 2003), 171–88.

Alfred's literary representation of Rome shows his ambivalent attitude towards its past. Whilst its former horrors and sufferings are not to be belittled, Rome also provides *exempla* of wisdom and faith. In his allusions to Rome and its citizens in his *Boethius*, Alfred seems often to have had in mind his own kingdom, one in which wisdom and faith must triumph in the face of constant barbarian destruction.

Other works composed in Alfred's reign attest to an awareness of the precedent of Rome and the perspectives it might throw on the situation in Anglo-Saxon England. The Old English translation of *Orosius* provides one example. The work, with its vision of a Christian purpose lying behind all history, clearly fitted neatly into Alfred's educational programme. But Orosius's primary aim in writing his work, which he outlines in his prologue, was very specific: to prove to his contemporary pagan audience of AD 417–18 that the sack of Rome by the Goths in 410 was not a result of the desertion of the old gods. Scholars have always assumed that this aim was irrelevant to the Old English translator, whose focus was more on the birth of Christ and the coming of Christianity.[41] But I would suggest that the theme of the original may well have prompted the selection of this work for translation. The gradual conversion to Christianity in England had entailed the repudiation of the pagan gods which the Anglo-Saxons had previously worshipped: Bede, *HE* II 13, in which Cefi destroys his own heathen temple and enclosure, provides a striking example of such repudiation.[42] But the Danish invasions of the second half of the ninth century brought about a severe test of that repudiation. The invasions must have exposed the Anglo-Saxons anew to heathenism and opened up the possibility of reversion to old beliefs.[43] These are of course exactly the types of responses which Orosius was confronting in his writing. The Old English author, with his translation of this work, implicitly suggests that abandoning pagan gods is no more the cause for the Danish attacks than it was for the sack of Rome by the Goths. His penultimate chapter, a free rendering of his source, could be addressed to a late ninth-century Anglo-Saxon audience rather than the Romans:

> Nugiet eow Romane mæg gescomian, cwæð Orosius, þæt ge swa heanlic geþoht sceoldon on eow geniman for anes monnes ege 7 for anes monnes geblote, þæt ge sædon þæt þa hæðnan tida wæron beteran þonne þa cristnan, 7 eac þæt eow selfum wære betere þæt ge

---

[41] See Whitelock, 'The prose of Alfred's reign', 90, and *Orosius*, ed. Bately, xciv; see also my discussion in 'Religious context: Pre-Benedictine Reform period', in *A Companion to Anglo-Saxon Literature*, eds P. Pulsiano and E. M. Treharne (2001), 135–50, at 141.

[42] *Venerabilis Baedae Opera Historica*, ed. C. Plummer (1896), I, 112–13.

[43] The threat to England's status as a Christian nation which the Danes represented extended well beyond the pre-Reform period. An explicit denunciation of the Danish gods, probably at least partly motivated by the same fear of backsliding, is found in Ælfric's sermon *De Falsis Diis* (*Homilies of Ælfric: A Supplementary Collection*, ed. J. C. Pope, 2 vols, EETS OS 259 and 260 (1967, 1968), II, 667–724)), and in Wulfstan's reworking of part of that sermon (*The Homilies of Wulfstan*, ed. D. Bethurum (1957), 221–4).

eowerne cristendom forleten 7 to þæm hæðeniscan þeawum fenge þe
eowre ieldran ær beeodon.[44]

If, for Orosius, the sack of Rome by the Goths was to be seen as confirming
Rome's place within an universal Christian scheme, so, implies the Old English
translator, the Danish attacks on Anglo-Saxon England should actually be viewed
as part of God's long-term plan for the establishment of England as a glorious
and successful Christian nation.

Other Alfredian works also relate Rome and England in various ways.
Bede's *Historia Ecclesiastica*, which was translated in Alfred's reign, directly
linked Anglo-Saxon England's Christian history with that of Rome.[45] Gregory's *Dialogi*, translated by Werferth Bishop of Worcester, may have attracted
attention because of, in Keynes's and Lapidge's words, 'an obvious parallel
between the Lombard invasions in sixth-century Italy which shattered Gregory's longing for tranquillity, and the Viking attacks in late-ninth-century England
which similarly destroyed Alfred's tranquillity'.[46] Certainly the Preface to
Werferth's translation, purportedly by Alfred himself though Malcolm Godden
has recently cast doubt on his authorship,[47] articulates Gregory's view that
contemplating the virtues and miracles of holy men can provide comfort
amidst 'þas eorþlican ymbhigdo' ('these earthly anxieties') and 'þas eorðlican
gedrefednesse' ('these earthly troubles').[48] The *Old English Martyrology*, which
may arguably have been composed in Alfred's reign,[49] includes, according to
Jane Roberts's recent analysis, a particular preponderance of saints linked with
Rome.[50]

Why might Alfred and his circle have expressed in so many different ways
their sense of the vitality of the link between Anglo-Saxon England and Rome?
To some extent this must be merely the articulation of a close connection
between the two which had existed since the arrival of Augustine. The evidence,
Veronica Ortenberg suggests, sustains 'a view of Rome during the Anglo-Saxon
period as, in the first place, a repository of books and relics, further a font of

---

[44] *Orosius*, ed. Bately, 156; trans.: 'Now may you Romans be ashamed, Orosius said, that you
should have entertained so disgraceful an idea, from fear of one man and the sacrifices of one man,
as to say that the heathen times were better than the Christian, and also that for yourselves it would
be better to abandon your Christianity, and adopt the heathen customs that your ancestors formerly
observed.'

[45] See in particular R. Vaughan, 'The past in the middle ages', *Journal of Medieval History*, 12
(1986), 1–14, at 8–9.

[46] Keynes and Lapidge, *Alfred*, 293, n. 2.

[47] M. Godden, 'Wærferth and King Alfred: the fate of the Old English *Dialogues*', in *Alfred
the Wise*, eds Roberts and Nelson, 35–51, at 36–7.

[48] *Dialogues*, ed. Hecht, 1.

[49] See J. M. Bately, 'Old English prose before and during the reign of Alfred', *ASE*, 17 (1988),
93–138, at 114; and C. Rauer, 'The Sources of the *Old English Martyrology*', *ASE* (forthcoming).

[50] J. Roberts, '*Fela martyra* "many martyrs": a different view of Orosius's city', in *Alfred the
Wise*, eds Roberts and Nelson, 155–78.

spiritual benefits, and not least a major attraction for her artistic treasures and liturgical splendour'.[51] To educated Anglo-Saxons, Rome was the centre of civilization and Christianity. Roman liturgy underpinned Christian observances in Anglo-Saxon England. Journeys to and from Rome were frequently undertaken by Anglo-Saxon pilgrims, merchants or others.[52] Large collections of relics from Rome were kept in English churches.[53] A fascination with imperial Rome too had revealed itself from at least the eighth century in the terminology used in Mercian charters and the imperial-style effigies appearing on coins.[54] An interest in Rome in the literary works from the Alfredian period is not intrinsically surprising. But I would suggest that the extent and type of allusions to Rome in these writings attest to a particular concern on the part of Alfred and his advisers to affirm the closeness of the relationship between England and Rome.

What circumstances might have motivated this impulse in the vernacular writings of the Alfredian court? Evidence from contemporary letters written during the period of Alfred's reign suggests that the relationship between Anglo-Saxon England and Rome was under some strain. The pervasive focusing by Alfred and the other Old English authors on parallels between Anglo-Saxon England invaded by Danes and Rome besieged by barbarians may reflect the part played by the Danish invasions in this estrangement.

The scanty epistolary evidence surviving from Alfred's reign does not do justice to the apparently active level of cross-Channel communication at that time. To the early part of Alfred's reign can be attributed the correspondence from Pope John VIII, written between about 874 and 878. The pope is openly critical of the Anglo-Saxons' failure to conform to appropriate religious standards. In a letter to Burgred, king of Mercia, he decries various sexual transgressions amongst the Mercians; the letter must have been written shortly before Burgred's flight to Rome reported in the *Anglo-Saxon Chronicle* annal for 874.[55] In a letter to Ethelred, archbishop of Canterbury, and Wulfred, archbishop of York, the pope urges the clergy to replace their lay habits by tunics reaching to the ankles.[56] In a third longer letter, apparently written in response to correspondence from Ethelred, the pope urges Ethelred to defend the church against all those who attempt to abuse it, including the king (to whom the pope mentions having written separately).[57]

[51] V. Ortenberg, *The English Church and the Continent in the Tenth and Eleventh Centuries: Cultural, Spiritual, and Artistic Exchanges* (1992), 148.

[52] For a recent discussion, see Keynes, 'Anglo-Saxon entries'.

[53] Ortenberg, *English Church*, 161.

[54] M. Hunter, 'Germanic and Roman antiquity and the sense of the past in Anglo-Saxon England', *ASE*, 3 (1974), 29–50.

[55] *Councils and Synods with other Documents relating to the English Church I A.D. 871–1204*, eds D. Whitelock, M. Brett and C. N. L. Brooke (1981), 1–2; trans. *EHD*, 880 (no. 220).

[56] *Councils and Synods*, 2–3; trans. *EHD*, 881 (no. 221).

[57] *Councils and Synods*, 4–6; trans. *EHD*, 881–3 (no. 222).

The allegations of sexual impropriety and lay disregard of church privileges in these letters conform to some extent, as Janet Nelson has shown, to the types of complaints made also about the Franks at the end of the ninth and beginning of the tenth centuries.[58] More surprising in the letters' contents, perhaps, is the scanty attention paid to the Danish attacks on England, given their frequency and ferocity in this period. Once the pope alludes indirectly to the Danes acting as divine punishment for the Mercians because of their sins, and once he expresses sympathy with the daily hardships Ethelred sustains. But his criticisms of English conduct, clerical and lay, are apparently independent of any effects that the Danish invasions may have had on England.

A later group of letters, written between about 886 and the early 890s, offers evidence of continuing communication between the Continent and the Anglo-Saxons. A letter from Archbishop Fulk of Reims to King Alfred, written probably in 886, refers more than once to a letter from Alfred requesting his help in ecclesiastical matters.[59] Fulk can be seen here as a representative of the papal viewpoint: not only was Reims in close contact with Rome at this time over its desire to be recognized as an apostolic see,[60] but also characteristic of the late ninth century was what Walter Ullmann calls 'the merging of papal and episcopal views ... the confluence of Rome and Rheims'.[61] Fulk is generous in his praise of Alfred's kingship. But it is clear that England has been the target of considerable criticism from abroad for the decline in its religious standards, particularly amongst the ecclesiastical orders. Fulk, apparently echoing Alfred's own words, describes the decline of the ecclesiastical order in England: 'qui in multis, ut dicitis, sive frequenti inruptione vel inpugnatione paganorum, seu vetustate temporum, vel incuria prelatorum, vel ignorantia subditorum conlapsus est'.[62] Other letters by Fulk from around 890 to Alfred and to Plegmund, archbishop of Canterbury, of which only abstracts survive, also imply, through their praise of the recipients, a pejorative attitude towards the English more generally. Thus Plegmund is congratulated by Fulk for his attempts 'pro abscidendis et extirpandis incestuosis luxuriae fomentis ... quae in ea gente videbantur inolevisse', and Alfred is praised for his determination to stamp out unchristian practices: 'quod perversissiman sectam, paganicis erroribus exortam et in illa

---

[58] J. L. Nelson, '"A king across the sea": Alfred in continental perspective', *TRHS*, fifth series 36 (1986), 45–68, at 62.

[59] The possibility that the letter was a fabrication was advanced by Nelson in '"A king across the sea"', at 48–9, and by Smyth, *King Alfred the Great*, 257–9; the genuineness of the letter has recently been asserted by J. L. Nelson, '" ... *sicut olim gens Francorum ... nunc gens Anglorum"*: Fulk's letter to Alfred revisited', in *Alfred the Wise*, eds Roberts and Nelson, 135–44.

[60] See Nelson, 'Fulk's Letter', 139–40, and Nelson, 'The Franks and the English', 148–50.

[61] W. Ullmann, *The Growth of Papal Government in the Middle Ages: A Study in the Ideological Relation of Clerical to Lay Power* (1970), 142.

[62] *Councils and Synods*, 8; trans. *EHD*, 883 (no. 223): 'which, as you say, has fallen in ruins in many respects, whether by the frequent invasion and attack of pagans, whether by the great passage of time or the carelessness of prelates or the ignorance of those subject to them'.

gente tunc usque relictam, verbi mucrone satageret amputare'.[63] Alfred's efforts to bring scholarly clerics into his court and to institute an educational programme have clearly earned praise, but Fulk's comments give some indication of just how severely the deterioration in Anglo-Saxon England has been viewed from abroad.[64]

One other letter, apparently written by Pope Formosus in the early 890s, sheds light on the attitude of Rome towards England in the latter part of Alfred's reign.[65] Someone, notes David Dumville, 'had informed the papacy that the English hierarchy had been insufficiently active against the threat posed by invaders'.[66] The response by Pope Formosus to the bishops of England is couched in no uncertain terms: 'Auditis nefandorum ritibus paganorum vestris in partibus repullulasse, et vos tenuisse silentium, ut canes non valentes latrare, gladio separationis a corpore Dei ecclesiae vos ferire deliberavimus.'[67] The letter, while giving some indication of just how low the reputation of the English clergy had sunk in Rome, is again written after an improvement in the situation: the pope goes on to explain that he has reconsidered, given that the bishops have begun to renew 'semina verbi Dei olim venerabiliter iacta in terra Anglorum'.[68]

These later letters suggest that the problems of the falling off in religious observance and the inadequate missionary efforts in the face of pagan invasions attracted vehement criticism. The particular difficulties experienced by Anglo-Saxon England in responding to Danish invasions have been ascribed by Janet Nelson to 'the relative underdevelopment of church–state relations in the English kingdoms as compared with the Continent'.[69] Whereas church and state in the Carolingian Empire tended to act together against the Danish invaders, the

---

[63] *Councils and Synods*, 13; trans. *EHD*, 887 (nos 224 and 225): 'to cut off and extirpate the incestuous heats of lasciviousness ... which would seem to have sprung up in that race'; 'he was concerned to cut down with the sword of the word that most perverse opinion, arisen from pagan errors, until then surviving among that people'.

[64] Alfred's Preface to his translation of Gregory's *Cura Pastoralis* attests to Alfred's awareness of, and concern for, England's status abroad: 'me com swiðe oft on gemynd ... hu man utanbordes wisdom & lare hieder on lond sohte, & hu we hie nu sceoldon ute begietan gif we hie habban sceoldon'; see *Pastoral Care*, 3; trans.: 'it has very often come into my mind ... how wisdom and teaching were sought in this land and how we now had to obtain them from abroad if we were to have them.'

[65] Although the letter survives only in post-Conquest sources, the first part of it is accepted as genuine; see *Councils and Synods*, 35.

[66] D. N. Dumville, 'King Alfred and the tenth-century reform of the English Church', in his *Wessex and England from Alfred to Edgar: Six Essays on Political, Cultural, and Ecclesiastical Revival* (1992), 185–205, at 191.

[67] *Councils and Synods*, 36; trans. *EHD*, 890–91, no. 227: 'Having heard that the abominable rites of the pagans have sprouted again in your parts, and that you kept silent "like dogs unable to bark", we have considered thrusting you from the body of the Church of God with the sword of separation.'

[68] *Councils and Synods*, 36; trans. *EHD*, 891, no. 227: 'the seed of the word of God once admirably sown in the land of the English'.

[69] Nelson, '"A king across the sea"', 67.

locally controlled Anglo-Saxon churches were more amenable to negotiation with them. This may have been in some respects to Alfred's political advantage, but it laid his country open to severe papal criticism. Alfred also included pagans in his entourage, as Asser's list attests.[70] In the eyes of Rome, Anglo-Saxon England became over-tolerant towards heathenism, both in relation to the Danish settlers and the practices of its own people.

But the later letters also suggest that Alfred, with the help of his advisers, did succeed in stemming the tide of papal hostility. The awareness of Rome and its links with England evident in the vernacular writings associated with his reign – the *Anglo-Saxon Chronicle*, the translations of *Boethius*, *Orosius*, Bede's *History*, and Gregory's *Dialogues*, and the *Old English Martyrology* – offer evidence of how just how much this relationship mattered to Alfred's court. When the *Anglo-Saxon Chronicle* annalist for 889 reports that there was no expedition to Rome but that King Alfred sent couriers with letters, he was not, I would suggest, merely filling an empty space with platitudes, but rather acknowledging a relationship which had enormous implications for England's attempt to establish itself as a significant force in Christian history in the late ninth century. Even the most apparently objective annals of the *Anglo-Saxon Chronicle* show us, in the words of Matthew Innes and Rosamund McKitterick, 'the extent to which the recording of a people's past acted as an expression of that people's identity'.[71]

---

[70] Asser, c. 76, 60.

[71] M. Innes and R. McKitterick, 'The writing of history', in *Carolingian Culture: Emulation and Innovation*, ed. R. McKitterick (1994), 193–220, at 193.

Chapter 5

Ædificia nova: treasures of Alfred's reign

Leslie Webster

Quid loquar, wrote Asser tantalizingly of the gold and silver treasures instigated by Alfred, [*de*] *aedificiis aureis et argenteis incomparabiliter, illo edocente, fabricatis?*;[1] but like jesting Pilate he did not stay for an answer to his own rhetorical question. Would that he had, for this task would then have been much easier. We must make do with only the most general descriptions of the products of gold and silver made by Alfred's craftsmen – those [*operatores*] ... *ex multis gentibus collectos et comparatos propemodum innumerabiles ... in omne terreno aedificio edoctos.*[2] This word *aedificium* occurs twice more in Asser's account – in chapter 56, where it is used to describe the many excellent treasures (*aedificia optima*) bestowed by Alfred on Guthrum on the occasion of the latter's baptism,[3] and in chapter 76, where the king is described as 'giving instructions to all his goldsmiths and craftsmen' and making to his own design (*sua machinatione*) *aedificia ... venerabiliora et pretiosiora nova* 'which far surpassed any tradition of his predecessors'.[4] The precise sense of the word *aedificium* has prompted some discussion, since it is normally used in the sense of 'building'; but it is clear from these contexts, as Keynes and Lapidge argue, that Asser is using it in primarily the sense of 'precious object', with perhaps an implication of 'construction' where craftsmen and design are mentioned.[5] The general impression Asser gives is thus clear enough; these are, as is fitting for the works of a king, wonderful and precious constructions, whether of gold or silver, or in other media; they are the

---

[1] Asser, c. 91, 76–7.

[2] Ibid., c. 101, 87.

[3] Ibid., c. 56, 47; and see footnote, 47.

[4] Ibid., 59; see also Keynes and Lapidge, *Alfred*, 91.

[5] It has been suggested that *ædificium* denotes an Insular house-shaped shrine; a closely related continental example discarded in late ninth- or early tenth-century Winchester shows that similar types were current in Æthelwulf's and Alfred's time (D. Hinton, S. Keene and K. Qualman, 'The Winchester reliquary', *Medieval Archaeology*, 25 (1981), 45–77; *The Golden Age of Anglo-Saxon Art 966–1066*, Exhibition Catalogue, The British Museum, eds J. Backhouse, D. Turner and L. Webster (1984), no. 12). However, while this could – at a pinch – be a plausible interpretation of the *aedificia optima* presented to Guthrum at his baptism, the more general contexts of the other occurrences of this word make it unlikely that it denotes anything so specific. Deshman's suggestion that some edificatory element may also be present in the word is tempting, but stretches the contemporary semantic range; R. Deshman, 'The Galba Psalter: pictures, texts and context in an early medieval prayerbook', *ASE*, 26 (1997),109–38, esp. 132–3.

products of many-skilled craftsmen assembled from many races; and in particular, those artefacts made to the king's own design or instructions are novel and exceptional as well as better than anything that went before. The only other probable reference to precious metalwork actually commissioned by Alfred comes in the famous allusion to the *æstels* in his Preface to the translation of the *Regula Pastoralis* sent out to each of his bishops; we are told only that each *æstel* is worth 50 mancuses, a formidable sum, which has traditionally prompted the reasonable inference that these objects were made of precious materials.[6] Thus far – and no further – the available documentary information on the metalwork of Alfred's court. In the face of the dearth of more informative descriptions, however, one may take some wry comfort from the fact that the only textual reference to the decoration of manuscripts associated with Alfred is to one which certainly antedates his reign – the book of English poetry with its beautiful illuminated initial which inspired the young Alfred to learn to read.[7]

Imprecise as the available sources are, I shall nevertheless concentrate in what follows on the small corpus of fine metalwork attributable to Alfred's circle; for as the few documentary descriptions imply, lavishly illuminated manuscripts and fine ivory carving in the manner of the Carolingian court schools seem, for reasons we shall return to, not to have been a prominent feature of Alfred's court – and certainly none survive today. But first I should admit to an underlying premise. What we know about the culture of Alfred's court and his own background and interests shows a consistent pattern of continental influences and contacts, particularly with the adjacent Frankish kingdoms. In such a climate, his *aedificia nova,* and the foreign craftsmen who made them, can be seen to draw on images and ideas associated with the Carolingian *renovatio* – though these ideas and influences were reworked into something very different in tone and purpose, as will be seen.[8]

However, it is also strikingly clear that this metalwork reveals the impact of Alfred's own tireless curiosity and inventiveness, repeatedly commented on by Asser, and manifest in the king's own writings. On the one hand, this curiosity is seen in his interest in God's created physical universe, exemplified by the incorporation into the Alfredian translation of *Orosius* of the famous passage about the voyages of Ohthere and Wulfstan in northern seas, the first of which at least was orally recounted to the king by the traveller himself. Another possible result of Alfred's lively interest in this encounter with the northern world may relate to the gift of walrus tusks which Ohthere presented to the king – the first documentary reference to this valuable commodity.[9] It is certainly from this

---

[6] Keynes and Lapidge, *Alfred*, 75.

[7] Asser, c. 23, 20.

[8] L. Webster, 'The legacy of Alfred', in *Golden Age*, eds Backhouse, Turner and Webster, 18–19, draws attention to a significant Carolingian influence on artefacts associated with Alfred's reign; see also J. Nelson, 'Alfred's Carolingian contemporaries', Chapter 17 in this volume.

[9] *Two Voyagers At The Court of King Alfred: the Ventures of Ohthere and Wulfstan, together*

point onwards that this fine-grained, dense and luminous carving medium replaced coarser bone and antler in the Anglo-Saxon carver's repertoire, giving rise to the great series of ivory carvings of the tenth and eleventh centuries. No such ivories can – as yet – be attributed to the period of Alfred himself, but he must have been aware of the potential of this new medium, as the account implies, and we may reasonably suspect that it was in his reign that its use was first encouraged and promoted.

On the other hand, Alfred's inexhaustible thirst for spiritual wisdom and knowledge was an equally important factor in the generation of new kinds of treasures – the same impulse that, for instance, drove the king to create his *enchiridion* in which he collected all manner of prayers, psalms and other matter which caught his interest.[10] The curiosity and inventiveness join forces with the spiritual quest in his creation of the candle-clocks – as David Pratt has ingeniously argued[11] – and, it is also clear, in the creation of the *æstels*, which were of course designed to be used in conjunction with close study of the *Regula Pastoralis*. These embodied ideas are true *aedificia nova*.

However, a review of what may be reasonably identified as surviving examples of Alfredian court metalwork will not detain us too long. In addition to the existing canon of the Alfred and Minster Lovell Jewels, the Fuller Brooch and Abingdon sword have in more recent years been generally attributed to the circle of Alfred, sharing as they do a distinctive use of highly visible and portable symbolic iconographies of a kind close to Alfred's own ideas about spiritual education and Christian kingship.[12] Latterly, the likely corpus has expanded steadily in small but surprising ways.

Alfredian artefacts may be divided into two groups: those which appear to be new inventions, true *aedificia nova*; and those which adopt traditional forms, but with new or unusual iconography.

The starting-point can only be the Alfred Jewel, which by virtue of its inscription, *Ælfred mec heht gewyrcan*, is reasonably attributed by most to Alfred's court workshops (Fig. 1). It is a complex and subtle piece, consisting of a filigree-enriched gold framework which encloses a reused Roman polished crystal, overlying an enamelled plate with a human image holding two flowering staffs. The apex of the jewel terminates in a decorated beast head, from the jaws of which issues a short and slender tubular socket, 4 mm in diameter. Round the sides of the jewel runs the inscription, ingeniously executed in openwork to enable the translucent properties of the crystal to show to best advantage. The

---

with the Description of Northen Europe from the Old English Orosius, ed. N. Lund and trans. C.Fell (1984), 19–20, and see 58–60.

[10] Asser, cc. 88 and 89, 73–5.

[11] D. Pratt, 'Persuasion and Invention at the Court of Alfred the Great', in *Court Culture in the Early Middle Ages. The Proceedings of the First Alcuin Conference*, ed. C. E. Cubitt (Turnhout, 2003).

[12] *Golden Age*, eds Backhouse, Turner and Webster, 19.

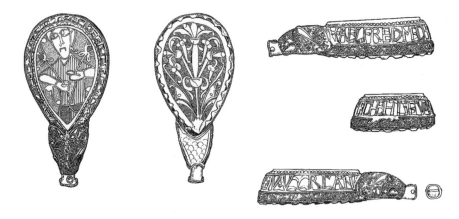

Fig. 1   The Alfred Jewel (from the drawing by P. Clarke). Reduced

flat back-plate is held in place by a dog-toothed frame, and is decorated with an
incised tree-of-life motif. The jewel is 64 mm in length, and the gold content of
the metal is 84.1 per cent. The jewel, since 1718 a principal treasure of Oxford
University, and now in the Ashmolean Museum, was found in 1693 close to
Athelney in Somerset, one of Alfred's monastic foundations.[13]

The jewel's function has been the subject of considerable debate, with
opinion tending to concur in favour of identifying it as the handle of one of the
precious *æstels* sent out at Alfred's command with the copies of his translation
of Gregory's *Regula Pastoralis*, one to each diocese of his kingdom. I shall not
rehearse the well-known and generally accepted arguments for the identification
of the word *æstel* as a manuscript pointer; in such an interpretation, the jewel
would have contained a short rod of some now-perished organic material in the
slender socket, and would have lain on the page, its flat base enabling it to be
moved about easily from word to word – to use David Pratt's happy analogy,
rather like a computer mouse. It should be borne in mind, however, that though
extremely plausible, and very probably correct, this remains not the only possible interpretation; the most convincing alternative proposal is that it could have
formed the head of a slender staff or wand of office carried by some official of
Alfred's court. As to the all-important iconography, to which we shall come later
on, it will be seen that most of the likely options would be entirely appropriate to
either of these functions. Whichever the case, there is no doubt that this object

---

[13] D. Hinton, *A Catalogue of the Anglo-Saxon Ornamental Metalwork in the Department of
Antiquities, Ashmolean Museum* (1974), no. 23, 29–48; Keynes and Lapidge, *Alfred*, 203–6;
Backhouse, Turner and Webster, *Golden Age*, no. 13; G. Kornbluth, 'The Alfred Jewel: reuse of
Roman *spolia*', *Medieval Archaeology*, 33 (1989), 32–7; *The Making of England: Anglo-Saxon Art
and Culture AD 600–900*, Exhibition Catalogue, The British Museum, eds L. Webster and J.
Backhouse (1991), no. 260; Pratt, 'Persuasion and invention', n. 22.

type appears to be without precedent until Alfred's reign, and to be precisely of it; the substantial corpus of fine metalwork from the eighth and early ninth centuries, and from the tenth and eleventh centuries contains nothing else to compare. Indeed, so far as I can tell, the nearest parallels from western Europe are the Torah pointers of sixteenth-, seventeenth- and eighteenth-century synagogues – slender rods which terminate in a small pointing hand, whence their Hebrew name, *yad*, hand.[14] It is also likely that the extreme lexical rarity of the word *æstel* implies that these too were new creations, born of the king's ardent campaign of renewal, and his own inventive and curious cast of mind. The very singularity of these objects suggests the creative force of the king's own personality, as Asser so clearly describes it.

The special nature of the Alfred Jewel may then reasonably be taken into account when considering the small group of other artefacts which are linked to it by form, content and construction. First among these is the Minster Lovell Jewel, also in the Ashmolean Museum (Fig. 2).[15] A simpler piece than the Alfred Jewel, it none the less shares with it a number of features. Found at Minster Lovell, Oxfordshire, in or about 1860, it consists of a round enamel set in a gold frame with filigree and granulation, as on the Alfred Jewel. The *cloisonné* enamel inlay is closely similar in both technical quality and in colour range to that on the Alfred Jewel. The enamel decoration consists of a stepped cross set within a cross with expanded terminals, of Insular type. A slender socket, diameter 5 mm, is attached below the base of the cross, and the flat back is plain. The jewel is 30 mm in length, and its gold content is 77.4 per cent.

A more recent addition to this group is the Bowleaze Jewel, found by a detectorist in debris from a cliff fall at Bowleaze Cove, Weymouth, Dorset in 1990, and now in the British Museum (Fig. 3, a–c).[16] It consists of a circular domed gold head with simple filigree and granulation, with, at its centre, a blue glass cabochon set in a collar; a short and slender socket, diameter 4.5 mm, is attached as before. The flat back-plate is missing. The jewel is very close in size and form to the Minster Lovell Jewel; it is 28 mm long and the gold content is 83 per cent. While it lacks the elaborate filigree and enamel of the previous two jewels, it is clearly linked to them in size and construction; and the use of blue glass may also be linked to the dominant use of blue enamel in the other two.

The final member of this group, the so-called 'Wessex' Jewel (Fig. 4, a–c), was found in 1997, also by a detectorist, near Cley Hill, Warminster, Wiltshire.[17] It is now in the Salisbury Museum. A rather different combination of the by-now familiar elements can be seen on it. Like the Alfred Jewel, it consists of a

---

[14] *Catalogue of the Permanent and Loan Collections of the Jewish Museum, London*, ed. R. D. Barnett (1974), nos 148–79, pls 66–7; E. Martyna (ed.), *Judaica: w zbiorach Muzeum Narodowego w Warszawie* (Warsaw, 1993),100–107.

[15] Hinton, *Catalogue*, no. 22; *Making of England*, eds Webster and Backhouse, no. 259.

[16] *Making of England*, eds Webster and Backhouse, no. 258.

[17] Christie's, South Kensington, *Sale Catalogue 21 April 1999*, lot 144.

Fig. 2   The Minster Lovell Jewel (photo: Ashmolean Museum). Enlarged

filigree-embellished gold framework which encases a reused rock-crystal. The crystal is approximately circular, pierced centrally, and flattened at front and back. Unlike the Alfred Jewel's flawlessly polished crystal, it exhibits considerable abrasion in places, giving it a somewhat opaque aspect. The form and wear patterns suggest that it is a reused Anglo-Saxon amuletic bead, probably from a necklace or a sword attachment, a type current in the late fifth and sixth centuries.[18] The slender frame which holds it consists of strips set cross-wise on the front of the jewel, where a blue glass cabochon is set centrally, at the crossing point of the strips; these are attached to a similar band running round the circumference of the jewel; the whole is secured by a rod which runs through the piercing at the centre of the crystal, and is attached to a gold disc with a lightly

---

[18] A. Meaney, *Anglo-Saxon Amulets and Curing Stones*, British Archaeological Reports, British Series, 96 (1981), 77–82. Examples of these are not recorded beyond the seventh century. A strikingly similar use of such a crystal consists of a gold and garnet framed pendant, found in the Isle of Ely and dated to the early seventh century; T. Lethbridge, 'Jewelled Saxon pendant from the Isle of Ely', *Proceedings of the Cambridge Antiquarian Society*, 46 (1953 for 1952), 1–3. It is uncertain whether this apparent gap in usage reflects a discontinuity of retrieval, or a genuine break in usage.

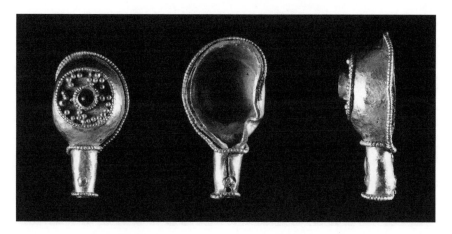

Fig. 3, a–c   The Bowleaze Jewel (photos: British Museum). Enlarged

incised cross, which covers the piercing's exit on the underside. A distinctive slender socket, diameter 5 mm, is attached at the base of the frontal cross. The jewel is 44 mm long, and the gold content of the frame is 86 per cent. Although this piece, unlike the other three, does not have a flat metal back, the flattened underside of the crystal and the flat gold disc beneath it would have enabled it to be slid as easily across a page as the others.

Quite clearly, the many technical and morphological cross-links between these – crystal, enamel, blue glass, filigree and granulation, similar gold content, socket size, flat bases – show beyond doubt that they form a closely related group. If we accept the Alfredian connection of the Alfred Jewel, and its most likely function, then these should all be accounted products of Alfred's court workshops. The fact that *all* were found at places in Alfred's Wessex can also hardly be coincidental. Though they clearly demonstrate a hierarchy of value (the Bowleaze Jewel at least being a mancus or two short of 50), there is nothing incompatible with them having a similar function, and emanating from the same workshop, at the same time, to the same novel programme.

If then these are *æstels* or even the terminals of staffs of office, what ideas lie behind their exceptional construction? The use of crystal *spolia* in two of them is particularly striking. Classical and early medieval lore about precious stones refers to the crystal's translucency, its clarity and whiteness, and may associate it with ice and fire; used particularly in early Frankish and Anglo-Saxon amuletic contexts, it was evidently thought to have special properties, though it is uncertain what exactly these might have been.[19] Perhaps pertinently,

---

[19] For example Isidore, *Etymologiarum libri XX*, XVI.13, ed. W. Lindsay (1911); Meaney, *Anglo-Saxon Amulets*, 90–96.

Fig. 4, a–c   The 'Wessex' Jewel (photos: British Museum). Actual size

Elias, patriarch of Jerusalem, who corresponded with Alfred and sent gifts to him, is also recorded in Bald's *Leechbook* as having recommended to Alfred a certain white stone which is said to protect, among other things, against all strange diseases;[20] did Alfred's interest in crystal somehow relate to this piece of lore, which in turn was of possible relevance to the mysterious internal disease from which Alfred suffered?[21] More plausibly, the translucency of crystal could in any case certainly link it to ideas about seeing clearly and understanding, with which Alfred was much concerned, and which would be entirely appropriate to a pointer designed to be used with an exemplary text such as the *Regula Pastoralis*. Since the shape of the reused crystal has also dictated the shape of the artefact in the two larger jewels, it may be significant that the other two adopt a closely similar circular form when freed from the necessity of accommodating a given component.

For one of these, the Minster Lovell Jewel, the iconography is immediately evident; the cross-within-a-cross pattern is a doubly concentrated image which strongly suggests a specifically religious context of usage. The Warminster piece also bears two crosses: one on its face and the other, less formally, on its underside; more suggestive, however, is the use of domed blue glass insets here and on the Bowleaze Jewel. The explanation may be quite simply that blue glass cabochons were regularly in use as small inlays in Anglo-Saxon ivory carvings and metalwork of the eighth and ninth centuries, and there is no more to their

---

[20] T. Cockayne (ed.), *Leechdoms, Wortcunning and Starcraft of Early England*, Rolls Series (3 vols, 1864–6), II.174–5, 290–91; Meaney, *Anglo-Saxon Amulets*, 92–3.

[21] Asser, cc. 25, 74, 91; A. Meaney, 'Alfred, the Patriarch and the white stone', *AUMLA, Journal of the Australian Universities Language and Literature Association*, 49 (1978), 65–79; Keynes and Lapidge, *Alfred*, 255–6, 270.

presence here than that.[22] But it is significant that they most often appear not prominently as a central feature, as here, but as insets for eyes, whether human, or more often, animal; could these two circular artefacts, each with a prominent blue glass setting at its centre, thus represent the *oculus* – specifically that inner eye with which Alfred was so concerned?[23] And here at last may come a potential link to the iconography of the Alfred Jewel itself. David Pratt's paper, referred to above, makes a very convincing case for placing the Alfred Jewel and its analogues, together with the Fuller Brooch, firmly in the context of Alfred's preoccupations with spiritual and temporal wisdom.[24] The images with prominent eyes on the Alfred Jewel and the Fuller Brooch, interpreted as personifications of Sight,[25] have been convincingly associated by Pratt with Alfred's many references in his own writings to *modes eagan*, the mind's eyes, the essential conduit through which we may seek and attain wisdom.[26] By extrapolation, Pratt convincingly argues that all these interlinked artefacts are emblematic of the Alfredian commitment to a search for spiritual wisdom. However, this argument may be further extended, by tracing here another image of wisdom in the Alfred Jewel, to be discussed below.

Of the second class of objects, that is, those that employ traditional forms to emphasize a new iconography, the Fuller Brooch has already been mentioned (Fig. 5). This severely beautiful silver disc brooch, which unfortunately lacks a provenance, bears an image of the Five Senses, with Sight pre-eminent.[27] Around the central bust of Sight are full-length personifications of the other four Senses in attitudes appropriate to their nature. This central group is surrounded by a zone of roundels representing *sensate* creation – humans, birds and quadrupeds, interspersed with geometric elements. Originally dated to the mid-ninth century by Bruce-Mitford, as noted earlier, it has more recently been recognized as a product of Alfred's reign, on grounds both of style and intellectual content. Though this type of brooch – a broad silver disc divided into many fields punctuated by bosses – is current from the beginning of the ninth century, the Fuller Brooch differs uniquely from its fellows in having a complex programme of figural decoration, rather than one formed exclusively of zoomorphic or vegetal motifs. It is not difficult to see how such an unusual item, carrying a very structured message about the pursuit of wisdom, might have made a suitable emblem not just of temporal status but also an exemplar of the search for spiritual wisdom upon which earthly power depends.[28]

---

[22] For example *Making of England*, eds Webster and Backhouse, nos 141,178, 179, 189, 194.

[23] Pratt, 'Persuasion and invention'.

[24] Ibid.

[25] E. Bakka, 'The Alfred Jewel and sight', *Antiquaries Journal*, 46 (1966), 277–82.

[26] Pratt, 'Persuasion and invention'.

[27] R. Bruce-Mitford, 'Late Anglo-Saxon disc brooches' in *Dark Age Britain: Studies presented to E.T. Leeds*, ed. D. Harden (1956), 171–201, esp. 173–90; *Golden Age*, eds Backhouse, Turner and Webster, no. 11; *Making of England*, eds Webster and Backhouse, no. 257.

[28] Pratt, 'Persuasion and invention'.

Fig. 5   The Fuller Brooch (photo: British Museum). Actual size

A recent find which certainly relates to the brooch stylistically is a late ninth-century strap-end found near Cranborne, Dorset – another Wessex provenance (Fig. 6).[29] Here a man or boy clambers upwards through the stems and branches of a vine, knife in hand and mouth agape as if to bite at the grape bunch dangling before him. The implication could not be clearer – he is about to cut the grapes and eat them. The pose is so graphic, and the image so very different from the normal repertoire of Anglo-Saxon strap-ends of this type, that one might indeed wonder if this could be another image of Taste. The more elaborate strap-ends sometimes appear in sets of four;[30] perhaps this and three

---

[29] In private possession, and unpublished.

[30] For example *Making of England*, eds Webster and Backhouse, no. 249, and a recent find of a set of four large decorated silver strap-ends from near York: *Treasure Annual Report 1998–1999*, Department for Culture, Media and Sport, 2000, 43–5, Fig. 76.

Fig. 6   Strap-end, Cranborne, Dorset (drawing: Nicholas Griffiths). Actual size

others, with Touch, Hearing and Smell, were to be worn *en suite* with a buckle or brooch bearing the image of Sight – appropriate accoutrements to have been made and worn in a context of Alfredian thought.

But another possibility presents itself, and one which could even co-exist iconographically with the former; the boy in the vine suggests the *ego sum vitis vera* of John 15: 1–10, where Jesus commands the faithful to 'dwell in me, as I in you'; the harvested grape becomes the eucharistic wine, Christ's own blood from which whoever drinks, dwells continually in Christ (John 6: 56). A closely similar scene appears on the cross-shaft from Codford St Peter, Wiltshire, where a young man with a flask in one hand and a fruiting vine branch upraised triumphally in the other, the grape bunch dangling by his head, symbolizes the same theme.[31] This remarkable sculpture has no other parallels, and given its Wessex provenance, we may speculate on a connection between the two, at least in terms of a shared tradition, or a shared interest in this unique presentation of the theme. The cross-shaft is usually stylistically dated to the early ninth century, because of its leaf forms, but the vine branch with its cusped junctions and pendulous sprigs is related to the tree-of-life motif on the back of the Alfred Jewel, which lends some credence to a later date.

The last of these pieces which might be assigned to Alfred's circle is the Abingdon sword, now in the Ashmolean Museum, and another Wessex find (Fig. 7).[32] Although in general form and technique the sword is a typical ninth-

[31] *Making of England*, eds Webster and Backhouse, no. 208.
[32] Hinton, *Catalogue*, no. 1.

Fig. 7 Sword-hilt, Abingdon, Berkshire (after *Archaeologia* L, pl. 27). Reduced

century type, its decorative scheme singles it out as uncharacteristically subtle and complex, compared with other contemporary swords. Its fleshy plant orna- ment certainly belongs to the end of the ninth century and relates it to the Fuller Brooch, and to the leaf forms of the Alfred Jewel back-plate. The iconography is subtle: the upper guard bears on one side the figures of a man and an eagle, and on the other, a calf and a stylized lion. These undoubted evangelist symbols, unparalleled on any other weapon, would form fitting decoration for the sword of a Christian warrior in Alfred's own image.

In discussing the unusual forms and distinctive iconographies of these pieces which, in their various ways, might be linked to the culture of Alfred's court and to the king's own spiritual interests and concerns, we should not however overlook the hints of a pre-existing royal tradition of using exotic iconographies, visible in surviving earlier products of the house of Wessex. The two royal donative rings associated with Alfred's father, Æthelwulf, and his sister, Æthelswith, are unique survivals, both evincing an acquaintance with themes more prominent in the Carolingian world than in Anglo-Saxon England at that time (Fig. 8, a–b).[33] The Æthelwulf ring bears the king's title, *Aethelwulf rex*; the accompanying decoration has usually been identified as the early Christian image of two peacocks flanking the tree of life, but comparison with a very similar motif in the late eighth-century *Godescalc Evangelistary*, commissioned by Charlemagne, makes it clear that this is in fact an elliptical image of peacocks at the fountain of life, a rare baptismal image that also occurs in another manuscript associated with the court school of Charlemagne, the early ninth-century Gospels of Saint-Médard of Soissons (Fig. 9).[34] It is not an image which occurs elsewhere in Anglo-Saxon art. Æthelwulf's daughter's ring bears inside the inscription *Ethelswith regna*, showing that it most probably dates to after her marriage to Burgred of Mercia at Chippenham in 853; it also carries an image of the *Agnus Dei*. Before the tenth and eleventh centuries, this is an exceptionally rare motif in Anglo-Saxon contexts.[35] The image is, however, again represented in manuscripts associated with the Carolingian court schools; the Adoration of the Lamb appears again in the Saint-Médard Gospels, and in the Codex Aureus of St Emmeram, commissioned by Charles the Bald *c.* 870.[36] These rings are unusual and distinctive artefacts which make striking use of continental baptismal and salvation iconography, and which were both quite possibly known to Alfred at first hand. Could they, for instance, have commemorated the respective marriages of father and daughter in 856 and 853? They were in any case evidently prestige objects made for presentation and to symbolize the premier-league status of the house of Wessex, signalling authority with more than a nod to the Carolingian dynasties across the Channel. They certainly make one long to know what exactly Æthelwulf's lavish gifts presented to Benedict III on the occasion of his visit to Rome in 855 might have looked like – among them, according to the entry in the *Liber Pontificalis*, 'a fine gold crown

---

[33] D. M. Wilson, *Anglo-Saxon Ornamental Metalwork 700–110 in the British Museum*, Catalogue of Antiquities of the Later Anglo-Saxon Period, 1 (1984), nos 31 and 1.

[34] Paris, Bibliothèque Nationale, Nouv. acq. lat. 1203, fol. 3v, and Paris, Bibliothèque Nationale lat. 8850, fol. 6v; F. Mütherich and J. Gaehde, *Carolingian Painting* (1977), 24, 34, pl. 2.

[35] Only two other pre-tenth-century examples are known, both from seventh/eighth-century Northumbria; in the *Codex Amiatinus*, and among the destroyed sculptures from Hoddam, Dumfries.

[36] Paris, Bibliothèque Nationale lat. 8850, fol. 1v, and Munich, Bayerische Staatsbibliothek, Clm. 14000, fol. 6r; Mütherich and Gaehde, *Carolingian Painting*, 24, 39, pl. 27, 108–9, pl. 38.

Fig. 8, a–b The rings of Queen Æthelswith (top) and King Æthelwulf of Wessex (bottom) (photo: British Museum). Enlarged

Fig. 9   The Godescalc Evangelistary, f. 3v (Paris, Bibliothèque Nationale,
Nouv. acq. lat., 1203; after Schramm and Mütherich, *Denkmale der
deutsche Könige und Kaiser*, fig. 8 [Munich 1962])

weighing 4lb', two gold beakers, a sword bound with gold, four silver gilt Saxon bowls, and various decorated garments.[37]

Another, more shadowy account of Æthelwulf's munificence, and of his continental interests, exists in a charter dated November 857 (Sawyer 318) confirming the gift of lands at Rotherfield, Hastings, Pevensey and London to the monastery of Saint-Denis, which also records other gifts from the king – of gold, of a silver vessel, and of cloths to decorate the shrine of Saint-Denis.[38] Though the text as it survives (the earliest manuscript is thirteenth century) is certainly not authentic, it may be based on a genuine record, as Atsma and Vézin have argued.[39] The existence of an extremely rare church dedication to St Denis at Rotherfield lends some credence to the possibility that this charter reflects some genuine tradition of grants to the French abbey.[40] If so, the implication is that Æthelwulf had visited the shrine when in Francia. Certainly, Æthelwulf would have had good reason, in 857, to have been generous to Saint-Denis; he had only the previous year married Judith, daughter of Charles the Bald, who himself had a special veneration for St Denis – of which more shortly.

Of course, Alfred was not only exposed to Frankish and Roman influences through his father's contacts; as a boy, he made two visits to Rome, in 853 and 855/6, both now confirmed by the Alfredian entries recently identified by Simon Keynes in the Brescia *Liber Vitae*.[41] These trips undoubtedly took him through Francia, and on the second of these, it is clear that he spent some time at the court of Charles the Bald, where his father married Judith on the return leg in 856. When he came to institute his own *renovatio*, it was naturally to Frankish advisers that he turned – initially to Fulco of Reims, and then to the Frankish scholars, Grimbald of Saint-Bertin, and John the Old Saxon, who presumably came from the eastern kingdom.[42] Much has been made of the likely texts they might have brought to Alfred's attention – Sedulius Scottus's *De Rectoribus Christianis*, and Hincmar's *De Ordine Palatii*, for example.[43] Asser's emulation of Einhard's *Vita Karoli*, his use of Frankish Latin terms, and his evident up-to-date knowledge of Frankish affairs may, as Keynes and Lapidge suggest, simply

---

[37] *The Lives of the Ninth-Century Popes from AD 817–891 (Liber Pontificalis)* Liverpool University Translated Texts for Historians, 20, trans. R. Davis (1995).

[38] E. Barker, 'Sussex Anglo-Saxon Charters, part II', *Sussex Archaeological Collections*, 87 (1948), 112–63, esp. 132–5 (S 318).

[39] H. Atsma and J. Vézin, 'Le dossier suspect des possessions de Saint-Denis en Angleterre revisité (VIIIe–IXe siècle)', *Fälschungen im Mittelalter*, MGH Schriften 33 (5 vols, Hanover, 1988), IV, 211–36.

[40] Barker, 'Sussex Anglo-Saxon charters', 132–5.

[41] S. Keynes, 'Anglo-Saxon entries in the *Liber Vitæ* of Brescia', in *Alfred the Wise: Studies in Honour of Janet Bately on the Occasion of Her Sixty-fifth Birthday*, eds J. Roberts and J. Nelson, with M. Godden (1997).

[42] Keynes and Lapidge, *Alfred*, 26–7.

[43] S. Keynes, 'Alfred the Great and Æthelred the Unready', *TRHS*, fifth series 36 (1986) 195–217, esp. 209.

derive from contact with Grimbald;[44] alternatively, they at least suggest the possibility that contacts between Alfred's court and Francia were regular and ongoing – as indeed Asser's reference to importing skilled foreign craftsmen may also indicate. We may detect visible indications of such contacts in the Carolingian reliquary which was excavated in a late ninth-century pit at Winchester a few years ago, and in the Carolingian-style wall-painting, also from Winchester, which was found in an excavation level which dates it to before 903.[45]

In an intellectual context where Alfred could also receive medical prescriptions from the patriarch of Jerusalem,[46] it is easy to see that the exchange of news and ideas with courts nearer home could have been regularly maintained, even in the difficult years of Viking activity – indeed, perhaps particularly so, when Charles and Alfred faced the same enemies, and perhaps found common cause in thinking about how an effective king should conduct himself in these circumstances.[47]

At one level, Charles the Bald – 'a Carolingian renaissance prince' as Wallace Hadrill described him, with all the ruthlessness as well as ostentatious artistic patronage that that implies – projects a rather different image of kingship from the godly austerity that Asser presents to us. The sumptuous manuscripts and lavish artefacts associated with Charles's reign signal a conscious assimilation of Roman and biblical exemplars; to take just one example, the Vivian Bible, made at Tours in *c*. 845/6, places the image of Charles among God's first chosen people, indicated by David, Solomon and Josiah, to symbolize that God's mission is entrusted to a second chosen race, the Franks.[48] The grandeur and sense of destiny implied by this and other court manuscripts associated with Charles are indeed a far cry from the striking dearth of illuminated manuscripts from Alfred's reign, and the modest quality of those – very different – texts that survive.[49] Even allowing for disparate conditions of loss and retrieval, this seems to reflect a real difference not only in wealth but also in cultural tradition between the two courts, and very probably, a real difference in personality as well as kingship style between the two kings. The grand bibles and psalters made

---

[44] Keynes and Lapidge, *Alfred*, 54–5.

[45] Backhouse, Turner and Webster, *Golden Age*, nos 12 and 25. A number of finds of secular Carolingian metalwork from Wessex, including a fine silver-gilt harness fitting from Wareham, support this picture: Webster and Backhouse, *Making of England*, no. 256.

[46] *Leechdoms*, II, ch. 64.

[47] As Wallace-Hadrill observed, in some sense the *Chronicle* for Alfred's reign marches in step with the *Annals of Saint-Bertin*, both contemporary records of two kings conscious of their own dynastic need 'built against a background of common experience, ... which was the war against the *pagani*'. J. Wallace-Hadrill, 'The Franks and the English in the ninth century: some common historical interests', in *idem*, *Early Medieval History* (1975), 201–16.

[48] Paris, Bibliothèque Nationale lat. 1, fol. 422v.

[49] For example Bodleian Library, MS Hatton 20; E. Temple, *Anglo-Saxon Manuscripts 900–1066*, A Survey of Manuscripts Illuminated in the British Isles, 2 (1976), no. 1.

for Charles were unique marvels, which elevated and distanced the king in all his power and glory; while the manuscripts which Alfred engineered were intended for circulation, and to bring his court and clergy nearer to his personal thinking. This is equally evident in the *aedificia* of both monarchs. Nevertheless, there are striking convergences, and ones which have significant implications for some of the artefacts associated with Alfred's court.

A number of objects, apart from manuscripts and their bindings, are associated with Charles the Bald, all of them exceptionally luxurious, and of superb craftsmanship. Prime among these is a remarkable series of gifts to the Abbey of St Denis made during Charles's lifetime, or bequeathed in his will. Despite the troubled years of mid-century, including the sack of the abbey in 865, the treasury at Saint-Denis in the ninth century has been described as one of the most important ensembles of precious objects in the West.[50] Charles became lay abbot of the monastery in 867, but his particular devotion to it can be presumed to pre-date this event by some years (and may gain corroboration from that dubious charter which includes reference to Æthelwulf's gifts to Saint-Denis in 857). There is certainly plenty of material evidence for Charles's interest in the monastery. The contents of the medieval treasury at Saint-Denis have been the recent subject of two brilliant major autopsies by Danielle Gaborit-Chopin.[51] This is indeed a tangled tale of abbatial agendas, elliptical inventories, muddled antiquarians and revolutionary zeal, too complex to dissect in detail here; in summary, however, a core of extraordinary and sumptuous items can be identified as having been given or bequeathed to the monastery by Charles. Chief among these are: the Sassanian 'dish of Solomon', the Antique 'cup of the Ptolemies' and the paten of serpentine associated with it; the gold altar frontal, the great gold jewelled cross, and the mighty 'escrain' or shrine. Of these, three and a fragment survive today to give an impression of the unusual quality of this metalwork, amplified by engravings of the pre-revolutionary treasury, made by Dom Michel Félibien at the beginning of the eighteenth century.[52] Some are antique and eastern trophies, others are new creations; all are extraordinary, and interlinked by technical signatures and in one case, an inscription, as well as by early tradition.

First, the object known today as the Chosroes Dish, first described in the fourteenth century in the *Grandes Chroniques de France* as an unsurpassed treasure, 'so marvellously wrought that in all the kingdoms of the world there is no other so subtle' (Fig. 10).[53] This is in fact a sixth/seventh century Sassanian piece of great magnificence, constructed from a gold framework set with garnet

---

[50] D. Gaborit-Chopin, in *Le Trésor de Saint-Denis*, eds D. Alcouffe, D. Gaborit-Chopin and others, Exposition Musées du Louvre (Paris, 1991), 44.

[51] D. Gaborit-Chopin, 'L'orfevrerie cloisonnée à l'époque carolingienne', *Cahiers Archéologiques*, 29 (1980–81), 5–26; Gaborit-Chopin in *Le Trésor de Saint-Denis*, 11–118.

[52] Gaborit-Chopin, in *Le Trésor de Saint-Denis*, figs. 7–11.

[53] Ibid., no. 10.

Fig. 10   The Chosroes Dish (Paris, Cabinet des Medailles; after Cabrol and
Leclerc, *Dictionnaire d'archéologie chrétienne et de Liturgie*, fig.
2819 [Paris 1913])

and rock-crystal cameos, and green glass, surrounded by a distinctive border of
semi-cylindrical garnets in gold cells. At its heart lies the crystal image of the
enthroned Sassanian king, most probably identified as Chosroes II (591–628). It
is not recorded when this came to Saint-Denis, but the gem-encrusted gold
border added in the second half of the ninth century to the first-century serpentine dish is clearly modelled on the outer border of the Chosroes Dish.[54] The
distinctive use of small heart-shaped garnets and other technical traits on this
mount is in turn shared with the destroyed early medieval fittings from the first-
century chalcedony cantharus with Dionysiac scenes, known as the cup of the

---

[54] Ibid., no. 12c.

Fig. 11   The Coupe des Ptolemées, showing lost Carolingian mounts (Paris,
Cabinet des Medailles; after Félibien)

Ptolemies (Fig. 11).[55] This prized vessel was recommissioned as a chalice in the
early Middle Ages, in tandem with the serpentine dish, which served as a paten
to the chalice. The lost mounts on the cup bore a possibly contemporary inscription (*hoc vas Christe tibi mente dicavit tertius in francos regmine Karlus*) which
links it directly to Charles the Bald.[56] The mounts for these two exotic late
antique items were thus evidently made under Charles the Bald's royal patronage, perhaps at Saint-Denis itself. Both are by this association also dependent on
the Chosroes Dish as a source of technical inspiration, thus indicating that,
however and whenever that extraordinary object arrived in Francia, it was present
and admired in the time of Charles, who is thought to have given it to the
treasury at Saint-Denis himself.

A similar network of technical details unites these pieces with other major
works by tradition associated with Charles the Bald – the lost great altar cross,
with its spectacular settings of sapphires, garnets and pearls, and the equally
destroyed golden altar with its similar range of gems and also enamels.[57] These
have left no trace, other than one small fragment, possibly from the cross,
Félibien's engraving and the National Gallery's famous *Mass of St Giles*. But

---

[55] Ibid., no. 11.

[56] Ibid., 83–7, esp. 86; in the context of Saint-Denis, the inscription referring to Charles the
Third denotes Charles the Bald, rather than Charles the Simple.

[57] Gaborit-Chopin, 'L'orfevrerie cloisonnée', 22–6; Gaborit-Chopin, in *Le Trésor de Saint-
Denis*, 44, 49–50, fig. 3, 43.

one other closely related item in this group of artefacts associated with Charles the Bald does in part survive, and has left a detailed record. This most remarkable of constructions is the item decribed at the beginning of the tenth century as the *escrain Kalles* – that is, the shrine of Charles the Bald. This too vanished into the revolutionary melting-pot, but we are fortunate that its crest was spared, and that a magnificent watercolour was also made by Etienne-Eloi de Labarre, before its destruction (Fig. 12).[58] Over one metre high, this amazing object, with its tiers of arches, its pendant crowns and other jewelled settings, shares distinctive technical and compositional elements with the jewelled cross and altar of Charles, and with the mounts on the paten and cup; and beyond these, its links to other metalwork datable to the second half of the ninth century – such as the inlays on the bindings of the Psalter of Charles the Bald, the Lindau Gospels and the Codex Aureus of St Emmeram – confirm the sense of a corpus of metalwork associated with Charles's involvement with St Denis. All display a powerful interest in the symbolic, whether in the assimilation of the Dionysian iconography of the cup to the cult of St Denis (in a way which seems to parallel the equivalent contemporary attribution of writings by the Greek Dionysius to St Denis),[59] or the reinvention of the Sassanian king as Solomon. These supremely luxurious items enshrine an intellectual complexity as well as glamour, and one well in keeping with what we know of Charles's own learning and education.[60]

They are indeed, also *aedificia nova*; but what relevance could these splendid and unusual artefacts have to Alfred's programme of renewal? None can be reliably associated with datable events within the reign of Charles the Bald, and therefore there is no clear chronology for their presence in the royal or monastic treasury. Speculation about whether the boy Alfred could have seen any of them during his stay at the Frankish court in 855/6, let alone on his earlier passage to and from Rome in 853, must remain just that. With a huge leap of faith and imagination, the dubious 857 Æthelwulf charter might just about imply a context for Alfred to have had access in 856 to treasures already present in the shrine of Saint-Denis, but it would be futile to press this slender clue too hard. And in truth, we don't need this; in a context of documented intellectual contacts with Francia and Alfred's significant importation of foreign craftsmen, it is surely very likely that detailed accounts of the extraordinary constructs associated with Charles, and his evident desire to make good the losses suffered by Saint-Denis under the Viking raids, were current in Alfred's circle, and indeed, came to the king's own receptive ear.

And here, we may return to the *æstels*. They are, as we have noted, unique in the Anglo-Saxon repertoire, and make striking use of unusual materials. The

---

[58] Gaborit-Chopin, in *Le Trésor de Saint-Denis*, nos 13a,b.

[59] Wallace-Hadrill, 'A Carolingian renaissance prince: the Emperor Charles the Bald', *PBA*, 64 (1978), 155–84, esp. 164.

[60] Ibid., 155–84; R. McKitterick, 'Charles the Bald (823–877) and his library: the patronage of learning', *EHR*, 95 (1980), 28–47.

Fig. 12 The 'Escrain' of Charles the Bald (after de Labarre)

elaborate *cloisonné* enamels have often been identified as Carolingian in inspiration, and are certainly not of a type seen in England before the late ninth century; *cloisonné* enamel with a similar colour range occurs on Saint-Denis objects made in the later ninth century, some possibly for Charles the Bald.[61] Equally, the bold use of rock-crystal spolia in two of the jewels is unparalleled in Anglo-Saxon work of this period, but resembles the well-attested reuse of precious stones in objects from the Saint-Denis treasury – most ostentatiously on the *escrain*, where the unusual use of elegant *à jour* frames to maximize translucency of the sapphires, aquamarines and amethysts also invites comparison with the openwork construction of the frames which hold the two Anglo-Saxon crystals. Rock crystal itself was highly prized at Charles's court, as the great crucifixion crystal, another of his gifts to Saint-Denis, demonstrates.[62] In such a context, it is tempting to conclude that knowledge and description of objects such as the *escrain* were influential in the physical design of the *æstels*. More contentiously, perhaps, there may also be an intellectual link.

Both kings, in the long-standing early medieval tradition of using Old Testament exemplars in the exercise and presentation of kingship, make much reference to King Solomon, the archetypally wise ruler, whose example showed that only through the pursuit of wisdom can true temporal rewards be earned.[63] One of Hincmar's improving gifts to Charles the Bald was a commentary on the Song of Songs, 3: 9–10, known as the *Ferculum Salomonis*; while Sedulius Scottus's *De Rectoribus Christianis*, written for Charles in 869, lays emphasis on Solomon's dream at Gihon, in which God granted the king unsought earthly power, because of his expressed pursuit of wisdom alone. The great bibles associated with Charles also make prominent reference to Solomon. The Codex Aureus of St Emmeram, made for the king *c.* 870, bears an image of the monarch enthroned, with an inscription linking him to his biblical ancestors, David and Solomon; while the great San Paolo Bible contains a full-page frontispiece to Proverbs, showing Solomon enthroned, above which are smaller images depicting Solomon's journey to Gihon on David's mule, and his anointing – potent images in a bible presented to Charles shortly after his coronation at Metz in 869.[64] Charles later presented this bible to Pope John VII, on the occasion of of his imperial coronation in Rome in 875; it has also been suggested that the ivory throne the new emperor presented on the same occasion could have signified reference to Solomon's ivory throne (1 Kings,10: 18).[65]

---

[61] For example D. Gaborit-Chopin, 'Note sur l'émail cloisonné de Saint-Denis', *Cahiers Archéologiques*, 38 (1990), 95–8.

[62] Gaborit-Chopin, in *Le Trésor de Saint-Denis*, no. 17; G. Kornbluth, *Engraved Gems of the Carolingian Empire*, no. 18,100–106, figs 18–1–12.

[63] Pratt, 'Persuasion and invention'.

[64] Munich, Bayerische Staatsbibliothek, Clm. 14000, fol. 5v; Rome, Abbazia di San Paolo, f.l.m., fol.188v; Mütherich and Gaehde, *Carolingian Painting*, 27–8, 108, 119, pls 37 and 44.

[65] Wallace-Hadrill, 'A Carolingian renaissance prince', 177.

Alfred's devotion to wisdom literature is well known, and needs no detailed description here; his love of the psalms, which he also translated, and of other sapiential works is recorded by Asser, and his own writings themselves frequently make use of wisdom themes – as when, in his translation of Boethius's *Consolation of Philosophy* he recasts the dialogues between Boethius and the Lady Philosophy into a debate between Wisdom and the Mind. Wisdom was also actively enjoined upon his bishops, ministers and thegns. Celebrated for his wisdom both in his day, and indeed in medieval tradition long after his death, he was directly compared by Asser to Solomon,[66] and there can be little doubt that Solomon was a conscious exemplar for the king, and widely acknowledged as such. David Pratt's argument, noted above, that the Fuller Brooch and the Alfred Jewel are both intimately linked with the cult of wisdom at Alfred's courts, is thus wholly convincing. Might one take this a step further, and see in the image on the Alfred Jewel not just a message about searching for wisdom with the mind's eye, but an image of Solomon, embodiment of kingly wisdom? The conscious influence of Carolingian court metalwork is visible in the manner and construction of the jewel; could it also be linked to the prominence of Salomonic reference in Charles's court?

Central to this possibility is the famous dish of Chosroes, known throughout the Middle Ages and beyond as the cup of Solomon (Fig. 10). It is easy to see how the central image of the enthroned eastern ruler was read as Solomon, and how such a magnificent dish could represent the idea of the spiritual and worldly riches of the biblical king. We have seen too, that this object was certainly known, and its craftsmanship emulated, at the court of Charles the Bald, for whom it must have carried a special resonance, in view of his own interest in Solomon. The crowned king sits on his lion throne, as if in judgement; his hands are together on the hilt of his sheathed sword, and from his shoulders two textile bands flutter diagonally upwards. Could this perceived image of Solomon in some way have served as inspiration for the image on the Alfred Jewel? The dish was justly famous throughout the Middle Ages, and significantly, was one of the very few items of gold and precious stones to have been spared in its entirety in 1793. This is an object which was venerated, which no one who saw it would ever forget, and which must certainly have been the subject of oral as well as written accounts. We might reasonably suppose that descriptions of this potent image of wise and godly kingship could have reached Alfred's ears, without having to propose the more risky suggestion that he saw it with his own eyes as a boy. A hypothetical account of this from one of his Frankish mentors, perhaps, or from a visitor to Alfred's court, would not necessarily have delivered a wholly exact idea of the image; by such a process, the bands fluttering diagonally upwards above the shoulders could have become

---

[66] Asser, c. 76, 59–62; and for the continuing medieval association of Alfred with sapiential matter, as in the twelfth-century text, *The Proverbs of Alured*, see B. Dickins and R. Wilson, *Early Middle English Texts* (3rd edn, 1956), 77–8.

assimilated to the existing Insular convention of Christ and other scriptural figures holding two diagonal flowering staffs,[67] and the crown with its central orb to the curious configuration in the centre of the figure's hair. The scrolls on which the figure's arms appear to rest may even be schematic representations of a throne's arms. Of course, the two images are not at all alike in form, but we are in the world of substance, not form, ideas not imitations; here the use of crystal in both, and the pose of authority assimilated to Anglo-Saxon traditions, are more significant than exactitude.

Whatever the answer, in the nature and originality of its iconography and construction the jewel represents the authentic voice of Alfred; and this innovative, thought-provoking quality is also matched in the excellent, if by Carolingian standards, more austere tone of those other pieces of precious metalwork which we may count as products of Alfred's circle. These are true *aedificia nova*, fitting testimonies to his devout commitment to spiritual wisdom and its temporal exercise, and precious witness to the brilliance of energy and invention which characterized his visionary programme of renewal.[68]

---

[67] As, for example, in the Lichfield Gospels, p. 221, and the Book of Kells, fol. 202v; J. Alexander, *Insular Manuscripts From the Sixth to the Ninth Century, A Survey of Manuscripts Illuminated in the British Isles*, 1 (1978), nos 21 and 52.

[68] My thanks are due to many friends and colleagues for inspiration and advice at various stages in the gestation of this paper; I would particularly like to mention James Graham-Campbell, Nicholas Griffiths, David Howlett, Lawrence Keen, Simon Keynes, Jinty Nelson, David Pratt, David Wilson, Patrick Wormald and Barbara Yorke.

ALFREDIAN LITERATURE

Chapter 6

The Alfredian canon revisited: one hundred years on

Janet Bately

Had this paper been composed for a conference a century ago, in 1899, its title might have been precisely the same – the Alfredian canon revisited, but the hundred-year review would have been very different, as would the views expressed in it on the contents of that canon and its chronology. For the starting-point would have been a list of texts named by William of Malmesbury as the work of the king: translations of Orosius's *Historiarum adversum Paganos Libri VII*, Gregory the Great's *Cura Pastoralis*, Bede's *Historia Ecclesiastica Gentis Anglorum*, Boethius's *De Consolatione Philosophiae*, an Enchiridion or handbook, and a translation of the psalms, still in progress at the time of the king's death.[1]

The first four of the works named by William of Malmesbury had long been identified with translations into Old English, of which manuscript copies still survived, and these were taken to form the core of the canon, along with Alfred's introduction to his law-code[2] and a first-person preface to a translation of Gregory's *Dialogorum Libri IV*, described by no less an authority than Alfred's biographer, Asser, in his *Life of Alfred* as commissioned from Bishop Werferth of Worcester.[3] By the end of the nineteenth century, Alfredian authorship had been claimed for two further translations. The first was a work given the title 'Blooms by King Ælfred'[4] by its first editor, but subsequently renamed Alfred's *Soliloquies*.[5] The second was a prose rendering of the first fifty psalms in the

---

[1] See D. Whitelock, 'William of Malmesbury on the works of King Alfred', in *Medieval Literature and Civilization: Studies in Memory of G.N. Garmonsway*, eds D. A. Pearsall and R. A. Waldron (1969), 78–93, at 85.

[2] For which see now P. Wormald, *The Making of English Law: King Alfred to the Twelfth Century* (1999).

[3] Asser, c. 77. For convenience rather than through conviction I have adopted the spelling *Werferth* in preference to *Wærferth* (except in quotations), throughout.

[4] So, for example, *Soliloquies*, 83, '(H)er endiað þa blostman þære forman boce'.

[5] 'The blooms of King Alfred', ed. O. Cockayne, in *The Shrine: A Collection of Occasional Papers on Dry Subjects,* nos 11–13 (1869–70), 163–204. Earlier, however, R. Pauli, *König Ælfred und seine Stelle in der Geschichte Englands* (Berlin, 1851), 239–40, had expressed doubts as to Alfred's authorship of this work. For summaries of the literature on this and other Alfredian topics see now G. G. Waite, *Old English Prose Translations of King Alfred's Reign*, Annotated Bibliogra-

twelfth-century Paris Psalter, which scholars sought to identify with the translation which, according to William of Malmesbury, the king was working on at the time of his death.[6] By 1899, however, with most of these texts available in modern editions, the composition of the canon was coming under very close scrutiny. Indeed, the author of our hypothetical paper would probably have discarded from it the psalms of the Paris Psalter. The association of these with Alfred had been firmly rejected as recently as 1894 by J. D. Bruce,[7] and with such success that it was not for another half century that the possibility of Alfredian authorship was to be seriously reconsidered.[8] What is more, by 1899 Alfredian authorship of the verse rendering of Boethius's meters, which replaces the original prose version in one of the two surviving manuscripts, had been rejected by Alfred Leicht and its text assigned a Kentish provenance by Eduard Sievers.[9]

Whether or not the OE *Bede* was retained in the literary canon would have depended on our author's reaction to the linguistic arguments put forward by Thomas Miller in 1890 and 1898, that the translator 'belonged to the North Midland district', and so could not be the West Saxon king.[10] For amongst the unconvinced was Charles Plummer, who in his edition of the *Chronicle*, 1899, could still refer to 'Alfred's Bede' without feeling any need for comment or justification. Indeed, if he did have a concern, it was with chronology, and with whether 'Alfred's Bede' was later or earlier than 'Alfred's Orosius'.[11] Moreover, Jacob Schipper, in his own edition of the *Bede*, 1897–99, was at that very time occupied with producing explanations for the Mercian element which in his view allowed for overall Alfredian authorship for the work, while slightly earlier, in 1893, J. W. Pearce had tried to square the circle by suggesting that the *Bede*

phies of Old and Middle English Literature VI, 2000. This bibliography, a draft of which Dr Waite generously sent me as I was finalizing my paper for the Southampton conference, has been invaluable to me in checking references and seeking out oversights. The first part of my paper necessarily covers some of the same ground as Waite's comprehensive and excellent historical introduction. However, I have been careful not to rework my own draft in the light of his material, and I believe that I have not compromised either his or my own independence.

    [6] See R. Wülker, *Grundriss zur Geschichte der angelsächsischen Litteratur, mit einer Übersicht der angelsächsischen Sprachwissenschaft* (Leipzig, 1885), 435–6.

    [7] J. D. Bruce, 'The Anglo-Saxon version of the book of psalms commonly known as the Paris Psalter', *PMLA*, 9 (1894), 43–164. A. S. Cook, *Biblical Quotations in Old English Prose Writers: Edited with the Vulgate and other Latin Originals, Introduction on Old English Biblical Versions, Index of Biblical Passages and Index of Principal Words* (1898), xl, sees the case for Alfred's authorship of 'all the prose Psalms extant' as not proven.

    [8] J. I'a Bromwich, 'Who was the translator of the prose portion of the Paris Psalter?', in *The Early Cultures of North-West Europe (H.M. Chadwick Memorial Studies)*, eds C. Fox and B. Dickins (1950), 289–303.

    [9] A. Leicht, 'Ist Koenig Aelfred der Verfasser der alliterierenden Metra des Boetius?', *Anglia*, 6 (1883), 126–70. Sievers's opinion is reported in *Boethius*, ed. Sedgefield, xli n.1.

    [10] *Bede*, ed. Miller, II.1 x; cf. I.1. lix, where Lichfield is named as 'a possible birthplace for the old English version of Bede'.

    [11] *Two of the Saxon Chronicles Parallel*, ed. C. Plummer (2 vols, 1892–99), cviii.

was 'the joint work of several translators', with Alfred possibly responsible only for the 'extremely literal' capitula and parts of Book I.[12]

As for texts associated with the king, rather than actually composed by him, our hypothetical author might well have been persuaded by the claims of Oswald Cockayne, that the 'Book of Martyrs' that he was editing was 'of þe age of Ælfred' and 'not only of Ælfreds [sic] time, but formed also under his direction',[13] though only a year later, in 1900, he would have been given pause for thought by George Herzfeld's arguments for a date of composition nearer to 850 than the end of the century.[14] In the nineteenth century indeed it was as much chronology as content that was controversial,[15] though some scholars were confident enough to attempt to date the texts fairly closely. So for Joseph Bosworth, the *Boethius* was translated in 888, the *Bede* in 890 or 891, the *Orosius* in 893, and lastly the *Pastoral Care* between 897 and 901.[16]

Today the literary canon is generally accepted as consisting of *Pastoral Care, Boethius*,[17] *Soliloquies,* and the prose psalms, along with prefatory material to the laws. The OE *Orosius* joins the *Dialogues* as 'Alfredian' only in the sense that there are reasonable grounds for supposing that, like that translation, it dates from Alfred's reign and might well have been composed as part of Alfred's plan for the restoration of learning – one of those books, in the words of Alfred, that it was most necessary for all men to know.[18] Although Elizabeth Liggins has suggested that the king may have composed the short passage in the *Orosius* containing the 'lament of Babylon', I do not find her linguistic arguments convincing.[19] Attempts to reinstate the *Bede* in the canon have failed, with Miller's views now prevailing; although as recently as 1972, Sherman Kuhn was still endeavouring to explain away its Mercian dialect features, his arguments, based on analyses of word-pairs, do not stand up to close scrutiny.[20] On the

---

[12] *Bede*, ed. Schipper; J. W. Pearce, 'Did King Alfred translate the *Historia Ecclesiastica*?', *PMLA*, 8 (1893), Appendix, vi–x.

[13] *The Shrine*, VI, 'Yule week', 29–35 and VIII, 'King Ælfreds Book of Martyrs', 44–158, at 45 and 148.

[14] *Martyrology*, ed. Herzfeld, xxxii and xxxv.

[15] See the useful chart in Wülker, *Grundriss*, 393.

[16] *Orosius*, ed. Bosworth, ix–x.

[17] With the possible exception of the verse meters: see below, p. 112.

[18] See the matched pair of articles dealing with Alfredian syntax and lexis respectively in *Anglia*, 88 (1970), namely E. M. Liggins, 'The authorship of the Old English *Orosius*', 289–322, and J. Bately, 'King Alfred and the Old English translation of *Orosius*', 433–60, also *Orosius*, ed. Bately, lxxiii–lxxxii.

[19] Liggins, 'The authorship', 321, with reference to *Orosius* 43.33–44.6. Indeed in some details, such as the use of the construction *gelice 7*, it agrees with the rest of the text against the canon.

[20] S. M. Kuhn, 'Synonyms in the Old English Bede', *Journal of English and Germanic Philology*, 46 (1947), 168–76 and *idem*, 'The authorship of the Old English Bede revisited', *Neuphilologische Mitteilungen*, 73 (1972), 172–80. In this article Kuhn repudiates his earlier opinion that *Bede* was an early work written while Alfred was still a novice ('Synonyms', 176), now

other hand, we have had Simeon Potter disputing Alfred's responsibility for the *Pastoral Care* in its final form ('It is impossible to think for a moment that this accurate, scholarly, painstaking work was done by the man who wrote [*Orosius*, *Boethius* and *Soliloquies*]'), and postulating as author a collaborator other than Werferth, or 'another differently composed group of collaborators'.[21] More recently, on ANSAXNET, F. Ann Payne has expressed doubts about Alfred's authorship of the *Soliloquies*. And there are of course those who have questioned whether Alfred was capable of undertaking any of the translations attributed to him even with substantial help, claiming that his actual personal participation could have been relatively limited. As Alfred Smyth observes:

> There may be less of Alfred to be found in works ascribed personally to him, and there may be more of the king's influence in works such as the Anglo-Saxon Chronicle ... than has been recognized hitherto. We can never exclude the possibility that his scholarly helpers had a hand in shaping those prefaces written in the king's name, or conversely, that they did not implement his wishes in the production of a work such as the Chronicle.[22]

As for chronology, the nineteenth-century minority view that the *Boethius* was composed later than the *Pastoral Care*[23] is now generally accepted as based on much sounder foundations than that which put the *Boethius* right at the beginning of Alfred's literary career – though scholars are now less certain that 'the "Blooms" must have been written later than the "Boethius"',[24] with opinion leaning towards the view that Alfred could have been working on both works simultaneously.[25] It may be that in the next hundred years, with the aid of computer-generated materials, it will be possible to reach firmer views on the chronology of the canon. I personally rather doubt it, particularly since so much depends on interpretation and often on very limited materials.

---

seeing it as Alfred's final composition, when he 'had little leisure for polishing his work' ('Authorship', 179–80). See, in response, D. Whitelock, 'The Old English Bede', *PBA*, 48 (1962), 57–90, at 58–9, and G. G. Waite, 'The vocabulary of the Old English version of Bede's *Historia Ecclesiastica*' (doctoral thesis, University of Toronto, 1984).

[21] S. Potter, 'On the relation of the Old English Bede to Werferth's Gregory and to Alfred's translations', in *Věstniku kralovske česke společnosti nauk*, ed. I. Roč (Prague, 1930, separately printed, 1931), 52 and 55.

[22] Smyth, *Alfred*, 541. I remain very much a sceptic as regards Alfred's direct involvement with the *Chronicle*.

[23] For this order see Wülker's chart, cited above, n. 15.

[24] F. G. Hubbard, 'The relation of the "Blooms of King Alfred" to the Anglo-Saxon translation of Boethius', *Modern Language Notes*, 9 (1894), 161–71, at 170.

[25] See, for example, A. J. Franzen, *King Alfred* (Boston, MA, 1986), 82–5. Incidentally, although she sees the *Pastoral Care* as probably the earliest of Alfred's translations, Dorothy Whitelock pointed out in her unpublished draft of a book on King Alfred that the relative closeness of the *Pastoral Care* to its original is not in itself conclusive: 'Alfred found less reason for making changes or additions to the Cura Pastoralis than in the Boethius and Soliloquies. It was more easily intelligible than they were and he was not in disagreement with the views expressed.'

Work on the constituent elements of the canon is in my opinion likely to centre on detail, on refinements of the parameters and on the identification of possible areas of collaboration or multiple authorship. The question of multiple authorship is very much a live issue, prompted in part by Alfred's own acknowledgement of help with the rendering of the *Pastoral Care*, in part by modern scholars' interpretation of what the *Life of Alfred* seems to be saying about Alfred's knowledge of Latin, or lack of it. So claims of more than one translator at work have been made for the *Boethius*,[26] some variations of usage within the *Pastoral Care* have been taken as evidence of the input of Alfred's advisers,[27] while for Kirby, 'although Alfred may have been able to comprehend the content of the books he caused to be translated, his precise role in the work of translating is to some degree imponderable'. Indeed he goes further and suggests that

> the passages inserted in the Old English Boethius (in particular) reflect not the contributions of the king advising his subjects on virtues and vices but his ecclesiastical entourage taking advantage of the unique opportunity afforded to instruct the king in good conduct by appropriate interpolations.[28]

Who the primary author of the Alfredian canon was, an Alfred or an Æþelred or indeed an Æþelþryþ, is not of course a matter that can be settled by a linguistic study. Theoretically at least the extent to which this primary author – King Alfred – relied on or was influenced by others, whether individuals, or, as has been suggested, a committee, is another matter, though any attempt to determine the degree to which such help might have affected the language of Alfred's works is fraught with difficulties. There are many unknowns, beginning with the extent of Alfred's vocabulary (and indeed his knowledge of Latin) before he started to translate, and the possibility (likelihood?) that he dictated a first – rough – draft, which was then turned into a fair copy by a secretary. Did his helpers comment on, alter, or correct his drafts, causing the introduction into the text of their own lexical preferences? (One wonders what scholars trained in literal translation, such as those responsible for the OE *Dialogues* and *Bede*, might have made of the free renderings of, say, the *Boethius*.) And might not Alfred's own vocabulary have developed over the years, just as Godden has shown Ælfric's to have done[29] – perhaps even more rapidly and radically, given their very different starting-points in terms of prior literary experience? Then there is the complication of the possibility of later scribal alteration, whether accidental or deliberate. (For examples of this we have to look no further than

[26] C. M. Warrick, 'The two translators of the Old English Boethius' (doctoral thesis, University of Indiana, 1967).

[27] R. W. Clement, 'The production of the *Pastoral Care*: King Alfred and his helpers', in *Studies in Earlier Old English Prose*, ed. P. E. Szarmach (Albany, 1985), 129–52. I hope to return to the question of the vocabulary of the *Pastoral Care* shortly.

[28] D. P. Kirby, 'Asser and his Life of King Alfred', *Studia Celtica*, 6 (1971), 12–35, at 34.

[29] M. R. Godden, 'Ælfric's changing vocabulary', *English Studies*, 61 (1980), 206–23.

the surviving manuscript copies of the *Bede*, the *Pastoral Care* and the *Dialogues*.)

And finally there is the problem of patchy cover, an inevitable consequence of the limited nature and extent of the corpus that has come down to us. Two simple illustrations of this are provided by the collocation *eala ea(w)* and the term *domere*. *Eala ea(w)* is unique to Alfred and to his translation of Boethius, where it occurs four times.[30] *DOE* records seven instances of *domere*, six of them in Alfredian texts – prose psalms, *Pastoral Care*, *Boethius* and the prefatory material to the laws. The seventh occurs in two post-conquest manuscripts of a homily drawing on Vercelli X, other versions of which use the more common *demere*.[31] Our records surely do not reflect the real distribution of this word.[32] So the presence of *eala eaw* or *domere* in some hypothetical newly discovered text might lend support to a theory of Alfredian authorship, but would not of itself prove it. As I observed many years ago, it is easier to demonstrate that a piece of writing is not by a particular Anglo-Saxon author than that it is, a comment which applies only too well to the first of three short pieces of Alfrediana which are the subject of the rest of this paper, the preface to the *Boethius*.

One hundred years ago Sedgefield could claim of this preface, which begins with the statement that King Alfred was the translator of this book and which relates how the king revised his original prose translation, that 'the consensus of critical opinion seems to be against Alfred's authorship; but nothing has been clearly proved one way or the other'.[33] Sedgefield was, of course, writing at a time when the verse rendering of Boethius's meters was generally supposed not to be the work of the king, in which case the preface, claiming Alfredian responsibility for it, had to be a forgery, a theory now generally fiercely rejected.[34] However, what the most recent investigations into the language of the verse meters[35] seem to me to show is that there is nothing to indicate that Alfred could not have been responsible for the versification, not that there is good evidence to assume that he was. The waters are of course

---

[30] An instance of *eala wa* at *Boethius*, 73.22 is Sedgefield's reconstruction of [ ]*ala wa*, with space left in the MS for an enlarged capital. However, the guide letter in the margin is *w*. For *wa la wa* see also *Soliloquies*, 76.9.

[31] See *Old English Homilies from MS Bodley 343*, ed. S. Irvine, EETS OS 302 (1993), VII. 128, 'Hwær is domeræ domselt?', and *The Vercelli Homilies*, ed. D. G. Scragg, EETS OS 300 (1992), X. 235, 'Hwær is demera domstow?' For Vercelli X see further J. Wilcox, 'Variant texts of an Old English homily', in *The Preservation and Transmission of Anglo-Saxon Culture*, eds P. E. Szarmach and J. T. Rosenthal (Kalamazoo, 1997), 335–51.

[32] See J. Bately, 'Here comes the judge: a small contribution to the study of French input into the vocabulary of the law in Middle English', in *Placing Middle English in Context*, eds I. Taavitsainen et al., *Topics in English Linguistics* (Mouton, 2000), 255–75.

[33] *Boethius*, ed. Sedgefield, xxxix.

[34] See Waite, *Bibliography*, section 10. Sedgefield himself (*Boethius*, xl–xli) keeps his options open.

[35] See, for example, *Alfred's Metres of Boethius*, ed. B. Griffiths (1991), 19–49.

muddied by the fact that the preface as we have it (in both surviving manu-scripts)[36] is in a form which fits the version in London, British Library, MS Cotton Otho A.vi (s. x med.), where the meters are rendered in poetic form, but not Oxford, Bodleian Library, MS Bodley 180 (s. xii[1]), which gives them in prose. Moreover, as Sisam[37] and others have shown, it is patently made up of some unquestionably Alfredian materials,[38] embedded in a framework whose syntax and vocabulary is neutral in terms of authorship, as typical of, for instance, Ælfric as of the Alfredian canon.

If it is entirely Alfred's own work (a second edition in modern terms, as Eric Stanley has put it),[39] then in its unoriginality it surely shows an untypical 'want of wit' on the king's part. But the Alfredian materials could equally well have been incorporated by an amanuensis of Alfred's, or even a reviser/scribe working after Alfred's death, bringing an older preface up to date, perhaps, or putting together a new one.[40] However, one section of the text gives cause for thought:

> *Boethius* 1.6–10 Ða bisgu us sint swiþe earfoþrime þe on his dagum
> on þa ricu becoman þe he underfangen hæfde, 7 þeah ða þas boc
> hæfde geleornode 7 of lædene to engliscum spelle gewende, 7
> geworhte hi eft to leoðe, swa swa heo nu gedon is.

Bill Griffiths sees this as either a historical parenthesis or a note on the further rendering of the text into verse and concludes that it 'could therefore be an interpolation, innocent in intent, and not indeed meant to sound like Alfred's own words, nor including much of that "Alfredian" phraseology that Sisam notes'. (Sisam himself had considered the possibilities of this part being an early interpolation, but concluded that 'the effect of remoteness must be dis-counted.'.)[41] Griffiths's arguments are ones with which I am very much tempted to agree. However, there is in this section one linguistic feature that does seem to point to Alfred, though it is a *hapax legomenon* and quite possibly coined by

---

[36] In the fire-damaged Cotton MS now known only from material in Junius's transcript.

[37] K. Sisam, 'The authorship of the verse translation of Boethius's metra', in *idem*, *Studies in the History of Old English Literature* (1953), 293–7, at 295–7; Griffiths, *Alfred's Metres*, 39.

[38] Cf. for example, *Boethius*, 1.2–6, 'Hwilum he sette word be worde, hwilum andgit of andgite, swa swa he hit þa sweotolost 7 andgitfullicast gereccan mihte for þam mistlicum 7 manigfealdum weoroldbisgum þe hine oft ægðer ge on mode ge on lichoman bisgodan', and *Pastoral Care*, 7.17–20, 'ða ongan ic ongemang oðrum mislicum & manigfealdum bisgum ðisses kynerices ða boc wendan on Englisc ... hwilum word be worde, hwilum andgit of angi[e]te ...'

[39] For example, Stanley, 'King Alfred's prefaces', *Review of English Studies*, NS 39 (1988), 349–64, at 360; also M. R. Godden, 'Editing Old English and the problem of Alfred's Boethius', in *Editing of Old English: Papers from the 1990 Manchester Conference*, eds D. G. Scragg and P. E. Szarmach (1994), 163–76, at 165: 'it is generally, and surely rightly, accepted as his own work'.

[40] For examples of intimate knowledge of the wording of someone else's work we need to look no further than Ælfric: see M. Godden, 'Ælfric and the vernacular prose tradition', in *The OE Homily and its Backgrounds*, eds P. E. Szarmach and B. F. Huppé (Albany, 1978), 99–117.

[41] Griffiths, *Alfred's Metres*, 38–9.

the writer for the occasion. That is the compound *earfoþrime*. *DOE* lists twenty compounds in *earfoþ* plus noun or adjective.[42] Fifteen of them are singletons, while six are recorded from verse only. However, no fewer than one quarter of these twenty compounds are found – and found only – in the Alfredian canon, *earfoþrime* there having the companionship of *earfoþdæde* (*Pastoral Care*), *earfoþfere* (*Soliloquies*), *earfoþhawe* (*Boethius* prose and verse), *earfoþtæcne* (*Boethius* verse). Like *eala eaw*, the compound *earfoþrime* reflects a demonstrably (but not uniquely) Alfredian mannerism, and its presence in the preface would seem to support the view that we may have here at the very least an underlying trace of an original composition by Alfred. Overall, its Alfredian credentials are linguistically impeccable. The question is how much of what we have was actually put together in this place by Alfred himself.

Of the second of my short passages, the prose preface to the OE *Dialogues* found in two of the three surviving manuscripts, the converse is true. Everything points away from Alfred. Unlike the preface to *Boethius*, which is mainly in the third person, it is in the first person throughout, thus purporting to be the king's own composition. It begins:

> Ic Ælfred geofendum Criste mid cynehades mærnysse geweorðod, habbe gearolice ongyten 7 þurh haligra boca gesægene oft gehyred, þætte us, þam þe God swa micle heanesse worldgeþingða forgifen hafað, is seo mæste ðearf, þæt we hwilon ure mod betwix þas eorþlican ymbhigdo geleoðigen 7 gebigen to ðam godcundan 7 þam gastlican rihte.[43]

However, over the years attention has been drawn to stylistic features that put its authenticity very much in doubt. The first sceptic that I know of was Simeon Potter, in the 1930s. The opening sentence, he says, 'does not sound like the voice of the King and may have been worded by Werferth'. And he adds in a note: 'It is certainly unlike the other businesslike and unpretentious prefaces by Alfred.'[44] Potter does not elaborate on his claim at this point. However, in the same study he provides statistical information that is relevant to the use of the dative absolute construction *geofendum Gode*:[45]

OE	Dative absolutes	Latin ablative absolutes
Bede	100	558
Dialogues	123	265
Pastoral Care	1	100
Orosius	5	318
Boethius	0	64

---

[42] I exclude compounds in *-lic*.

[43] Reading of MS C: see *Dialogues*, 1.1–12.

[44] Potter, 'Relation', 40.

[45] Ibid., 21–3.

(Potter might also have noted here, but does not, that the preface's *geofendum Criste* is paralleled by *gifendum drihtne* in the body of the *Dialogues.* [46])

The atypicalness in an Alfredian context of this opening sentence was also noted by Dorothy Whitelock in 1979, seemingly independently of Potter, when she voiced the suspicion that 'Werferth or one of his clergy had a hand in the composing of Alfred's preface'. She compared its flamboyant opening with a description of Ealdorman Æthelred of Mercia in 883 (BCS 551) as 'inbryrdendre Godes gefe gewelegod 7 gewlenced mid sume dæle Mercna rices'.[47] Finally and most recently, Malcolm Godden, commenting on Dorothy Whitelock's observation, has cited a number of features of language and style that 'would suggest that [the author] was Wærferth himself, and that he had more than just a hand in it':

> [L]inguistically and stylistically it shows all the hallmarks of Wærferth's writing rather than Alfred's own. The obsessive use of word-pairs – *ongyten and gehyred, geleoðigen and gebigen, godcundan and gastlican, sohte and wilnade, þeawum and wundrum, mynegunge and lufe* – is a well-known characteristic of Wærferth, Alfred's own use of them being more moderate and more discriminating; *sohte and wilnade* occurs as a pair only once otherwise in the Old English prose corpus, and that is in the Old English *Dialogues*; and *ymbhigd-* as a stem occurs in the *Dialogues* and other anonymous works but not in Alfred's own – the words he uses in his own prefaces are *woruldðing* and *weoruldbisgo.*[48]

Collectively these arguments are quite sufficient to convince me, and doubtless others, that the preface to the *Dialogues* is not the work of Alfred himself, a conclusion that is fully borne out by a detailed linguistic analysis.

As with the preface to the *Boethius*, the bulk of the vocabulary (and indeed the syntax) is 'standard' OE, found in a wide range of texts from more than one period. However, what features of potential significance there are all point firmly away from Alfred, and like the stylistic features mentioned above (the word-pairs, the dative absolute construction), but with one exception, are paralleled in the body of the *Dialogues*. Two of these are the use of the noun *ymbhigd* and the verb *gehycgan*. The first of these words, as Godden has pointed out, is not found in the Alfredian canon. (The Alfredian word is *ymbhoga.*[49]) It was to be replaced in Oxford, Bodleian Library, MS Hatton 76, a copy contain-

---

[46] Cf. also the gloss to the *Regularis Concordia* 1.88 'Christe largiente: Criste gyfendum' in H. Logeman, 'De consuetudine monachorum', *Anglia*, 13 (1891), 365–448 and 15 (1893), 20–40.

[47] D. Whitelock, 'Some charters in the name of King Alfred', in *Saints, Scholars and Heroes*, eds M. H. King and W. M. Stevens (Collegeville, MN, 1979), 79–98, at 90. 'Mid Godes gife' of course corresponds to the Latin formula *Dei gratia.*

[48] M. Godden, 'Wærferth and King Alfred: the fate of the Old English *Dialogues*', in *Alfred the Wise*, eds J. Roberts and J. L. Nelson, with M. Godden (1997), 35–51, at 36–7.

[49] It occurs in *Pastoral Care, Boethius, Psalms*; also, occasionally, in *Dialogues*. For the related *oferhygd-* see H. Schabram, *Superbia: Studien zum altenglischen Wortschatz. I. Die dialektale und zeitliche Verbreitung des Wortguts* (Munich, 1965).

ing a revised version of *Dialogues* Books I and II, by *carfulnys*.[50] The second of my two words, *gehycgan*, was left unchanged by the reviser, though two other instances of it were removed from the body of the translation in favour of *geþencan*. It is never found in the prose of the canon. Four occurrences of the form in the *Boethius* verse meters are all apparently there to fulfil the demands of alliteration and poetic variation, and since *gehycgan* is of not uncommon occurrence in OE verse may have been adopted as a piece of poetic diction. A third word in this category is *geleoþien*. This is one of a group of verbs based on the root *līþ-*,[51] all found in the *Dialogues* but never used in the Alfredian canon,[52] and indeed very rarely recorded elsewhere. An instance in *Dialogues* of *toleoþod* for Latin *laxatur* was replaced by *tolæten* in the revised version. However, the verb survives into Middle English, where the Middle English Dictionary (*MED*) entry 'lēthen' reports instances mainly from the west midland and north-west midland areas.

The exception is the adverb *gearolice*. This is yet another word recorded only a handful of times in surviving texts. Apart from this instance, it is found in two Vercelli homilies (nos X and XVI), both identified by Donald Scragg[53] as Mercian in origin, in Blickling Homily X (also with Mercian characteristics) and in two poems, *Elene* and *Deor*. Its normal collocation is with *witan* or, as here, *ongietan*. It is never found in the body of the Alfredian translations, though significantly it occurs once as a variant reading in contents list/chapter heading xx of the *Pastoral Care*.[54] At the same time, however, it is never found in the body of the *Dialogues* as it has come down to us. In both the canon and the *Dialogues* the verbs *witan* and *ongitan* are regularly collocated with adverbs such as *geare, georne, geornlice*.[55]

How are we to explain this difference in usage between the preface and the body of the text? If we rule out accidents of transmission and limitations of record, then we must consider the possibility that the preface is not the work of the primary translator of the *Dialogues*,[56] named in the *Life of Alfred* as Werferth. There are two alternatives. The first is that we have here the usage not of Werferth himself but of someone collaborating with him – one of the true friends referred to in the preface itself, possibly drawn from the ranks of Werferth's clergy, as Dorothy

---

[50] See D. Yerkes, *The two versions of Wærferth's translation of Gregory's Dialogues: an Old English Thesaurus* (Toronto, 1979). *Ymbhydiglican* is similarly replaced by *carfullice*.

[51] *Aliþian, toliþian* and *onliþian*.

[52] For *Pastoral Care*, 151.2, *geliþod* see *An Anglo-Saxon Dictionary Based on the Manuscript Collections of the Late Joseph Bosworth. Supplement by T. Northcote Toller* (1921), s.v. **geliþian**.

[53] *Vercelli Homilies*, ed. Scragg.

[54] Bately, 'Book-divisions and chapter-headings in the translations of the Alfredian period', festschrift article, forthcoming, also *idem*, a paper on multiple authorship of *Pastoral Care* (in progress).

[55] In *Boethius* also collocated with *openlice, eað, fullice, sweotole*.

[56] Godden, 'Wærferth and King Alfred', 37, comments on the striking consistency of the *Dialogues*' translation methods.

Whitelock has suggested, with the same kind of literary training and with a similar linguistic background. In this context it should be noted that none of the items of vocabulary that point away from Alfred is exclusive to the *Dialogues*. The use of dative absolutes, certainly a mannerism of *Dialogues*, is also characteristic of the *Bede*, as Potter observed,[57] and of some ninth-century charters,[58] while the use of word-pairs[59] is paralleled both in the *Bede* and in a number of homilies, including Vercelli X, with the collocation *sohte 7 wilnade* as much a feature of the *Bede* as of *Dialogues*.[60] *Woruldgeþingþ* occurs also in multiple MSS in Vercelli X, *ymbhygd* in Blickling XII, with related forms in Vercelli X and the Mercian life of St Chad. The verb *gehycgan* is found in the *Bede* and in Vercelli XIV, with *hycgan* in Blickling IV and a version of Vercelli X, *gearolice*, as we have seen, in Vercelli and Blickling homilies.[61] Only the verb *geleoþian* is not recorded from texts of this group. But, given its limited distribution pattern on the one hand and its survival into Middle English on the other, it must surely be supposed that, as with *domere*, the word's actual currency must have been wider. There is no reason why it should not also have been part of the vocabulary of a colleague of Werferth's, a term of general use in his circle.[62]

The second alternative – and one that in my view cannot lightly be dismissed – is that the preface was written for Alfred by someone actually in the king's entourage, one of Alfred's amanuenses or scholarly helpers, a Mercian perhaps, or at least trained in Mercia, writing directly at Alfred's command.

It is, in contrast, the question of date not dialect or idiolect that is central to my third and last discrete unit, the prayer located at the end of the *Boethius* in Oxford, Bodleian Library, MS Bodley 180. Humfrey Wanley, in the early eighteenth century, had catalogued this as a separate work with the title *Oratio ad Deum*. Sedgefield, reporting this, claimed that it was not written in the same hand as that of the main text, but none the less included it in his edition.[63] Neil Ker described the prayer as 'written more roughly and with a finer pen', yet saw it as 'probably in the main hand'.[64] It is included in Keynes's and Lapidge's *King Alfred* as the concluding prayer of the *Boethius*.[65] However, already in 1980 Dorothy Whitelock was writing to ask me my opinion:

---

[57] See, for example, Waite, 'The Vocabulary', *passim*; Potter, 'Relation', 23.

[58] See, for example, renderings of the Latin formula *regnante domino*, A. J. Robertson, *Anglo-Saxon Charters* (1939), nos XI, XII and XVIII.

[59] To the forms cited by Godden from the body of *Dialogues* might be added 327.16 *gehyrað 7 ongytaþ*; 179.4 *wundrum 7 þeawum*.

[60] See *Bede* 420.4 and 450.7; also 204.25, *wilnian 7 secan*; *Dialogues*, 236.3, *gewilnode ... 7 sohte*.

[61] For other locations for these words see the *DOE* microfiche concordance.

[62] Cf. the rare term *cynehad*, recorded only in the canon and in *Bede*.

[63] *Boethius*, ed. Sedgefield, xv. He did not, however, include either its forms or those of the contents list in his glossary.

[64] N. R. Ker, *Catalogue of Manuscripts containing Anglo-Saxon* (1957), 359.

[65] Keynes and Lapidge, *Alfred*, 137. *DOE* also includes its forms as part of Alfred's *Boethius*.

> Has anyone ever bothered to consider whether it is genuine? It looks to me like the sort of prayer anyone might have written and fathered on to Alfred. But if it were by Alfred, I should be interested in his special regard for St Michael. Why should it refer to the *gehyrsumnes* of St Michael? Was he specially noted for obedience? I may be revealing abysmal ignorance ...

I incorporated part of my reply in a footnote to a paper on the authorship of the prose psalms, saying that the prayer 'in my opinion does not belong to the *Boethius* and does not represent Alfred's work'.[66] A new query, this time from Professor Abels, caused me to return to the question of Alfredian authorship, now greatly aided by two new invaluable tools, the Toronto concordance and the Thesaurus of Old English.[67] What follows is a brief summary of my more significant findings:

1.   The hard core of the text is as usual what we might call basic OE, non-specific in terms of dialect, idiolect and date. However, a handful of words stand out from the rest:

1.1   First of all a cluster of words never found either in the Alfredian canon or in *Dialogues* or *Bede*: *trewnes; galnes; gehyrsumnes; gewissigan*. The first of these, *trewnes*, is a *hapax legomenon*.[68] The others in this group are all typical of late West Saxon.

Galnes. This noun is of frequent occurrence in the works of Ælfric and is also found in Wulfstan and in the post-Benedictine revival Vercelli Homilies XIX and XX, with the related words *galscipe* in a group of late texts, including Wulfstan's. The normal term in 'early'/Alfredian texts is *wrænnes* (found in *Pastoral Care, Boethius, Psalms, Orosius*), along with the adjective *wræn* (*Orosius* and *Dialogues*), though *Pastoral Care* has a single instance of *gægolbærnes* and *Bede* the adjective *gæglisc*.

Gehyrsumnes. This is another term never found in the Alfredian translations but a feature of Ælfric and other late texts. Early texts have the form *h(i)ersumnes,* used a number of times in *Pastoral Care* and occurring also in *Orosius, Dialogues, Bede* and the *Anglo-Saxon Chronicle* entry for 828.

Gewissigan. The verb *gewissian* is found in the works of Ælfric,[69] Byrhtferth and Wulfstan, but never in Alfredian and other texts of early origin. Ælfric also frequently uses the variant *wissian*. In contrast *Dialogues, Pastoral Care* and Alfred/Ine's Laws all have the verb *wisian*.[70]

---

[66] Bately, 'Lexical evidence', 79, n. 65.

[67] *A Thesaurus of Old English*, by J. Roberts and C. Kay, with L. Grundy, King's College London Medieval Studies, 11 (2 vols, 1995).

[68] *Getreownes* is also a *hapax legomenon*. See *Vercelli*, ed. Scragg, IV.279 and cf. *Pastoral Care*, 421.21, *his treowa 7 his hiersumnesse*.

[69] Sharing with the prayer the collocation *gewissian to þinum/his/Godes/willan*.

[70] *Gewisian* is used also by Wulfstan.

1.2 **Toforan**. Not found in the Alfredian translations (which use the form *beforan*), this is a mainly 'late' feature, though a handful of instances are also found in early Mercian texts.[71] It is used by Ælfric, and occurs in Vercelli XX and XXI, homilies which Scragg dates to the late tenth century. It is also a feature of the revised version of *Dialogues*, where on several occasions it replaces *beforan*. In the *Anglo-Saxon Chronicle*, the related construction *foran to*, introducing dates, first appears in annals for the second decade of the tenth century.[72]

1.3 Providing some support for a theory of non-Alfredian authorship, though not totally unrepresented in the canon, are three other words: *wiþerwinna*, *costnung* and *geþanc*. None of these is typically Alfredian. I shall be discussing in another place the distribution of *geþanc* in *Pastoral Care*.

2. Stylistically the prayer is characterized by a formal use of parallelisms. It has a fondness for what might be called lists or strings, with five phrases introduced by *for* at the beginning, a string of six descriptions of God at the end, and six imperatives. 'Mid clænum geþance' is paired with 'mid clænum lichaman', *gesewenlicum* with *ungesewenlicum*, *wyrhta* with *waldend*,[73] while 'to þinum willan 7 to minre sawle þearfe' occurs twice. It is of course very possible that an as yet unidentified Latin prayer is responsible for all of these features. Cumulatively, however, the effect is one untypical of Alfredian texts.

The onus, then, is on those who would see the prayer as the work of Alfred to produce some evidence other than manuscript proximity for this attribution. If the prayer had been preserved in a different context, it is hard to believe that anyone would have labelled it as Alfredian on the basis of its language. Moreover, the probability is that that language would have been described as typically late OE.

So, looking back over one hundred years of scholarship, what conclusions may we draw about progress in defining and delimiting the Alfredian canon? At the macro-level, there are some confident inclusions and some firm exclusions. At the micro-level we have a number of theories, likelihoods, possibilities, assumptions, albeit all necessarily based on very limited evidence. It would appear that the prayer at the end of the *Boethius* is a late text that has nothing to do with Alfred. The prose preface to the *Dialogues* was written for the king, either by an amanuensis, or possibly by a Mercian working on the project, though probably under the king's instructions. The prose preface to the *Boethius* continues to pose a number of problems. However, it not only contains no feature which could not be Alfredian, but also includes one compound of a type which occurs more frequently in the king's known works than in any other text or group of texts that has come down to us today.

---

[71] *Dialogues*, 82.4; *Bede*,196.29.

[72] See also *The Blickling Homilies*, ed. R. Morris, EETS OS 58, 63 and 73 (1874–80), III and XII, and *Martyrology*, 72.17.

[73] The collocation *wyrhta 7 waldend* is found in a number of late OE texts.

In the preface to the *Soliloquies*, the author – Alfred – wrote of going to the forest (the works of the Church Fathers) to collect materials with which to construct a dwelling place.[74] A thousand years later scholars turned to surviving Old English manuscripts in an attempt to rebuild what they took to be the Alfredian canon. What view future generations will take of the relatively minor adjustments and alterations that we have made to these at the end of the twentieth century can only be a matter for conjecture – but as Alfred himself said, let others with many a wagon take over our tasks.[75]

---

[74] *Soliloquies*, 47.1–4.
[75] Ibid., 47.6–12.

Chapter 7

The form and function of the preface in the poetry and prose of Alfred's reign

Allen J. Frantzen

The Place of the Preface in Old English

Notorious for overpraising the accomplishments of King Alfred, Anglo-Saxonists may, in one area at least, have underestimated the literary achievement of his reign. As Alfred and his contemporaries translated works into the vernacular, they also created prefaces for works that did not have them. No prefaces accompany the Latin texts of the *Historiarum adversus Paganos Libri VII* of Orosius,[1] the *Soliloquia* of Augustine,[2] the *Consolatio Philosophiae* of Boethius,[3] or the *Dialogi* of Gregory the Great.[4] Although Gregory's *Liber Pastoralis* came equipped with a prefatory letter, Alfred must have thought it was inadequate for his purposes, since he placed it after two prefaces of his own.[5] For the preface to the law-code Alfred had a precedent in the preface to Ine's laws. But the law-code is not a translation, and Ine's preface (which survives only in the form transmitted by Alfred) can scarcely be compared to Alfred's monumental introduction.[6]

Alfred and his contemporaries obviously believed that the texts they translated could not stand alone, even though most of these works had formerly done so. Indeed, the preface seems to have been a signature preoccupation of Alfred and his court. Other well-known vernacular texts from the period do not have prefaces, including the Old English *Martyrology*, the Old English *Orosius*, and the *Anglo-Saxon Chronicle*.[7] The *Life of St Chad* is replete with borrowings from

---

[1] *Pauli Orosii Historiarum adversus Paganos Libri VII*, ed. C. Zangemeister, CSEL 5 (Vienna, 1882).

[2] Augustine, *Soliloquia*, Migne, *PL* 32, 869–904.

[3] *Boethii Philosophiae Consolationis Libri Qinque*, ed. W. Weinberger, CSEL 67 (Leipzig, 1934).

[4] Gregory the Great, *Dialogorum libri V*, Migne, *PL* 77 (Paris, 1862), 148–433. The Latin original of Gregory's text does not have a preface, despite Colgrave's and Mynors's reference to the 'preface' to this work. See B. Colgrave and R. A. B. Mynors (eds and trans), Bede, *HE*, xxx.

[5] Gregory the Great, *Regula Pastoralis*, Migne, *PL* 77 (Paris, 1862), 13–128. For the Old English translation, see *Pastoral Care*, ed. Sweet, 2–9 (Alfred's prefaces), and 22–5 (Gregory's).

[6] Liebermann, *Gesetze*, I.15–123.

[7] *Martyrology*, ed. Kotzor. *Orosius*, ed. Bately. D. Dumville and S. Keynes, *The Anglo-Saxon Chronicle: A Collaborative Edition* (23 vols, 1983–).

earlier Latin saints' lives as well as Bede's *History* (sources which include prefaces) but lacks a preface of its own.[8] The prefatory evidence from the edition of the Mercian translation of Bede's *Ecclesiastical History* is misleading. Thomas Miller placed the word 'praefatio' before Bede's letter, although the Old English manuscripts he prints do not include the heading.[9] Prefaces in another prominent Mercian text, Wærferth's translation of the *Dialogues* of Gregory, include a prose preface in Alfred's voice and a verse preface that salutes the king as a treasure-giver.[10] Malcolm Godden has argued that the prose preface was probably not written by Alfred; at the same time, it could not have been written without his influence.[11] Jane Roberts has recently underscored the view that 'there is a distinct lack of any positive evidence' for 'a Mercian school of translation' before Alfred's reign.[12] There is certainly no evidence for a Mercian tradition of vernacular prefaces.

Strange, then, given the importance that Alfred's learned circle attached to the preface, to see the ambivalence with which the genre has been handled. Anglo-Saxonists have often read the prefaces independent of the texts they accompany, especially the prose preface to the *Pastoral Care*.[13] Alfred's prefaces draw attention partly because they are seen as original, even autobiographical statements – a faulty assumption, as Alfred Smyth has pointed out.[14] In reference to the law-code, Patrick Wormald has observed that all idiosyncrasies of Alfred's translations are not necessarily, as Wormald craftily puts it, 'instances of the infiltration of the king's ideas' into his texts.[15] The lure of autobiography is not the only reason that some of the prefaces have been thoroughly studied; mere length has played a part in their popularity. Unlike the texts themselves, the prefaces are short and easily anthologized. The preface to the law-code, of course, is not; hence its neglect.[16]

---

[8] R. Vleeskruyer, *The Life of St. Chad: An Old English Homily* (Amsterdam, 1953).

[9] *Bede*, ed. Miller, 1:2.

[10] For the Old English, see *Dialogues*, ed. Hecht.

[11] M. R. Godden, 'Editing Old English and the problem of Alfred's *Boethius*', *The Editing of Old English*, eds D. G. Scragg and P. E. Szarmach (1994), 163–76.

[12] J. Roberts, 'On the development of an Old English literary tradition' (Inaugural Lecture from the Department of English, King's College, London, 1998), 13, citing K. Sisam, *Studies in the History of Old English Literature* (1953), 31.

[13] This is not to deny the value of collecting an author's prefaces, as Jonathan Wilcox has done with the prefaces of Ælfric. See J. Wilcox (ed.), *Ælfric's Prefaces*, Durham Medieval Texts 9 (1994). Indeed, given the deplorable editorial state of Alfred's works generally, an edition of Alfred's prefaces would be well worth undertaking.

[14] Smyth, *Alfred*, 585, 595–7.

[15] P. Wormald, *The Making of English Law: King Alfred to the Twelfth Century* (1999), 420.

[16] Based on a random sample of sources old and new. *Sweet's Anglo-Saxon Reader in Prose and Verse*, rev. D. Whitelock (1967), includes the preface to the *Pastoral Care* but no excerpts from the text, the prose preface to the translation of the *Consolation* and five excerpts from the text (4–7). Keynes and Lapidge, *Alfred*, includes the prefaces to the *Pastoral Care*, the *Consolation* and the *Soliloquies*, as well as to the *Dialogues* as translated by Wærferth (123–53) and Wulfsige's preface to this work, and excerpts from the laws, but not the preface. In *An Anglo-Saxon Reader* (New York,

Sometimes Alfred and his associates wrote both prose and verse prefaces for the same works. It is reasonable to assume that they did so for a purpose. Yet the verse prefaces to the translations of the *Pastoral Care, Consolation of Philosophy*, and Gregory's *Dialogues* are usually printed as prose, as if the Anglo-Saxons' choice of genre had no consequences.[17] James Earl's analysis of Alfred's 'talking poems' is a welcome corrective to this tendency.[18] Elsewhere disregarded, genre ossifies in the *Anglo-Saxon Poetic Records*, where the verse preface to Alfred's translation of Boethius appears as the 'proem' to a text called the *Meters of Boethius* (itself an editorial excerpt from the *Consolation*).[19] The most conspicuous victim of prefatory ambiguity is, of course, the preface to the law-code. Attenborough omitted most of it because it had 'no bearing on Anglo-Saxon law'.[20] Only small sections of the introduction have been translated by Whitelock and by Keynes and Lapidge.[21] Hence, as Wormald has demonstrated, readers have missed almost entirely the ideological significance of the king's legislation as literature.[22]

How has the preface come to be regarded either as secondary or as an end in itself? Hegel thought of prefaces as 'a kind of chit-chat external to the very thing it appears to be talking about'. But, as Derrida pointed out, Hegel situated this observation in a preface, thus making the preface essential even as he dismissed it.[23] By adding a preface, an author implies the need for a supplement to the text. Any supplement, no matter how conventional, simultaneously strengthens and weakens the work to which it is attached. It explains the text but also calls attention to the need for an explanation. The so-called 'preface' to *Beowulf* is an example. The first of the poem's forty-three fitt numbers appears only after fifty-two lines of the text.[24] Henry Bradley argued that these fifty-two lines

---

1927), Milton Haight Turk included part of the preface to the law-code and excerpts from the laws (51–6) as well as the prefaces to the *Soliloquies* (86–7) and the *Pastoral Care* (67–70).

[17] As by Sweet (ed.), *Pastoral Care*, 8–9; see also Hecht, 2, and, after Hecht, M. Godden, 'Wærferth and King Alfred: the Fate of the Old English *Dialogues*', in *Alfred the Wise,* eds J. Roberts and J. L. Nelson, with M. Godden (1997), 35–6.

[18] J. W. Earl, *Thinking about 'Beowulf'* (Stanford, 1994), 87–99.

[19] G. P. Krapp (ed.), *The Paris Psalter and the Meters of Boethius*, 4 (New York, 1932), 153. See comments on the manuscript evidence in pages xxxv–xxxvi. Malcolm Godden's reconstructed opening pages of one manuscript of Alfred's translation of Boethius is a recent and welcome attempt to recover evidence about the early state of this text: Godden, 'Editing Old English', 172–6. K. Kiernan's ultraviolet photographs of the manuscript and a planned edition of this heavily damaged manuscript will do much to reveal the interrelation of poetry and prose in the translation; D. Hayes is preparing an edition of the manuscript based on these photographs, discussed in 'Building Electronic Editions of Badly Damaged Manuscripts,' 35th International Congress on Medieval Studies, Kalamazoo, Michigan, 5 May 2000.

[20] Attenborough, *Laws.*

[21] *EHD*, pp. 407–17; Keynes and Lapidge, *Alfred*, 163–70.

[22] Wormald, *The Making of English Law*, 416–29.

[23] J. Derrida, *Dissemination*, trans. B. Johnson (Chicago, 1981), 10–12.

[24] All references are to the edition by F. Klaeber, *Beowulf and the Fight at Finnsburg* (3rd edn, Lexington, MA, 1953), see p. 3 for the first fitt number.

were the beginning of a different poem, that *Beowulf* as it stands actually begins with the first fitt, and that its syntax was altered slightly to splice the two together.[25] In a similar vein, R. W. Chambers suggested that the glory of the ancient Danish kings recounted in these lines belonged outside the poem proper and this material, which he called 'prologue or preface', was 'simply left outside the numbering'.[26] Bruce Mitchell and Fred Robinson, the poem's most recent editors, comment that these lines 'may be taken as a prologue or prelude'.[27]

Three words have been used to describe this poem's first fifty-two lines: preface, prologue, and prelude. Of these three terms, the last is the least conventional, for it implies analogies to music and performance rather than literature. However, none of these words moves us very far from the other two. 'Preface' is defined in the *Oxford English Dictionary* not only as 'the introduction to a literary work, usually containing some explanation of its subject, purpose, and scope, and the method of its treatment' (II. 2) but also as a 'prologue' (3). Both 'prologue' (q.v., 1) and 'prelude' (2) are defined as a 'preface'. There is an advantage to pursuing the musical analogy implied in 'prelude' and in extending it to another word for the preface, 'overture', which is nowhere called a 'preface' in the *OED*. A 'prelude' is what is played before (*prae* + *ludere*). An 'overture' literally designates an opening (*overture*) and is both a musical and a structural metaphor. As a musical introduction, the overture is described as 'often containing or made up of themes from the body of the work, or otherwise indicating the character of it'.[28] As a literary introduction, the overture can be assigned a similar task. I propose to contrast 'overture' to 'prelude' and to use some of the differences between them to explore Alfred's ideas about the prefaces to his work.

Differences between musical preludes and overtures can be seen in the use of these terms by Richard Wagner, who gave preludes to *Lohengrin*, *Tristan und Isolde*, *Parsifal*, and *Der Ring des Nibelungen* and overtures to *Tannhäuser* and *Der Fliegende Holländer*. In his discussion of Wagner's operas, Ernest Newman describes the prelude to *Tristan* as 'the slow musical elaboration of a single bitter-sweet mood'. The prelude leads up to the main part; it sustains its own logic and mood, bittersweet or otherwise. An overture, Newman writes, tells 'the story of the opera by the succession and interplay of leading motives',[29] thus following the logic of the plot. With its own logic and argument, the prelude leads into but does not encapsulate the work. The overture does just that: an

---

[25] For a summary of Bradley's views, expressed in the *Encyclopedia Britannica* (11th edn), see R. W. Chambers, *Beowulf: An Introduction to the Study of the Poem with Discussion of the Stories of Offa and Finn*, 3rd edn, with a Supplement by C. L. Wrenn (1959), 293–5.

[26] Chambers, '*Beowulf*', 296.

[27] B. Mitchell and F. C. Robinson (eds), *Beowulf: An Edition* (1998), 49, n. 51.

[28] All definitions are taken from the *Oxford English Dictionary*. In defining 'overture', the *OED* notes that the first use in reference to music was in 1667 and that the word was used in reference to a poem by Swinburne in 1870.

[29] E. Newman, *The Wagner Operas* (Princeton, 1949), 127, 207.

epitome in two senses, it is both a précis of the work's main ideas – its 'story' or narrative – and a segment typical of the whole.

One can, in fact, demonstrate that the first fifty-two lines of *Beowulf* are not a prelude leading up to the main matter but instead an overture that introduces a sequence anticipating most of the poem's main ideas. The opening theme is the glory of kings ('þeodcyninga þrym', l. 2), juxtaposed to another theme, the jural role of violence and terror. This is how Scyld Scefing came to power (ll. 4–6a) and how power is won by both Hrothgar and Beowulf (see ll. 64–7, for example). Miserable beginnings are overcome by generosity (ll. 6b-8a, 43–6); Beowulf too has unpromising origins (ll. 2183b-89b). Patrimony and inherited tradition assert the dominance of the male in a homosocial world, but references to birth implicitly assert the role of the female, in the overture (ll. 12–16a) and wherever sons are mentioned. In the community whose glory is imagined in these lines – as elsewhere in *Beowulf* – protection and security are given in exchange for loyalty (ll. 7a–11, 20–25); the price of stability is, as always, violence. The overture ends, appropriately, with a funeral (ll. 34–51), as does the poem. Lines 1–52 can, therefore, be said to 'tell the story' of *Beowulf* before the poem itself speaks.

Both preludes and overtures lead seamlessly into the first scenes of the operas I have named, but preludes and overtures are structurally and affectively different. They prepare the audience in different ways. In an analysis of the relations between texts and readers, narrative theorist Roland Barthes described some texts as 'writerly', others as 'readerly'.[30] It will be useful to coordinate the distinction between overture and preface with Barthes's terms. 'The goal of a literary work (of literature as work)', Barthes writes, 'is to make the reader no longer a consumer, but a producer of the text.'[31] The 'readerly' text is a product in which the reader is merely a passive receiver. The 'writerly' text is partly produced by the reader. For Barthes, traditional novels, filled with conventions that clue the reader's response, are 'readerly' because the conventions do much of the reader's work. Experimental fiction, on the other hand, is 'writerly' because it forces the reader to 'write', to exert effort in order to make sense of the work. Overtures can be seen as readerly. They seek to familiarize the reader with the content about to be exposed and are dependent on the structure ('the story', the narrative sequence) of the works they epitomize. Preludes can be seen as writerly rather than readerly because they advance a single idea whose relation to the whole, although clearly thematic, is, structurally and otherwise, unspecific. The prelude places more demands on the reader, for its relation to the whole remains somewhat enigmatic – as if the writer were talking to himself, the reader or listener simply overhearing. The overture, in contrast, speaks directly to the audience about the work.

---

30 R. Barthes, *S/Z*, trans. R. Miller (1974). See also J. Harris, 'The plural text/the plural self: Roland Barthes and William Coles', *College English*, 49 (1987), 158–70.

31 Barthes, *S/Z*, 4.

Latin Prefaces

The distinction between prelude and overture can be seen in some Latin prefaces that might have been known to Alfred and his helpers. The most common form of the preface in early Anglo-Saxon England before Alfred – whether called 'prefatio', 'proemium', or 'prologus' – was the preface to a saint's life. For a sample of such works, I examined prefaces to lives written by Felix[32] and Eddius Stephanus,[33] the authors of the anonymous *Life* of Cuthbert and *Life of Gregory the Great*,[34] and to Bede's life of Cuthbert,[35] and, for balance and variety, the prefaces to Bede's *Historia Ecclesiastica* and to Gregory's *Regula Pastoralis*. I identified five features common to the Latin prefaces: the greeting to the work's patron; advice offered to the reader, sometimes in the form of a warning; commentary on the author's working method; the modesty topos, asserting the author's unworthiness; and the text's rhetorical density, measured by the use of figures of speech, usually metaphors.

Each of these features suggests a distinct relationship between reader and writer. A greeting to the patron is found in all the saints' lives I examined. The patron is, of course, a reader to whom the author speaks directly. But in the minds of all *other* readers, the relationship between the author and patron is exclusive. In this greeting the author speaks over the heads of many readers to one or two who are more important than any others. It would be difficult to imagine a more self-conscious attempt to set the writer apart from the audience and put the reader on guard. The warning to the reader does not necessarily address the audience directly, but can do so, and not in a reassuring way. Gregory's preface to the *Pastoral Care*, actually a letter to Bishop John, warns of unworthy or unprepared readers, who 'must be deterred from the precipitate venture'.[36] Prefaces to the Latin and prose Old English lives of Guthlac anticipate a sceptical response to the *Life* and warn readers of the dangers of intellectual blindness.[37] Unworthy readers are put on the defensive as the intellectual distance between author and reader is emphasized.

A third feature is commentary on the author's working methods. In the *History*, for example, Bede says that in order to remove doubts from the reader's mind he will 'make it [his] business to state briefly from what sources [he has] gained [his] information'.[38] This topos was borrowed from the first book of Gregory's *Dialogues*.[39] Authors of saints' lives were usually at pains to demon-

---

[32] B. Colgrave (ed. and trans.), *Felix's Life of Guthlac* (1956).

[33] Colgrave (ed. and trans.), *The Life of Bishop Wilfrid by Eddius Stephanus* (1927).

[34] Colgrave (ed. and trans.), *The Earliest Life of Gregory the Great* (1985), 32.

[35] Colgrave (ed. and trans.), *Two Lives of St. Cuthbert* (1940).

[36] H. Davis (trans.), *St. Gregory the Great: Pastoral Care* (Westminster, MD, 1950), 12.

[37] Colgrave, *Felix's Life of Guthlac*, 63.

[38] Colgrave and Mynors, *Bede's Ecclesiastical History*, 2.

[39] See Colgrave, *Two Lives of Cuthbert*, 341; Bede admired and used the *Dialogues* and listed

strate the authority of their reports and to stress the reliability of their witnesses. One who did not was the author of the anonymous life of Gregory, who also omits a warning to the reader; he makes no comment on his working method either in his proemium or his second preface, the 'prefaciuncula'.[40] Statements that underscore the writer's preparation and the validity of his claims, like the warning to the reader, emphasize the distance between the author and the audience.

Closely akin to commentary on method is the author's use of the modesty topos. Felix, Eddius Stephanus, and the anonymous writer of the life of Cuthbert used this device, which entered the canon from the *Life* of Anthony by Athanasius.[41] Describing the familiar, double-barrelled protestation of 'unworthiness and incapacity', Colgrave notes that not all authors took the commonplace seriously.[42] It was widely imitated none the less. Alcuin used it in his *Life* of Willibrord, as did Odo of Cluny in the *Life* of Gerald of Aurillac, two examples of many.[43] There are exceptions, including the Whitby *Life* of Gregory, Bede's *History*, and Gregory's preface to the *Pastoral Care*. Within the readerly–writerly dynamic, the modesty topos is a paradox. Even as it is qualified by the modesty trope, the author's authority is asserted, his prominence enhanced by protestations of unworthiness.

Figurative language, the fifth distinguishing trait, is potentially the most writerly of all these features, especially when the figures of speech are obscure or erudite. Of the texts I examined, only two exploit figurative language – the prefaces to the *Cura Pastoralis* and to Felix's life of Guthlac. Prominent in Felix's preface are nautical metaphors (the ship; the stream) that emerge in Alfred's verse preface and epilogue to the *Pastoral Care*.[44] Felix also describes 'the waters of genius', 'the flowers of rhetoric', and 'the meadows of literature' (all in two lines), and, less cheerfully, the 'veils' over the minds of readers and the 'blackness of ignorance'.[45] The preface to the *Regula Pastoralis* characterizes pastoral duties as 'burdens' from which Gregory has sought to conceal himself. Gregory's text claims to proceed in an orderly way, 'step by step' across

---

it prominently among Gregory's works in the *History*, see Book 2, ch. 1, 126–8. For Gregory's statement, see the translation by Edmund G. Gardner (n.d.), 5.

[40] Colgrave, *The Earliest Life of Gregory the Great*, 73.

[41] Colgrave, *The Life of Bishop Wilfrid by Eddius Stephanus*, 3; Colgrave, *Felix's Life of Guthlac*, 65.

[42] Colgrave, *The Earliest Life of Gregory the Great*, 140, n. 1.

[43] The translation of Alcuin's *Life* of Willibrord by C. H. Talbot omits the preface: C. H. Talbot, *The Anglo-Saxon Missionaries in Germany* (1954). A version of the preface is supplied by T. F. X. Noble and T. Head (eds), *Soldiers of Christ: Saints and Saints' Lives from Late Antiquity and the Early Middle Ages* (University Park, 1995), 191, 296–7.

[44] Colgrave, *Felix's Life*, 62–3. See Earl, *Thinking about 'Beowulf'*, 96–7.

[45] Colgrave, *Life of St. Guthlac*, 62–3. See R. Waugh, 'Literacy, royal power, and king–poet relations in Old English and Old Norse compositions', *Comparative Literature*, 49 (1997), 289–315.

the 'threshold' of discourse.[46] Eddius Stephanus refers to 'the path to virtue' and to the 'envious pricks of the ancient foe'.[47] Significantly, the two prefaces densest in figurative language (Gregory's and Felix's) are also the most forceful in challenging the reader.

The Latin prefaces I have described are rich in conventions and intertextual borrowings. How effectively they prepare readers for the texts that follow – how well they function as either prelude or overture – is another matter. With the exception of the preface to the *Regula Pastoralis*, these prefaces say little about the form or content of the works themselves. Felix, for example, might be said to outline the life of Guthlac because Felix says that he will describe the saint's birth, life before taking vows, and the end of his life. But such commentary, hardly specific, occupies only a brief moment of the extended preface.[48] By contrast, the preface to the mid-ninth-century anonymous *Life* of Willehad, Alcuin's slightly older contemporary, not only shuns self-effacing protestations but offers a theological rationale for writing a saint's life.[49] Like an overture, it prepares the reader for the narrative to come. Among the Latin prefaces I have surveyed, only the preface to the *Regula Pastoralis* anticipates the whole work in both theme and form. Gregory writes, 'The book is divided into four separate treatises, that it may bring its message to the mind of the reader in an orderly manner.'[50] Gregory then names the function of each part – how to attain dignity, how to live with dignity, how to teach with dignity, and how to perceive and control one's own faults. There, in the preface (the overture), is the *Pastoral Care* in miniature. Most hagiographic prefaces are, in the framework I have been using, closer to preludes than is Gregory's preface, and are therefore more writerly than readerly.

Vernacular Prefaces

Hagiographic prefaces were presumably known to Alfred but did not exercise an obvious influence on his work. Asser used such prefaces, although he did not attach one to his life of Alfred.[51] Because the Latin tradition is highly literate, the authors of hagiographic prefaces could speak in the coded language of rhetorical conventions. Such precedents would not have sufficed for Alfred, an author who struggled to find a voice and who 'wrote' (a figurative term in relation to his work) as part of a team of which he was probably not the most learned member. Not an obvious believer in the merits of imitation, he

---

[46] See Davis, *St. Gregory the Great: Pastoral Care*, 20–21.
[47] Colgrave, *The Life of Bishop Wilfrid by Eddius Stephanus*, 2–3.
[48] Colgrave, *Felix's Life of Guthlac*, 62–3.
[49] Noble and Head (eds), *Soldiers of Christ*, 281.
[50] Davis, *St. Gregory the Great: Pastoral Care*, 20.
[51] W. H. Stevenson (ed.), *Asser's Life of King Alfred* (1904).

represented himself as a pioneer in learning for the laity, even as he took the clergy to task for their scholarly deficiencies. He had only a few learned cohorts to address, and his prefaces therefore could not play off the vast Latinate tradition to which hagiographic prefaces belong. Obviously Alfred had no need to greet a patron. He used the epistolatory mode in which this greeting usually occurs only in the *Pastoral Care*, a text directed to his social inferiors, bishops who seem to be regarded as thegns.[52] Alfred also used the modesty topos once – although, as we will see, there is disagreement on this score – and only once warns the reader, both these examples in the prose preface to his translation of Boethius. Only two features in Alfred's prefaces are consistent with the Latin tradition: figurative language, a rich and some-times confusing aspect of the prose associated with the king, and commentary on the author's working methods.

Given the readership sketched in the preface to the *Pastoral Care*, and Asser's well-known comments on the king's efforts to improve the rudimentary education of his courtiers,[53] we might expect Alfred's prefaces to be more readerly than writerly, more like explanatory overtures than meditational, intro-spective preludes. But as I read them, Alfred's prose prefaces merely gesture at helping the reader grasp the form and content of the translations that follow. Each prose preface, like a prelude, ruminates on themes related to the text (and is in some cases demonstrably inspired by it), with interspersed comments on the environment in which the text was translated. Hence, in Barthes's language, Alfred's prose prefaces are predominantly writerly; they force the reader to produce explanations and connections not supplied by the author. The verse prefaces address the works' aims more directly, and hence are readerly. It is worth comparing the affective differences of these genres in the translations of the *Pastoral Care* and the *Consolation of Philosophy*, which have one preface in prose and another in verse. In some manuscripts both works contain an elaborate suite of prefatory material consisting of multiple prefaces and chapter headings. The manuscript evidence of the translation of the *Pastoral Care* shows prefatory material composed in two parts, a prose and verse preface written at about the same time and, after the chapter headings, Gregory's own preface. The manu-script evidence of the *Consolation*, although notoriously difficult to decipher, suggests a similarly elaborate plan.

The prose and verse prefaces to the *Pastoral Care*, taken together, refocus the text and give Gregory's work a distinctly secular purpose. Neither preface

---

[52] Bernard Huppé observed some time ago that the preface to the *Pastoral Care* was indebted to the epistolatory tradition. On the role of bishops, see Smyth, *Alfred*, 533–4.

[53] According to Asser, c. 106 (trans. Keynes and Lapidge, *Alfred*, 110), Alfred ordered ealdormen, thegns and reeves who were illiterate from childhood and who could not learn on their own to be read to by members of their families or even freemen or slaves. Alfred was assiduous about the education of his sons and daughters and supposedly taught the sons of his officials himself (c. 75, 90–91).

addresses the spiritual concerns of Gregory's letter to John or of the *Pastoral Care* itself. Indeed, the prose preface plainly subordinates the church to the king, as many commentators have observed. A singular attempt to explain conditions governing the production of the text, this preface does not directly address the concerns of Gregory's text. Both the preface and the main text are generally about the role of teaching and teachers. But Gregory speaks to pastors about practical matters of the cure of souls, while Alfred's notion of good teaching is aimed at secular or social rather than spiritual goals.

The verse preface, although by no means a paraphrase of the prose, is also secular in its emphasis. The poem owes more to the heroic than to the sacred tradition of Old English verse. Alfred portrays Gregory as the Lord's warrior ('drytnes cempa', 4b) who acquired or won over most of mankind for the guardian of heaven ('moncynnes mæst gestrynde rodra wearde', 8–9a), as if the pope were a thegn who conquered nations for his lord.[54] Gregory is seen as a leader praised not only for the wisdom of his mind ('gleawmod', 6b) but for his hoard of cunning thoughts ('searoðonca hord', 7b), which has helped him achieve most glorious fame ('mærðum gefrægost', 10b). This last bit of praise appears in a string of superlatives as befitting a Roman emperor as a pope ('Romwara betest, monna modwelegost, mærðum gefrægost', 9–10b).

In relation to the audience, one might argue that the verse has an effect opposite to that of the prose. If the prose preface belabours the difficulties of a reform of learning, the verse preface celebrates a direct and seemingly untroubled line of authority from Gregory to Augustine to Alfred and adds two not unremarkable details. We learn that Alfred ordered more such (books) so that he could send them to his bishops:

> … heht him swelcra ma
> brengan bi ðære bisene, þæt he his biscepum
> senden meahte, forðæm hi his sume ðorfton,
> ða ðe lædenspræce læste cuðon (ll. 13b–15b)

> he [Alfred] ordered that more of the same [i.e., books] be brought to
> him according to this example, so that he might send them to his
> bishops, for some of them needed them [the books], those who could
> hardly read Latin.

The implication is that the bishops had better buckle down if they expect to meet the king's expectations. The prose preface is far more tactful in indicting ignorance in the kingdom.

Both literally and figuratively Alfred's prefaces are detached from the *Pastoral Care.* Two early manuscripts are especially revealing of the circumstances in which the prefaces were produced. The two prefaces in Hatton 20 were written, Sisam says, 'in hands which do not appear in the contents and the

---

54 See Smyth, *Alfred*, 555, on the verse preface to the *Pastoral Care* and its relation to the text. All quotations from the verse preface are from *The Anglo-Saxon Minor Poems*, 110.

text'.[55] The use of 'hands' here underscores the fact that the prose and verse prefaces were written by different scribes. Evidently the verse preface was not ready when the prose preface was finished, and neither was ready when the text itself was complete. The translation of the work and the writing of the prefaces were undertaken as separate projects. In both the Hatton manuscript and in Cotton Tiberius B.xi., the two prefaces occupy a bifolium that could be attached to the text later. Thus they constitute a material preface as well as a literary one. This dissociation of the prefaces from the earliest exemplars is at least symbolic of the gap between the prefaces and the translation itself.

The prose and verse preface are complementary preludes to the *Pastoral Care*. Nothing in either text refers to the structure or even the specific pastoral content of the text itself. The overture comes in Gregory's own preface, which refers to the work's four-part structure and describes the 'threshold' of the larger discourse. Gregory's preface is somewhat diminished in effectiveness in part by the list of chapter headings that precedes it. Gregory's text itself is subtly altered by Alfred. Gregory warns readers who are unprepared for his discourse and who 'must be deterred from the precipitate venture at the very threshold of this our discourse'. The preface is imagined as an antechamber or a passage leading to a doorway beyond which the work lies. In Alfred's rendering, Gregory's threshold becomes 'the very door of this book' ('fram ðære dura selfre ðisse bec', p. 25, l. 11).[56] Alfred also transforms Gregory's step-by-step progression explicitly into a metaphor for ascent. 'I wish this discourse to rise in the mind of the learners as on a ladder ('hlædre', p. 23, l. 17), by steps, nearer and nearer, until it [the discourse] firmly stands on the upper floor (in the upper room) of the mind which learns it.' Alfred adds the image of the mind as an upper chamber, the destination to which the idea climbs. The figure of the ladder is not used here to link heaven and earth – that is, the disciples and the God they contemplate – but to join two levels of learning. The ladder is referred to later in the *Pastoral Care*; Alfred also used this image in the *Soliloquies* to describe how the one who wishes to perceive wisdom with his mind's eye must approach wisdom step by step, as one who wants a good view must mount a sea cliff on a ladder.[57] The ladder was a figure for mystical ascent derived from the story of Jacob and already familiar in patristic writing – for example, the letters of Jerome. It is also used in the *Dialogues* of Gregory the Great.[58] Alfred's additions enhance the readerly qualities of Gregory's preface but do not strengthen the ties between

---

[55] K. Sisam, *Studies in the History of Old English Literature* (1953), 142–3. N. R. Ker, however, does not designate two hands for the Hatton prefaces; *Catalogue of Manuscripts Containing Anglo-Saxon* (1957), 387–8.

[56] All quotations taken from the Hatton manuscript as edited by Sweet, *Pastoral Care*, and given by line and page number in the text.

[57] *Pastoral Care*, c. 16, ed. Sweet, 100–101. See *Soliloquies*, ed. Carnicelli, 'swilce he on sume hlædre stige and wylle weorðan uppe on sumu(m) sæclife' (78).

[58] See *Dialogues*, Book 7, II. 25–9.

Gregory's preface and the *Pastoral Care*; they do not transform the prelude into an overture.

The second work for which Alfred prepared two prefaces is the *Consolation of Philosophy*, but here the manuscript evidence is less clear. The only surviving copy of the prose preface refers to a form of the work in verse and prose; it is attached to Oxford, Bodleian Library, Bodley 180, which is the later of the two surviving manuscripts (but which contains what is always called the earlier form of the text, with the meters in prose only).[59] The now-fragmentary manuscript, British Library, Cotton Otho A.vi, contains the meters in Old English verse. The only copy of the verse preface is found in the transcript of this manuscript made by Junius before the Cotton Library fire.[60] Two longer prefaces accompany this translation, both describing the historical context of Boethius and his political plight. Earl regards the poetic form of this preface as the first meter to the *Consolation*, and describes it as 'a verse development of a wholly original prose version not based on Boethius'.[61] Since it is numbered as the first meter (in the metrical version) and the first chapter (in the prose version), this text should not perhaps be considered a preface. On the other hand, it is not part of the text of Boethius, and I see no middle ground between a preface and the translation that follows.

I am concerned with the first two of these four texts, since they give rise to surprisingly discordant impressions of Alfred as a writer. The prose preface, with its much-quoted comment about 'word for word translation', is flat-footed, a meagre tissue of clichés:

> Ælfred kuning wæs wealhstod ðisse bec, and hie of boclædene on englisc wende, swa hio nu is gedon. Hwilum he sette word be worde, hwilum andgit of andgite, swa swa he hit þa sweotolost and andgitfullicast gereccan mihte for þam mistlicum and manigfealdum wordum and bisgum þe he hine oft æfðer ge on mode ge on lichoman bisgodan.

> King Alfred was the translator of this book and turned it from Latin into English as it is now done. Now he set forth word by word, now sense by sense, as he most clearly and intelligently was able to do

---

[59] See Godden, 'Editing Old English', for a summary of the manuscript evidence, 163–6.

[60] Only two words from the metrical preface can be attested from the fragments of the Tiberius manuscript, but obviously it too contained both prefaces; see *The Anglo-Saxon Minor Poems*, cviv and the calculations in Ker, *Catalogue*, 257–8. Ker notes that the 'writing on fol. 4+6, 8 is smaller, and the number of lines to the page was probably as much as 30', while the pages of the main text contained 'probably' not more than fifteen lines each. Fol. 6+4 contains the preface (Sweet, p. 4, l. 10, to p. 8, l. 5), about forty-five lines of type. I calculate that thirty lines of Old English become twenty-two lines of type in Sweet's edition. These forty-five lines of type would then account for about sixty lines of Old English, or two written sides. The main text seems to have taken up fifteen lines per page, that is, to have been written in larger script than the prefaces, which were written in smaller script to fit on to the bifolium.

[61] Earl, *Thinking about 'Beowulf'*, 88.

amid the various and manifold worldly cares that often troubled him in mind and body.[62]

The debt to both the verse and the prose prefaces of the *Pastoral Care* seems clear. It is little more than a recasting of some key ideas from that text, and has no more relation to the *Consolation* than the prefaces to the *Pastoral Care* have to that text. Even as a prelude the prose preface to the *Consolation* is weak, 'readerly' in the extreme, one might say, for from the start one has the feeling that one has already read it. In her contribution to this volume (Chapter 6), Janet Bately comments on the banality of these phrases, which, as she says, could have been written by almost anybody, for example, a scribe imitating Alfred's ideas and style.[63]

The prose preface to the *Consolation* has two features that, as I have noted above, are not found in other prefaces associated with Alfred's translations: Alfred's only use of the modesty topos and his only attempt to warn the reader. However, the warning is not the traditional admonition to a reader who might not be worthy of the text. Instead, the preface excuses the translator and warns that the reader is not to blame him (Alfred, presumably) if the reader can do a better job with the text than Alfred could. The author also asks the reader not to hold him responsible for errors, a request made in none of the other prefaces, and concludes on the stoic if banal note that each man can only do his best with what he has. I find this uncharacteristically timid and weak and doubt on these grounds alone that Alfred was responsible for it.

My assessment of the prose preface differs from that of Godden, who has argued that this preface is Alfred's because it requests prayers and uses the modesty topos. Godden distinguished the preface to the *Dialogues* of Gregory the Great from the prefaces to Alfred's works because it contrasts 'to the modest third-person references in the king's preface to his own works'.[64] Alfred was a modest author, but these third-person references do not strike me as modest. 'King Alfred sends words of greeting in a loving and amicable way': these words follow the inscription to the *Pastoral Care*. 'King Alfred was the translator of this book': these are the first words of the *Consolation of Philosophy*. 'Now I, King Alfred, have collected these laws': these are not exactly the *first* words of Alfred's law collection, which begins three folios earlier, but Alfred's 'ic' is the third first-person pronoun in the text, an exceptional case, since the other two belong to God.[65]

The poor quality of the prose preface to the translation of Boethius is all the more evident when it is compared to the verse preface.

---

[62] For the Old English, see *Boethius*, ed. Sedgefield, 1 (my translation).

[63] See Bately, 'The Alfredian canon revisited', above, pp. 107–20.

[64] Godden, 'Editing Old English', 36.

[65] In *The Parker Chronicle and Laws (Corpus Christi College, Cambridge, MS. 173)*, eds R. Flower and H. Smith, EETS OS 208 (1941), Alfred's 'ic' appears between the first two numbered sections of the code, on fol. 39b of a text that begins on fol. 36a.

Ðus Ælfred us ealdspell reahte,
cyning Westsexna, cræft meldode,
leoðwyrhta list. Him wæs lust micel
ðæt he ðiossum leodum leoð spellode,
monnum myrgen, mislice cwidas ...

Thus King Alfred told us old tales,
the king of the West Saxons displayed skill,
the poet's art. It was a great pleasure to him
that he proclaimed poems to the people,
a delight to men, in different sayings.

Alfred is portrayed as a teller of old tales ('ealdspell') who took pleasure in proclaiming poems to his people and delighting them with different kinds of speech. 'Cwidas' means 'sayings', but also 'tale', 'report', 'expression of thought' and 'discourse'. As Earl writes, the poem offers 'just a hint of the dramatic structure' of the *Consolation* itself. Earl also argues that the verse preface is a projection of Alfred's voice into the text, which assimilates it, so that Alfred cuts himself off from his own voice and allows the book to speak as a text, not as an object.[66] Although I do not want to encourage adding to our already rich stock of roles for this all-purpose king, I would like to rejoin the king's voice to these poems, and to imagine that he declaimed them. There is no reason why he or any literate figure would not have participated in a tradition of public proclamation. Even without an autobiographical link, the verse preface is more overture than prelude. It not only casts the author (Alfred) as a poet but suggests something of the 'different discourses' ('mislice cwidas') of the *Consolation* that follows.

I do not have the space to explore the preface to the *Soliloquies*, justly famous for its figurative richness, or to the law code, which I too now neglect. But a brief examination suggests that in their relations to the texts that follow they too are more like preludes than overtures, making strong thematic connections rather than structural connections to the translations. The preface to the *Soliloquies* describes mental processes of assimilation and reformulation that are part of a spiritual quest; the *Soliloquies* itself is about such a quest. The preface is richly material and concrete; the same cannot be said for Augustine's text, but Alfred inserted sharp images into the text (just as he did with the *Consolation*), and in this way adapted the Latin text to suit the tenor of his preface to it (just as he adapted Gregory's preface to the *Pastoral Care* to make it seem more of a piece with his own thought).[67] Like the prose preface to the *Pastoral Care*, this preface might be said to offer a parallel to rather than a précis of the Latin text.

What stands out in a review of Alfred's prefaces in the context of my discussion of preludes and overtures – and the qualities of readerly and writerly

---

66 Earl, *Thinking about 'Beowulf'*, 90, 95.

67 See A. J. Frantzen, *King Alfred* (Boston, 1986), 14–16 (preface to the laws) and 71–2 (preface to *Soliloquies*).

communication – is the apparent originality of the vernacular texts. If preludes are situated at one end of a continuum and overtures at the other, Alfred's prefaces clearly favour the prelude as a model. Hagiographic prefaces are deeply conventional and, therefore, readerly. Alfred's prefaces are not conventional. For him and his assistants, the Latin prefaces might well have been writerly rather than readerly. If Alfred and his helpers understood the conventions of hagiographic prefaces, they did not choose to imitate them. Instead, they wrote prefaces that favour the model of the prelude. Like the Latin prefaces, the vernacular prefaces are, with respect to the texts that follow, writerly: they do little to prepare the reader for the translation itself. None of them offers the reader significant assistance with either the form or the content of that text; only one of them, the verse preface to the *Consolation*, even gestures at such assistance. Yet there was precedent for this assistance, as we see in Gregory's preface to the *Pastoral Care*. Alfred's best prefaces are in verse; they communicate directly with the reader as hearer ('Listen who will' reads the last line of the verse preface to the *Consolation,* 'Hliste se þe wille', 10b). Here too there is an irony. Some Latin texts also have both prose and verse prefaces, but the distinction between them does not parallel the distinction between Alfred's prefaces in prose and verse. Alcuin's *Life* of Willibrord, like Bede's *Life* of Cuthbert, took both prose and verse forms, and Alcuin tells us why. One version, Alcuin said, 'walk[ed] along in prose' and was for public reading in church, while the other, 'running with the muse of poetry', was to be read by Beornrad's pupils 'over and over again privately in their rooms'.[68] Commenting on these texts, Michael Lapidge notes that 'the difficulty of their diction makes them unapproachable except through long, careful and meditative study'.[69] With Alfred's prefaces the purposes are reversed. The prose prefaces to the *Pastoral Care* and the *Soliloquies* are complex and require careful reading. The verse prefaces to the *Pastoral Care* and the *Consolations*, on the other hand, are vigorous statements with a public, performative quality.

The apparent originality of the vernacular prefaces might be attributed to Alfred's emerging idea of himself as both reader and writer. I would not choose to frame the debate solely in modern terms of writer and self, however, or of overture and prelude. I would emphasize instead the facts of textual production that the fragmentary corpus of prefaces reveals. These texts represent work by committee, rushed and incomplete, that mixes what might be Alfred's words with words written on his behalf, in his voice and person. It would be a mistake to fit these prefaces into a paradigm of an elaborate, finished introductory sequence such as is attested by the oldest manuscripts of the *Pastoral Care*; the assembly of those prefaces on a separate bifolium appears to have been a special effort. It would also be a mistake to form these texts into a complete picture of

---

[68] Alcuin's *Life* of Willibrord, trans. Noble and Head, *Soldiers of Christ*, 191–2.

[69] M. Lapidge, 'The saintly Life in Anglo-Saxon England', in *The Cambridge Companion to Old English Literature*, eds M. Godden and M. Lapidge (1991), 259.

educational reform with Alfred at its nexus, a gesture that merely echoes the king's claim in the prose preface to the *Pastoral Care*. It would, I think, be more profitable to speculate on these prefaces as performances, trying to imagine how the double prefaces and the complex preface to the law-code were received and enacted in public. Surely that is better than enlisting the prefaces as further testimony for a plan to publish 'certain books most necessary for all men to know'.

Scholars have used this famous phrase from the preface to the *Pastoral Care* to weld the translations into a syllabus, with slots for philosophy, theology, church history, world history, and so forth.[70] It seems preposterous that of all the theological books he might have translated, Alfred would have chosen the *Soliloquies*, that he would not have translated Bede's *History* himself (or at least said that he did), and that he would have allowed a marginally competent companion to struggle with Gregory's *Dialogues* (which, unlike the *Soliloquies*, really is a useful text).[71] Perhaps we should simply assume that the court's scholars translated the books they had on hand and that they hoped that readers – and what did readers have to choose from? – would make a virtue of necessity and accept these books as 'most necessary to know' because they had the king's imprimatur. Intending no disrespect to the great scholarship invested in Alfred's cause in the last hundred years, I suggest that we have been too willing to take the king at his word.

Let us think instead about the lived experience of the reader regarding a manuscript that contained not only prose and verse prefaces by Alfred and an extended list of chapter headings but also a preface by Gregory. Was the verse memorized or extracted for proclamation? The headings might have merely visual clues that performed the work of the overture as they specified structure. Alfred's prefaces themselves are not formally complex, but their incorporation into codices that include inscriptions, prose prefaces, verse prefaces and chapter headings is formally intricate. It is necessary, then, to situate each preface in the context of its manuscript, taking visual as well as aural clues from the mixture of genres each presents. It is well to undertake such reading free of preconceptions about the coherence of the king's prefaces, much less of his entire corpus. Such analysis will be especially productive if we find richer ways of conceptualizing the prefaces themselves as both text and performance. Thinking of these prefaces as preludes and overtures is, I believe, a way to begin that process.

---

[70] Frantzen, *King Alfred*, 106–8.
[71] See the case made by Godden, 'Wærferth and King Alfred', 44–8.

Chapter 8

The player king: identification and self-representation in King Alfred's writings

Malcolm Godden

If we can say anything at all about King Alfred's taste in literature, it is that he loved the dialogue as a form. He apparently began his literary programme by persuading Wærferth, bishop of Worcester, to translate the *Dialogues* of Gregory the Great, which are cast as an exchange between Gregory himself and his friend the deacon Peter. He went on to produce his own adaptation of Boethius's *De Consolatione Philosophiae*, which is cast as a dialogue between Boethius and Philosophy, and about the same time produced a work loosely based on the *Soliloquies* of Augustine, which take the form of a dialogue between Augustine and Reason. Even when he wrote his preface to the *Pastoral Care*, he could not resist casting his own thoughts in the form of an internal dialogue. But when literary dialogues between the author's persona and an interlocutor are appropriated by another author, as Alfred does with Boethius and Augustine, we get some interesting effects and dilemmas. Who is now the I-figure in these texts? And who is speaking through the two interlocutors? The effect in the two works is to create a double dialogue. If Boethius the author splits himself, as it were, between Philosophy and a representation of himself which we might call Boethius the prisoner, Alfred then introduces himself as a third party engaged in a dialogue with Boethius the author, speaking at times through the first speaker, Wisdom, and at times through the second, called 'Boetius' or Mod; and similar effects are evident in the *Soliloquies*.

The process involves some complex games of identification and self-representation, in which pronouns like I and you have variable signifieds. That Alfred was perfectly familiar with such devices and multiplicities of voice is evident from his introductions to his version of the psalms, where he can tell us, for instance, 'when David sang this psalm, he lamented to the Lord that there should be so little loyalty in his days, and so little wisdom in the world; and so does each righteous man who sings it now, he sings it about his own times, and so did Christ about the Jews, and so did King Hezechiah about Rapsaca king of the Assyrians'.[1] Or we

---

[1] *Psalms* 13.1; 'Ða Dauid þisne þreotteoðan sealm sang, þa seofode he to Drihtne on þam sealme, þæt æfre on his dagum sceolde gewurðan swa lytle treowa, and swa lytel wisdom wære on worulde; and swa deð ælc rihtwis man, þe hine nu singð, he seofað þæt ylce be his tidum; and swa dyde Crist be Iudeum, and Ezechias be Rapsace, Assiria cyninge.'

might note how, in the *Pastoral Care*, Alfred begins with a third-person reference to himself, quickly switches to his own voice, though fictionalized perhaps, then speaks in the voice of the book in the metrical prologue, and finally speaks in Gregory's voice for the rest. Whom he is addressing is not mentioned at the outset, but he ends by addressing 'Iohannes'. Such authorial switches of voice and character in the *Boethius* and *Soliloquies* raise questions about the positioning of the works and of course about the whole programme of using Alfred's apparent writings to identify his own position, especially on the subject of kingship.

In the Latin text of the *De Consolatione* Boethius plays a literary game with the reader at the outset. The work opens with a poetic lament in which the author is apparently addressing his readers and complaining of his misery: 'I used to sing of happiness', he says, 'now (*nunc*) I can only make poems about grief.'[2] But the prose text that follows insists on a readjustment, a rethink of our relation to the text: 'While I was thinking these thoughts to myself in silence, and set my pen to record this tearful complaint, there seemed to stand above my head a woman.'[3] The narrator reveals that the opening verses are not addressed to any audience but were an interior monologue, a thought articulated in silence (*tacitus*) by the character Boethius at some moment in the past, and communicated now by the author to the reader as a record of that past event; the *nunc* of the opening verses is not the now of the literary present when the author addresses the reader but really the 'then' of the prison dialogue. And we relocate ourselves as the readers of a philosophical prose text rather than the audience of a poetic lament.

Alfred in his version disposes of this literary device by writing an introductory account of Boethius that leads into the opening verses, making it abundantly clear that the song of woe belongs to that past event when Boethius the prisoner met Wisdom, and is not an address by the author to the reader.[4] But he evidently noted the game being played, and sets up his own ambiguities about the I-figure and his situation. In the Latin text this speaker is just called I, *ego*, meaning the persona of the author, described as lying on his couch or bed in grief, in some place of exile from the court and power. The Old English text has a parallel figure, described as lying on the floor in a prison cell, who then reports the appearance of Wisdom and the ensuing dialogue with him.[5] In the

---

[2] I paraphrase Boethius, *De Consolatione Philosophiae*, ed. L. Bieler, CCSL 94 (Turnhout, 1957), Book I, metre 1.

[3] *De Consolatione* I pr.1; 'haec dum mecum tacitus ipse reputarem querimoniamque lacrimabilem stili officio signarem, astitisse mihi supra uerticem uisa est mulier.' The translation is by S. J. Tester, printed in *Boethius: the Theological Tractates [and] the Consolation of Philosophy* (Cambridge, MA and London, 1973).

[4] For the text see *Boethius*, ed. Sedgefield, 7–8.

[5] Despite the tradition of reading the *De Consolatione* as prison-literature, Boethius does not in fact seem to represent himself at any point as a prisoner, only as an exile from court. The various *Vitae* of Boethius that circulated with his work in later times, to one of which Alfred was no doubt indebted for his view of the author, sometimes represent him as exile, sometimes as prisoner; see

first two books the Old English text designates the speaker in the dialogue pretty consistently as *þæt mod*, 'the mind', no doubt to underline the interior nature of the dialogue. We presumably understand this to be the mind of Boethius the prisoner, but the term perhaps allows a degree of separation from both Boethius and Alfred. In books 3 to 5, the second speaker is mainly designated *ic*, 'I', meaning the author, though occasionally as 'Mod'. But from time to time he is designated more specifically as 'Boetius'. If the use of 'Mod' as a name for the speaker serves to generalize or universalize the dialogue, and the use of *ic* perhaps suggests a generalized author-persona who need not quite be either Boethius or Alfred, the use of 'Boetius' pulls us back sharply to an awareness of a voice belonging to a specific individual in particular circumstances; and this applies not only to the fictionalized second speaker but to the author Boethius and his whole work, since we are fully aware that the work as a whole is in some sense his and purports to derive from the personal experience that the work describes.

That is all the more true of the passages in the Old English text which refer to the specific experiences or circumstances of Boethius. Alfred gives us the introductory account of the author but then omits in silence the whole discussion of his political fortunes and downfall which occupies Book I prose 4 of the Latin text – not surprisingly, perhaps, since it gives such a different picture of the political situation from the one which Alfred had given in his own introduction, as we shall see. Then in chapter 10 we return to his specific situation: the speaker is identified again as 'Boetius' and Wisdom points out to him that what he has lost was not worth having and that he still retains the real good of this world – his father-in-law Symmachus, his virtuous wife and his two sons, who are the image of their father and politically successful as ealdormen. The passage reminds us as readers that the whole philosophical argument voiced by Wisdom is specific to the situation of the historical Boethius, but there are also some troubling dramatic ironies here. Any reader of Gregory's *Dialogues*, in Latin or Old English, would have recalled the vision reported in Book 4, when a hermit saw the soul of Theoderic the Ostrogoth, Boethius's king, being thrust into Hell, by way of the mouth of Etna, by the spirits of two of his earlier victims, Pope John and the senator Symmachus, Boethius's father-in-law and patron – Waerferth adds the comment that Symmachus was innocent.[6] Tradition also records that Theoderic had the two sons of Boethius killed, but perhaps it would be improper to import that piece of information. Even so, Alfred and his associates knew from the *Dialogues* that Symmachus was killed by Theoderic and probably knew from other traditions (such as the *Vitae* or the *Liber Pontificalis*) that Boethius was eventually killed by him too. The consolation offered by Wisdom – that Symmachus and the rest of his family are alive and well, and show that real good survives

---

Anicii Manlii Severini Boetii Philosophiae Consolationis Libri Quinque, ed. R. Peiper (Leipzig, 1871), xxx–xxxiv.

6 *Dialogues*, ed. Hecht, 306.

misfortune – thus appears to later readers as rather cold comfort, even though Boethius may well have thought when he wrote the *De Consolatione* that these goods, and indeed his own life, would remain to him though he was exiled from power and his supposed friends had deserted him. Alfred and his readers knew better, and Wisdom's authority seems somewhat undermined by that limitation. One wonders too about the Old English text's emphasis on the tribulations of marriage and family shortly afterwards in c. 11 (24.7–14) and again in c. 31, which contrast unexpectedly with Wisdom's idealization of domestic bliss. The little passage on Boethius's family seems to have a curiously distancing effect, objectifying the author and reminding the Anglo-Saxon readers of their distance from the work and the circumstances that inspired it.

More significant, though, are the references to Boethius's political fortunes. In the Latin text Boethius represents himself as a statesman who has sought to use his political position to do good for his country and people but has been undermined by political rivals and condemned by the very senate that he had tried to preserve, and thus been ousted from power, fame and fortune. He scarcely mentions the king, Theoderic the Ostrogoth, and then rather neutrally, as the ultimate authority who needs to be swayed or persuaded by the statesman; his enemies are his rivals, the other counsellors and officers, not the king. And he strongly rejects the charge that he had wanted to depose or oust Theoderic and restore Roman liberty.

The Old English text presents Boethius as the victim of an unjust tyrant king Theoderic, whom he had tried to topple by calling in the forces of the eastern emperor and who had responded by throwing him into prison. Boethius is here a courtier whose power-relations are with the king, not the senate or rivals. All three references to Theoderic in the Old English text are introduced there without prompting from the Latin text. They seem to represent a deliberate process of characterizing the speaker as the historical Boethius, rather than an everyman figure, and more particularly as the counsellor and victim of a wicked king. The first reference is of course the introduction, which tells of Theoderic's injustice to the righteous figure who tries to resist him. Then in chapter 16 the Old English text introduces a second reference to Theoderic. Wisdom, following Boethius's Philosophy, argues that power and status are false goods, and asserts that when they are acquired by evil men their effects are evil, since such tyrant kings use power to destroy and devastate the kingdoms subjected to them and those around them. But in the Old English text Wisdom introduces Nero and Theoderic as examples – 'when power and status fall to the worst and least worthy people, as it has done now to this same Theoderic and formerly to the emperor Nero, and also to many like them'.[7]

---

[7] *Boethius*, ed. Sedgefield, 34.20–24; 'Hwæt, se eower wela þonne and se eower anweald, þe ge nu weorðscipe hatað, gif he becymð to þam eallra wyrrestan men, and to þam þe his eallra unweorðost bið, swa he nu dyde to þis ilcan Þeodrice, and iu ær to Nerone þæm casere, and oft eac to mænegum hiora gelicum.'

Nero is presumably mentioned because he is the subject of Book II metre 6, which comes two pages later in the Old English text, but Theoderic has not been mentioned since the introduction. Wisdom goes on almost immediately to refer to 'your ancestors' the Roman senators who drove out the proud king Tarquin because of his arrogance. The passage serves to emphasize that Wisdom is speaking in the long ago to the sixth-century Roman, not in the here and now of Anglo-Saxon kingship. But it also makes the point, forcefully, that the speaker, and thus the writer of the text, has himself had particular experience of Philosophy's general truth about the relationship of royal power to moral depravity, and represents a people who had a long history of resistance to the tyranny of kingship.

The third reference to Theoderic is in c. 27 (62.8 and 13). In the Latin text Philosophy refers allusively to a certain Decoratus, an unworthy or corrupt politician with whom Boethius could not have been induced to serve – another example of the truth that morality and power do not naturally go together. It's another characteristic reference to Boethius's rivals in politics. Equally characteristically, the Old English version substitutes a reference to Theoderic. Wisdom addresses the speaker firmly as Boetius:

> But tell me now, I ask you, Boetius, why you had such manifold evils and so much hardship in power while you had it, or why you unwillingly lost it? Was it not because you would not consent in all things to the will of the unjust king Theoderic? Because you perceived him to be in all things unworthy of rule, shameless and perverse, without any good quality? Therefore we cannot easily say that the evil are good, though they have power. You would not have been driven from Theoderic, nor would he have rejected you, if you had approved of his folly and his injustice as much as his foolish favourites did.[8]

It is a puzzling question as to how Alfred got here from Decoratus the corrupt politician, though it may have started with reading *decorato* as an adjective. There may be some influence from Boethius's long account of his political fortunes and fate in Book I, which the Old English text had initially passed over, but that has nothing about his relationship to the king, and it is the senate that has condemned him according to that account. This exchange between Wisdom and 'Boetius' is a clear instance of Alfred fictionalizing, creating a narrative which nicely fits the dramatic situation that he has imagined but for which there is no warrant in his source. It alludes to the duty of the good counsellor to speak

---

8 Ibid., 62.2–14; 'Ac gesege me nu, ic ascige ðe, þu Boetius, hwi þu swa manigfeald yfel hæfde and swa micele uneðnesse on þam rice, þa hwile þe ðu hit hæfdest, oððe forhwy þu hit eft þinum unwillum forlete? Hu ne wasð þu þæt hit næs for nanum oðrum ðingum buton forðæmðe þu noldest on eallum ðingum bion geþwære þæs unrihtwisan cyninges willan Þiodrices? forðæmðe ðu hine ongeate on eallum þingum unwyrðne þæs anwealdes, swiðe sceamleasne and ungeþwærne, buton ælcum godum þeawe. Forþam we ne magon nauht eaðe secgan þæt þa yfelan sien gode, þeah hi anweald habban. Ne wurde þu ðeah na adrifen from Ðeodrice, ne he ðe na ne forsawe, gif þe licode his dysig and his unrihtwisnes swa wel swa his dysegum deorlingum dyde.'

his mind rather than flatter, and again strongly characterizes the speaker as Boethius the victim of a tyrant king.

What seems to me particularly striking in these references to Theoderic is the fact that Alfred goes out of his way to characterize the I-figure who operates within the text and claims authorship of it as someone with a particular history and position, and one which is so sharply different from Alfred's own. 'Boetius' here is the honest courtier, serving under a tyrant king and himself trying to resist tyranny, and being punished for his honesty; Alfred is of course a king himself, exercising power and presumably dismissing courtiers himself from time to time and imprisoning his advisers. It is, moreover, a world where kings generally are tyrants and illustrate the vanity of power and fame. We have Nero and Tarquin as tyrant kings, and evil and injustice are said to dominate from their thrones (chapter 4). The passage in Book IV metre 2, on proud kings who are really subject themselves to their passions, is rewritten in the Old English version in a way that stresses their arrogant and unjust character and their inner worthlessness.[9] And the story of Ulysses is radically rewritten to make him an archetype of the bad king, neglecting his men for the love of Circe.[10]

The degree to which the Old English writer has got inside the character of the honest courtier rather than the king, and appropriated his voice, is evident a little later from chapter 29:

> 'Do you think (says Wisdom) that the company of the king and the wealth and power that he gives his favourites can make anyone prosperous or powerful?' I answered, 'Why not? What is sweeter and better in this present life than serving the king and being close to him, and then the wealth and power?'[11]

Wisdom in reply demonstrates the emptiness and ephemerality of such pleasures, since history tells us that many a king has lost power and wealth. If one looks back to the Latin to see where all this is coming from, one sees that in Book III prose 5 Boethius has introduced the topic of the false good of kingship and intimacy with kings, and deals first at length with kingship and its insecurities, and then turns to the parallel insecurity of a king's counsellors. Alfred certainly uses some of that material on kingship but he has made the position of the courtier the primary issue. And when he comes to the arguments Boethius had offered on the insecurity of the courtier or counsellor, he expands on them substantially, enlarging on the murder of totally innocent advisers by Mark

---

[9] Ibid., 111.12ff.

[10] See S. Irvine, 'Ulysses and Circe in King Alfred's *Boethius*: a classical myth transformed', in *Studies in English Language and Literature: 'Doubt wisely': papers in honour of E.G. Stanley*, eds M. J. Toswell and E. M. Tyler (London and New York, 1996), 387–401.

[11] *Boethius*, ed. Sedgefield, 65.2–7; 'Hweðer þu nu wene þæt þæs cyninges geferræden and se wela and se anweald þe he gifð his deorlingum mæge ænigne mon gedon weligne oððe wealdendne? Ða andsworede ic and cwæt: Forhwi ne magon hi? Hwæt is on ðis andweardan life wynsumre and betere þonne þæs cyninges folgað and his neawest, and siððan wela and anweald?'

Antony and Nero and emphasizing the horrors and perils of serving a cruel king. The parallel with the story of Boethius himself as told in the Old English text is hard to miss, and once again we find Alfred working harder than Boethius himself had done to objectify the perspective as that of the unjustly condemned courtier. It is reasonable perhaps that Alfred should think sympathetically of a king's followers, but striking even so that he should cite serving a king as a false good.

All this makes all the more prominent the one important moment in the Old English work when the I-figure does seem to speak not as courtier but as king: the passage in chapter 17 on the means of government and the three estates. In the Latin Boethius speaks briefly about power and fame in his own character as a counsellor (I translate very literally): 'You yourself know that the desire for mortal things did not dominate me at all. But I wanted the material for governing things, so that my qualities should not decay in silence.'[12] He is apparently justifying his political ambitions on the grounds that it was not the pursuit of a false good but the wish to manifest his own virtues – a curiously solipsistic justification of political activity. The Old English version greatly expands this reply, and the I-figure seems to speak as king: 'I desired tools and material for the work that was entrusted to me ... the tools and material for a king to rule with are as follows ... and so I sought the material for ruling with, so that my skills and governance should not be forgotten'.[13] In context the passage is doubly inappropriate. Why is Boethius the courtier speaking as a king and defending the power and position of kings? Only in the previous chapter the I-figure has been firmly identified as 'Boetius', the victim of a tyrant king, the descendant and heir of Roman senators who had cast out earlier tyrant kings, living in a world where kings seem always to be tyrants or figures of empty pride. And, second, what is Boethius the wretched prisoner doing lecturing Wisdom with such apparent authority? It is I think the only place in the whole work where the I-figure does so; his role is normally to act as the representative of delusion or misfortune.

It is possible to get round the apparent identification of the speaker as a king, if we treat the central ten lines of his reply, on the specific tools of kingship and using third-person reference, as a kind of parenthesis, giving the readers information in a manner extraneous to the dialogue rather as Wisdom does elsewhere in the work, explaining matters of ancient history or astronomy. Then we could just about read the rest as Boethius the consul or *heretoga* talking

---

12 *De Consolatione*, II, pr. 7.1; 'Tum ego: scis, inquam, ipsa minimum nobis ambitionem mortalium rerum fuisse dominatam; sed materiam gerendis rebus optauimus, quo ne uirtus tacita consenesceret.'

13 *Boethius*, ed. Sedgefield, 40.9–27; 'tola ic wilnode þeah and andweorces to þam weorce þe me beboden was to wyrcanne; ... Þæt bið þonne cyninges andweorc and his tol mid to ricsianne ... Forþy ic wilnode andweorces þone anweald mid to reccenne, þæt mine cræftas & anweald ne wurden forgitene & forholene.'

about his own kind of involvement in politics and arguing that he had merely sought the means of performing the duties entrusted to him and manifesting the wisdom that was within him. Since the previous chapter has already mentioned that kings in Rome were replaced by *heretogan*, whom the people also tried to expel, it would be possible to think of *heretogan* as supreme rulers in some periods. The adverb *Forþy* at line 25 would then refer not back to the account of a king's needs but forwards only: 'the reason why I sought the material by which to exercise power was so that my skills and governance should not be forgotten and ignored'. Even so, one would have to say that the Boethius figure has no business discussing the tools of kingship at all, certainly not in such positive terms, since the text has consistently represented kings as tyrants and figures of vanity and Boethius is meant to be defending his own kind of power, as consul or *heretoga*. There seems to be for once another voice here, engaged in a kind of dialogue with the author of the Latin text, with Wisdom and with Boethius the rejected courtier, as if the king is suddenly allowed to speak for his side.

The argument seems somewhat confused, conveying an uncertainty as to what exactly the speaker is defending himself against. It looks at first as if he is justifying political or royal power on the grounds that it was not sought but entrusted to him, but what he actually says is 'I have not eagerly sought earthly power, I have just sought tools and material for the work entrusted to me', defining these as clerics, fighting men and workmen to occupy his land, and the physical necessities required to support and equip them, as if by justifying his desire for subordinates and for material things he is defending himself against the earlier criticism of those who seek false goods such as wealth and status. But while it is plausible enough to argue that governance depends on the support of the population, and they in turn on the means to live, it is difficult to see how Alfred or Boethius could claim responsibility for populating the land or providing food and clothing for the population. One might read the passage as an implicit riposte to Wisdom's picture of tyrant kings in the previous chapter. Those are described as devastating and destroying their own and neighbouring kingdoms, like fire or flood or volcano; the speaker here offers a view of kingship that emphasizes the opposite, suggesting perhaps that a true king or a good king is one who sees his subjects as aids to good government and is concerned with preserving and supporting them rather than destroying them.

But what kind of authority does the passage have? As I said, it is the only instance where the I-figure seems to have any authority, or to be offering a view other than one characterized as deluded. If this is an idealization of kingship, however, it is apparently undermined by the speaker's defence of kingship or political power as an opportunity to win fame for himself and publicize his own wisdom, and that is in turn challenged by a critique of such false aspirations, since Wisdom immediately replies to the I-figure's defence by arguing, as Philosophy does in the Latin text, that such desire for reputation is the last infirmity of noble minds. Quite how thoroughgoing is this rejection of the speaker's position is a matter of continuing dispute and perhaps in the end personal judgement. Lapidge and Keynes point to the critique of fame as grounds for not treating the means of government passage as the king's personal credo; Smyth has more recently argued that in the Old English text at least the attack is only on the pursuit of immoderate or unjustified fame and that the passage on the means of government and the desire for fame is one in which 'the genuine Alfred summarizes his personal attitude towards kingship'.[14] One might indeed note that Wisdom himself had earlier offered an encomium on fame (c. 13). But clearly this defence of kingship, if it is one, is heavily qualified by the surrounding text in at least three ways: the sustained emphasis throughout the work on kings as tyrants; the I-figure's total lack of authority in all passages except this one; and the association of kingship with aspirations for the false good of fame. And if it is to be understood as an Alfredian or royal voice, it is in conflict with the strenuous efforts elsewhere in the text to identify the I-figure as Boethius the courtier. One might also add that what the speaker offers is a thoroughly secular notion of fame as immortality and that the recurrent references in the Old English text elsewhere to an after-life as a balance to the injustice of this world might have suggested a stronger defence of a king's engagement in the active life than this, even within the terms implied by Wisdom. (That is, Alfred has appropriated the flawed defence of a political life made by Boethius when he could have offered a much more cogent one, in terms of either the importance of maintaining justice or the pursuit of personal salvation.) And although the speaker seems to be adopting the voice of a king or ruler at this point, the views reflected in the passage arguably make better sense as a courtier's advice to a king than as a king's defence of his position.

To sum up on the Old English *Boethius*, then, it is a commonplace that in selecting the *De Consolatione* to translate and adapt King Alfred was choosing a work that had not yet begun to be the seminal text of the Middle Ages that it later became and one that expressed assumptions and philosophical positions that could scarcely be more distant from those that characterized late ninth-century Christian England and Europe. Though he adapted it extensively to his own world picture, its philosophy remains otherworldly and on occasion that philosophy is challenged or undermined by both speakers within the dialogue of the Old English text. The occasional identification of the I-figure, and therefore the author, as 'Boetius', and a Boethius with very specific experiences from which the work arises, is a reminder – one firmly embedded in the text – of its distance from Alfred's own world. Second, the Old English version creates as its central character and speaker a person called 'Boetius' who is the victim of a tyrant king, a Roman politician or courtier operating in a world of tyrant kings, and invites us to see things from his perspective. If there is an Alfredian voice favouring kingship, it is buried deep in contexts which work hard against it.

---

[14] Keynes and Lapidge, *Alfred*, 298; Smyth, *Alfred*, 584.

The resonance of the picture of tyranny in the Old English text is hard to determine. Knowing that Alfred is author, or thinking that we do, we might say that the picture of tyranny offered in the work serves to differentiate Boethius's world from his own – his own readers, he may be saying, live under a much more benevolent monarchy – but that necessarily also differentiates and historicizes the philosophical position, since it so evidently emerges from the experience of tyranny. Alternatively the picture of tyranny may be seen as a universal condition of humanity, but that is not what one would expect from Alfred. Or we might say, as Alfred Smyth suggests, that the tyranny has a contemporary parallel in the violence and display of Norse kings;[15] but it is hard to feel there were real parallels to be drawn between them and a Nero or Tarquin, and the effect would again be to delimit and objectify the philosophical position. One possible answer to the question why the Old English *Boethius* emphasizes tyranny so much is that Theoderic is, as the prologue makes clear, a usurping king supplanting the true line of the Roman emperors; in Alfredian terms, then, the picture of tyranny relates not to legitimate West Saxon kings but perhaps to Anglo-Saxon and Norse usurpers. But nothing more is said about Theoderic being an illegitimate king after the prologue, and the tyranny is exemplified not only by Theoderic but also by Nero and Mark Antony and other Roman kings and emperors, by Ulysses and by kings in general.

The particular interest in the concern with the courtier's voice in the *Boethius* is that something similar seems to be happening in the *Soliloquies*. There too we find a sustained interest in the courtier's or adviser's perspective, and an imaginative concern with the plight of the counsellor ousted from his king's favour and imprisoned. In the Latin text, Augustine presents the work as a dialogue between himself and something that he calls Reason. The Old English text begins (at least as we have it in its acephalous state) with a prologue in the Old English author's voice and then presents the rest as the work and words of Augustine. Initially it is a dialogue between Reason and *Mod* but the latter is always referred to as *ic*. As with the Old English *Boethius*, one can see the Old English author actively engaged in preserving and accentuating the identification of the speaker as the original author Augustine. There is the reference to 'Alippius your servant'.[16] There is the reference to the speaker's present age of thirty-three, and his rejection of material things at the age of nineteen, and his present unmarried status and his determination never to marry.[17] These references are all from the source, but Alfred also introduces the single most striking passage in the whole work, the reference to the emperors Theodosius and Honorius. Reason says to the Augustine figure, using a secular analogy for trusting in divine revelation: 'You have a lord whom you trust in all matters better than yourself, and so has many a servant who has a less mighty lord than

---

[15] Smyth, *Alfred*, 592.

[16] *Soliloquies*, ed. Carnicelli, 58, line 7.

[17] Ibid., 72–3.

yourself ... if he told you of something that you had not heard or seen before, wouldn't you trust him? ... And do you think that Honorius the son of Theodosius is wiser or more truthful than Christ the son of God?' And Augustine replies: 'Honorius is very good and his father was better, a virtuous and wise man of the true line of lords ... I honour them as one should an earthly lord, but I honour Christ as the lord of lords.'[18]

There is no possible prompt for this in Augustine's *Soliloquies*, which has in any case been left behind by this stage. As the editors say,[19] Alfred has presumably written this in the mistaken belief that Augustine wrote his *Soliloquies* in the reign of Honorius, 395–423, though in fact the work is generally thought to have been written during the reign of his father Theodosius I, in 386–7. There have been various suggestions as to why he did this,[20] but it still seems to me that the likeliest prompt is Orosius. His *Historia* gives a similar encomium on Theodosius at VII.34, and one on Honorius at VII.42, and indicates that Honorius was reigning at the time of writing.[21] Since Orosius ends his work by addressing Augustine, who inspired the work, it is not surprising that Alfred thought that Augustine was also writing during the reign of Honorius, and that Honorius was the good son of an even better father. And since it was in the reign of Honorius that Alaric and the Goths sacked Rome, it would have provided for Alfred a nice link to the event with which the Old English *Boethius* begins and the Old English *Orosius* ends, and which, according to the *Anglo-Saxon Chronicle*, ended Roman rule in Britain.

Sources and historical circumstances aside, there are two major issues surrounding this curious detail. It is, first of all, a literary device to add verisimilitude to the argument, as Carnicelli and others have said;[22] more precisely, to remind us firmly that the speaker and writer of this text is Augustine of Hippo in the fifth century, not Alfred or anyone else in the ninth. But it lends verisimili-

---

18 Ibid., 87.18–89.13; 'Ða cwæð heo: hwæt, ic wat þæt ðu hefst ðone hlaford nu todæg ðe þu treowast æt elcum þingum bet þonne þe siluum, and swa hefð eac manig esne ðara þe unricran hlaford hefð þonne ðu hefst ... Hu þincð þe nu gyf se þin hlaford ðe hwilc spel segð þara ðe þu nefre ær ne geherdest, oððe he þe segð þæt he hwethwugu gesawe þæs þe ðu nefre ne gesawe? Ðincð þe hweðer þe awuht æt his segene tweoge, forðam þu hyt self ne gesawe? ... Ac ic wolde þæt þu me sedest hweðer þe ðince Honorius, Þeodosius sunu, wisra oððe unleasera þonne Crist, godes sunu? Ða cweð ic: nese, la nese, ne nawer neah. ... Honorius is swiðe god, þeah his feder betere were; he wes swiðe æfest and swiðe rædfast and swiðe rihte mines hlafordes kynnes ... . Hi ic wille wyrðian swa swa man worldhlaford sceal ... and þe oðre ðe þu er embe sprece, swa swa heora hlafordes, and swa man þone kyng sceal, þe byð kyng ealra kcynga.'

19 Ibid., 103.

20 See, e.g., M. McC. Gatch, 'King Alfred's version of Augustine's *Soliloquia*: some suggestions on its rationale and unity', in *Studies in Earlier Old English Prose*, ed. P. E. Szarmach (Albany, 1986), 17–45, at 34–5; J. Bately, 'Evidence for knowledge of Latin literature in Old English', in *Sources of Anglo-Saxon Culture*, ed. P. E. Szarmach, Studies in Medieval Culture, 20 (Kalamazoo, 1986), 35–51, at 45 and nn. 51–2.

21 Orosius, *Historiae aduersum paganos*, ed. K. Zangemeister, CSEL 5 (Vienna, 1882).

22 *Soliloquies*, ed. Carnicelli, 103.

tude to a complete fiction; this is not in fact Augustine speaking in any sense, and not an argument one can imagine him using. Alfred presumably knows that what he is saying here, through Reason and Augustine, was not said by Augustine but wants us to think so, and that perhaps is odd in a work concerned essentially with the nature of truth. It is not in fact an argument that he needs to distance himself from, as far as one can see, nor one that particularly needs concrete illustration by naming the lords in question.

Second, the passage presents Augustine as a courtier or intimate of the emperor; Honorius is a personal lord who often tells Augustine things that he doesn't otherwise know, and whom Augustine trusts because he is a good lord, and Augustine's friends are the thegns of that lord. The notion that in reality Honorius knew anything Augustine did not is unlikely, and I have not found any evidence that the bishop had ever met Honorius or given any indication of a personal relationship with him. What evidence there is for his dealings with the emperor would suggest exasperation with his vacillation rather than trust. Alfred has apparently imagined Augustine as someone who would have had a close personal and dependent relationship with his king. And this leads us to the next point.

In apparent contrast to this emphasis on Augustine as the author of the dialogue and speaker in it, is the series of well-known passages on kingship and lordship in the Old English *Soliloquies*, passages often anthologized as evidence of Alfredian views, and discussed by Waterhouse and Smyth amongst others.[23] All are introduced by the Old English writer rather than derived from his sources, and used as analogies or metaphors for the theological argument, and they are evidently at odds with Augustine's real identity as bishop or teacher of rhetoric, an individual not engaged in issues of kingship and lordship. The one analogy that might be said to deal with lordship and does derive from the source rather makes the point: Augustine's friend Alippius becomes 'Alippius þin cniht', emphasizing the translator's fascination with service. Almost all these passages involve an analogy with the courtier or the follower of a king or lord. The series starts with the reference in the prologue to a man who has built a house on land granted by his lord; we then have the analogy of receiving your lord's writ; the importance of the lord's friendship; the many roads to the king's court and the many types of subject who live under one king; believing what your lord tells you as Augustine believes his lord Honorius; the guilty man seeing the king who has condemned him, and his favourites; the man in a king's prison able to see his friends outside but unable to be helped by them; the king's favourite who is exiled and returns. All these invite the reader to see things from the perspective of the follower or courtier rather than the lord or king; and more importantly, in all but the first (the one in the prologue) Reason is inviting the Augustine-figure

---

[23] *EHD*, 917–19; Keynes and Lapidge, *Alfred*, 138–52; R. Waterhouse, 'Tone in Alfred's version of Augustine's *Soliloquies*', in Szarmach, *Studies*, 47–85; Smyth, *Alfred*, 588–94.

to see things from that perspective, and the Honorius passage requires us to see that perspective as appropriate to Augustine's own social position.

Two brief allusions seem to challenge this pattern by suggesting the perspective of a king rather than a courtier, since they refer to the need to have enough wealth to support followers. The difficulty is that they are closely tied to an identification of the speaker as Augustine. In Book I the speaker says to Reason:

> I rejected wealth long ago; I am 33 now, and I was 19 when I decided
> not to love riches, and to seek to have no more than I needed in order
> to live, and to support and keep the people that I ought to support.[24]

It is this last part, from 'and to support', that the Old English text adds. The speaker then denies any desire for a wife, asserting that it is better for priests not to marry, and reiterates the point that he desires no material things beyond what he needs to support his body's health and strength, plus what he needs to support others whom he has to look after. One is of course reminded strongly of the means of government passage in the Old English *Boethius*, with its similar emphasis on needing the materials to support a king's followers. But if, as commentators argue, the double emphasis in the *Soliloquies* on needing enough to support others is an Alfredian and royal perspective, it remains the case that the text attaches that sentiment and the responsibility to a speaker whom the text at the same point identifies as a celibate priest of thirty-three called Augustine. And since the text has already converted Augustine's friend Alippius into his *cniht* or servant, it would perhaps be natural for an innocent reader to interpret these details as a reference to Augustine's need to support his household rather than a king's need to support his thegns.

To sum up on the *Soliloquies*, the Old English text is engaged in creating a speaker who is strongly realized as Augustine: a priest who has forsworn marriage and material things, who refers to his own other works and lives under the emperor Honorius. He is nevertheless not entirely the Augustine of tradition, but is an intimate of the emperor and addressed as if he is a courtier and repeatedly offered analogies between his own relationship with God and the relationship of courtiers and retainers, such as himself, with a king or lord. And of course this realization of the personality behind the philosophical argument is doubly fictional since so little of the argument is derived from Augustine's work anyway.

What we notice most in both works is a curious act of historical imagination. Alfred takes a literary dialogue from the late antique world of the Roman empire and appropriates it to his own ninth-century concerns, language and world-picture; but at the same time he develops the personae of the authors

---

[24] *Soliloquies*, ed. Carnicelli, 72.12–17; 'gefirn ic hyt hohgode þæt ic hine sceolde forseon. Ic hæbbe nu XXXIII wintra, and ic hæfde ane les þene XX þa ic erest hyt gehogede þæt ic hine ealles to swiðe ne lufige ... ne æac maran getilige to haldænne, þonne ic gemetlice bi beon mage, and þa men on gehabban and gehealdan þe ic forðian scel.'

within those works in ways which emphasize at times to the reader their otherness, their subjecthood, their sheer historical rootedness in their own times and experience. The sense of a dialogue with voices from the past, the awareness that these are texts and views that emerge from a different, Roman world, is an essential feature of both works. Yet those authorial identities owe as much to Alfred's own imagination and experience as to any historical reality or tradition, and the imagined authors are often given responsibility for views and arguments that owe little or nothing to Boethius or Augustine. At the same time, the perspective or mind-set that characterizes these works is not entirely what one would expect from Alfred. As everyone has said, especially in discussions of authorship, both works are imbued with analogies drawn from the world of a king and express sensitivities associated with kingship. The unexpected thing is that, with one problematic exception (the passage on the means of government in the *Boethius*), these analogies express the perspective not of a king but a courtier, a mind that is familiar with how it feels to be favoured or not favoured by the whim of a king, or to be dependent on a superior, or to be the subject of a tyrant king flattered by his favourites, or with the many different routes to a court, or the importance of recognizing a king's writ. Both texts show a remarkable sympathy with the position of the thegn or adviser cast out of his king's favour. If we did not know already that a king was the author we might well suppose that it was one of his associates at court. Whether that is because Alfred had discussed these texts with his associates so often that he got used to the analogies and perspectives that they used, or because he had himself grown up under a series of rather daunting kings from his own family, or because the works were largely conceived and written by one of his courtiers, is hard to say.

ALFREDIAN GOVERNMENT
AND SOCIETY

Chapter 9

Alfredian government: the West Saxon inheritance

Nicholas Brooks

The emphasis in the title of this chapter lies on the word 'inheritance'. The underlying question is: how far were Alfred's governmental and administrative practices devised by the king himself with the aid of his court advisers, or were they standard procedures that he had inherited from previous West Saxon kings? Was Alfred an innovator in government or merely an able transmitter of an old inheritance? We have recently been reminded of the antiquarian myth-making that turned King Alfred into the founder, not only of the University of Oxford, but also of hundreds and tithings, of the royal navy, of county councils and of much else that was held sacred in the British political, constitutional and educational worlds between the thirteenth and the nineteenth centuries.[1] But more recent historians have also found signs of new beginnings in the rule of King Alfred. Thus the late Henry Loyn saw this reign as marking the watershed between the primitive early Anglo-Saxon polities and what he understood as the 'territorial state' of later Anglo-Saxon England;[2] while Patrick Wormald has conceived the reign as a starting-point for 'the making of English law'.[3] But it must be confessed that, despite the interpretative models of such luminaries, it is still not easy to assess Alfred's impact upon royal government. We can see something of the king's political and military activities in the pages of the *Anglo-Saxon Chronicle* and of Asser's *Life of Alfred*; we can see the results of his administration in the surviving coins bearing his name and in the boroughs that resisted Danish assault in the later 880s and early 890s. But it is singularly difficult to say anything about the governmental processes involved.

There is, moreover, reason to believe that the administration of the core West Saxon shires (Fig. 13) of Hampshire, Wiltshire, Dorset and Somerset by ealdormen appointed by the king had been in existence throughout the ninth century, that is since the reign of Alfred's grandfather, Ecgberht (802–39). Very

---

[1] S. D. Keynes, 'The cult of King Alfred the Great', *ASE*, 28 (1999), 225–356, esp. 230 (hundreds and tithings), 235–7, 244–5, 260–69 (University of Oxford); B. A. E. Yorke, 'Alfredism', below, pp. 362–80, esp. 364, 371–6.

[2] H. R. Loyn, *The Governance of Anglo-Saxon England, 500–1087* (1984).

[3] P. Wormald, *The Making of English Law: King Alfred to the Twelfth Century, I: Legislation and its Limits* (1999).

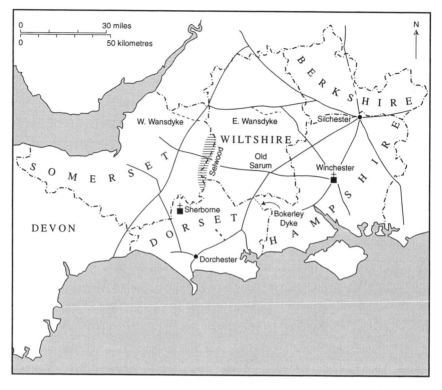

Fig. 13   The shires of the early West Saxon kingdom, showing Roman roads and linear earthworks (after Yorke)

possibly it goes back further to the 750s, when the *Chronicle* first mentions Hampshire (*Hamtunscir*), and when *praefecti* or *principes* first attest the charters of West Saxon kings.[4] It is even possible that the structure of shires run by ealdormen actually dates from the reign of King Ine (685–725); in that case the references in Ine's laws to *scirmen*, and to ealdormen and their *scirs*, could be accepted as referring to this same system.[5] Otherwise we must regard them either as a later updating (perhaps when the code had been appended to Alfred's lawbook) or as referring not to the shires familiar to us in later times but rather to an older system of smaller units of lordship known under various names in different parts of England (*regiones*, *provinciae*, lathes, leets, rapes, Danelaw

---

[4] H. M. Chadwick, *Studies on Anglo-Saxon Institutions* (1905), 282–90; A. T. Thacker, 'Some terms for noblemen in Anglo-Saxon England, c. 650–900', in *Anglo-Saxon Studies in Archaeology and History II*, eds D. Brown, J. Campbell and S. C. Hawkes, British Archaeological Reports, British Series 92 (1981), 201–36; B. Yorke, *Wessex in the Early Middle Ages* (1995), 84–93.

[5] Laws of Ine, cc. 8, 36.1, 39, ed. Liebermann, *Gesetze*, I, 92, 104–6.

hundreds and so on), but as 'shires' in northern England and south-eastern Scotland.[6]

Of the operation, regularity and procedures of these courts, of the appointment and dismissal of their officers, of the arrangements for the capture of criminals and of the enforcement of law upon recalcitrants – in short of the machinery of an incipient state – Alfred's laws tell us nothing. We are left to conclude that whatever new regulations Alfred and his *witan* may have ordered to be enforced,[7] they did not alter long-standing arrangements by which local folk-moots under king's reeves and 'shire'-moots under the king's ealdormen administered the law for their districts. Such royal agents (or their sons) might need to be bullied to attend King Alfred's school in order to resuscitate (or to create) the ability to read his laws in English;[8] they might even need to be dismissed for treachery; but the fundamental administrative machinery of the kingdom was, it would seem, an ancient one which Alfred (like his son) left intact. Seemingly he had no reason to make specific reference in the *Domboc* to what was long established and well understood.

Alongside the paucity of evidence for government in the laws and in the Burghal Hidage, we also find a scarcity of acceptable royal charters or diplomata from Alfred's reign. Only ten have any call upon our attention.[9] No good case can therefore be made for Alfred as an effective administrative reformer, let alone as a 'founder' of English (or even of West Saxon) government. His gifts of leadership may have lain in man management, on the field of battle and in intellectual discourse, rather than in bureaucratic reform. Indeed there is a temptation to suspect that the king's rule was indeed both simple and primitive. Certainly there is an attractive informality about a king who corroborated the key judgement of one of his ealdormen in a dispute over a substantial estate at Fonthill while washing his hands in his chamber at Wardour (Wiltshire).[10] Al-

---

[6] G. W. S. Barrow, 'Pre-feudal Scotland: shires and thegns', in *idem*, *The Kingdom of the Scots* (1973), 1–68.

[7] The preface to Alfred's own code specifically refers to the regulations of earlier kings which he rejected and ordered to be observed in other ways: 'on oðre wisan bebead to healdanne': Liebermann, *Gesetze*, I, 46.

[8] Asser, c. 106, pp. 92–5. In this paper I have cited this work as an authentic work of Asser. The attempt of Smyth, *Alfred*, to discount it as a forgery produced at Ramsey *c*. 1000 has been decisively rejected by S. D. Keynes, *JEccH*, 47 (1996), 529–51, M. Lapidge, *The Times Higher Education Supplement*, 8 March 1996, 20, D. Howlett, *EHR*, 112 (1997), 942–4, and D. Pelteret, *Speculum*, 73 (1998), 263–5.

[9] Only two charters of Alfred survive as possible originals: BCS 536 (S 344) and BCS 576 (S 350); another, which is only preserved in a late cartulary text, may be a copy of an authentic charter: BCS 567 (S348). Seven other diplomata of Alfred are (in varying degrees) spurious in their present form, but may have been drafted using documents of the reign: BCS 550 (S 345); BCS 561 (S 346); BCS 564 (S 347); BCS 549 (S 352); BCS 565 (S 354); BCS 581 (S 355); BCS 568 (S 356).

[10] Harmer, *Documents*, no. 18 (S 1445); there is a full discussion of this Old English account in S. D. Keynes, 'The Fonthill letter', in *Words, Texts and Manuscripts: Studies in Anglo-Saxon Culture Presented to Helmut Gneuss* (1992), 53–97.

fred was not, perhaps, a man who needed to take refuge in elaborate trappings of government procedure and the formalities of etiquette.

Some elements in the organization of the West Saxon court certainly do go back to the reigns of Alfred's father, Æthelwulf, and of his grandfather, Ecgberht (802–39). Restricting the royal succession in 839 to Æthelwulf, the nearest heir of Ecgberht, and to Æthelwulf's sons at the subsequent royal deaths in 858, 860, 865 and 871 marks the successful stabilization of a new dynasty. One element in this decisive change from the previously much more fluid succession arrangements was a process of committing the archbishops of Canterbury and all the 'Saxon' bishops (of London, Selsey, Winchester and Sherborne) to the support of Ecgberht's dynasty. The allegiance of these bishops was secured at a council held at Kingston in 838 and in subsequent confirmations at Wilton and *æt Astran* in 839; the process, it would seem, led to a new manner of treating the south-eastern territories of Kent, Essex, Surrey and Sussex as a single kingdom held as an appanage by a son of the king.[11]

The assemblies of the kings with their West Saxon nobles, lay and ecclesiastical, were not only occasions for the affirmation of loyalty to a chosen heir, but also for the exercise of royal government. Professor Keynes has recently identified a coherent single tradition in the diplomatic of the extant West Saxon royal charters in the period from *c.* 840 to 899.[12] Whereas in Kent, in Sussex, or in the Hwiccan territory of Mercia, diocesan writing offices seem to have been responsible for drafting the bulk of the extant ninth-century royal charters, Keynes has shown that grants in the name of King Æthelwulf and of his sons relating to land in Hampshire, Wiltshire, Berkshire, Somerset or Dorset share certain common features in their formulation. This common diplomatic tradition may plausibly be attributed to the work of ecclesiastics serving in the king's following or household. Certainly there is no trace in Wessex of any distinction between a Winchester and a Sherborne diplomatic, such as we can show throughout the ninth century between the charters granting estates in the dioceses of Canterbury and Rochester, even when Kent was under West Saxon rule.

It is instructive that these West Saxon charters show the ninth-century kings meeting their leading subjects – bishops, ealdormen (*duces*), and the king's thegns (*ministri*) – in great councils or witans held on the great Christian festivals, especially on St Stephen's day (26 December) following the celebration of Christmas and on Easter Sunday. These formal councils appear to have gathered at a relatively small number of royal vills or centres. Dorchester is

---

[11] For the council of Kingston in 838, see BCS 421 (S 1438) and the discussion in N. P. Brooks, *Early History of the Church of Canterbury* (1984), 136–7, 146–7, 197–200 and 323–5 and S. D. Keynes, 'The West Saxon charters of King Æthelwulf and his sons', *EHR*, 109 (1994), 1109–49, at 1112–14. For the political consequences in the south-east, see *idem*, 'The control of Kent in the ninth century', *Early Medieval Europe*, 2 (1993), 111–31 and C. Cubitt, *Anglo-Saxon Church Councils c. 650–850* (1995), 236–8.

[12] Keynes, 'West Saxon charters'.

much the most favoured venue in the extant documents; but [Sout]hampton, Winchester, Kingston, Amesbury, Somerton, Micheldever, Woodyates, and the unidentified royal vills of *Suðtun* (one of the many Suttons) and *Andredeseme* (in the Weald?) also appear. The records of these major meetings of the royal court in ninth-century Wessex take us to the political heart of the kingdom and to its major formal occasions. These charters record gatherings where (we may suppose) major issues of politics, warfare, peace-making and law-making were also resolved and more generally where royal power and patronage were exercised.

The majority of the extant West Saxon charters of the period from 839 to 871 are grants to important lay nobles, mostly of the rank of ealdormen, and usually granting them substantial estates within their own ealdormanries. A grant by King Æthelred of ten hides of land at Wittenham (Berkshire) to *princeps* Æthelwulf in the year 862 may serve as a good example of the rewards for service received by the high nobility of ninth-century Wessex.[13] We only know of such grants, of course, if the estates later happened to come into the hands of the Church; in this case Wittenham and its charter passed into the possession of the reformed monastery of Abingdon. The beneficiary of the charter, Ealdorman Æthelwulf, had been the Mercian ealdorman of Berkshire; he had attended the witans of the Mercian kings, Wiglaf and Berhtwulf, at least from 836 until *c.* 845; but when the shire had been handed over to West Saxon control in the 850s, Æthelwulf had transferred his allegiance to the West Saxon dynasty and had thenceforth attended West Saxon councils. He was to die fighting alongside King Æthelred and his brother, the ætheling Alfred, against the *mycel here* at Reading in 871. That his family felt that his roots remained Mercian may be suggested by the fact that after the battle his body was spirited away for burial at *Northworthig* (Derby);[14] but there is no hint in the *Chronicle* that his loyalty to the West Saxon dynasty, rewarded by such grants, had ever wavered.

If we turn from the gatherings of the itinerant West Saxon court to the administration of the kingdom at the local level, then here too we find that Alfred inherited and continued an existing system, namely of shires with smaller districts (*regiones*) within them. The ealdorman presided over the shire court and led the shire army; the king's reeve presided over the *regio* and over the king's *tun* at its heart. Crucial to the whole system was the assessment of the free *ceorls*, or 'warland' peasants, and of their family land-holdings ('hides') grouped for administrative purposes in round figures of tens and hundreds.[15] This assess-

---

13 BCS 505 (S 335) = S. E. Kelly, *The Charters of Abingdon*, Anglo-Saxon Charters, VII (2000), no. 15. The charter is attributed to King Æthelred (865–71) but dated 862 and witnessed by Bishop Swithun of Winchester who died in 862 or 863. Keynes ('West Saxon charters', 1129–31) has shown that its formulation is acceptable and suggested that dynastic arrangements may have been more complex at that time than the *Anglo-Saxon Chronicle* might suggest, that is, that Æthelred may have exercised some royal power at the same time as his elder brother, Æthelberht.

14 Æthelweard IV 2, p. 37. For his career, see Keynes, 'West Saxon charters', 1127.

15 R. Faith, *The English Peasantry and the Growth of Lordship* (1997), 89–125.

ment system was the key to the early medieval king's ability to exploit the land he ruled. It was fundamental for the levying of food-rents (Ine's law-code specifies the *feorm* that was due to the king from ten hides),[16] for the exaction of service in the army (one man from five hides?) and for many labour-services (which are likely to have always required one warland peasant from every hide): for bridge- and borough-building, for the construction of royal palaces, churches, causeways and roads, for drainage schemes in marshlands and for a host of other 'public' or communal duties.[17]

The artificiality of the assessment is apparent in the two earliest English administrative documents, namely the 'Tribal' and Burghal Hidages. The so-called 'Tribal Hidage', perhaps of the seventh century, assigns 300 hides (or multiples of 300) to small peoples and larger figures of 7, 15, 30 or 100 thousand hides to kingdoms. The Burghal Hidage assigns hidage figures to each borough, most of which are round numbers of several hundred hides. Both documents seem to witness a world in which the assessment of peoples and territories was fixed by rulers rather than deriving from the actual size of the free population or the extent of the ceorls' arable holdings. The fact that Bede's *Ecclesiastical History* gives different figures for some of the Tribal Hidage peoples reinforces the suggestion that the assessments were subject to political manipulation and had been imposed from the top down. Thus where the Tribal Hidage had assigned 600 hides to the *Wihtware*, Bede tells us that the Isle of Wight was assessed at 1200 hides at the time of its conquest by Cædwalla of Wessex.[18]

The Burghal Hidage seems to bring us closer to territorial reality in allocating specific numbers of hides to the maintenance and defence of some thirty West Saxon boroughs.[19] It is tempting to interpret the hidage figures for individual boroughs as representing coherent burghal districts responsible for the long-term maintenance and defence of the boroughs. If we were to assume that the districts were indeed both contiguous and contemporary, with every hide of land in the West Saxon kingdom sending one man to a borough, then it would be clear that the hidage assessment in the Burghal Hidage was very much

---

[16] Ine, cc. 70.1, ed. Liebermann, *Gesetze*, I, 118–20.

[17] I am much indebted to the work in progress of Andrew G. Bell, which will transform our understanding of the survival of public services by warland peasants in the thirteenth and fourteenth centuries.

[18] Bede, *HE* IV 14. For the Tribal Hidage, see D. Dumville, 'The Tribal Hidage: an introduction to its texts and their history', in *The Origins of Anglo-Saxon Kingdoms*, ed. S. R. Bassett (1989), 225–30 and A. R. Rumble, 'An edition of the Burghal Hidage together with recension C of the Tribal Hidage' in Hill and Rumble, *Defence of Wessex*, 18–23.

[19] Now at last properly edited by A. R. Rumble in *The Defence of Wessex: the Burghal Hidage and Anglo-Saxon Fortifications*, eds D. Hill and A. R. Rumble (1996), 14–36. For an argument that the hidage figures cannot be used to calculate the size of the Anglo-Saxon fortifications, see N. P. Brooks, 'The administrative background to the Burghal Hidage', ibid., 128–50, at 129–32 (reprinted in *idem, Communities and warfare, 700–1400* [2000], 114–37, especially 116–20).

heavier than the assessment of the same shires almost two centuries later at the time of the Domesday survey (1086). It is certainly clear that the Burghal Hidage does not list the boroughs in shire order and that there is no simple relationship between the burghal districts and the shires of Domesday Book. Since the shire system in the West Saxon heartland was much older than the reigns of Edward the Elder and of his father Alfred, the absence of any explicit reference in the Hidage to the shire system or to the involvement of ealdormen in supervising the work is curious. At least since the reign of Alfred's father, King Æthelwulf, estates in the shires of the West Saxon heartland had been obliged to contribute to boroughwork (*arcis munitio*); outwith Wessex we find the Mercian ealdorman, Æthelred, organizing the construction of the borough at Worcester and being involved in the laying out of the new borough at London (*Lundenburh*).[20] The fact that in the eleventh century throughout England earls still enjoyed one-third of the profits of justice in burghal courts – the so-called 'earl's third penny' – may most easily be explained as a recompense for ealdormen's involvement in setting up the boroughs and their defences at the start of the English urban revival.[21] We should therefore expect a system of burghal defence to have been supervised and implemented in their shires by the ealdormen.

Many historians have sought to elucidate the relationship of the Burghal Hidage assessment with that of the Domesday survey.[22] Since the Hidage assigns many more hides to the forts than Domesday Book allocates to the same shires, it has naturally been supposed that the tenth and early eleventh centuries must have seen some reductions in assessment, through the operation of 'beneficial hidation', that is, through the granting of reductions to favoured districts or lords, whether lay or ecclesiastical. Exactly such a reduction can be seen on numerous manors in Domesday Book between 1066 and 1086. Such changes in the assessment system might fit with the apparent 'top-down' quality of the system and with the existence of widely variant assessments in our earliest records. But much the most important contribution to this discussion has been that of Professor Peter Sawyer, who pointed out that in Sussex, Hampshire,

---

[20] For the appearance of the clause reserving the obligation of boroughwork in West Saxon charters from the 840s, see N. P. Brooks, 'The development of military obligations in 8th- and 9th-century England', *England before the Conquest: Studies presented to D. Whitelock*, eds P. Clemoes and K. Hughes (1971), 69–84, at 80–81, reprinted in *idem, Communities and Warfare*, 32–47, at 43–5. For Ealdorman Æthelred's role in the borough at Worcester, see Harmer, *Documents*, no. 13 (S 223); for his involvement at London, see D. Keene, 'Alfred and London', below, pp. 235–49. Æthelred's involvement, however, may have been a relic of the role of earlier Mercian kings rather than an anticipation of the role of shire ealdormen.

[21] F. M. Stenton, *Anglo-Saxon England* (3rd edn, 1971), 534–5.

[22] F. W. Maitland, *Domesday Book and Beyond* (1897), 187–8, 229–30, 502–6, 524; H. M. Chadwick, *Studies on Anglo-Saxon Institutions* (1905), 204–19; J. Brownbill, 'The Burghal Hidage', *Notes and Queries* 11th series, 4 (1911), 2–3; J. Tait, *The Medieval English Borough* (1936), 15–25; D. A. Hinton, 'The fortifications and their shires', *Defence of Wessex*, eds Hill and Rumble, 151–9.

Dorset, Wiltshire, Berkshire and Surrey there does appear to be a close relation between the Domesday assessment of the shire and the assessment in the Burghal Hidage of those boroughs that were to have a continuing existence as urban centres after the Viking threat had receded.[23] Thus the five Burghal Hidage boroughs in Sussex (*Eorpeburnan*?, Hastings, Lewes, Burpham and Chichester) have a combined assessment of 4344 hides, but without the failed boroughs of *Eorpeburnan* and Burpham the assessment totals 3300 hides, which is notably close to the Domesday total for the shire of 3225. In Hampshire, Twynham and Portchester may have dropped out, leaving the continuing boroughs of Winchester (2400) and Southampton (150) with a total very close to the Domesday shire's 2588 hides. In Dorset, Bredy failed to emerge as a town, leaving Shaftesbury and Wareham's total (2300 hides) very close to Domesday's 2321. In Wiltshire, Chisbury failed as a lasting borough, but the total for Wilton, Malmesbury and Cricklade (4100 hides) is close to the Domesday shire's 4050. In Berkshire, Sashes never became a town, leaving Wallingford's 2400 hides close to the Domesday total of 2473, while in Surrey, Eashing dropped out, leaving Southwark's 1800 hides to be found from the 1830 hides of the Domesday shire.

In his attempt to explain these correspondences Sawyer suggested that when the Viking threat eased, there may no longer have been any need to maintain and garrison emergency forts like Burpham, Sashes or Eashing; in consequence the hidage assessment of the shires could be safely reduced. But it seems very unlikely that the hidage assessments of whole shires would be determined in relation to boroughwork alone. Hidage, as we have seen, served as a means to assess not only work on boroughs, but also service in the army, food-rents and a wide range of public and seigneurial services; it is very unlikely that kings and lords would have been willing to reduce the pool of communal labour available to them just because there was less need for boroughwork. If that is so, then we should rather recognize the Burghal Hidage as a remarkable exercise in getting a quart out of a pint pot. That is to say, Alfred and his son would seem to have succeeded in maintaining the established boroughs where West Saxon *ceorls* had been accustomed to labour for at least a couple of generations; and they also managed not only to garrison these centres on a permanent basis but also to construct a series of additional forts to meet the Viking threat.

It is perhaps easiest to understand the huge new burdens shouldered by the warland peasants at this time by considering one shire as an example. It is likely that for at least thirty years before Alfred's reign the 2500 or so hides of Hampshire had had to produce annually that number of warland peasants to maintain the Roman defences of Winchester (2400) and the newer (presumably Anglo-Saxon) earthworks of *Hamtun* (150) in good repair. An attempt has been

---

[23] P. H. Sawyer, *From Roman Britain to Norman England* (1978), 227–8. I follow here the interpretation of Sawyer's figures which I set out at length in Brooks, 'Administrative background', Hill and Rumble (eds), *Defence of Wessex*, 128–50, at 129–38.

made to locate the Burghal Hidage borough of *Hamtun* at the tiny late-Roman promontory fort of Clausentum at Bitterne, though the hypothesis has neither archaeological nor place-name evidence to commend it. There is every reason to suppose that *Hamtun*, which had already given its name to the shire a century earlier, was indeed the settlement beside the Test underlying the medieval town of Southampton. Topographically *Hamtun* is quite distinct both from the adjacent short-lived eighth-century open trading settlement of *Hamwic* on the bank of the Itchen and from Clausentum to the north.[24]

The Burghal Hidage may suggest, however, that in the emergency of Alfred's and Edward the Elder's reigns the same peasants who had hitherto performed boroughwork at Winchester and *Hamtun* had been required to become permanent garrisons, *burhware* or burgesses, of Winchester and Southampton. Some of them may have also had for some years their labour diverted to the construction of the defences of a fort at Twynham, between the rivers Stour and Avon, and to the repair of the walls of the late-Roman 'Saxon Shore' fort of Portchester, which King Edward acquired from the bishop of Winchester in 904.[25] The fact that Portchester seems never to have become an urban settlement in late Anglo-Saxon England, and that Twynham never developed a mint and was merely mentioned as a borough with 31 houses in Domesday Book in the course of a routine manorial entry, suggests that the warland peasants of Hampshire had been reluctant to devote much of their time and energies to these two emergency boroughs; both could serve as places of refuge, but their prospects for permanent urban occupation were bleak. None the less it was surely the settlement of a permanent garrison derived from the Hidage figure of 2400 men at Winchester and of 150 at Southampton which began the transformation of those two settlements into real towns, that is, into lasting centres of specialized labour, rather than mere places of emergency refuge. In other words, some or all

---

[24] For recent syntheses of the archaeological evidence for Hamwic, see A. Morton, *Excavations in Hamwic, I*, Council for British Archaeology, Research Report, 84 (1992), esp. 20–77; *Excavations at Hamwic, II*, ed. P. Andrews, Council for British Archaeology, Research Report, 109 (1997). Archaeological evidence for the beginnings of settlement beneath medieval Southampton is inevitably more sparse than from Hamwih, where large-scale excavation has been possible. There is a convenient recent summary by M. Brisbane in *The Blackwell Encyclopaedia of Anglo-Saxon England*, eds M. Lapidge, J. Blair, S. Keynes and D. Scragg (1999), s.v. Southampton. *Hamtun* was the place where the West Saxon witan met on 26 December 825 (BCS 390 [S 272] and BCS 389 [S 273]) and in *c.* 901 (BCS 596 [S 360] and BCS 602 [S 370]), which implies a place capable on occasions of accommodating a substantial assembly of nobles and their attendants. The attempt to locate *Hamtun* at Clausentum is based on the mistaken belief that we must seek a site with defences of a length equivalent to the Burghal Hidage figure of 150 hides. See D. Hill, 'The Burghal Hidage – Southampton', *Proceedings of the Hampshire Field Club and Archaeological Society*, 24 (1967), 59–61.

[25] BCS 613 (S 372). King Edward granted Bishop Denewulf 40 hides at (Bishop's) Waltham in return for the same amount of land at Portchester. It cannot be assumed that the use of Portchester as an emergency borough had to await the king's acquisition of the estate. In Domesday by 1086 Twynham borough has 39 houses (*masurae*) but is only entered under the manor (DB i, 38v, 44r).

of the *ceorls* who had to garrison Southampton and Winchester may have been intended from the start to become burgesses (*burhware*). The only way to persuade warland peasants to take on the huge burden of garrison work is likely to have been to give them an economic interest in the nascent borough through the prospect of personal self-advancement. At Winchester, though not yet at Southampton, many seasons of excavation have enabled us to see how the labour of the *burhware* transformed the intra-mural space through the laying down of a grid of streets with many wagon-loads of flints and gravel, through setting out the boundaries of the burgage plots and constructing the first town houses within them.[26]

If thanks to the Burghal Hidage and Domesday Book we can hope to detect how Alfred may have exploited the hides of his warland peasants both to garrison the West Saxon boroughs and to construct new ones, it is much more difficult to identify, let alone to map, the fundamental rural territories within which these *ceorls* had attended the folk-moots and where they had rendered services at the king's *tun* or 'royal vill'. One approach to the early administrative districts of Wessex may be through study of the medieval hundredal meeting-places. The early researches of the Swedish scholar, O. S. Anderson, suggested that many of these were very ancient sites indeed and were likely to have served as the meeting-places of courts long before the emergence of the hundred system in the middle years of the tenth century. It may be worth revisiting and mapping those places most likely to have been ancient court-sites.[27]

Another means of identifying early administrative territories was that of J. E. A. Jolliffe and of his follower K. P. Witney, namely by counting hides (in Kent *sulungs*) in Domesday Book in order to detect early territories which still retained some uniformity in their pattern of assessment in 1086.[28] Their method is

---

[26] The seminal article of M. Biddle and D. Hill, 'Late Saxon planned towns', *Antiquaries Journal* 51 (1971), 70–85 drew attention to features in the layout of late Saxon Winchester which can be found in the topography of other Burghal Hidage sites and which suggest the birth of urbanism. For overall summaries of the Winchester evidence, see M. Biddle (ed.), *Winchester in the Early Middle Ages*, Winchester Studies, 1 (1976), and *idem*, 'Winchester: the development of an early capital', in *Vor- und Frühformen der europäischen Stadt im Mittelalter*, eds W. Schlesinger and H. Steuer (Göttingen, 1973), 229–61. For an important discussion of the relative fortunes of *Hamtun* and Winchester, see B. A. E. Yorke, 'The bishops of Winchester, the kings of Wessex and the development of Winchester in the ninth and early tenth centuries', *Proceedings of the Hampshire Field Club and Archaeological Society*, 40 (1984), 61–70, now reprinted in *Anglo-Saxon History: Basic Readings*, ed. D. A. E. Pelteret (2000), 107–20.

[27] O. S. Anderson, *English Hundred-Names* (3 vols, Lund, 1935, 1939, 1939).

[28] J. E. A. Jolliffe, 'The hidation of Kent', *EHR*, 44 (1929), 613–14 and *idem*, *Pre-feudal England*, 44–6 identified a dozen hypothetical early lathes assessed at 80 or 160 sulungs in Domesday Book. K. P. Witney corrected some of Jolliffe's errors, but retained his interpretation in his *Kingdom of Kent* (1982), 52–60, 236– 8. The reservations of G. Ward, *Archaeologia Cantiana*, 45 (1933), 290–94, about Jolliffe's use of evidence are developed in my 'The creation and structure of the kingdom of Kent', *The Origins of Anglo-Saxon Kingdoms*, ed. S. R. Bassett (1989), 55–74, at 71–2.

not without circularity of argument, but if I have been right to argue here that much of the Domesday assessment of the West Saxon shires goes back at least to the ninth century, then there may be greater potential for local studies of its structure and functions than has yet been realized.

Another form of Kentish enquiry that might be imitated in Wessex is the highly distinctive work of Alan Everitt in identifying early estate-centres from traces of manorial and ecclesiastical dependence that survived in late medieval records and in particular in the historical and topographical survey of the great eighteenth-century Kentish antiquarian, Edmund Hasted.[29] By this means Everitt detected about fifty such *tunas* in Kent, which were all located on the best soils for arable farming. Not all can have been king's *tunas* under royal reeves; nor can they have all been the centres of early 'lathes'. But Everitt's approach may be producing a more real pattern of landed power in which not only the Kentish kings but also the secular nobility and the leading churches had their own estate-centres. We may reconstruct the administration of Wessex erroneously if we focus exclusively upon royal vills and construct model territories dependent only upon them.

Another productive approach to the geography of early medieval lordship has been the study of the boundaries of ancient ecclesiastical parishes as they are recorded in the Tithe Awards from the 1840s. It is clear that the parishes established in England in the twelfth century and in essence mapped in the Tithe Awards, followed estate boundaries that very often already existed in the tenth century when so many of the perambulations set out in Anglo-Saxon royal charters were writtten.[30] In consequence a number of scholars have been tempted to suggest that the creation of 'bookland estates' by grants of royal charters marked a crucial phase in a process which saw the break-up of the old larger land units of less intensive lordship and the emergence of the manor and of nucleated villages with open-field systems of agriculture.[31] 'From the *regio* to

---

[29] A. Everitt, *Continuity and Colonization: the evolution of Kentish settlement* (1986), draws much of its evidence from E. Hasted, *History and Topographical Survey of the County of Kent* (12 vols, 1797–1801).

[30] There are convenient surveys of the huge volume of work identifying Anglo-Saxon charter bounds in N. P. Brooks, 'Anglo-Saxon charters; a review of the work of the last twenty years', *Anglo-Saxon England*, 3 (1974), 213–34, at 223–4, now reprinted in *idem, Anglo-Saxon Myths* (2000), 181–202, with a postscript on 'Anglo-Saxon charters 1973–1998', 202–15, with subsequent work on boundaries surveyed at 214–15. F. A. Youngs Jr, *Guide to the Local Administrative Units of England, I Southern England; II, Northern England*, Royal Historical Society, Guides and Handbooks, 10 and 17 (1979, 1991).

[31] Some of the more important recent reviews of the evidence are: H. S. A. Fox, 'Approaches to the adoption of the Midland system', *The Origins of Open-Field Agriculture*, ed. T. Rowley (1981), 64–111; C. C. Taylor, *Village and Farmstead: A History of Rural Settlement in England* (1984); D. Hooke (ed.), *Medieval Villages: A Review of Current Work*, Oxford University Committee for Archaeology, Monograph 5 (1985); *The Rural Settlements of Medieval England*, eds M. Aston, M. Austin and C. C. Dyer (1989); C. Lewis, P. Mitchell-Fox and C. C. Dyer, *Village, Hamlet and Field: Changing Medieval Settlements in Central England* (1997), 1–37.

the manor' might be seen as the economic and administrative agenda of late Anglo-Saxon England. And King Alfred might be thought to stand, if not at its beginning, at least prominently in its early stages.

But this interpretation of parish boundaries as defining one stage in the fragmentation of the larger land units has been challenged by the work of Desmond Bonney in Wiltshire. He sought to relate the evidence of the ancient ecclesiastical parishes in that county to a variety of relic features in the landscape: to barrow burials, to Roman roads, to linear eathworks of Iron Age or Dark Age origin. His view that the coincidence of pagan Anglo-Saxon burials and barrows on parish boundaries suggested that the boundaries had preceded the burials has proved controversial.[32] But his work on the relationship of parish boundaries in north Wiltshire to the Iron Age boundary bank known as Grims Dyke and to the huge Dark Age earthwork of East Wansdyke is altogether more compelling.[33] Bonney showed that in north-eastern Wiltshire the parish boundaries respect and follow the course of the relatively modest Grims Dyke meticulously. Evidently this Iron Age boundary earthwork remained in use as an administrative (and doubtless an estate) boundary down to the twentieth century. But in the north-west of the county we find a very different pattern in relation to East Wansdyke (Fig. 14). The parish boundaries, which had followed the course of the Roman road at the western end of the dyke, pay no attention at all to the massive dyke. The parishes of Alton Barnes, Alton Priors, Overton and All Cannings all had small portions of their territory on one side or the other of the dyke in a manner that seems highly improbable if this huge landscape feature had existed when these boundaries were first established. The estates or land units that these parish boundaries define were laid out at a time when the Roman road to the west existed but when the Wansdyke itself had apparently not yet been built. 'Estates', 'townships' or land units with these boundaries must therefore have already existed in the fifth or sixth century when East Wansdyke was constructed and have remained of significance in the era when bookland estates were being created in the tenth century and parishes established in the twelfth. Late Anglo-Saxon bookland estates may therefore often have concerned land divisions that were in whole or in part far more ancient.[34]

---

[32] D. Bonney, 'Pagan Saxon burials and boundaries in Wiltshire', *Wiltshire Archaeological and Natural History Magazine*, 61 (1966), 25–30; *idem*, 'Early boundaries and estates in southern England', *English Medieval Settlement*, ed. P. H. Sawyer (1979), 41–51. For critical views see M. Biddle, 'Hampshire and the origin of Wessex', in *Problems in Economic and Social Archaeology*, eds G. de G. Sieveking et al. (1976), 324–41, at 328; A. Goodier, 'The formation of boundaries in Anglo-Saxon England: a statistical study', *Medieval Archaeology*, 28 (1984), 1–21; M. G. Welch, 'Rural settlement patterns in the Early and Middle Anglo-Saxon periods', *Landscape History*, 7 (1985), 13–25.

[33] D. Bonney, 'Early Boundaries in Wessex', *Archaeology and the Landscape: essays for L.V. Grinsell*, ed. P. J. Fowler (1972), 168–86, at 174–80.

[34] This seems to concur with the detailed work of P. J. Fowler, *Landscape History and Local Archaeology in Fyfield and Overton, Wiltshire*, Society of Antiquaries of London, Research Report (2000), which appeared too late for discussion in this chapter.

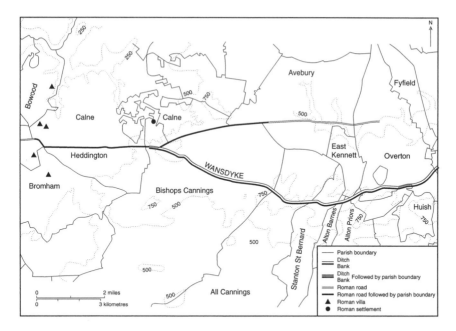

Fig. 14   Parish boundaries in the vicinity of East Wansdyke (after Bonney)

An alternative and equally promising approach to identifying early medieval territorial units has been the attempt to identify the minsters or mother churches of seventh- and eighth-century England. These churches had *parochiae* ('minster parishes') over which they had pastoral authority. It has been suggested that in Wessex the minster churches were always on royal estates, that they were founded by kings in, or close to, their royal *tun* or 'vill', and that their *parochiae* were normally coterminous with the *regiones* administered by reeves from the king's *tunas*.[35] Probable mother churches can be detected because their nineteenth-century parishes were often unusually large, because in medieval times they were often served by more than one priest and because in late medieval or early modern records traces of their superiority over other churches may be found in such matters as tithes, oblations, burial and baptismal rights. In reconstructing the parishes and minster parishes of Hampshire, Patrick Hase is properly cautious about suggesting that this scheme ever existed at one moment in time or that every detail of his interpretation can be relied upon (Fig. 15). But he does suggest that much of this system was introduced quite rapidly in the late seventh and early eighth centuries, that is presumably under bishops Hædde (676–705) and Daniel (705–44 or 745) of

---

[35] P. H. Hase, 'The development of the parish in Hampshire, particularly in the 11th and 12th centuries' (unpublished Cambridge PhD. thesis, 1975), 1–15.

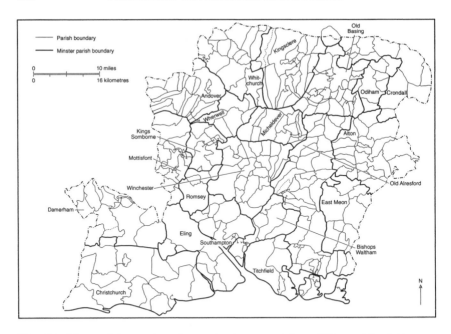

Fig. 15   The parishes and conjectural minster parishes of Hampshire (after Hase)

Winchester. Similar conclusions have been propounded for other areas of England.[36]

One of the minster parishes identified by Hase in central Hampshire was that of Micheldever, which still had an unusually large valley and downland parish at the time of the Tithe Awards and whose church still had rights over chapels at Popham, East Stratton and Northington in the later Middle Ages. He therefore suggested that Micheldever had been a minster and that its *parochia* may also have originally extended over the group of villages to the east, all called after the name of the small stream of the Candover (Brown Candover, Chilton Candover and possibly Preston Candover) and of the adjacent small vills comprising the tiny Domesday hundreds of Bermondspit and Mainsborough.[37] Was Hase's conjectural minster parish of Micheldever coterminous with a *regio* that had been adminis-

36 J. E. A. Jolliffe, *Pre-feudal England: the Jutes* (1933), esp. 41–6; Barrow, 'Pre-feudal Scotland' (as n. 6); much of the best recent work is found in *Minsters and Parish Churches: the Local Church in Transition 950–1200*, ed. J. Blair (1988) and *Pastoral Care before the Parish*, eds J. Blair and R. Sharpe (1992). See also J. Blair, *Early Medieval Surrey: Landholding, Church and Settlement Before 1300* (1991); S. R. Bassett, 'The administrative landscape of the diocese of Worcester in the tenth century', in *St Oswald of Worcester: Life and Influence*, eds N. Brooks and C. Cubitt (1996), 147–73; D. M. Hadley, *The Northern Danelaw, c.800–1100* (2000), 94–164.

37 Hase, 'Development of the parish', 297–300.

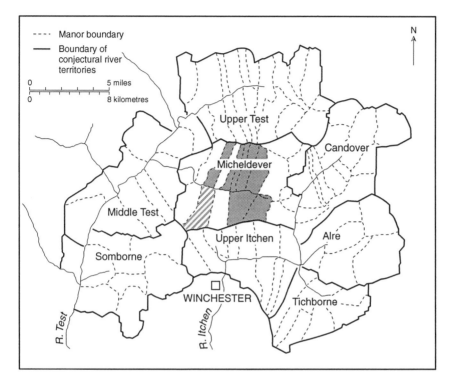

Fig. 16 Conjectural river-valley units of central Hampshire (after Klingelhofer), showing the manors of Micheldever and Wonston

tered from the villa regalis of Micheldever where in 862 King Æthelred I had granted Wittenham to Ealdorman Æthelwulf? A slightly different 'archaic hundred' of Micheldever has been proposed by Eric Klingelhofer, who has suggested that the early *regiones* of central Hampshire comprised river-valley territories with the divisions at the watersheds (Fig. 16). He would locate one upon the Micheldever stream, and others on the Upper Itchen (i.e. the Worthies), on the Candover and on the Middle and the Upper Test valleys.[38]

What is certain is that two centuries later, by the early or middle years of the eleventh century, Micheldever was a substantial manor and also the centre of a private hundred belonging to the abbey of New Minster in Winchester. At that

---

[38] E. Klingelhofer, 'Settlement and land-use in Micheldever Hundred, 700–1100', *Transactions of the American Philosophical Society*, 81/3 (1991); *idem, Manor, Vill and Hundred: the development of rural institutions in early medieval Hampshire*, Pontifical Institute of Mediaeval Studies, Toronto, Studies and Texts, 112 (Toronto,1992), 19–24, 65–6, 71–5, 88–112, 128–62. Klingelhofer's work is full of interesting detail, but is confusing in its presentation and uncritical in its use of sources. The same applies to his earlier 'Settlement and land use in Micheldever'.

time the monks forged a charter purporting to be a grant by King Edward the Elder of one hundred hides at Micheldever to the abbey in the year 901.[39] But the charter is not a grant of a single consolidated territory, but of seven separate estates. For six of them the charter provides detailed perambulations of their bounds (Fig. 17), whose language and formulation suggests they had been composed at different times between the mid-tenth and mid-eleventh centuries. The monks apparently wished to administer these once separate possessions as a single immunity. The core manor of Micheldever lay at the heart of this assemblage of estates and two separate but nearby strips of land at Cranbourne and Candover were to be regarded as part of the manor throughout the central and later Middle Ages; other properties assigned to the hundred hides of Micheldever were the distant New Minster properties of *Rige leah*, Durley and Curdridge. There is no evidence that these outlying parts had any ancient association with Micheldever. They do not seem, for example, to have provided specialized pasture or timber rights, in the manner of outlying members of some 'discrete' or 'multiple' estates whose antiquity has been asserted with some plausibility.[40] Rather the monks of New Minster seem to have forged the charter in order to assert their title to a grouping of estates that they were gathering in the early eleventh century. By the time of Domesday Book and in the later forged 'Golden' foundation charter of the New Minster, the manor and hundred of Micheldever had grown yet again with further New Minster acquisitions.[41]

If we cannot use the forged Micheldever charter to establish the extent of an ancient *regio* administered from the royal vill, then we have to look for less clear hints elsewhere. One relic of an early Micheldever territory may be found in a charter of the year 904 by which King Edward the Elder granted 10 hides 'at Micheldever' to the refectory of the community of St Peter's, Winchester, seemingly to the Old Minster. The bounds establish that the estate granted was actually the township of Wonston in Barton Stacey hundred, that is that part of the parish of Wonston which lies to the south of the Micheldever stream (Fig.

---

[39] BCS 596 (S 360). There is a full edition of this charter with a lengthy interpretation of the boundaries in N. P. Brooks, 'The oldest document in the college archives? the Micheldever forgery', *Winchester College: Sixth-centenary Studies*, ed. R. Custance (1982), 189–228. The charter has now been re-edited in S. Miller, *Charters of New Minster, Winchester*, Anglo-Saxon Charters, 9 (2001), no. 3. I am grateful to Mr P. R. Kitson for advice on the dating of the different Old English boundary clauses.

[40] G. R. J. Jones, 'Early estate organization in England and Wales', *Geografiske Annaler*, 43 (1961), 174–81; *idem*, 'Settlement patterns in Anglo-Saxon England', *Antiquity*, 35 (1961), 221–32; *idem*, 'Multiple estates and early settlement', *English Medieval Settlement*, ed. P. H. Sawyer (1979), 11–40. See also D. Hooke, 'Early medieval estate and settlement patterns: the documentary evidence', *Rural Settlements of Medieval England*, eds M. Aston, D. Austin and C. C. Dyer (1989), 9–30. For a critique see N. Gregson, 'The mutiple estate model: some critical questions', *Journal of Historical Geography*, 11 (1985), 339–51.

[41] See Brooks, 'Micheldever forgery', 194–6, 216–18; Klingelhofer, 'Manor, Vill and Hundred', 156–62. The 'golden charter' is BCS 604 (S 370). In 1066 the manor and hundred of Micheldever comprised 106 hides (DB i.42).

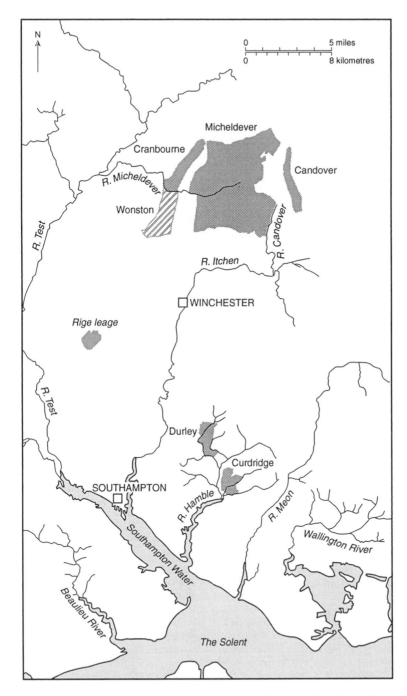

Fig. 17 The 100-hide estate of Micheldever as claimed by the New Minster in S360, together with the 10 hides 'at Micheldever' (Wonston) granted by Edward the Elder in 904

17);[42] it is separated from the New Minster's hundredal manor of Micheldever by the Bishop of Winchester's manor and parish of Stoke Charity, which may also have once been known under the name 'Micheldever'.[43] It is therefore very possible, as Klingelhofer has suggested, that many of the vills on either side of the Micheldever stream had previously formed a larger unit named from the stream; their later names may have been used concurrently for early component portions of that unit or may have been formed after the old territory was carved up into separate bookland estates or manors.

The fact that the place-name Micheldever is an early topographic name of Celtic, that is Brittonic, origin reinforces Klingelhofer's suggestion since a number of early estate-centres are known to have been named from such features. The earliest reference to Micheldever is the form *mycendefr*, found in the charter of 862 which establishes the derivation of this stream-name from Primitive Welsh *micn*, 'bog', and *dubro*, 'water'; the first element was later altered by popular etymology to Old English *micel*, 'large'.[44] Clearly 'boggy stream' is a much more accurate description for the Micheldever than 'great water'.

A hint that the early district dependent upon Micheldever may, however, have been larger than either Hase or Klingelhofer supposed is found in the boundary clause of the core Micheldever estate in the forged 901 charter to the New Minster (Fig. 18). The twenty-seventh point in the perambulation is the *gemot hus* ('moot-house'), which can be located precisely at the crossing point where the Roman road from Winchester to Silchester (A33) meets the ancient downland drove-road to Alresford, the Lunway or 'lundenwey'. An inn (Lunways Inn) has stood at this cross-roads at least since the eighteenth century.[45] Cross-roads are of course characteristic sites for hundredal meeting-places, though the

---

[42] BCS 604 (S 274). The interpretation of its bounds as excluding the vill of Sutton Scotney and being bound on the north by the Micheldever stream was first established by R. Forsberg, *A Contribution to a Dictionary of Old English Place-Names* (Uppsala, 1950), 202. It is curious that S 274 is preserved in the cartularies of the New Minster rather than of the cathedral. There may have been an unrecorded transfer of Wonston from the New to the Old Minster, or perhaps confusion arose from the name Myceldefer so that the charter was believed to refer to the New Minster manor.

[43] A little-studied list of Old Minster properties in Old English, BCS 1161 (S 1821), perhaps from the time of Bishop Æthelwold (963–84) includes both 10 hides at Myceldefer (i.e. Wonston) and 50 hides at Wealtham and Myceldefer (Bishop's Waltham and ? Stoke Charity). See Klingelhofer, *Manor, Vill and Hundred* (1992), 158–9, who suggests that the bishop's holding in 1066 of ten hides at Stoches in Domesday Book (DB i.40c) may refer to Stoke Charity rather than to Stoke by Hurstbourne.

[44] E. Ekwall, *English River Names* (1928), s.v. For the naming of large early estates from rivers and other topographical features and for the association of names in *-tun* with the fragmentation into bookland manors in the tenth and eleventh centuries, see M. Gelling, *Signposts to the Past* (1978), 123–5 and W. J. Ford, 'Some settlement patterns in the central region of the Warwickshire Avon', *English Medieval Settlement*, ed. Sawyer, 283–6.

[45] For the identification of the bounds see Brooks, 'Micheldever forgery' (as in n. 39), 202, 218.

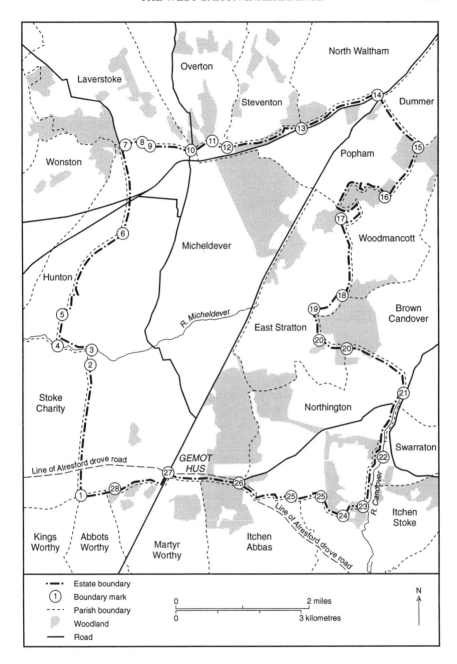

Fig. 18 Interpretation of the bounds of the core estate at Micheldever (the first boundary clause in S360), showing the position of the *gemot hus* at no. 27

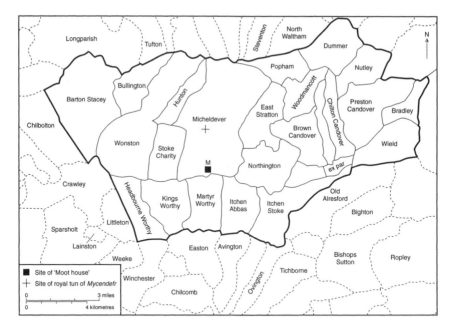

Fig. 19   Conjectural reconstruction of the early *regio* of Micheldever

charter's reference to the meeting-'house' (rather than to an open-air meeting-place) is unique. Hundredal meeting-places, however, were normally sited more centrally within their territories, so the location of the moot-house here on the hundredal and manorial boundary may suggest that it may once have served a territory which had extended further south. Micheldever's early territory may therefore have included the Worthies (Headbourne, Kings and Martyr Worthy). Anderson's suggestion that the tiny Domesday hundreds of Bountisborough (comprising the parishes of Itchen Abbas, Itchen Stoke, Swarraton and Godsfield) and Mainsborough (comprising the parishes of Brown and Chilton Candover and of Woodmancott) are relics left high and dry by the eleventh-century creation of the New Minster private hundred of Micheldever has much to commend it. Some or all of the hundred of Barton Stacey may have been a similar relic on the west.[46]

It may therefore be that the early *regio* of Micheldever should be reconstructed on a larger scale and with its *gemot hus* built at its heart (Fig. 19). We would then be looking at a territory which in 1066 was assessed at some 289 hides,[47] perhaps a relic of a small folk unit of 300 hides such as we find in the

---

[46] Anderson, *English Hundred-Names: South-Western Counties*, Lunds Univ. Arskrift, new series, section 1, vol. 35, no. 5 (Lund, 1939).

[47] The 1066 assessments are as follows in Domesday Book: 1. Barton Stacey hundred: Barton Stacey 7½ hides, Bransbury 4h, Newton Stacey 1h, Norton 1h, Sutton Scotney 5h, Wonston 10h,

Tribal Hidage. No such conjecture could convince us without much fuller analyses of the early administrative structure of the whole of Hampshire (and indeed of other West Saxon shires) using the full range of evidence that has been briefly summarized here – ecclesiastical, manorial, topographical and documentary. My purpose is to propose a programme for future researchers, not to suggest that early Wessex had indeed been divided into 300-hide folk units, rather than into Hase's minster parishes or Klingelhofer's river-valley 'archaic hundreds'. The example of Micheldever surely warns us to keep our options open and to resist imposing any single interpretative model. It may well be that more than one pattern of early lordship, of folk units and *regiones* coexisted in the early Middle Ages and may be recoverable in some parts. But it is also possible that many of the constituent units of these territories, the townships, some of which were to re-emerge as bookland estates in the tenth century and as ecclesiastical parishes by the twelfth, were of very ancient origin indeed (at least as far as their boundaries were concerned). The locations of settlements and the forms of agricultural exploitation could and did change in the early medieval period, but they often did so within established boundaries.

Such traces of archaic boundaries in the English landscape hint at governmental continuities from the 'middle Saxon' period and in some respects from a far more distant past, perhaps from the Celtic Iron Age. When King Alfred sought to administer his kingdom, he was working within an old system of lordship, of courts, territories and warland peasants. We find no truth in the medieval myth that he invented the hundred and tithings of England; nor did he give any new shape to the West Saxon shires; nor, it would seem, to the ancient hidage assessment that formed the basis of public obligations. His achievement lay rather in getting more service out of his nobles and out of the *ceorls* on the warland than his predecessors had managed, in getting boroughs not only built but also garrisoned, and thereby in making the first tentative steps taken towards an urban future. The burdens he imposed may have given an early twist of the ratchet to the developing feudal régime of manors, boroughs, nucleated settlements and open-field systems and to the growth of seigneurial lordship over the rural population. A programme of systematic research may yet reveal much more of the structure of local government and local power that Alfred inherited in Wessex, but it does not seem likely that we will detect much administrative innovation to be attributed to the great king. The pressing military, religious and educational concerns that so dominated his thoughts and those of his advisers were not, it would seem, an appropriate seedbed for fundamental governmental reform.

Headbourne Worthy 3h 1v, Kings Worthy [6h], Martyr Worthy 3h + ? Stoke Charity 10h. 2. Micheldever hundred: Micheldever (including Drayton, Popham and Stratton) 106h, Abbots Worthy 7h. 3. Mainsborough hundred: Brown Candover 20h, Chilton Candover 10h (including Woodmancott). 4. Bountisborough hundred: Abbotstone 9h, Itchen Abbas 12h, Itchen Stoke 8h, Wield 10h, Yavington 3h. 5. Bermondspit hundred: Preston Candover 19h 1v, Dummer 5h, Ellisfield 8h, Farleigh Wallop 4h, Herriard 5h, Nutley 5h, Sudberie 2½ h.

Chapter 10

The power of the written word: Alfredian England 871–899

Simon Keynes

I start with a truth which I'm sure we all hold to be self-evident. We have at our disposal an extraordinary variety of written sources for the reign of King Alfred the Great, ranging from extended 'literary' works produced for polemical or didactic purposes, such as the *Anglo-Saxon Chronicle*, Asser's *Life of King Alfred*, and the large corpus of Alfredian prose, to the variety of 'documentary' records which originated in the service of more strictly utilitarian ends, such as the treaty between Alfred and Guthrum, the king's law-code, his will, and the small corpus of the king's charters. It is sometimes suggested that this truth is an accident of survival, and that if we happened to have similar material for Offa, or for Æthelstan, we would see that there was not so much difference between them all. The fact is we don't, and there was. The variety of written sources for Alfred the Great is at once the product, the expression, and the symbol of what was so distinctive about Alfred's kingship and royal government. The régime did not have to invent the technology, but it did need the will and the wherewithal to exploit it, and to foster conditions in which the product might thrive. What we seem to encounter at King Alfred's court is the feverish activity of a small group of men who were eager to generate verbiage in the king's interests, to control its dissemination, and to ensure at the same time that it would reach a wide public. The modern analogies spring readily to mind. Just as advocates of the Internet, in the present day, have to overcome the passive resistance of the inveterate technophobe, so too did Alfred have to prevail over those among his ealdormen, reeves and thegns who (as Asser put it), 'either because of [their] age or because of the unresponsive nature of [their] unpractised intelligence',[1] were slower than others to take advantage of new opportunities. Nor is it inappropriate that the most immediately recognizable symbol of the age should be an object identified as an *æstel*, or reading-aid; and in so far as we now have four such objects, each of a different type or grade, it would appear to follow that the reading-aid was as ubiquitous in Alfredian Wessex as the mobile telephone, or the computer mouse, has become in Tony Blair's Britain. Of course, the objects in question may have been status symbols, fashion accessories, or gadgets of some other kind; but

---

[1] Asser, c. 106, p. 94, trans. Keynes and Lapidge, *Alfred*, 110.

leaving them aside, there should be an organizing principle behind such a variety or profusion of written material, and a sense, therefore, in which those in the king's circle perceived the potential of the written word in securing their political objectives, and were able then to harness and to exploit its power.

It would not be inappropriate briefly to review the place which the use of the written word has come to occupy in Alfredian studies; and it may be instructive, at the same time, to see how matters which we now take for granted assumed their present shape and form. Almost exactly fifty years ago, the late Michael Wallace-Hadrill published a seminal article in which he had occasion to pronounce on the modern perception of King Alfred the Great: 'We hold that Alfred was a great and glorious king in part because he tells us he was.'[2] In Wallace-Hadrill's view, it was in the second half of the ninth century that the 'full force of Frankish example hit England'. He found it lurking, for example, in the *Anglo-Saxon Chronicle* (dynastic propaganda for the royal House of Wessex, in the manner (as he saw it) of the Royal Frankish Annals), and of course in Asser's *Life of King Alfred* (a portrayal of kingship heavily influenced by Einhard's *Life of Charlemagne*). Indeed, he suspected 'Carolingian influence upon Alfred in almost every direction', in matters military, liturgical, educational, literary and artistic, instancing the promotion of the vernacular (an interest known to have been shared by Charlemagne), and the codification of law. The point was that Alfred sought to compensate for his 'profound sense of dynastic insecurity', under intense Viking threat, by turning to Frankish spin-doctors ('the experts on kingship') – and with their help cultivating a sense of the past calculated to make people aware of their common interests and identity, and projecting an image of the king intended to encourage them to give him their enthusiastic support. Wallace-Hadrill's article was published only seven years after the first appearance of Sir Frank Stenton's *Anglo-Saxon England*, and in retrospect it can be seen to represent a turning-point in Alfredian studies, after which nothing was quite the same again. It is an early manifestation of what is now an utterly orthodox attitude towards the primary sources, by which we take nothing at face value, and give all due attention instead to matters of authorship, date and literary genre, and to circumstances of publication and transmission, considering at the same time whether or not a source seems to convey a particular message to a chosen audience for a hidden (or unhidden) purpose. Wallace-Hadrill's argument made little impression, however, on Dorothy Whitelock, whose translation of the *Chronicle*, first published in 1955, was reissued in its definitive form in 1961.[3] Whitelock registered Stenton's view that the *Chronicle* was a

---

2 J. M. Wallace-Hadrill, 'The Franks and the English in the ninth nentury: some common historical interests', *History*, 35 (1950), 202–18, at 216–17. The operative words were subsequently altered to 'in part because he rightly implies this', in J. M. Wallace-Hadrill, *Early Medieval History* (1975), 201–16, at 213.

3 *EHD*, no. 1; *ASC*, trans. Whitelock and others (1961). Wallace-Hadrill sent an offprint of his article to Whitelock, 'with best wishes', on the cover of which she wrote: 'the one with the nonsense about Alfred.'

'private' compilation, by a south-western ealdorman, and thus felt unable to up-hold 'the confident attribution of the work to Alfred's instigation'; one senses, however, that she was well aware of its place in an Alfredian scheme, and that she may have wanted to keep the options open.[4] Wallace-Hadrill's line was picked up and developed by Peter Sawyer, in his *Age of the Vikings* (1962), after which it became axiomatic, in certain circles, that the *Chronicle* was West Saxon dynastic propaganda, emphasizing the failure of the Mercians and praising the achieve-ments of Æthelwulf and his sons.[5] Wallace-Hadrill returned to the field in his deeply influential Ford Lectures (1970), on 'Early Germanic Kingship', pursuing the continental analogies in ways which introduced new dimensions into the perception of Anglo-Saxon history, and, in Alfred's case, making particularly suggestive remarks about the law-code.[6] Yet it was two papers published at the same time, in 1971, which determined the further development of Alfredian stud-ies, transforming Wallace-Hadrill's bandwagon into a fully articulated lorry: one by the late R. H. C. Davis, on the *Anglo-Saxon Chronicle*,[7] and the other by David Kirby, on Asser's *Life of King Alfred*.[8] As Davis put it, Alfred's reign 'presents the historian with an interesting problem, since he is confronted with the possibility that almost all the sources may have originated with either Alfred himself or his immediate entourage'.[9] He proceeded to test the 'objectivity' of the *Chronicle*, and found, seemingly to his surprise, that it was pro-Alfredian: 'not a survey of all Anglo-Saxon history, but an account of King Alfred's ancestors, the kings of Wessex', conveying the impression that 'the house of Cerdic always emerged victorious', and calculated to indoctrinate his people 'with loyalty to himself and enthusiasm for his cause'. Davis was curiously reluctant to accord Asser's *Life of King Alfred* any place in his scheme, presumably because of his lingering doubts about the authenticity of the work; but Kirby had no such reservations, and brought the *Life of King Alfred* firmly and most effectively back into the reckon-ing. The *Life* was seen as a work based on earlier reports which Asser had sent back to the members of his own community at St David's, but augmented, in 893, with additional material in praise of the king, and with material translated from the *Anglo-Saxon Chronicle*. The work was intended in this form not only for the benefit of an audience or readership in Wales, for it was directed in addition towards a much wider audience in Alfred's own kingdom; and its purpose was to emphasize the king's greatness, to publicize his achievements, to extol his virtues,

---

[4] *ASC*, trans. Whitelock, xxii–xxiii; cf. Swanton, xviii.

[5] P. H. Sawyer, *The Age of the Vikings* (1962), 20. Stenton complimented Sawyer on his 'original account of the *Chronicle*, as a work to be judged for its intrinsic character' (letter from FMS to PHS, 15 Oct. 1962, quoted here by kind permission of Professor Sawyer).

[6] J. M. Wallace-Hadrill, *Early Germanic Kingship in England and on the Continent* (1971), esp. 124–51, at 148–50.

[7] R. H. C. Davis, 'Alfred the Great: propaganda and truth' (1971), reprinted in his *From Alfred the Great to Stephen* (1991), 33–46.

[8] D. P. Kirby, 'Asser and his Life of King Alfred', *Studia Celtica*, 6 (1971), 12–35.

[9] Davis, 'Alfred the Great: propaganda and truth', 33 and 41.

to insist upon the importance of obedience, and, in general, to make 'all the points that the West Saxon king wished to stress'. It followed, in effect, that Alfred was all done with mirrors: his supposed greatness was the product of his own propaganda, and the reality was by implication significantly different.

In the past twenty-five years or so Alfredian studies have advanced much further, in ways which combine to ensure that we now have a far more sophisticated understanding of the king, and of the period in which he moved. The advance has been the collective and cumulative achievement of scholars working in several different disciplines, and it is striking how work in one discipline seems often to depend, in some respect, on work in one or more of the others; of course, the fact that it should be so itself expresses a fundamental truth about the age of Alfred, which is in turn a function of the king's own distinction. In retrospect, it is perhaps the archaeologists who can claim a significant part of the credit for setting King Alfred on his way. The excavations at Winchester, throughout the 1960s, did as much for Alfred as they did for Bishop Æthelwold, by heightening awareness of the place traditionally regarded as the 'capital' of Wessex; but it was perhaps more so the identification of Alfredian towns and fortifications on the ground which gave substance to his activities in defence of his kingdom, and in the same process transformed the 'Burghal Hidage' from a curiosity to an administrative text of the utmost historical importance.[10] There was no danger, then, of losing sight of the successful warrior who (in Ælfric's words) 'often fought against the Danes, until he won the victory and protected his people';[11] and the less danger, therefore, of forgetting the thoroughly practical and resourceful king who tried his hand at everything from naval architecture to horology. Yet perceptions of Alfred as leader of his people in war also depended on the prevailing perception of the Vikings, and of the nature of the threat they represented. The instruments of divine punishment for the sins of the English people had come to be regarded as the prime agency of their decline: as cause, rather than effect. The Vikings were then reinvented in the 1960s as salesmen pressing their wares on somewhat unappreciative customers, in natural extension (as the saying went) of normal Dark Age activities; but just as their threat seemed to be diminishing to the point of non-existence, Wallace-Hadrill sounded his words of warning,[12] Alfred Smyth revived gory tales of the blood-

---

[10] N. Brooks, 'The unidentified forts of the Burghal Hidage' (1964), reprinted in his *Communities and Warfare 700–1400* (2000), 48–68; M. Biddle and D. Hill, 'Late Saxon planned towns', *Antiquaries Journal*, 51 (1971), 70–85; *The Defence of Wessex: the Burghal Hidage and Anglo-Saxon Fortifications*, eds D. Hill and A. R. Rumble (1996).

[11] 'swa swa wæs Ælfred cining, þe oft gefeaht wið Denan, oþ þæt he sige gewann 7 bewerode his leode': from *Judges* (Epilogue), in *The Old English Version of the Heptateuch / Ælfric's Treatise on the Old and New Testament and his Preface to Genesis*, ed. S. J. Crawford, EETS OS 160 (1922), 416; *EHD*, no. 239 (i).

[12] J. M. Wallace-Hadrill, 'The Vikings in Francia' (1974), reprinted in his *Early Medieval History*, 217–36, esp. 220, with reference to the notion that the Vikings should be seen as 'little more than groups of long-haired tourists who occasionally roughed up the natives'.

eagle sacrifice,[13] and Nicholas Brooks restored our faith in the size of their fleets and armies, and so in the impact which they had on their unfortunate victims.[14] The Vikings were promptly re-reinvented, in even softer focus, and attention was transferred to the private lives of those who had settled in Dublin and York, or stayed back home in Scandinavia.[15] So off they went with their ivory combs on their bone skates, in order to prepare themselves for the next board-game. Fortunately, no one was fooled, or at least not many, or for very long. Patrick Wormald soon gave expression to his belief that the Vikings, if not exactly mad, 'were probably bad, and certainly dangerous to know'.[16] The excavations at Repton showed what it meant, in the 870s, when the Danish army settled down for the winter, and thus provided a most important corrective.[17] Archaeologists also showed what was meant when Alfred 'occupied' London, in 886;[18] numismatists, for their part, transformed our understanding of the ninth-century economy, and of the way we can look at relations between Mercia, Wessex and Kent;[19] and historians wondered what it all meant in terms of their own.

Here we come back to the use of the written word. It is generally assumed, with good reason, that most things which moved in Alfred's reign were driven by those who operated within the royal court, although we can but wonder what particular contribution was made by Wærferth of Worcester, Plegmund from Mercia, Asser of St David's, Grimbald of Saint-Bertin, John the Old Saxon, and all the others (known or unnamed). Initially, it was a matter of establishing the 'Alfredian' corpus, and clarifying the relationship between its various component parts – accomplished in the 1960s and 1970s, primarily by Dorothy Whitelock and Janet Bately.[20] In this process Alfred may have lost the Old English *Bede*

---

[13] A. Smyth, *Scandinavian Kings in the British Isles 850–880* (1977).

[14] N. Brooks, 'England in the ninth century: the crucible of defeat' (1979), reprinted in his *Communities and Warfare 700–1400*, 48–68.

[15] J. Graham-Campbell and D. Kidd, *The Vikings*, Exhibition Catalogue (1980).

[16] C. P. Wormald, 'Viking studies: whence and whither?', *The Vikings*, ed. R. T. Farrell (1982), 128–53, at 148.

[17] M. Biddle and B. Kjølbye-Biddle, 'Repton', *The Blackwell Encyclopaedia of Anglo-Saxon England*, eds M. Lapidge, J. Blair, S. Keynes and D. Scragg (1999), 390–92, with further references.

[18] M. Biddle, 'London on the Strand', *Popular Archaeology*, 6.1 (July 1984), 23–7; A. Vince, 'The Aldwych: mid-Saxon London discovered', *Current Archaeology*, 8 (1984), 310–12; and many later publications on the same theme.

[19] M. Dolley, 'Ælfred the Great's abandonment of the concept of periodic recoinage', *Studies in Numismatic Method presented to Philip Grierson*, eds C. N. L. Brooke, B. H. I. H. Stewart, J. G. Pollard and T. R. Volk (1983), 153–60; H. Pagan, 'Coinage in southern England, 796–874', *Anglo-Saxon Monetary History: Essays in Memory of Michael Dolley*, ed. M. A. S. Blackburn (1986), 45–65; and M. Blackburn, 'The Anglo-Saxons and Vikings: eighth-tenth centuries', in P. Grierson and M. Blackburn, *Medieval European Coinage, with a Catalogue of the Coins in the Fitzwilliam Museum, Cambridge*, I: *The Early Middle Ages (5th–10th Centuries)* (1986), 267–326. For another perspective, see J. R. Maddicott, 'Trade, industry and the wealth of King Alfred', *Past and Present*, 123 (1988), 3–51.

[20] D. Whitelock, 'The prose of Alfred's reign' (1966), reprinted in her *From Bede to Alfred:*

and the Old English *Orosius*,[21] though neither work was necessarily removed from his circle; but the restoration to the Alfredian canon of the vernacular rendering of the first fifty psalms of the Psalter was ample compensation, not least because it afforded a vital insight into the king's perception of his predicament, and showed how he may have conceived his response.[22] Lest one should be inclined to dismiss Alfredian prose as so much hot air, which God forbid, one should also remark, in this connection, that attention has been drawn (by Leslie Webster) to the strikingly 'intellectual' component in the decoration of late ninth-century metalwork, and that it has been shown more recently (by David Pratt) that the complex iconography of the Fuller Brooch, in particular, can be most readily understood in relation to ideas seen floating around at Alfred's court.[23] Another major development was represented by Malcolm Parkes's analysis of the Parker manuscript of the *Anglo-Saxon Chronicle*, promoting Grimbald as the Frankish spin-doctor responsible for introducing a tradition of 'West Saxon historiography', and advancing a claim for Winchester to be regarded as the intellectual power-house of the Alfredian revival.[24] It is difficult indeed to dissociate the production of the *Chronicle* from the circle of learned men around the king, and Stenton's south-western ealdorman has taken what may prove to be his last bow. It remains far from clear, however, whether the *Chronicle* should be assigned to Grimbald, at Winchester, or to a party or parties unknown, perhaps working somewhere else; one might add that the interpretation of the 'common stock' of the *Chronicle* along Wallace-Hadrill's lines, as West Saxon dynastic propaganda, has also been called into question, for much can be made of its more extended historical scope and of its wider political outlook.[25] Another major source has also undergone a transformation. Patrick Wormald soon began

---

Studies in Early Anglo-Saxon Literature and History (1980), no. VI; J. M. Bately, *The Literary Prose of King Alfred's Reign: Translation or Transformation* (1980), reprinted as Old English Newsletter, Subsidia 10 (Binghamton, NY, 1984); A. Crépin, 'King Alfred's Cultural Policy', *Bulletin des Anglicistes Médiévistes*, 20–21 (1981–2), 294–308.

[21] D. Whitelock, 'The Old English Bede' (1962), reprinted in her *From Bede to Alfred*, no. VIII; and *Orosius*, ed. Bately.

[22] J. Bately, 'Lexical evidence for the authorship of the prose psalms in the Paris Psalter', *Anglo-Saxon England*, 10 (1981), 69–95; see also Keynes and Lapidge, *Alfred*, 31–2 and 153–60. The possibility that the continuous translation of the psalms in the Paris Psalter represented the work of King Alfred had been raised by J. M. Kemble in 1833: see *John Mitchell Kemble and Jakob Grimm: a Correspondence 1832–1852*, ed. R. A. Wiley (Leiden, 1971), 34.

[23] L. Webster, 'The Legacy of Alfred', *The Golden Age of Anglo-Saxon Art 966–1066*, eds J. Backhouse, D. H. Turner and L. Webster, Exhibition Catalogue (1984), 18–19; D. Pratt, 'Fuller Brooch', *Blackwell Encyclopaedia of Anglo-Saxon England*, eds Lapidge and others, 196–8.

[24] M. B. Parkes, 'The palaeography of the Parker manuscript of the *Chronicle*, laws and Sedulius, and historiography at Winchester in the late ninth and tenth centuries', *ASE*, 5 (1976), 149–71. For Grimbald himself, the classic study remains P. Grierson, 'Grimbald of St Bertin's', *EHR*, 55 (1940), 529–61; see also J. Bately, 'Grimbald of St Bertin's', *Medium Ævum*, 35 (1966), 1–10.

[25] D. Whitelock, 'The importance of the battle of Edington' (1978), reprinted in her *From Bede to Alfred*, no. XIII; Keynes and Lapidge, *Alfred*, 39–42.

to work his magic with the law-code,[26] and has since shown precisely where it stands in the tradition of law-making, and what it represents in relation to the development of the king's power over his people.[27] It is otherwise Asser himself who catches our attention, if only because he is the only one among them who has left us with an extended account of the king. I have nothing to say about the authenticity of his 'Life of King Alfred', except to remark that the debate, which has now raged for well over 150 years, is testimony, of a kind, to the importance of the text itself in determining the way we regard the king.[28] So far is Asser's 'Life' from being the rock on which the legend of Alfred depends, that if you don't like his portrayal of Alfred, warts and all, and if you prefer the traditional image of the king, then you have to denounce the 'Life' as a forgery. In fact we should have no difficulty whatsoever in accepting Asser's portrayal of Alfred for precisely what it is; though it remains necessary, and thoroughly worthwhile, to approach Asser's 'Life' in its literary and linguistic contexts, and not least to consider its purpose, and its intended audience. It was suggested many years ago that Asser intended his 'Life' for an audience in Wales (perhaps his friends at St David's);[29] and although there are many who are more inclined to believe that the 'Life' was intended to be read at the king's court,[30] there is something to be said for holding firm to the older view.[31] Whatever the case, it is essentially

---

[26] P. Wormald, '*Lex scripta* and *verbum regis*: legislation and Germanic kingship, from Euric to Cnut' (1977), reprinted in his *Legal Culture in the Early Medieval West: Law as Text, Image and Experience* (1999), 1–43.

[27] P. Wormald, *The Making of English Law: King Alfred to the Twelfth Century*, I: *Legislation and its Limits* (1999).

[28] T. Wright, 'Some historical doubts relating to the biographer Asser [in a letter to Sir Henry Ellis, 18 November 1841]', *Archaeologia*, 29 (1842), 192–201; cf. Asser, xcvi–cx. V. H. Galbraith, 'Who wrote Asser's *Life of Alfred*?', in his *An Introduction to the Study of History* (1964), 85–128; cf. D. Whitelock, *The Genuine Asser*, Stenton Lecture 1967 (1968), reprinted in her *From Bede to Alfred*, no. XII. Smyth, *Alfred* (1995); cf. S. Keynes, 'On the authenticity of Asser's *Life of King Alfred*', *JEccH*, 47 (1996), 529–51; Abels, *Alfred*, 18–26, and M. Lapidge, 'Asser's reading', this volume, Chapter 2.

[29] Asser, ed. Stevenson, lxxix ('he speaks of England and the English as if he were addressing his own countrymen'); M. Schütt, 'The literary form of Asser's *Vita Alfredi*', *EHR*, 72 (1957), 209–20, at 210; D. Whitelock, 'Recent Work on Asser's Life of Alfred', *Asser*, ed. Stevenson (1959 reprint), cxxxii–clii, at cl–cli; Keynes and Lapidge, *Alfred*, 41–2 and 56.

[30] For example D. P. Kirby, 'Asser and his Life of King Alfred', 26–33; J. Campbell, 'Asser's *Life of Alfred*', *The Inheritance of Historiography 350–900*, eds C. Holdsworth and T. P. Wiseman, Exeter Studies in History 12 (1986), 115–35, reprinted in his *The Anglo-Saxon State* (2000), 129–55; and A. Scharer, 'The writing of history at King Alfred's court', *Early Medieval Europe*, 5 (1996), 177–206.

[31] S. Keynes, 'King Alfred and the Mercians', *Kings, Currency and Alliances: History and Coinage of Southern England in the Ninth Century*, eds M. A. S. Blackburn and D. N. Dumville, Studies in Anglo-Saxon History 9 (1998), 1–45, at 41–4. Asser's *Life of King Alfred* (written in 893) complemented the *Anglo-Saxon Chronicle* (first published *c.* 892) by making the account of the king's wars accessible to non-English readers, and by elevating the struggle against the Danes to the level of a holy war (Christians against pagans), so that the Welsh could more readily identify with the king's cause. It also established his credentials as 'ruler of all the Christians of the island of Britain', in other words as their overlord. Yet it has proved difficult to demonstrate that the text was

Asser's perception of the king which has now come into its own: we can compare him with Offa, or with Æthelstan, but the more instructive analogy is with Solomon. Alfred without Asser might lose his warts; but he would also lose the dimension which enables us to understand what he was all about, and which thereby prevents him from being reduced to a story-book hero.

If Alfred the Great is now seen, more than ever before, as the product of his own publicity machine, we might ask ourselves where did this perception of the power of the written word come from, and on what did it depend?[32] The text which best shows how contemporaries viewed the pattern of events in the eighth and ninth centuries is almost painfully familiar: the letter addressed by the king to each of the bishops in his kingdom, prefixed to copies of the translation of Pope Gregory's *Regula pastoralis*.[33] The rhetoric is compelling. A period of great happiness and prosperity (in the late seventh century) was followed by years of neglect and decline (in the eighth century), leading to the situation which had come to obtain by the early ninth century, when churchmen could read English perfectly well, but not Latin, and when they had lost access, therefore, to so much of the wisdom contained in Christian writings. This decline prompted the expression of divine anger in the form of Viking invasions (in the mid-ninth century), with consequent loss of the 'wealth' (*wela*), apparently referring to the treasures and books (*maðmas ond bocas*) which had accumulated in churches throughout the land. There were very few men south of the Humber who were capable of comprehending their Latin service-books, and for all Alfred knew there were not many beyond the Humber either; moreover, those south of the Humber seem to have been in Mercia, for Alfred could not recollect any, south of the Thames, when he became king in 871. In much the same vein, Asser alludes to Alfred's repeated complaints about the absence of competent scholars in Wessex (chs 24–5), remarks on the necessity for the recruitment of scholars from outside the kingdom (chs 76–9), and describes Alfred's 'Handbook' in terms which imply that its compilation was the germ of the larger programme of translation (chs 87–9).[34] The received view arises when

actually known in Wales. It is important to note, therefore, that the *Life* was known to Gerald of Wales, who quoted a substantial extract from chs 14–15 in his *Vita regis et martyris Æthelberti* (M. R. James, 'Two Lives of St Ethelbert, King and Martyr', *EHR*, 32 (1917), 214–44, at 222–36). The discussion of this point in Keynes and Lapidge, *Alfred*, 57–8, following Asser, lxiii–lxiv, overlooked the full version of Gerald's text, as printed by James.

[32] For the association between words and power in Old English literature, see S. Lerer, *Literacy and Power in Anglo-Saxon Literature* (Lincoln, NB, 1991); see also J. Neville, *Representations of the Natural World in Old English Poetry*, Cambridge Studies in Anglo-Saxon England 27 (1999), 113–14 and 196–8.

[33] *Pastoral Care*, ed. Sweet, 2–9 (text), and *EHD*, no. 226 (translation). See also D. N. Dumville, 'King Alfred and the tenth-century reform of the English Church', in his *Wessex and England from Alfred to Edgar* (1992), 185–205, at 186–98, and N. Guenther Discenza, '"Wise wealhstodas": The Prologue to Sirach as a model for Alfred's preface to the *Pastoral Care*', *Journal of English and Germanic Philology*, 97 (1998), 488–99.

[34] The book was already full when Alfred first showed it to Asser; so they decided to expand

the two sources are merged: an absence of competent scholars anywhere in Alfred's kingdom (south of the Thames) at the time of his accession; an influx of scholars to Alfred's court from outside Wessex (specifically from Mercia, Wales, and the Continent); and a fresh start in the late 880s, which by definition owed little or nothing to Wessex and Kent. Alfred goes on in his letter to indicate what he hoped to accomplish by translating certain carefully chosen books from Latin into English: all free-born young men now in England (*on Angelcynne*) would be taught how to read in English, and those intended for holy orders would be taught Latin. Modern scholars are able to put their own constructions upon the king's letter, and might suppose, for example, that Alfred was encouraging his bishops to undertake their own programmes of translation, or that he was urging them to establish cathedral schools;[35] but the simplest interpretation is that the king was directing a single programme from the centre, and that he had his own school in mind.[36] It is tempting, at the same time, to read the letter more loosely as an indictment of the woeful standards of literacy which obtained in Wessex and Kent at the time of Alfred's accession. Of course it was in Alfred's interest, at a time of crisis, to exaggerate the extent of decline in order to stress the need for reform; of course he resorted to hyperbole when we might have preferred him to stick to ascertainable facts; and of course there was more activity in the ninth century than the letter might seem (on a literal reading) to imply.[37] The fact remains, however, that there was a marked decline in the quantity and quality of books produced during the second and third quarters of the ninth century.[38] Further questions arise: did the decline affect only book production in Latin; or did it extend to lower levels of 'pragmatic' literacy in Latin, and indeed to any form of literate activity in English? Moreover, a larger issue is at stake. Did the extensive, expert and intelligent use of the written word in the latter part

---

it, and at the same time, on 11 November 887, they conceived the idea to translate a passage into English, 'and thereupon to instruct many others'.

35 A. Meaney, 'King Alfred and his secretariat', *Parergon*, 11 (1975), 16–24, at 16; Bately, *The Literary Prose of King Alfred's Reign*, 5; J. Morrish, 'King Alfred's letter as a source on learning in England in the ninth century', *Studies in Earlier Old English Prose*, ed. P. E. Szarmach (Binghamton, NY, 1986), 87–107, at 88–90; Dumville, 'King Alfred and the tenth-century reform of the English Church', 194; and Smyth, *Alfred the Great*, 559–66. D. A. Bullough, 'The educational tradition in England from Alfred to Ælfric: teaching *utriusque linguae*' (1972), reprinted in his *Carolingian Renewal: Sources and Heritage* (1991), 297–334, at 298–301, rightly stresses the significance of Alfred's determination to promote both Latin and the vernacular.

36 Alfred's remarks about education can be interpreted in relation to Asser's remarks about the king's educational programme. The school attended by Æthelweard and others (Asser, c. 75) is presumably the school which received a grant from the royal treasury (Asser, c. 102); but it would appear that special arrangements were made for Edward and Ælfthryth, and some others, within the king's household (Asser, cc. 75, 76).

37 Morrish, 'King Alfred's letter'. See also Smyth, *Alfred*, 549–53.

38 H. Gneuss, 'King Alfred and the history of Anglo-Saxon libraries' (1986), reprinted in his *Books and Libraries in Early England* (1996), no. III, 29–49, at 36–7; Dumville, 'King Alfred and the tenth-century reform of the English Church', 188, n. 14.

of Alfred's reign represent a new beginning, drawing under external influence on resources and traditions from outside his ancestral kingdom?[39] Was it a matter, in other words, of decline, collapse, and revival? Or might there have been a sense in which the Alfredian régime was able to draw on its own West Saxon inheritance – by no means a tradition of great scholarship and book production, but perhaps something more practical and down to earth, perhaps not seen by us, and perhaps not covered by the king's letter to his bishops?

Effective use has been made, in this connection, of the incompetent draftsmanship, dreadful Latinity, and inferior handwriting of the surviving corpus of single-sheet charters produced in the third quarter of the ninth century, in ways which strike me as one of the most compelling demonstrations of the value of charter evidence for purposes of cultural history, albeit, in this instance, of culture in decline.[40] The process reached its nadir with a notorious charter, dated 873, written by a Canterbury scribe who seems to have been challenged in most of those faculties which would have associated him with the rest of mankind.[41] (Professor Brooks characterized the scribe in question, with impeccable understatement, as a bit longsighted and forgetful; Professor Lapidge remarked, more directly, that the scribe's ignorance of Latin appears to have been total.) Where else, indeed, might one expect to find decent standards of literacy, if not at the metropolitan see of Canterbury?[42] I would not for a moment wish to challenge the construction that is put upon these wonderfully lamentable documents, but wish simply to register a plea that the evidence should be kept in perspective, lest we otherwise lose sight of some larger issues. The charter evidence adduced in support of the 'decline of learning' comes largely from Kent, notably from the archives of Christ Church, Canterbury, and applies (of course) to an aspect of pragmatic literacy in Latin. Yet a situation which obtained in the eastern extremity of Alfred's extended kingdom, albeit in the church of the successors of St Augustine, is not necessarily representative of the situation which might have obtained in what was regarded by contemporaries as the 'more important' western part of the kingdom;[43] or for that matter in the kingdom of the Mercians,[44]

---

[39] D. N. Dumville, 'English Square Minuscule script: the background and earliest phases', *Anglo-Saxon England,* 16 (1987), 147–79, at 155–69, esp. 156–8.

[40] See Brooks, 'England in the ninth century', 15–16; N. Brooks, *The Early History of the Church of Canterbury: Christ Church from 597 to 1066* (1984), 170–74, at 172; Dumville, 'English Square Minuscule script: the background and earliest phases', 156; and M. Lapidge, 'Latin learning in ninth-century England', in his *Anglo-Latin Literature 600–899* (1996), 409–54, at 446–54.

[41] BCS 536 (S 344), of which there are facsimiles in *The Making of England*, eds L. Webster and J. Backhouse (1991), 261 (no. 236), and Smyth, *Alfred*, pl. 20.

[42] Brooks, 'England in the ninth century', 16; *Church of Canterbury*, 172.

[43] For this distinction (Asser, c. 12), see further below, n. 53.

[44] The quality of Mercian charters produced in the central decades of the ninth century demands further consideration. BCS 524 (S 214) is a charter of King Burgred, dated 869, which is preserved in what would appear to be its original single-sheet form; see S. Keynes, 'Mercia and Wessex in the Ninth Century', *Mercia: an Anglo-Saxon Kingdom in Europe*, eds M. P. Brown and C. A. Farr (2001), 310–28.

and of course it would not necessarily apply to standards of literacy in the vernacular.[45]

I have argued elsewhere that a very distinctive diplomatic tradition can be recognized in ninth-century Wessex, which can be seen extending from the 830s into the early 870s, and that this tradition, and whatever it implies, should be distinguished from the separate arrangements which existed for the production of charters in Rochester and Canterbury.[46] It is apparent, moreover, that this 'West Saxon' tradition has a palaeographical dimension, in the sense that texts which belong to the tradition, extant in their original single-sheet form, are seen to have been written in a no less distinctive kind of script. The script has recently been characterized, by Dr Julia Crick, as a 'West Saxon minuscule', displaying features found already in the eighth-century hand of St Boniface, yet still found one hundred years later in an interesting group of texts, of which some are putatively 'West Saxon', and of which others are of origin unknown.[47] Specimens of this 'West Saxon minuscule' found in the documentary record comprise the work of three scribes: (i) a scribe who wrote the Wilton 839 endorsement on the archbishop's copy of the Kingston 838 agreement,[48] and the long, thin copy of the Kingston 838 agreement + Wilton 839 endorsement;[49] (ii) a scribe who wrote the æt Æstran 839 endorsements on the same two documents; and (iii) a scribe who wrote King Æthelwulf's charter for himself, dated 847 [= 846], which happens to be the earliest surviving original with a vernacular boundary clause, affording an instance, therefore, of Latin and vernacular texts occurring in association with each other.[50] Specimens in books include a ninth-century Southumbrian manuscript of Phillipus's Commentary on Job (Bodley 426), which has often been linked to these charters, and some ninth-century glosses to the eighth-century Blickling Psalter (New York, Pierpont Morgan Library, M.776).[51] The latest surviving and dated specimen of this type of script is the charter of King Æthelwulf for himself, issued in December 846, on which basis one might choose to associate the script with the second quarter of the ninth century, leaving plenty of time for decline in the decades which followed. It is the case,

---

45 See S. Kelly, 'Anglo-Saxon lay society and the written word', *The Uses of Literacy in Early Mediaeval Europe*, ed. R. McKitterick (1990), 36–62, at 46–8 and 52–7, stressing that the use of vernacular was pre-Alfredian. For pertinent comment on the situation, see D. N. Dumville, 'English libraries before 1066: use and abuse of the manuscript evidence', *Anglo-Saxon Manuscripts: Basic Readings*, ed. M. P. Richards (New York, 1994), 169–219, at 194–5, and Dumville, 'Motes and beams: two insular computistical manuscripts', *Peritia*, 2 (1983), 248–56, at 254–5.

46 S. Keynes, 'The West Saxon charters of King Æthelwulf and his sons', *EHR*, 109 (1994), 1109–49; see also *Charters of Shaftesbury Abbey*, ed. S. E. Kelly, Anglo-Saxon Charters 5 (1996), 17–18, and nos 3–6.

47 J. Crick, 'The case for a West Saxon minuscule', *Anglo-Saxon England*, 26 (1997), 63–79.

48 BCS 421 (S 1438, MS. 1).

49 BCS 421 (S 1438, MS. 3).

50 BCS 451 (S 298). For further details, see Keynes, 'West Saxon charters', 1112–14 and 1116–18.

51 See Crick, 'The case for a West Saxon minuscule'.

however, that the West Saxon charters continue with what I would regard as strength and purpose into the 850s and 860s; so, if only one or two of them had chanced to survive in their original form, we might well have had a continuation of stately 'West Saxon' minuscule to set up for comparison with the wretched specimens of demented chicken tracks from Kent.

It may be instructive at this point to dwell for a while on the nature of the kingdom represented by these 'West Saxon' charters of the 850s and 860s, in the period immediately preceding the accession of King Alfred the Great. The map (Fig. 20) depicts southern England in the ninth century, before the invention of the 'kingdom of the Anglo-Saxons' in the early 880s (and with apologies to the Viking fleet lost at sea off Swanage in 877). There is a basic distinction to be drawn between three separate political orders. First, a 'Mercian' polity, with its centre of power in the west midlands, not as yet a territorial unit divided into shires, but with influence presumed to extend eastwards to Lindsey, spreading over the constituent peoples known collectively as the Middle Angles, and reaching south-eastwards towards the fleshpots of London; though ecclesiastical, economic and political interests may have been beginning to encourage Londoners to look for leadership towards the king of the West Saxons.[52] Second, the kingdom of the East Angles, minding its own business in typical obscurity. And third, south of the Thames, the 'kingdom of the West Saxons and other southern peoples', being the notional combination of a 'more important' (*principalior*) western part, comprising the ancient shires of Wessex,[53] and an eastern part comprising the ancient political divisions of Surrey, Sussex, Kent and Essex. It was from his 'royal palace', at Wilton, where the West Saxon council had ratified the Kingston agreement in 839, that King Æthelwulf issued the so-called 'Decimation' charters in 854; but although he moved freely between the two parts of his kingdom, he made little attempt to merge them into one, and, in 856–8, had a document drawn up to record the intended division of the kingdom after his death.[54] Charters of the distinctively 'West Saxon' type continued to be issued in the period 858–71, in the names of King Æthelbald (858–60), King Æthelberht (860–65), and King Æthelred (865–71).[55] They are

---

[52] S. Keynes, 'The control of Kent in the ninth century', *Early Medieval Europe*, 2 (1993), 111–31, at 129–30.

[53] Asser, c. 12. For the view that Asser's distinction was between the eastern and western parts of Wessex, not between Wessex and the south-eastern provinces, see D. P. Kirby, *The Earliest English Kings* (1991), 201. For the view that *principalior* meant 'more royal', see J. Nelson, in R. Balzaretti, J. Nelson and J. R. Maddicott, 'Debate: Trade, industry and the wealth of King Alfred', *Past and Present*, 135 (1992), 142–88, at 163.

[54] The document itself is lost, but was mentioned by Asser, c. 16. A document described by Alfred as his father's will was read at a council at *Langandene* in 871 (Keynes and Lapidge, *Alfred*, 175).

[55] Keynes, 'West Saxon charters', 1118–31. BCS 504 (S 335), dated 862, and BCS 508 (S 336), dated 863, were drawn up in the name of King Æthelred, who did not become king until 865; but the charters are from different archives (respectively Abingdon and the Old Minster, Winches-

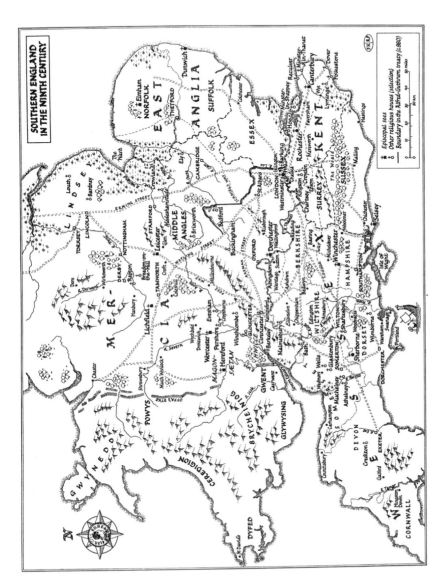

Fig. 20   Map of southern England in the ninth century

not documents of the greatest complexity, or diplomatic distinction, but nor are they indicative or symptomatic of a kingdom in a state of terminal decline. It may be difficult to assess the Latinity of these charters, or to make very much, linguistically, of the vernacular bounds, for the simple reason that the texts have been transmitted to us by much later copyists, at Abingdon, Shaftesbury, Glastonbury and Winchester; but further work on these texts may yet reveal some evidence of the distinctive usages of their draftsmen and scribes. There is no compelling evidence which might connect the charters with the scriptorium of one, or other, or both, of the episcopal sees in Wessex (Winchester and Sherborne); and there are various considerations, as opposed to evidence, which encourage the view that the charters were drawn up by priests in the service of the king at the West Saxon court.[56] Indeed, it is worth remarking that the charters transport us into a world dominated not so much by Winchester and Sherborne, or by the ecclesiastical powers which they represent (which is what might be expected by analogy with Kent), as by the shire towns where meetings of the king and his councillors were held, such as Wilton, Dorchester, Somerton and Southampton, and by royal estates, like Amesbury and Micheldever. Or so, at least, it seems to me. The essential point is, however, that several, perhaps even numerous, charters were issued in Wessex in the crucial third quarter of the ninth century; and that the continuity of what is so recognizably a 'West Saxon' diplomatic tradition, from the 830s into the 870s, suggests in turn that the use of the associated 'West Saxon minuscule', or something developed from it, might itself have extended all the way to the eve of King Alfred's accession in 871. It is most unfortunate, of course, that not one of these 'West Saxon' charters issued in the third quarter of the ninth century survives in its original form, to set beside Mercian and Kentish charters of the same period, or (and perhaps more to the point) to set *between* the 'West Saxon Minuscule' of the second quarter of the ninth century and the minuscule practised at Alfred's court in the 890s (represented by two contemporary manuscripts of the OE *Pastoral Care*). The point is, however, that the charters stand for a literate tradition in ninth-century Wessex which is all too easily overlooked.

My main purpose in this paper is to emphasize the existence of this West Saxon tradition of 'pragmatic' literacy in Latin and the vernacular, and to ask (no stronger than that) whether it might have contributed in any way to the programme of revival undertaken by Alfred in the late 880s. The problem, of course, is to ascertain whether the West Saxon tradition of pragmatic literacy reached forwards from the 860s, through the dark years of the 870s, and thence onwards into the 880s and beyond. Was the situation in Wessex, in the early 870s, quite as bleak as a literal reading of Alfred's letter might suggest? To what

---

ter), and tend therefore to support each other. Æthelred may have acted as a form of sub-king in Wessex, during Æthelberht's lifetime. For further discussion of S 335, see *Charters of Abingdon Abbey*, ed. S. E. Kelly, 2 vols, Anglo-Saxon Charters 7–8 (2000), no. 15.

[56] Keynes, 'West Saxon charters', 1131–4.

extent had there ever been a breach in tradition, necessitating something which approximated to a fresh start?[57] In some respects there can be no doubt that new influences were at work in Alfred's kingdom. We have people from Mercia, from Wales, and from the western and eastern Frankish kingdoms; we have inspiration from the Bible, from various other writings, and much else besides. Yet perhaps we should not forget that there were also some West Saxons at King Alfred's court. In King Alfred's law-code we have an ancient West Saxon tradition, not to mention an even more ancient but separate Kentish tradition, which merge in the 880s with an ostensibly 'Mercian' tradition, and with material derived from the Old and New Testaments. There are other features of the Alfredian polity which trace their origins back to the reign of King Æthelwulf (839–58), King Ecgberht (802–39), or King Ine (688–726). One thinks of shires, and other administrative or military arrangements; the network of royal estates and towns, and other aspects of the organized economy; the structure of the nobility, and other aspects of secular society; the response to Viking raids; and so on. Is it too much to ask, in these circumstances, whether there might have been any such continuity which might provide at least part of the background for the Alfredian use of the written word?

Michael Clanchy has stressed the contrast between the variety of documentation surviving from the post-Conquest period, and the pitiful scraps from Anglo-Saxon England.[58] It is important, none the less, to assess the Anglo-Saxon evidence in relation to different levels of literate activity at court, ranging from incidental manifestations of 'pragmatic' literacy, in the routine procedures of royal government, to the organized production of books. At the bottom level, it is clear that the use of the written word for utilitarian or practical purposes was widespread in the ninth century; and a particularly strong case can be made in respect of vernacular documents.[59] It is only appropriate, therefore, that when Alfred wished to make a point about readiness to follow the unfamiliar message contained in holy scripture, he devised an analogy involving readiness to follow the unknown intention represented by a lord's *ærendgewrit* and his seal, which depended in turn on the presumption that this method of communication was commonplace.[60] The analogy was presumably apposite in the 890s, and may or

---

[57] On the reform of script in the late ninth century, see Dumville, 'English Square minuscule script', 156–9, and D. N. Dumville, *A Palaeographer's Review: the Insular System of Scripts in the Early Middle Ages*, I, Kansai University, Institute of Oriental and Occidental Studies, Sources and Materials Series 20.1 (Suita, Osaka, 1999), 119–20.

[58] M. T. Clanchy, *From Memory to Written Record: England 1066–1307*, 2nd edn (1993), esp. 26–32 and 65–7.

[59] For a most effective exposition of the evidence, see Kelly, 'Anglo-Saxon lay society and the written word', 46–62.

[60] Keynes and Lapidge, *Alfred*, 141. At issue is Augustine's difficulty in renouncing familiar, worldly or tangible things in exchange for unfamiliar Christian concepts. Augustine remarks that if an unfamiliar thing was as familiar to him as something he could see, he would embrace the one and renounce the other. Reason is taken aback by this simplistic remark, remarking (in effect) that

may not have been so before. Unfortunately, written communications of the ephemeral kind would have had little or no chance of preservation; and as if it is not bad enough to have lost the letters exchanged between Alfred and Asser, or between Alfred and the patriarch, or the inventories of property at Congresbury and Banwell, or the letters despatched to Rome with the king's couriers,[61] we know nothing whatsoever of the routine messages, letters of appointment, and other administrative orders which must have passed from the centre to the localities. All that we have in its original form, from King Alfred's reign, is the will of Ealdorman Alfred, drawn up during the archiepiscopate of Æthelred, archbishop of Canterbury, and belonging, therefore, to the period 871 × 888.[62] The document is of singular historical importance not least because it is central to our understanding of the differences between bookland and folkland,[63] and it is of considerable linguistic interest as an example of a regional dialect in the late ninth century.[64] Nor should one overlook its potential significance as a physical object. Its script was cited by Professor Dumville in connection with the reformed minuscule of the *Pastoral Care* manuscripts (circulated in the early 890s); although, as he recognized, it could be five, ten or even fifteen years earlier, in which case 'it would be necessary to revise conventional wisdom in respect of late-ninth-century attempts to reform the Insular minuscule of southern England'.[65] It is no less significant that the hand of the main text, on the face, is different from the hand of the Canterbury witness-list, on the dorse; for this evidence of two-stage production suggests that the document might have been drawn up 'locally' and then ratified on a separate occasion by a scribe operating on behalf of the archbishop of Canterbury. No less important is the will of King Alfred himself, drawn up in his capacity as king of the West Saxons; interesting not least because it emerges that written copies of an earlier version of his will had been drawn up, distributed to various parties, and then taken back again and destroyed.[66]

---

if Augustine were to receive his lord's letter and seal (i.e. a message in written form, authenticated by an impression of a seal), instructing him to do something unfamiliar, he would have no difficulty in following the instruction, and would not stay put. For further discussion of Alfred's letter and seal, see also Clanchy, *Memory*, 31, 310 and 311–12.

[61] Asser, cc. 79, 81 and 91; *ASC, s.a.* 889.

[62] BCS 558 (S 1508), from BL Stowe Charter 20. For a facsimile of face and dorse, see W. B. Sanders, *Facsimiles of Anglo-Saxon Manuscripts*, 3 vols, Ordnance Survey (1878–84), iii. 20; for a facsimile of the face only (without the witness-list on the dorse), see *The Making of England*, eds Webster and Backhouse, 264 (no. 239).

[63] *EHD*, no. 97.

[64] See *The Oldest English Texts*, ed. H. Sweet, EETS OS 83 (1885), 451–3 (Charters, no. 45), and Harmer, *Documents*, 128–30 (cited as 'Kentish'). See also M. Gretsch, 'The language of the Fonthill Letter', *ASE*, 23 (1994), 57–102, at 76–7, for observations which extend its interest in relation to other documents preserved in their original form.

[65] Dumville, 'English Square Minuscule script', 157–8.

[66] BCS 553 (S 1507), recently edited in *Charters of the New Minster, Winchester*, ed. S. Miller, Anglo-Saxon Charters 9 (2000), no. 1. See also *The Making of England*, eds Webster and Backhouse, no. 240, with facsimile of the text in the *Liber Vitae* of the New Minster, Winchester.

It has to be admitted, on the other hand, that the king's Latin diplomas make a very poor showing for the 870s, and that while they reveal much about the cultural and political state of affairs at Alfred's court in the later 880s and 890s, the evidence as a whole falls a very long way short of what we should like for a reign of such importance.[67] Pity the monks of Athelney, and for that matter the nuns of Shaftesbury, who had to scrape the barrel for something which they could pass off as a foundation charter.[68] Why should this be so? Can it be that much of the evidence was destroyed by the Vikings? Or is it yet another manifestation of the decline of Latin learning? We should, I think, look at the paucity of West Saxon charters across the *whole* of the period from *c.* 860 to *c.* 925, and for an explanation which would account for the continuation of the phenomenon from Alfred's reign into that of Edward the Elder, when a crisis of literacy should not have been the problem. The answer may be, quite simply, that for various reasons fewer charters were produced in Alfred's reign, and that other factors conspired to reduce almost to nothing the chance that any would be preserved.[69] A profusion of charters would indicate that a king was selling land or privileges in order to raise money in the short term; a dearth of charters might well be capable of a similarly mechanistic explanation. Under the strained conditions which obtained in the late ninth and early tenth centuries, it may be that the natural inclination of those in positions of power (whether king, ealdorman, or sheriff) was to take estates of bookland into their own hands, and to retain them for purposes of their own; and one need not doubt that some religious houses lost out in this process, as well as laymen, for one reason or another.[70] It may be, moreover, that the kings (Alfred and Edward) were reluctant to dispense with the revenues which accrued to them from the enjoyment of their rights over folkland, and that accordingly they were less inclined than usual to create new estates of bookland. Of course it would still have been possible to transfer existing estates of bookland from one pair of hands to another, since older charters would suffice for that purpose, and, under special circumstances, to issue replacement charters for charters which had been lost; but there would have been little call for the conversion of folkland into bookland, and so for the

---

[67] See D. Whitelock, 'Some charters in the name of King Alfred', *Saints, Scholars and Heroes*, eds M. H. King and W. M. Stevens, 2 vols (Collegeville, MN, 1979) I, 77–98, and Keynes, 'West Saxon charters', 1134–41.

[68] For the alleged foundation charter for Athelney, see S. Keynes, 'George Harbin's transcript of the lost cartulary of Athelney abbey', *Proceedings of the Somerset Archaeological and Natural History Society*, 136 (1992), 149–59, at 155; and for that of Shaftesbury (S 357), see *Charters of Shaftesbury Abbey*, ed. Kelly, no. 7.

[69] For further discussion, see S. Keynes, 'Edward, King of the Anglo-Saxons', *Edward the Elder*, eds N. J. Higham and D. H. Hill (2001), 40–66.

[70] For further discussion, see R. Fleming, 'Monastic lands and England's defence in the viking age', *EHR*, 100 (1985), 247–65, and D. N. Dumville, 'Ecclesiastical lands and the defence of Wessex in the first viking age', in *idem, Wessex and England from Edgar to Alfred: Six Essays on Political, Cultural, and Ecclesiastical Revival* (1992), 29–54.

production of new charters. It is also possible under such strained conditions that laymen followed the example of their king in being less inclined to dispose of their property outside the immediate family,[71] and so had no need on their own account to procure charters converting folkland into bookland. One does wonder, moreover, whether political developments from the mid-920s onwards might have rendered many older title-deeds obsolete, leaving us only with random remnants of the earlier order. We should hesitate, therefore, before interpreting the scarcity of Alfredian charters as evidence of an incapacity to produce such charters in the first place.

From the almost non-existent low-grade documentary records of this kind we move up a gear, or two, to the king's law-codes. Pride of place, at least in a chronological sense, would appear to belong to the treaty between Alfred and Guthrum, assigned by historical convention to the late 880s,[72] pushed back by some commentators (for reasons which are tenable, though not compelling) to 878,[73] and by at least one other (for reasons which arise from reconsideration of numismatic evidence bearing on the status of London) to *c.* 880.[74] The text of the treaty is transmitted in a seemingly 'official' version, and in a seemingly 'local' variant form;[75] and if its existence presupposes that Alfred's government had some capacity for literate activity at the time of its production, it should be noted that both of the 'revisionist' dates place it some time before the Alfredian revival got under way. We then encounter the stately *domboc* itself: the product of deep thought, intensive research, and great political vision. The view that the *domboc* was drawn up (in or) after 893 depends simply on the fact that no mention of it was made by Asser, writing in that year;[76] but the possibility remains that it represented an aspect of the legal activity which is implicit in the

---

[71] See Keynes and Lapidge, *Alfred*, 309, n. 24.

[72] *EHD*, no. 34 (886–90), following F. M. Stenton, *Anglo-Saxon England*, 3rd edn (1971), 260–62; see also R. H. C. Davis, 'Alfred and Guthrum's Frontier' (1982), in his *From Alfred the Great to Stephen*, 47–54, and Keynes and Lapidge, *Alfred*, 171–2 and 311–13. See also *The Making of England*, eds Webster and Backhouse, no. 242, with facsimile.

[73] Dumville, 'The treaty of Alfred and Guthrum', in his *Wessex and England from Alfred to Edgar*, 1–27, at 13–23, followed by Wormald, *Making of English Law*, 286, n. 105. The principal reason given for the new dating (given that the conventional *termini* depend upon considerations which are less than secure) is the desirability of associating the extant treaty with a recorded act of peace-making; and the best option is the 'Treaty of Chippenham', made between Alfred and Guthrum in the immediate aftermath of the battle of Edington in 878 (*ASC*), sometimes known as the 'Treaty of Wedmore'.

[74] Keynes, 'King Alfred and the Mercians', 31–4. The consideration which in my view indicates a date in or after 880 is the fact that Guthrum acts 'for all the people who are in East Anglia', suggesting that the treaty was drawn up following Guthrum's departure from Cirencester in late 879 (*ASC*) and the settlement of his army in East Anglia (*ASC*, *s.a.* 880). Cf. Dumville, *Wessex and England*, 20, with the comments of Nicholas Brooks and Niels Lund reported in n. 97.

[75] Keynes, 'Royal government and the written word', 233–4; Wormald, *Making of English Law*, 285–6.

[76] Wormald, *Making of English Law*, 120–25, 281 and 286.

closing chapters of Asser's 'Life', and that it might therefore have been drawn up
c. 890.[77] It would be interesting indeed to know what these texts looked like in
their earliest forms: by whom were the copies made, by what agency were they
circulated, and to what use were they put by those who received them.

It quickly becomes self-evident, when we reach the summit, that the extraordinary programme of translations prepared under King Alfred's direction
presupposes the existence of an organized body or network of scribes, made
responsible for the production and multiplication of books; though whether all
books received the same treatment is obviously another matter. The arrangements which existed for the publication of the Old English *Pastoral Care*,
completed in or after 890 (appointment of Archbishop Plegmund) and before
896 (death of Bishop Swithwulf), or perhaps before the autumn of 892 (if
Alfred's expressed hope for 'peace enough' suggests that he was writing before
the hope was dashed by the return of the Danish army),[78] can, of course, be
reconstructed in fascinating detail, from a combination of explicit indications in
the surviving manuscripts themselves, complemented by more subtle and complex considerations arising from textual and palaeographical analysis.[79] Copies
of the translation are known to have been despatched to Archbishop Plegmund
(Canterbury), Bishop Swithwulf (Rochester), Bishop Wærferth (Worcester),
Bishop Hehstan (London), and Bishop Wulfsige (Sherborne). We may imagine
that other copies reached Bishop Denewulf (Winchester), Bishop Wulfred
(Lichfield), Bishop Alhheard (Dorchester), Bishop Wighelm (Selsey), and Bishop
Edgar (Hereford). Other religious houses in Alfred's kingdom may have received
copies of their own. It is far from clear, however, how all this activity was
organized. Asser referred in passing to King Alfred's scribes,[80] but did not
consider it his business to enlarge any further. In the verse preface to the OE
Pastoral Care, we read that Alfred translated the book into English, 'and sent me
south and north to his scribes [*writerum*]', commanding them 'to produce more
such (copies) from the exemplar [*be ðære bysene*], so that he could send them to
his bishops', because those who knew least Latin could do with a translation.[81]
It would appear to follow that the king used a dispersed network of scribes, and
that copies were distributed to various places for the production of further
copies, so that each of the ten bishops in the kingdom might receive one. Other
evidence suggests that there was a 'headquarters', where a master copy was kept

---

77 Asser, cc. 105–6; Keynes and Lapidge, *Alfred*, 39, 163 and 304.

78 Cf. Abels, *Alfred*, 232–3.

79 K. Sisam, 'The publication of Alfred's Pastoral Care', in his *Studies in the History of Old
English Literature* (1953), 140–47; N. R. Ker, as cited below, n. 82; D. M. Horgan, 'The relationship between the O.E. MSS. of King Alfred's translation of Gregory's *Pastoral Care*', *Anglia*, 91
(1973), 153–69; D. M. Horgan, 'The Old English *Pastoral Care*: the scribal contribution', *Studies*,
ed. Szarmach, 109–27; and R. Clement, 'The production of the Pastoral Care: King Alfred and his
helpers', *Studies*, ed. Szarmach, 129–52.

80 Asser, cc. 24–5.

81 Keynes and Lapidge, *Alfred*, 127.

or where the master copies were kept, and where a record was maintained of copies which had been made and despatched to their intended recipients. It is not immediately clear what this might signify: a network of scriptoria attached to religious houses in different parts of Alfred's extended kingdom, at Canterbury, Winchester, Sherborne, Worcester, and so on; or some form of central or royal writing-office, based at a particular royal estate, perhaps (though by no means necessarily) at Winchester, and linked in some way to other writing-offices at royal estates elsewhere; or a hybrid scheme, linking the court to particular churches and particular royal estates.

Two late ninth-century manuscripts of the OE *Pastoral Care* survived into modern times: Tiberius B. xi, in the library of Sir Robert Cotton, and Hatton 20, in the Bodleian Library at Oxford.[82] The Cotton manuscript would rate as the more important of the two, were it not for the fact that it was badly damaged in the fire at Ashburnham House in October 1731, and its remnants all but destroyed in a fire at the British Museum in July 1865.[83] Vital information about it can, however, be derived from surviving fragments of the manuscript itself, from a complete transcript of it made by Franciscus Junius in the seventeenth century, and from a description made by Humfrey Wanley in the early eighteenth century; all of which information has been brought together and most skilfully interpreted by Neil Ker.[84] The main text, which began on what would later become fol. 3, was written by one scribe (**A**), writing a large, elegant hand; now represented by a single leaf, carrying parts of chs 49–50, which was detached from the rest of the manuscript probably in the sixteenth or early seventeenth century, and which survives in Kassel. A second scribe (**B**), writing a smaller

---

[82] BL Cotton Tiberius B. xi, described by N. R. Ker, *Catalogue of Manuscripts Containing Anglo-Saxon* (1957), 257–9 (no. 195), and Oxford, Bodleian Library, MS. Hatton 20, described ibid., 384–6 (no. 324). For facsimiles, see *The Pastoral Care: King Alfred's Translation of St. Gregory's Regula Pastoralis*, ed. N. R. Ker, Early English Manuscripts in Facsimile 6 (Copenhagen, 1956).

[83] For the fire of 1731, see S. Keynes, 'The reconstruction of a burnt Cottonian manuscript: the case of Cotton MS. Otho A. I', *British Library Journal*, 22 (1996), 113–60, at 113–16. For the fire of 1865, see A. Prescott, '"Their present miserable state of cremation": the restoration of the Cotton library', *Sir Robert Cotton as Collector: Essays on an Early Stuart Courtier and his Legacy*, ed. C. J. Wright (1997), 391–454, at 419–21.

[84] *The Pastoral Care*, ed. Ker, esp. 12–15; Ker, *Catalogue*, no. 195. One small detail can be added to the story. In 1697 Humfrey Wanley wanted to establish 'the true Saxon character of King Alfred's time'; and, suspecting that the manuscript in the Bodleian Library might be of that period, needed to confirm his judgement by comparing its script with the script of what he presumed to be Archbishop Plegmund's copy in the Cottonian library. So he made arrangements for the engraver John Sturt to go to the Cottonian library, and to make a facsimile of the script in Tiberius B. xi: a continuous passage of a few lines, and a representative alphabet. See *Letters of Humfrey Wanley: Palaeographer, Anglo-Saxonist, Librarian 1672–1726*, ed. P. E. Heyworth (1989), 77–9. Alas, Sturt's facsimile does not survive; but in a plate of scripts in Hickes's *Thesaurus*, published in 1703–5, we find an alphabet from Tiberius B. xi placed above an alphabet from Hatton 20. The alphabet extends our knowledge of the script of the 'main' scribe (**A**) in Tiberius, otherwise represented by the Kassel leaf, and by the Preface in Hatton 20.

hand (represented only by miserable fragments), added the prose preface, on a separate bifolium placed at the beginning of the book, starting on the verso of fol. 1, ending half-way down verso of fol. 2, and leaving a blank space where the intended recipient of the copy would be named.[85] A third scribe (**C**) added the verse preface (on 2v). A vernacular note in yet another hand (**X**) was written on the recto of fol. 1, to the effect that copies of the manuscript had been given to Archbishop Plegmund, to Bishop Swithwulf (d. 893 × 896), and to Bishop Wærferth. The presence of such a note at the front of the book is taken (not unreasonably) to imply that this was a master copy of the manuscript, presumably kept at Alfred's 'headquarters', where scribes **A–C** were active. The copy despatched from HQ to Wærferth, bishop of Worcester, is, of course, that which survives to this day as Oxford, Bodleian Library, MS. Hatton 20.[86] Again, it is possible to get a detailed sense of the nature of the operation from Ker's close analysis of the manuscript, and what emerges is most intriguing. The text itself was written by two scribes, working in collaboration with each other. The first scribe (**D**) wrote the greater part of the text, in a hand characterized as 'unpractised' (with a number of 'experimental' letter forms, errors and corrections). The second scribe (**E**), writing a script which is better and more upright, took over for short passages, including the final page. Most interestingly, the prose preface was added on a bifolium placed at the beginning of the book, by the same scribe (**A**) who had written the main text of the Cotton manuscript; this scribe also made some contemporary corrections to main text as written by scribe (**D**). The verse preface, on 2v, was added by scribe (**D**), after some further practice.

When studied in relation to each other, the two *Pastoral Care* manuscripts are thus able to transport us into the midst of an organized team of at least six scribes, showing how they worked together and how they performed their appointed tasks with differing degrees of skill. The details can be reformulated in terms of each contributing member of the team: scribe (**A**) wrote the main text of the Cotton manuscript, made corrections to the text of the Hatton manuscript, and added the prose preface in the Hatton manuscript; scribes (**B**) and (**C**) added the prose and verse prefaces to the Cotton manuscript; scribe (**D**) wrote the main text of the Hatton manuscript, in collaboration with the rather superior scribe (**E**), and added the verse preface, thereby completing scribe (**A**)'s contribution. A sixth scribe (**X**) hovered behind them, keeping track their work. If two manuscripts produce evidence of at least six collaborating scribes, how many scribes might have been represented in ten manuscripts, or more? And this is just the OE *Pastoral Care*. There is one further point, which takes us back, in a sense, to the lowest level of literate activity. Neil Ker noted that the scribes involved in the production of the *Pastoral Care* manuscripts knew more or less what they were

---

[85] Fragments of the two leaves of the preface survive as BL Cotton Tiberius B. xi, fols 8 and 4 + 6, reproduced in *The Pastoral Care*, ed. Ker.

[86] *The Pastoral Care*, ed. Ker, 17–23; Ker, *Catalogue*, no. 324; *The Making of England*, eds Webster and Backhouse, no. 235.

doing, as if they had some experience in relatively undemanding tasks; but in his judgement (arising from the uneven quality of the membrane, the inconsistent arrangement of leaves in a quire, observable irregularities in pricking and number of lines, and variation in script), the scribes do not appear to have been well trained or much experienced in the procedures of book production. Ker suggested, therefore, that the production of the *Pastoral Care* manuscripts was an extension of the activity of scribes who had previously been engaged in producing charters.[87] One only wonders what charters Ker might have had in mind.

For as long as we continue to think in terms of a total collapse of literacy in the late ninth century, as something which is suggested by Alfred's remarks in the letter accompanying his translation of the OE *Pastoral Care*, and as something duly reflected in the atrocious quality of surviving single-sheet charters in the third quarter of the ninth century, then we shall continue to think in terms of a revival which owed everything to external influence, and to which any residual West Saxon tradition had rather little to contribute. There is no doubt that the West Saxons had much to learn from the Mercians;[88] and that, one suspects, is what the kingdom of the Anglo-Saxons was all about. There is also no doubt that the English had much to learn from the Continent, as has been shown by Michael Wallace-Hadrill, Janet Nelson, Anton Scharer, and many others.[89] No one could deny the potential significance, at Alfred's court, of Grimbald of Saint-Bertin and John the Old Saxon: after all, Grimbald and John must have been prominent among those who brought books from the Continent to England in the 880s,[90] and it was through their teaching that the king's outlook (*ingenium*) was (in Asser's tantalizing phrase) 'very considerably broadened'.[91] I am simply wishing, however, to put two propositions side by side: that West Saxon practices should not be judged, in the ninth century, by Kentish evidence; and that the Alfredian programme of the late 880s and 890s must have involved quite an extaordinary amount of scribal activity, which cannot have come out of the blue. It was Neil Ker's suggestion that the scribes of King Alfred's writing-office had learnt their trade doing charters; and it seems to me that the West Saxon diplo-

---

[87] *The Pastoral Care*, ed. Ker, 19.

[88] Cf. Keynes, 'The reconstruction of a burnt Cottonian Manuscript: the case of Cotton MS. Otho A. I', 141.

[89] See, in particular, Wallace-Hadrill, *Early Germanic Kingship in England and on the Continent*; 124–51; J. L. Nelson, 'A king across the sea: Alfred in continental perspective' (1986), 'Reconstructing a royal family: reflections on Alfred from Asser, Chapter 2' (1991), and 'The Franks and the English in the ninth century reconsidered' (1997), all reprinted in her *Rulers and Ruling Families in Early Medieval Europe: Alfred, Charles the Bald, and Others* (1999), nos I, III and VI; and Scharer, 'The writing of history at King Alfred's court'.

[90] Keynes and Lapidge, *Alfred*, 265, n. 195; Dumville, 'English Square Minuscule script', 154–5.

[91] Asser, c. 78. For Grimbald, see above, n. 24. For John the Old Saxon, see M. Lapidge, 'Some Latin Poems as Evidence for the Reign of King Athelstan' (1981), reprinted in his *Anglo-Latin Literature 900–1066* (1993), 49–86, at 60–71; see also D. Howlett, *British Books in Biblical Style* (Dublin, 1997), 493–504, esp. 497.

matic tradition, taken in conjunction with a residual Mercian tradition and a revived Kentish tradition, give us a fair impression of where they had come from, and of what they were bringing together.

Where does this leave us? I have emphasized the extent to which the Alfredian régime depended for the advancement of its purposes on exploiting the power of the written word: represented by the charters, the treaty, the law-code, the *Chronicle*, Asser's *Life*, the translations, and so on. This is hardly controversial, though it should be recognized that it is distinctively *Alfredian*, and not a matter of chance. I have suggested, in addition, that the notion that Alfred's use of the written word depended on a *revival* of literacy in the late 880s, which drew its strength from *outside* Wessex and Kent, should perhaps be modified, in order to take account of the possibility that there may have been a significant degree of dependence on practices which were deep rooted in Wessex, if largely unseen. Yet what of the organizing principle behind all this activity in court circles, and what of its driving force? The Alfred we need to leave behind is the Alfred who, having fought his way through the 870s, was so busy in the 880s that he had to wait until the 890s before he could begin to indulge himself in a bit of reading and writing. The temptation we must resist is to stand back and admire a multiplicity of 'different' Alfreds, as if he were a king with a series of different identities: the soldier, the law-maker, the statesman, the educator, and the scholar, not to mention the ship-builder, the candleclock-maker, the hypochondriac, and so on. The genuine Alfred of the late ninth century was not Alfred the Great, but the integrated Alfred, for whom all these things were inseparable aspects of his determination to discharge the responsibilities of his high office for the good of his subjects and in the service of God.

Chapter 11

Alfred's coinage reforms in context

Mark Blackburn

The development of the monetary system was one of the first aspects of government to attract Alfred's attention. By the end of the first decade of his reign, he
had effected two radical reforms, restoring the fineness of the coinage and
expanding the mint network, while introducing a new weight standard, new
classical designs and a new denomination, the halfpenny. These were achievements indeed in a period when for much of the time his kingdom was under
attack or threat of attack from Viking invaders.

The classic account of Alfred's coinage is that of Dolley and Blunt,[1] but
subsequent work, based in part on new finds, has led to a revision of the
chronology and of some mint attributions, indicating that the Vikings did not
have control of London in the years prior to Alfred's 'restoration' of the city in
886 and prompting a somewhat different interpretation of the coinage reforms.
Even since the review of 1998,[2] further new finds have been made which have
led to a modification of our ideas on some points. These will be considered
below, but the main purpose of this paper is to take a longer view of the
development of the coinage during the ninth and tenth centuries, and so to assess
Alfred's contribution to it. By way of preamble, it should be said that before
Domesday Book there is very little documentary evidence for the way in which
the monetary system operated. What follows is drawn almost entirely from an
interpretation of the surviving coins, evidence which is surprisingly rich and
happily growing year by year.

Ninth-century Background

The basic monetary framework in England had been developed in the seventh
and eighth centuries, and owed much to Frankish precedent, although there were

---

[1] R. H. M. Dolley and C. E. Blunt, 'The chronology of the coins of Ælfred the Great 871–
99', in *Anglo-Saxon Coins. Studies presented to F. M. Stenton,* ed. R. H. M. Dolley (1961),
77–95.

[2] M. Blackburn, 'The London mint in the reign of Alfred', in *Kings, Currency and Alliances.
History and Coinage of Southern England in the Ninth Century,* eds M. A. S. Blackburn and D. N.
Dumville (1998), 105–23; S. Keynes, 'King Alfred and the Mercians', in *Kings, Currency and
Alliances,* eds Blackburn and Dumville, 1–45, esp. 14–18 and 29–30.

significant differences.[3] In the early ninth century the currency in England comprised a single denomination – the silver penny – which was struck at a handful of mints located in major commercial centres with access to international trade (that is, Canterbury, Rochester, London, York and probably Ipswich).[4] Intermittently there was also a mint in Wessex, probably at Southampton or Winchester, although in terms of output it was of secondary importance.[5] The fact that the main mints were located in the east or south-east of the country in part reflects a long-term monetary trend – throughout the Middle Ages more coinage was available in those regions than in the west and north – but the distribution of mints was also influenced by their proximity to the ports that brought in continental silver, which was the principal source of metal for the coinage. Since the later eighth century, it seems to have been obligatory for foreign coins to be reminted into local money before they could be used in England. And here lay the fundamental reason for royal interest in the coinage: a fee of between 5 per cent and 25 per cent would have been charged for minting, the profits from which could be a significant source of revenue for the crown.[6] The existence of a sound currency would, of course, also have facilitated government – the collection of tithes, tolls, taxes and fines – as well as the economy generally.

In a well-managed monetary system it was desirable to have a uniform currency that could circulate freely throughout all parts of the state, although at times local interests might conspire against this to encourage regional currency areas and reminting with a distinctive local coin design. The classic example of a uniform currency was that established by Charlemagne (768–814) and Louis the Pious (814–40). In a monetary reform of *c.* 794 Charlemagne had succeeded in establishing one uniform coinage for the whole Carolingian kingdom – some forty mints from Pisa to Dorestadt and from Mainz to Rennes were producing coins of more or less identical design and of the same weight and fineness. In 822/3 Louis the Pious gave the principle its ultimate expression by dropping the name of the mint from the coin inscription and replacing it with a standard formula, *'Christiana religio'*, so that even today numismatists find it impossible

---

[3] P. Grierson and M. Blackburn, *Medieval European Coinage 1. The Early Middle Ages (5th–10th Centuries)* (1986), especially chs 8 and 10.

[4] C. E. Blunt, C. S. S. Lyon and B. H. I. H. Stewart, 'The coinage in southern England, 796–840', *British Numismatic Journal,* 32 (1963), 1–74; H. E. Pagan, 'Coinage in southern England, 796–874', in *Anglo-Saxon Monetary History*, ed. M. A. S. Blackburn (1986), 45–65.

[5] See discussion below, pp. 208–12.

[6] There is no evidence for the level of minting fees in the ninth century, but 5 per cent (one shilling in the pound) was a typical fee in England in the later Middle Ages, while in the later tenth and eleventh centuries it has been estimated that it may have been as high as 25 per cent; C. E. Challis (ed.), *A New History of the Royal Mint* (1992), 132–5; C. S. S. Lyon, 'Variations in currency in late Anglo-Saxon England', in *Mints, Dies and Currency. Essays Dedicated to the Memory of Albert Baldwin*, ed. R. A. G. Carson (1971), 101–20, esp. 118; C. S. S. Lyon, 'Some problems in interpreting Anglo-Saxon coinage', *ASE*, 5 (1976), 173–224, at 205–8.

to distinguish between the products of many of the mints in this coinage.[7] The hoards show how easily the coinage moved across the Empire,[8] and it is fair to say that such a large common currency in Europe was only achieved again with the introduction of Euro coins in 2002. On the Continent Charlemagne's ideal of a single currency was lost after 840 as power was fragmented following the division of the Empire between Louis's four sons.[9] In England the reverse was the case, for the ninth and tenth centuries saw steps being taken towards the establishment of a strong unified currency, a state that was finally achieved by Edgar in the 970s.[10] A phrase in the law-code III Edgar ch. 8, and reiterated later, reflects this aspiration: 'one coinage shall be current throughout all the king's realm, and no-one shall refuse it'.

After Offa's reform of the 760s, most Anglo-Saxon coins carried the name of the king, the few exceptions being those struck under episcopal rights granted by the crown. However, although the king was the source of authority for all minting, it is debatable what degree of control the court exercised over it in practice. The moneyers were surely licensed by the crown and standards of weight and fineness must have been prescribed centrally, yet in other respects they seem to have enjoyed a degree of independence. Many of the coin designs were personal to particular moneyers, and there was little attempt to bring uniformity to the appearance of the coinage during most of Offa's reign.[11] After a further reform in *c*. 792 the obverse was more or less standardized on three lines of inscription, although there was still some latitude in the choice of reverse designs. More significantly, it is clear that moneyers were *not* royal officials appointed from people close to the court. In the late eighth and earlier ninth centuries, when control of Kent and East Anglia switched repeatedly between Mercian or West Saxon and local rulers, the mints continued to operate without significant interruption and the same moneyers worked for successive rival kings.[12] From this we can infer that the moneyers were not political appointees, but local people probably of some stature among the commercial community. Indeed the very location of the principal mints in or near ports facing the Channel or North Sea implies that the coinage was economically, rather than politically, driven.

That certain aspects of the coin designs were laid down is evident from the coin inscriptions. We find that the form of the king's name is more standardized

[7] S. Coupland, 'Money and coinage under Louis the Pious', *Francia*, 17/1 (1990), 23–54.

[8] Coupland, 'Money and coinage', 34–5.

[9] D. M. Metcalf, 'A sketch of the currency in the time of Charles the Bald', in *Charles the Bald: Court and Kingdom*, eds M. T. Gibson and J. L. Nelson (2nd edn, 1990), 65–97.

[10] K. Jonsson, *The New Era. The Reformaton of the Late Anglo-Saxon Coinage* (Stockholm, 1987).

[11] C. E. Blunt, 'The coinage of Offa', in *Anglo-Saxon Coins*, ed. Dolley, 39–62.

[12] The point is well illustrated by Tables 3.1 and 3.2 in I. Stewart, 'The London mint and the coinage of Offa', *Anglo-Saxon Monetary History*, ed. Blackburn, 27–43. Many examples from later reigns could also be given.

than that of the moneyer and sometimes it is in a different dialect, as Bibire has shown.[13] For example, the coins of Berhtwulf of Mercia (840–52), which were struck at London, invariably spell the king's name BERHTVVLF or -VLF, with Anglian smoothing of the first element which is indicative of a Mercian or Northumbrian dialect, whereas none of the eleven moneyers' names on the reverses shows any sign of Anglian smoothing, and where the form is diagnostic it is always in what appears to be a Kentish dialect. This implies that the die-cutter was given a model which included the obverse inscription defined by the Mercian court, but for the moneyer's name he drew on his own native Kentish or London dialect. Little is known about the dialect used in London during the Anglo-Saxon period – indeed the coins may be the only evidence to survive.

While there was some central regulation of the coinage during the first half of the ninth century, there was still considerable variety in the designs and appearance of the coins – not only as between different mints but even between moneyers of the same mint. By the late tenth century, however, the monetary system was completely different.[14] The currency was very uniform: a standard design was used by all moneyers and at all mints, now vastly increased in number and distributed throughout England. The coinage was systematically withdrawn and replaced by a new type every few years. It had become a highly sophisticated fiscal tool, closely managed from the centre. The changes had come in stages over the preceding 150 years, and the reforms of Alfred's reign played a significant role. But the process had gathered momentum in the mid-ninth century, under Alfred's father, Æthelwulf (839–58), and brothers, Æthelberht (858/60–65) and Æthelred I (865–74).

Monetary reorganizations were often accompanied or implemented by a complete recoinage (*renovatio moneta*), although there could be other purely economic or fiscal reasons for renewing the currency. If one looks at the pattern of recoinages over the Anglo-Saxon period (Fig. 21), it is clear that before Edgar's reform these were unusual. There had been only one in the seventh century and two in the eighth century, yet there were no less than five recoinages between 850 and 880, after which there was not another in England for almost a century. The period 850–80 thus stands out as one of intense activity. The reason for this series of recoinages is not entirely clear. One factor was economic conditions. There appears to have been a silver shortage in western Europe indicated by a debasement of coinage of Northumbria from the 820s, and in the West Frankish kingdom and southern England from the 840s.[15] Just as the West Frankish debasement was brought to an end by Charles the Bald's major recoinage

---

[13] P. Bibire, 'Moneyers' names on ninth-century Southumbrian coins: philological approaches to some historical questions', in *Kings, Currency and Alliances*, eds Blackburn and Dumville, 155–66.

[14] Challis (ed.), *A New History*, 49–68.

[15] D. M. Metcalf and J. P. Northover, 'Coinage alloys from the time of Offa and Charlemagne to *c.* 864', *Numismatic Chronicle*, 149 (1989), 101–20.

Fig. 21   Recoinages in Wessex and Mercia

of 864, so some of the English recoinages of this period were clearly attempts to restore the fineness of the coinage which could not be maintained.[16] Even if this was a significant motivation for the recoinages, as indeed it was for Edgar's *c.* 973, it is evident that the opportunity was also taken to reform or develop the mint administration.

Some moves had already been taken by Offa and his successor Cenwulf (796–821) to bring greater uniformity in coin design among moneyers, for example, in Cenwulf's *Tribrach* type or his *Portrait-Cross and Wedges* type at Canterbury, but this was not sustained. The first time a single design was imposed on all moneyers at the two most active West Saxon mints, Canterbury and Rochester, was in Æthelwulf's *Doribi-Cant* type in the later 840s (Fig. 22, no. 1). Æthelwulf used the imaginative device of a monogram of the letters DORIBI, which could stand for both *Dorobernia* (Canterbury) and *Dorobrevia* (Rochester). His succeeding *Inscribed Cross* type (Fig. 22, no. 2) in the early or mid-850s likewise standardized the type at both mints, and provided a related design for the use of Archbishop Ceolnoth.[17] Similarly, the *Floriate Cross* issue (Fig. 22, no. 3), although surviving today in very small numbers, appears to have provided Wessex with a uniform currency in the early 860s. The designs were so consistent, being executed by a single die-cutter, that after the mid-850s we are unable to distinguish the output of Rochester, if indeed it remained an active mint.

That changes were afoot during the mid-ninth century is also indicated by a sharp increase in the number of moneyers operating at Canterbury and Rochester (Table 11.1). From a stable base of six to eight moneyers in the first four decades of the century, the number doubled in Æthelwulf's reign, and more than doubled again under Æthelberht. Pagan has suggested that this last increase might have been intended to facilitate a recoinage called not at the beginning but a few years into the *Inscribed Cross* issue.[18] This would be unusual, for the

---

[16] D. M. Metcalf and J. P. Northover, 'Debasement of the coinage in southern England in the age of King Alfred', *Numismatic Chronicle*, 145 (1985), 150–76.

[17] Opinions vary on the date for the introduction of the *Inscribed Cross* (or *Open Cross*) type and the weight to be attached to the moderate discontinuity of moneyers at its inception: C. S. S. Lyon, 'Historical problems of Anglo-Saxon coinage (2). The ninth century', *British Numismatic Journal*, 37 (1968), 216–38, at 229; Pagan, 'Coinage in southern England', 57–60.

[18] Pagan, 'Coinage in southern England', 59–60.

Table 11.1   Number of moneyers at Canterbury and Rochester

Date	No. of moneyers (approx.)
c. 800	6
c. 825	8
c. 840	8
c. 845	12
c. 855	14
c. 860	35
c. 870	20
c. 890	12

introduction of a new type was normally an inherent part of a *renovatio moneta*. Other reasons for an increase in minting activity can be suggested, such as a growth in continental trade, but we should not assume that an increase in moneyers would have been reflected in a comparable growth in mint-output. Die-studies of these coinages through which we might test this have yet to be carried out (indeed for some issues too few coins are available), but the evidence of single finds suggests that the size of the currency may have been stable or even declining in this period. If this is borne out, it would imply that the recruitment or licensing of additional moneyers under Æthelwulf and Æthelberht was not prompted by economic necessity but resulted from a fundamental reorganization of the mints in the mid-ninth century. The two are not mutually exclusive. Economic expansion can, of course, prompt an administrative reorganization, as undoubtedly occurred at London in the 860s when the complement of moneyers grew from one to some thirty, following a decade or so when the mint was barely active.[19] By merely relaxing the quota on the number of moneyers allowed at the mints, the king could have increased his revenue from fixed fees and the supply of dies,[20] even if for some it may have transpired that the business of minting was not profitable enough to make it worthwhile.

The recoinage in Wessex of *c.* 867 marked another major development. By adopting the Mercian *Lunettes* type, which had been struck by Burgred (852–74) since the 850s, Æthelred I was establishing a monetary union between the two kingdoms. As well as standardizing the type, there also seems to have been

---

[19] H. E. Pagan, 'Coinage in the age of Burgred', *British Numismatic Journal*, 34 (1965), 11–27.

[20] We have no evidence from the ninth century to indicate the way in which moneyers accounted for their receipts from minting, but Domesday Book shows that in the eleventh century it was through a combination of fixed fees, farms (that is, an estimate of likely annual income), and possibly direct accounting for revenue; P. Grierson, 'Domesday Book, the geld *de moneta* and *monetagium*: a forgotten minting reform', *British Numismatic Journal*, 55 (1985), 84–94.

an agreement to introduce a new alloy with a higher tin content.[21] Although previously West Saxon, Mercian and even East Anglian coins had mixed freely, there was now a common uniform currency circulating between Chester and Dover, Exeter and Lincoln, based on coins that were being produced almost exclusively at the south-eastern mints of London and Canterbury. The Anglo-Saxons were thus moving ever closer to the classic monetary system implemented by Charlemagne and Louis the Pious, but ironically now lost in the Frankish world.

Dramatic monetary changes had therefore been taking place in the lead-up to Alfred's accession. The benefits of a uniform currency were appealing to the West Saxon kings, and in the process Æthelwulf and his sons had found it necessary to reform the administration of the mints. The substantial increase in the number of moneyers and the closer control of them evident from the imposition of uniform coin designs suggest a change in their relationship with the king. In this process, one of the most important features of the moneyer's contract, the way in which he accounted for minting profits, may well have come under scrutiny too. One suspects that in this period the kings were not only trying to make coin circulation more efficient, for the benefit of trade and the convenience of government, but were also seeking to maximize their revenue from the mints. Increasingly the coinage was becoming a fiscal tool, and the initiatives started under Æthelwulf and extended by his sons Æthelberht and Æthelred would be built upon by Alfred and his successors.

Alfred's Two Recoinages

Alfred's principal monetary reforms were initiated during the first ten years of his reign, in which period he effected two comprehensive recoinages, the main features of which are summarized in Table 11.2. The first, in *c.* 875, must have been very demanding both economically and politically. The *Lunettes* type that he had inherited in 871 and continued in his earliest years was struck to standards of fineness and weight that were far lower than those set by Offa at the end of the eighth century. The reason for the weakening of the coinage has often been attributed to the effects of the Viking campaign in England, especially after 865, but, as indicated above, it now appears that western Europe had been experiencing a general shortage of silver which prompted a debasement of the coinages. Charles the Bald had restored the quality of the West Frankish coinage in 864, and Alfred followed suit a decade later though by then the task was much greater. There was five times more silver in a new *Cross-and-Lozenge* coin than in one of the poor *Lunettes* coins that these replaced. So for every five or even six pennies brought in by people they would receive one new one in exchange.

---

[21] Metcalf and Northover, 'Debasement', 161–3, 165.

Table 11.2   Principal monetary developments during Alfred's reign

---

Recoinage of c. *875*

- initial restoration of the weight and fineness of the penny to *c.* 1.35 g and 95 per cent fine
- new classical designs
- expansion of the mint network connected with or anticipating the establishment of the burghal system
- a reduction in the number of moneyers?
- continued monetary alliance with Mercia

Recoinage of c. *880*

- establishment of a new heavier weight standard for the penny at *c.* 1.6 g
- introduction of a new halfpenny denomination
- special issues at Mercian mints (London, Gloucester and Oxford) to mark Alfred's assumption of control
- further expansion of mint network (and continuing)

Prices at market would have adjusted rapidly, but one wonders how easily people would have coped with a five-fold revaluation of the penny in the case of payments stipulated in contracts and leases, penalties laid down by law, or outstanding debts. Political historians should thus be aware of the strength of government exercised by Alfred in implementing this recoinage, as early as the mid-870s, surely one of the most difficult periods of his reign. The second recoinage, in *c.* 880, was less radical economically, involving only a 20 per cent increase in the weight of the penny. The fact that there are no documentary references to 'new pennies' in either of these periods, surely reflects a dearth of surviving records rather than a heavy reliance on oral transactions.

Before deciding on a simple restoration of Offa's standards of *c.* 1.35 g and *c.* 95 per cent fine silver in *c.* 875, Alfred appears to have toyed with the alternative idea of moving to the current Carolingian weight standard of *c.* 1.75 g, for a unique surviving coin of a transitional *Geometric-Quatrefoil* type is struck at this weight.[22] Some five years later, in his second recoinage, Alfred turned his attention once again to an adjustment in the weight standard, this time increasing it not to the full Carolingian standard but to an intermediate *c.* 1.6 g. This was to remain the theoretical standard for the penny in Wessex and Mercia until Edgar's monetary reform. Interestingly, when Viking coinages were established in the Southern Danelaw in the 880s and the Northern Danelaw in the 890s, they opted for the previous 1.35 g standard, presumably as this was the

---

[22] M. Blackburn and S. Keynes, 'A corpus of the *Cross-and-Lozenge* and related coinages of Alfred, Ceolwulf II and Archbishop Æthelred', in *Kings, Currency and Alliances,* eds Blackburn and Dumville, 125–50, at 130.

system familiar to the indigenous Anglian populations there. It is possible that Alfred's reform of *c.* 880 was part of a general revision of weights and measures, in which case one might hope to find signs of a different system in use in the Danelaw from that elsewhere in England.

The penny had been the sole denomination in England since its introduction in the seventh century. In Francia a half-denier or 'obol' had been produced since Pepin the Short's reform of *c.* 755, but nothing similar was adopted here until Alfred's second recoinage of *c.* 880. Then halfpennies corresponding in design to the current pennies, but smaller in size and of half the weight, were produced for the first time. They are very scarce today, probably because smaller denominations are not normally hoarded as savings, but their counterparts from mints in the Danelaw copying Alfred's halfpennies are more prolific. Because these were struck to the lighter Danelaw standard, they were for a time mistakenly regarded as one-third pennies.[23] Halfpennies continued to be produced for about a century, but they were superseded, after Edgar's monetary reform, by a new practice of simply cutting pennies into halves and quarters to provide small change.

Ninth-century coin designs were on the whole fairly stylized. There was considerable variety and originality in the choice of geometric types which occupied the reverse and occasionally the obverse of coins, but the portrait side was essentially a crude reworking of a bust that had strayed far from its classical origins. To find, as we do in Alfred's reign, and within a period of just five years (*c.* 875–80), a series of new coin types where elements of the design have been deliberately and carefully copied directly from Roman coin prototypes is quite extraordinary.[24] Some of the geometric reverse designs that accompany these were also carefully chosen, borrowing elements from Offa's and Æthelwulf's coinages. There must have been someone in Alfred's court with a flair for coin design and a particular interest in Roman coins, which would have turned up in hoards then, just as they do today. One wonders whether this same individual inspired the comment recorded in the *Anglo-Saxon Chronicle s.a.* 418 that 'In this year the Romans collected all their treasures which were in Britain and hid some in the ground ... '. This interest in Roman Imperial coinage is another indication of the cultural sophistication of Alfred and his court.

Apart from the changes of weight and fineness, Alfred's reign is most notable for initiating an expansion of the mint network. The classic pattern of mints located at or near the east-coast ports was broken. At the beginning of Alfred's reign, in the *Lunettes* coinage, we can recognize just two mints operating in Wessex and Mercia – Canterbury and London. During the short second phase of the coinage (*c.* 875–80) at least four further mints appear – Winchester, one at another location in Wessex, one in southern Mercia (Oxford?) and one in north-west Mercia, perhaps at Chester. During the last two decades of the reign

---

[23] P. Grierson, 'Halfpennies and third-pennies of King Alfred', *British Numismatic Journal*, 28 (1955–7), 477–93.

[24] Blackburn, 'The London mint', 113–14.

(c. 880–99) mint-signed issues attest mints at Exeter and Gloucester as well as Canterbury, London and Oxford, and non-mint-signed issues imply the existence of several others the locations of which are uncertain. By the year 900 there were at least nine established mints and possibly a few more. The process of expansion was continued by Alfred's successors.[25] Edward the Elder doubled that number to at least seventeen mints, and Athelstan brought it to almost thirty (even more if you add the mints in the reconquered Danelaw). There was a close connection between boroughs and mints: each borough was entitled to operate a mint, though not all did so. The logic was that a mint, like the tolls received from the operation of a market, could provide a revenue to help maintain the borough. The expansion of the mint network, then, had a parallel in the establishment of the new fortified towns or boroughs.[26]

In the Danelaw under Viking rule there were radical monetary changes taking place from the 880s onwards, with new mints producing large coinages and a currency that was quite distinct from that of Wessex and Mercia. In terms of the broad economic development of England, the Danelaw coinages are highly significant, although they will not be considered here.[27]

Continuity at the West Saxon Mint(s)

In 1998 it was argued that the Winchester mint was opened in the mid-870s following a break in minting of some thirty-five years in Wessex proper.[28] This appears to coincide with Alfred's replanning of the city, which on archaeological evidence Biddle dates to around 880.[29] Two coins have since come to light to bridge that thirty-five year period of inactivity, and suggest that there may have been a greater degree of continuity in minting than had hitherto been suspected.

Most coins of West Saxon kings were struck for them in the sub-kingdom of Kent, at Rochester or Canterbury. In Wessex itself coinage was thought to have been produced in three discrete periods. During the first half of the eighth century a prolific coinage of the small early pennies ('sceattas') was struck in Hamwic, where they have also been found in large numbers.[30] At the turn of the

[25] C. E. Blunt, B. H. I. H. Stewart and C. S. S. Lyon, *Coinage in Tenth-Century England* (1989), ch. 3.

[26] M. Blackburn, 'Mints, burhs and the Grateley code, cap. 14.2', in *The Defence of Wessex. The Burghal Hidage and Anglo-Saxon Fortifications*, eds D. Hill and A. R. Rumble (1996), 160–75, at 162–5.

[27] M. Blackburn, 'Expansion and control: aspects of Anglo-Scandinavian minting south of the Humber', in *Vikings and the Danelaw*, ed. J. Graham-Campbell et al. (2001), 125–42.

[28] Blackburn and Keynes, 'A corpus', 143.

[29] M. Biddle, 'The study of Winchester: archaeology and history in a British town, 1961–83', *PBA,* 69 (1983), 93–135, at 119–23.

[30] D. M. Metcalf, 'The coins', in *The Coins and Pottery from Hamwic*, ed. P. Andrews, Southampton Finds 1 (1988), 17–59.

century a small coinage was struck for Beorhtric (786–802), known today from three extant specimens, and during a third phase of activity spanning perhaps the late 820s to early 840s, coins were produced for Ecgberht (802–39) and Æthelwulf. Ecgberht's coins were of two types.[31] One with a monogram of SAXON in the obverse field, completing the legend +*Ecgberht rex Saxon(iorum)*, was struck by at least five moneyers (Beornehart, Bosa, Ifa, Tideman and Tilred), while the second type, with the full *Saxoniorum* in three lines, is known for one moneyer (Eanwald). Of Æthelwulf only a single coin from the West Saxon mint was known, also by the moneyer Eanwald, with a slightly different SAXON monogram on the obverse and a cross-and-wedges design on the reverse (Fig. 22, no. 5).[32] This issue was seen as a continuation of Ecgberht's coinage, and dated 839–c. 843,[33] although the cross-and-wedges reverse design could suggest an association with the period c. 843–8 when Rochester used this device.

A second specimen of Æthelwulf's *Saxon* type by a new moneyer Osric (Fig. 22, no. 6) came on the market in 1996, and has been acquired by Stewart Lyon.[34] The legends read:

Obv. +AEÐELVVLF REX, around SAXON monogram
Rev. +OS•RI•C MONETA (NE ligatured), cross and four wedges.
Weight 1.26 g. Die-axis 180°.

The letter forms and style of die-cutting generally are similar to those of the other specimen. Osric may have been a successor to Eanwald, rather than his contemporary, but there is no stylistic reason to think that the coins are far apart in date.

The other new coin is a penny of Æthelred I's rare *Four-Line* type, by the same moneyer Osric (Fig. 22, no. 7). It was found more than twenty years ago, on 3 October 1979, by Jeremy de Montfalcon at Stanmore, Hants. He had shown the coin shortly after that at the British Museum, but it has never been published, save that it is the basis for a mistaken entry in the second edition (1980) of North's *English Hammered Coinage*, where Osric is said to be known as a moneyer in Æthelred I's *Lunettes* type.[35] Through the good offices of Dr Gerald Dunger, in 1999 the coin was reported to the Corpus of Early Medieval Coin

[31] C. E. Blunt, 'The coinage of Ecgbeorht, king of Wessex, 802–39', *British Numismatic Journal*, 28 (1955–7), 467–76, at 474–5.

[32] R. H. M. Dolley and K. Skaare, 'The coinage of Æthelwulf, king of the West Saxons, 839–58', in *Anglo-Saxon Coins*, ed. Dolley, 63–76, at 70–71, and pl. VIII, 20.

[33] Grierson and Blackburn, *Medieval European Coinage 1*, 287, 294–5.

[34] Bought A. H. Baldwin and Sons, 1996. I am grateful to Mr Lyon for drawing this coin to my attention and discussing its significance with me, as well as giving permission to publish it here. His collection is deposited on long-term loan at the Fitzwilliam Museum.

[35] J. J. North, *English Hammered Coinage 1. Early Anglo-Saxon to Henry III c. 600–1272*, 2nd edn (1980), no. 623. I am grateful to Jeffrey North and Marion Archibald for helping to resolve this error. In the ninth century a moneyer Osric is only known from the two coins discussed above.

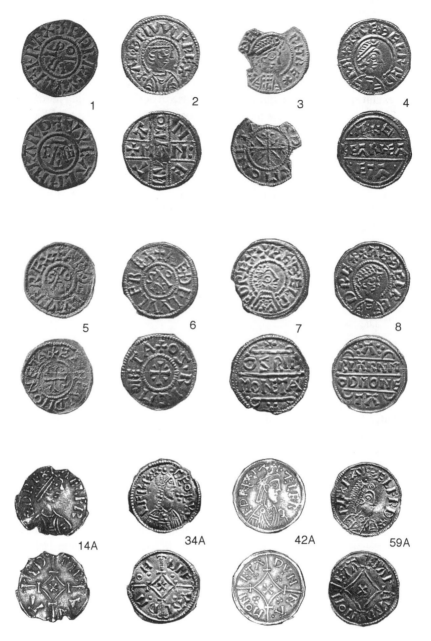

Fig. 22   Coins from Æthelwulf to Alfred

These coins, which illustrate the discussion, are in the Fitzwilliam Museum, Cambridge, unless otherwise indicated. The last four are described in the Appendix to this chapter.

1   Æthelwulf, *Doribi/Cant* type, *c.* 848–51, Rochester, moneyer Wealhheard.
2   Æthelwulf, *Inscribed Cross* type, *c.* 852/5–58, Canterbury, moneyer Manna.
3   Æthelberht, *Floriate Cross* type, *c.* 863–65, Canterbury, moneyer Dudda.
4   Æthelred I, *Lunettes* type, *c.* 867–71, Canterbury, moneyer Bearhea.
5   Æthelwulf, *Saxon* type, 840s, Southampton/Winchester, moneyer Eanwald (Keary and Grueber, *Catalogue of English Coins* (as n. 38), no. 25).
6   Æthelwulf, *Saxon* type, 840s, Southampton/Winchester, moneyer Osric.
7   Æthelred II, *Four-Line* type, *c.* 865–67, Southampton/Winchester, moneyer Osric.
8   Æthelred II, *Four-Line* type, *c.* 865–67, Canterbury, moneyer Biarnmod.
14A   Alfred, *Cross-and-Lozenge* type, *c.* 875–80, Canterbury, moneyer Tirwald.
34A   Ceolwulf II, *Cross-and-Lozenge* type, *c.* 875–80, London, moneyer Liafwald.
42A   Alfred, *Cross-and-Lozenge* type, *c.* 875–80, South Mercian mint (Oxford?), moneyer Dunna (Baldwins).
59A   Alfred, *Cross-and-Lozenge* type, *c.* 875–80, London, moneyer Liafwald (Spink).

Finds by Mr de Montfalcon, who still retained the piece, and it has since been acquired by the Fitzwilliam Museum, Cambridge.[36] The legends read:

Obv. +AE•ĐELR / ED REX
Rev. + / OSRIC / MONETA (NE ligatured) / •.•
Weight 1.17 g, chipped. Die-axis 270°.

The other known specimens of this *Four-Line* issue are all in a consistent style that is clearly the work of the Canterbury die-cutter (for example Fig. 22, no. 8), and the evolution of the bust from Æthelberht's *Inscribed Cross* and *Floreate Cross* types (Fig. 22, nos 2–3) to Æthelred's and Alfred's *Lunettes* type (Fig. 22, no. 4) can be seen clearly.[37] The new coin of Osric is quite unlike these. The eye, nose and hair are formed in a different way; the king is shown bare-headed, whereas on the Canterbury coins he wears a diadem; and the shoulders and drapery have a very different composition. On the Osric coin the lettering is larger, and hence more crowded; the As have both a cross-bar and top-bar, and most distinctively the *eth* (Đ) has the bar through the curved front rather than the upright back. This is a form later associated particularly with the west Midlands, but it is occasionally found at southern mints, as on some early Rochester coins of Æthelwulf.[38] The design of the reverse takes the same basic form as the Canterbury coins, but rather than using the top and bottom lunettes to complete the inscription, on the new coin they are decorated with a cross and three pellets, so that it is in fact a two-line rather than four-line legend. The dies are clearly the work of a different artist and were probably produced for a different mint. Although some twenty years may separate the two Osric coins, they surely represent the same moneyer operating at the West Saxon mint. This attribution is reinforced by the findspot of the *Four-Line* Osric coin, for Stanmore is now a suburb of Winchester, on the Southampton side of the city.

The significance of the Æthelred coin is not simply that it shows the West Saxon mint to have been in operation in *c.* 865–67, but that there was some continuity with the mint of the 840s. We cannot tell whether coins were produced there in the intervening period, but the fact that Osric's right to exercise the office of moneyer was preserved over the twenty-year period strongly implies that they were. If so we could expect one day to find an *Inscribed Cross* issue for Æthelbald of Wessex (858–60). The continuity of moneyer also implies that the mint of the 860s was in the same town as that of the 820s–840s, even if it does not resolve the question whether this was Southampton or Winchester. The perceptive arguments rehearsed by Dolley in 1970 remain as forceful as

---

[36] Accession no. CM.519–2000. I am very grateful to Mr de Montfalcon for making the coin available for publication and acquisition.

[37] Lyon, 'Historical problems', 230–34, and pl. 23, 8–11.

[38] C. F. Keary and H. A. Grueber, *A Catalogue of English Coins in the British Museum. Anglo-Saxon Series* (2 vols, 1887/93), I, 16, nos 37–9.

ever.[39] The significance of Southampton *(Hamwic)* in the eighth and ninth centuries has been emphasized by further archaeological excavations there, while those in Winchester have reinforced the radical nature of the Alfredian redevelopment of the city. This would have been a thoroughly appropriate occasion to move the mint from the commercial *wic* to the newly fortified burgh. One's hesitation over firmly accepting this, however, is caused by the small scale of the ninth-century West Saxon coinage, which evidently was not driven by the sort of commercial demand one might have expected in *Hamwic*.

In short, there is growing evidence for some continuity in minting in Wessex during the middle decades of the ninth century, a period when our knowledge of the coinage is generally weak because relatively few specimens survive. By contrast, the *Lunettes* coins of *c.* 867–75 are reasonably plentiful thanks to dozens of hoards prompted by the activity of the great Viking army, and the fact that no West Saxon issue has been identified in this type, suggests that minting there was exiguous or had ceased. By any reckoning, then, the *Cross-and-Lozenge* coinage of the later 870s from Winchester marks a significant revival, and one that we can fairly associate with the other initiatives Alfred was pursuing in rebuilding the city.

Alfred, Ceolwulf and Control of the London Mint

It is reasonable to suppose that the initiative for the two coinage reforms came from Alfred, given his record for innovation in other spheres, but the recoinage of *c.* 875 also affected Mercia, and its king, Ceolwulf II (874–*c.* 879), evidently agreed to continue the monetary alliance established by Burgred before him. Whether this agreement was part of the original arrangements of 874/5 was called in question by the realization that the majority of the surviving coins of Ceolwulf were struck towards the end of his reign.[40] It is apparent from the progressive degradation in style away from the Roman prototype that Alfred's coins preceded those of Ceolwulf at the two mints they shared, namely London and another in southern Mercia (Oxford?). This sequence is somewhat surprising – for it implies that after Burgred's expulsion in 874 mints in southern Mercia recognized Alfred as their king, and only acknowledged Ceolwulf's authority towards the end of his reign. This analysis of the material remains basically sound, but a new coin of Ceolwulf recently found shows that the situation was more complicated than we had thought. This is one of four recent finds of *Cross-and-Lozenge* coins which are described in the Appendix below.

The new Ceolwulf coin appeared in the coin trade at the end of 1998, along with one of Alfred by the same moneyer (Appendix, nos 34A and 59A

---

[39] M. Dolley, 'The location of the pre-Ælfredian mint(s) of Wessex', *Proceedings of the Hampshire Field Club and Archaeological Society*, 27 (1970), 57–61.

[40] Blackburn, 'The London mint', 116–20; Keynes, 'King Alfred and the Mercians', 17–18.

shown in Fig. 22). Coin finds of this type are exceptionally rare, and it is likely that they are strays from the small Pitstone, Buckinghamshire, hoard of 1996.[41] They are by the prolific London moneyer Liafwald. The Ceolwulf coin (Fig. 22, no. 34A) is quite unlike the nine other Ceolwulf coins of London style.[42] The bust is more refined, with details that are much closer to the original Roman prototype. Within the sequence of London dies we published, this one belongs at or near the beginning, alongside the first *Cross-and-Lozenge* coins of Alfred. There is also a difference in the spelling of the king's name, which is CEOLVVLF on the new coin but CIOL- on the other (later) London coins. The reverse is unusual in having small hooks at the end of each cross-arm, a detail that has been copied from contemporary coins of Canterbury, in what we termed the Canterbury B style. The new Ceolwulf coin seems to belong to an early experimental phase of London die-cutting.

The implications of this new coin are significant. It remains the case that most of the coins struck in London immediately after Burgred's exile in 874 were in the name of Alfred, and that these were followed in the later 870s by coins in Ceolwulf's name. However, it is now evident that at the beginning of this new coinage (*c.* 875) some coins were also struck at London for Ceolwulf II. In addition to the new *Cross-and-Lozenge* coin of fine style, I would now attribute to London at this same period the *Two Emperors* coin of Ceolwulf II. Simon Keynes and I had hesitated over whether this was contemporary with Alfred's specimen and from the same London mint, for three reasons: the style of die-cutting on the two coins is very different, the Ceolwulf *Two Emperors* coin has the CEOL- spelling rather than the CIOL- of other known London coins, and London did not otherwise appear to be working for Ceolwulf at the beginning of this coinage. Two of these three arguments have been dispelled by the new coin – the CEOL- spelling is now attested and there is an early Ceolwulf coin. Since the moneyer of the *Two Emperors* coin is known at London in other types, it seems reasonable to attribute this to London as well.

This reinterpretation to some extent enhances Ceolwulf's status, for he can now be seen as a partner with Alfred in the initial recoinage, continuing the monetary alliance that Burgred had formed with the West Saxons. But for all that it does not lessen Alfred's role in affairs. It remains the case that for a period in the mid-870s the great majority of the coins struck at the Mercian mint in London were in the name of Alfred. This would imply that it was from Alfred that they derived their authority to strike coins and to him that they accounted for most of their profits. It will be remembered that the coinage reform of *c.* 875 would have been hard to implement economically, and have required strong

---

[41] Blackburn and Keynes, 'A corpus', 127, 142–3. The reconstructed hoard would now comprise five coins, four of Ceolwulf and one of Alfred, all of the London moneyer Liafwald and in fine condition.

[42] I am grateful to Stewart Lyon, who has acquired the coin, for discussing its style and significance with me.

political control. Its acceptance in London, the most productive mint in England, would have been critical to the success of the whole reform. Alfred may have seized the initiative, and in negotiating the terms of the recoinage with Ceolwulf have insisted that he (Alfred) had a role in implementing the recoinage in London. The fact that the die-cutter of Alfred's *Two Emperors* coin, also from London, accorded him the unusual title *rex Anglo(rum)* ('king of the English') may reflect the die-cutter's perception that Alfred was the superior king politically.

After Ceolwulf's demise *c.* 879 the London mint passed once again to Alfred, as did the rest of English Mercia. Alfred's second recoinage followed soon after this, *c.* 880, and the new coinage was of the so-called *Two-Line* or *Horizontal* type. Significantly, at three mints the new *Two-Line* design was not used initially, but instead there were special issues which combined Alfred's name with that of the mint. The mints were London, Oxford and Gloucester, Mercian towns that had recently come under Alfred's control, as the coins appear to have been proclaiming. The use of the coinage for political propaganda was very unusual in the Anglo-Saxon period, but Alfred perhaps knew of one clear precedent; when his grandfather Ecgberht conquered Mercia in 829 and struck coins at London using the title *rex M(erciorum)* and the mint name *Lundonia civit(as)*.

Conclusions

Alfred implemented some important monetary reforms during the first decade of his reign. In doing so he was building on developments in mint administration that had been overseen by his father and brothers – Æthelwulf, Æthelberht and Æthelred. Together they had achieved a uniform currency for all Wessex and Mercia, that was being struck by an increased number of moneyers in both kingdoms. However, they had allowed the intrinsic value of the penny to decline, probably because of an international shortage of silver. In Alfred's early years it declined still further, but in a bold reform he restored the weight and fineness to the levels set by Offa, and then raised the weight further to establish a new standard for the English penny. Alfred's other major contribution to the development of the monetary system was to extend the mint network, a policy continued by his successors – particularly Edward the Elder and Athelstan. This gave people greater access to mints and exchanges, while also providing an income to support the fortified boroughs, including those in the reconquered Danelaw many of which had already enjoyed mints under Scandinavian rule. While pursuing this expansion during the first half of the tenth century, standardization of design went by the board and regional coin types developed. The find evidence from England is too thin to be certain, but it hints at the development of regional circulation areas where the local coin type was dominant. Standards of weight and fineness also began to decline again, though not as severely as in the early

870s.[43] Only with Edgar's monetary reform of *c.* 973 was the value of the penny again restored and a single uniform currency for all England established. A comparison between pre-reform hoards such as Tetney and post-reform ones such as Oakham and Chester (1914) brings home just how much more mobile coinage had become.[44] The products of local mints naturally dominate most finds, but coins from every part of the country are now generally represented as well.

Parallels have been drawn between the carefully managed system of periodic recoinages that lasted for 150 years after Edgar's reform and the series of recoinages that occurred between 850 and 880.[45] Dolley identified not five *renovatio monetae* in this period but seven, and credited Æthelwulf with being the architect of a 'policy of periodic recoinage', which, he said, Alfred abandoned in the 880s because of the changing political and economic climate caused by the settlement of the Danelaw. But the parallel is not to be pressed. After Edgar's initial reform, the late Saxon and Norman recoinages were effectively a tax-gathering scheme of the highest sophistication, and one which was to have a profound influence on the monetary systems of several states of northern and central Europe. The ninth-century recoinages, on the other hand, each probably involved some economic or administrative reform of the monetary system. They are likely to have been *ad hoc* events arranged in order to change or develop some aspect of the coinage, whether it be the weight or fineness, uniformity of design to improve accountability and facilitate circulation, or implementation of a monetary alliance with Mercia. These were significant developments, but seen in context they were only a step towards the goal that was later to be achieved by Edgar.

---

[43] Blunt, Stewart and Lyon, *Coinage in Tenth-Century England* (n. 25 above), 235–45.

[44] Jonsson, *The New Era* (n. 10 above), 102–6. As usual, local mints are better represented,

[45] M. Dolley, 'Ælfred the Great's abandonment of the concept of periodic recoinage', *Studies in Numismatic Method*, ed. C. N. L. Brooke et al. (1983), 153–60.

Appendix

Additions to the Corpus of Cross-and-Lozenge *Coins*

The following coins, illustrated in Fig. 22 (nos 14A, 34A, 42A and 59A), are additions to M. Blackburn and S. Keynes, 'A corpus of the *Cross-and-Lozenge* and related coinages of Alfred, Ceolwulf II and Archbishop Æthelred', *Kings, Currency and Alliances*, eds Blackburn and Dumville, 125–50. The numbering below follows the sequence of the original article, and comparative coins are also cited from that source.

Canterbury style B
King Alfred
14A. *Moneyer*: Tirwald
Obverse: +AELFR EDREX (starting above head)
Reverse: TIR VV A LD, with central saltire and no border, the cross-arms ending in two vestigial cusps.
Weight: 1.06 g, chipped. *Die-axis:* 0°.
Provenance: Lyon collection (deposited Fitzwilliam Museum); bt Baldwins 2000, in stock, since 1999 or earlier; without provenance.
Comment: New dies. This is the second specimen of the type for this moneyer. The obverse is close in style to no. 12, while the reverse can be compared to no. 15, although the treatment of the ends of the cross-arms is novel.

London style
King Ceolwulf
34A. *Moneyer*: Liafwald
Obverse: +·CEOLVV LFREX· (starting above head)
Reverse: LIF VAL DM ON (N reverse barred), cross-arms have cusps at ends.
Weight: 1.45 g, slight chip. *Die-axis:* 0°.
Provenance: Lyon collection (deposited Fitzwilliam Museum); bt Spink (*Numismatic Circular* February 1999, no. 326); acq. Dec. 1998 with no. 59A; no provenance, but probably a stray from the Pitstone, Buckinghamshire hoard, *c.* 1996.
Comment: This is an important coin. It is in a finer style than any of Ceolwulf's other *Cross-and-Lozenge* coins and comparable with the best of Alfred's (e.g. nos 26–8), which would appear to put it among the earliest *Cross-and-Lozenge* coins of London. The reverse is influenced by Canterbury style B dies (e.g. no. 11), but the letter forms and the presence of MON show that it is not made by the Canterbury die-cutter. It is interesting that the reverse of no. 11 is not among the earliest of the Canterbury style B dies, for the quatrefoil border has been diminished to a pair of cusps at the end of each cross-arm. With so few dies known it is dangerous to propose a chronology for such developments, but the evidence of this new coin perhaps suggests that the *Cross-and-Lozenge* type started earlier at Canterbury than London.

Winchester style
King Alfred
42A. *Moneyer*: Dunna
Obverse: +ÆLFR EDREXSA (starting above head)
Reverse: DVN NA· MON ETA, with central saltire and trefoils of pellets in quarters pointing inwards.
Weight: 1.46 g.
Provenance: Baldwins, acq. Jan. 2000; found near Winchester, *c.* 1999.
Comment: New dies. Stylistically this coin falls between nos 42 and 43 of Dunna, but it is closest to a coin of Wulfred (no. 51) which has a very similar bust and inward pointing trefoils on the reverse. This specimen supports the observed sequence of striking. Four coins of Dunna are now known, the three earlier in the name of Alfred and the latest in the name of Ceolwulf II, suggesting the mint was in southern Mercia, possibly at Oxford.

Other styles
King Ælfred
59A. *Moneyer*: Liafwald
Obverse: +ÆLFRDx REXSAI (starting above head)
Reverse: LIAF VAD MON ETA (N reverse barred)
Weight: 1.17 g.
Provenance: Spink (*Numismatic Circular* March 1999, no. 743); acq. Dec. 1998 with no. 34A; no provenance, but probably a stray from the Pitstone, Buckinghamshire hoard, *c.* 1996.
Comment: Although a coin of the prolific London moneyer, Liafwald, this piece is in a style that is otherwise only known from a coin of Eadwulf (no. 59, but note that on pl. 10 of Blackburn and Keynes, 'A corpus' the obverses of 59 and 60 were transposed in error). That specimen is of good weight (1.38 g), while this is very light, which might arouse suspicions that it is an imitation. However, weights of London coins could be very variable (cf. die-duplicates, nos 40–41 weighing 1.49 g and 1.21 g). This seems, then, to be the work of a second London die-cutter. When in the issue this die-cutter was operating is not clear; arguments can be advanced to support an early or a late date, but none is conclusive.

Chapter 12

The origin of Alfred's urban policies

David Hill

> What of the cities and towns he restored and the others which he built where none had been before? (*De civitatibus et urbibus renovandis et aliis, ubi nunquam ante fuerant, construendis?*: Asser, c. 91)

A consensus has emerged in modern standard works that the continuous history of Anglo-Saxon and medieval towns began with Alfred, who founded a majority of the Anglo-Saxon urban sites, and that these were usually laid out in rectilinear street patterns to reflect their functions of defence, trade and refuge. This 'burghal system' was backed by military reforms and included the early warning of the beacons.[1] Nowhere was this to be seen more clearly than in the 'type site' of Winchester.[2] As a result of a series of brilliant excavations by Martin Biddle we were convinced in the 1970s that all *herepaths* lead to Winchester. This has generally been accepted, and voices against this view are rare, though David Sturdy has questioned the Alfredian origin of the rectilinear plan.[3]

This simplified view has been carried too far by some archaeologists and urban historians. The fact of the rectilinear street plan together with the idea that late Saxon towns have square fortifications can lead to erroneous interpretations such as that of the plan of Axbridge.[4] In a similar way because of a feeling that Alfred is the origin of the burghal system attempts have been made to re-date the *Burghal Hidage* to an earlier date by some forty years,[5] a 'daring' view refuted by Dumville.[6]

---

[1] D. Hill and S. Sharp, 'An Anglo-Saxon beacon system', in A. R. Rumble and A. D. Mills (eds), *Names, Places and People: An Onomastic Miscellany for John McNeal Dodgson* (1997), 157–65.

[2] M. Biddle and D. J. Keene, 'The late Saxon *Burh*', in M. Biddle (ed.), *Winchester in the Early Middle Ages,* Winchester Studies 1 (1976), 449–69.

[3] D. Sturdy, *Alfred the Great* (1995), 255.

[4] M. Biddle and D. Hill, 'Late Saxon Planned Towns', *Antiquaries Journal*, 51 (1971), 70–85; M. Batt, 'The Burghal Hidage – Axbridge', *Proceedings of the Somerset Archaeological and Natural History Society*, 119 (1974), 22–5.

[5] R. H. C. Davis, 'Alfred and Guthrum's frontier', *EHR*, 97 (1982), 803–11.

[6] D. N. Dumville, 'The treaty of Alfred and Guthrum, Appendix: The date of the Burghal Hidage', in *idem, Wessex and England from Alfred to Edgar* (1992), 24–7.

The Alternatives – Indigenous and Pre-existing

It would seem reasonable to review the sources for Alfred's policies, plans and strategies; clearly Alfred was not simply a lonely genius. We are faced with the question of whether Alfred derived some of his ideas or whether they came from his innate genius. Clearly his military reforms, his literary and intellectual endeavours, his ship designs, and his reforms of the coinage all point to a remarkable and original approach.

There were in the eighth century a range of sites which had at least one of Stenton's criteria for an Anglo-Saxon town – a wall, a mint and a market. The age of Offa has been renamed, and Stenton's 'Age of Mercian Supremacy' has become Hodges's 'Age of the Emporia', with Southampton, London *wic*, Ipswich and York. It should also be noted that there was throughout early medieval Europe a rebirth of towns and fortifications, a pattern into which Alfred's efforts must fit.

How far indigenous urban development had progressed is demonstrated by a charter, Offa's charter of 786,[7] which among the appurtenances of a great estate appends a *vicum in aquilone parte venalis loci*. It would be anticipating to examine further the ninth-century charters but it is clear that here we have an occupied *burh* which has most of the attributes of an Anglo-Saxon town, streets, market, wall, refuge, and tenurial heterogeneity, before the year 800, three-quarters of a century before Alfred's works. S 1182 (762) can be translated in part:

> † In the name of our Lord Jesus Christ.
> I, Dunwald, the thegn of King Ethelberht of glorious memory ... assign after my death a residence (*villam*) which is situated in the market place at the Queen's Gate of the city of Canterbury (*ad QUENEGATUM urbis DOROVERNIS*) and which Hringwine now holds – the same which the aforesaid king granted with other small lands in his own right for me to possess with his tribute, and to give to whomsoever I should wish ... . This land is surrounded by these boundaries: in the south, having three perches in extent, and thence west a most straight line divides the land of the king and this for 23 perches as far as the walled enclosure (*maceria*) which adjoins the city wall on the north side, having 33 rods.

In the same reign comes Offa's Dyke, in the centre of which is the burh of Hereford. In a series of important excavations the early history of the site has been elucidated. After a battle between the Welsh and Offa in 760 at Hereford ('Army Ford'), an important route centre and a gateway into Wales, it is likely that Offa fortified the site. The defences covered a rectangular fifty-acre site. There are two phases of early defence, a small (marking-out) bank and ditch followed by a rampart of gravel with a larger ditch.[8]

---

[7] S 125.

[8] S. Bassett, 'Burhs in the age of the Mercian Supremacy', in *Æthelbald and Offa*, eds D. Hill and M. Worthington (forthcoming).

In the centre of the Mercian kingdom lies Tamworth. It may be important that under the fortifications attributed to 913 an earlier ditch has been found which has been given an Offan context. It is not considered by the excavator to have been defensive and was five feet deep by eight feet wide at the top.[9] Recent work has revealed an important mill but the palace of the charters has not been discovered. Similarily Winchcombe in what is now Gloucestershire has an early ditch under its later Saxon fortifications.[10]

There was also a long tradition of fortification in Dark Age and Middle Saxon Britain. By the reign of Offa we have charter evidence of fortress building and maintenance, and also the archaeological evidence of at least two large defended settlements, the possibility of a minimum of four forts, a possible palace site at Kingsbury by Saint Albans and a complex system of frontier defences. In Mercia at least there was the expertise to build burhs, and in four old Roman centres the models for town life. It may well be that from Mercia came the germ of burh building and the marrying of fortress constructions with the foundation of town life that has been so confidently attributed to Alfred, Wessex and the mid- to late ninth century. The range of urban sites would appear to be indicated in a unique entry in Simeon of Durham *s.a.* 764:

> In the same year many towns, monasteries and villages in various
> districts and kingdoms were suddenly devastated by fire; for instance
> the calamity struck Stretburg, Winchester, Southampton, the city of
> London, the city of York, Doncaster and many other places ...

Apart from topography and archaeology there is also the evidence of the charters. Anglo-Saxon royal diplomas granted estates with general immunities but usually excepted three obligations: (i) service with the army; (ii) the building of fortresses and (iii) the construction of bridges. In a fundamental article Nicholas Brooks has traced the development of these military obligations, emphasizing that the first recorded instance of the reservation of the obligation to defend or maintain fortresses is to be found in a general grant of privileges to the Mercian churches by Æthelbald of Mercia at the synod of Gumley in 749.[11] The king reserves 'vel necessariis defensionibus arcium contra hostes non sunt renuenda' ('the necessary defence of fortresses against enemies'). The king of the Hwicce reserved the defence of fortresses in 767 and 770,[12] and Offa in a charter dated 793 × 796 frees from all works except the usual three, which includes *arcium munimentum*,[13] and

---

9 J. Gould, 'Third report of the excavations at Tamworth, Staffs.: the western entrance to the Saxon borough', *South Staffordshire Archaeological and Historical Society Transactions*, 10 (1969), 37.

10 Bassett, 'Burhs'.

11 N. J. Brooks, 'The development of military obligations in eighth- and ninth-century England', in P. Clemoes and K. Hughes (eds), *England before the Conquest: Studies in Primary Sources Presented to Dorothy Whitelock* (1971), 69–84; the privilege is BCS 178 (S 92).

12 S 58 and 59.

13 S 139.

as with other diplomas it is emphasized that these burdens are laid upon the whole people without exceptions. At the synod of Clofeshoh in 792 Offa is recorded as freeing the churches in Kent of all burdens

> nisi expeditione intra Cantiam contra paganos marinos cum classis migrantibus vel in australes Saxones si necessitas cogit, ac pontis constructionem et arcis munitionem contra paganos itemque fines Cantwariourum.[14]

By 811 the charters are adding the obligation to destroy pagan forts in addition to the construction of forts against the Vikings.[15] After 822 the three obligations become general in the charters. It is not until 846 that we have a West Saxon charter of undoubted authenticity with a reservation clause but it is possible that it was not until the reign of Æthelbald (855–60), when all three burdens began to be reserved in West Saxon charters, that an obligation to build fortifications was first regularly exacted in Wessex. What evidence there is points to the obligation of fortress work starting in Mercia and spreading, not reaching Wessex until the mid-ninth century.

By 800 we can see the use of a core of towns such as Canterbury and Rochester, York and London as thriving communities with mint, market and wall. They certainly were clearly distinguishable from the surrounding agricultural settlements. At Saxon Southampton we seem to have that institution beloved of geographers, a trading settlement which is purely an organic growth trading with the whole of Europe and itself a settlement which lived from its trade both local and distant.

The early part of Alfred's reign does not provide a great deal more in the way of information. On the return of the Danes with a fleet in 875 they were met by Alfred with a naval force and defeated. It is clear that Alfred was using a mobile defensive strategy similar to that employed by Charlemagne, but the greatest threat to Wessex was the Great Army already established in the Midlands, and they *slipped away* into Wareham in 876.[16] The terms of the *ASC* leave one to wonder what there was at Wareham to 'slip into'. Asser states quite categorically that

> the aforesaid army of the Danes, leaving Cambridge at night entered a castle (*castellum*) called Wareham where there is a *monasterium* of holy virgins between the rivers Frome and Trent ... placed in a most secure situation, except that it was exposed to danger on the western side from the nature of the ground.[17]

If one feels, with Dorothy Whitelock and with Keynes and Lapidge, that one can accept Asser as a primary source, then this testimony cannot be ignored

---

[14] S 134.

[15] S 1264 (811) and 186 (822).

[16] *ASC, s.a.* 876.

[17] Asser, c. 49.

and we can see that the description of Wareham is correct. These earthworks have been excavated, but it is in the nature of archaeological evidence that it will rarely allow exact dates to such structures; all that can be said is that the primary bank is 'possibly after *c.* 700'.[18] If it is a pre-Alfredian work then we can, as at Hereford and, perhaps, Tamworth, postulate the 'de novo' works as starting much earlier than has been previously thought. *Burhs* are often held to be Alfredian simply because of the nature of the documentary evidence. On the other hand Wareham *may* mark the beginnings of Alfred's building policy.

A similar situation may be shown to exist at Exeter, the site to which the Danes fled in 877. Here the *ASC* states:[19]

> King Alfred rode after the mounted army with the English army as far as Exeter, but could not overtake them before they were in the fortress (*fæstene*) where they could not be reached.

The meaning of the word *fæstene* is not precise but it may imply the circuit of the Roman walls, which were usually referred to in other terms, or some other, intra-mural, work, using a portion perhaps of the Roman walls. Æthelweard states that they 'laid out a camp in winter-time in the city of Exeter', but whether this comes from an original source other than the *ASC* is doubtful.[20] The possibility remains that the defensive work at Exeter dates to a period before 877.

One possibility is that Alfred was inspired by a literary model; with Alfred's known interests there is a possibility that the details of town planning came to him through some classical text. Unfortunately, though Vegetius was known in Alfred's England, there is no known text which discusses rectilinear patterns.

A Continental Model?

We have problems with the sites which were built or reoccupied by the Danes, Norwegians or Vikings. Until the famous sequence of round forts found at the close of the tenth century in Denmark and Scania, Viking forts that are proven by archaeology in England are rare. It has been suggested that the model for West Saxon fortifications had been taken from the Vikings, but the timing of their constructions is against this, and the town sites are too late to form models. There are problems with the sites that have been located; there are few of them and their sizes are very variable. We have Biddle's discoveries in Repton,[21] but if

---

18 R.H.C.M. (England), 'Wareham west walls', *Medieval Archaeology*, 3 (1959), 120–38, at 137.

19 *ASC s.a.* 877.

20 Æthelweard, 42.

21 M. Biddle and B. Kjølbye-Biddle, 'Repton and the Vikings', *Antiquity*, 66 (1992), 36–51.

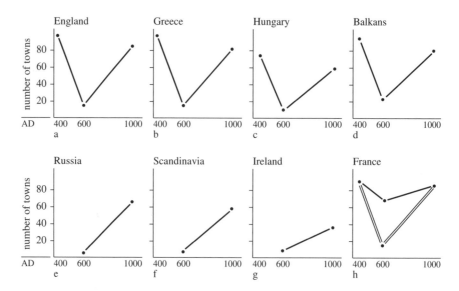

Fig. 23   Graphs showing numbers of European towns, 400–1000

one translates the length of the wall there using the *Burghal Hidage* calculation, the size of the Viking army ('the Great Army') appears much too small. In other cases, for example Fulham, we are not certain that we are looking at the Viking encampment, so calculations are difficult.[22] There is still the unexamined work at Shoebury.

There is a clear resurgence of towns in Europe in the period 700–900 (see Fig. 23),[23] and Alfred's reign lies in the centre of that expansion; in other words the spirit of the period favoured the re-emergence of urban sites whether or not Alfred was in charge. The rebuilding of town walls and the construction of new fortresses within the Carolingian Empire were not begun until the 860s, when Charles the Bald began a programme of fortification 'iuxta … aliarum gentium consuetudinem';[24] there are clear parallels with English military obligations. In the first half of the ninth century, by contrast, we hear of Frankish bishops destroying city walls in order to use the stone for cathedral and chapter buildings.[25]

---

[22] P. Arthur and K. Whitehouse, 'Report on excavations on Fulham Palace moat, 1972–1973', *TLMAS*, 29 (1978), 45–72, at 54–7.

[23] D. Hill, 'Unity and diversity – a framework of European towns', in R. Hodges and B. Hobley (eds), *The Rebirth of Towns in the West, 700–1050*, Council for British Archaeology Research Reports, 68 (1988), 8–15.

[24] *Edictum Pistense* (862), c. 27, in *Capitularia regum Francorum II*, eds A. Boretius and V. Krause, MGH Capitularia regum Francorum 2 (Hanover 1890–97), 321–2.

[25] Brooks, 'Military obligation', 81.

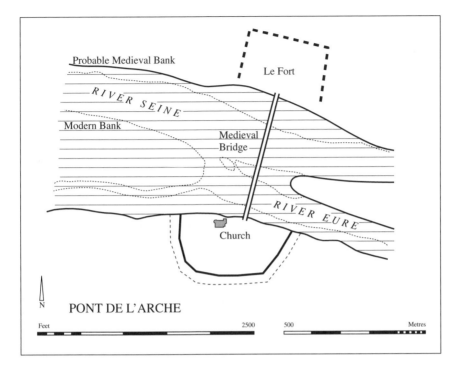

Fig. 24   Pont de l'Arche

Of all these works, however, the one best known to me is Pont de l'Arche (Fig. 24).[26] The plan of this site is remarkable in that the works (of which only the northern half survives) have a rectangular plan. That the site was known to the élite of Wessex is very probable, and it is also likely that this regular figure pre-dates the West Saxon double or bridge sites. This site or its as yet undiscovered analogues would appear to have been the model for West Saxon rectangular sites such as Cricklade and sites such as Bedford, Hertford, London/Southwark and others. These numerous sites consist of a blocking of a river by two facing fortifications linked by a fortified bridge.

---

[26] J. Hassall and D. Hill, 'Pont de l'Arche: Frankish influence on the West Saxon burh?', *Archaeological Journal*, 127 (1970), 188–95; B. Dearden and D. Hill, 'Charles the Bald's bridge-works at Pitres (Eure): Recent excavations at Pont de l'Arche and Igoville', *Haute-Normandie Archaeologique*, 1 (1988), 63–70.

The Alternatives – the Vatican City

There is a record of an inscription on a stone above the eastern gate at Winchester:[27]

> Traveller, whoever present here, see this gate,
> pour forth due praises to the thunderer on high for
> Christ's servant Swithun, once the Bishop, through whose
> great solicitude and care the lovely structure of this bridge
> was built to the praise of Christ and the beauty of the
> City of Winchester when the sun in its course had turned
> 800 years and had unfolded fifty nine years in addition after
> the mercy of Christ was incarnate,
> and when the seventh indiction was turning its course.

Now neither the stone nor the gate survive, but there are indications that this inscription did exist. It should be noted that the indiction is correct for 859; Swithun died in 862. There is no reference to his sanctity and it might therefore be that this is evidence of a mid-ninth-century restoration of the defences of Winchester. No motive is immediately apparent for a forgery of this nature. Later traditions link Winchester's walls and gates to Swithun.

Alfred is claimed to have travelled twice to Rome, once with his father Æthelwulf, king of the West Saxons (839–58), between early 855 and late 856. In August 846 a Saracen fleet sailed into the mouth of the Tiber and overpowered the new fortifications and towns that had been built there. From the estuary they moved on to Rome. The walls were too strong for the invaders and in the fighting that followed Saxons, as well as Lombards, Frisians and Franks who were resident in the schools, died defending the city. Outside of these walls stood St Peter's and the Vatican and when the resistance was overpowered the monuments of western Christendom were desecrated. Europe was rocked by reports that the grave of the prince of the Apostles had been rifled, the contents of his coffin scattered and everything of value removed from the Vatican Hill.

Pope Sergius decided to fortify the whole of the Vatican Hill and to surround St Peter's. He therefore wrote to the emperor Lothar for advice and assistance. Lothar himself in a capitulary in November or December of 846 bewailed the fact that the Roman Church should have fallen into the hands of the infidel. He directed that St Peter's should be enclosed with a wall and that money should be sent from every part of the Empire.[28] However it was not until the accession of Pope Leo IV that the work was taken in hand in a systematic manner. The enclosure on the Vatican Hill came to be known as the Leonine City (Fig. 25). The walls were built in a horseshoe from the mausoleum of Hadrian, which was fortified, right around the whole of St Peter's. The forty-foot-high

---

[27] See also the text in A. Audrey Locke (ed.), *In Praise of Winchester: An Anthology in Prose and Verse* (1912), 129.

[28] P. Llewellyn, *Rome in the Dark Ages* (2nd edn, 1993), 264–5.

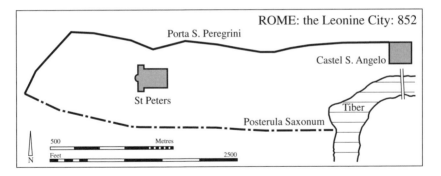

Fig. 25 Rome: the Leonine City, 852

walls were built of tufa and tiles and contained forty-four towers and three gates.[29] The work was carried out by gangs from the estates of the church. These *miltiae* had a section of the twelve-foot-thick wall assigned to them and worked under their *corrector*. The completed sections were marked with inscriptions.[30]

On 27 June 852 the city of Rome, led by Pope Leo IV, celebrated the completion of the work; the entire clergy processed barefoot and with ash-strewn heads around the walls, the procession being led by the seven cardinal bishops sprinkling the walls with holy water. At each of the three gates the procession stopped, and the pope invoked blessings on the work. The gates were surmounted with Latin inscriptions which in thirteen lines of verse commemorated the erection of that gate.[31] The southern of these gates was known as the *Saxonum posterula* ('postern of the Saxons'), as it stood next to the *xenodochia*. Here in a series of hostels the Saxon community lived a separate life. Their close-packed settlement was called their *burh*, which led on to the present place-name surviving in Rome of *borgo*. It is recorded that their native habit of building in wood appears to have been followed, for the area was devastated by a series of disastrous fires during the course of the ninth century.

In the year following the consecration of the Leonine walls Alfred came to Rome for his first visit, and it was probably at the Saxon School he stayed. When he returned with his father King Æthelwulf in 855 it was here they stayed, for the royal pair lived in Rome for a year during which King Æthelwulf restored the Saxon School.[32] It is not merely a flight of fancy to see the two, father and son, passing through the Postern Gate of the Saxons and having pointed out to them, and translated, the inscriptions recording their erection. Certainly they

[29] H. K. Mann, *The Lives of the Popes in the Early Middle Ages: The Popes During the Carolingian Empire, Leo III to Formosus, 795–891, II – 795–858* (1925), 264–6.

[30] Llewellyn, *Rome in the Dark Ages*, 264–5.

[31] Asser, ed. Stevenson, 245.

[32] C. Plummer, *The Life and Times of Alfred the Great, Being the Ford Lectures for 1901* (1902), 75–6.

would have been told in great detail the events of the previous decade and the part played in them by the trained bands of the Saxon School. The walls of the Leonine City would still be pristine and still be a major topic of wonder and conversation. In 856 they returned home, pausing one imagines at the *xenodochia* which existed in Pavia, to arrive in Wessex in the mid-winter of 856–7.

Is it at present a fantasy to link the work on the Leonine City carried out by the bishop of Rome, and entered by gates bearing Latin inscriptions, with the work claimed to have been carried out in Winchester by its bishop, Swithun? The evidence consists of a copy of a ten-line Latin verse claimed to have been an inscription on the east gate of the city recording work completed in 859, two years after Æthelwulf's return and seven years after the completion of the Leonine City. Persistent traditions have always linked Swithun with the restoration of the walls of Winchester and the inscription may be an important addition to our evidence of the refortification of Winchester.

August 846	Sack
27 June 852	Dedication
853	Alfred's first visit
Early 855 to late 856	Æthelwulf's visit
859	Swithun's bridge and gate

The careful delineation of the walls of the Leonine City by Gibson and Ward-Perkins shows the crenellations in the later heightening.[33] These appear to be designed for a ballista or similar machine. It is remarkable that at Exeter city wall Blaylock and Parker discovered late Saxon work surviving for over 100 metres.[34] Sitting on top of the Roman wall, which had been cut down by removing weathered and unstable material, the crenellations are about 1.2 metres wide and 1 metre tall, with the apertures averaging about 1.6 metres. There is an apparent link between the design of the refurbished wall at Exeter and the walls of the Leonine City.[35]

---

[33] S. Gibson and B. Ward-Perkins, 'The surviving remains of the Leonine Wall' and 'The surviving remains of the Leonine Wall, part II: the passetto', *Papers of the British School at Rome*, 47 (1979), 30–57 and 51 (1983), 222–39.

[34] S. R. Blaylock and R. W. Parker, *Exeter City Defences: Fabric Recording of the City Wall in Northernhay Gardens Adjacent to Athelstan's Tower, 1993–4*, Exeter Museums Archaeological Field Unit, report 94 (1994), 46 and figures 1–3; see also I. Burrow, 'The town defences of Exeter', *Report and Transactions of the Devonshire Association*, 109 (1977), 13–40.

[35] D. Hill, 'Athelstan's urban reforms', *Anglo-Saxon Studies in Archaeology and History*, 11 (2001), 173–85.

Alfred's Own Works

With the occupation of Wessex in 878 we start to find specific mentions of the construction of defensive works. Alfred retreated into the heart of Somerset 'and afterwards at Easter, King Alfred made a stronghold (*geweorc*) at Athelney, and he and the section of the people which was nearest to it proceeded to fight from that stronghold against the enemy'.[36] At this time there were other bands of West Saxons resisting the Danish occupation; that of the ealdorman of Somerset 'in a certain wood' and that under the ealdorman of Devon, Odda, at a site in North Devon:[37]

> and the Danes sailed to Devon, where with twelve hundred others, he met with a miserable death, being slain while committing his misdeeds, by the king's servants, before the Castle of Cynuit (*arcem Cynuit*) into which many of the king's servants, with their followers, had fled for safety. The pagans, seeing that the castle was altogether unprepared and unfortified, except that it had walls in our own fashion, determined not to assault it, because it was impregnable on all sides except the eastern, as we ourselves have seen, but they began to blockade it, thinking that those who were inside would soon surrender either from famine or want of water, for the castle had no spring near it.

It is not clear where this site is to be located. A strong claim has been made for Countisbury in North Devon,[38] where the camp has a strong topographical similarity to the site mentioned, but the clear statement that there was no spring close by would seem to rule out the camp of Countisbury, as there is a spring and small stream flowing within the circuit. It may also be considered on more general grounds an improbable place for the ealdorman of the shire to rally his people, as it is tucked away on the far north east corner of the shire; a more central position in the populated valleys of the Taw or Torridge might seem more appropriate, perhaps the Pilton Camp of the *Burghal Hidage*. The point for us is that there existed in North Devon a refuge for some part of the people which was in use in the early part of the reign and which Æthelweard calls a 'certain fortress'.[39]

The crisis of 878 ended with the battle of Edington and the kingdom of Wessex being granted a respite from the Danes. It is during this respite that we should expect a great reorganization of the defences, and we know that some work did take place, but it should not be forgotten that there were already defences and that they had played a part in the survival of the kingdom. Evidence does exist for Alfred's founding of Shaftesbury in 880, the earliest evidence for foundation we have.

---

[36] *ASC, s.a.* 878.

[37] Asser, c. 54.

[38] J. E. B. Gover, A. Mawer and F. M. Stenton, *The Place-Names of Devon* (1931), 62–3; *ASC*, ed. Plummer, ii. 93; but see also Asser, ed. Stevenson, 265.

[39] *quodam castro*: Æthelweard, 43.

How many *burhs* Alfred built and when they were constructed is not certain, but there is enough to show an outline of the process, to assign at least a complete overhaul of the existing system and the addition of a large number of innovations. The most important statements come from Asser. In a panegyric on the achievements of Alfred, the bishop, following the format of Einhard's *Life of Charlemagne*, outlines his works:[40] 'What of the cities and towns he restored, and the others, which he built where none had been before?' It should be noted that although this is a panegyric there is no attempt to claim that Alfred brought towns or fortifications to Wessex for the first time. The part of the king, the direct authority, and the hierarchy that organized the actual work is well brought out by a section later in the same chapter:

> but if, among these exhortations of the king, his orders were not carried out because of the slackness of the people, or of things begun late in time of need were unfinished and of no profit to those who undertook them – for I may tell of fortresses ordered by him and still not yet begun, or begun too late to be brought to completion – and enemy forces broke in by land and sea, or as so often happened on every side.

Asser then goes on to point out the consequences, the loss of 'fathers, wives, children, servants, slaves, handmaids, their labours and all their goods', which brings repentance and they 'regret that they have carelessly neglected the king's orders, and with one voice praise the king's wisdom, and promise to fulfil with all their strength what they have before refused, that is with regard to the building of fortresses and the other things for the common profit of the whole kingdom.'

The word used for *burh* by Asser is either *castellum* or *arx*, and is clearly used for sites where he is not referring to Roman sites and does not wish to use *civitas*; one of these is recorded in *ASC* in its account of the campaign for 892,[41] when the Danes rowed up the river Lympne as far as the Weald, four miles from the estuary. There they stormed a fortress (*abrǣcon an ge weorc*); inside that fortress (*f(ǣst)enne*) there were a few peasants and it was only half made.

There is therefore evidence that the king was restoring cities, presumably Roman, building new towns, ordering fortifications which were to act as a refuge for a cross-section of the population, that these fortifications and towns were instituted by him, although usually constructed by local men, presumably ealdormen, and that the construction was still under way when Asser wrote in 892.

From Asser and other sources there are further fragmentary indications which, taken together, show how far the system of fortifications and towns was developing. Already Canterbury, Rochester, Winchester, Clausentum(?), Wareham,

---

[40] Asser, c. 91, 75: 'De civitatibus et urbibus renovandis et aliis, ubi nunquam ante fuerant, construendis?'

[41] *ASC, s.a.* 892.

Exeter, Athelney and *Arx Cynuit* have been shown to have been in operation before the expansion of the system usually assigned to the period 878–92.[42] Before the next *ASC* reference to *burhs* in 885 there are two sets of references in Asser which point to *burh* foundation; both are concerned with monastic foundations. Alfred founded a monastery at Athelney, perhaps around 880, which was defended, for we are told that Athelney

> is surrounded on all sides by very great, swampy and impassable marshes, so that no one can approach it except by punts, or by a bridge which has been made with laborious skill between the fortresses (*arces*). At the western end of this bridge a very strong fort (*arx*) has been placed of most beautiful workmanship by the king's command.[43]

Here we see again the royal nature of the *burh*. The western fortress can be identified on the ground as a promontory burh at Lyng,[44] whilst the rest of the description would seem to be interpretable on the ground with the line of the causeway leading to the island of Athelney, now Athelney Hill. The other fortress is apparently to be sought on the western height of that hill, the site of the abbey being well known from both the ploughed-up stone remains and the documentary references. It may be that the second, eastern, fortress or *burh* does not coincide with the refuge *burh* built in 878.

Asser also refers to the building of the abbey at Shaftesbury. This is not the place to discuss the inscription excavated at the turn of the century, but there is a strong and early tradition that the *burh* was founded by Alfred in 880 which in no way is at odds with what we know of the reign. Asser, talking of the foundation of the monastery, states that it was built 'by the east gate of Shaftesbury'.[45] The *ASC* then resumes with the account of the siege of Rochester by the Danes, 'who built works around themselves' before the siege was raised by the arrival of Alfred and his army. London had been in the hands of Alfred in 883 and in 886 London was restored and, apparently, repopulated; we are told by Asser that it was honourably rebuilt and made habitable.[46] Alfred entrusted the burh (*burg*) of London to the ealdorman of Mercia Ethelred, who was in some semi-autonomous position under Alfred and in control of those parts of Mercia not occupied by the Danes.

In 892 the Danes again attacked Wessex, and it is here that one may see the Alfredian system in operation. The initial landing was unsuccessfully opposed because there was an incomplete *burh* on the Lympne, and the Danes were able to set up fortifications, one at Milton Royal, near Sittingbourne in Kent, the

---

[42] F. M. Stenton, *Anglo-Saxon England* (3rd edn, 1971), 264–5.

[43] Asser, c. 92, translated in *EHD*, 273.

[44] D. Hill, 'The Burghal Hidage – Lyng', *Proceedings of the Somerset Archaeological and Natural History Society*, 111 (1967), 64–6.

[45] Asser, c. 98.

[46] Asser, c. 83.

other at Appledore. The two forts were watched by the army and by the men from the *burhs*. This is the first mention of the new kind of force, the garrison of the *burhs* apparently operating as a separate organization and dependent therefore on a series of *burhs*. The mounted men who had already been mentioned in the accounts of the Wareham campaign of 876–7 acted as scouts and attacked small parties of Danes:[47] 'The king divided his army into two, so that always half were at home, half on service, apart from the men that guarded the *burhs* (*butan þæm monnum þe þa burga healden scolden*)'. The garrisoning of the *burhs* and the *burhs* themselves were now an important element in the defence of the realm, as can be seen in the *ASC*'s remark: 'and the King's thegns who were at home in the fortresses assembled from every borough east of the Parrett ... '.[48] The term used for fortresses is not consistent: *geweorcum* and *byrig* are used indiscriminately. In 894 the citizens (*burgware*) of Chichester put the Danes to flight and killed many hundreds of them when they were attempting to ravage in Sussex.[49]

In 895 Alfred fought a campaign which is of great interest to us. The Danes had turned up the River Lea, presumably to avoid the bridge which may be expected to have been built at this period between Southwark and London. They then built a fortress twenty miles above London which was attacked by a mixed party of the *fyrd* and the citizens' *burg wara*, apparently from London; the Saxons were defeated with the loss of four of the king's thegns. Alfred then came up at harvest time and camped in front of the *byrig* of London to allow the people to get in the harvest.

> Then one day the king rode up along the river, and examined where the river could be obstructed, so that they could not bring the ships out. And then this work was carried out: two fortresses (*ge weorc*) were made on the two sides of the river. When they had just begun that work (and had encamped for that purpose), the enemy perceived that they could not bring the ships out. Then they abandoned the ships and went overland till they reached Bridgnorth on the Severn and built that fortress.[50]

This passage not only shows Alfred making the decision to build a *burh*, but acting as his own chief engineer and selecting the site; it is also a fine example of the use of a 'bridge *burh*'.

Apart from the mention of the *wic gerefa* of Winchester dying in 896,[51] there are no further mentions of *burhs* or towns in the *ASC* for the reign of Alfred, but there are a few signed coins from the reign which show minting at London, Canterbury and Winchester, with Exeter begining to strike coins from

---

[47] *ASC, s.a.* 876.

[48] *ASC, s.a.* 893.

[49] *ASC, s.a.* 894.

[50] D. Whitelock, *The Beginnings of English Society* (1951), from *ASC, s.a.* 895.

[51] *ASC, s.a.* 896.

around 894. If we follow Stenton's definition of an Anglo-Saxon town as having a wall, a mint and a market, then perhaps we could assume that Exeter was a 'town'. That we have only a small part of the evidence for the *burhs* set up by Alfred is clear. For example Bath is a mint very early in the reign of Edward the Elder, and the reeve of Bath was sufficiently important to have his obit recorded in the *ASC*, *s.a.* 906. Christchurch was seized in the brief civil war that opens Edward the Elder's reign, but as Portchester did not come into royal hands until 904,[52] and so became available for refurbishing and adding to the defences of the realm, it would be unsafe to assume that all the *burhs* listed in the Burghal Hidage of *c.* 919 were built by Alfred. Some were built before his reign, some known from his reign did not survive to be recorded, and some were founded after his death.

Sufficient evidence for this system of garrisoned *burhs* in Wessex and south-west Mercia exists for us to agree that 'the details of the scheme are only known from the document of Edward's reign which is generally known as the "Burghal Hidage". But there is good reason to believe that its outline was laid down by Alfred.'[53] Asser did not claim at any point that Alfred had initiated or invented an urban policy. Clearly we know about 'the cities and towns he restored' (for example London) 'and the others which he built where none had been before' (for example Shaftesbury); we also know that he built forts (for example the unfinished fort in the Weald). The policy of expansion could very well have been under way in the reigns of his brothers, perhaps by 859 as a result of their experiences in Rome, or expanded as a result of knowledge of such Carolingian sites as Pont de l'Arche. Blackburn's point that the first two of the coinage reforms took place under Alfred's brothers and predecessors should alert us to the fact that Alfred was deeply involved with the surviving written sources for the period and on such as Asser we depend for evidence of Alfred's town policies.[54]

---

[52] S 372.

[53] Stenton, *Anglo-Saxon England*, 265.

[54] Blackburn, Chapter 11 in this volume.

Chapter 13

Alfred and London

Derek Keene

This paper is a response from a London historian to recent discoveries and interpretations concerning what we can now see as one of the defining episodes in London's history: Alfred's attitude to, control and organization of the place. That episode has much to tell us about the relationship, both then and now, between London and the state. These reflections do not offer new evidence or detailed interpretations, which are published elsewhere. They are based on the numerous contributions made by other scholars: archaeologists at the Museum of London and elsewhere, whose patient observations, careful chronologies and interpretative insights have reformed our understanding of London in this period; Tony Dyson, whose close examination of the documents concerning the city waterfront has done the same; and Mark Blackburn, Simon Keynes and others, whose reshuffling of the coinage and of relations between Wessex and Mercia has provided a new chronology and context for documented events. Taken together, these findings amount to one of the most striking clusters of paradigm shifts to have taken place in English historical studies in recent years.[1]

While historians wrestle with textual niceties and story-telling, archaeologists sometimes come up with the big picture. In this case their contribution has been to demonstrate that in Alfred's time or thereabouts London entirely changed its shape and focus. In attempting to understand this dramatic change, historians should remember that while the evidence recovered from archaeological strata of this period in London reveals sequences of events, absolute chronologies remain imprecise and may change as interpretation of the material moves forward. Texts tell us that between the seventh and the ninth centuries London was a busy, and presumably populous, commercial place, visited by merchants from overseas.[2] Archaeology demonstrates that this activity cannot have been within the city walls, which in the Roman period had sheltered the greater part of London's business. Renewed commercial life was associated with a suburban district to the west of the city. Here there was a large, dense and well-organized settlement extending over some 60 hectares from the National Gallery and

---

[1] Of two recent general studies, Abels, *Alfred*, pays due regard to Alfred's concern for London, while Smyth, *Alfred*, does not.

[2] For London in this period, see: M. Biddle, 'A city in transition: 400–800', in *The City of London From Prehistoric Times to c.1520*, ed. M. D. Lobel, The British Atlas of Historic Towns, 3 (1989), 20–29; A. Vince, *Saxon London: An Archaeological Investigation* (1990).

Seven Dials down to the river, and east to Chancery Lane and beyond. This was the *wic* or *vicus* of London, a name that seems to be preserved in the modern name Aldwych, first recorded in the late twelfth century as *vetus vicus* or *Aldewich*.[3] At its peak this settlement contained a resident population of several thousand people, probably well over 5000 since its extent was at least a quarter of the area covered by the city of London from about 1200 onwards. In its first phase the settlement seems to have been primarily commercial, but from the later seventh century onwards many of its inhabitants were engaged in specialized crafts.[4] Such a town needed an elaborate infrastructure of exchange to sustain it. Landing-places on the river frontage below the steeply shelving ground rising up to The Strand were presumably among its key installations. The Strand itself was probably the principal thoroughfare, and at least one street has been identified leading north from it. Inside the city walls, by contrast, there is very little evidence for settlement during this period and large areas seem to have been entirely empty. St Paul's Cathedral was probably the main focus of activity. It is noteworthy that city finds from this period tend to lie between St Paul's and the river.[5] The river thus served to convey supplies and distinguished visitors to the cathedral, as well as merchant vessels upstream to the *wic*, where there was probably also a vigorous downstream river trade. If there was a royal palace in the city it was probably close to St Paul's, perhaps within or adjoining the enclosure known as *Paulisburi*.[6] Place-names in the city denote the existence of other élite enclosures, but most of those names probably originated no earlier than the eleventh or twelfth century. One exception, represented by the modern name Lothbury (behind the Bank of England), may incorporate a short form of the personal name Hlothere, borne by a seventh-century king of Kent.[7] Lothbury,

---

[3] J. E. B. Gover, A. Mawer and F. M. Stenton, *The Place-Names of Middlesex*, English Place-Name Society, 18 (1942), 166. See R. Coates, 'New light from old wicks: the progeny of Latin *vicus*', *Nomina*, 22 (1999), 75–116.

[4] R. Cowie, 'A gazetteer of Middle Saxon sites in the Strand/Westminster area', *TLMAS*, 39 (1988), 37–46 (covers finds to 1991); R. Cowie and R. Whytehead, 'Lundenwic: the archaeological evidence for middle Saxon London', *Antiquity*, 63 (1989), 706–18; R. Cowie, 'Archaeological evidence for the waterfront of middle Saxon London', *Medieval Archaeology*, 36 (1992), 164–8; R. L. Whytehead and R. Cowie, with L. Blackmore, 'Excavations at the Peabody site, Chandos Place, and the National Gallery', *TLMAS*, 40 (1989, published 1993), 35–176; D. Bowsher and G. Malcolm, 'Excavations at the Royal Opera House: Middle Saxon London', *TLMAS*, 50 (1999), 4–11; D. Keene, 'London, 600–1300', in *The Cambridge Urban History of Britain*, vol. 1, *Middle Ages*, ed. D. M. Palliser (2000), 187–216; D. Keene, 'Industrial organisation in English towns, 650–1150', in *Labour and Labour Markets Between Town and Country (Middle Ages–19th Century)*, eds B. Blondé et al. (Turnhout, 2001), 53–74.

[5] Vince, *Saxon London*, Fig. 8.

[6] The location of the (or any) royal palace within the city is a complex subject worthy of fundamental reassessment. For an eleventh-century indication that it lay immediately to the north of St Paul's, see R. H. C. Davis, 'The College of St Martin-le-Grand and the Anarchy, 1135–54', *London Topographical Record*, 23 (1972), 9–26. For other suggestions, see below.

[7] Biddle, 'City in transition', 23; E. Ekwall, *Street-Names of the City of London* (1954), 194–7.

where one high-status object of eighth-century date has been found, may thus denote an early focus of authority within the walls at some distance from St Paul's. Kentish laws of about 680 refer to the king's hall at London,[8] but that was almost certainly in the suburban settlement since the hall said to be in the *wic* (*þonne tæme he to wic to cyngæs sele*) and the activities of the king's 'wic-reeve' (*wicgerefa*) were associated with it. The commercial district of London thus contained its own administrative focus from an early date.

One explanation of this distinctive pattern of city and suburb may be that the entire walled city had come to be seen as a reserved enclosure associated with the exercise of power. Of more practical significance, however, was the fact that the substantial remains of the Roman riverside wall and other buildings probably rendered it difficult to bring the city into use again as a site of trade. Open land immediately upstream was much more freely accessible from the river.

During the ninth century the greater part of the *wic* settlement was abandoned. Our understanding is partial since we know little about sites close to The Strand itself, where, if anywhere, some survival and continuity might be expected. The outlying church of St Martin-in-the-Fields may have survived from the early settlement, and it is possible that other churches did too.[9] To the north of The Strand, however, there is no evidence indicating habitation later than the ninth century, and the latest surviving remains of houses are overlaid by a type of soil which indicates that agriculture was the predominant activity there until the seventeenth century, when building began again. The recent excavation at the Royal Opera House suggests that contraction and desertion constituted a two-stage process, associated perhaps with general economic disruption inflicted by the Viking marauders, whose first recorded attack on London (*Lunde(n)ne*) was in 842,[10] and with a local defensive response to the invasions. In this neighbourhood near its northern limit, the settlement either contracted from north to south along the street which ran through the site, or was truncated when what seems to have been a defensive ditch was dug across it on an east–west line. This ditch was a prominent feature in the mid-ninth century when, perhaps about 851, a 'purse-hoard' of Northumbrian coins was buried in soil which appears to have constituted its southern berm. Unfortunately, the precise stratigraphical association between the hoard, the ditch and other archaeological features is not clear.[11]

From the tenth, or perhaps the later ninth, century onwards it is clear from the distribution of datable buildings, streets and finds that the main focus of settlement and business in London was within the walls.[12] But London did not

---

[8] Attenborough, *Laws*, 22–3.

[9] Biddle, 'City in transition', 28; Vince, *Saxon London*, 61.

[10] *ASC 'A'*, ed. Bately, 42; *'B'*, ed. Taylor, 31; *'C'*, ed. O'Keefe, 55; *'D'*, ed. Gubbin, 21.

[11] Bowsher and Malcolm, 'Excavations'; discussion of coins in G. Malcolm and D. Bowsher with R. Cowie, *Middle Saxon London: Excavations at the Royal Opera House, 1989 to 1999*, Museum of London Archaeological Services Monograph 15, 2003, 128–9, 278–84.

[12] Vince, *Saxon London*, Figs 14, 17, 24.

suddenly regain its former standing as a major concentration of people and trade. Thus, while there is evidence for inland trade between London, the Thames Valley and the Danelaw from the early tenth century, the city's overseas commerce appears not to have revived until much later.[13] The intramural settlement grew especially rapidly from the eleventh century onwards, and we know that new streets were added to the existing system, both within and without the walls, between the late tenth and the early thirteenth centuries.[14] Even about 1200, when the city's population may have neared 40,000, large parts of the area within the walls were sparsely settled, especially towards the north and east.[15]

This new appreciation of its changing shape makes a vital contribution to interpreting the texts concerning London in the ninth century. At that time the name 'London' seems to have denoted the entire place, within which there were two physically distinct elements. One was the extramural settlement which, when it was distinguished from the whole, was denoted by the terms *wic* or *port*. The other was the area within the Roman walls, denoted by the terms *civitas* or *burh*, which came more frequently to be used in accounts of the defence of London during the late ninth century.[16]

If we are to understand London in the reign of Alfred, we must place it in its geographical context, both commercial and strategic. Perhaps the best characterization of London's context, then as now, is as a metropolis on the margin – marginal both to the inland territory of Britain and to continental Europe, but well connected by road, river and sea to both. The key to London's success lies in its role as an interchange, dealing in goods, information, money and ideas, and often processing or adding value to those commodities before distributing them elsewhere. Middle England, however, is almost always an influence looming in the background. From the seventh century onwards, London was a powerful attraction to rulers whose heartlands lay at a distance in Kent, Wessex and Mercia. Mercian interests prevailed (although they may not necessarily have excluded those of Wessex), and London achieved a key position in an axis of power and circulation which extended from the Midlands down the Thames Valley to the estuary and to highly commercial districts in eastern Kent and overseas.[17] As in other periods, London offered distinct advantages as a strategic node in such a system, attractive to rulers as a source of income, goods and power, and as commanding vital routes. As the Viking menace grew, West Saxons and Mercians buried their differences, and control

---

[13] L. Blackmore, 'Aspects of trade and exchange evidenced by recent work on Saxon and medieval pottery from London', *TLMAS*, 50 (1999), 38–54.

[14] D. Keene, 'The character and development of the Cheapside area; an overview', *TLMAS*, 41 (1990), 178–94, esp. 178–82; T. Dyson, 'King Alfred and the restoration of London', *London Journal*, 15 (1990), 99–110, esp. 99–100.

[15] Keene, 'London, 600–1300'.

[16] For a summary discussion of the use of these terms, see Biddle, 'City in transition', 27–8.

[17] Keene, 'London, 600–1300'; S. Keynes, 'The control of Kent in the ninth century', *Early Medieval Europe*, 2 (1993), 111–31.

of London, once a matter of rivalry, became one of mutual concern. The two kingdoms were linked by royal marriages and came to share a common monetary system. London nevertheless remained within the Mercian sphere. During the 860s and 870s the output of its mint appears to have been greater than that of the Canterbury mint under West Saxon control, although of an increasingly debased coinage. By the 860s, however, the bishop of London appears to have moved into the orbit of the West Saxon king.[18]

The Viking storming of London in 851[19] seems to have been important for these developments and has implications for the royal intervention there later in the century. The *Chronicle*'s terms (*Lundenburg, Lundenburh*) suggest that the walled city was attacked, perhaps because it was a seat of authority where there was a great store of wealth. That does not preclude an assault on the suburb, however, or the possibility that the suburb itself was protected by a defensive work. The scale of the disaster is indicated by the slump in Mercian coin output and presumably prompted King Burgred in 853 to enter an especially close alliance with Wessex.[20] In reasserting control over London, as his coins indicate that he did, Burgred perhaps assigned rights there to men of power whom he could trust. That may be the underlying purpose of a charter attributed to 857 by which he sold to the bishop of Worcester, who already enjoyed some freedom from toll in London, for his own use or that of the city of Worcester, a profitable little estate in the *vicus* of London which had formerly been purchased from a reeve called Ceolmund.[21] Along with the property, or perhaps just for use within it, went the weights and measures customarily used in the town (*portus*). It seems likely that the site, formerly associated with a reeve, lay within the suburban settlement or *wic*, and possible that it had a role in the regulation of trade. The property was said to be not far from the west gates of London, a description which may indicate a situation in the settlement which lay across the Fleet in front of Newgate and Ludgate. The description could indicate a site just within the walls between the two gates, but the reference to the *vicus* favours an extramural site.[22] It is possible that the property remained in the possession of the bishop and church of Worcester and roughly corresponded to property in The Strand, including the church of St Mary, which was restored to them at the beginning of the twelfth century. The Strand property, where the bishops of Worcester later had their London house, was within the area now occupied by

---

[18] S. Keynes, 'King Alfred and the Mercians', in *Kings, Currency and Alliances*, eds M. A. S. Blackburn and D. M. Dumville (1998), 1–45.

[19] ASC '*A*', ed. Bately, 44; '*B*', ed. Taylor, 31; '*C*', ed. O'Keefe, 55.

[20] Keynes, 'Alfred and the Mercians', 7–9.

[21] BCS 492 (S 208); S. Kelly, 'Trading privileges from eighth-century England', *Early Medieval Europe*, 1 (1992), 3–28, esp. 12.

[22] Biddle, 'City in transition', 29; Kelly, 'Trading privileges', 12, suggests that the reference to the *portus* indicates that the property lay within the city rather than the suburb, but that seems less likely. The charter is often discussed as if it referred to a single west gate rather than the plural: cf. E. Ekwall, *Street-Names*, 38.

Somerset House, an ideal location from which to oversee the *wic* and its business.[23]

In 871–2, the first year of Alfred's reign, the Danes wintered in the city of London (*Lundenbyrig*).[24] Some part of the area within the walls, if not the whole of it, would have made an ideal winter refuge. According to the latest views on the coinage, there is no reason to believe that the invaders undertook any more prolonged occupation of London between that year and Alfred's death. The output of the London mint continued, and there is a notable continuity in the group of London moneyers from the later part of Burgred's reign through the successive phases of Alfred's coinage. The Danes drove Burgred from the kingdom in 874, but Alfred succeeded him in control of London and reformed the coinage. One of Alfred's London issues early in this phase represents him as 'king of the English' and another as 'king of the Saxons and Mercians'. This may be an early articulation of ideas concerning English unity against the enemy, but it may be no more than an acknowledgement by Mercians in London and its region that Alfred was the *de facto* ruler, at least until the outcome of the Danes' appointment of Ceolwulf as king of Mercia became clear. Alfred is not so styled on coins from his Wessex mints at that time. A year or two later, about 877–8, Alfred apparently recognized Ceolwulf's control of Mercia and London. This may reflect the formal division of Mercia by the Danes in 877 and the fragmentation of authority in Wessex during very difficult years for Alfred. Ceolwulf's rule in London, indicated by his production of coin, continued to be effective until he disappears from view in 879–80.[25]

What these royal activities imply for the physical settlement of London is difficult to say. They may only have affected the city within the walls, where moneying was probably concentrated close to the seat of royal authority. This is suggested by a coin weight of the period (?876–80) found on the north side of St Paul's churchyard, in the area where the citizens' folk-moot is known later to have met.[26] In the later topography of the city this was a highly significant location, set between the cathedral and a possible site for the royal palace and opening east into Cheapside, the city's principal business street. Goldsmiths, who would have included moneyers, clustered at the west end of Cheapside, in an association with the seat of power which resembled that of their counterparts

---

[23] R. R. Darlington (ed.), *The Cartulary of Worcester Cathedral Priory*, Pipe Roll Society new series 38 (1968 for 1962), nos 53, 70–72. One reference to the restored church of St Mary (no. 53; T. Hearne (ed.), *Hemingi Chartularii Ecclesiae Wigornensis* (1723), 427–9) implies that it was within the walls close to the church of St James Garlickhithe, but that is probably a confusion since there was no church of St Mary close to that of St James.

[24] *ASC 'A'*, ed. Bately, 49; *'B'*, ed. Taylor, 35; *'C'*, ed. O'Keefe, 60; *'D'*, ed. Gubbin, 25.

[25] M. Blackburn, 'The London mint in the reign of Alfred', in *Kings, Currency and Alliances*, eds Blackburn and Dumville, 105–23; Keynes, 'Alfred and the Mercians'. For a less favourable view of Alfred's position in London at this time, see Smyth, *King Alfred*, 48–50.

[26] Blackburn, 'London mint', 116; L. Webster and J. Backhouse (eds), *The Making of England: Anglo-Saxon Art and Culture, A.D. 600–900* (1991), 286 (no. 264).

in Winchester.[27] The years around 880 were the period in which Alfred's broader defensive strategy, involving the establishment of walled centres of refuge and of mints at inland towns, began to be put into effect. At the same time Londoners may have begun to use the walled city as a place of refuge, perhaps even colonizing whatever installation the Danes had made for their overwintering. The distribution of London coin hoards is suggestive on this point. A hoard attributed to about 842 from the Middle Temple is clearly associated with the western commercial settlement, as are the recently discovered hoard of about 851 from the Royal Opera House, a hoard of about 872 from Waterloo Bridge and perhaps another of the same date from Westminster Bridge. Two other hoards, from within the city walls at Bucklersbury and in Thames Street, indicate that the shift of settlement from suburb to city was under way by about 880 since they contain coins of the special 'London Monogram' type which Alfred probably issued to mark his resumption of control of London after Ceolwulf's death.[28]

Coins provide little help with disentangling the next stage. A newly appreciated annal for 883 is usually translated to mean that in that year the English (presumably Mercians and Saxons) encamped against the Danes at London (*sæton wið þone here æt Lundenne*) and that the outcome was an English military success following a short-lived Viking occupation of the city.[29] But does the *Chronicle*'s phrase necessarily imply a siege rather than some more peaceful form of meeting?[30] And need the Vikings have been in the city rather than some place nearby?

Next come the famous events of 886. Asser notes that Alfred restored the city of London and made it habitable again (*Lundoniam civitatem honorifice restaurauit et habitabilem fecit*).[31] This seems to be a clear reference to resettlement within the walls and perhaps to refurbishment of the city's defences. The corresponding account in the *Chronicle* (*gesette Ælfred cing Lundenburh*)[32] is now usually taken to mean that Alfred 'occupied' London, perhaps following a siege, and in the tenth century its verb was translated as 'besieged' (*obsidetur*).[33] But *gesettan* can equally well denote a settling of people or the physical ordering

---

[27] C. N. L. Brooke and G. Keir, *London 800–1216: the shaping of a city* (1975), 277–8; M. Biddle (ed.), *Winchester in the Early Middle Ages: An Edition and Discussion of the Winton Domesday* (1976), 397–400.

[28] Blackburn, 'London mint', 110n., 120–22; M. Blackburn and H. Pagan, 'A revised checklist of coin hoards from the British Isles *c.* 500–1100', in *Anglo-Saxon Monetary History: Essays in Memory of Michael Dolley*, ed. M. A. S. Blackburn (1986), 291–313, esp. 294.

[29] *ASC 'B'*, ed. Taylor, 38; *'C'*, ed. O'Keefe, 63; *'D'*, ed. Gubbin, 28. Keynes, 'Alfred and the Mercians', 21–3.

[30] Cf. the range of meanings indicated in J. Roberts, C. Kay and L. Grundy, *A Thesaurus of Old English* (2 vols, 1995), 2, 1319.

[31] Asser, c. 83, p. 69.

[32] *ASC 'A'*, ed. Bately, 53; *'B'*, ed. Taylor, 39; *'C'*, ed. O'Keefe, 64; *'D'*, ed. Gubbin, 29.

[33] Keynes, 'Alfred and the Mercians', 21–3.

of a place,[34] and thus correspond precisely to Asser's Latin. Asser's statement that this restoration followed the burning of towns and the slaughter of people may refer to the events of 885, when Rochester had been besieged, rather than to any recent assault on London (in 886, or even in 883). Alfred acknowledged the essentially Mercian character of London and entrusted the city (*burh*) to Æthelred, a powerful figure and probably a member of the Mercian royal house who nevertheless had already acknowledged Alfred's authority and at that time or soon afterwards married Alfred's daughter. A later account states that Alfred gained control of the area surrounding London and of that part of Mercia that Ceolwulf had held.[35] That territory may have corresponded to the 'lands belonging to London (*Lundenbyrig*) and Oxford' which Alfred evidently entrusted to Æthelred, and which on the latter's death in 911 passed to Alfred's son.[36] As ealdorman of Mercia Æthelred from 886 occupied a position very like that of the ealdormen governing other former kingdoms which had been brought within the orbit of Wessex earlier in the ninth century. Æthelred's control of this territory was always under the authority of the English king, who from time to time took direct action there. Moreover, unlike his immediate predecessors as rulers of Mercia, Æthelred did not issue coins, a clear indication of the limits to his power.

These events reveal the strategic significance of London as a forward defence in a militarized zone. The reordering of the city may also have formed part of an ideological programme intended to promote it as a symbol of unity against a common enemy. The *Chronicle*'s account of 886 states that those 'English people' (*Angelcyn*) not under the rule of the Danes on that occasion submitted to Alfred. Asser's use of the word *honorifice* and Alfred's more general concern to emphasize the common cause of Mercians (Angles) and Saxons suggests that the occasion was one of special ceremonial significance, involving the deployment of a buzz word (*Angelcyn*) whose potential to shape a collective identity resembled that of 'Britons' in much later, but certainly comparable, historiographical circumstances. Moreover, London's 'neutral' position between Wessex and Mercia made it the ideal site at which to proclaim such a message. It has even been suggested that Alfred had a larger vision for London as a royal seat, and in that connection may have revived an earlier proposal to shift the metropolitan see to the city.[37] On the other hand, we should allow the possibility that the ideological aspect of these events was elaborated in subsequent literary accounts rather than fully articulated at the time.[38] In any case, ambitious plans

---

[34] Roberts, Kay and Grundy, *Thesaurus*, 2, 1311–12.

[35] B. Thorpe (ed.), *Florentii Wigornensis monachi chronicon ex chronicis* (2 vols, 1848–9), vol. 1, 267.

[36] *ASC 'A'*, ed. Bately, 64; '*C'*, ed. O'Keefe, 73; '*D'*, ed. Gubbin, 38.

[37] S. Foot, 'The making of *angelcynn*: English identity before the Norman Conquest', *TRHS*, sixth series 6 (1996), 25–47; J. L. Nelson, 'The political ideas of Alfred of Wessex', in *Kings and Kingship in Medieval Europe*, ed. A. J. Duggan (1993), 125–58.

[38] Cf. Smyth, *Alfred*, 108–9.

to elevate London as a political and ecclesiastical centre, if they existed at all, appear to have been dropped before the end of the reign. Whatever the political and ideological significance of the 'restoration' of London in 886, the security of London required constant attention through the 890s. This is demonstrated by Viking activities in the vicinity and their forts on the Thames estuary and the river Lea, as well as by the Londoners' role in assaulting them. It was in these years rather than earlier in Alfred's reign that London served as an effective stronghold in the forefront of resistance.

What did the 'restoration' of the city amount to? Were the perhaps few remaining inhabitants of the *wic* shifted *en masse* to new houses within the walls? Or was the whole process more gradual, involving the recruitment of a now dispersed population to inhabit and build the city? A gradual development seems most likely, but perhaps following some predetermined plan. By the years 893 and 895 the 'citizens' (*burgwara*) of London, presumably dwelling within the walls, had become a distinct and sufficiently numerous body of people to be effective in military action. They participated in attacks on the forts at Benfleet and on the Lea and brought back hostages and ships to the city. Indications from other towns, including Winchester, suggest that restoration would involve the laying out of a regular pattern of streets, with a principal market street at the core, and perhaps the apportionment of plots of land and economic rights to powerful lords.[39] The latter is especially well recorded in two London documents. They are not entirely above suspicion, but their content is circumstantially convincing and their dates may be correct.[40] Thus in 889 Alfred, in association with Æthelred as *subregulus*, granted to the bishop of Worcester an enclosure in London known to the citizens as 'at the old stone building' called *Hwaetmundestane*. This has been convincingly identified with a block in the city on the river frontage adjoining the important commercial landing-place later known as Queenhithe. Within the property the bishop was to have weights and measures, for the use of which he could exact a charge. He could also exact tolls on transactions within his land, but outside in the public street and on the 'commercial foreshore' (*ripa emtoralis*), where ships presumably beached at low tide, tolls were payable to the king. The purpose of this grant seems to have been to provide the bishop with a facility comparable to that which Burgred had sold to his predecessor in the *wic* in 857. The dimensions of the plot are given; it was bounded at one end by a public street (identifiable as the later Great Trinity Lane) and at the other by the city wall, presumably the Roman riverside wall. The second record concerns a conference at Chelsea in 898–9 regarding the planning (*instauratio*) of London, and involving Alfred, Archbishop Plegmund

---

[39] M. Biddle and D. Hill, 'Late Saxon planned towns', *Antiquaries Journal*, 51 (1971), 70–85.

[40] BCS 561, 577–8 (S 346, 1628). The essential discussions are: T. Dyson, 'Two Saxon land grants for Queenhithe', in J. Bird, H. Chapman and J. Clark (eds), *Collectanea Londiniensia: Studies in London Archaeology and History Presented to Ralph Merrifield* (London and Middlesex Archaeological Society Special Paper 8, 1978), 200–215; Dyson, 'King Alfred'.

of Canterbury, Æthelred and Æthelred's consort. Two adjacent plots of land were assigned, one to the archbishop and the other to the bishop of Worcester, the latter presumably identical with his acquisition in 889.[41] The plots were separated by a public street running up from the river and bounded by narrow lanes to west and east. The plots adjoined the wall, beyond which they had mooring or beaching rights for ships (*navium stationes*) according to their width.

Twelfth-century and later records of property-holding on the waterfront corroborate the existence of the bishop's and the archbishop's earlier holdings on these sites. The stated dimensions of the plot granted in 889 indicate that its proportions correspond with those of the block bounded by Thames Street, Bread Street Hill, Great Trinity Lane, and Little Trinity Lane as recorded on the Ordnance Survey map at 1:2500 scale surveyed in 1873. The published interpretation of the dimensions makes them fit that block by attributing to the perch measure used a significantly shorter length than the conventional 16 feet 6 inches.[42] On the other hand, it seems equally possible that a perch of conventional length was used and that the 'mismatches' in width are to be accounted for by some imprecision in measurement, by the irregular outline of the block and by subsequent shifts in the frontages of what were in origin probably wide and uncertainly defined streets. The 'mismatch' in length could be explained if the riverside wall, which has not been observed in the immediate vicinity, lay somewhat to the south of its commonly estimated position.

These assignments of large blocks of land to two of the king's most influential supporters and intellectual associates seem designed to secure their position in London, to promote trade and to ensure the orderly development of the city. Worcester and Canterbury are also significant in this context since they represent poles on the main axis of Mercian authority with which London had long been associated, suggesting that the restoration of London was part of a wider political strategy. Plegmund, who became archbishop in 890, had a Mercian background and his involvement in London may have marked the end of any plans to elevate its see to metropolitan status. The two plots assigned in 898–9 were said to be at 'Æthelred's hithe' (*Æderedes hythe*), a name which denotes the landing-place later known as Queenhithe and which links the sub-king to the control of an important site serving London's crucial river trade. Presumably his rights were limited to the facilities on the foreshore, at one of the few locations on London's later river frontage where there was open access from the river to a public market. These events reveal Æthelred acting in association with Bishop Wærferth in a way which resembles their partnership in the establishment of the *burh* at Worcester at about the same time.[43] The apparent absence of the bishop of London from events associated with the refoundation of the city is striking.

---

[41] Kelly, 'Trading privileges', 12–13 and n. 27 doubts aspects of Dyson's interpretation, but offers more complex and less convincing alternatives.

[42] Dyson, 'Two Saxon land grants', 208–9.

[43] *EHD*, 540–41.

His extensive territorial rights in London, within and without Bishopsgate and between St Paul's and the river, may already have been long established,[44] although it is possible that they were reordered during the 880s. There are few other clues as to land apportionment within the walls at that time.

These two documents of 889 and 898 indicate the existence of streets forming some sort of grid and perhaps created since 886. Certainly none of the streets involved had known Roman predecessors. The street between the two plots, later Bread Street, ran directly up from the river to Cheapside. Although not recorded by name until much later, and only indirectly indicated by archaeological evidence of the late ninth or tenth century, Cheapside bears a striking resemblance to the market streets that formed spinal elements in some other 'Alfredian' street plans. It was wide, occupied a well-drained site and ran directly east from St Paul's, a situation which suggests its importance from an early date. Only one other street, now known as Bow Lane and lying a block east from Bread Street, ran uninterruptedly up from the river to Cheapside, and there is some archaeological evidence from near its Cheapside end that it dates from the late ninth or early tenth century. These streets indicate economic functions and relationships, and seem intended to link river trade with the city's internal market. In contrast to patterns in some other towns, this layout was not replicated to the north of Cheapside. The main area of initial settlement was thus clearly associated with the western half of the city within the walls, the established focus of power, and with the area between Cheapside and the river, as is further demonstrated by the presence of at least one cross-street (represented by Great Trinity Lane and its continuations to east and west) on an east–west line. Almost precisely halfway between that cross-street and Cheapside is Atheling Street ('the street of the prince', now Watling Street), aligned on Ludgate and perhaps owing its name to the fact that it led into the enclosure around St Paul's. These features suggest that Atheling Street was an integral feature of the early plan or predated it.[45]

The hunt for grids and extended linear features has had a sorry influence on London street studies,[46] but there are some indications that streets were laid out on a regular pattern in the other half of the city, to the east of Walbrook, at the end of the ninth or in the tenth century. Archaeology suggests that Fish Street Hill, leading up from London Bridge, could be of this date, as could Botolph Lane two blocks to the east and running directly up from the river to Fenchurch Street. A block further east, St Mary's Hill likewise runs up to Fenchurch Street. Perhaps principles similar to those which informed the relationship between Cheapside, Bow Lane and Bread Street were employed in laying out this area.

[44] P. Taylor, 'The bishop of London's City Soke', *Bulletin of the Institute of Historical Research*, 58 (1980), 174–82.

[45] Keene, 'Cheapside area'; Dyson, 'King Alfred'; Ekwall, *Street Names,* 81.

[46] Cf. T. Tatton-Brown, 'The topography of Anglo-Saxon London', *Antiquity*, 60 (1986), 21–8; G. Milne, 'King Alfred's plan for London?', *London Archaeologist*, 6 (1990), 206–7.

Fenchurch Street and Lombard Street, and perhaps also Cornhill, probably originated in this period, their position being in part dictated by the Walbrook crossing
at the east end of Cheapside, on which they converged. Eastcheap, on the other
hand, which is sometimes claimed as the eastern equivalent of Cheapside, almost certainly postdates the streets running up to Fenchurch Street.[47] There is
thus a suggestion of an intended downstream focus of trade and settlement in
Alfred's London, as well as an upstream one at Æthelred's Hithe. London Bridge
itself may well have been constructed at this time, or reconstructed for the first
time since the Romans. The earliest archaeological features identifiable as part
of the bridge structure are no older than late tenth century,[48] but the reference to
Suthringaweorc in the Burghal Hidage suggests that the bridgehead settlement
of Southwark, and presumptively the bridge, existed by the early tenth century
and were part of the Alfredian scheme.[49] As well as carrying traffic across the
river, a bridge would have served to defend the main residential and commercial
area in the western part of the city against raiders coming up the Thames, an
arrangement which has parallels elsewhere in England and overseas. One other
seemingly regular group of streets in the eastern part of the city, but above the
bridge, may have originated under Alfred or soon after. This consists of the
modern Cannon Street and the streets set at right angles to it. Cannon Street may
postdate Fish Street Hill and antedate Eastcheap, but otherwise its date is far
from clear.

One major feature probably dating from the restoration of the city is the
boundary of its jurisdiction. The early boundary, which survives on the east side
of the city and against Moorfields to the north, followed a line 200 to 300 yards
in front of the city wall and probably marked out a killing-ground for the
purposes of defence. There was a similar boundary at Winchester.[50] By 1200 the
city's extramural jurisdiction had been greatly extended to the west and north
outside the city gates, to more or less its modern line. On the west side the early
boundary corresponded to the river Fleet and a tenth-century description of the
Westminster Abbey land which then included the site of the *wic* identified that
part of the boundary as 'London fen', a precise characterization of the valley
bottom. Another description of the same part of the boundary identifies it as 'the
alderman's boundary', a name which may preserve a memory of Ealdorman
Æthelred as ruler of the city.[51]

Where did Æthelred base himself when in London? He may have lodged
near St Paul's, if that is where earlier and later kings dwelled. A place-name and

---

[47] *London Journal*, 20 (1995), 108.

[48] B. Watson, T. Bingham and T. Dyson, *London Bridge: 2,000 Years of a River Crossing*
(Museum of London Archaeological Services Monograph 8, 2001), 57–60.

[49] D. Hill and A. R. Rumble (eds), *The Defence of Wessex and Anglo-Saxon Fortifications*
(1996), 120, 218; for problems, see Dyson, 107 and n. 57.

[50] Biddle (ed.), *Winchester in the Early Middle Ages*, 257, 260–68.

[51] M. J. Gelling, 'The boundaries of the Westminster charters', *TLMAS*, n.s. 11 (1953), 101–4.

legends, however, offer clues concerning a possible different location.[52] There is a twelfth-century story that the parish church of St Alban, Wood Street had once been the chapel of King Offa of Mercia, the founder of St Alban's Abbey. The chapel was said to have adjoined the royal palace, the liberty of which had been reduced to a single small house.[53] This story may have been a fiction designed to bolster the abbey's claim to the church of St Alban, which may have been of no great antiquity and which the abbey was then in the process of losing to the monks of Westminster.[54] A few yards away stood the church of St Mary Aldermanbury. That church took its name from the house called Aldermanbury to which was attached a small estate comprising churches and other property rights.[55] This estate is first recorded 1123 × 32 as the 'soke of *Aldremanesburi*'.[56] The name, later transferred to a street, occurs in both plural and singular forms. If plural, the reference is probably to the aldermen of the city wards whose Guildhall, subsequently the heart of civic government, stood close by. If originally singular (as in the case of the first record), the reference could be to the enclosure of the most singular alderman in London's history, Ealdorman Æthelred himself.[57] Wood Street, leading to Cripplegate, may have been the earliest of the streets to the north of Cheapside and could have served, along with Bread Street almost directly in line to the south, to link Æthelred's inland base with his hithe on the river frontage. A sixteenth-century text from St Paul's Cathedral refers to property in Aldermanbury as having been the 'place' of King Ethelbert of Kent, the founder of St Paul's.[58] These references to Ethelbert and Offa may indicate no more than wishful thinking, but they could derive from a memory of the neighbourhood, some of whose topographical features reflect the plan of the former Roman fort on the site (Aldermanbury adjoined the site of the east gate of the fort) as a seat of royal or public authority under Æthelred and possibly earlier. The recent identification of the Roman amphitheatre, just south-east of the fort, as a feature which survived with sufficient presence to influence the medieval pattern of streets in the neighbourhood, has added a further element to the discussion. This is the possibility that the *arena* was a space which came to

---

[52] Discussed in outline in T. Dyson and J. Schofield, 'Saxon London', in *Anglo-Saxon Towns in Southern England*, ed. J. Haslam (1984), 285–313, esp. 306–8.

[53] H. T. Riley (ed.), *Gesta Abbatum monasterii sancti Albani, a Thoma Walsingham, regnante Ricardo secundo, eiusdem ecclesiae praecentore, compilata*, Rolls Series 28 (3 vols, 1867–9), 1, 55; R. Vaughan, *Matthew Paris* (1958), 182–4.

[54] E. Mason (ed.), *Westminster Abbey Charters, 1066–c. 1214*, London Record Society 25 (1988), 145–6 (mistranslates the St Alban's record).

[55] J. C. Davies (ed.), *The Cartae Antiquae Rolls 11–20*, Pipe Roll Society 71 (1960 for 1957), no. 339.

[56] H. W. C. Davis, 'London lands and liberties of St Paul's, 1066–1139', in *Essays in Medieval History Presented to T.F. Tout*, eds A. G. Little and F. M. Powicke (1925), 45–59, at 56.

[57] F. M. Stenton, *Norman London, an essay* (1934), 12 (favours the originality of the plural form); Ekwall, *Street Names*, 195.

[58] W. Page, *London, its Origin and Early Development* (1929), 129.

be used for civic assembly, regulated by whoever controlled the site of authority at Aldermanbury, and that the Guildhall itself was the descendant of some earlier high-status structure forming part of the amphitheatre.[59] This would place an important stage in the evolution of London's civic topography in the time of Alfred or earlier, but much remains uncertain about these possible connections. The former *arena* appears to have been unused between the fourth or fifth centuries and the eleventh, when houses were built on the site, which can hardly have served as a place of assembly at that time. The earliest part of the Guildhall structure so far observed seems to date from no earlier than the mid-twelfth century.[60] Nor do we know for certain that the building was used as the city Guildhall until the thirteenth century: a 'guildhall' mentioned 1123 × 32 need not have been the civic building.[61] Moreover, weighing against all the arguments concerning the existence of an early royal residence, site of authority or seat of city government in the neighbourhood, is the body of archaeological evidence, which indicates that settlement spread slowly to the north of Cheapside and that there is little sign of activity in the vicinity of Aldermanbury before the eleventh or twelfth century. It may have been in the twelfth and thirteenth centuries, and not under Alfred or earlier, that the administration of the city came to be based in this district within the walls.

Conclusion

Under Alfred London experienced a major transformation, which undoubtedly took place under royal patronage and control. A disrupted and contracting trading settlement was relocated or re-established within the walls, which had hitherto contained, so far as we can tell, only seats of episcopal, royal and perhaps other authorities. The outlines of the commercial infrastructure (markets, streets and landing-places) which shaped the city's later growth were laid out, although the extent of that activity is far from clear. Though undertaken by a king of Wessex, these actions can be seen as part of a continuing Mercian tradition of managing London through the extended ninth-century crisis of invasion and warfare. So extreme was the crisis that the programme for London came to be driven by the common interest of Wessex and Mercia. Notions of competition between the two kingdoms for the control of London may be inappropriate. Nevertheless, Wessex became the dominant power, to which Mercian authority was subordinated. Coinage indicates the complexity of the process, a period of joint currency being followed by one of separate but parallel currencies associated with London. In the end, however, the Mercian right to issue money was terminated. As experi-

---

[59] Biddle, 'City in transition', 23–4.

[60] N. Bateman, 'The London amphitheatre', *Current Archaeology*, 137 (1994), 164–71; N. C. W. Bateman, 'The London amphitheatre: excavations, 1987–1996', *Britannia*, 28 (1997), 51–85.

[61] C. M. Barron, *The Medieval Guildhall of London* (1974), 15.

ence in the European Union teaches us today, there are few more significant forms of regalian emasculation than losing one's coins. In 886, Alfred may have exploited his control of London to proclaim a new sense of English identity, intended to over-ride former national loyalties. He perhaps had plans for the city as a royal centre, but they did not last long. Indeed, despite its overwhelming size, wealth and power, London did not conclusively emerge as the English capital until the late thirteenth century. In the late ninth its enduring Mercian character prevailed. Indeed, Ealdorman Æthelred left a more distinct memory in the city with the place-name 'Æthelred's hithe', still in use in the twelfth century, than did Alfred himself. By the end of the reign it seems that Winchester had emerged as the site for memorializing Alfred's house, through the foundation of great churches, gifts and burial.[62] Alfred himself was buried in Winchester. We do not know where Æthelred lies.

---

[62] Smyth, *Alfred*, 512.

Chapter 14

Succession and inheritance: a gendered perspective on Alfred's family history

Pauline Stafford

The story we have of Alfred's family history is largely the story Alfred chose to tell us. It is preserved now in Asser's *Life* in particular, for whose content Alfred himself was an important source, and in Alfred's will, in which the king recited a series of agreements and arrangements about family land.[1] Another version is to be found in the West Saxon genealogical material. This too was compiled in Alfred's reign in circles close to the king to defend Alfred's claim to the throne. It was then incorporated into the *Anglo-Saxon Chronicle*.[2] All of these accounts are arguably teleological, explaining how the late ninth-century situation had been arrived at, and making Alfred the end towards which the West Saxon family was inexorably moving. All are certainly retrospective, and potentially heavily edited, versions of the family's past, and the resulting problems for reconstructing Alfred's family have been recognized.[3] The purpose of this paper is to revisit and extend the analysis of those problems, particularly for the period pre-871. Janet Nelson's article cited in note 3 has already suggested that asking about the women as well as the men of the family may be a way forward. I want to give that new key of gender another turn in an attempt to unlock and remember more of the ninth-century family story Alfred rewrote and forgot.

Some general observations on gender and the early English sources are a necessary preliminary. The documents overtly concerned with land and landholding can roughly be divided into two. On the one hand, there are the diplomas or royal charters, largely in Latin and concerned ostensibly with direct royal patronage. On the other a range of texts, usually but not always in the vernacular, is concerned with the passing on of land within families, or between individuals and churches, thus with inheritance, bequests and the disputes these can produce.[4] This distinction is heavily gendered. Women are almost, but not

---

1 Asser; the will is in Harmer, *Documents*, no. 11.

2 D. Dumville, 'The West Saxon genealogical regnal list and the chronology of early Wessex', *Peritia*, 4 (1985), 21–66.

3 For example as note 2 Dumville and J. L. Nelson, 'Reconstructing a royal family: reflections on Alfred from Asser, chapter 2', in *People and Places in Northern Europe, 500–1600*, eds N. Lund and I. Wood (1991), 47–66, with particular attention to Alfred's maternal kin.

4 See, for example, Harmer, *Documents*, no. 4 (S 1197) – Lufu's arrangements; Harmer,

completely, absent from the diplomas, whether as grantors, grantees and to a lesser extent as witnesses. The ninth century as presented by the diplomas is largely a world of men, granting and receiving land and witnessing these transactions. By contrast, the second group of texts is full of women. A high proportion of them deal with complicated arrangements for succession to land and disputes about it, and they involve women – as bequeathers of land, as legatees, as claimants. They involve women as actors as well as passive receivers in the world of land-holding.

This division can be explained in various ways. At first sight it supports a simple sharp distinction in the ninth century between a public world of patronage and politics, recorded in the diplomas, almost entirely masculine, and a private world of family and its arrangements, with a marked feminine presence and roles. It is also a reminder of the contentious nature of women's claims on land in the ninth century, of the reality of those claims, but also of their secondary and contested nature, their vulnerability, which requires protection and documentation. But the division is also certainly textual, between on the one hand the already highly formalized Latin diploma and on the other the more flexible documentation of bequest and dispute. I do not wish to imply that this is a division between texts which simply describe the world, my second group, and those whose formality hides it, the first. It is too easy to assume that the more complex a document is, the more, by virtue of its very complexity, it is a transparent window on to a transaction. The second group provides, for example, no simple guide to family structures and claims. These documents have usually been produced precisely in order to construct family, to emphasize some claims and repress others in the interests of bequeathors or recipients – and this, of course, includes the will of king Alfred, which belongs in this group. Conversely the diplomas themselves, with their recitation of almost entirely male witness lists and their stress on the passing of land between men, may hide women and family, but they must have helped construct, even if they do not simply describe, a masculine political, public world.

But recognition of the division and awareness of its textual nature is a warning. There is clearly an important sphere of family and land which the diplomas obscure. It is one where land is claimed, and where claims can be overridden, or debated, emphasized or suppressed, but one where all these are difficult manoeuvres. It is a sphere of tension and dispute as well as of accepted rules and consensus. And it is not a sphere where men simply pass on claims among themselves, nor where fathers simply pass on claims to eldest sons – but one where there is scope for arrangement and where women as well as men may

---

Documents, no. 5 (S 1195) and the associated S 1198, ed. S. E. Kelly, *Charters of St Augustine's Abbey, Canterbury and Minster-in-Thanet*, Anglo-Saxon Charters, 4 (1995), no. 24 and compare the two charters for the same family, both for men, Kelly, *St Augustine's*, no. 21 (S 300) and BCS 507 (S 332); Harmer, *Documents*, nos 8 (S 1202), 9 (S 1204a) and 10 (S 1507) – all concerning Ealdorman Alfred and his family.

be involved. There may be a public sphere of men and politics, but in so far as it is itself concerned with land, patronage and inheritance it cannot be hermetically sealed from this other – and vice versa. Indeed the language of separate spheres, useful as it is, is also misleading, suggesting as it does two separable, distinct worlds. Two partial perspectives on the same world might be a better way of conceptualizing it. Consideration of the nature of our documentation is thus a reminder that Alfred, as a late ninth-century king, would have lived, acted and justified his actions not simply in the sphere or ideology of public politics, but also in that other familial context. However, in so far as there is a sharp distinction between the two groups of documents, awareness of the nature of the documentation should make us particularly sensitive to any disturbance of that distinction. If women appear in the Latin diplomas, we should be doubly alert to the probability that something of interest may be happening.

In addition to the documentation overtly concerned with land and its transmission, what for want of a better word we might call the record sources, there are also other more obviously narrative sources, more obviously concerned with a family's history, and more obviously giving a construction of the past from the present's perspective. As far as Alfred is concerned, these are the West Saxon genealogical material, Asser's *Life* of the king, and in some ways the *Anglo-Saxon Chronicle* – which is part history, and part commentary on the genealogy.

In these documents too there are gendered distinctions. The *Chronicle* is overwhelmingly masculine: women are rarely mentioned. The genealogical material, again, is overwhelmingly masculine, even though patently concerned with the world of family and inheritance.[5] Alfred traced his descent, and specifically his claim on the throne, through the male paternal line.[6] This material clearly echoes the priority given to 'rihtfedren' kin, kin in the paternal line, found in many of the documents concerned with land and family.[7] It is a reminder, if such were needed, that Alfred's own major – though not necessarily only – family concerns would be with males in the paternal line. It should also be a reminder of the extent to which family is constructed from the present's perspective. The genealogical material is not in any sense a total picture of the family's past, but an edited version of that past leading directly to Alfred. Had some other king been on the throne at the end of the ninth century, it might have been written differently. More important, it is no guide to the range of other claims on family

---

5 The presence of Ine's sisters, here and in the *ASC*, is unusual. It may be that they were included in the 'regnal lists', which Dumville thinks were less amenable to manipulation later, 'West Saxon genealogical regnal list', 61. Their appearance, and its possible link to the impact of Christian conversion, requires more attention.

6 On this agnatic bias in early England, T. Charles-Edwards, 'Anglo-Saxon kinship revisited', in *The Anglo-Saxons: From the Migration Period to the Eighth Century, An Ethnographic Perspective*, ed. J. Hines (1997), 171–210. Cf. Dumville, 'West Saxon genealogical regnal list', 23 and n. 5 on the legitimating function of the genealogies in the *ASC*.

7 Harmer, *Documents*, no. 10 (S 1508), and *ASC 'A', s.a.* 755 and 784.

inheritance, whether through the paternal or maternal line, through male or female, which existed at any one point either in Alfred's present or in the immediate past. It was, as Dumville has shown, susceptible to manipulation and rewriting. Alfred's genealogy was recast in the later ninth century. The first generations, the founding fathers of the line were, in some versions, rewritten. Mythical male origins conferred special legitimation. Rewriting of them suggests again how far inheritance, family and succession were important to some people in Alfred's Wessex. Women in the family's past could, as we shall see, be used rather differently.

The source most concerned with family, however, and most concerned with women in the family, is Asser's *Life* of the king. This might be considered natural in a biography, though we should be wary of reading the genre ahistorically. Concern with a king's family life has a different significance in the ninth century than it might have in, for example, a nineteenth-century biography. As Sharer has argued, Asser's account of Alfred's family is not a series of vignettes of the private man. Asser's *Life* is biography as a Mirror of Princes, where the king's ability to rule must be demonstrated, and in which family, household and their management are an integral part of that rule.[8] It is also a source close to Alfred himself, who is cited as Asser's informant. This is arguably Alfred's story of his own family. We should not read Asser as the 'obvious' or 'only possible' story of Alfred and the ninth-century West Saxon family. It too is a constructed story, where choices have been made of what to include and what to omit. Those choices were not unconstrained by past events. They engaged with a past which could not simply be rewritten. As Asser himself reveals, some of those past events were still living debated issues. Indeed what he seems to have been *forced* to confront and explain, as for example in events of the 850s, is as interesting as what Asser *chose* to discuss – if those two can be separated. Asser was engaging with a debated and thus debatable past, and it is Alfred's version of it we are hearing – with Asser's 'spin'. And if the story he told was not 'natural and obvious', *a fortiori* the unusual presence of women within it was even less so. Given the predominantly masculine nature of all other ninth-century West Saxon stories, even family stories, Asser's stories about women might repay particular attention.

Thus the documentation and its nature point to the importance of family and inheritance in the ninth-century world, which might be obscured by a superficial reading of certain types of document, for example the diplomas. We should be warned against reading any of this documentation as a transparent window on ninth-century reality, whether the reading is of narrative sources like Asser, or apparently more neutral ones like wills or diplomas. And it suggests that we might be particularly attentive to what one might call 'women out of place' – or rather women *in* the documents.

---

[8] A. Scharer, 'The writing of history at King Alfred's court', *Early Medieval Europe*, 5 (1996), 177–206, at 185ff.

Charters are a key source for reconstructing the ninth century as it happened, as opposed to the ninth century as it was later remembered.[9] The rare appearances of women in West Saxon charters highlight three dates in ninth-century Wessex before Alfred's accession in 871: 854, 858–60 and 868.[10] In 854, the date of the famous second decimation charters, Æthelwulf, Alfred's father, made some sort of landed arrangements concerning churches. In a document related to these his daughter, Æthelswith, appears. In most of them his two youngest sons, Æthelred and Alfred himself, also witness for the first time.[11] The years 858–60 are the dates of the reign of Æthelwulf's eldest surviving son and successor, Æthelbald, in Wessex. Only two charters survive in any form from his reign; both are witnessed by his wife and queen, his father's widow, Judith.[12] In 868 Alfred's sister Æthelswith, queen of the Mercians, appears in a West Saxon charter, making a grant in her own name. In the same year, Wulfthryth, wife of Alfred's older brother, the reigning king Æthelred I, is named as a witness, as are two unidentifiable king's sons, Beorhtferth and Oswald.[13] These rare appearances of women arguably highlight important dates and arrangements in the history of the West Saxon family and its inheritance, arrangements to which Alfred himself alerts us, but whose full significance he does not always choose to clarify.

The year 854 is when Æthelwulf made some sort of landed arrangements which had significance for the churches of his kingdom.[14] The appearance of male and female family members in charters now links those arrangements with a larger series of decisions concerning royal land and family, made prior to Æthelwulf's departure for Rome in 855. Æthelwulf had five sons and at least one daughter. He had made provisions for his two eldest sons during the first decade of his reign. Æthelstan, probably his eldest son, had been made a king in Kent soon after his father's accession.[15] Æthelbald was also given some recognition, if not some formal role, in the course of the 840s.[16] By c.

---

[9] S. Keynes, 'The West Saxon charters of King Æthelwulf and his sons', *EHR*, 109 (1994), 1109–49, at, for example, 1128–9.

[10] For more discussion of the appearances of Alfred's daughter Æthelflæd in charters after 871, see my 'Political Women in Mercia, Eighth to Early Twelfth Centuries', in *Mercia, an Anglo-Saxon Kingdom in Europe*, eds M. P. Brown and C. A. Farr (London, 2001), 35–49.

[11] Æthelswith, BCS 480 (S 1862), dated Wilton, Easter 854; the Æthelbald *dux* here is probably Æthelwulf's son, Keynes, 'West Saxon charters', 1122 and n. 3.

[12] BCS 495 (S 1274) and *Charters of Shaftesbury Abbey*, ed. S. E. Kelly, Anglo-Saxon Charters 5 (1996), no. 3 (S 326).

[13] BCS 522 (S 1201), Æthelswith's grant, also witnessed by Oswald, Burgred and Alfred; BCS 520 (S 340), Wulfthryth, Oswald and Alfred; BCS 873 (S 539), witness of the Mercian ætheling.

[14] Keynes, 'West Saxon charters', 1119–22.

[15] BCS 426 (S 287), AD 839 – a contemporary charter from Kent.

[16] *Charters of Sherborne*, ed. M. A. O'Donovan, Anglo-Saxon Charters (1988), no. 3 (S 290), dated 841, *recte* Christmas 840, with two different witness lists. In the earlier one, apparently of 840, Æthelbald is 'filius regis'; in BCS 538 (S 319), ?844 and BCS 451 (S 298), 847, original preserved at Winchester, he witnesses second as 'filius regis'. Some change, perhaps formalization

850 both older sons were prominent in the defence against the Vikings. In 851 the *Anglo-Saxon Chronicle* notes two victories, in both of which it stresses the role of Æthelwulf's sons: Athelstan's victory in Kent, Æthelwulf and Æthelbald's joint one at *Acleah*. This is Athelstan's last appearance in any document. There are no charters between 851 and 854. His disappearance during these years was presumably one factor prompting a rethinking of family arrangements. A second was the marriage in 853 of Æthelwulf's daughter Æthelswith to the Mercian king, Burgred, with the need to provide for her dowry. Æthelred and Alfred, her younger brothers, appear in charters of 854 for the first time, and with the same title used of Æthelbald in the 840s. At about this date, the fourth brother, Æthelberht, was given some authority and the title of king in, though not necessarily of, Kent. The period 853/4 has all the appearance of a general family settlement. This is the possible, if not probable, date for the making of Æthelwulf's will, in which land in Wessex was settled jointly on the three brothers, Æthelbald, Æthelred and Alfred.[17] Such a settlement may have involved an element of joint rule, on the Carolingian model.[18] Whatever was happening in these years, it involved the emergence of Æthelwulf's younger

---

of his status seems to occur *c*. 850 when he appears as 'dux filius regis' before his brother Athelstan; Kelly, *St Augustine's*, no. 21 (S 300). It is probably he who appears in the 854 charters as 'dux', in first place after the bishop; see for example BCS 468 (S 304), 473 (S 309), 475 (S 310), 476 (S 311).

[17] Asser, c. 16 firmly places the will after the return of Æthelwulf from Rome and mentions a division of the kingdom and a settling of the inheritance on sons, daughter and kinsmen. Keynes and Lapidge, *Alfred*, 33 suggest that this is the arrangement to which Alfred refers in his will. But if that included, as it seems to have done, extensive lands in Wessex, it is not easy to see how Æthelwulf would have been in a position to make such sweeping inheritance arrangements after 855, D. Dumville, 'The ætheling, a study in Anglo-Saxon constitutional history', *ASE*, 8 (1979), 1–32. Did Æthelwulf remake his will after 856, giving Æthelred and Alfred lesser lands in the east, referred to in the will of Alfred as lands received while Æthelbald was king? Is Asser confusing (deliberately?) two wills? He may have been particularly concerned to suggest that the arrangements which implied some sort of joint inheritance and thus succession for the three brothers were post-856, that is, had not been undone. The omission of Æthelberht, the fourth brother, from the joint arrangements for the three brothers has been seen as critical to the dating of the will, arguing that it must postdate his appointment as king of Kent, and thus be after Æthelwulf's return from Rome in 856. However, his appointment as king, with some sort of responsibility in Kent, was almost certainly prior to the departure for Rome, and should probably be seen as part of the arrangements of 853–54. Æthelberht is apparently absent from the 'decimation charters', though he may be the 'dux Æthelbryht' who witnesses them. But he appears as 'rex' alongside his father in two Kent charters, one of which is certainly to be dated to 855: Campbell, *Rochester*, 23 (S 315) and BCS 467 (S 316). Æthelwulf himself is king of Kent in both charters. Simon Keynes suggested that Æthelwulf did not give his sons the sort of position in Kent which he enjoyed under his father Ecgberht: 'The Control of Kent in the Ninth century', *Early Medieval Europe*, 2 (1993), 111–31, at 125. But this situation also underlines how far he was stressing the kingship, or potential kingship, of all his sons in the mid-850s.

[18] J. L. Nelson, 'The Franks and the English in the ninth century reconsidered', *The Preservation and Transmission of Anglo-Saxon Culture*, eds P. Szarmach and J. T. Rosenthal (Kalamazoo, 1997), 141–58, at 146.

sons, with consequent implications for the hopes and expectations of his eldest son, Æthelbald.

When Alfred remembered the events of these years, he recalled a significant milestone on his route to the crown, namely his visit to Rome and consecration there by the pope in 853. The wider family context of 853–54 throws new light on that consecration, illuminating both Alfred *and* his brother Æthelred. The reorganization of inheritance in these years involved both these young princes. Both had been raised closer to kingship, their family claims stressed. If consecration by the pope was designed to underline and strengthen those decisions, potentially contentious ones, both sons would have required it. One of the two non-English sources which may allude in any way to these events suggests that both were, indeed, involved.[19] Alfred remembered 853, but selectively – it was only his own consecration which he retailed. By the time Asser wrote, the events and intentions of 853/4 had taken on a particular meaning due to Alfred's own accession, appearing as an element in the long-term designation and choice of Alfred. By now any consecration or involvement of Æthelred in 853 was irrelevant to Alfred; in view of the rival claims of his own and Æthelred's sons, it may even have been something which he chose to forget. But 853/4 was not so Alfred-centred, nor geared merely to *his* eventual succession. The fate of Alfred *and* his brother was at stake.

In 855 Æthelwulf left for Rome, a journey which had often signalled abdication for earlier kings. Æthelwulf, however, returned, in the late autumn of 856, and with a new wife and a consecrated queen, Judith. During his absence his eldest son Æthelbald rebelled. It is difficult now to be certain what prompted what in these years. Did Æthelbald's actions signal opposition to his father's return, were they a response to his father's absence, to the marriage,[20] or equally likely, to the arrangements of 853/4 themselves? What *is* clear is the result. The kingdom was divided on Æthelwulf's return between father and son, and Æthelwulf was relegated to the less-valued eastern portions. When Æthelwulf died in 858, Æthelbald succeeded to the whole of Wessex, and married Judith, his father's widow and queen. She appears as a witness in both the surviving charters of his reign.

Judith's charter witnesses mark a radical departure from previous West Saxon practice. They have more in common with the elevation of the king's wife as queen and her charter witnesses in late eighth- and ninth-century Mercia. In raising Judith in this way, Æthelbald may have been following the practice of his

---

[19] S. Keynes, 'Anglo-Saxon entries in the *Liber Vitae* of Brescia', *Alfred the Wise*, eds J. Roberts, J. L. Nelson and M. Godden (1997), 99–119 – recording *both* sons in N. Italy; see especially 112–13.

[20] Cf. P. A. Stafford, 'Charles the Bald, Judith and England', *Charles the Bald, Court and Kingdom*, eds M. Gibson, J. L. Nelson and D. Ganz (2nd edn, 1990), 139–53, and M. J. Enright, 'Charles the Bald and Æthelwulf of Wessex: the alliance of 856 and strategies of royal succession', *Journal of Medieval History*, 5 (1979), 291–302.

father's last years; no genuine charters of Æthelwulf after 856 survive as a guide to Judith's status then. He may have been copying his sister's prominence in Mercia. In either case he was not acting like a man who intended the succession to pass to his younger brothers. Whatever else such an elevation did, it stressed vertical succession from father to son at the expense of wider kin claims. Judith's position must raise questions about Æthelbald's commitment to any earlier decisions made in favour of Æthelred and Alfred.

Division of the kingdom, Æthelwulf's relegation – underlined by his burial at Steyning to the east of Wessex – if not the raising of a wife as queen were events which shook the political world of mid-century Wessex. They continued to have serious implications during Alfred's reign. As the youngest brother with surviving nephews, sons of his older brother(s), if not other male relatives, Alfred faced pressing questions of his own succession and inheritance. The events of the 850s were unwelcome family ghosts. They raised the precedent of arguments for division. They had demoted the father on whose will and intentions Alfred built his own claims, and they may have overridden arrangements for younger sons, and thus raised questions about claims based on them. Alfred was concerned about the 850s. It was probably he who moved his father's body from Steyning to Winchester, removing any stigma attached to the burial.[21] It may be no accident that in the *Anglo-Saxon Chronicle* Æthelwulf's prestigious pedigree appears at the end of his reign, not at the beginning, legitimizing Alfred's father even – especially – after his demotion. And in his recitation of the family agreements and decisions which Alfred makes at the opening of his own will, Æthelbald's accession and reign are conspicuous by their absence. The loaded nature of that omission is suggested not merely by the rest of the will, which implies new arrangements made now,[22] but by the attention which Asser paid to these years, to queens and to the delegitimization of Æthelbald. The

---

[21] Reference to Steyning as the place of burial comes from the version of *ASC* which lay behind the Annals of St Neots; the body lay at Winchester according to *ASC 'A'* and other versions. Alfred may have moved the body there; see *The Liber Vitae of the New Minster and Hyde Abbey, Winchester*, ed. S. Keynes (Copenhagen, 1996), 16, n. 4. Steyning was left to Alfred's nephew, a surviving son of Æthelred. Was Alfred concerned about a link between the body, land and inheritance? The only surviving copy of Alfred's will is from New Minster, Hyde, to which Edward the Elder moved *his* father's body.

[22] When Alfred details the meeting at Swinbeorg, where he and Æthelred came to agreement about their children, he makes a distinction between the lands which Æthelwulf had settled on all three brothers jointly and those which Æthelred and Alfred were given by their father while Æthelbald was still alive – perhaps referring to a new landed arrangement made after 856, more suited to the new circumstances. Had Æthelbald now taken control of all the joint lands, leaving his father to make new provisions for his younger brothers? Such a rearrangement would also explain why, when Æthelberht took over Wessex on Æthelbald's death in 860, he also took all the lands once promised to his three brothers, which by that date were in Æthelbald's own hands. Steyning, in Æthelwulf's eastern portion of the kingdom, was confirmed to Æthelred's son in Alfred's will. Was it thus part of the land which was given to Æthelred and Alfred 'in Æthelbald's day', which it had been agreed at Swinbeorg should go to the sons of the first brother to die?

story of Eadburh, to which I shall return, was placed here. The last stages of
Æthelwulf's reign and that of Æthelbald upset the picture of a ninth century
leading inevitably to Alfred. Alfred's actions and his telling of the ninth-century
story in Asser and his will suggest the extent of his concern with the long
shadow which they cast.[23]

The next appearance of royal women in diplomas was in 868. Wulfthryth,
wife of Æthelred I, witnesses as 'queen/*regina*' in this year. Æthelswith, Alfred's
sister and the Mercian queen, witnessed a West Saxon charter, and made a grant in
her own name of land in Wessex. And, as in 854, other family members appear: an
Oswald, king's son; a rare Mercian ætheling, Beorhtferth, and Alfred himself. And
again this was a year of royal marriage, in this case of Alfred himself to a Mercian
royal woman, Ealhswith – probably a descendant of King Coenwulf.[24] Marriage
marked an important transition in adult life, and Asser may imply that Alfred
received some special status now, becoming 'secundarius'.[25] Whatever their public political significance, the events of this year seem once again rooted in family.
Rather, they may once again point to the inextricable linking of the two.

The events of this year can be seen as a milestone of the far-sighted West
Saxon public policies of the ninth century: alliance with Mercia, in which both
Æthelred and his brother Alfred took equal and amicable part, marked by the
presence of the Mercian royal family in Wessex, a year of fraternal designation
in which Æthelred underlined his brother's claims and status.[26] In the long term
these events did become crucial to the drawing together of Wessex and Mercia.
Through Ealhswith, Alfred, and the couple's future children, would gain claims
and legitimacy in Mercia, making Alfred himself, and their daughter Æthelflæd
who married Æthelred II of Mercia in 887, acceptable there. But this longer
term is a rewriting of the past by subsequent history. The significance of any
events changes over time; their full potential is not planned, let alone determined, by their initial participants. Taking into account all the familial aspects of
this year, 868 looks more complex.

Alfred's marriage has not received all the attention it deserves.[27] Alfred's
wife was not from the current Mercian royal family, into which his sister was

---

[23] Were other family members also involved in 856–58? Was Ealhstan, bishop of Sherborne,
supporter of Æthelbald, a descendant of Ecgberht's sister, Ealhburg, or of his father, Ealhhelm?

[24] Keynes and Lapidge, *Alfred*, 241; her brother Æthelwulf seems to be acting as heir of
Coenwulf in BCS 575 (S 1442).

[25] Asser, c. 29, first uses the term in relation to the wedding; cf. the attempt to broaden it to a
wider date in c. 42.

[26] S. Keynes, 'King Alfred and the Mercians', *Kings, Currency and Alliances: History and
Coinage of Southern England in the Ninth Century*, eds M. A. S. Blackburn and D. N. Dumville
(1998), 1–45, at 9–10. *ASC 'A'* speaks of Burgred seeking help from Æthelred and Alfred in this
year. This is not inconsistent with family divisions; and it is, in any case, itself a retrospective
interpretation.

[27] Though see Nelson, 'Reconstructing', 65–6 and 'Monks, Secular Men and Masculinity
c. 900', *Masculinity in Medieval Europe*, ed. D. M. Hadley (1998), 121–42.

married, but from an earlier and sidelined royal house.[28] Marriage brought allies to a young prince as much as, if not more than, to the kingdom his brother ruled. It entailed property arrangements. Alfred himself refers in his will to the number of times he importuned his brother to divide up the inheritance. Marriage would have been just such an occasion, and in itself a legitimate opportunity to press claims. His sister Æthelswith's grant of land within Wessex in that year points to some reassertion of her dowry, in response perhaps to new family rearrangements. The year 868 may signal Alfred's impatient self-assertion rather than an amicable, far-sighted arrangement between him and his brother. Æthelred's charters do not point to close relations between the brothers after 865. Alfred is a rare witness of his brother's, admittedly sparse, charters. Were Alfred and Æthelred at one in 868? Was Alfred forcing his brother's hand in his favour, demanding an enhanced position in Wessex, or at least securing one in response to the changed situation his marriage had brought? How far was Alfred fishing Mercian troubled waters in 868? Are the appearances of the Mercian royal family, including Alfred and Æthelred's sister, in charters of this year an indication of enhanced general alliance, or a specific reaction to this changed situation, which had aligned Alfred with a rival dynasty at a time of Viking pressure and defeat? Was anxiety not alliance their provocation? Was Æthelred affirming his own Mercian alliances, with his sister and her husband? Is 868 an indication of tensions within the West Saxon family up to the very eve of Alfred's accession?

The fact that Æthelred chose this year to forefront his wife, Wulfthryth, as queen points to the need to ask such questions. This was not usual in ninth-century Wessex, and as in the 850s, it had direct implications for the succession, and particularly for the sons of Æthelred and Wulfthryth. If Alfred's status changed in 868, if his position were strengthened and his determination to press his own claims underlined, Wulfthryth's appearance was a simultaneous reminder that Æthelred's own sons were still to be remembered and protected. The year 868 may mark the arrangement signalled in Alfred's will, whereby the two brothers effectively eliminated from the succession the sons of whichever died first; Alfred's position of strength in that year fits with the enormity of that decision. Æthelred's gamble with his sons' future was hedged by the stress on their birth and the status of their mother. The tense atmosphere of these years, in which his own ambitions could be seen to threaten both family unity and Mercian links, would not be a version of the past Alfred would be anxious to recount in his sanitized view of the family history.[29]

---

[28] The current ruling family, into which Æthelswith had been married and to which Burgred and perhaps the ætheling Beorhtferth belonged, was the so-called Mercian 'B' dynasty; see P. Wormald, 'The ninth century', *The Anglo-Saxons*, ed. J. Campbell (1982), 138 and Keynes, 'King Alfred and the Mercians', 11, n. 40 and 39, n. 168. A son of a Beorhtsige ætheling died fighting alongside Alfred's nephew at the battle of Holme, against Alfred's son and heir Edward the Elder. Members of this family seem to have felt no love for Alfred and his successor.

[29] It is possible, however, that some echo of it survives in the 871 entry in *ASC* and account of these same events in Asser. The death of Æthelred was certainly opportune from Alfred's point of

West Saxon/Mercian marriages and queens were to the fore in 868, as in the 850s. Both are the subject of one of the most famous family stories of ninth-century Wessex, that of Eadburh. She was the daughter of Offa of Mercia and wife of the West Saxon king Beorhtric. Beorhtric had driven out Alfred's grandfather Ecgberht, then ruled until his accession. Her story was told in great detail in Alfred's day, including, perhaps especially, by Alfred himself, who often related it.[30] This was not the ninth century which Alfred forgot, but one which he seemed determined to remember. Although Asser gives the fullest version, it is also referred to in the *Anglo-Saxon Chronicle*.[31] On the death of Ecgberht, there is no genealogy (just as there is none at his accession), but there is a reminder that he was driven out by Offa and Beorhtric, and that Beorhtric helped, because he had married Offa's daughter. In 787 the *Chronicle* had recorded that marriage, and followed mention of it immediately by reference to the arrival of the first Viking ships. From 737 to 853 Eadburh is the only woman in the *Chronicle*. In a source which rarely mentions women she gets two mentions, and star billing from Asser. Eadburh was bad news, but she was certainly news. In 853, the *Chronicle* records Æthelswith's Mercian marriage, and in 855 it features Judith.[32] It is in relation to Judith and the dramas of the 850s that Asser tells his famous story.

Eadburh's story is the tale of why the West Saxons did not have queens, and it is a cautionary tale. The wicked queen Eadburh poisoned her way round her husband's court, ending up by accidentally poisoning Beorhtric himself. She fled with treasure to the Carolingian court, where she showed her stupidity by opting for Charlemagne's son, when offered the hand of the great king himself. Following lust rather than enlightened self-interest, she thus ended up in a nunnery, only to be ejected as a result of accepting the advances of one of her own countrymen. She came to a fitting end in poverty and begging in Pavia.

It is a good story, but an odd one – at least as told by Asser. It is in some ways anti-Mercian – or rather anti-Offa,[33] as it is in the laconic treatment in the

---

view, and together with the events of 868 may have left rumbling discontent. The treatment of Æthelred in these accounts, both the celebration and the veiled criticism, may reflect divided opinion.

[30] Asser, c. 13.

[31] *ASC 'A'*, s.a. 836 and 787.

[32] The only other references to women in the ninth-century *ASC* will be again to Judith, *à propos* the succession to the Carolingians in 885, and the death of Æthelswith in exile in Pavia in 888. In 900 Æthelred I's son's capture of a nun as part of his bid for power in Wessex is mentioned, as are the deaths of Ealhswith's brother, Athulf, 902 and of Ealhswith herself in 904. Ealhswith was never mentioned in the *ASC* during her husband's reign, only after his death, in the reign of her son, Edward the Elder. In every case except 888 the succession/inheritance context of references to women is obvious. It may be that 888 itself should be re-examined in this light, not least for the continued interest within Alfred's Wessex in his Mercian-married sister, and the possible claims of her, her children and any survivors of this family *vis-à-vis* Alfred's own daughter's marriage to a Mercian ruler. Cf. n. 28 above.

[33] She is a tyrant like her father: Asser, c. 14.

Chronicle, where its narrative association is with Offa, Viking attacks and the expulsion of Ecgberht, father of the ninth-century West Saxon dynasty. Like Alfred's marriage, it is a reminder that West Saxon/Mercian relations were not merely between kingdoms, but between a shifting succession of families. It is anti-queen – it is told to explain the West Saxon practice of not having queens – yet Asser labels this practice 'perverse and detestable'.[34] The whole tale and its telling places a question mark over why Alfred laid such stress on a story which successfully justified such a 'detestable' custom.

The simple answer is that this was how it happened, but there are problems with accepting this. The Carolingian aspects look to be at best a garbling or distorted retelling of events, whilst the overall moral nature and even the details of poisoning and treasure fit a pattern of stories about queens which cumulatively tell us much about their household power and its sources, but which are individually difficult to interpret.[35] The story has some of the qualities of myth, not of history. It was certainly a good story and it might be argued that Asser told it as such. This is merely a reminder, however, of the extent to which all stories, even good ones, are constructed. Where and how they are told is significant, not least when they involve women and are incorporated in a *Life* which was also a Mirror of Princes.[36] A good story which Alfred often told is presumably more than his regular ninth-century after-dinner party piece.

What we seem to have in Asser is a final version of an old tale, which had grown and accumulated meanings in its telling. Its first version may be as old as the reign of Ecgberht, with Eadburh as a convenient scapegoat for feelings against those who had driven out Ecgberht, a familiar female role.[37] As an in-marrying wife, close to the heart of West Saxon rule, but distinct from it by virtue of her foreign birth, Eadburh could readily function in this way. She was thus established at the accession of Ecgberht's family as an evil female presence, almost an inversion of the founding fathers, a touchstone of non-West-Saxonness. If kin going back to Cerdic legitimized anyone to whom it was attributed, Eadburh could tarnish everything her story touched.

The story seems to have been told again in the 850s,[38] and it was perhaps now that it acquired its specifically anti-queenly slant. Those who were opposed to Æthelwulf's return seem to have used it. The fact that Ecgberht and Æthelwulf had not previously seated a queen beside them now became a defining characteristic of West Saxon monarchy, underlined by Eadburh and her evil reputation.

---

[34] Asser, c. 13.

[35] On these see P. Stafford, *Queens, Concubines and Dowagers* (2nd edn, 1998) and 'Queens and Treasure', *Treasure in the Middle Ages*, ed. E. Tyler (2000), 61–82.

[36] On women in stories see Philippe Buc, 'Italian Hussies and German Matrons', *Frühmittelalterliche Studien*, 29 (1995), 207–25.

[37] Cf., for example, the role of Brunhild, and the story about her, in seventh-century Francia – and comment by I. Wood, *The Merovingian Kingdoms, 450–751* (1994), 134–5.

[38] Note that it does not matter to my argument if it was first told now, since the elements within it have the functions already suggested whenever they were first put together.

It justified opposition to a king returning home with a young queen, by elevating the issue of queenship to a point of principle. But the interest of the story lies not merely in its genesis and first development, but in Alfred's interest in it and its continuing relevance to him. It points first to the continuing importance in Alfredian England of the 850s and the issues they had raised. Asser makes it clear that people were still rehearsing rival arguments about the 850s and Æthelbald's rebellion.[39] Division and his father's demotion were difficult questions for Alfred, but live ones. To relate them to queens and wicked women was perhaps preferable to any stress on the changing inheritance arrangements to which they were related. If the 850s had to be faced, better for Alfred to remember queens, who, if they undermined Æthelwulf to some extent, also usefully tarred Æthelbald, who continued his father's practice.

The story also had relevance to the events of 868. As a narrative device Eadburh the evil woman from an earlier Mercian marriage was a perfect counterpoint to Alfred's own Eadburh, his virtuous Mercian royal mother-in-law.[40] As he chose to present it later, his became the right sort of Mercian marriage for a West Saxon king. A *West Saxon* royal marriage, whether in 868 or later, invoked West Saxon royal tradition, at least as the 850s had defined it. The West Saxons did not have queens, and Ealhswith, Alfred's wife, was not a queen – unlike, for example, Wulfthryth, Æthelred I's wife. Did Alfred thus link himself with the Æthelwulf of pre-856, who had married Alfred's own, non-queenly, mother? One can only wonder how the story might have played with that other queen of 868, his Mercian royal sister, *Queen* Æthelswith.[41]

Traditional as it was, however, the practice of not having a queen must have become increasingly problematic in the last decades of the ninth century. Queens had been consecrated by now, including, perhaps, in West Francia the wife of one of the new kings of 888. News of this was reaching England.[42] Asser's statement that West Saxon practice was unusual makes somewhat better sense *c*. 890 than in 856. Neither Alfred's wife nor his mother had been consecrated or raised as queens.[43] The issue of the succession loomed increasingly large. Where did the status of Ealhswith leave the claims of her and Alfred's son,

---

[39] Asser, c. 12.

[40] D. Howlett, *British Books in Biblical Style* (1997), 394–5 and Asser, c. 29.

[41] Eadburh's death, at Pavia, like Æthelswith's, may be no more than coincidence, but its mention is rather pointed. How warm were relations between Æthelswith and Alfred after 868? Did she have children, with claims on the Mercian – or West Saxon – thrones? There is no sign that Alfred supported any of her husband's family after 875; his relations with Burgred's supplanters were, however, cordial.

[42] *AF*, trans. Reuter, 115, n. 2 – material recorded in *ASC, s.a.* 887 can have been written no earlier than 889, when events it records together now were complete.

[43] Since Alfred was not king at the time of his marriage to Ealhswith, he could not have made her queen in 868. If his eldest son Edward were born or conceived before his accession, to raise Ealhswith as queen after 871 could have introduced dissension and rivalry among his own sons, re-ranking the claims of any sons born after her elevation.

Edward, especially *vis-à-vis* his cousin, Æthelwold, whose mother had been recognized as queen in 868? In these circumstances the story may have gained a new lease of life, told against Alfred's nephew.[44] It may have served to assert an important negative, that a West Saxon king's wife and mother of his heir need not be a queen, though she must, like Ealhswith, be a king's *wife*.[45] Alfred may, on occasions, have made West Saxon virtue out of circumstance, but by the 890s, if not before, the dangers for his sons must have become increasingly apparent. West Saxon practice which Alfred had previously upheld may have begun to appear 'detestable', and in the last decade of his reign Alfred may have seen the advantages for his son in having a queen.[46] Eadburh and her story would finally have been outliving their usefulness.

The story we have of the ninth-century West Saxon royal family is Alfred's, and the dominance of the Alfredian sources means that we shall never recapture the tale in all its alternative versions. But the story of Eadburh and the appearances of women and other family members in charters points to some of the picture we have lost. They suggest alternative readings of the 850s and 868, with a West Saxon family neither totally united nor especially fraternal, with arrangements made and unmade, and with Alfred far from always the favoured heir. They reinforce the hints in Alfred's will of family tensions and the importance of succession and inheritance issues as late as the 880s and 890s, and they point to the continuing significance of the 850s and the family's earlier history in the arrangements of these decades. Looked at from this perspective, ninth-century Wessex looks more like the Carolingians, or like its own tenth-century English successor – messier and more contingent, driven not only by diplomacy and plans for unity, but also by family accident, rivalries, arguments and alliances. It may not be quite the Wessex Alfred chose to tell us about; but it is one, I believe, he would recognize only too well.

---

[44] B. Yorke, 'Edward as Aetheling', in *Edward the Elder 899–924*, eds N. J. Higham and D. H. Hill (2001), 25–39.

[45] Asser makes a point of the legitimacy of the marriage in 868: c. 29 mentions betrothal and marriage; c. 74 *nuptias* 'solemnly' celebrated.

[46] A new *ordo* for the consecration of a queen may have been reworked in England late in Alfred's reign, perhaps for a wife of Edward. It was based on the so-called Erdmann/Sens Ordo: R. A. Jackson, *Ordines Coronationis Franciae. Texts and Ordines for the Coronation of Frankish and French Kings and Queens in the Middle Ages* (Philadelphia, 1995), no. XIII. J. L. Nelson 'Early medieval rites of queen-making and the shaping of medieval queenship', *Queens and Queenship in Medieval Europe*, ed. A. Duggan (1997), 301–15, 309, n. 42, and 310–11 for its likely use for Theodrada, wife of Odo. The English version made changes, by returning to the original in the case of the abbess's prayer, *eadem*, 'The second English Ordo', *Politics and Ritual in Early Medieval Europe* (1986), at 367, n. 22. She argues for a probable date in the 890s, though the range is late ninth/early tenth century. If it is pre-900, was Alfred hedging his bets by preparing for the consecration of his son's queen? Was Edward making such preparations, perhaps even in resistance to his father? For differing views see Nelson, 'Reconstructing' and Yorke, 'Edward'.

Chapter 15

Alfred the Great, the *micel hæðen here* and the viking threat

Richard Abels

King Alfred's greatness is rooted in his military successes against viking invaders. Certainly, victory on the battlefield was the *sine qua non* for Alfred's political and cultural achievements. To appreciate Alfred's accomplishments, one must first understand the nature of the military threat that he faced and overcame. This would seem a simple enough task. The historical consensus is that Alfred fought a series of wars against a unified viking army, referred to in the *Anglo-Saxon Chronicle* as the *micel hæðen here*; the only real area of scholarly disagreement has been over the size of that army. But despite this near unanimity there is good reason to question the received opinion about the nature of the viking threat and, in particular, of the *micel hæðen here*.[1]

In this paper, I will suggest that the authors of the *Anglo-Saxon Chronicle* characterized viking war bands as *heres* in order to distinguish them from 'real armies', that is, legitimate, organized military forces, and that this distinction was drawn as well by the authors of a number of contemporary Frankish annals. I will further argue that the viking forces operating in England in the 860s through 890s were composite bands that on occasion coalesced temporarily for mutual gain, but which were constantly in flux in terms of their leadership and personnel. Alfred had to contend not with a single viking army, but with various individual bands that occasionally operated together but often pursued their own interests. In other words, the *micel here* may have been 'great' in size, but it was not an 'army'.

The traditional account of Alfred's dealings with vikings, exemplified by Sir Frank Stenton's magisterial *Anglo-Saxon England*, emphasizes that Alfred successfully weathered three major invasions of Wessex by a ruthless, capable and disciplined enemy.[2] The nature of 'the Viking threat' in England, assert

---

[1] The impetus for this paper was Janet Nelson's invitation in her review of my *Alfred the Great: War, Kingship and Culture in Anglo-Saxon England* (1998) to rethink the 'Vikings' as a historical construct. *TLS*, 14 May 1999, 23: hence my use of lower-case 'v'. I would like to thank David Appleby, Robin Fleming, Carroll Gillmor, Christine Grainge and Ernest Tucker for commenting on earlier drafts of this paper and for helping me think through the evidence and clarify my arguments.

[2] F. M. Stenton, *Anglo-Saxon England*, 3rd edn (1971), 245–55; M. Wood, *In Search of the Dark Ages* (1987), 104–25. See also N. Brooks, 'England in the ninth century: the crucible of defeat', *TRHS*, fifth series, 29 (1979), 1–20; P. Wormald, 'The Ninth Century', in J. Campbell, P. Wormald and E. John, *The Anglo-Saxons* (1982), 144–51; Smyth, *Alfred*, 51–146.

Stenton et al., changed radically in 865 with the advent of what the *Anglo-Saxon Chronicle* termed 'a great heathen army' (*micel hæðen here*). What had hitherto been local, uncoordinated raids by small bands of vikings now coalesced into a viking army bent on conquest. Over the next thirteen years this force, led by the supposed sons of Ragnar Lothbrok, Ivar the Boneless, Halfdan, and, perhaps, Ubbe, changed the very fabric of English politics and society.[3] In part because of this army's 'remarkable unity of command',[4] cohesion and discipline, the great army was able to systematically defeat and conquer Northumbria (867), East Anglia (869) and Mercia, where they first established a puppet ruler, Ceolwulf II, before taking control of the eastern half in 877. The only native kingdom and royal house to survive was that of Wessex, and this was due to King Alfred, who, much like Winston Churchill in 1939, stood alone against an ever more threatening and dangerous foreign invader. Stenton, indeed, may have had this comparison in mind; the first edition of *Anglo-Saxon England*, after all, was published in 1943. Michael Wood in his popular 1979 BBC programme, *In Search of the Dark Ages: Alfred the Great*, made the parallel visually explicit by introducing Alfred to his viewers while standing in Churchill's communications centre for the Battle of Britain.

True to the spirit of the *Anglo-Saxon Chronicle*, Stenton's narrative reaches its climax in Alfred's near defeat and final triumph at Edington in the winter and spring of 878. The dénoument has the Army's leader, Guthrum, accept baptism and Alfred's spiritual kinship, and so become a legitimate king of East Anglia with a proper Christian name, 'Æthelstan'. While these events were transpiring, however, a new viking army entered the Thames and made camp at Fulham, where it overwintered in 878. By November 878 it had departed for the Low Countries. The *Anglo-Saxon Chronicle* for the 880s follows the movements of this new 'great army' on the Continent with obsessive care, apparently with the knowledge that it would return to England in 892 to fight what Alfred Smyth calls King Alfred's Last War. That war presented Alfred with a composite viking enemy capable of fighting a cohesive war on three fronts, and savvy enough to threaten Alfred with a classic double pincer attack.[5] Even if one does not go as far as John Peddie or Paddy Griffith in applying modern military scientific analysis to viking warfare,[6] the received account of Alfred's dealings with the vikings has him fighting wars against Danish armies.

The very terms 'war' and 'armies', however, are charged with meaning. The questions we ought to ask are whether the viking forces that Alfred engaged were, in fact, 'armies' and what he fought were 'wars'. The danger, of course, is to fall into anachronism. No ninth-century *exercitus* or *fyrd* would have met the

---

[3] See, for example, Smyth, *Alfred*, 63.

[4] Stenton, *Anglo-Saxon England*, 246. But cf. the more cautious assessment of H. Loyn, *The Vikings in Britain*, Historical Association Studies (1994), 40.

[5] Smyth, *Alfred*, 123.

[6] J. Peddie, *Alfred, Warrior King* (1999); P. Griffith, *The Viking Art of War* (1995).

specifications of a modern army in terms of chain of command, communication, discipline, cohesion, order, training, or pay. But did Alfred and his Carolingian contemporaries recognize the viking forces they fought as similar in character to the *fyrds*, *folc* and *exercitus* they led? The temptation is to say of course they did. The authors of the *Anglo-Saxon Chronicle*'s entries for the 860s through the 890s consistently use the term *here* to describe viking forces. Indeed, the *Chronicle* from 865 on refers to *se here*, and the use of the definite article gives the impression that, as far as the chronicler(s) was concerned, Alfred and his Frankish contemporaries in the 880s and 890s faced a single, unitary force bent on conquest. If *here* indeed meant 'army', as its Germanic cognate apparently did,[7] then there can be little doubt that, as far as the chronicler was concerned, Alfred fought a 'great heathen army'.

Here has traditionally been translated as 'army', and by the late tenth and early eleventh centuries it could mean precisely that. Ealdorman Æthelweard translated the *Chronicle*'s *here* with *exercitus*, and Ælfric of Eynsham rendered *exercitus* as *here* in his grammar and in several of his homilies and saints' lives.[8] Even ninth-century and earlier Insular authors, on occasion, translated *here* into Latin as *exercitus*. The Welshman Asser regularly did so in his *Vita Ælfredi Regis*, though, interestingly, he tended to qualify it with the addition of *paganorum* even where *hæthen* is lacking in the original.[9] Alfred himself used *here* on four occasions in his *Pastoral Care* for host, though he chose *fyrd* to render army in his translation of the forty-third psalm.[10] In certain compound words, such as *heregeatu* and *herepath*, *here* also apparently carried a general military connotation.

None the less, it is equally clear that the authors of the *Chronicle* saw a difference between a *here* and what they called a *fyrd* or, sometimes, a *folc*. As has been frequently observed, the *Chronicle* entries for Alfred's and Edward's

---

[7] See D. H. Green, *Language and History in the Early Germanic World* (1998), 84–90. In the Carolingian capitularies, the fine for failing to answer a summons to the host (*exercitus*) was termed *heribannum* (analogous to Anglo-Saxon *fierdwite*): F. L. Ganshof, *Frankish Institutions under Charlemagne*, trans. B. and M. Lyon (New York, 1968), 68, 160–61 n. 66 (references to capitularies). Cf. *fierdwite* in Anglo-Saxon laws: *Ine*, c. 51; *II Cnut*, cc. 12, 65.

[8] Æthelweard, *s.a.* 860 and *passim*. A. Di Paolo and R. L. Venezky, compilers, *A Microfiche Confordance to Old English* (1980), s.v. *here*. *Here* is among the words used in Old English poetry to denote an army. See, for example, *Widsith*, l. 120, in *The Anglo-Saxon Poetic Records, III: The Exeter Book*, eds G. P. Krapp and E. V. K. Dobbie (1936), 153, and *Exodus* ll. 13, 323 in *The Anglo-Saxon Poetic Records, I: The Junius Manuscript*, ed. G. P. Krapp (1931), 91, 100, where Moses is called *herges wisa*.

[9] See, for example, Asser, cc. 49, 50, 58, 60, 61, 69, and *ASC, s.a.* 876, 878, 879, 880, 881, 884.

[10] *Pastoral Care*, 18.129.7, 21.161.24, 46.433.14, 54.433.27. For example, Gregory the Great, *Regulae Pastoralis Liber* II 7, *PL* 77, col. 30, lines 10–13: 'Languente enim capite membra incassum vigent, et in exploratione hostium frustra *exercitus* velociter sequitur, si ab ipso duce itineris erratur.' Cf. *Pastoral Care*, c. 18: 'sua eac bið se *here* eal idel, ðonne he on oðer folc winnan sceal, gif se *heretoga* dwolað'. See also Paris Psalter, no. 43, ed. Richard Stracke (http://www.aug.edu/augusta/psalms/psalm43.htm): *on fyrd* for *in virtutibus*.

reigns, by and large, reserve *here* for the Northmen.[11] Only in two places does the chronicler apply the term to a force levied by Alfred in the annals for 875, where Alfred takes a *sciphere* out to sea to fight against seven viking ships, and for 885, where the king is said to have dispatched a *sciphere* to ravage East Anglia, apparently in retaliation for the East Anglians having broken the peace by aiding a *here* that attacked Rochester. More typical is the entry for 917:

> Þa eft æfter þam þa giet *gegadorode micel here* hine of Eastenglum & of Mercna lande & foran to þære byrig æt Wigingamere & ymbsæton hie utan & fuhton lange on dæg … Þa æfter þam þæs ilcan sumeres *gegadorode micel folc* hit on Eadweardes cynges anwalde of þam niehstum burgum þe hit ða gefaran mehte & foron to Temeseforda … . Þa æfter þam þæs forhraþe *gegadorode micel folc* on hærfest ægþer ge Cent ge of Suþrigum ge of Eastseaxum ge æghwonan of þam nihstum burgum & foron to Colnecesastre & ymbsæton þa burg … Þa æfter þam þa giet þæs ilcan hærfestes *gegadorode micel here* hine of Eastenglum ægþer ge þæs *landheres* ge þara *wicinga* þe hie him to fultum aspanen hæfdon … Þa þæs forhraþe þæs ilcan hærfestes for Eadward cyning mid Westsexna *fierde* to Passanhamme … & him cirde to Þurferþ eorl & þa holdas, eal se *here* þe to Hamtune hierde norþ oþ Weland & sohton hine him to hlaforde & to mundboran.[12]
> (Italics added)

Here the Chronicler's language carefully parallels the *micel here* assembled (*gegadorode*) by the foe with the *micel folc* assembled by the English, and contrasts the West Saxon *fierd* that King Edward brought to Passenham with the various Danish *heres* that submitted to it.

This care leads one to think that *here* was a term of art for the compilers of these entries. The key is a much-quoted legal text, *Ine* c.13 §1: *Ðeofas we hatað*

---

[11] *Here* appears in the *ASC* only four times before the coming of the Danes, in entries for 603, 606, and 684, 685 in the 'E' recension (and as later additions to 'A'). In the first case it refers to the Scots who fought against the Northumbrians at Degastan; in the second, to Welsh forces at Chester; and in the third and fourth, to King Ecgfrith of Northumbria's attack upon the Irish. M. Swanton, *The Anglo-Saxon Chronicle* (1996), xxxiii–xxxiv, combines *here*'s two meanings and renders it as 'raiding-army'.

[12] *ASC 'A'*, ed. Bately, *s.a.* 917, trans. Swanton, *s.a.* 920, pp. 102–3 (but changing Swanton's translation of *folc* from 'tribe' to 'army'): 'Then yet again after that, a great raiding-army gathered from East Anglia and from the land of Mercia, and went to the stronghold at Wigingamere and besieged it, and fought it long into the day … Then after that, the same summer, a great army [*folc*] gathered together in King Edward's domain, from the nearest strongholds who could travel to it, and went to Tempsford … Then very quickly after that a great army [*folc*] gathered together in harvest-time, both from Kent and from Surrey and from Essex, and from the nearest strongholds everywhere, and went to Colchester and besieged the stronghold … Then yet again after that, the same harvest-time, a great raiding-army gathered together from East Anglia, both from the raiding-army occupying the land and from those vikings whom they enticed to help them … Then very quickly after this, the same harvest-time, King Edward went with a West Saxon army to Passenham … and Jarl Thurferth and the holds turned to him, together with all the raiding-army which belonged to Northampton, as far north as the Welland, and sought him as their lord and protector.' For *folc* meaning 'army', see Green, *Language and History*, 90–95.

oð VII men; from VII hloð oð XXXV; siððan bið here. 'We say "thieves" if the number of men does not exceed seven, "band" for a number between seven and thirty-five. Anything beyond this, [we call] a *here*.' Some historians, myself included, have used this law to argue for the small size of armies in early Anglo-Saxon England under the assumption that *here* means 'army'.[13] But as F. L. Attenborough saw, here and in clause 15, *here* is best translated as a 'raid'.[14] Ine was not waxing philosophical about the essentially similar nature of the thief and the soldier, but was merely distinguishing the quantity of marauders. Ine legislated about both *heres* and *fyrds*,[15] and for him, as for the chronicler, only the latter meant 'army'.

Micel here, then, merely meant a large band of raiders. The *Chronicle's* language underscored the destructive activity (*hergung*, pillaging) and, perhaps, the illegitimate character of the forces that harried Alfred's realm. *Here*, after all, is linguisitically cognate with the verb *hergian*, to ravage. Alfred's choice of *here* in his translation of Boethius to describe the forces of the unrighteous king who crushes all his neighbours points in the same direction.[16] In this context, the use of *sciphere* for the naval force that Alfred sent against the East Anglians in 885 is the exception that proves the rule, since its manifest purpose was a punitive expedition to harry the treacherous East Anglians.

The authors of the *Chronicle* intended their readers to think that a single *micel here* operated in England between 865 and 878, and that the *here* that wintered at Fulham in 878 was also the *here* that devastated Francia throughout the 880s before returning to England in 892. The consistent use of the definite article gives the desired impression. The reason, I think, is clear. The *Chronicle* may not be modern propaganda, but, as R. H. C. Davis observed almost three decades ago, it is ninth-century propaganda meant to present a specific image of its hero, King Alfred.[17] The stories of Edington and of Alfred's heroic defence against a hydra-headed foe in the 890s are more focused and dramatic if Alfred is shown as defeating a single great heathen force than fighting against several different viking gangs.

Viking activity in England in the second half of the ninth century was probably less organized and systematic than the chronicler and modern historians would have one believe. As Alfred Smyth has wisely observed, 'It is unlikely ... that the invaders of East Kent in 892 consisted of precisely the same army

---

13 R. P. Abels, *Lordship and Military Obligation in Anglo-Saxon England* (1988), 35. Cf. P. H. Sawyer, *The Age of the Vikings* (1962), 120, who concluded, 'If a *here* could be three dozen men, it would be as well not to call it an "army".'

14 Attenborough, *Laws*, 40. Cf. Liebermann, *Gesetze*, II.2, 499–500 (s.v. *Heer*).

15 *Ine*, c. 51. Cf. *Alfred*, c. 40 §1.

16 *Boethius*, Lay no. 25: 'and se hlaford ne scrifð, ðe ðæm waldeð, freonde ne feonde, feore ne aehtum'. The author of *Orosius* seems to reserve *here/sciphere* for aggressors and invaders. For example Marcellus in Sicily ([I] x, ed. Bately, p. 5, line 4), the forces of Pharaoh (I 7, p. 26, line14), the forces of the Amazons (I 10, p. 30, lines 2, 5, 8), Agesilaus in Asia Minor (III 1, p. 54, line 34).

17 R. H. C. Davis, 'Alfred the Great: propaganda and truth', *History*, 56 (1971), 169–82.

which had been at Fulham in 879, tested the defences of Rochester in 885, and had [according to the *Anglo-Saxon Chronicle*] supposedly campaigned up and down the Meuse, Scheldt, Seine, and Marne as one fighting force throughout the 880s.'[18] I would only omit the 'precisely'. The fuller contemporary Frankish sources present a far different vision of vikings than does the *Chronicle*, one that invites us to rethink Alfred's dealings with vikings. The *Annals of Saint-Bertin, Saint-Vaast, Saint-Wandrille* and *Fulda* reveal a Francia beset with numerous different viking bands in various locales under a multitude of leaders, who occasionally joined forces. Did the Frankish chroniclers regard these viking war bands as 'armies'? Some undoubtedly did. The author of the *Libellus miracularum s. Bertini* reports, for instance, that the Danish fleet that entered the Scheldt in April 891 'was called by everyone "the great army" [*magnus exercitus*]'.[19] That so many Frankish writers refrained from characterizing viking forces as 'armies', however, is certainly suggestive. In the *Annals of Saint-Bertin*, for instance, Prudentius only once has a Dane leading an *exercitus*. The Dane in question, Roric, was not only a member of the Danish royal house, but had once held the *vicus* of Dorestad from the emperor Lothar. The 'army' he raised from his native land was intended to 'persuade' Lothar to restore his benefice.[20] Roric, though called a 'pirate' in the *Annals of Fulda*, is hardly typical of viking chieftains.[21] By contrast, Prudentius repeatedly refers to various *exercitus* of Frankish and Breton rulers. For him, Northmen were quite simply *piratae*.[22] Indeed, in his annal for 846 Prudentius contrasts some 'Danish pirates' (*piratae Danorum*) who extorted tribute from the Frisians with an unnatural pack of wolves in the Aquitaine that 'gathered together in groups of up to 300, in the manner of an army [*in modum exercitus*], formed a sort of battle-line and marched along the road, bravely standing *en masse* against all who tried to resist them'.[23] Hincmar, who in the end *may* have come to see the vikings as an organized military threat

---

[18] Smyth, *Alfred*, 113.

[19] *Libellus miraculorum s. Bertini*, c. 6, ed. O. Holder-Egger, MGH SS 15 (Hanover 1887), 512. Given that the *Anglo-Saxon Chronicle* was composed soon after this event, one might think that its author's choice of *se micel here* was influenced by such reports from Francia. If so, the chronicler carefully chose his language to convey not only the size but the 'nature' of the viking forces. I would like to thank Christine Grainge for having called my attention to this text and for allowing me to see her as yet unpublished translation.

[20] *AB, s.a.* 850, 841; *AF, s.a.* 850; *AX, s.a.* 851.

[21] In 855 Roric returned to Denmark, apparently with the blessings of Lothar, to strive for the throne. He settled for territorial concessions from the new Danish king Horic. For Roric's careers as raider and 'faithful man' to King Louis and King Charles the Bald, see *AB, s.a.* 855, 867, 870, 872; *AF, s.a.* 857, 873, 882

[22] For example, *AB, s.a.* 838, 843, 846, 851, 853, 854, 856, 857, 858, 859. Cf. *AV, s.a.* 881, 886.

[23] *AB, s.a.* 846: 'Luporum incursio inferiorum Galliae partium homines audentissime devorat, sed et in partibus Aquitania in modum exercitus usque ad trecentos ferme conglobati et per viam facto agmine gradientes, volentibusque resistere fortiter unanimiterque contrastare feruntur' (trans. Nelson, 62).

intent on bringing the 'kingdom under their control',[24] never calls a viking force
an 'army' (*exercitus*) or host (*hostis*, his preferred usage), reserving those terms
for Carolingian rulers. Most usually in Saint-Bertin and other ninth-century
chronicles, the Franks raise armies to fight Northmen and each other. What
seems to have characterized an *exercitus*, at least for Prudentius, was the force's
size, organization, ability to coordinate military actions, and the legitimacy of
the authority that had assembled it.[25] Prudentius and Hincmar, I think, were
drawing a distinction along the lines of *here* and *fyrd*: for them an *exercitus*
implied not only organized force but regality. By labelling his forces as an
exercitus, Prudentius, who sympathized with Roric, was lending the Danes'
raiding a patina of legitimacy.

The relevance of the Frankish sources to Alfred's reign seems clear. The
same vikings who established strongholds on the Seine, Loire, Somme and
Meuse criss-crossed the Channel in search of plunder; we have no reason to
believe that they organized their forces any differently when they reached British
shores. If so, the great heathen army that 'systematically conquered' most of
England between 865 and 878 and its successor, 'the army' that left Fulham in
879, campaigned throughout Francia in the 880s and returned to England for yet
another go in 892, may be the inventions of historians influenced by preconceptions about 'the Vikings' and early medieval 'armies' and misled by the narrative
strategy of the *Anglo-Saxon Chronicle*.

Ninth-century Frankish chroniclers and authors of saints' lives, much like
Asser and the compilers of the *Anglo-Saxon Chronicle*, were predisposed to view
vikings in theological and moral terms, as 'the rod of God's wrath' to chastise his
faithless people.[26] Their successes, in Hincmar's words, 'manifested a divine
judgement, for what had been done by the Northmen obviously came about by
divine, not human, power'.[27] The description of vikings as *pagani* and *hæthenan*
clearly places the struggle on a moral plane. But even the apparently neutral
characterization of vikings as *Nortmanni*, which is how they most often appear in
the *Annals of Saint-Bertin*, *Fulda* and *Saint-Vaast*,[28] hints at a moral dimension to
the devastation, echoing as it does the language of Jeremiah (1: 14), 'Out of the
north evil shall break forth upon all the inhabitants of the land', a verse quoted
with regularity by English and Carolingian ecclesiastical writers from Alcuin on to
explain the spiritual significance of the depredation of these new Babylonians.[29]

---

[24] *AB, s.a.* 882. Hincmar uses *scara* in this entry to describe a Viking force. Elsewhere he uses
the term for a contingent of troops: *AB, s.a.* 866, 868, 869, 871, 876, 880, 882.

[25] As implied by the description of the 'army-like' wolfpack in *AB, s.a.* 846.

[26] S. Coupland, 'The rod of God's wrath or the people of God's wrath? The Carolingian
theology of the Viking invasions', *JEccH*, 42 (1991), 535–54.

[27] *AB, s.a.* 881: 'divino manifestante iudicio, quia quod a Nortmannis fuerat actum, non
humana sed divina virtute patratum extiterit' (trans. Nelson, 222).

[28] Coupland, 'Rod', 541.

[29] H. Zettel, *Das Bild der Normannen und der Normanneneinfälle in westfränkischen,
ostfränkischen und angelsächsichen Quellen des 8. bis 11. Jahrhunderts* (1977), 193–6.

For the most part, Prudentius, Hincmar, Rudolf, Regino, and the others were uninterested in differentiating among the various viking bands that raided the territories around their monasteries and sees. It sufficed that they were all 'Northmen' or 'pagans'. Locusts, after all, are merely locusts; one does not distinguish particular swarms. But more than Asser or the authors of the *Anglo-Saxon Chronicle*, the Frankish chroniclers were aware that their enemy's true name was legion.

A careful reading of the *Annals of Saint-Bertin* and other Frankish sources suggests that various and disparate companies of vikings operated along the rivers of Francia in the second half of the ninth century. These often acted individually, but on occasion joined forces, at least temporarily, to seize larger prey, as is attested by the well-recorded Siege of Paris in 885–86.[30] For the most part, the chroniclers merely recorded the presence or activity of Northmen or Danish pirates in a region, but, on occasion, they indicate that these were composite forces. In 858, while Bjorn, '*dux* of a part of the pirates on the Seine' (*partis piratarum Sequanae insistium*), was swearing fidelity to Charles the Bald at his palace of Verberie, another 'part' of those 'pirates' was capturing the abbot of St-Denis.[31]

The Frankish chroniclers were also capable of distinguishing between the kings and princes of their neighbours to the north, the Danes, and those Danes, including royalty, who had turned to piracy.[32] King Horic I of Denmark sent envoys to the emperor Louis in 838 to assure him that, out of loyalty, he had ordered the capture and execution of the 'pirates' who had plundered Walchern and Dorestad in the previous year.[33] After being received back as a *fidelis* by the emperor Lothar in 850, the Danish royal pretender Roric not only gave up his pirate ways, but pledged that as lord of the Frisians, 'he would faithfully handle the taxes and other matters pertaining to the royal fisc, *and would resist the piratical attacks of the Danes*' (emphasis added).[34] Even non-noble Danes could resist pirate attacks. When in 873 a 'certain Northman of royal stock' named Rudolf descended upon the Ostergau in Frisia, local resistance to his attack was led by 'a Christian Northman who had long lived among the Frisians'.[35]

---

[30] *AV, s.a.* 885–6; Abbo of Saint-Germain-des-Prés, *Bella Parisicae Urbis*, ed. Anton Pauels (1984), ll. 27–38 (pp. 24, 26). A Danish king, Sigifrid, was in command of the besieging forces.

[31] *AB, s.a.* 858 (trans. Nelson, 86).

[32] For examples of Frankish dealings with Danish royals, see *AB, s.a.* 831, 834, 839, 847, 854, 855. Cf. *AB, s.a.* 838, 841, 846, 847; *AF, s.a.* 852, 873 for Danish Vikings.

[33] *AB, s.a.* 838. Horic hoped to persuade Louis to grant him rule over the Frisians and Obodrites, but Louis, according to Prudentius, found the request offensive, perhaps because he suspected that Horic himself was behind the piratical attacks. Horic desired to control the Frisians in part to prevent *their* attacks on his people: *AB, s.a.* 839, 847.

[34] *AF, s.a.* 850: 'ea conditione, ut tributis caeterisque negotiis ad regis aerarium pertinentibus fideliter inserviret, et piraticis Danorum incursionibus obviando resisteret' (trans. Reuter, 30).

[35] *AF, s.a.* 873.

The story of Rudolf as told in the *Annals of Fulda* is especially interesting for what it reveals about Frankish–Danish relations in the late ninth century. Prior to its notice of Rudolf's attack, the *Annals* report that King Sigifrid and his brother Halfdan had sent embassies to Louis the German to make peace over border disputes, regularize trade between the kingdoms, and to petition the Carolingian king to treat them 'as if they were his sons, while they for their part would venerate him as a father for all the days of their life'. Rudolf's demand for 'tribute' from the inhabitants of the Ostergau and the locals' response that they were not bound to pay tribute to any man other than King Louis and his sons clearly shows that this was a dispute over territorial lordship, perhaps even a response to Sigifrid's settlement of the border with Louis. To characterize Rudolf, clearly a Danish royal pretender, as a 'viking' would be misleading.

The nature of ninth-century viking warbands and their leaders is perhaps most clearly revealed by the careers of two Northmen who operated on both sides of the Channel, Weland and his more famous contemporary Hæsten. Theirs was not a simple story of heathen predators and Christian prey, but, rather, a complicated tale of aspiration to acceptance, conversion, negotiations with predatory Frankish princes, and mutual betrayals.

Weland was the leader of an unsuccessful raid on Winchester in 860 reported in both the *Anglo-Saxon Chronicle* and the *Annals of Saint-Bertin*.[36] The latter permits us to track in unique detail the movements of this particular viking band and its leader before and after this foray, and to glimpse the complex political realities that shaped the interaction between vikings and native rulers.[37] Weland, apparently, had been leading a band of vikings that had established itself the previous year on the river Somme. There they had come to an agreement with King Charles the Bald to drive off or kill a different band of vikings who had built a fortress on the island of Jeufosse in the Seine, from which they had conducted raids deep into the countryside.[38] Charles agreed to pay the Somme vikings three thousand pounds of silver, weighed out under their watchful eyes – these would-be mercenaries no more trusted Charles than he them – and they undertook to drive out the Seine vikings. While Charles raised the cash by taxing the treasures of churches and the houses and moveable wealth of landholders and merchants, the Somme vikings took hostages from the Franks and struck out across the Channel. Their rough reception at the hands of the West Saxons persuaded them to return to Francia where, under the leadership of Weland, they finally fulfilled their bargain with Charles.

While King Charles raised silver and gathered livestock and corn for his viking allies so that the realm would not be looted, Weland's forces blockaded

---

[36] *ASC, s.a.* 860; Asser, c. 18.

[37] *AB, s.a.* 859–61.

[38] C. Gillmor, 'Aimoin's *Miracula Sancti Germani* and the Viking raids on St. Denis and St. Germain-des-Prés', in *The Normans and their Adversaries at War*, eds R. Abels and B. Bachrach (2001), 103–27.

the Seine vikings in their stronghold and starved them into submission.[39] The survivors agreed to pay Weland 6000 lb of gold and silver, and then, surprisingly, joined up with him. With winter coming on, Weland's forces split up into smaller bands (*sodalitates*) to winter among the various ports and abbeys of the Seine basin. After one of the bands burnt Meaux, Charles raised an army and stationed troops along both banks of the Oise, Marne and Seine.[40] Weland and the leaders of the other viking bands agreed to return their captives and depart the kingdom. The great fleet broke up into smaller bands. Some sailed to Brittany to take service with the Breton chieftain Salomon, while others signed on with Salomon's rival, Robert the Strong of Anjou.

Weland himself returned to Charles's court within the year, having apparently lost command of his fleet. He swore fidelity to Charles and, along with his wife and entourage, accepted baptism, presumably in order to secure the Frankish king's favour. In an odd turn of events, the viking chieftain was accused by one of his own men of 'bad faith' and of having sought baptism 'as a trick'. He proved his accusation by killing Weland in single combat in the presence of Charles and his court. One suspects that Charles 'set up' Weland. Though the Frankish chronicles constantly condemn Danish treachery, more than one Northman met a treacherous end at the hands of Frankish allies.[41]

Hæsten, the leader of an eighty-ship fleet that made base at Milton Regis in 892, was a far more celebrated viking chieftain[42] and played a more central role in Alfred's story, but his and Weland's careers share significant similarities. He apparently had a long and successful career as a viking chieftain in Francia before he came to England. He first appears in the sources as one of the leaders of a combined viking–Breton raid up the river Sarthe into Anjou in 866. For some years after that he led a viking band based on the Loire, which profited not only from pillaging monasteries and villages but from offering its services to local counts in their interminable border wars.[43] He relocated to northern France and the Lowlands in the 880s and was sufficiently prominent to draw the personal attention of King Louis III of West Francia, who bought peace from him in 882. In 890, as the leader of a band of vikings based at Argoeuves-sur-Sommes, he entered into a 'woeful compact' with the abbot of St-Vaast that allowed him to roam freely over the lands of the abbey in return for his promise

---

[39] *AB, s.a.* 861.

[40] Nelson, *Charles the Bald*, 206. C. Gillmor, 'War on the rivers: Viking numbers and mobility on the Seine and Loire, 841–886', *Viator*, 19 (1988), 83, interprets *sodalitas* to mean the crew of a single viking ship.

[41] For example, *AF, s.a.* 852, 885: the murders of Heriald and Godafrid.

[42] *The Gesta Normannorum Ducum of William of Jumièges, Orderic Vitalis, and Robert of Torigni* I, 4–10, ed. and trans. E. M. C. van Houts, Oxford Medieval Texts, 2 vols (1992–95), i.17–27. See F. Amory, 'The Viking Hasting in Franco-Scandinavian legend', in *Saints, Scholars and Heroes: Studies in Medieval Culture in Honour of Charles W. Jones*, eds M. H. King and W. M. Stevens, 2 vols (1979), ii. 265–86. See also Smyth, *Alfred*, 116–19.

[43] Regino, *s.a.* 867 [for 866], 874.

to spare (and perhaps protect) the monastery. He used the 'peace' to prepare a surprise attack on the monks in connivance with a second viking band at nearby Noyon.[44] As Smyth observes, the recorded activities of Hæsten make it impossible for him to have been with the *Chronicle*'s *here* either at Fulham or later, as it ravaged its way across northern Francia in the 880s.[45]

The careers of Weland and Hæsten shed a great deal of light upon the nature of the viking threat faced by King Alfred. The vikings who ravaged Francia and Britain in the mid- and late ninth century were not a 'people' and their warbands were not well-regulated 'armies'. Though the chronicle sources often label viking fleets as 'Danish' or 'Northmen', these terms better describe the leaders rather than their crews, who probably were a heterogeneous and variable lot. By the 850s many Scandinavians (and others) practised piracy as a profession, not unlike the members of the Free Companies of the Hundred Years War or the buccaneers who plundered merchantmen and sacked towns throughout the Caribbean in the late seventeenth century. Weland's viking *here* in 860–61 was clearly a composite force made up of various independent *liðs*, including perhaps an opportunistic sixty-ship fleet and, eventually, the remnants of the very vikings whom Weland had contracted to destroy.[46] Weland's *here* dissolved after the captains and their men split up the loot.[47] Like skeins of particularly nasty migrating geese that join together under one leader, only to break up and reform under another, such viking *heres* represented fluid and shifting combinations of smaller fleets. As prominent as they are in our sources, Hæsten and Weland were merely two viking chieftains among many.

If we reconsider Alfred's dealings with vikings in light of the Frankish sources, we can see that the actual threat he faced was different from what has often been depicted. For one thing, the *Chronicle*'s *micel hæthen here* may have been less well organized and cohesive than Stenton, Smyth, Peddie and others thought. The *micel here* was probably constantly changing in terms of its personnel and leadership from the time it first began to gather in East Anglia in 865. Even before the *Anglo-Saxon Chronicle* has the *here* 'sharing out' the kingdoms of the Northumbrians, East Anglians and Mercians, individual viking bands probably departed with their loot, with newly arrived vikings taking their place. The *micel sumorlida* that opportunistically combined forces with the Reading vikings in 871 is a case in point. By 874 what may have been left was a mere

---

[44] *AV, s.a.* 890. See Smyth, *Alfred*,116.

[45] Smyth, *Alfred*, 116.

[46] *AB, s.a.* 861. W. Vogel, *Die Normannen und das fränkische Reich bis zur Gründung der Normandie, 799–911* (1906), 184. Cf. Gillmor, 'War on the rivers', 84, who argues that the text actually describes a portage operation of sixty small boats. For the meaning of *lið*, see N. Lund, 'The Danish perspective', in *The Battle of Maldon, A.D. 1991*, ed. D. Scragg (1991), 119–30.

[47] Cf *Libellus miraculorum s. Bertini*, cc. 6–7, which describes how a force of 550 'young men who deemed themselves to be more active and daring than the others' secretly broke away from the *magnus exercitus* at *Cirisiacus* to try their hand at freebooting, only to be cut to pieces by the defenders of St-Omer.

remnant of the *here* that had fought in York in 867. Certainly, the physical dimensions of the viking encampment at Repton do not encourage one to think in terms of a 'great army'.[48] Nor can we be certain about the *micel here*'s leadership. The prominence given in the *Chronicle* and medieval sagas to Halfdan and Ivarr may simply be in recognition of their personal successes, just as the *Chronicle* singles out Guthrum from Oscetel and Anwend, the other two 'kings' associated with him in the annal for 875.[49] The mention of Guthrum reminds us that there were at least several viking 'kings' in the *micel here*, including the obscure Bacgseg, about whom we know nothing other than that he died fighting the West Saxons in 871, as well as various named and unnamed 'earls' (jarls), each of whom probably was the captain of a fleet.

Alfred may not even have faced the *Chronicle*'s *micel here* in the crisis that began in 876 and climaxed two years later in the battle of Edington. Guthrum first appears in a historical source in the *Anglo-Saxon Chronicle*'s entry for 875, where he is said to have led part of the viking force at Repton in association with two other 'kings'. When he came to England is unknown, as is his previous career, since he is not mentioned in any continental source. That he and his two partners arrived with the *micel sumorlida* in 871 is sheer speculation. By 874, however, they had joined forces with Halfdan to seize the Mercian royal vill of Repton and drive the surprised Mercian king Burgred into exile.[50] But within a year, the forces had split, with Halfdan returning to Northumbria and the three kings relocating to Cambridge. Presumably, this was the viking *here* that slipped past the West Saxon *fyrd* into Wareham in 876, and which returned to Wessex in the winter of 878. Oscetel and Anwend disappear as suddenly from the *Chronicle* as they appeared. The chronicler is clear that in the crisis of 878 Alfred faced a single enemy leader, the viking king Guthrum.

The *Chronicle* account emphasizes Alfred's military victory over Guthrum and Guthrum's submission to Alfred and his consequent conversion to Christianity.[51] What I find equally intriguing is that Alfred chose to deal with Guthrum rather than destroy him and his forces. Alfred's grandfather Egberht was celebrated in the *Chronicle* for having 'conquered everything south of the Humber'.[52] Alfred chose not to emulate him. He did not follow up his victory at Edington by leading an expedition into East Anglia or Mercia. Rather, he expanded his

---

[48] M. Biddle and B. Kjølbye-Biddle, 'Repton and the Vikings', *Antiquity*, 66 (1992), 36–51; *eidem*, 'Repton and the "great heathen army", 873–4', in *Vikings and the Danelaw: Papers from the Proceedings of the Thirteenth Viking Congress, Nottingham and York, 21st-30th August 1997*, eds J. Graham-Campbell, R. Hall, J. Jesch and D. N. Parsons (2001), 45–96. Martin Biddle (personal communication) regards the entrenched area as an emergency fortress rather than the winter camp itself. But cf. Asser, c. 35, where it appears Haldan and Bagsecg had their entire camp at Reading defended with a rampart built between the Thames and Kennet.

[49] *ASC, s.a.* 875, 878.

[50] *ASC, s.a.* 874, 875.

[51] Asser, c. 56 (trans. Keynes and Lapidge, *Alfred*, 84–5).

[52] *ASC, s.a.* 829.

authority through negotiation. Alfred as always was being practical. By raising Guthrum from the baptismal font and recognizing him by treaty as a legitimate king of the East Angles, Alfred was acting no differently from his Carolingian contemporaries.[53] Louis the Pious and his successors saw an advantage in establishing exiled members of the Danish royal house as counts in areas vulnerable to viking raiding. A number of Danish chieftains, beginning with Louis the Pious's endowment of the exiled Danish king Harald Klak in 826, were entrusted with the care of Frisia.[54] Louis conferred the *vicus* of Dorestad as a benefice on the Northmen Roric and his kinsman Harald, and Lothar confirmed the grant to Roric, explicitly on condition that he would defend it against Danish 'pirates', though only after Roric had forced his hand by seizing the emporium.[55]

Alfred, I believe, saw Guthrum in similar terms, as a useful ally against future viking incursions. In the aftermath of Edington, while the newly converted Guthrum and his army sojourned in Cirencester in territory belonging to his ally, the Mercian King Ceolwulf II, a viking fleet sailed up the Thames past London and encamped at Fulham, on the 'Mercian' north banks of the river. Though Asser implies that these newcomers joined Guthrum, the silence of the *Chronicle* suggests that they were independent players, perhaps remnants of the viking band that Louis III and Carloman II had defeated on the Loire in November 879.[56] Indeed, their presence on the Thames may have persuaded Guthrum to look to his interests in East Anglia. In 880 he returned to East Anglia, where he 'settled and shared out the land'.[57] The Fulham vikings, perhaps in response, sailed for Ghent soon after Guthrum's return.

The arrival of this new fleet and the death or deposition of Ceolwulf II sometime around 879 or 880 formed, I believe, the backdrop for the famous treaty between Alfred and Guthrum that divided between them what had once been Mercia. By the terms of this treaty Alfred was to succeed to Ceolwulf's kingdom of western Mercia and Guthrum was to incorporate the eastern part of Mercia into an enlarged kingdom of East Anglia.[58] Alfred, moreover, was to

---

[53] For Carolingian kings insisting that Danish followers convert, see Abels, *Alfred*, 164–5.

[54] Rimbert, *Vita Anskarii*, c. 7, ed. G. Waitz, MGH SRG 55 (Hanover, 1884) (trans. C. H. Robinson, *Anskar: the Apostle of the North* (1921), 38). On Lothar I's grant of Walchern to Harald in 841–42, and Charles the Simple's negotiations with the still pagan Seine vikings in the mid-890s, see E. Searle, *Predatory Kinship and the Creation of Norman Power, 840–1066* (1988), 41–2.

[55] *AF, s.a.* 850.

[56] Asser, c. 58; *ASC, s.a.* 879.

[57] *ASC, s.a.* 880.

[58] See R. H. C. Davis, 'Alfred and Guthrum's frontier', *EHR* 97 (1982), 803–10, reprinted in *idem, From Alfred the Great to Stephen* (1991), 47–54. Cf. D. Dumville, 'The treaty of Alfred and Guthrum', in *idem, Wessex and England from Alfred to Edgar* (1992), 1–28. Ceolwulf has often been portrayed as a 'puppet' king on the basis of the *Anglo-Saxon Chronicle*'s characterization of him as 'a foolish thegn' who gave hostages and swore oaths to the Danes that he would be their man and would be ready to hand over his kingdom to them on demand: *ASC, s.a.* 873. This clashes, however, with the charter and numismatic evidence that presents Ceolwulf as Burgred's legitimate successor and Alfred's partner in coinage. The *ASC*'s presentation may have been designed to

have control over London and its mints, at least for the time being. What Alfred gained, or so he believed, was a buffer against future viking attacks on Kent and up the Thames. In the event, Guthrum proved less reliable than Alfred had hoped. East Anglian Danes joined a viking *here* in 885 in an attack on Rochester. Alfred's anger at the East Anglians for breaking the peace they had contracted with him manifested itself in a punitive *sciphere* to East Anglia, Alfred's only foray as king against the Danes outside the confines of his kingdom.

Alfred, on the whole, however, must have felt satisfied with the deal that he had made with Guthrum. He apparently tried similar negotiations with Hæsten in 892. As I have argued in my book, it is unlikely that Hæsten's forces at Milton Regis were in any way associated with the larger viking fleet that had earlier made camp at Appledore.[59] The most reasonable interpretation of Alfred's dealings with Hæsten, which included standing sponsor at the baptism of the viking chieftain's sons, was that he was attempting to negotiate an arrangement. Alfred realized the problems involved in fighting on two fronts, and perhaps hoped that Hæsten would play Weland to his Charles the Bald. Alfred, we know from Asser, counted Danes among the members of his court – ironically, he would have been less likely to demonize the Danes than have their Christian descendants and some modern historians – and it is not inconceivable that he saw Hæsten as a possible recruit. If that was Alfred's thinking, he was to be disappointed. Despite his best efforts, he found himself fighting the two viking bands at Milton Regis and Appledore as well as an opportunistic *here* from Danish Northumbria. Though the events of 892–95 have been treated by historians as a war on several fronts, it seems more probable that Alfred faced something similar to what Hincmar records in 882, several different viking *heres* trying to take advantage of the activities of the others, so that it appeared as if a single, hydra-headed enemy was attempting to take over the kingdom. What the members of these *heres* seem to have been most interested in, however, was obtaining loot, *feoh*, that they could use to purchase land in East Anglia and Northumbria. Those who failed in this reluctantly crossed the Channel to the Seine to continue their careers as pirates.[60]

The defensive system that Alfred created in the 880s and 890s was designed to defend against the simultaneous attacks by different *heres*, precisely as happened in 892–95. Each *burh* was permanently garrisoned, with Roman roads and rivers allowing troops to assemble from neighboring *burhs* for larger expeditions. Alfred's mobile field force complemented this system. Alfred did not design this system so much to prevent conquest as to minimize the possibility of raiding. *Heres* could enter his kingdom, but if they did, they were unlikely to make it back to their ships with their booty. As a result, Alfred was able to fight

---

discredit Ceolwulf and justify his deposition. Certainly, Ceolwulf's abasement before his pagan masters is meant to contrast with Alfred's heroic resistance.

[59] Abels, *Alfred*, 287–92.
[60] *ASC*, *s.a.* 896.

vikings simultaneously in the eastern, northern, and western frontiers of his kingdom. It was not Alfred but his son Edward who saw the possibility of using this system for aggression, conquest and settlement.

It is well to remind ourselves that the word 'viking', *wicenga*, was not a synonym for Dane, Norwegian, or Scandinavian. It meant pirate – not warrior or soldier. Relatively few Scandinavian males in the ninth century probably went a-viking, and not all vikings were Scandinavians. The viking *heres* that Alfred and his English contemporaries faced were no different from those that operated in Francia. The raiding bands depicted in the Frankish chronicles did not suddenly gain cohesion, discipline, strategy and organization when they reached the shores of Britain. The period 892–95 was not a prefiguration of the Battle of Britain or 1066, or even of 1015, for that matter. As in Francia, viking leaders could and did join together for mutual benefit, but once they had their profit, these forces would once again dissolve. The main difference, of course, is that some of these viking chieftains were able to conquer and control territories in England. This is not to be minimized. It meant that a new and different society and culture emerged in what was to be called the Danelaw. But the conquests were not systematic; nor were they effected by what Christian chroniclers would have deemed 'armies'. If we seek a modern analogy for Alfred confronting vikings, it is not Churchill facing down a German invasion but George W. Bush desperately trying to objectify terrorism in order to deal with it in a proper military manner.

Chapter 16

Alfred's new longships

Edwin and Joyce Gifford

Many attempts have been made to decipher the enigmatic description of Alfred's longships in the *Anglo-Saxon Chronicle* of 896.[1] This interpretation follows ten years of our research on the characteristics of Saxon ships,[2] including the building and sailing of half-scale models of the well-recorded remains of two vessels: the magnificent 27-metre Anglian ship found in Mound One at Sutton Hoo in Suffolk built about 600 (Fig. 26) and the modest 14-metre Graveney trader (Fig. 27), from Kent of *c.* 900. Although 350 years separate them, the construction methods and the characteristic shapes of the hull cross-sections of these two ships are so alike (Fig. 28) that we can assume a continuous tradition of ship-building throughout this period in south-east England.

The trial results of the half-scale model of the Sutton Hoo ship (Fig. 29), were particularly significant as they indicated that the sailing performance of the full-size ship could have been remarkable, being able to reach and run, in winds of Force 4 and above, at speeds of 10 knots or more over an arc of 200° and to average 7 knots when on passage with favourable winds. This would have resulted in journey times such as these:

Rendlesham, Suffolk to Canterbury	0.5 day
Canterbury to France	0.5 day
Suffolk to York	1.5 days
Suffolk to Jutland	3 days

The 0.6-metre draft would have allowed the ship to be sailed with confidence in shallow coastal waters and, helped by the bold sheer at bow and stern, to beach-land even in high surf when necessary.

This combination of high speed, shallow draft and surf beach-landing would have made the Sutton Hoo ship safe for the waters of the east coast of England, the southern North Sea and the north-west coasts of Europe, all of

---

[1] Keynes and Lapidge, *Alfred*, 119.

[2] E. and J. Gifford, 'The sailing characteristics of the Saxon ships, as derived from half-scale working models with special reference to the Sutton Hoo ships', *International Journal of Nautical Archaeology*, 24 (1995), 121–31; E. and J. Gifford, 'The sailing performance of Anglo-Saxon ships', *Mariner's Mirror*, 82 (1996), 131–53.

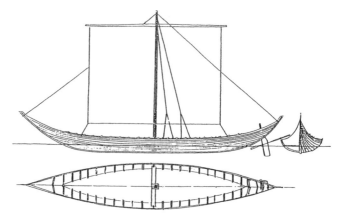

Fig. 26   Sutton Hoo ship. 7th cent. 38 oars. 27 × 4.5 × 1.2 × 0.6 m. 10 knots
sailing, 6 knots rowing

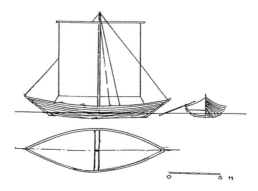

Fig. 27   Graveney ship. 10th cent. 38 oars. 13.4 × 4.0 × 1.0 × 0.5 m. 7 knots
sailing

which are bordered by creeks, sand banks and beaches to which she could safely
run before a rising gale.

   Anglo-Saxon ships were not at an intermediate state of development by
shipwrights searching blindly in the Dark Ages, but were fully resolved designs,
difficult to improve upon even with today's knowledge. The building, sailing and
testing of half-scale models has expanded our understanding of their performance and seaworthiness from an intuitive appreciation to a conviction based on
measurement, which has substantially changed the previously held views on
Anglo-Saxon seafaring. Æthelstan (Alfred's kinsman) could have become familiar with this tradition when he became under-king of Kent in 836 and could have
used the 38-oar Anglian type of longship when he captured nine Danish ships at

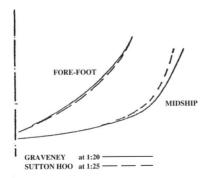

Fig. 28   Sutton Hoo and Graveney ships: comparison of critical sections

Sandwich in 851. Similar ships could have been used by Alfred in his early actions.

During this early period of random raiding, the attackers always had the advantage of surprise when landing on sparsely populated coasts, so the defenders would rarely have been able to stop them at sea but could only respond to the alarms given by beacons or messengers by racing to catch the raiders on the beach or chase them as they were leaving. For this they needed fast, shallow-draught ships at strategic places round the coast, probably based at or near burghs. The map (Fig. 30) shows that the coastal burghs are rarely more than 25 miles apart and that in south-east Kent the then navigable Wantsum Channel between Reculver and Sandwich would have allowed rapid movement between Gravesend and Sandwich, both of which had well-sheltered waters and beaches from which ships could be quickly launched to intercept or pursue raiders.[3] We believe that after the Saxons started to combat the raiders with ships of the Sutton Hoo Anglian type, they would have realized that faster vessels, with larger crews, would give better results. We believe that the much-studied entry in *ASC* for 896 gives clear clues to the characteristics of these new longships:

> The same year the raiding-armies in East Anglia and Northumbria greatly harassed Wessex along the south coast with predatory bands, most of all with the warships they had built many years before. Then King Alfred ordered longships to be built to oppose the warships; they were well-nigh twice as long as the others, some had 60 oars, some more; they were both swifter and steadier, and also higher than the others; they were neither of Frisian design nor of Danish, but as it seemed to himself that they might be useful.[4]

---

[3] D. Hill, *Atlas of Anglo-Saxon England* (1981), 86; T. Tatton Brown, 'Anglo-Saxon towns of Kent', in *Anglo-Saxon Settlements*, ed. D. Hooke (Oxford, 1988), 213–32, at 213; P. Bennett, personal communication.

[4] *ASC*, trans. Keynes and Lapidge, *Alfred*, 118–19.

We understand that the scribe for this part of the *ASC* has a reputation for accuracy, so we have looked carefully at each phrase with the eyes of boat-builders and sailors.

'*the warships they had built many years before*'. These were probably light, shallow, easily beachable raiders of 20 to 30 oars similar to the Danish warship of 950,[5] found at Ladby, with its presumed complement of 60 and speeds of nine knots under sail and five knots under oar.

'*they were well-nigh twice as long as the others, some had 60 oars*'. The scribe is precise in giving the dimensional increase to be in length only; the ships were not twice as *large*. Doubling the number of oars does not double the overall length of the ship as the bow and stern sections remain the same, so the phrase '*well-nigh twice as long*' has an authentic ring.

'*both swifter and steadier*'. These characteristics would follow from in-creased length.

'*also higher than the others*'. This suggests that the increase in construc-tion-depth to give the strength required for the longer hull was obtained by increasing the freeboard rather than the draught. This would mean that the longer ships could still operate in shallow water in pursuit of the Danes and be easy to beach. The additional freeboard would give better protection to the crew, with the oars working through oar-ports rather than against tholes on the gunwhale. With this method of mounting the oars, the crew could apply full power astern so that the ship could be equally fast in both directions and even turn in its own length, both useful characteristics in narrow waterways.

'*neither of Frisian design or Danish, but as it seemed to himself that they might be most useful*'. We suggest that Alfred's 60-oar longships were a straight-forward 'stretch' of the length of the 300-year-old 38-oar 27-metre Anglian type to 37 metres, with the same beam and draught, giving greater speed while still being able to navigate the shallow waters of the English coast (Fig. 31). This method of increasing the performance of a proven design has a long tradition in ship-building.

The *ASC* appears to give the earliest reference to 60-oar longships in northern Europe, as was recognized by H. Shetelig, the great Norwegian mari-time historian when he wrote in 1951:[6]

> This King Alfred had created a new type of vessel built for war at sea, in order to keep the Vikings away from the coast. This fleet was the foundation of a sea power, which was kept up by the later Kings of England. By the middle of the next century it was stated that the fleet had 3,600 ships and that it was ordered out each year for manoeuvres. King Alfred's ships were not, properly speaking, Viking ships: on the contrary, they were a fleet used for coastal defence against the Vikings. But this is the first we hear in western Europe of

---

[5] A. C. Sorensen, 'The Ladby ship', *Newsletter from Roskilde*, 10 (1998), 19.

[6] A. W. Brøgger and H. Shetelig, *The Viking Ships* (Oslo, 1951, repr. 1971), 135.

Fig. 29   Half-scale model of the Sutton Hoo ship at 7 knots on the River
Deben

> a type of ship which in Norse terminology would be called a longship
> – in this case a ship of 30 thwarts (60-oars) or rather more ... thus we
> know that the first longships in Western Europe were used in Eng-
> land during King Alfred's struggle against the Vikings.

A narrow 64-oared longship has been found recently at Hedeby[7] and can
be tree-ring-dated to 958 (Fig. 32). Olav Trygvason is recorded as building a 60-
oar ship in 995,[8] but this was of the battleship type, which was deeper, heavier
and slower than the longship and so not suitable for the pursuit of hit-and-run
raiders.

Our research with the half-scale model of the Sutton Hoo ship[9] has provided data for us to calculate that Alfred's new longships could have carried a
complement of 140 men at speeds of 12 knots when sailing and 7 knots under

[7] O. Crumlin-Pedersen, *Viking age ships and shipbuilding in Hedeby Schleswig*, Ships and
Boats of the North, 2 (Roskilde, 1997), 81–99.

[8] Brøgger and Shetelig, *Viking Ships*, 146–51.

[9] See n. 2.

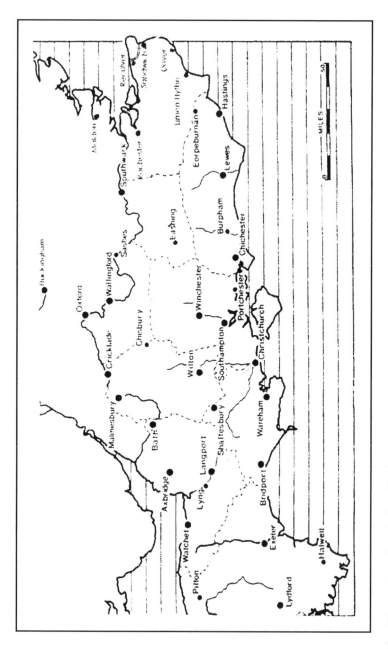

Fig. 30   Map to show burghs in Alfred's time

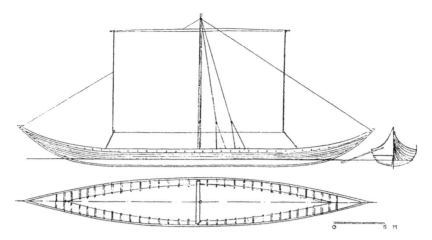

Fig. 31   Alfred's ship (postulated), 9th cent. Length shown to same scale as
Figs 26 and 27. 60 oars. 37 × 4.6 × 1.4 × 0.6 m. 12 knots sailing, 7
knots rowing

oar. Such speeds would have enabled the English ships, if stationed at 20-mile
intervals, to reach the stricken beach well within two hours of the alarm, either
to catch the raiders ashore or to run them down as they were leaving. With the
speed and capacity of Alfred's new ships, combined with the strengthening of
fortifications and signalling systems along the coast, is it surprising that the
Danish raids dwindled for so many years?

Postscript

Since presenting this paper we have read M. J. Swanton's paper on Alfred's
ships,[10] and wish to comment on certain points raised and to correct some
widely held misconceptions amongst scholars unfamiliar with ship design and
structural engineering and inexperienced with boat handling. In particular, a
misconception that may have arisen through the power of poetic metaphor is the
idea that flexibility in a ship is a good thing. Anyone who has suffered the agony
of rowing in an old, 'flexible' clinker eight will remember the joy of rowing in a
new, stiff boat. A flexible hull is not good for oarsmen, for sailors, or for
beaching.

One of the innovations that transformed the quality of clinker boats during
the first millennium was the use of trenails (wooden pegs) for fastening planks
to the frames rather than lashings, which were used in Scandinavia until the end

---

[10] M. J. Swanton, 'King Alfred's ships: text and context', *ASE*, 28 (1999), 1–22.

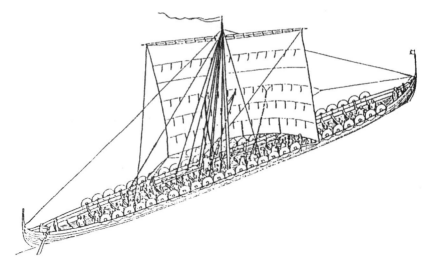

Fig. 32   Hedeby ship. 10th cent. 64 oars. 31 × 2.7 × 1.5 m. Speeds not known

of the millennium. Because of its use in famous ships, such as the Norwegian *Gokstad*, this lashing technique has acquired an unwarranted reputation, along with the supposed virtue of flexibility. We suggest that it was probably used to allow movement of the green planks during drying, to avoid splitting, especially in pine boats. But the use of willow trenails instead of lashings makes for much stiffer hulls, while permitting some shrinkage of the planks, and made possible the building of longer, lighter vessels such as the Sutton Hoo ship with its length of 27 metres.

We have no problem with the OED definition of *unwealt* as steadiness.[11] In nautical terms this means resistance to heeling or rolling of the whole ship and is often referred to as stiffness. But this is not the same as structural stiffness of the hull, which refers to its resistance to twisting. Likewise we agree with the translation of *hieran* as higher, since a longer ship needs additional height to give increased longitudinal strength. Two additional topside planks only are sufficient for this purpose and would entail negligible increase in draught. A square sail stepped amidships imposes no excessive loads on a hull, even when tacking, provided that an adequate mast step is fitted and its use is by no means restricted to a following wind, as has been demonstrated by our trials[12] and those of Crumlin-Pedersen and Vinner.[13]

---

[11] *Oxford English Dictionary*, 2nd edn, vol. 19, col. 862: '*Walt*. [O.E. *Wealt* found only in *unwealdt* – steady] of a ship, unsteady, crank'.

[12] See n. 2.

[13] O. Crumlin-Pedersen and M. Vinner, *Roar og Helge of Roskilde* (Roskilde, 1993), 29.

We do not know whether the Anglo-Saxons practised ramming, but when a small, open boat crossed the bows of our Sutton Hoo half-scale model and caused a collision, our long, curved bow slid over the small boat's gunwale, pushing it down into the water and swamping it, without any permanent damage to either craft. This was an unplanned but effective demonstration.

The lack of information about the success or failure of Alfred's innovatory ships is frustrating, but the recent discovery of a 64-oar longship at Hedeby, dated to 958, indicates that the design concept outlasted Alfred.

Glossary

Draught	Depth of the ship below the waterline
Freeboard	Height of the gunwhale above the waterline
Gunwhale	The upper edge of the hull
Oar-ports	Circular holes in the side of the ship through which the oars passed. These could be closed with wooden shutters when under sail
Reach, to	To sail across the wind
Run, to	To sail down wind
Tholes	Shark's-tooth-shaped pieces of oak fastened to the top of the gunwhale to locate the oars and resist the forward thrust. A strop of rope or leather was used to prevent the oar slipping aft on the recovery part of the stroke

ALFRED AND
CONTEMPORARY RULERSHIP

Chapter 17

Alfred's Carolingian contemporaries

Janet L. Nelson

'We have heard much of the destructive effects of the Vikings … in the ninth century: we forget that for most of Europe …, it was the Franks who were the Vikings.'[1] If I focus more narrowly in this paper, I begin by invoking that larger perception of Franks and also Anglo-Saxons (they too were perfectly capable of being Vikings). I present a series of snapshots which either bring Alfred and his Carolingian contemporaries into a single frame, or pair them like pictures in a diptych (for genealogies, see Figs 33 and 34).[2] The self-representations and ideologies of Carolingian rulers can never be understood apart from the audiences and constituencies – Frankish, Anglo-Saxon, and even Viking Vikings – for whom they played and at whom the royal actions were directed. But my focus is on kings, and on regarding contemporaries as a useful means of assessing Alfred's distinctiveness.[3]

Alfred almost certainly met at least one Carolingian king, and maybe two. The one he met was Charles the Bald, the one he maybe met was Louis II of Italy. The occasion was Alfred's second journey to Rome and back in 855–56. Though he had already visited Rome in 853 when sent to the pope by his father King Æthelwulf, and may have visited Carolingian royal courts en route, there is no direct evidence to that effect. Simon Keynes has recently highlighted the implications of certain Anglo-Saxon names in the Brescia *Liber Vitae*. We can be reasonably sure of the reality of Alfred's second visit to Rome in the company of his father – a journey well documented, as far as Æthelwulf is concerned, in both West Frankish and Roman sources.[4] Brescia is not too far from Pavia, Louis II's capital, and it seems very likely that a royal pilgrim and his *familia*

---

[1] T. Reuter, 'Plunder and tribute in the Carolingian Empire', *TRHS* fifth series, 35 (1985), 75–94, at 91.

[2] I use the word Carolingian(s) to refer to members of that family, not to their contemporaries at large.

[3] For earlier comparative approaches, see H. M. Cam, *Local Government in Francia and England* (1912); J. M. Wallace-Hadrill, *Early Germanic Kingship in England and on the Continent* (1971); J. L. Nelson, '"A king across the sea": Alfred in Continental perspective', *TRHS* fifth series, 36 (1986), 45–68, and 'Charles le Chauve et les utilisations du savoir', in *L'École carolingienne d'Auxerre*, eds D. Iogna-Prat, C. Jeudy and G. Lobrichon (Paris, 1991), 37–54, repr. in Nelson, *Rulers and Ruling Families in Early Medieval Europe* (1999), chs I and VII.

[4] S. Keynes, 'Anglo-Saxon entries in the *Liber Vitae* of Brescia', in *Alfred the Wise. Studies in Honour of Janet Bately*, eds J. Roberts and J. L. Nelson (1998), 99–119.

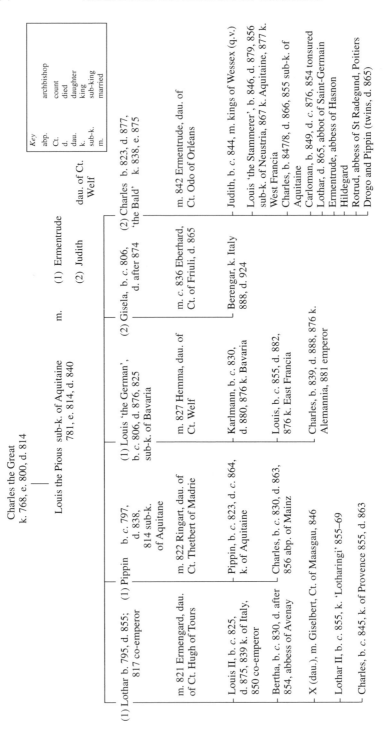

Fig. 33 Carolingians and descendants

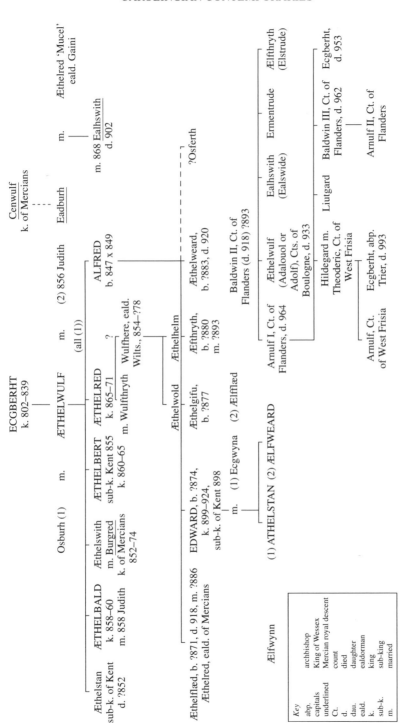

Fig. 34 Alfred's family

would have stopped to visit. As for Charles the Bald, Æthelwulf spent well over two months in his company before marrying his daughter, Judith, on 1 October 856. Alfred at some point must surely have been presented to this prestigious new kinsman. What impression, if any, did these Carolingians leave on a six- or seven-year-old? 'Kings seated on high seats ... girt about with a great company of thegns decked with belts and gold-hilted swords and wargear of many kinds ... ': could those images of 'unrighteous kings' be the grown man's recollection of real live Carolingians?[5] Frankly, we have no idea of what those childhood experiences meant to Alfred. Louis II and Charles the Bald may have repelled as well as attracted an imaginative little boy, and left a lasting memory, if not model, of royal wealth and power. Were the royal residences at Verberie, or Pavia, only Cheddar, or Winchester, writ large?[6] Or were Carolingian and Cerdicing courts qualitatively different? I shall return to these questions towards the end of this paper.

If Alfred lived at his father's court after Æthelwulf returned to Wessex with his new bride in 856, could Judith have been the 'mother' who, according to Asser, offered a book of Saxon songs to whichever of her 'sons' could learn it first?[7] On the whole this identification seems unlikely, though not for the reason given by Stevenson and Stubbs, namely that the 'light Frankish princess' – 'light' because of her subsequent career as a widow who married her stepson, then, widowed anew, eloped with a young nobleman – was unlikely to have been interested in Old English poems.[8] In fact, Judith might well have wanted to learn Old English, and songs would have been a fine learning medium.[9] Further, the age-gap between herself and Alfred could only have been some four or five years: unless Judith was a stereotypically wicked stepmother, why should they not have enjoyed Saxon songs together? Judith's identification as the 'mother' of Asser's story is unconvincing for chronological reasons, however. By late 856, two of Alfred's elder brothers were no longer living at their father's court but had been set up with courts and kingdoms of their own. The story as it stands has to be fitted into the early 850s, and that raises other difficulties, without being

---

[5] *Boethius*, ed. Sedgefield, 128. I am well aware that Alfred's authorship of the Lays, that is, of the verse sections of the Old English version of Boethius's *Consolation of Philosophy*, is debatable. See Janet Bately, Chapter 6 in this volume. The passage quoted may nevertheless give a rough idea of an Alfredian image.

[6] For Cheddar in Alfred's time, see P. Rahtz, *The Saxon and Medieval Palaces at Cheddar*, British Archaeological Reports, British Series 65 (1979), 99–107; for Winchester, see M. Biddle, *The Study of Winchester: Archaeology and History in a British Town, 1961–1983*, 93–135. Cf. also J. Maddicott, 'Trade, industry and the wealth of King Alfred', *Past and Present*, 123 (1989), 3–51, at 4, 45; Nelson, 'Debate: Trade, industry and the wealth of King Alfred', *Past and Present*, 135 (1992), 153–4, and Maddicott, ibid., 174–5.

[7] Asser, c. 23, 20, trans. Keynes and Lapidge, *Alfred*, 75.

[8] Stevenson, *Asser*, 222–3, also referring to W. Stubbs's introduction to his edition of William of Malmesbury's *Gesta Regum*, Rolls Series, 2 vols (1887–89), ii, p. xlii.

[9] I am grateful to Rosemary Lewin for this point.

wholly impossible.[10] Whatever Judith's attitude to her young stepson, she could well have brought Carolingian cultivation to the West Saxon court.[11] She surely came with an entourage. It may be no coincidence that the first West Saxon charter to demand fortification work (*arcis munitio*), a grant of Æthelbald to Winchester in 858, is also attested by *Judith regina*.[12] Nor may it be coincidental that soon after Judith's return to Francia, after Æthelbald's death, Charles the Bald required in the Edict of Pîtres (June 864) that all incapable of military service 'must work at new cities and bridges ... according to the custom of antiquity and of other peoples (iuxta antiquam et aliarum gentium consuetudinem ad civitates et pontes ... operentur)'.[13] Mid-ninth-century West Saxon courts evidently had their own access-routes to Romanness, through Rome itself and through books and stylistic models brought thence to England since the days of Gregory the Great, and also through the relatively recent model of Mercian contacts.[14] In other words, the explanation for parallels between Carolingians and Cerdicings may lie in independent borrowings from Roman practice, past and present, rather than in contemporary imitation of the Frankish metropolis by the West Saxon subaltern. Both West Frankish and West Saxon rulers were experimenting – as Charlemagne had done – with strategies that were at once dynastic and imperial, that is, with representations of their own royal authority as that of a king over a family of kings and/or successor to the powers and responsibilities of Christian emperorship. If Æthelwulf's marriage to Charles the Bald's daughter in 856 was intended by Charles to suggest his own hegemonial status, Æthelwulf himself, only a little earlier, had planned something similar within his own family, including *his* son-in-law, the Mercian king Burgred.[15] It was not just the fact of being recorded in the same 853 *Chronicle* entry that

---

[10] *Pace* Smyth, *Alfred*, 181–5; cf. Keynes, 'On the authenticity of Asser's Life of King Alfred', *JEccH*, 47 (1996), 529–51, at 536; see further Stevenson, *Asser*, 222–5. If Alfred himself was the source, this story could embody a layer of memory with fact and fancy superimposed.

[11] The bishop of Bristol (G. F. Browne), 'Alfred as a religious man and educationalist', in A. Bowker ed., *Alfred the Great* (1899), 71–99, at 77–8.

[12] S 1274; see N. P. Brooks, 'The development of military obligations in eighth- and ninth-century England', in P. Clemoes and K. Hughes, eds, *England before the Conquest: Studies presented to Dorothy Whitelock* (1971), 69–84, at 81, and now S. Keynes, 'The West Saxon charters of King Æthelwulf and his sons', *English Historical Review*, 109 (1994), 1109–49, at 1123, 1127–9. This implication of Keynes's case for S 1274's authenticity was kindly pointed out to me by Emma Beddoe.

[13] MGH Capit. no. 272, c. 27, pp. 321–2; cf. Nelson, 'The Franks and the English in the ninth century reconsidered', in P. E. Szarmach and J. T. Rosenthal, eds, *The Preservation and Transmission of Anglo-Saxon Culture* (Kalamazoo, MI, 1997), 141–58, repr. in Nelson, *Rulers and Ruling Families in Early Medieval Europe* (1999), ch. VI, at 147–8.

[14] See Nelson, 'Carolingian contacts', in *Mercia: an Anglo-Saxon Kingdom in Europe*, eds M. P. Brown and C. A. Farr (2001), 126–43.

[15] *AB*, s.a. 856, 73, trans. Nelson, 83; *ASC 'A'*, s.a. 853, ed. Bately, 45 (all references hereafter are to Bately's edition); Nelson, 'The Franks and the English in the ninth century reconsidered', 143–6.

linked the sending of Alfred to Rome and the marriage of his sister to Burgred. Alfred at this point was one among Æthelwulf's intended or hoped-for successors: a potential king of part of the expanded West Saxon realm. In 858, Æthelbald's Winchester charter, issued with his new Carolingian queen at his side, was a statement of exalted regnal claims in a new register. Where this left Alfred, only time would tell.

In 868, Alfred married Eahlswith and successfully requested divine replacement of his earlier heaven-sent illness by an affliction more compatible with the duties of this new state. In this same year, his rather older Frankish contemporary 'the divorce-raddled Lothar II', as Karl Leyser memorably called him, complained that Nicholas I (d. 867) had been unimpressed by 'our openhearted and pure defence' of what the pope considered bigamy at best. Lothar continued to suffer ecclesiastical censure as one 'to whom no wife was conceded nor concubine allowed (cui nec uxor conceditur nec concubina permittitur)'.[16] Lothar hoped that Nicholas's successor would prove more sympathetic. Lothar was, and is, an awful example of a king with 'an unruly [private] body', 'a prisoner of patrimonial concepts of rule'. His misdemeanours in the bedroom could not be judged in isolation from his (public) action in royal household and realm.[17] Yet Carolingian and Cerdicing experience also taught that a king capable of wielding the smack of firm government could get away with murder. No king was immune to moral criticism, but a powerful one could silence it as long as he lived, and even mute it retrospectively. Bishops did not always find it politic to seek surveillance of Christian bedchambers, and those assembled at Attigny in 822 refused to judge when Louis the Pious referred to them an allegation of 'dishonourable and dishonouring (inhonesta) sexual practices' by a noblewoman against her husband.[18] Æthelbald contracted an incestuous but advantageous marriage with his stepmother, and got away with it, at almost the same time as Lothar's unruly body began to raise difficulties. Lothar's problems were caused by his vulnerability in the cruel game of Carolingian family politics. His uncles were made wicked, from Lothar's standpoint, by intra-familial competitiveness and the necessarily expansive aspirations of lordship. Even so, Lothar might with luck have salvaged a realm of sorts, had time not run out on him. What Alfred might have learned from such eventful histories

---

16 For Alfred's request, Asser, c. 74, pp. 54–7, trans. 88–90; for Lothar II's complaints, Regino of Prüm, Chronicon, ed. F. Kurze, MGH SSrG (Hanover, 1890), s.a. 868, p. 95; Concilium Aquisgranense, 862, ed. W. Hartmann, MGH Concilia IV (Hanover, 1998), p. 75. See S. Airlie, 'Private bodies and the body politic in the divorce case of Lothar II', Past and Present, 161 (1998), 25, n. 73; K. Leyser, Communications and Power in Medieval Europe, ed. T. Reuter, 2 vols (1994), I, 44.

17 Airlie, 'Private bodies', 33, 37 and passim.

18 Airlie, 'Private bodies', 23; but cf. the 822 case recalled by Hincmar, De divortio Lotharii regis et Theutbergae reginae, ed. L. Böhringer, MGH Concilia IV, 1 (Hanover, 1992), 141–2: the bishops 'sent her back to the judgement of the laymen and the conjugati so that they would judge between her and her husband because they were knowledgable in such cases … '.

was, precisely, a sense of the importance of luck and timing, and, as R. W. Southern remarked in another context, of how far one could go.[19]

In 871, the year of Alfred's accession, three notable Carolingian reigns, in West Francia, East Francia and Italy, had been under way for about thirty years. There was some correlation between length and effectiveness.[20] Charles the Bald and Louis the German had recently carried out the plan they had plotted in 868, and divided Lothar II's kingdom between them. That meant excluding their great-nephew, Lothar's son Hugh, whom they declared the son of a concubine, and hence not throne-worthy, though Lothar had married Hugh's mother in a great public ceremony in 862.[21] It also meant excluding Lothar's elder brother Louis II of Italy, despite his outraged protests. All these were disputes and choices as between Carolingians – and there were plenty of Carolingians. Charles had a son and two grandsons; he had also remarried after his first wife's death in October 869, and already fathered a little daughter. Louis the German had three sons, and a grandson, Arnulf.[22] There were at least two other adult Carolingians in the male line: Pippin and Herbert, great-great-grandsons of Charlemagne, grandsons of Bernard of Italy.[23] The dynasty was flourishing. No one could imagine a non-Carolingian king of the Franks.[24] Here – so it may have looked to Alfred – was a *stirps regia* to die for.

Yet Alfred's attitudes to his own close kin were as inevitably ambiguous as his Carolingian counterparts'. In the very year of Alfred's marriage, his brother King Æthelred's wife attested a charter as *regina*, thus staking a strong claim for her two young sons to inherit their father's kingdom. If Charles and Louis in 869–70 had ignored *their* nephews' claims, just such a ruthless exclusion was imperative for Alfred when his brother Æthelred died in 871. Alfred explicitly and publicly overrode his nephews' claims to important family property, and implicitly but no less certainly excluded them from a share in the kingdom.[25] Alfred's action may seem spectacularly bare-faced, but

---

[19] Southern's remark was made *à propos* an assessment of how far the Investiture Contest changed the workings of secular power: *The Making of the Middle Ages* (1953), 140.

[20] See Carolingian family-tree, Fig. 33, p. 294. Distinctive names denoted membership of the *stirps regia*, hence expressed and reinforced the family's identity. Eric Goldberg's forthcoming book illuminates the kingship of Louis the German. Cf. Nelson, *Charles the Bald* (1992), and N. Staubach, *Rex christianus* II: *Hofkultur und Herrscherpropaganda im Reich Karls des Kahlen II: die Grundlegung der 'religion royale'* (Cologne, 1993). Louis II of Italy still awaits a monograph.

[21] *AB, s.a.* 862, 93–4, trans. Nelson, 102.

[22] St Arnulf of Metz was an ancestor of the Carolingians. The name reappeared in the dynasty in the mid-ninth century: O. G. Oexle, 'Die Karolinger und die Stadt des heilige Arnulf', *Frühmittelalterliche Studien*, 1 (1967), 250–364.

[23] *AB, s.a.* 877, 215, trans. Nelson, 201 and n. 10.

[24] S. Airlie, '*Semper fideles*?: Loyauté envers les Carolingiens comme constituant de l'identité aristocratique', in *La royauté et les élites dans l'Europe carolingienne*, ed. R. Le Jan (Lille, 1998), 129–44.

[25] In his will, Alfred asks the witan 'to expound the law', expressing concern 'lest any man should should say that I treated my young kinsmen wrongfully, the older or the younger. And then

contemporary aristocrats, familiar with the exigencies of family politics, found it possible to understand, condone, and cloak with legitimacy. In early 878, when Viking pressure on Wessex was greater than ever, large numbers of West Saxons, among them Ealdorman Wulfhere of Wiltshire, accepted the lordship of the Viking leader Guthrum. If Wulfhere was the brother-in-law of Æthelred, hence maternal uncle of Alfred's nephews, the changed scenario, as compared with 871, becomes explicable. The nephews' added value in terms of years had altered calculations and loyalties.[26] Alfred certainly faced an external threat in 878, but compounding and inseparable from it, and more serious still, was an internal, that is, West Saxon, one from a rival descent-line of the royal family itself. That *combined* threat made Alfred's position in the early months of 878 so desperate, his victory at Edington so necessary.

Nor, despite their relative longevity, and glamour, were the Carolingians more secure from intra-familial conflict than the Cerdicings.[27] Disputes between Carolingians necessarily meant the political involvement of regional aristocratic families, often the wife's kin of the royal rivals, for it took a Carolingian and a married-in noblewoman to produce a new descent-line. Furthermore, in 869–70, a promising Carolingian kingdom, Lotharingia (it already had a name) had been extinguished and divided, with disturbing consequences for some of its leading men. As for Aachen, most splendid of all Carolingian palaces, a capital of sorts until 869: it seemed unlikely ever to recover its earlier glory and function. Louis the German was to visit it more or less annually after 870 until his death in 876; thereafter the visits of East Frankish Carolingian kings were to be rare indeed, for they were intent on consolidating other political centres in Frankfurt and Regensburg, just as Charles, his hopes of Aachen dashed, was making his own West Frankish *sedes* at Compiègne on the Oise.[28] These were signs of separate development. As for Louis II, definitively deprived by his uncles of his fraternal rights in Lotharingia, his imperial title meaning *de facto* no more than rule in Italy, he was making the most of Lombardy; but he had no son, and the future of his kingdom was already beginning to interest his uncles and cousins, then others too.[29]

The demise of Lotharingia found no echo in the *Anglo-Saxon Chronicle*. It was a different story after November 884 when part of a Danish *here* that had been ravaging Picardy crossed from Boulogne to Rochester.[30] Now – suddenly – the *Chronicle* recorded the death of Charles the Bald's grandson Carloman in a

---

they all pronounced what was right and said: "Now everything has come into your possession ... '",
Keynes and Lapidge, *Alfred*, 175.

[26] Nelson, "'A king across the sea'", 53, 54, 56.

[27] Airlie, '*Semper fideles?*', 131–6.

[28] C.-R. Brühl, *Fodrum, gistum, servitium regis* (Cologne, 1968), 24, n. 75; *idem, Deutschland–Frankreich: die Geburt zweier Völker* (Cologne, 1990), 393, 405–6, 491–2.

[29] G. Sergi, 'The Kingdom of Italy', in *The New Cambridge Medieval History*, vol. III, ed. T. Reuter (1999), 346–51.

[30] The month is known from the *AV*, *s.a.* 884, 55.

hunting accident in December, noted the death of his brother Louis the year before, and spelled out the sequel: 'Charles [the Fat] succeeded to all the western kingdom between the Mediterranean and the North Sea and the English Channel, even as his great-grandfather had had it, except for Brittany.' Then follows a little genealogy back five generations from Charles to Pippin, Charlemagne's father.[31] The annal for 887–88 continues this authorial interest in the Carolingians:

> Charles king of the Franks died, and Arnulf his brother's son deprived him of the kingdom six weeks before his death. And then the *rice* was divided into five, and five kings were consecrated thereto: that, however, was done with the consent of Arnulf; and they [that is, the other four] declared that they should hold it [that is, each kingdom] at his [Arnulf's] hand (*to his honda healdan sceoldon*) ... because not one of them was born thereto on the paternal side, except him alone.[32]

The *Chronicle*'s emphasis here is unique. I think it reflects a combination of information received via Fulk of Rheims in 888 (but not before the spring of that year)[33] and a spin supplied at Alfred's court. At this point, and this really could be the nearest we have to contemporary evidence, Alfred may well have shared Fulk's sense that a hegemonial Carolingian empire persisted.[34] Asser made the point metonymically: *regnum in quinque partibus conscissum est sed tamen principalis sedes regni ad Earnulf iuste et merito provenit.*[35] Only with hindsight, writing at least a decade later, did Regino present 888 as a total and definitive splitting of the Empire; yet, curiously, modern historians have consistently privileged Regino's account. The *Anglo-Saxon Chronicle* may give a partisan, indeed a Fulkish, view of 888 but it is a contemporary view. Its West Saxon spin was a reference, echoed by Asser, to rights passing uniquely in the paternal line: this was something Alfred himself presented in his will as *comme il faut* as far as his own personal lands were concerned.[36] One of the other claimants of 888, Berengar, was of Carolingian descent on his mother's side; and indeed this had recently been the basis of Charles the Fat's scheme in 887 to adopt his first cousin twice-removed, Louis of Provence, the son of Louis II's daughter

---

[31] *ASC 'A'*, s.a. 885, 52.

[32] *ASC 'A'*, s.a. 888, 53. The annalist reckons the year at this point from September.

[33] *AV*, 65 shows that only then did Fulk switch his support from Guy to Odo as king of the West Franks.

[34] It is certainly true that the next passage in the *ASC* annal referring to the wars between Guy and Berengar for the Italian kingdom must have been written in or after 889 (oddly enough *AV*, 65, shows a similar retrospective touch); but there is nothing to suggest the same for the sentences quoted above. Reuter, *AF*, s.a. 888, 115, n. 2, notes that the *Chronicle* account is *ex post facto*; but that is equally true of Regino of Prüm; see below.

[35] Asser, c. 85, 71–2; Keynes and Lapidge, *Alfred*, 98, translate: 'five kings were consecrated and the empire was torn up into five parts. Nevertheless, the principal seat of the realm fell to Arnulf – rightly and deservedly ... '.

[36] Will, in Keynes and Lapidge, *Alfred*, 178.

Ermengard.[37] To admit regnal claims through Carolingian women was to open up a Pandora's box. Yet there were good reasons why the 'rules' of patrineal descent and legitimate birth were being bent. Like the claims of the illegitimate Carolingian Arnulf, claims through women were, up to a point, viable now because of the sudden, appalling, dearth of legitimate Carolingian male heirs in the paternal line: no fewer than ten had died between 875 and 888. Alfred, relative upstart though his dynasty was and of shady origins, did not share this problem either in 888 or a few years later, when his will shows him stalked by a band of æthelings, not all of them legitimate.[38]

Yet potential claims through Carolingian women may have had a certain allure even for Alfred. Among the associates whom Fulk of Rheims had taken with him to seek Arnulf's blessing for the West Frankish king Odo in April 888 was Count Baldwin II of Flanders, grandson of Charles the Bald through Judith who had eloped with Baldwin I of Flanders in 862. They seem to have planned to seek the protection of a friendly Viking warlord in Frisia, and perhaps that is just what they did. Certainly Hincmar of Rheims, who was also on terms with the Viking in question, wrote to him, and to the bishop of Utrecht, urging them on no account to harbour the fugitive pair. Judith's father grudgingly came round to the idea a year later, after a lot of papal politicking, and allowed Judith and Baldwin to be 'joined in holy matrimony'.[39] By the late 880s, Judith's son was one of the big players in West Frankish politics. Significantly, Baldwin II became the husband of Alfred's daughter Ælfthryth. The marriage is usually dated after 893 on the grounds that Asser, writing in 893, doesn't mention it, but it could have been a shade earlier. The naming of the couple's first son Arnulf might have been a tactful compliment in 891 or 892 to the recent victor of the Battle of the Dyle in October 891 (it would still, of course, have been a tactful compliment at any time in the mid- to late 890s). But the name was perhaps more probably an evocation of St Arnulf of Metz, hence of Baldwin's Carolingian descent through his mother Judith. The naming of the couple's second son, Æthelwulf, and of two of their daughters, Eahlswith and Ælfthryth, shows their mother's pride in her own royal ancestry, and her grandson's and great-grandson's name Ecgberht was to extend this theme.[40] One of the earliest examples of

[37] *AF, s.a.* 887, Bavarian Continuation, 115, trans. Reuter, 113 with n. 6; see the incisive analysis of S. MacLean, 'The Emperor Charles the Fat', University of London Ph.D. dissertation, 2000, ch. 6.5.

[38] For Alfred's ancestry, see now A. Scharer, 'The writing of history at King Alfred's court', *Early Medieval Europe*, 5 (1996), 177–206, at 178–85; for the evidence of his will for the 890s, Nelson, 'Reconstructing', 59–63.

[39] *AB, s.a.* 862, 863, 87–8, 103–4, trans. Nelson, 97–8, 110; Hincmar, *Epistolae*, nos 155, 156, ed. E. Perels, MGH Epp. 8 (Berlin, 1939), 120; and see S. Reynolds, 'Carolingian elopements as a sidelight on counts and vassals', in B. Nagy and M. Sebók eds, ' ... *The man of many devices who wandered full many ways* ... ', *Festschrift in Honor of János M. Bak* (Budapest, 1999), 340–46.

[40] Fig. 34, 295. See E. Freise, 'Die "Genealogia Arnulfi comitis" des Priesters Witger', *Frühmittelalterliche Studien*, 23 (1989), 203–43. Cf. above, n. 22.

a Frankish count's wife having the title *comitissa* in documents is Ælfthryth (though only after her husband's death in 918).[41] Like her older sister Æthelflæd, Ælfthryth made sure that no one forgot she was a king's daughter.

By the mid-ninth century, the Cerdicings may have envied the time-depth of the Carolingian dynasty, and the Carolingians' success in representing their dynasty's rule as divinely authorized, a fact and frame of Frankish life. Carolingian family-consciousness impressed Alfred and his contemporaries. Alfred's own father had bought into it, perhaps driven by dynastic difficulties of his own. In the late 880s, Carolingian imperial authority still seemed a going concern. Reformulated in hegemonial terms, it had been experimented with extensively by Charles the Bald, both in what we call sub-kingdoms but they called *regna* ruled by the king's sons under some paternal surveillance, and, by looser extension, in relations with Bretons and West Saxons and Scandinavian warlords in Frisia and Francia too.[42] Charles the Fat continued the experiments in the 880s, as did Arnulf from 888 on.[43] By then, Carolingian dynastic tragedies had shocked contemporaries on both sides of the Channel. They did not, though, cause loss of confidence in the dynasty as such, nor in Carolingian hegemonial empire in general: on the contrary, hegemony could work just as well if the subordinate rulers were not themselves Carolingians. Affinal kin-ties via hypergamy were fine, as long as you had enough daughters. There was also friendship, which was not an early Ottonian invention.[44] *Amicitia*, like *consortium* or *fraternitas*, was a familiar *and unequal* relationship in the ninth century too. Arnulf was the friend of Odo in 888 in the same way that Alfred was the friend of Æthelred a year or two before and Hywel and co. a year or two later.[45]

By 899, Carolingian dynasticism seemed to be enjoying a new lease of life in all of the three main successor-states. In East Francia, Arnulf's campaigning season on the eastern frontier was a success; and he had a six-year-old son 'named Louis after his grandfather'.[46] In West Francia, Charles the Bald's grandson and namesake had been consecrated to a reunited kingdom on 28 January 898, a choice of date – the anniversary of Charlemagne's death – that suggested larger aspirations.[47] In Italy, Berengar was energetically restoring his maternal

---

41 R. Le Jan, *Famille et pouvoir dans le monde franc. Essai d'anthropologie sociale* (Paris, 1995), 360.

42 Nelson, 'The Franks and the English in the ninth century reconsidered', 143–6.

43 See S. MacLean, 'Charles the Fat and the Viking Great Army: the military explanation for the end of the Carolingian Empire', *War Studies Journal*, 3 (1998), 74–95; R. Schieffer, *Die Karolinger*, 2nd edn (Stuttgart, 1997), 187–93.

44 G. Althoff, *Verwandte, Freunde und Getreue. Zum politischen Stellenwert der Gruppenbindungen im früheren Mittelalter* (Darmstadt, 1990), 96–114, offers an excellent discussion, but overstates the differences between earlier and later Carolingians, and between West and East Frankish Carolingians in the early tenth century.

45 *AV*, s.a. 888, 66; Asser, c. 80.

46 *AF*, s.a. 893,122, trans. Reuter, 125; *AF*, s.a. 899, 133, trans. Reuter, 138–9.

47 B. Schneidmüller, *Karolingische Tradition und frühes französisches Königtum. Unter-*

grandfather's kingdom.[48] If Alfred knew of these events, there is no evidence as to how he viewed them. But it seems clear that when Alfred's son Edward, perhaps in 917 (917 × 919) arranged the marriage of his daughter Eadgifu/ Otgiva to Charles of West Francia, he expected this alliance with an apparently powerful king to bring political rewards.[49]

Ideological strategies are nothing without tactical nuts and bolts. In the second half of the ninth century, as earlier, Carolingian kings actually governed their realms, if in more or less spasmodic and indirect ways. Much power was regional, as it always had been. Yet assemblies, and the making of appointments, or at least ratification of successions, to high offices, gave kings leverage in a world of aristocratic networks and rivalries. Charles the Bald, Louis the German, Charles the Fat, Arnulf all put into effect threats to remove and replace faithless counts.[50] Carolingians tried, with mixed success, to control the marriages uniting their own offspring with noble partners, and occasionally intervened in the aristocratic marriage-market. Kings could threaten aristocrats indirectly, via ecclesiastical sanctions, with loss of marital and martial rights as punishment for major crimes: definitive and very public forms of dishonour.[51] Evidence from all three of the main kingdoms shows kings threatening men who failed to perform public duties with the ritual humiliation, the *harmscar*, of publicly carrying a saddle (or dog) on their backs.[52] Louis the German actually imposed this punishment on a group of Allgäu landowners in 853.[53] Alfred's governmental methods were comparable. He deprived Ealdorman Wulfhere of Wiltshire of office and lands for 'deserting ... both his lord King Alfred and his country in spite of the oath which he had sworn to the king and all his leading men'.[54] He threatened other ealdormen and reeves with loss of their posts. Nothing like the *harmscar* is known for Wessex, however: Asser suggests that Alfred humiliated the recalcitrant in less formal and ritualized ways.[55]

Carolingian kings had acquired large and thriving kingdoms not only by encouraging Franks to behave like Vikings but by exacting goods and services from Frankish *homines*, especially better-off ones. This is where your *rex* can be

---

suchungen zur Herrschaftslegitimation der westfränkisch–französischen Monarchie im 10. Jahrhundert (Wiesbaden, 1979), 123–4.

[48] G. Arnaldi, 'Berengario I', in *Dizionario biografico degli Italiani* 9 (Rome,1967), 1–26.

[49] See Nelson, 'Eadgifu', *The New Dictionary of National Biography* (forthcoming).

[50] Nelson, 'Kingship and royal government', in *The New Cambridge Medieval History,* vol. II, ed. R. McKitterick (1995), 383–430, at 406–22.

[51] Ibid., 399–400, 428–9.

[52] M. de Jong, 'Power and humility in Carolingian society', *Early Medieval Europe,* 1 (1992), 29–52.

[53] Louis the German, Diploma 66, ed. P. Kehr, MGH Diplomata regum ex stirpe Karolinorum I (Berlin, 1932–4), 92.

[54] *EHD*, 541–2, no. 100 (S 362).

[55] Asser, c. 106, 93–4, trans. Keynes and Lapidge, *Alfred*, 109–10; Asser, c. 91, 78, trans. 101–2.

studied as *homo economicus*.[56] Charles the Bald collected *annua dona*, in bullion, cash and kind, at his great summer assemblies. He also levied occasional contributions to pay off tributes to Vikings in the 850s and earlier 860s, and again in 876 and 877. His *renovatio monetae* in 864 was an extra form of taxation, at once symptomatic and productive of healthy royal finances. Dues and services were heavily imposed on the estates of the royal fisc. Churches and church property contributed to all the above, both to the exceptional demands for contributions to tributes, and to regular requirements for *stipendia* to reward troops for the king's army. Last but not least, payments came into the royal treasury for offices conferred, authorizations for markets or fortification-building permitted, favours bestowed, charters granted. So assiduous was Charles in collecting all these payments that rebels in 858 could claim that 'anything left to his subjects after the pagans had plundered them from outside … Charles destroyed from inside by crafty savagery …': a backhanded compliment to the bite of royal fiscality.[57] Similar but slimmer evidence for financial exactions comes from Lotharingia in the 850s and 860s. From the East Frankish kingdom, there is predictably much less evidence, for coinage was minted there on a very much smaller scale. The conditions that allowed a partly monetized economy to flourish existed in north-west Europe. In this respect, Charles and Alfred operated, so to speak, in the same market.[58] For them, collecting tributes was a viable defence policy: they could pay off Vikings when necessary, as Louis of Italy apparently could not pay off Saracens. The obligation to build (or maintain) and man fortifications was presupposed by Alfred's system of *burhs*, which, despite shortcomings recorded in Kent in 892, seems to have worked effectively in Wessex in 893–96.[59]

Kings who extracted wealth from their people were expected to distribute good things in return. The idea that Carolingian kings in the second half of the ninth century, especially but not only in West Francia, were excessively lavish granters of royal lands has long been one of the explanations offered for the decline of the monarchy: allegedly a kind of cyclical decline to which early medieval realms were generally prone. But these kings were in fact cautious and discriminating land-givers, notwithstanding the scale of their fiscs and realms. It is well over 1200 km from Rennes to Rome, or from Utrecht to Rome; well over 1000 km from the Meuse to Mosberg on Lake Balaton.[60] The logistical problems of getting an Anglo-Saxon prince and an entourage twice

---

[56] For what follows, see Nelson, *Charles the Bald* (1992), ch. 2.

[57] *AF, s.a.* 858, 49–50 , trans. Reuter, 42.

[58] See A. Verhulst, *Rural and Urban Aspects of Early Medieval Northwest Europe* (1992); idem, *The Rise of Cities in North-West Europe* (1999), ch. 3; R. Hodges, *Towns and Trade in the Age of Charlemagne* (London, 2000).

[59] *ASC 'A', s.a.* 892, 893–6.

[60] C. Bowlus, 'Imre Boba's reconstructions of Moravia's early history and Arnulf of Carinthia's *Ostpolitik* (887–892)', *Speculum,* 62 (1987), 552–74, at 569–70.

to Rome in 853 and 855 should be set against those of getting Charles the Fat
and an army across the Alps twelve times between 879 and 886. As for land-
grants, there was an important difference between heartlands (*Kerngebiete*)
where royal estates were concentrated, and more distant regions (*Fernzonen*),
where there were fewer royal estates that distance in any case made harder to
control. Further, magnates need to be distinguished from humbler *fideles* as
recipients of royal land: the grants of Charles the Bald and Arnulf, many of
them quite small-scale, in the Seine basin or Bavaria respectively, were mostly
made to *fideles*, some explicitly said in the charters to have served the king
well, and the grants were concentrated in the early difficult years of their
reigns. These Carolingians, remember, also confiscated lands: that was the
corollary of being able to fire as well as hire.[61] Grants given in more distant
regions, as by Charles the Bald in Septimania or Arnulf in Pannonia, enhanced
the regional power of magnates who were powerful anyway: duchies, or territorial princes, were no novelty in this period.

The vast majority of Carolingian land-grants were made for churches. Yet,
given that the Church, from the outset, was the great institutional prop of
Carolingian monarchy, such grants did not represent a net loss to royal resources, provided that kings could still extract prayers, gifts, and military or
other service from the churches concerned.[62] In the case of Louis II of Italy, 56
of his 69 charters (and 43 of the 44 lost ones mentioned in other documents)
were for ecclesiastical beneficiaries, only 3 (and 1 of the lost ones) for lay
beneficiaries.[63] Charles the Bald, Charles the Fat and Arnulf could all generally
rely on their churchmen and all were able to stage imposing assemblies to
display the Church's support: 42 archbishops and bishops attended Charles the
Bald's assembly at Ponthion in July 876; Charles the Fat's assembly at Ravenna
on 6 January 880 was clearly large though no attendance list is extant;[64] 25
archbishops and bishops attended Arnulf's assembly at Tribur in May 895.[65]
True, all three rulers suffered from individual defections: that of Bishop Liutward

---

[61] See R. Schieffer, 'Karl III, und Arnulf', in K. R. Schnith and R. Pauler, eds, *Festschrift für
Eduard Hlawitschka zum 65. Geburtstag* (Kallmünz, 1993), 133–49, at 140. Cf. also Nelson,
Charles the Bald, 257–9, 261–3, 267–8.

[62] Nelson, 'Kingship and royal government', 388–92, 422–3.

[63] Ten other charters were for Louis's wife, sister, and daughters. Of Louis the German's 171
charters, only twelve are grants to individuals, and seven of those (marked *) were to churchmen
(DD LG 10,* 12,* 19, 30,* 38,* 45, 46, 83,* 98,* 99, 108, 165*). Karlmann in his three-year reign
made four grants to individuals out of 28 charters (DD Km 1,18, 23, 25; the first three of those
being to clerics)], Louis the Younger in his six-year reign, three out of 24 charters (DD LY 2, 11,
20). Cf. MacLean, 'Charles the Fat', chs 4.2, 5.3. Charles the Bald made 50 grants to individual
laymen out of 354 charters in a 37-year reign, 18 per cent of the total compared to the East Frankish
7 per cent: Nelson, *Charles the Bald*, 267–8.

[64] *MGH Capit.* 2, ed. A. Boretius (Hanover, 1897), no. 230, 123–6, see P. E. Schramm, *Kaiser,
Könige und Päpste*, II (Stuttgart, 1968), 294.

[65] *AF, s.a.; Capitularia regum Francorum II*, eds A. Boretius and V. Krause, MGH Capitularia
regum Francorum 2 (Hanover 1890–97), no. 252, 196–249.

of Vercelli signalled Charles the Fat's downfall in 887, that of Abbot Bernard of St-Gall troubled Arnulf in 890, while that of Archbishop Wenilo of Sens caused crisis for Charles the Bald in 858.[66] Churchmen could be suspected of more intimate betrayal, as when Bishop Liutward was alleged in 887 to have been the lover of the queen.[67] These were exceptions. In the causes of Carolingians, bishops generally served, fought, and sometimes died.

Compare Alfred. As a land-granter, he was notably discriminating. Of scarcely more than a dozen extant grants, the beneficiaries of six were laymen. Four, including two thegns and two ealdorman, received lands in 'border' shires: Wiltshire, Berkshire and Kent.[68] One of the thegns paid Alfred '50 mancuses of gold' for his estate. It would be anachronistic to see the grant as a sale, but the gift:counter-gift ratio was very strongly tilted in the king's favour.[69] Alfred's bishops were accused *en masse* by continental critics of sexual misconduct. But massed West Saxon bishops are something of a contradiction in terms.[70] These men were few, and very dependent on royal support. Alfred classed bishops as among his thegns – his followers. He cheerfully passed on to them the burden of tribute payments to Vikings, yet complained that they had been 'careless', excessively involved in 'worldly affairs'.[71] Such involvement, including in some cases military as well as fiscal obligations, was just what the king demanded of them.

So far, comparison has suggested more similarities than differences between Alfred's régime and those of his Carolingian contemporaries. There was a large difference of scale, however, and this had important consequences. Though lacking the intimacy of an Irish *tuath* (people, kingdom), Wessex was small enough to permit and foster relatively close and frequent contacts between the king and the élite. War intensified these in Alfred's kingdom. Like Charlemagne and Louis the Pious, Alfred dispensed annual gifts (in cash or kind) to his

---

[66] Liutward: MacLean, 'Charles the Fat', 189–205, and for the alleged sexual misconduct, Bernard: M. Borgolte, *Die Grafen Alemanniens in merowingischer und karolingischer Zeit* (Sigmaringen, 1986), 263, 265; Wenilo: Nelson, *Charles the Bald*, 188–92. Regino of Prüm, *Chronicon*, s.a. 888, ed. F. Kurze, MGH SSrG (Hanover, 1890), 127. For the wider dimensions of such accusations, see G. Bührer-Thierry, 'La Reine adultère', *Cahiers de Civilisation Médiévale*, 35 (1992), 299–312 and Airlie, 'Private bodies'.

[67] P. Stafford, *Queens, Concubines and Dowagers. The King's Wife in the Early Middle Ages* (Athens, GA, 1983), 95; and cf. now T. Reuter, 'Der Uota-Prozeß', in *Kaiser Arnolf: das ostfränkische Reich am Ende des 9. Jahrhunderts*, eds F. Fuchs and P. Schmid (Munich, 2002), 247–64.

[68] S 348 (North Newnton is only some ten miles south of the Wiltshire border), 355, 356, 350. The others are S 345 and 347. Keynes, 'Charters', 1134–40, lays firm foundations for further work on the documents' political implications.

[69] S 355.

[70] Nelson, '"A king across the sea"', 61–7.

[71] *EHD*, 532–3, no. 94 (S 1278 = Birch 533/4; Worcester 872); Preface to *Pastoral Care*, trans. Keynes and Lapidge, *Alfred*, 125–6.

entourage.[72] But, as far as I know, not a single extant precious object might qualify as a Carolingian analogue to the Alfred Jewel. If this absence is no coincidence, it is hardly symptomatic of poverty. Carolingians, later in the ninth century as earlier, had rich treasuries and invested lavishly in church ornament. Perhaps such giving reflects the style of mature Carolingian monarchy: a style characterized by increased liturgification, by increasingly intimate bonds with specially favoured churches, and by a more distant relationship between king and *fideles* than had prevailed in Charlemagne's day. The image of *familiaritas* purveyed in the *De ordine palatii* was written, perhaps in 812/813, by Adalard, in the light of his experience of Charlemagne's court. The less familiar image of mature Carolingian government was a function of changed operations and partially reconfigured political structures. The Carolingians of the later ninth century, though they held assemblies, did so less often than before. The repeated regular cooperation of Charlemagne and his *fideles* in annual campaigns (remember those Franks were like Vikings) and during Charlemagne's imperial years, in the huge frenetic effort of governmental correction, was long past. Instead, regional powers, vigorously shaken up and reallocated by Charlemagne, had got bedded down again.[73] Magnates stayed in their territories, organized frontier campaigns of their own. Kings did not see their great men so often. With the aid of churchmen, kings set about demonstrating their uniqueness; and in Italy and in East as well as West Francia, they went in for forms of ruler-representation that amplified distance rather than closing it.

With kings on high seats amidst – but above – a great company of those who served, we are back where we started: with the mind's eye of Alfred. Early medieval kingship displayed many common traits, attributable to shared ideological inheritances, analogous circumstances and responses to the same challenges. For all that, there remains a contrast between Alfred and his continental contemporaries. Charles the Bald, and other Carolingians of his generation and the next, preferred high seats and splendid crown-wearings, the exclusive signs and symbols of a monarchic style on the way to becoming Ottonian. Alfred's political practice is harder to reconstruct, since the annalistic evidence is skeletal, charters are scarce, capitularies and royal letters virtually non-exist-

---

[72] *De ordine palatii,* l. 360 (c. 22), ll. 440–46 (c. 27), eds T. Gross and R. Schieffer, MGH Fontes iuris Germanici antiqui (Hanover, 1980), 72, 80, and for authorship and date, see Nelson, 'Aachen as a Place of Power', in F. Theuws and M. de Jong, eds, *Topographies of Power in Early Medieval Europe* (Leiden, 2001), 217–41; Notker the Stammerer, *Gesta Karoli* II, c. 21, ed. H. Haefele, MGH SSrG (Berlin, 1959), 92, and for the date and context of Book II, see MacLean, 'Charles the Fat', 231–6; Alfred's Will, trans. Keynes and Lapidge, *Alfred*, 173–8.

[73] K.-F. Werner, 'La genèse des duchés en France et en Allemagne', *Settimane di studio del Centro italiano di studi sull'alto medioevo,* 27 (Spoleto, 1981), 175–223; cf. M. Innes, *State and Sociey in the Early Middle Ages* (Cambridge, 2000), esp. chs 6, 7; C. La Rocca and L. Provero, 'The dead and their gifts: the will of Eberhard, count of Friuli, and his wife Gisela, daughter of Louis the Pious (863–864)', in F. Theuws and J. L. Nelson, eds, *Rituals of Power from Late Antiquity to the Early Middle Ages* (Leiden, 2000), 225–80.

ent. Yet there are entrées via Asser's *Life* and Alfred's own writings, including not least the prefatory section of his will. Much of the best recent work by historians has approached Alfred through these texts. The political style that emerges was one of intimacy and directness. It involved engagement with the élites of the kingdom, all the king's men. We can picture Alfred in the landscape of a relatively small kingdom in which communications were manageable. Whereas it took Charles the Bald or Arnulf several days of hard riding even to get from one end of the heartland to another, and many more days to travel between peripheral zones, you could walk, if fit, from Reading to Winchester – that is, from top to bottom of Wessex – in a strenuous day. To assemble West Saxons, even West Saxons and Kentishmen, was a quite different logistical proposition from organizing the councils of Ponthion or Tribur. 'If your lord's letter [of summons] and his seal [authenticating the letter or its bearer] came to you', Alfred asked, 'would you not thereby know his intention?' Alfred was interested in the seal first and foremost as a bond.

The surviving artefacts commissioned by Alfred's Carolingian contemporaries, above all by Charles the Bald, as Leslie Webster conclusively shows, were intended to link the ruler with his patron saint or with God. Housed in shrines, they became part of the arcana of monarchy.[74] As far as this world went, they were not media, nor were they designed to stimulate a traffic-flow. Alfred too commissioned artefacts: astonishingly, we have not only Asser's textual testimony to these commissions but the material testimony of no fewer than four surviving objects. Generations of Alfredian specialists had perhaps grown so familiar with the Alfred Jewel and the Minster Lovell Jewel that in a sense they took them for granted. A lucky conjunction – the coming to light of two more analogous objects in addition to the two 'jewels' long known, and the fresh inquiry of a young scholar, David Pratt – has refocused attention on the artefacts' function and context as well as their form.[75] These were the tokens of a court society with a difference, where gifts were signs of distinction yet equally of solidarity. The prefatory letter to the Old English version of the *Pastoral Care* records the giving of just such objects to bishops; but the four jewels' survival makes it reasonable to infer that other, lay, thegns and other, lay, rectors received similar gifts (did the differential adornment of the jewels indicate a kind of ranking?). This king honoured his leading men, lay and ecclesiastical alike, with *æstels*, that is, with precious book-markers, precise symbols of a shared learning enterprise and of royal encouragement to success therein. Alfred wished to represent himself not only as a lord with intent, but as a student among students of wisdom, as a learner of Latin for translation purposes, a user of the vernacu-

---

[74] See Chapter 5 in this volume; cf. MacLean, 'Charles the Fat', ch. 6: 7.

[75] D. Pratt, 'Persuasion and invention at the court of Alfred the Great', in C. Cubitt, ed., *Court Culture in the Early Middle Ages* (Turnhout, 2003), forthcoming. The Alfred Jewel proclaims itself commissioned by Alfred; the case for linking the other three jewels with Alfred rests on stylistic and functional similarities.

lar in order to communicate widely with 'free-born men'. It is nothing less than a wonder that so much of Alfred's personality is revealed in his and Asser's surviving writings. No less of a wonder are the four jewels, signs of a king persuasive and inventive, with a mind of his own. He knew what the Carolingians of his own time did, and chose, nevertheless, a distinctive style and vision of rulership. If he had a Carolingian model, it was perhaps, rather than any contemporary, an imagined Charlemagne.

Chapter 18

Alfred the Great and Arnulf of Carinthia: a comparison

Anton Scharer

We may remind ourselves first of all of some relevant dates: Alfred was born in 849, acceded to the throne in 871 after three of his brothers, and died on 26 October 899. Arnulf, an extramarital (not illegitimate) son of Karlmann and the noblewoman Liutswind was born around 850, became king in November 887 (ousting his uncle Charles the Fat), emperor in 896, and died on 8 December 899.

At the outset some note must be taken of the seemingly more private side of these almost exact contemporaries. Under the year 899, the Regensburg continuation of the *East Frankish Annals* (the so-called 'Annals of Fulda'), a source close to the court, reports:

> Then a scandal, and worse, a crime, unheard of for many years, was published about Queen Uota: that she had yielded her body to a lustful and wicked union. She cleared herself of the accusation at Regensburg in the month of June with 72 oath-helpers before the judgement of the leading men who were present. At the same time, and in the great public meeting held in the great town of Regensburg the king was attacked by paralysis and fell ill; this was because a poison had been administered to the king by men and women so that he should become paralysed by it. One of these was called Graman, who was convicted of high treason and beheaded at Ötting; another fled into hiding in Italy, and a third was a woman called Ruodpurc, who was found by strict investigation to have been the instigator of the crime, and perished on the gallows at Aibling.[1]

This extraordinary case has (to my knowledge at least) not found much favour with latter-day commentators. Over a century ago the most knowledgeable

---

[1] *AF*, trans. Reuter, 138–9, ed. Rau, 172: 'Tum vero multis temporibus inauditum scelus et, quod non oportuit, facinus de regina Uota divulgatum est, id est ut corpus suum inlecebroso ac iniquo manciparet coniugio. Quod ipsum Radaspona urbe mense Iunio iuxta primorum presentium iudicium LXXII iurantibus difinitum comprobatur. Ipso quoque tempore eiusdem magni et communis civitate Regia placiti rex paralisy solutus infirmatus est; secundum autem ut regi nocuum quoddam a viris ac feminis daretur, ut inde paraliticus efficeretur. Quorum unus vocabatur Graman, qui reus maiestatis convictus et ideo Otinga decollatus est, alter vero fuga lapsus in Italia latuit; et alia quoque femina nomine Ruodpurc, quae eiusdem sceleris auctrix deprehensa certa examinatione inveniebatur, Eipilinga in patibulo suspensa interiit.'

expert in the field, Ernst Dümmler, suggested with true professorial gravity that there may never have been a very close relationship between Arnulf and Uta, considering the emperor's former liaisons and the preference he is said to have held for the offspring of these affairs.[2] A more satisfactory present-day explanation would be to assume that a disenchanted faction of the nobility which may have taken issue with the emperor's policy of promoting members of his wife's family, the Frankish 'Konradiner', tried to stir up trouble. Arnulf's predecessor and uncle Charles the Fat had stumbled over a similar situation;[3] in his case it marked one of the stages in the loss of power. Arnulf, however, mastered this assault and even set out on a campaign later in the summer. What has all this to do with Alfred, you may ask? It sets him in perspective.

The 'Annals of Fulda' call Uta, Arnulf's wife, only once by name, that is when they report on the scandal that I have been talking about. On a few other occasions she is not named but referred to as queen. What may superficially look like some kind of intentional slighting on the part of the annalist is made up for by the fact that in a number of her husband's charters Uta is mentioned as having intervened (*interventu dilectissime mee coniugis Ote ...*)[4]. Now in Anglo-Saxon royal charters of the time we lack this kind of evidence: interventions or petitions are not recorded; furthermore the corpus of some 160 genuine charters[5] of Arnulf looks impressive if compared to the charters issued in the name of Alfred: seventeen, forgeries included![6]

Moreover, the *Anglo-Saxon Chronicle* fails to mention Alfred's wife during his lifetime, and Asser, though reporting on Alfred's wedding and the wife's Mercian ancestors, never tells her name. Eahlswith only features in Alfred's will and even here her role is a minor one, as Janet Nelson has so clearly discerned:[7] 'Thus, at the time the Will was drawn up, Ealhswith's stock with her husband seems not to have been particularly high. In 892/3, the silence of the ASC and

---

[2] E. Dümmler, *Geschichte des ostfränkischen Reiches* (2nd edn, 3 vols, Leipzig, 1888), III, 462–63, but see now the fundamental and illuminating reappraisal by T. Reuter, 'Der Uota-Prozeß', in *Kaiser Arnolf: das ostfränkische Reich am Ende des 9. Jahrhunderts*, eds F. Fuchs and P. Schmid (Munich, 2002), 249–64, which came to my knowledge only after I had given this paper.

[3] Regino, *s.a.* 887, ed. Rau, 274/6.

[4] Quotation from *Diplomata Arnulfi*, ed. P. Kehr, MGH Diplomata regum Germaniae e stirpe Karolinorum 3 (2nd edn, Berlin, 1955) no. 154 (9 June 897); attention should also be drawn to the following instances: nos 44 (3 May 889), 107a, 170 (13 December 898), 171 and especially 176 (2 July 899).

[5] This is without taking account of the pieces which have a genuine basis but must be classified as 'verunechtet' ('falsified').

[6] See S 342a-357 and Simon Keynes, 'The West Saxon charters of King Æthelwulf and his sons', *EHR*, 109 (1994), 1109–49, esp. 1134ff.

[7] J. L. Nelson, 'Reconstructing a royal family: reflections on Alfred, from Asser, chapter 2', in *People and Places in Northern Europe 500–1600. Essays in Honour of Peter Hayes Sawyer*, eds I. Wood and N. Lund (1991), 47–66, at 65. This article is reprinted in her *Rulers and Ruling Families in Early Medieval Europe: Alfred, Charles the Bald, and Others*, Variorum Collected Studies Series (1999), no. III.

Asser tells a similar tale.' It is only after Alfred's death that Ealhswith emerges from obscurity.[8] However, the case of Uta reveals the dangers of publicity, of being talked about. One must not forget that apart from the one incident Arnulf's queen also kept a rather low profile. Obviously, problems in the royal family struck at the roots of the early medieval state.

But let me focus on Alfred again. In the story of the king's illness and suffering, as told by Asser, Alfred's wedding in Mercia marks a decisive stage:

> after the feasting which lasted day and night, he was struck without warning in the presence of the entire gathering by a sudden severe pain that was quite unknown to all physicians. Certainly it was not known to any of those who were present on that occasion, nor to those up to the present day who have inquired how such an illness could arise and – worst of all, alas! – could continue so many years without remission ... Many, to be sure, alleged that it had happened through the spells and witchcraft of the people around him; others, through the ill-will of the devil ...

Others, Asser goes on to say, saw the illness caused by fever, 'still others thought that it was due to the piles'.[9] In Arnulf's case the attack of illness (paralysis) had also taken place in public, but here is no weighing and considering of possible causes, no room for suggestions of spells and witchcraft; it is poison for which two wretched culprits, perhaps those behind the accusations against the queen, have to die. Both instances witness to the climate of fear and suspicion at court.

Now that we have touched on the subject of Arnulf's and Alfred's 'illnesses', a few considerations may be called for. In the discussion of Asser's *Life of Alfred* those critics who unreasonably threw doubt on the authenticity of the biography have taken especial offence to the portrayal of the suffering king. Two statements will suffice: 'the hagiographical picture of Alfred as a neurotic invalid is irreconcilable with all we really know about him'[10] and 'This image of the invalid and neurotic Alfred, clutching his childhood book of prayers, keeping secret nightly vigils prostrated in prayer in remote churches, and storming Heaven for diseases to mortify his flesh, must be one of the last medieval fictions still taken seriously by modern scholars'.[11] The defenders of the *Life*'s originality have far too long tried to avoid the subject and only recently taken it more seriously by showing that illness and suffering were just another means of proving Alfred to be the elect. This image, elaborated by Asser, but reflecting the intellectual currents at the court, none the less derived from some sort of malady on the part of the king (for which there is evidence independent of Asser).

---

[8] Nelson, 'Reconstructing a royal family', inferring from this evidence 'that Ealhswith was a consistent supporter of Edward', her son.

[9] Asser, c. 74, 54–5 (translation taken from Keynes and Lapidge, *Alfred*, 88–9).

[10] V. H. Galbraith, *An Introduction to the Study of History* (1964), 113.

[11] Smyth, *Alfred*, 202.

Besides, comparison with Arnulf shows that attacks of illness neither overthrew the emperor, nor prevented him from governing and conducting military campaigns in the eyes of his contemporaries, though, admittedly, the evidence is scarce and not very detailed. On his way back from Rome in 896, where he had been crowned emperor, Arnulf wanted to attack Spoleto, the stronghold of Angeltrude, the widow of his former opponent Wido. According to the *East Frankish Annals* (this is a contemporary account!), 'before he arrived at his destination he was held back by a severe illness in his head, and broke off the plan unfinished and hurried back as fast as possible through the valley of the Trent and returned to Bavaria in May'.[12] Early in the following year there is again mention of his illness: 'He himself held a general assembly at the town of Regensburg, and because of his illness decided to spend the winter in Bavaria in hidden places.'[13] And indeed, for the period from the end of January to the beginning of May 897 we lack any other indications of his whereabouts.[14] After holding a general assembly in Tribur in July, Arnulf went to the monastery of Fulda to pray.[15] One feels inclined to view this as having something to do with Arnulf's illness, but this is a matter of speculation. Perhaps the Cadmug gospel book was returned to Fulda on the same occasion.[16] The final climax in Arnulf's record of illness at the public meeting in Regensburg (June 899) has already been mentioned. None the less the emperor went on a campaign later in the summer against a rebellious count who had his stronghold far east of Regensburg, in Mautern, a town on the Danube in present-day Lower Austria. Owing to his ill-health Arnulf advanced and attacked successfully by boat.[17] The final years of the languishing emperor have been interpreted as bearing the mark of declining royal authority. Of course, the benefit of hindsight may encourage such a view; but, we must not forget, Arnulf did not share his uncle's fate.

---

[12] *AF*, ed. Rau, 166 (trans. Reuter, 134): 'Sed antequam ad locum destinatum pervenisset, gravi infirmitate capitis detentus inperfectum reliquit ... ' Regino of Prüm, another contemporary witness (his *Chronica* reaches to 906 and was dedicated to Adalbero, bishop of Augsburg, in 908) has this to say: 'Inde [that is from Rome] revertens paralisi morbo gravatur [sc. Arnulf], ex qua infirmitate diu languescit' (ed. Rau, 304). This is the only reference by Regino to Arnulf's failing health.

[13] *AF*, ed. Rau, 168–70 (trans. Reuter, 136–7). 'Ipse vero habito generali conventu urbe Regino propter gravitudinem corporis in Baioaria secretis locis hiemare disposuit.'

[14] *AF*, trans. Reuter, 136, n. 2, who interprets this as 'a significant sign of decline in royal authority'. *Regesta Imperii I. Die Regesten des Kaiserreichs unter den Karolingern 751–918*, 2nd edn by E. Mühlbacher (Innsbruck, 1908), 777, no. 1928a (cited henceforth as *RI* with number).

[15] '... Fuldense cenobium causa orationis petiit': *AF*, ed. Rau, 170 (trans. Reuter, 137).

[16] H. Löwe, *Die Karolinger vom Vertrag von Verdun bis zum Herrschaftsantritt der Herrscher aus dem sächsischen Hause. Das ostfränkische Reich,* Wattenbach–Levison, Deutschlands Geschichtsquellen im Mittelalter, Vorzeit u. Karolinger, 6. Heft (Weimar,1990) 662. P. E. Schramm and F. Mütherich, *Denkmale der deutschen Könige und Kaiser,* Veröffentlichungen des Zentralinstituts für Kunstgeschichte in München 2 (Munich, 1962) 138 and 268, no. 59.

[17] '... rex ... decrevit navigio, quia iam tunc infirmus corpore fatigaretur, civitatem Mutarensem, in qua ipse Isanricus intus erat, aggredi': *AF*, ed. Rau, 172 (trans. Reuter, 139).

Thus King Alfred's suffering, however much it may have been created by Asser, by the court and by the king to give the impression of Alfred as the chosen and elect, is brought into a contemporary context. Alfred's tribulations had started in his youth: 'when in the first flowering of his youth before he had married his wife, he wished to confirm his own mind in God's commandments, and when he realized that he was unable to abstain from carnal desire, ... ' he engaged in ascetic exercises and prayed 'that Almighty God through His mercy would more staunchly strengthen his resolve in the love of His service by means of some illness which he would be able to tolerate – not, however, that God would make him unworthy and useless in worldly affairs'. In due course the young Alfred 'contracted the disease of piles through God's gift'.[18] Evidently Asser had borrowed from Gregory the Great's account of (the young) Benedict who, tormented by an overpowering carnal desire, had wanted to leave the solitude (eremus), but divine grace had come to his rescue: he threw himself in the thornbushes, the outer wounds extinguishing the inner fire (passion).[19] Louis the Pious had, in similar circumstances to Alfred's, fearing to be carried away by his ardour, contracted a marriage, as one of his biographers tells.[20] Commenting upon this, the most recent editor wrily remarks that at the time of his wedding Louis had already fathered two children from one or two liaisons.[21]

These are no mere incidents: they are testimony to the randy, promiscuous way of life of the aristocratic youth; they also show the slow and hesitant progress of the church's concept of marriage;[22] and lastly they have something to do with the dynamics of succession (or coming to power). There were 'traditional' forms of matrimony ('Friedelehe') which in the eyes especially of latter-day churchmen would perhaps have qualified as little more than liaisons. Arnulf himself originated from such a relationship between Karlmann, son of Louis the German, and a certain Liutswind.[23] And Arnulf had two sons, Zwentibold and Ratold, and a daughter, Ellinrat, from at least two partnerships of this kind. Once on the throne, he concluded a legal matrimony out of political necessity and thereby a shadow was cast on the legitimacy of his offspring by other women. Generally, such a scheme can be observed with sons of the royal family whose chances of gaining the kingship seemed slight, as in the case of Arnulf, or who came to power fairly late.[24] Against such a background the identity of Osferth,

---

[18] Asser, c. 74, ed. Stevenson, 56 (translation in Keynes and Lapidge, *Alfred*, 89–90).

[19] Gregory the Great, *Dialogi* II 2, ed. U. Moricca, Fonti per la storia d'Italia 57 (Rome, 1924), 78–9.

[20] Astronomus, *Vita Hludowici imperatoris*, c. 8, ed. E. Tremp, MGH SRG 64 (Hanover, 1995), 306–8.

[21] Ibid., 307, n. 114.

[22] For these matters see W. Hartmann, *Die Synoden der Karolingerzeit im Frankenreich und in Italien*, Konziliengeschichte, Reihe A: Darstellungen (Paderborn, 1989), 444–45, 469–73 and, with regard to the synod of Tribur (895), 369–70.

[23] Cf. *Diplomata Arnolfi*, 87 and 136, 129 and 204.

[24] Implied by B. Kasten, *Königssöhne und Königsherrschaft: Untersuchungen zur Teilhabe*

'kinsman of King Alfred', becomes an interesting question. And hence Janet Nelson's suggestion that he may have been an illegitimate son of King Alfred cannot be dismissed out of hand.[25] Osferth appears as witness in charters and he features in Alfred's will.[26]

This brings up one of the key problems not just of the early medieval state, but ultimately of every state governed by a monarch: who is to succeed when the ruler dies, and what are the mechanisms of succession? Alfred's will is a pointer in that direction, and the whole problem can be observed in some detail in Arnulf's moves to safeguard the succession of his sons. How high on Arnulf's agenda this question ranged can be guessed from the fact that as early as the end of May 889, at a general assembly in Forchheim,

> there was a discussion about the state of the kingdom, and it was agreed that the leading men of the Franks should confirm by oath, like the Bavarians, that they would not withdraw from the rulership and government of his sons, that is of Zwentibold and Ratold, who had been born to him by concubines. This some of the Franks refused to do for a time, but at length they satisfied the king's will and did not refuse to give their right hands on it, but with the reservation that this should only hold good if he did not have an heir by his lawful wife.[27]

Now these measures were taken only one and half years after Arnulf had come to power, and the leading men of the Bavarians had given their consent by oath even before that. The situation which the Franks had anticipated, the birth of an heir by Uta, Arnulf's lawful wife, occurred in the autumn (September/October) of 893.[28] And Arnulf reacted swiftly to the new line-up in the succession and the diminished chances of his older issue. After having returned from his first

---

am Reich in der Merowinger- und Karolingerzeit, MGH Schriften 44 (Hanover, 1997), 517, 543–4, 547.

[25] Nelson, 'Reconstructing a royal family', 59–60, with special reference to S 1286; S. Keynes, 'The Fonthill letter', in *Words, Texts and Manuscripts. Studies in Anglo-Saxon Culture Presented to Helmut Gneuss on the Occasion of his sixty-fifth birthday*, eds M. Korhammer, with K. Reichl and H. Sauer (1992), 53–97, at 93, n. 164 'could not bear to contemplate' this idea. On Osferth see also Keynes and Lapidge, *Alfred*, 322, n. 79.

[26] Keynes and Lapidge, *Alfred*, 174–78 and 313–26, at 177, providing a translation with commentary of Harmer, *Documents*, no. 11, 15–19.

[27] *AF*, ed. Rau, 148 (trans. Reuter, 118): 'Exeunte mense Madio rex apud villam, quae dicitur Forahheim, generale conventum habuit; ibique disputans de statu regni sui consultum est, ut eodem tenore primores Francorum prout Baioarii iuramento confirmarent, ne se detraherent a principatu vel dominatu filiorum eius, Zwentibulchi quidem et Ratoldi, qui ei de concubinis erant nati. Quod quidam Francorum ad tempus rennuentes, tandem regie satisfacientes voluntati dextram dare non recusabant, eo tamen modo, ut si de legali sua uxore heres ei non produceretur.'

[28] *RI*, no. 1891a; *AF*, ed. Rau, 156 (trans. Reuter, 125): Arnulf returning to Bavaria from a campaign against the Moravians comes to the queen at the vill of Ötting: 'De qua [*sc. Queen Ota*] ei non multum post filius nascebatur, quem Haddo Moguntiacensis archiepiscopus et Adalpero Augustae Vindelicae episcopus sacro fonte baptismatis chrismantes nomine avi sui Hludawicum appellaverunt.'

Italian expedition,[29] he held a general assembly in Worms early in June 894 and on this occasion tried to make Zwentibold king of Lotharingia, but failed to win over the Lotharingian magnates.[30] A year later he succeeded in this endeavour at a meeting again held in Worms. In the presence of the West Frankish King Odo and with universal assent, Zwentibold was ordained king and received (the rule over) Lotharingia.[31] Thus, by parcelling out a distinct unit of the realm to the oldest son he defused the succession problem. A similar move of Arnulf's with regard to his second son Ratold can be conjectured. On the hasty return (April/ May 896) from his second Italian expedition, mentioned above in connection with his illness, Arnulf left 'his little son called Ratold, who had been born to him by a concubine, at Milan to receive the fidelity of the Italian people'.[32] This probably indicates that Ratold's share may have been some kind of rule over Italy. However, the youngster had to withdraw and returned to his father; this is the last we hear of him.

Take by comparison the succession practice of the Cerdicings in the second half of the ninth century, with the principle of division (between Æthelbald and Æthelberht) and collateral succession in Wessex proper apparently having been laid down in Æthelwulf's will[33] and adapted, but observed, by his sons. A similar situation obtained with Louis the German, Arnulf's grandfather (d. 876), and his restless sons: division and collateral succession resulting ultimately in one brother getting the lot, namely Charles the Fat, Arnulf's 'wicked' uncle. Obviously such regulations were at the expense of and went against the succession chances of any nephews; to realize these they revolted, successfully in Arnulf's case, abortively in the case of Æthelwold,[34] who after Alfred's death posed a challenge to Edward the Elder.[35] That collateral succession worked (for a while) had also to do with the chance effect of very short reigns: Alfred's brothers ruled for about five (Æthelbald and Æthelberht) and six years (Æthelred) respectively, too short a time apparently to successfully found a 'dynasty', a new core family to hold on to kingship as Alfred managed to do.[36] Arnulf tried the same, but ultimately failed: he was succeeded by a 'child' of six. And the early death of this Louis in 911 meant the end of the line.

Alfred's will refers (not just once, but on a few occasions) to the consent of the 'witan'. The chief men feature likewise in the king's laws, in his treaty with Guthrum and in his charters. How to win over, handle, reward and control

---

[29] About the first four months of 894: *RI*, no. 1892f–1897b.

[30] Regino, ed. Rau, 300; *RI*, no. 1897f.

[31] *RI*, no. 1908a.

[32] *AF*, transl. Reuter, 134; *RI*, no. 1918a.

[33] As preserved in Alfred's will (ed. Harmer, *Documents*, 16, and trans. Keynes and Lapidge, *Alfred*, 174 and the comment 314, n. 3) and Asser, c. 16, 14–15; trans. Keynes and Lapidge, *Alfred*, 72–3 and 236–7, n.33.

[34] Son of Æthelred.

[35] *ASC*, *s.a.* 900, 902, 903.

[36] J. L. Nelson, 'The political Ideas of Alfred of Wessex', in her *Rulers and Ruling Families*, 150.

the aristocracy, higher and lower, was a key question of rulership. Alfred reflected on this in a much wider context, the threefold division of society, in his translation of Boethius's *Consolation of Philosophy*, where he makes Mind say:

> You know of course that no one can make known any skill, nor direct and guide any authority, without tools and resources; a man cannot work on any enterprise without resources. In the case of the king, the resources and tools with which to rule are that he have his land fully manned: he must have praying men, fighting men and working men. You know also that without these tools no king may make his ability known. Another aspect of his resources is that he must have the means of support for his tools, the three classes of men. These, then, are their means of support: land to live on, gifts, weapons, food, ale, clothing, and whatever else is necessary for each of the three classes of men.[37]

The fighting men are referred to as tools of the king, and are linked to Alfred's whole view of society, a very modern one at the time, that shows great awareness of the importance of providing the necessary resources. A thegn's expectations were not far from Alfred's mind, as we may judge from the Preface to the *Soliloquies*:

> but every man, when he has built a hamlet on land leased to him by his lord and with his lord's help, likes to stay there some time, and go hunting, fowling and fishing; and to employ himself in every way on that leased land, both on sea and land, until the time, when he shall deserve bookland and a perpetual inheritance through his lord's kindness.[38]

For examining how this worked in practice the evidence is unfortunately slender.[39] There are indications of a 'massive transfer of landed wealth from ecclesiastical to lay hands' in Kent as a result of the Viking raids[40] and there are hints of Alfred secularizing some Abingdon lands (presumably in order to give them out to his thegns) which would fit into the same context;[41] likewise the case of Ealdorman Wulfhere, who forfeited his lands for treason,[42] because these lands would come up for regranting. These developments were accompanied by other measures of a 'disciplinary' nature, partly advertised in a 'public relations' manner: the importance attached to loyalty and to keeping oath and pledge in Alfredian literature and law, the 'new' treason law and the introduction of a general oath of loyalty.

A glance at Arnulf's actions in this respect is, in view of the more abundant charter evidence, revealing. The first year of his reign is marked by a burst

---

[37] *Boethius*, 40; trans. Keynes and Lapidge, *Alfred*, 132.

[38] Translation from Keynes and Lapidge, *Alfred*, 139.

[39] Fundamental here is Nelson, 'Political ideas', 150–52.

[40] N. Brooks, *The Early History of the Church of Canterbury* (1984), 206.

[41] Nelson, '"A king across the Sea": Alfred in continental perspective', in her *Rulers and Ruling Families*, 45–68, at 61, n. 82; see also 58–9.

[42] S 362; *EHD*, 541–3, no. 100.

of donations for his clerical and lay supporters in the south-east of the realm, his power-base.[43] Moreover, in a survey of royal property-donations from Charlemagne to Lothar of Supplingburg (twelfth century), Arnulf takes the top position.[44] By applying carrot and stick he drew the leading men to his side. Open accounts were settled, sometimes late. Acting steadily and waiting for the chance to alter the balance of power, that is how Rudolf Schieffer has characterized Arnulf's 'Adelspolitik'.[45] This is also the impression gained from the cases of infidelity for which contemporary accounts, mainly charters, exist.[46] The consequences for the accused varied from the loss of life and property to the restitution of temporarily confiscated lands, doubtless reflecting the changing political constellations.

To work with, to be on good terms with the aristocracy was a prerequisite for major military actions. The magnates, lay and clerical alike, provided and led the contingents of mounted cavalry which were decisive in war. And Arnulf had seen action since his youth. The 'wild East', with many small conflicts and skirmishes escalating at times into major engagements and outright war (against the Moravians), had been his home ground and had shaped his experience.[47] He was noted as leading the Bavarians in his uncle's expedition against the Vikings in the summer of 882 (Elsloo).[48] The special role of the Bavarians from Arnulf's beginnings, his reliance upon their military strength, probably compares to some extent with Alfred's dependence on and trust in the thegns of Somerset.[49] Arnulf's ability to cope with conflicts in far-removed theatres of war (from present-day Belgium to Italy and Slovakia) can be set beside Alfred's tenacity in sustaining protracted campaigns. Both were successful against the Vikings, though one noted battle in Arnulf's case (October 891)[50] stands against Alfred's two wars. And whereas we know of Alfred's military reforms, nothing of this kind is heard about Arnulf.

The ruler's success depended to a large degree on how he realized kingship, on how he staged the play in which he starred and the plot of which was written by circumstance, the 'prevailing conditions', by dominant agents (for example the Vikings, the magnates and so on) and last but not least by himself and his entourage. Here belong all the means employed in the display of king-

---

43 R. Schieffer, 'Karl III. und Arnolf', in *Festschrift für Eduard Hlawitschka zum 65. Geburtstag*, eds K. R. Schnith and R. Pauler, Münchener Historische Studien, Abteilung Mittelalterliche Geschichte 5 (Kallmünz, 1993), 133–49, at 140.

44 Ibid., n. 54.

45 Ibid., 145.

46 See especially *Diplomata Arnolfi*, nos 81, 97, 120, 121 and 132 and *RI*, nos 1851, 1869, 1886a, 1892, 1893 and 1905 and the references there to Dümmler, *Ostfränkisches Reich*.

47 Cf. H. Wolfram, *Die Geburt Mitteleuropas, Geschichte Österreichs vor seiner Entstehung 378–907* (Vienna, 1987), 290ff.

48 *RI*, no. 1638a and following.

49 Asser, c. 55, 44–5; translation Keynes and Lapidge, *Alfred*, 84.

50 *RI*, no. 1865a.

ship, ranging from ritual to patronage in all its forms and to the propagation of certain ideas. In this respect Charles the Bald's court culture[51] had set the standard which was emulated and transformed by Alfred and his court.

The evidence in Arnulf's case looks slighter and more elusive. Of course, there is the powerful statement in regard to the king's position in the proceedings of the synod of Tribur (May 895),[52] the Poeta Saxo – he composed an epic poem on Charlemagne some time in the period 888–91 – invoked Arnulf, the founder of the dynasty, on behalf of his latter-day relative and namesake[53] and he had a few more nice things to say about Arnulf, by singling him out in direct comparison to Charlemagne.[54] If Arnulf was indeed a patron or addressee of the Poeta Saxo,[55] the poet's attempt to create an image of Charlemagne as the apostle of the Saxons and to further the sense of community between Franks and Saxons will have had a broader message. Its Gregorian connotations[56] can be paralleled with the much greater influence of Gregory's works on Alfredian court culture, and especially with the image of Gregory the Great as apostle of the English which stood at the root of such concepts of community as the English, 'Anglecynn' and Anglo-Saxons, both promoted by Alfred and his circle of 'intellectuals'.

Not very much is known about Arnulf as patron of art. Precious objects that he received as gifts or acquired, such as the 'Codex Aureus', a *de luxe* gospel book of Charles the Bald, and the 'ciborium', actually a portable altar with ciborium, he apparently gave to St Emmeram, his most favoured monastery and residence in Regensburg. The Cadmug Gospels, an eighth-century Irish pocket gospel book which tradition associated with St Boniface, he returned to Fulda.[57] This could give rise to the impression of gift-sharing rather than commissioning works of art on Arnulf's part, but the donation of the nunnery Susteren to the priest and 'illustris artifex' Siginand[58] for his services, as well as another one to an 'artifex' Eopreht, perhaps a masterbuilder,[59] are a salutary reminder of the king's activity as patron and of what was lost subsequently and

---

[51] See J. L. Nelson, *Charles the Bald* (1992) and N. Staubach, *Rex Christianus. Hofkultur und Herrschaftspropaganda im Reich Karls des Kahlen. Teil II: die Grundlegung der 'religion royale'*, Pictura et poesis 2/II (Cologne, 1993).

[52] *MGH Capitularia*, eds A. Boretius and V. Krause (2 vols, Hanover 1893–97), II, no. 252, 209ff.; *RI*, no. 1905b; Hartmann, *Synoden*, 367ff.

[53] Poeta Saxo, *De gestis Caroli magni imperatoris*, verses 135ff., ed. P. von Winterfeld, MGH Poetae 4 (Berlin, 1899), 58–9.

[54] Ibid., verses 415ff., 65.

[55] See H. Beumann, 'Poeta Saxo' in: *Die deutsche Literatur des Mittelalters. Verfasserlexikon*, vol. 7(2nd edn, Berlin, 1989) cols 766–9, especially 768.

[56] Convincingly uncovered by B. Bischoff, 'Das Thema des Poeta Saxo', in: *Speculum Historiale: Festschrift Johannes Spörl* (Munich, 1965), 198–203, esp. 201–3, though the Whitby *Life of Gregory the Great* should perhaps also be brought into the discussion.

[57] See generally Schramm and Mütherich, *Denkmale*, nos 52, 59, 60, 61, pp. 134ff.

[58] *Diplomata Arnolfi*, no. 85 (23 February 891).

[59] *Diplomata Arnolfi*, no. 77 (15 April 890) and the implications of no. 152 (5 May 897), already pointed out by Dümmler, *Ostfränkisches Reich*, III, 485–6.

not recovered by chance finds, such as the Alfred Jewel and the related 'prestige fittings'. These, however, and the Fuller Brooch can be related to themes in Alfred's writings, to the court culture.

Here we touch on the great difference. From a chance reference in a letter of Archbishop Fulk of Reims, Arnulf's assumed acquaintance with heroic poetry can be inferred,[60] probably a taste he shared with Alfred. But no literary pursuits of Arnulf's are recorded, no writings of his are known, nor any educational programme. It is only by what others say that a picture of Arnulf can be drawn; his own voice is mute and, unlike Alfred's, cannot be heard after eleven hundred years. What is the good, then, of comparing these two contemporaries, whose awareness of each other in the case of Arnulf remains unrecorded, in Alfred's rests on the important *Chronicle* entry for 887 and Asser's recast,[61] it may be asked. The point is to show, as I hope I have succeeded in doing, the extent of the common ground between these two kings, and thus the extent of the differences as well. Both Alfred and Arnulf knew what it meant to be a king in the second half of the ninth century, but Alfred, perhaps by a combination of vision and luck, managed to convey to us something of his experience of being a king, because he wrote about it.[62]

---

[60] Letter of Fulk to Arnulf from 893 on behalf of Charles the Simple, as related by Flodoard, *Historia Remensis ecclesiae,* IV 5, ed. M. Stratmann, MGH SS 36 (Hanover, 1998), 383; see also Dümmler, *Ostfränkisches Reich*, III, 384–6.

[61] Cf. esp. Nelson, 'Political ideas', 133–4.

[62] I wish to thank Janet Nelson for judicious comment and suggestions. All remaining errors are mine.

Chapter 19

Alfred's contemporaries: Irish, Welsh, Scots and Breton

Wendy Davies

On Monday 9 July 871, 'the year that King (*rex*) Salomon wanted to go to Rome but was unable to do so because his chief men (*principes*) would not let him, because of fear of the Northmen', Salomon walked the bounds of St Ducocca's little monastery in the *plebs* of Cléguerec 'down from Cléguerec hill to the great stones, along the public road to the mound at the crossroads below Silfiac church ... down the valley ... to the river Blavet'.[1] This followed the return of the property, which was substantial, to the abbot of Redon, Liosic, in Perret (north of Silfiac), before Salomon, his sons, four counts, the leader (*princeps*) of Poher, a bishop, an archdeacon, another abbot, and many others; it was returned by the 'tyrannical' machtiern Alfrit (*tyrannus et uere tyrannus* – *tyrannus* is the standard Latinization of 'machtiern' in this collection), who had appropriated the land and constructed a boundary bank or ditch (*fossata* and *finem*) around it; the occasion followed a court case brought by Liosic's recent predecessor Ritcand before Salomon in his court at Retiers, following at least two decades of complaint. Salomon later sent many gifts to St Peter's, in Rome, since his intended visit had been prevented.

Salomon was the ruler of Brittany at the time of Alfred's accession (857–74). He was a ruler who, as can be seen from the charter above, travelled the length of the country (Perret is just about in the middle of Brittany, and Retiers is in the far east of the country, well to the east of Rennes; see Fig. 35); he had defensive responsibility for it, he commanded a court of aristocrats, and he had diplomatic relations with the pope. He was a ruler of power and significance.

In this he was not alone among Alfred's western contemporaries. Alfred was born at a time of hero rulers in north-western Europe. In the mid-ninth century Kenneth (Cinaed) mac Ailpín was renowned in Scotland (843–58); he was not the first to rule Pictland in eastern Scotland and Dalriada in the west together, the two main components of the so-called 'unified' kingdom of Scotland, but he was the significant ancestor – the man regarded in tenth-century and

---

[1] *CR*, no. 247; a *plebs* was the primary unit of social organization and the predecessor of the fully developed parish; in the ninth century it was usually about 40–50 km^2 in area; see W. Davies, *Small Worlds. The Village Community in Early Medieval Brittany* (1988), 63–7.

Fig. 35   Map of Brittany

later tradition as the founder of the kingdom of Scotland.[2] (In fact, the polity was not called 'Scotland' at that stage but continued to be called Pictish in ninth-century sources and then was termed 'Alba' in the early tenth century.[3]) In Brittany in 849 Salomon's predecessor Nominoe was ruling (842–51), the first to rule the whole of Brittany, and ancestor of the dynasty that dominated the country through the ninth century and into the tenth.[4] In Wales Rhodri Mawr was ruling, one of several Welsh rulers at the time, but the only one to attract – at least from the twelfth century – the epithet *mawr*, 'great': a hero of resistance to the Vikings, ruler and extender of Gwynedd (north-west Wales), he was seen as

---

[2] 'Chronicles of the Picts', in *Chronicles of the Picts. Chronicles of the Scots*, ed. W. F. Skene (1867), 8. Cf. D. Broun, 'The origin of Scottish identity in its European context', in *Scotland in Dark Age Europe*, ed. B. E. Crawford (1994), 22–3.

[3] Broun, 'Origin of Scottish identity', 25–6.

[4] A. Chédeville and H. Guillotel, *La Bretagne des saints et des rois, V^e–Xe siècle* (Rennes, 1984), 227–78.

a significant ancestor, at the head of the genealogies of the rulers of Welsh Wales, north and south, for centuries thereafter.[5] And in Ireland, a land of very different political structures, with many kings and complex patterns of overkingship, the southern Uí Néill (that is, midland) ruler Máel Sechnaill mac Máel Ruanaid raided and took hostages across the whole of Ireland, even to the south coast, the first in any real sense to be an 'overking' of the whole of Ireland; emphasizing his political range, he was called 'king of all Ireland' (*ri Herenn uile*) by the Ulster annalist at his death in 862 and, unusually for an Irish overking at this time, he died peacefully.[6]

This, then, was a significant, and formative, period in political development in Celtic areas.

Rhodri Mawr was still ruling when Alfred became king. However, the others had been succeeded by other, but still prominent, rulers: Kenneth's son Constantine in 'Scotland'; Nominoe's brother's grandson Salomon in Brittany; and Máel Sechnaill's northern Uí Néill rival Aed (of the Cenél nEogain branch of the family) in Ireland, called 'king of Tara' by the annalist.[7] Some had direct contacts with Wessex; others did not. Some had courtly relationships with Alfred's world; others did not. They all shared a Viking problem, at different times and in different ways. I intend in what follows, therefore, to give you a brief sketch of the political structures within which Alfred's western contemporaries operated; to make some comments on their interactions with Wessex; and to consider their Viking problems.

Contemporary Polities in the West

Alfred's contemporary Celtic rulers may have numbered as many as one hundred and probably numbered at least fifty, made up as follows: a series of, respectively, single and joint rulers in Brittany, a few contemporary rulers in Scotland, several contemporary rulers in Wales, and many contemporary rulers in Ireland.

Scotland and Brittany were both regions where political developments of the mid-ninth century had, or are seen to have had, long-term consequences leading to the formation of a state, or quasi-state.

Brittany had been politically fragmented before this period, and had been at times notionally subject to Frankish kings, but institutions of government were rapidly developed after Nominoe, the 'originator', particularly under

---

[5] W. Davies, *Patterns of Power in Early Wales* (1990), 44–6; 'Descriptio Kambriae', I.2, I.3. in *Giraldi Cambrensis Opera*, vol. 6, ed. J. F. Dimock, Rolls Series (1868), 166–7; P. C. Bartrum (ed.), *Early Welsh Genealogical Tracts* (1966), 36, 46–7; J. E. Lloyd, *A History of Wales from the Earliest Times to the Edwardian Conquest* (2 vols, 1911), ii. 765–8.

[6] *AU*, AD 862; see F. J. Byrne, *Irish Kings and High-Kings* (1973), 262–7.

[7] *AU*, AD 864.

Salomon and under Alan I, the Great, who was ruling at the time of Alfred's death.[8] Although intermittently acknowledging the superiority of the West Frankish king in the tenth century and thereafter, and dropping the royal title of the later ninth century in favour of the more limited *dux*, Brittany in effect functioned as a separate state, with a very effective fiscal system, until the sixteenth century; since it kept its own laws and its own *parlement* and estates, it was in some respects separate until the French Revolution.[9] Although its rulers' relationship with the Frankish kings varied in the ninth century – sometimes dependents, sometimes allies, sometimes enemies – and although there are some doubts about the effectiveness of their authority in the far west, Brittany provides the best example of ninth-century Celtic political development: there is no hint that there was any Breton authority responsible for the whole country before the ninth century.

The 'origin' of the kingdom of Scotland is traditionally placed in the mid-ninth century, under Kenneth, who united Pictland in the east and Irish Dalriada in the west (although Pictish terminology continued in contemporary texts for some decades). This union certainly seems to have been anticipated by the periodic rule of both elements by a single Pictish or Dalriadic king in the eighth and early ninth centuries; and it is fashionable at the moment to argue that the union involved southern not northern Pictland in the mid-ninth century.[10] In other words, the physical extent of Kenneth's impact in the mid-ninth century is arguable; in any case the early kingdom clearly did not include the whole of present-day Scotland, for there were Scandinavian settlements in the North and Gall-Goídil (Irish-speaking foreigners) in the Hebrides;[11] both northern and western Isles came to be part of the kingdom of Norway in the central Middle Ages (see Fig. 36).[12]

However, despite those doubts, the basis for what would become the kingdom of Scotland appears to have been laid at this time: tenth-century chroniclers saw Kenneth as the significant ancestor.[13] Further, part at least of the British kingdom of Strathclyde seems to have been dominated by 'Scotland' from the late ninth century (that is the area around Dumbarton, near the mouth of the Clyde). By the eleventh century Scotland was a well-founded kingdom, with effective fiscal, judicial, military and administrative institutions.

---

[8] Chédeville and Guillotel, *La Bretagne*, 313–21, 368–74.

[9] Chédeville and Guillotel, *La Bretagne*, 402; J. Kerhervé, *L'État breton aux 14e et 15e siècles. Les ducs, l'argent et les hommes* (2 vols, Paris, 1987); A. Croix, *L'Âge d'or de la Bretagne 1532–1675* (Rennes, 1993).

[10] Broun, 'Origin of Scottish identity', 29; D. N. Dumville, *The Churches of North Britain in the First Viking Age* (1997), 36.

[11] Gall-Goídil, literally 'foreigners' and 'Gaels, that is, Irish'; hence either Irish who behaved like foreigners (Scandinavians) or Irish-speaking Scandinavians; see Dumville, *Churches of North Britain*, 26.

[12] B. E. Crawford, *Scandinavian Scotland* (1987), 51–8.

[13] M. O. Anderson, *Kings and Kingship in Early Scotland* (1973), 77, 196–7; Broun, 'Origin of Scottish identity', 22.

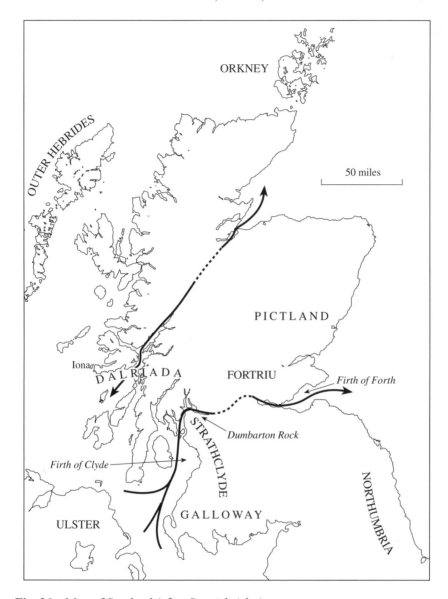

Fig. 36   Map of Scotland (after *Scottish Atlas*)

In Wales there is little to suggest institutional development at this period. There were several separate kingdoms in the region, of which Rhodri's kingdom, Gwynedd, was the largest, probably encompassing the whole of north Wales by 872. But there were at least four other Welsh kingdoms to the south, of which at least two had continuous histories into the late eleventh century; these political

Fig. 37   Map of the kingdoms of Ireland

units were, then, very small. Rhodri, and his son Anarawd especially, seem to
have been bent on territorial expansion for Gwynedd, Anarawd raiding the
kingdoms to the south (see Fig. 38).[14] While it is reasonable to compare this
with the behaviour of Irish overkings – raiding for tribute, taking hostages,
seeking submissions – and therefore to see the Gwynedd kings as would-be
'high-kings' of Wales, high-kingship was not the outcome of the raids; those

---

[14] Asser, c. 80, trans. Keynes and Lapidge, *Alfred*, 96.

who were raided looked outside Wales for protection and soon brought in foreign fighters, both Scandinavian and English, to help their resistance.[15] Although Rhodri's descendants established themselves in south-west Wales (Dyfed) in the tenth century, different branches of his family fought each other and contested for power and control, limiting governmental development in that period. The fiscal system was rudimentary; there was a high degree of anarchy in the tenth and eleventh centuries; powerful ecclesiastical immunities were established; and significant political action was sometimes taken by bands of aristocrats against the interests of kings.[16]

Ireland was again a contrast: in the ninth century it was still a land of many kings and tiny kingdoms (*tuatha*), some of whose kings were overkings, expecting tribute, attendance and (military) assistance from their subject kings, from whom they took hostages and to whom they gave gifts.[17] The overkingships were not – on the whole – institutionalized and were therefore very volatile: some had very short lives and succession was rarely straightforward. The ensuing political climate was consequently dominated by fighting and raiding, conflicts which involved – by the ninth century – some ecclesiastical institutions too. Kings could be abbots, especially in Munster (south-western Ireland): Olchobar, king of a *tuath* and Munster overking in 851, was also abbot of the monastery of Emly.[18] Despite this prevailing volatility, some of the separate kingdoms were absorbed by others and some of the many overkingships came close to being institutionalized: those of the north and middle (Uí Néill), south-east (Leinster), south-west (Munster) and west (Connacht). Moreover, the Uí Néill overkingship exercised by Máel Sechnaill in the mid-ninth century looked beyond the north and centre to the whole of Ireland, taking hostages and securing assistance from the 'provinces' beyond (see Fig. 37).

Máel Sechnaill did not *establish* an all-Ireland overkingship (which was not to happen until the eleventh century), and he did not secure the Uí Néill overkingship for his branch of the Uí Néill family, the Clann Cholmáin. However, he did establish a model – a pattern for other powerful kings to emulate. Many tried, but it took time for them to be consistently successful.

There were different kinds of polity, then, and different patterns of political development in the west, but Alfred's most prominent contemporaries in these four Celtic regions were all powerful men, who could command and control effective fighting forces. Their territorial range – the scale of their active

---

[15] Cf. D. N. Dumville, 'Anglo-Saxon and Celtic overkingships: a discussion of some shared historical problems', *Bulletin of the Institute of Oriental and Occidental Studies, Kansai University*, 31 (1998), 85, on the ninth-century end of Welsh political structures.

[16] W. Davies, *Wales in the Early Middle Ages* (1982), 106–12; Davies, *Patterns of Power*, 35–7, 41–7; W. Davies, 'Adding insult to injury: power, property and immunities in early medieval Wales', in *Property and Power in the Early Middle Ages*, eds W. Davies and P. Fouracre (1995).

[17] Byrne, *Irish Kings*, 41, 196–9; D. Ó Corráin, 'Nationality and kingship in pre-Norman Ireland', in *Nationality and the Pursuit of National Independence*, ed. T. W. Moody (1978).

[18] Byrne, *Irish Kings*, 214.

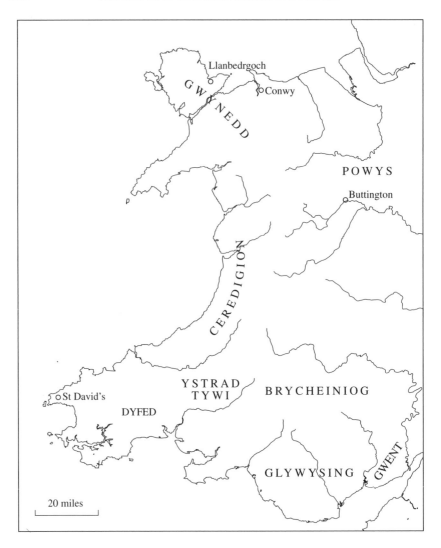

Fig. 38   Map of the kingdoms of Wales

rulership – was in most cases comparable to Alfred's Wessex. Brittany was directly so, being the same size of 'state'; the 'Scotland' of the later ninth century was a little smaller;[19] the overkingship of Ireland stretched even farther, although of course the basic units of kingship there were very much smaller. But

---

[19] Cf. Broun, 'Origin of Scottish identity', 29, who argues that the original Alba was smaller than Pictland.

Gwynedd, the largest kingdom of Wales, even when expanded to include Powys to the north-east and Ceredigion to the south, was clearly not of the same scale. This fact probably had a bearing on Asser's attitude to Alfred: in contrast to his experience at home, Alfred's Wessex was a great kingdom.

Interaction with Wessex

The last known king of Cornwall was drowned in the 870s; Asser was given the monastery of Exeter with a sphere of authority that included Cornwall; some of the inscribed stones of Cornwall commemorate people with English names; and Alfred's will included land in north-east Cornwall.[20] Although it can be maintained that it took Athelstan's campaigns in the south-west in the tenth century to finalize the integration of this country within the English kingdom, in essence the work was done in Alfred's reign. Once the kingdom of Cornwall had been incorporated in Wessex, of the kings of the west it was the Welsh who had the most direct interaction with it.

The elements of the story are well known. First, Alfred's biographer, Asser, was called from St David's in west Wales to Alfred's court. St David's was an ancient, and prestigious, monastic and episcopal house. After Asser came to the West Saxon court, he divided his time between St David's and Wessex, notionally six months on and six months off. In other words, he maintained contact with Wales and was himself a channel for continuing communication between Alfred's court and the rulers of Wales. Simon Keynes has reminded us that he thinks that the *Life of Alfred* was itself written for a Welsh audience.[21] Second, Rhodri, the great king of Gwynedd, was killed by the English in 878; this was presumably by the midland English, who had campaigned in north Wales throughout the ninth century and were defeated at Conwy in 881.[22] Third, according to Asser, the southern Welsh kings – that is, the kings of Dyfed, Glywysing, Gwent and Brycheiniog – sought Alfred's protection, accepted Alfred's *dominium*, and 'submitted' to him round about the mid-880s because they were being harried by the sons of Rhodri on the one hand from the north and by the Mercians on the other from the north-east (see Fig. 38).[23]

I do not think that *dominium* in this account means 'rule' in any practical sense, because there is no reflection in Welsh sources of any kind of English rule on the ground; however, the arrangement must have brought the Welsh rulers into close touch with the Wessex court – a relationship amply demonstrated in

---

[20] S. M. Pearce, *The Kingdom of Dumnonia. Studies in History and Tradition in South Western Britain AD 350–1150* (1978), 168–9; cf. E. Okasha, *Corpus of Early Christian Inscribed Stones of South-West Britain* (1993), 47–8.

[21] Keynes and Lapidge, *Alfred*, 56–7.

[22] Davies, *Patterns of Power*, 69.

[23] Asser, c. 80, trans. Keynes and Lapidge, *Alfred*, 96, and notes at 262–3.

the next two generations by well-recorded appearances of Welsh rulers with the king in England (although this was not sustained into the later tenth and eleventh centuries).[24] Almost certainly as a consequence, Welsh warriors joined the West Saxon troops which followed the Essex host to Buttington on the River Severn in 893, laying siege to the host for several weeks before defeating it; some of the Welsh, then, went to fight for the English. Ultimately Anarawd, Rhodri's son, joined the southern kings and had by 895 secured English assistance against Ceredigion and Ystrad Tywi (in west Wales); at that point English troops were inside Wales, campaigning and ravaging with the north Welsh.[25]

Beyond Wales and Cornwall interaction was not so direct. However, in a sense Breton and Irish rulers belonged to the same courtly world as that of the West Saxons. Just as Alfred travelled to Rome and went to the court of Charles the Bald, subsequently sending for continental scholars for his court, Breton and Irish rulers had comparable diplomatic relationships and scholarly exchanges. Erispoe of Brittany, Nominoe's son and successor (851–57), had his daughter betrothed to Charles's eldest son in 856; Salomon's son (who may have been sponsored by Charles at baptism in 864) swore fidelity to Charles; and Salomon himself received lands in Neustria from Charles.[26] Salomon, as we saw at the start, wished to make the journey to Rome and, though prevented from doing that, sent gifts to the pope. Both Louis the Pious and Charles patronized leading Breton monasteries such as Landévennec and Redon, with a notable consequent impact on their scholarly culture: most notable of all, Carolingian minuscule quickly replaced characteristically Insular forms of writing in Brittany, but favourite Carolingian authors were also copied and Carolingian-preferred texts of the Bible and the liturgy were adopted.[27]

Irish rulers were obviously more distant, but even so Charles the Bald received a delegation in 848, bringing gifts from the *rex Scottorum* (king of the Irish), Máel Sechnaill, and a request for safe passage to Rome for the travellers; Donnacán, the holy scholar, had died in Italy in 843. Irish scholars inhabited the courts, secular and ecclesiastical, of ninth-century western Europe – a marked and distinguished presence – and kept in intellectual touch with their homeland: a group of four such scholars on their way to the Continent were entertained in the Gwynedd court round about 840 and later wrote back to their teacher in Ireland about the cryptogram test they had encountered there. Notably, the three Irish who landed in Wessex in 891 headed straight for Alfred's court; the Irish, of all people, were accustomed to travel and to contacts abroad.[28]

---

[24] H. R. Loyn, 'Wales and England', *Welsh History Review*, 10 (1980–81), 283–301.

[25] *AC*, AD 894.

[26] Chédeville and Guillotel, *La Bretagne*, 288; J. L. Nelson, *Charles the Bald* (1992), 208; *AB*, s.a. 873.

[27] Chédeville and Guillotel, *La Bretagne*, 344; J. M. H. Smith, *Province and Empire. Brittany and the Carolingians* (1992), 162–77.

[28] D. Ó Cróinín, *Early Medieval Ireland 400–1200* (1995), 222–9; *ASC, s.a.* 891.

The northern world seems to have been more distant from Alfred's circle and from the Continent, although this impression may have more to do with the paucity of sources than any real difference. At least we know that the Carolingian scholar Walahfrid Strabo wrote a poem on the violent death of Blathmac, 'holy teacher' of Iona in Dalriada off the west coast of Scotland, and that Abbot Indrechtach of Iona died in England in 854, on his way to Rome.[29]

The Common Problem

All of these western and northern regions experienced Viking raiding in Alfred's lifetime and this caused problems for all of them, to differing extents and with different outcomes.

Raiding was a problem for the Bretons for most of Alfred's lifetime (although to a lesser extent in the late 870s and early 880s), and was often inextricably connected with those experienced by the West Frankish king. The Viking threat actively involved Breton aristocrats, sometimes working in independent groups, in alliance or in conflict, and was perceived as a problem by other Bretons, like those in the monastery of Redon: the abbot sought permission from the bishop to be excused from sending his priests to Vannes for ordination because of the dangers they might encounter on the road. Breton rulers themselves spent a great deal of time on campaign, culminating in the victories of Alan the Great against the Loire and the Seine Vikings in 888–90 both within Brittany and at St Lô in Normandy.[30]

Raiding in Ireland and Wales was problematic until the 870s, and then lessened. In Wales Rhodri won victories in 856, but was forced overseas to Ireland in 877. The problems came from the west and seem largely to have been a backlash of Viking activity in Ireland, where they were seriously disruptive for about forty years from 833, burning monasteries, capturing clerics for ransom and killing warriors. With fleets on the rivers and inland lakes of Ireland, there were many different groups of Vikings, although they were predominantly of Norse origin until the Danes arrived in 849. From 873, however, the so-called '40-year peace' dawned.[31]

From 839 Vikings raided from the west into the Pictish heartland in inland Scotland, killing members of the Pictish ruling family that year. Thereafter raids continued through Alfred's lifetime into the early tenth century, the raiders

---

[29] *AU*, AD 825; cf. C. Doherty, 'The Vikings in Ireland: a review', in *Ireland and Scandinavia in the Early Viking Age*, eds H. B. Clarke, M. Ní Mhaonaigh, R. Ó Floinn (Dublin, 1998), 310; *AI*, AD 854.

[30] Chédeville and Guillotel, *La Bretagne*, 297–321, 359–68; N. S. Price, 'The Vikings in Brittany', *Saga-Book of the Viking Society*, 22 (1989), 339–55.

[31] H. R. Loyn, *The Vikings in Wales* (1976), 4–8; *AU*, AD 856, 877; Ó Cróinín, *Early Medieval Ireland*, 233–55.

sometimes staying for long periods – Olaf (Amlaíb) spent three months in Fortriu in 866 – collecting tribute and causing devastation, and they took Dumbarton, royal focus of Strathclyde, in 870 (see Fig. 36).[32] Some at least of these raiders – like Olaf – were Dublin Norse; it has been argued that he and his allies dominated the kings of 'Scotland' for much of the later ninth and early tenth centuries;[33] indeed, it has recently been suggested that Scotland was the focus of an overkingship of Scottish and Irish Vikings at this time.[34] However, there clearly were other Viking groups involved in Scotland; the Gall-Goídil (Irish-speaking foreigners) came from the Hebrides, and the Danish Halfdan of Northumbria raided Galloway and Strathclyde in 875. Viking activity was politically disruptive in central Scotland for much of the period.

While the pattern of raiding was obviously different for these Celtic areas, so too were their experiences of Viking settlement. In Brittany there is no evidence of any ninth-century settlement. For Wales the evidence is very thin: Asser certainly speaks of Vikings overwintering in the south-west in 878; and for the longer term there are traces of some small-scale settlement in both the south and the north of the country. However, it is extremely difficult to tie any of this down to the ninth century.[35] At Glyn Farm, Llanbedrgoch, on Anglesey, currently being excavated, there are certainly structural phases of this period and indications of strengthening the fortifications and increases in population in the late ninth century. Whether or not any of this represents Viking, as opposed to native, activity is controversial; and, in any case, excavation is not yet finished.[36] By contrast, the heavy Norse settlement of the northern and western isles off Scotland, and northern parts of the mainland, seems to have begun by this time, leading by 1100 to linguistic change, together with the creation of the Scandinavian Earldom of Orkney and incorporation of the isles into the kingdom of Norway.[37] There was significant settlement in Ireland too, but of a quite different kind: a small number of strongpoints was established, controlling the hinterlands around them. Although they did not all survive into the central Middle Ages, several of those in the south of the country did so.[38] By the eleventh century the Limerick

---

[32] *AU*, AD 866, 870; A. O. Anderson, *Early Sources of Scottish History, AD 500–1286* (2 vols, 1922, rev. edn 1990), I, 292–312.

[33] A. P. Smyth, *Scandinavian York and Dublin* (2 vols, Dublin, 1975–79), I, 17–19, 35–6, 62–4, 93–7, 108; cf. Dumville, *Churches of North Britain*, 1–2, 29.

[34] D. Ó Corráin, 'The Vikings in Scotland and Ireland in the ninth century', *Peritia*, 12 (1998), 329–31, 333–7.

[35] Loyn, *Vikings in Wales*, 8–22; Davies, *Patterns of Power*, 51–6.

[36] M. Redknap, 'Glyn, Llanbedrgoch, Anglesey (SH 515 813)', *Archaeology in Wales*, 34 (1994), 58–60; ibid., 35 (1995), 58–9; ibid., 36 (1996), 81–2; ibid., 37 (1997), 94–6; ibid., 39 (1999), 56–61.

[37] Crawford, *Scandinavian Scotland*, 76–9.

[38] H. B. Clarke, 'Proto-towns and towns in Ireland and Britain in the ninth and tenth centuries', in *Ireland and Scandinavia*, eds Clarke, Ní Mhaonaigh, Ó Floinn, 341–68; P. F. Wallace,

Vikings were especially active in the Irish Sea, but more than a century before that the rulers of Viking Dublin were ranging widely over western and northern Britain as well as within Ireland; by the late tenth century Dublin, a Viking foundation, was a thriving urban centre, as the other surviving strongpoints were also to become. This urban development was something new for Ireland, in contrast to the long-established urban trends of southern England. This had important repercussions, both in respect of genuinely urban and commercial development and of the creation of a goal for would-be high-kings of Ireland: control of Dublin became essential for successful overkings in the eleventh and twelfth centuries, and those who contended for the position characteristically headed straight for the city.

Lastly, alliances. Interaction between Celtic rulers and aristocrats and Viking groups is very characteristic of the Viking period in the west. As was the case elsewhere in Europe, the Vikings were not a simple 'enemy'. Breton rulers, and other Bretons, at times allied with Viking leaders, both against other Vikings and against West Frankish rulers. So, Salomon fought *with* the Loire Vikings against Weland in 862 and *with* Haesten when he went to raid Poitou in 866; but he fought *against* Haesten *and* the Loire Vikings in 869 at Avessac, and with the Franks *against* the Vikings in the period 868–73.[39] The presence of active Viking groups on and around the Continent had a direct bearing on the relationship between Breton and Frankish rulers. Irish kings too allied with Viking leaders: Cerball, king of Ossory, allied with Olaf and Ivarr in 859; Aed of the northern Uí Néill allied with the Dublin rulers against the southern Uí Néill in the early 860s; Norse and Irish raided the ancient Irish sites of Knowth and Newgrange together in 863, to cite but a few examples. They intermarried too: Olaf married the daughter of Aed, and Cerball's daughter married a Dublin Viking.[40] This provided at least a complicating factor in Irish politics; though we no longer think that the Vikings destroyed 'classical' Irish society, they certainly fed the volatility of the Irish political process.

Even Anarawd of Gwynedd for a time allied with the Danish king of York – against the English – although Viking alliance is much more characteristic of tenth-century than of ninth-century Welsh history. (Scotland is uncertain: Godfrey of the Gall-Goídil may have worked with Kenneth, but the record is not contemporary.[41]) Alliance with Viking groups was therefore a major factor in determining political trends in the west. This seems to have been much more pronounced than it was in England. However, while there is certainly much less of alliance-

---

'*Garrda* and *airbeada*: the plot thickens in Viking Dublin', in *Seanchas. Studies in Early and Medieval Irish Archaeology, History and Literature in Honour of Francis J. Byrne*, ed. A. P. Smyth (Dublin, 2000), 273.

[39] *CR*, nos 242, 247; *AB, s.a.* 862, 866; Price, 'Vikings in Brittany', 348–53; Smith, *Province and Empire*, 105–7.

[40] *AU*, AD 859, 861, 862, 863; Byrne, *Irish Kings*, 263; Doherty, 'Vikings in Ireland', 301.

[41] Anderson, *Early Sources*, I, 267; Crawford, *Scandinavian Scotland*, 47.

making in the English record than in the Celtic, perhaps this is because the English record was dominated by the interests of the West Saxon court. James Campbell's comments on Viking alliances with the English may perhaps lead to a reassessment in the future.[42]

A Last Word

It is interesting that this Alfredian period was also a period of hero rulers in the Celtic west and north, much more consistently so than at any other period in the early Middle Ages. The rulers of Brittany, Wales and Scotland at this time have all been – and continue to be – heroes of school books, as King Alfred is. It may be suggested that that is more to do with modern myth-making than with ninth-century activity. Modern myth-making certainly plays a part in sustaining it: Breton independence movements since the nineteenth century have used stories of ninth-century rulers to emphasize their separate past; the maintenance and development of Scottish and especially Welsh political identities also draw from time to time on ninth-century heroes. However, the perspective is not merely modern: these rulers of the second half of the ninth century were seen as significant ancestors by medieval kings and their record-makers; and they were regarded as significant people by historians in the Middle Ages. Their fame began early: Rhodri was already 'Great' by the twelfth century, as Gerald of Wales makes clear. Not only that. Contemporary records made them distinctive too, in various ways, as indicated above.[43]

Why is it that the later ninth century provides the great heroes of the past in Celtic areas? It cannot be a reaction to and reflection of King Alfred, since several predated him. Perhaps it is more likely that it was a response to the legacy of Charlemagne. And resistance to the Viking aggressor gave the kings a prominence they would not otherwise have had; the Vikings unquestionably came from outside; the impact of aliens provoked at least the beginnings of a sense of identity.

I hope that this gives some context to Alfred in north-west Europe. While I do not wish to belittle his achievement, Alfred was clearly one of several Insular, western, rulers, of similar-sized polities. These were rulers who inhabited a courtly world where scholarship was valued and whose scholars moved between courts and churches across western Europe. They were rulers who were thrust into prominence by the need to deal with the Viking inrush. While differing in some respects, notably in their access to and control of coinage, these rulers were of the same cultural world as Alfred. Of course, they are not as dominant in the contemporary record as Alfred; but this is because the contemporary record

---

[42] See above, Chapter 1.

[43] See above, notes 5, 6, 13; and for Brittany, R. Merlet (ed.), *La Chronique de Nantes* (Paris, 1896).

in the Celtic west is much more miscellaneous in provenance: it was not so dominated by the ruler's court. I would like you to entertain the possibility, however, that these Celtic rulers were just as significant.

Chapter 20

The ruler as instructor, pastor and wise: Leo VI of Byzantium and Symeon of Bulgaria

Jonathan Shepard

The courts featuring in this paper lay at the far end of Europe from Alfred's Wessex. Their rulers at first sight have little in common with Alfred, and not much more to do with each other: on the one hand, the Byzantine emperors, spending most of their time in 'the reigning city', Constantinople; and on the other, in the steppe-like plains south of the lower Danube, the Bulgar khans, operating out of their principal towns and encampments, first Pliska and then (from the last years of the ninth century) Preslav.[1] The two rulers at the centre of attention are Emperor Leo VI (886–912) and Symeon of Bulgaria (893–927). As their regnal dates imply, they were half a generation younger than Alfred, being born respectively in the mid- and the early 860s, and it will be necessary to glance at their fathers, especially at Symeon's, Khan Boris-Michael.

The populations which these two pairs of fathers and sons governed were also rather disparate. On the one hand, there were Greek-speaking peasants, soldiers and officials, many of them possessing a fair degree of literacy and most of them referring to themselves as 'Romans', in line with their rulers' insistence that their capital, 'the New Rome', was the centre-point of legitimate rule on earth, having been relocated to the Bosporos by Constantine the Great. On the other hand, facing the Byzantines across more than one thousand miles of often mountainous borderlands, there were the Bulgars, whose forefathers had crossed the Danube in the late seventh century but who retained many features of their nomadic lifestyle, fighting tactics and political organization in the later ninth century, together with use of a distinctive form of the Turkic language. The khans, their chief landholders and their traders looked to the city of Constantinople as a source of enrichment, exporting linen, honey and other primary produce to exchange for luxury goods and, probably, such silver and gold as they could get past the Byzantine customs officials (who were supposed to halt the outflow of gold).[2]

---

[1] On Preslav's palace buildings, see M. Vaklinova, 'Preslavskiiat dvorets', in V. T'pkova-Zaimova and G. Danchev (eds), *Istoriko-arkheologicheski izsledvaniia v pamet na prof. Stancho Vaklinov* (Veliko T'rnovo, 1994), 45–58 and figs 1–11.

[2] Leo VI, *Das Eparchenbuch* 9.6, ed. and German trans. J. Koder (Vienna, 1991), 108–9.

On this economic plane, most conspicuously, the Bulgars occupied a kind of satellite role in relation to Byzantium.

It was probably the need for access to Constantinople's uniquely lucrative markets that prompted Khan Symeon to protest at the transfer of the Bulgars' trading staple from there to Thessalonica, a wealthy enough city but less easily reached by producers from the Danube plain. Symeon's protests were ignored and his next move, a resort to force, seems to have caught the Byzantine government by surprise: in 893 or 894 Symeon sent troops on to Byzantine soil, even though his father had received a Byzantine religious mission a generation earlier and the Bulgars had 'embraced the Christian faith and little by little adopted the customs of the Romans, giving up their savage and nomadic way of life together with their unbelief', in the words of Leo VI.[3] For three or four years a series of battles, truces and diplomatic manoeuvres ensued: the upshot, in 896 or 897, was a Bulgar victory over the main Byzantine army at the Battle of Bulgarophygon. Symeon came to terms with the Byzantines in 897 and ruled for a further thirty years. For much of that period, peace prevailed. In fact I would argue that open, full-scale, warfare was confined to, essentially, the years from 917 to 924, in comparison with quite lengthy stretches of peace. Only after suffering repeated Byzantine provocations and betrayals did Symeon begin to respond with full-scale campaigning and, eventually, style himself as 'emperor of the Bulgars and the Romans'.[4] Yet his reputation among the Byzantines during and after his lifetime was that of 'a typhoon of ambition', 'guilty of the shedding of much Christian blood'[5] in pursuit of the imperial throne at Constantinople upon which, allegedly, he had long set his sights. The Byzantine image of Symeon as a barbarous 'warmonger' has left its mark on modern interpretations.[6]

This brings us to the methodological difficulty besetting any comparison between rulership in Byzantium and Bulgaria, an imbalance in the source-materials. The imbalance is partly due to so many more Byzantine texts being to hand than Bulgarian ones. But it also stems from a difference in the type of sources available and the information which they provide. Byzantine sources offer a plausible narrative of events and generally represent Symeon as an aggressive, if sometimes gullible 'barbarian'. Greek chronicles and saints' *Lives* are fullest in their coverage of Symeon's invasions of Byzantine territory in the

---

[3] Leo VI, *Tactica*, 18.61, *PG* 107, col. 960.

[4] Symeon's successive titles are registered on his seal types: I. Iordanov, *Pechatite na preslavskite vladeteli 893–971* (Sofia, 1993), 9–12, photos on tables V-VI; *idem*, 'Nov pechat na Simeon I Veliki (893–927)', *Starini*, 1 (1999), 101–6; J. Shepard, 'Bulgaria: the other Balkan "empire"', in T. Reuter (ed.), *New Cambridge Medieval History, III* (1999), 567–85, at 573–8.

[5] I. Dujčev, 'On the treaty of 927 with the Bulgarians', *Dumbarton Oaks Papers*, 32 (1978), 274–5; *Vita* of St Luke the Younger, *PG* 111, col. 453.

[6] G. Ostrogorsky, *History of the Byzantine State*, trans. J. Hussey (1968), 262; W. Treadgold, *History of the Byzantine State and Society* (Stanford, 1997), 473–5; J. Shepard, 'Symeon of Bulgaria – peacemaker', *Annuaire de l'Université de Sofia St Kliment Ohridski*, 83 (1989), 9–10.

later years of his reign and make much of the devastation that they wrought. In contrast, there is nothing that could strictly be called annals or a 'chronicle' from the Bulgarian side, and the majority of texts of Bulgarian origin from the late ninth and earlier tenth centuries are not original works, but translations from the Greek, generally on religious themes. We are therefore liable to view events and régimes exclusively through Byzantine lenses, and to pay less attention to periods and activities that the Byzantine sources neglect, such as the lengthy peace from 897 onwards and the works of translation and study under way at Symeon's court during that period.

I shall not dwell further on the imbalance between the Byzantine and Bulgarian sources, nor is it my principal aim to rehabilitate Symeon as a 'peace-maker' rather than a warmonger, or fully to reassess his relations with Byzantium. Instead, the focus will be on the image of rulership which Symeon deliberately projected: a scholarly ruler dispensing 'justice', offering instruction and thus guiding his people towards knowledge of doctrine, righteousness and, ultimately, salvation. This brand of rulership was, I suggest, similar to that of Symeon's contemporary, Leo VI. Leo was already known in his lifetime as 'the Wise',[7] and his scholarly activities and authorship or sponsorship of a variety of texts have been expounded by T. Antonopoulou and S. Tougher. What has not, so far as I know, been pointed out is the close resemblance between Leo's style and actual practice of leadership and those of Symeon.[8] Each presented himself as, in effect, a 'philosopher king', combining the roles of sage, instructor and shepherd of his flock; and writings of each of them survive. Symeon's are exiguous in comparison with Leo's outpourings, but they convey something of his intellect and objectives. Sufficient material is available for a comparison between the two rulers' notions and styles of leadership. I shall only glance at how far their images had the intended effect on contemporaries and how far they matched reality. Finally there is the question of what accounts for this: is it just a coincidence arising out of quite separate situations, or is there some connection between the leadership styles of the two régimes and even, perhaps, with régimes still further afield?

Leo's reputation for being 'wise' was perhaps partly foisted on him by his father's strivings to establish his régime as legitimate. Basil I drew on and developed existing notions of Byzantine emperors as counterparts to the Old Testament kings David and Solomon, being well aware of the parallel between himself and David. David was, after all, an 'upwardly mobile' who had risen from obscurity and gained power at the expense of his former patron, much as Basil, the former groom and favourite of Emperor Michael III, had done: in 867 Michael was murdered in the palace *coup* that brought Basil to supreme power. A letter addressed to Photius early in Basil's reign asks for a commentary on

---

[7] S. Tougher, *The Reign of Leo VI (886–912): Politics and People* (Leiden, New York, Cologne, 1997), 110–12.

[8] Tougher notes in passing that Symeon was 'famed for his wisdom': *Leo VI*, 112.

three passages in the Book of Kings, 'concerning Saul, the anointing of David, and the wisdom of Solomon'.[9] Basil was much taken with the concept of the ruler as anointed and thereby rendered sacred and unassailable; among the relics of Old Testament kingship installed in his New Church beside the palace was the horn from which Samuel anointed David.[10] Subsequently, Photius wrote a couple of hymns comparing Basil with David and he probably also composed a panegyrical poem representing Basil as a 'new David', about to set forth and defeat the 'Davidic myriads' in the eastern borderlands.[11]

From this it appears that any son of Basil I would have invited comparison with Solomon, the learned and peace-loving son of David, especially if that son did not provide active military leadership or direct campaigns in person, as was in fact the case with Leo. But Basil himself was anxious that his children should, literally, be seen to be highly educated and that mastery of books, specifically holy books, should be a special trait of his *nouveau régime*. A mosaic in an imperial apartment showed Basil and his wife enthroned, and all their children. The boys were 'holding codices that contain the divine commandments', while the girls carried 'books of the divine laws'. The biographer of Basil, writing in the palace milieu, offers his interpretation: 'the artist wished to show that not only the male but also the female offspring had been initiated into holy writ and shared in divine wisdom; for even if their father had not at first been familiar with letters on account of the circumstances of his life, yet he caused all his children to partake of wisdom (*sophia*)'.[12] In part, the mosaic was an exercise in 'over-compensation', demonstrating that the second generation was steeped in book learning, even if the new dynasty's founding father was unlettered. But it also affirmed two special relationships – between book learning and the higher wisdom that comes from Scripture; and between God's law and imperial law-making. It is probably no accident that the children were shown in imperial vestments holding what were recognizably 'books of laws' or 'commandments'. The implication is that they possessed not merely learning, but special under-standing of divine precepts and that this made them outstandingly fit for rulership.

Leo VI did not merely live up to the expectations of piety and God-guided wisdom that his father's propaganda fostered. His personal predilections and talents converged with official rhetoric and the role his father had cast for him, to spectacular effect. Leo made a point of demonstrating that his wisdom, while stemming to a great extent from books, was multi-faceted, encompassing the

---

[9] Tougher, *Leo VI*, 125; G. Dagron, *Empereur et prêtre. Étude sur le 'césaropapisme' byzantin* (Paris, 1996), 205–6.

[10] P. Magdalino, 'Observations on the Nea Ekklesia of Basil I', *Jahrbuch der österreichischen Byzantinistik*, 37 (1987), 58–60; Dagron, *Empereur*, 217; L. Brubaker, *Vision and Meaning in Ninth-Century Byzantium* (1999), 185–91.

[11] A. Markopoulos, 'An anonymous laudatory poem in honor of Basil I', *Dumbarton Oaks Papers*, 46 (1992), 226–9, 230, line 70, 231, lines 212–14; Dagron, *Empereur*, 206.

[12] Theophanes Continuatus, 5.89, ed. I. Bekker (Bonn, 1838), 333–4; Tougher, *Leo VI*, 127.

things of this world as well as the next, and that such know-how could, in part, be dispensed to others. What marks him out from his predecessors on the throne since Late Antiquity is that he did not merely read numerous books: he also wrote them, on a massive scale. Many were collections of excerpts, laws or regulations,[13] or compilations lightly touched up. Leo may well have had assistants of one sort or another, but the product was put out under his name and bolstered his reputation as sage and overseer. Not long after his accession he wrote and, seemingly, actually delivered an oration that celebrated his father's achievements while also showing off his own command of rhetoric and classical Greek. The literary output carried on through the first half of his reign.[14]

No comprehensive study of Leo VI's writings is available,[15] while the holdings of the library or libraries in the palace are far from clear. But Leo was better placed than most writers to track down texts and appropriate them. He could also call upon experts, as when a former general was instructed to write a treatise on imperial expeditions.[16] Thus the palace figured as a kind of information node, both storing wisdom and disseminating it in prescriptive form. It may well be that the very bulk and heterogeneity of Leo's writings was deliberate: no one else could compete with the masses of information at his disposal. This enhanced Leo's reputation and thereby his authority as an unsurpassable know-all. There is, admittedly, no surviving explicit reference to the size or range of Leo's palace library, but the scholar Arethas joked that he was giving up book-collecting, now that the emperor presided over 'the wise undertakings' at court and broadcast 'the seeds of all good things'.[17] This statement, made in an oration, implies that the emperor had abundant books to hand. That Leo wished to hear such conceits is suggested by the number of court orations heaping praise on his 'wisdom'. A further indication is the fact that a treatise on court banqueting which Leo commissioned stresses that he is neither 'ignorant' nor 'lacking in wisdom', but 'most wise'.[18] The author, who, as master of ceremonies, was probably not especially intellectual, offers an important attestation of the image overarching life at court.

If Leo's library as such did not receive praise from contemporaries, it may be because books were regarded as necessary but not sufficient for generating

---

[13] See D. Simon, 'Legislation as both a world order and legal order', in *Law and Society in Byzantium: Ninth – Twelfth Centuries*, eds A. E. Laiou and D. Simon (Washington, DC, 1994), 18–25; G. Dagron, 'Lawful society and legitimate power', in ibid., 38–46.

[14] Tougher, *Leo VI*, 115–16, 167–72; *The Homilies of the Emperor Leo VI*, ed. T. Antonopoulou (Leiden, New York, Cologne, 1997), 9–11, 19–20.

[15] See *Homilies*, ed. Antonopoulou, 18–23; *eadem*, 'An epistolary attributed to Leo the Wise', *Jahrbuch der österreichischen Byzantinistik*, 47 (1997), 76 and n. 17.

[16] Constantine Porphyrogenitus, *Three Treatises on Imperial Expeditions*, ed. and trans. J. F. Haldon (Vienna, 1990), 44–5, 56 and n. 40, 94–7 (text), 180–82.

[17] Arethas, *Scripta minora*, ed. L. G. Westerink, II (Leipzig, 1972), 46; Tougher, *Leo VI*, 115.

[18] Philotheus, *Kleterologion*, ed. N. Oikonomides, *Les listes de préséance byzantines des IX et X siècles* (Paris, 1972), 84–5; Tougher, *Leo VI*, 115.

imperial wisdom. Divine intervention was needed to make an emperor truly wise, and the master of ceremonies, when elaborating on Leo's wisdom, states that he 'is honoured with the grace of God in thought and deed'.[19] Likewise a poem praising Leo as homilist terms him adorned by the *logos*, the Word of God, a finer ornament even than the purple.[20] The notion that Leo owed 'higher' wisdom to divine grace unavailable to ordinary mortals is expressed in an ivory which depicts the Mother of God adding a pearl to Leo's crown. The pearl is probably that of wisdom, the crown is an obvious emblem of imperial authority and the setting evokes St Sophia, a church closely linked with the palace.[21] There could scarcely be clearer visual expression of the special connection between majesty, piety and superlative wisdom. Whether the ivory comes from a sceptre or some other work of 'official art' or is merely some subject's token of loyalty is disputed among art historians.[22] It is in any case in key with one of Leo's most unusual productions, his sermons.

The very existence of these sermons is noteworthy, in that no earlier emperor seems to have composed any, let alone delivered them in person, since the time of Constantine the Great.[23] Leo was eager to show off his personal erudition and literary skills as well as his piety. The sermons above all demonstrate mastery of the rhetorical techniques of the encomium. They do not show particular interest in developing or expounding upon theological issues for their own sake.[24] But the prayers at the end of the sermons give him an opportunity to set out his ideology, and the emperor's role as helmsman of the ship of state or shepherd of his flock is a common theme: '(Reward me) by granting that in this life I guide with knowledge the flock entrusted to me, (O Thou) who has acquired pastoral knowledge to the highest degree'.[25] Leo represents himself as interceding with God on behalf of his subjects and repeatedly refers to David and Solomon.[26]

Most of Leo's sermons are very general, making no direct allusion to current events, although a few are plainly intended to serve a particular purpose.[27] On the whole he maintained the stance of moral arbiter, the 'praise of

---

[19] Philotheus, *Kleterologion*, 84–5; Tougher, *Leo VI*, 115.

[20] T. Antonopoulou, 'Verses in praise of Leo VI', *Byzantion*, 66 (1996), 281–4.

[21] K. Corrigan, 'The ivory scepter of Leo VI: a statement of post-Iconoclastic imperial ideology', *Art Bulletin*, 60 (1978), figs 1 and 2 on 408, 409–13; H. Evans and W. D. Wixom (eds), *The Glory of Byzantium. Art and Culture of the Middle Byzantine Era A.D. 843–1261* (New York, 1997), 201–2 and fig. 138.

[22] Corrigan, 'Ivory scepter', 407, 409–11; Evans and Wixom, *Glory of Byzantium*, 201–2.

[23] *Homilies*, ed. Antonopoulou, 40–41, 105.

[24] Ibid., 160–61, 192–3, 203–4, 215, 252–9.

[25] Cited in ibid., 73.

[26] Ibid., 78–9; *eadem*, 'Homiletic Activity in Constantinople around 900', in M. B. Cunningham and P. Allen (eds), *Preacher and Audience. Studies in Early Christian and Byzantine Homiletics* (Leiden, Boston, Cologne, 1998), 320.

[27] For example, a sermon justifying the installation of Leo's nineteen-year-old brother, Stephen, as patriarch in breach of canon law: *Homilies*, ed. Antonopoulou, 38, 245–6; Tougher, *Leo VI*, 15, 82–3.

good works [being] the seed of virtue'.[28] The majority of the sermons were delivered in St Sophia and the audience presumably consisted largely of members of the court and senior clergy. They would have been able to make something of the 'high-style' Attic Greek of the sermons. The giving of the sermons was, then, an Establishment occasion, replete with self-congratulation. Yet one should not underestimate the extent to which these occasions served to bond the emperor's officials and other notables with him, placing new, moral, inhibitions on the 'flock', which could not decently turn upon its 'shepherd'. Equally, one should not underrate the impact of the sermons on the street people of Constantinople, even if few could get into St Sophia, let alone understand the emperor's 'high-style' Greek. Popular sensibilities could run wild: so raucous was the crowd upon the arrival of the relics of St Lazarus in the City that Leo had to abandon plans to deliver a sermon in celebration.[29]

Besides the pastoral image pervading the sermons and preambles to Leo's decrees, there is a didactic aspect. Leo believed that knowledge gained from the writings of 'the ancients' could be applied to current affairs, and he did not recognize a sharp distinction between advice on practical matters and legislation. In both spheres he lays down the law on the strength of his superior wisdom, gained from the blend of book-learning and divinely vouchsafed truth that he alone possessed.[30] Thus in his treatise on *Tactics* he offers detailed guidelines on military matters, while obliquely conceding his own lack of campaigning experience.[31] He could hope that tabulating the rules of engagement would make his throne the more 'Solomonic' and unassailable.

The position of Symeon, khan and on occasion highly practical war-leader of the Bulgars,[32] differed greatly from Leo's, but the image that texts composed under his aegis project is not unfamiliar, and it left its mark on the Byzantine sources. In fact the fullest indication of Symeon's aspirations and lifestyle comes from the letters of Patriarch Nicholas Mysticus, written mainly in the period from 917 to 925. In a letter deploring the resumption of hostilities, Nicholas asks how Symeon of all people can be causing bloodshed and the destruction of churches:

> Symeon, who for his great wisdom, for the favour shown him by heaven, has led the Bulgar people to a height of glory, who more than any man detests wickedness, who honours justice, who abominates injustice, ... who differs from those who profess to live out of the world in no way except only in the exercise of the authority given to him by God.[33]

[28] *Laudatio of S. Trypho, Acta Sanctorum, Novembr.* IV (Brussels, 1925), 349; *Homilies*, ed. Antonopoulou, 43 and n. 44.

[29] Arethas, *Scripta Minora*, II, ed. Westerink, 15; *Homilies*, ed. Antonopoulou, 26, 36, 43–4.

[30] Dagron, 'Lawful society', 39, 46.

[31] Leo VI, *Tactica, praefatio*, 18.123, *PG* 107, cols 675–8, 975–6; Tougher, *Leo VI*, 167–72.

[32] Shepard, 'Symeon', 21 and n. 99 on 39.

[33] Nicholas Mysticus, Patriarch of Constantinople, *Letters*, eds R. J. H. Jenkins and L. G. Westerink (Washington, DC, 1973), 94–5.

Symeon is virtually the only person whom Nicholas addresses as 'wise',[34] and he assumes that Symeon will be familiar with early Byzantine history: 'I imagine that, with your seriousness of character, you apply the same seriousness to your study of ancient history.'[35] Nicholas also takes him for a constant reader of the works of St Paul: 'I know that day by day you water your fair soul in the life-giving streams of the doctrine of the blessed Apostle.'[36] These statements accord with an earlier letter to Symeon from a Byzantine diplomat: 'You have the sentiment of justice together with the sentiment of humanity, as is clearly attested by everyone.'[37] This letter was written within a couple of years of Symeon's accession and it suggests a certain consistency in Symeon's stance as ruler.

These letter-writers had their own agenda and were trying to flatter Symeon. But they geared their epithets to what they took to be Symeon's self-image, highlighting his virtues as a just and pious ruler. Patriarch Nicholas plays on his asceticism and devoutness, befitting one who had been a monk before coming to the throne. Symeon's sense of responsibility for his people before God is brought out in a letter of Nicholas to the archbishop of Bulgaria. Nicholas made a thinly veiled attempt to get the archbishop to excommunicate Symeon, in the event that Symeon did not make peace: 'You possess many means of persuasion which work together towards entreating him.' First of these persuaders is the grief of Christ at the Christians' mutual slaughter. Then, 'you have the holy churches into which he goes to commune with God on behalf of himself, his wife, his children and indeed of all that nation of which he is lord'.[38] Nicholas then refers to Holy Communion, 'which as he eats and drinks he has undoubting hopes that he is partaking of sanctification'. Nicholas would scarcely have bothered to write to the archbishop in these terms had he not been confident that Communion and prayers on behalf of himself and his people mattered greatly to Symeon.

If the Byzantine writers shed some light on Symeon's devout lifestyle linked to a sense of duty, it is a contemporary Bulgarian encomium that expands most fulsomely on the bookish basis of his reputation for 'wisdom' and piety. The encomium *In praise of Tsar Symeon* singles out for special praise Symeon's collection of 'all the most reverend sacred books': Symeon is said to appear to his nobles as 'a new Ptolemy', founder of the great library in Alexandria, and he has 'filled his palaces' with his books.[39] This feat is held to earn him eternal memory and, even, some sort of crown of sanctity. Presumably this is because of the uses to which Symeon is putting his books. He is commissioning transla-

---

[34] Nicholas Mysticus, 70–74; Tougher, *Leo VI*, 112.

[35] Nicholas Mysticus, 134–7, 32–5.

[36] Ibid., 162–3.

[37] G. Kolias, *Léon Choerosphactès magistre, proconsul et patrice* (Athens, 1939), 80–83.

[38] Nicholas Mysticus, 86–7.

[39] *Simeonov Sbornik (po Svetoslavoviia prepis ot 1073g.)*, eds P. Dinekov et al., I (Sofia, 1991), 202; F. J. Thomson, 'The Symeonic florilegium … ', *Palaeobulgarica*, 17 (1993), 52 (translation).

tions, and our encomiast has himself been ordered to translate 'this most difficult book' of 'the most wise' Basil of Caesarea, with instructions to convey the exact sense of the original.

The encomium receives some support from evidence of another project connected with Symeon. The preface to one of the extant selections of the works of John Chrysostom translated into Slavonic states:

> While he studied all books, old and new, canonical and uncanonical, above all holy writ, and while he understood the rules and customs of all the teachers and their wisdom, the pious tsar Symeon marvelled at the wisdom of the sermons of blessed John Chrysostom ... Reading through all his books, he chose sermons from them all and composed from them this single work, which he called the *Zlatostruy* ('Golden Streams').[40]

Apparently the supervisor of the project marked out the various Greek passages to be translated, using the Slavonic word for 'beginning'; the word was initially incorporated in the translated text.[41] The task of selection was carried out from a wide array of Chrysostom's works and F. Thomson has observed that this 'independent selection from Chrysostom's works ... is further proof of the excellent library at ... [Symeon's] disposal'.[42] Thomson concluded that Symeon himself made the original selection, while others did the actual work of translating. This tends to bear out the encomium's claims both for the extent of Symeon's collection of 'sacred books' and for his close involvement in translation work.

One might ponder the shades of meaning of the 'wisdom' that the preface to the *Zlatostruy* attributed to Symeon, but a further facet of his activities deserves highlighting. He did not confine himself to the role of reader of the Church Fathers in Greek and commissioner of translations. He also sought to edify and educate, as the encomium of *Tsar Symeon* brings out with another image: Symeon is 'a labour-loving bee' who gathers the thoughts of St Basil 'from every flower of his writings' into his 'wise heart' and then pours forth 'from his lips like sweet honey before his boiars' for their enlightenment.[43] Symeon is envisaged as acting independently of the translator, drawing directly upon St Basil's works and presenting a distillation to his nobles, presumably through a public address or extempore sermon. That he would have been conversant with the formal requirements of rhetoric is suggested by his education in Constantinople. According to Liudprand of Cremona, Symeon learnt there 'the rhetoric of Demosthenes and the syllogisms of Aristotle'.[44] In fact he was confident enough of his proficiency in formal public speaking to address the

---

[40] Cited in E. Georgiev, *Raztsvet't na b'lgarskata literatura v IX–X v.* (Sofia, 1962), 276.

[41] F. J. Thomson, 'Chrysostomica Palaeoslavica ... ', *Cyrillomethodianum*, 6 (1982), 22, 47.

[42] Ibid., 47, n. 161 on 55.

[43] *Simeonov Sbornik*, I, 202; Thomson, 'Symeonic florilegium', 52.

[44] Liudprand, *Antapodosis*, III 29, in *Opera omnia*, ed. P. Chiesa, CCCM 156 (Turnhout, 1998), 81.

Byzantine emperor at their meeting before their respective entourages on the Golden Horn in 924. He spoke then in fluent, if heavily accented, Greek.[45]

The image of Symeon as the orator and instructor at his court is consistent with another role ascribed to the ruler by John the Exarch. Offering a review of the human body in his treatise, *The Six Days* (*Hexaemeron*), John describes the mind as being like a 'lover of truth, a firm and perceptive judge or simply an emperor, sitting on his tall throne', speedily adjudging the messages relayed by the other senses, and accepting or rejecting their raw data.[46] One of John's sermons, composed for Christmas and addressing the notables of Preslav, warns of divine wrath befalling those who seek pleasure rather than penitence and are irreverent in church, and some of whom are equally disrespectful before the ruler.[47] These reprimands suggest an air of high moral seriousness at Symeon's court, as well as mixed reactions to it on the part of some nobles. They complement the encomium and other indications that Symeon supervised translation work and the copying of manuscripts. According to a marginal note to the Slavonic translation of St Athanasius's *Discourse against the Arians*, the translation was carried out on Symeon's orders in 906 and then, in the following year, a copy was made by Theodore Doksov, at Symeon's behest.[48] Doksov, a cousin of Symeon, had become a monk and lived in the vicinity of Preslav. This vignette suggests the extent to which fellow-members of the Bulgar ruling house were subsumed into a pious project under a didactic and *dirigiste* figure.

Nicholas Mysticus played upon the edifier in Symeon when he called him 'one who has the know-how and ability to teach virtue to others'.[49] One might take this to refer only to Symeon's edification of his scholars and nobles gathered at Preslav, preaching before the converted. But Symeon showed a sense of wider pastoral responsibilities, even while asserting moral ascendancy over his nobles. The works rendered into Slavonic under his aegis bear witness to this: besides the 'most difficult' writings of Basil and books of doctrinal exegesis, more straightforward texts were translated and collated in an accessible form. Already in the first year of Symeon's reign the so-called 'Didactic Gospel Book' was compiled. Its main section comprises a collection of translated Greek sermons expounding in plain words the Gospel readings prescribed for each Sunday through the year.[50] Symeon's patronage of pastoral work at grass roots is brought out in the *Life* of St Clement. Symeon was, it claims, impressed by reports of

---

[45] Dujčev, 'Treaty of 927', 278–9.

[46] John the Exarch, *Hexaemeron*, ed. R. Aitzetmüller, VI (Graz, 1971), 193–4. The emperor's intellectual dominance over his court features as a motif in Leo's sermons: *Homilies*, ed. Antonopoulou, 78.

[47] A. I. Iatsimirsky, *Iz istorii slavianskoi pis'mennosti v Moldavii i Valakhii XV–XVII vv.* (Pamiatniki Drevnei Pis'mennosti i Iskusstva 162) (St Petersburg, 1906), 57; Georgiev, *Raztsvet't*, 211.

[48] Georgiev, *Raztsvet't*, 331.

[49] Nicholas Mysticus, 136–7.

[50] Georgiev, *Raztsvet't*, 168–81.

Clement's powers as 'teacher of virtue', assigning him soon after his own accession to a see in the borderlands looking towards Thessalonica.[51] Clement set about training priests in the conduct of church services and expounding doctrine, a 'new Paul for the new Corinthians'.[52] He also wrote sermons, 'simple and clear works for all the festivals, which contained nothing deep or particularly wise, but which could be understood by even the stupidest Bulgar'![53] Many of Clement's sermons survive, and their interweaving of Bible stories with exegesis of basic doctrine tends to bear out the claims made for them by the *Life*.[54] Symeon seems to have set so much store by Clement's work that he refused the aged Clement's request to retire from his see in 916, saying that it would be 'an ill omen for my own loss of the imperial throne'.[55] That Symeon regarded learning as interlinked with pastoral care is suggested by the early tenth-century *Life* of another scholar in his circle, Naum. He was despatched from Preslav to what had been Clement's first sphere of activity, in the southwest of Bulgaria; the *Life* laconically states that 'the pious tsar Symeon sent Naum ... instead of him [Clement], to carry out instruction'.[56] There is no reason to doubt this further hint that Symeon wanted ordinary people to be instructed directly by scholars.[57]

These considerations should make us hesitate to dismiss outright the characterization of Symeon as 'simple and good, especially towards those showing sobriety of morals and a most Christian way of life'.[58] The *Life* of Clement rhetorically portrays him in a 'Solomonic' relationship to his father: showing 'zeal for the house of God' (Psalms 68: 10), he 'completed the unfinished work of his father and extended the holy preaching of the Gospel; through his foundation of churches everywhere he established orthodoxy as unassailable'.[59] Symeon himself seems to have emphasized that he was carrying on the work of Boris. The naming of his 'Golden and New Church' at Preslav may have been deliberately evocative of the Temple of Solomon, the New Jerusalem and the 'Nea' (New Church) built by Basil I in Constantinople.[60] At the same time Symeon reportedly compared his own work with that of Moses, carrying out God's will.[61] He thus laid claim to be guiding his entire people towards the Promised

---

[51] I. G. Iliev, 'The long life of Saint Clement of Ohrid. A critical edition', *Byzantinobulgarica*, 9 (1995), 99–100; D. Obolensky, *Six Byzantine Portraits* (1988), 27–8.

[52] Iliev, 'Life of Clement', 101.

[53] Ibid.

[54] Obolensky, *Six Portraits*, 30–31.

[55] Iliev, 'Life of Clement', 103. However, the episode could have been touched up, if not invented, by the hagiographer: Iliev, 'Life of Clement', 75–6, 117.

[56] I. Ivanov, *B'lgarski starini iz Makedoniia* (repr. Sofia, 1970), 306; Georgiev, *Raztsvet't*, 159.

[57] On the nature and date of the earliest *Life*, see Iliev, 'Life of Clement', 72–4.

[58] Ibid., 99.

[59] Ibid.

[60] P. Georgiev, 'Zlatnata ts'rkva v Preslav', *Preslav* (Sofia) 5 (1993), 14–19.

[61] Nicholas Mysticus, 176–7.

Land. Nicholas ridiculed this,[62] but his harping elsewhere on Symeon's zeal for justice and role as edifier suggests that he understood the basis for Symeon's 'Moses-posture' well enough. And if, as is quite likely, Symeon was responsible for the dissemination among his subjects of a translation of extracts from a Byzantine law-code, the 'Law for the Judgement of the People',[63] his professed concern for justice gained concrete form, and this may have encouraged self-identification with Moses.

Such is the basis for supposing a distinct resemblance between the leadership modes of Leo VI and Symeon. Each presented himself as a 'philosopher king', acting out the roles of uniquely wise man, instructor and pastor. Resemblance does not, of course, amount to identity, and terms such as 'wise' or 'pastor' may have had rather different connotations in the city of Constantinople from what they meant in Preslav or among the medley of peoples under Symeon's sway. Thus, for instance, translation-work had no part to play in Leo VI's court culture, and the tendency of his sermons was towards the metaphorical and elaborate literary devices. In contrast, lucid, accurate exegesis of doctrine and Church Fathers' sermons, capturing the meaning of the original, was what Symeon encouraged in his translators. And even though Symeon continued to reserve foremost position for the Greek language in court ceremonial, religious services and, apparently, official documents,[64] he clearly intended Slavonic to be the language of everyday written communications, religious study and sermons. This served a directly pastoral purpose, inculcating Christianity more thoroughly into all Symeon's subjects: it is around the end of the ninth century that cremations in urns, burials with horses and other distinctively pagan funerary rites disappear from Bulgarian burial-grounds, and not earlier.[65] Promoting a Slavonic written language also performed a political function, in that a monotheistic religion expounded in sermons using plain words focused the loyalties of Symeon's disparate subjects upon him as a new Moses, Solomon or (in John the Exarch's image) as the 'mind' of the body politic. Thus 'wisdom' and the role of the ruler as pastor-cum-instructor were for Symeon a means towards 'nation-building', whereas for Leo VI they were rather a means of upholding the empire's hegemony and reinforcing his own legitimacy, as unique intermediary between God and mankind.

Even so, the stance of Leo and Symeon specifically as *intellectual* leaders of their courts seems to me at once too similar and too distinctive to be sheer

---

[62] Ibid.

[63] On the controversy as to where the code was translated, see V. Vavřínek and B. Zástěrová, 'Byzantium's role in the formation of Great Moravian culture', *Byzantinoslavica*, 43 (1982), 182–5.

[64] V. Beshevliev, *P'rvo-b'lgarski nadpisi* (Sofia, 1992), 81–3; C. Hannick, 'Les nouvelles chrétientés du monde byzantin: Russes, Bulgares et Serbes', in G. Dagron, P. Riché and A. Vauchez (eds), *Histoire du christianisme des origines à nos jours, IV: Évêques, moines et empereurs (610–1054)* (Paris, 1993), 932–3.

[65] U. Fiedler, *Studien zu Gräberfeldern des 6. bis 9. Jahrhunderts an der unteren Donau*, I (Bonn, 1992), 239–41, 267–70 and plate 106, 282–3, 291–5, 305–16.

coincidence within a common Christian tradition. There are two quite solid, even unsurprising, reasons for the resemblance and also, maybe, a more speculative one. The latter has links with a communication that should bring us back to earth in Wessex. First, one must emphasize the fact that the late ninth-century Bulgarian Church was an offshoot of the Byzantine Church, having the same doctrine, rites of worship and type of hierarchy, while relying on Patristic Greek texts and more recent hagiography for exegesis of doctrine and other religious guidance. Given that the Bulgars were essentially receiving Byzantine religious instruction for the first generation after Khan Boris's conversion, it is not surprising that they partook of the cultural revival that Byzantium underwent from around the mid-ninth century onwards. There was a marked increase in literary activity and more fulsome recognition of the value of advanced learning in government circles around that time. Some senior churchmen became more willing to concede a role to higher learning as a means of access to the divine. Through mastery of classical Greek grammar, prose-style and some factual knowledge, one could better understand the Fathers' teachings and points of doctrine, thereby gaining a purchase on 'inner', spiritual, wisdom.[66] Having sharpened one's wits on the reasoning techniques of Aristotle and learnt the rules of rhetoric, one could also put the case for Orthodox belief and practice more effectively, not least against proponents of Judaism and Islam.[67]

Both Leo VI and Symeon were exposed to this cultural trend, and its towering figure had an impact on one, very probably on both, of them. This was Photius, who in the interval between his first and second spells as patriarch – in the earlier 870s – was tutor to the young Leo. Thereafter he remained on close, if sometimes adversarial, terms with Leo and Leo's father. Photius's erudition and ability were famed among contemporaries and are impressive by any standards. His *Bibliotheca*, a set of notices on works he had read of ancient, Patristic and subsequent Greek literature, runs to 280 titles. He reviews many works of classical history, philosophy and rhetoric that are now lost.[68] We have already encountered him as adviser to Basil I on the Book of Kings and as the probable author of a panegyric acclaiming Basil as a 'new David'. He demonstrated his devotion to books as a means to Orthodox wisdom by, for example, giving a lavishly illuminated codex of the *Sermons* of Gregory Nazianzen to Basil around 880.[69]

Photius also offered instruction to Boris of Bulgaria soon after his conversion to Christianity in 864, sending a long letter on Church history, doctrine and

66 P. Lemerle, *Le premier humanisme byzantin* (Paris, 1971), 159–76, 194–204, 243, 265, 302–7; N. G. Wilson, *Scholars of Byzantium* (1983), 79–88; Brubaker, *Vision*, 235–7.

67 Lemerle, *Humanisme*, 194, 202; K. Corrigan, *Visual Polemics in the Ninth-Century Byzantine Psalters* (1992), 43–61, 78–94. Brubaker, *Vision*, 214–17, 239, 262.

68 Wilson, *Scholars*, 93–111; Photius, *The Bibliotheca. A selection*, trans. N. G. Wilson (1994), 1, 6–12 (introduction).

69 L. Brubaker, 'Politics, patronage and art in ninth-century Byzantium', *Dumbarton Oaks Papers*, 39 (1985), 1–6, 11–12; *eadem*, *Vision*, 236–8, 412–14. See above, pp. 341–2.

precepts for a Christian prince. The principles of rulership that Photius puts forward apparently stem from classical writers such as Isocrates, Dio of Prusa and the encyclopedist Stobaios.[70] Photius enjoins Christian virtues such as frequent prayer, benefactions to the clergy, the building of many churches and encouraging people to attend them: 'through praying together, your nation will achieve greater unity and will obtain common salvation and well-being'.[71] But he also praises the more secular virtues of moderation and clemency. Lawfulness and legitimacy of authority are the two main props of a stable régime, which needs to be in concord with its subjects as well as with God. Boris is warned against 'tyranny' and arbitrary behaviour that results from ignoring the laws: 'those who cannot lead the people wisely easily resort to punishment'.[72]

This letter is erudite, says little explicitly about Bulgaria's particular circumstances, and is in Greek. One might therefore suppose it to have passed over Boris's head, in contrast with the detailed, case-specific letter sent to Boris by Pope Nicholas I.[73] However, the questions which Nicholas is answering bespeak anxiety as to correct forms of worship, seriousness, fear of sin and a sense of duty to impose the new cult on all his people. For example, Boris asked whether he had sinned in putting to death even the offspring of the leaders of the rebellion against his imposition of Christianity.[74] These qualms stem readily enough from the general maxims laid down in Photius's letter to Boris. Moreover piety, honouring virtue and behaving humanely with regard for 'justice' are qualities attributed to Symeon by a variety of sources, while his zeal for building and attending churches has been noted above (p. 349). This is not to claim that Symeon knew of Photius's letter, let alone that he, with his 'seriousness of character', consciously implemented its precepts (see above, p. 346). Symeon had other pathways to recent Byzantine writings, not least while a student in Constantinople in the 870s or earlier 880s; and others besides Photius were now championing book-based learning and philosophy as a means to understanding and serving God. It remains possible that Symeon, apparently a trainee monk while in the capital, met Photius, who was still corresponding with his father.[75] In any case, Photius's contribution to late ninth-century Constantinopolitan Church

[70] Photius, *Epistulae et Amphilochia*, eds B. Laourdas and L. G. Westerink, I (Leipzig, 1983), 1–39; L. Simeonova, *Diplomacy of the Letter and the Cross. Photios, Bulgaria and the Papacy, 860s–880s* (Amsterdam, 1998), 134, 137–41, 149.

[71] Photius, *Epistulae*, I, 22; Simeonova, *Diplomacy*, 127–30.

[72] Photius, *Epistulae*, I, 27; Simeonova, *Diplomacy*, 137–8.

[73] *Epistolae Karolini Aevi IV*, MGH Epistolae 6 (Berlin, 1925), 568–600.

[74] *Epistolae Karolini Aevi IV*, 577; H. Mayr-Harting, *Two Conversions to Christianity. The Bulgarians and the Anglo-Saxons* (Reading, 1994), 16–24; Simeonova, *Diplomacy*, 155, n. 164, 197–218.

[75] Photius, *Epistulae*, II (Leipzig, 1984), 220–21; III (Leipzig, 1985), 113–14; G. Dagron, 'L'Église et l'État (milieu IX–fin X siècle)', in G. Dagron, P. Riché and A. Vauchez (eds), *Histoire du christianisme des origines à nos jours, IV: Évêques, moines et empereurs (610–1054)* (Paris, 1993), 185–6.

life and political culture was immense.[76] Directly or indirectly, his scheme of learning is likely to have made an impression on the khan's young son. In fact Symeon may have been more receptive than Leo himself to the techniques favoured by Photius's circle. Such, at least, might be inferred from Liudprand's singling out of the 'syllogisms of Aristotle' among the subjects that he studied and it fits with the tenor of Symeon's correspondence with the envoy, Leo Choerosphactes: the latter expressly invokes the authority of 'the Stagirite', Aristotle, on a point of grammar.[77]

This brings us to a second fairly unsurprising reason for the resemblance between the political culture of Symeon's and Leo's courts. A spirit of rivalry pulsed between them. This was partly a matter of Symeon's discontent over his virtual satellite status. He seems to have been minded to expect Byzantine agents to perform proskynesis before him when bearing tribute payments, much as his own envoys would have had occasion to do during their frequent attendances at the emperor's court.[78] Symeon's throne-room at Preslav was clearly intended to hold its own against the *basileus*'s and so, seemingly, was the symbolism of buildings such as the 'Golden and New Church'.[79] Competitive wisdom was also in play. Leo exploited a solar eclipse to forecast to the Bulgars its details, minutely and accurately. He thereby showed extraordinary technical knowledge of the movements of the heavens and, by implication, a special relationship with their First Mover. Symeon seems to have brooded on this one-upmanship, for subsequently, while negotiating with Choerosphactes, he sought a prediction as to whether or not he would release his Byzantine prisoners-of-war. Leo VI replied through his envoy that Symeon would now free the prisoners. Symeon seized upon this: 'your emperor, for all his knowledge of the heavens, knows nothing at all about the future!'[80] Other letters evince his interest in logic-chopping and the possible ambiguities of statements.[81] The claims to foreknowledge of Leo, his contemporary, may have whetted Symeon's appetite for learning from books, most of them necessarily in Greek.

Undoubtedly, the current of political and religious culture ran strongly from Byzantium towards Bulgaria, but there was some counter-flow. It was not only in diplomacy and war that Symeon could give the *basileus* something to think about. Symeon's father had, towards the end of his reign, grandiosely refurbished a church in the valley of the Bregalnitsa and translated to it the relics of three of the Fifteen Martyrs of Tiberiopolis. The ceremony was followed by

---

[76] Dagron, 'L'Église', 171–6, 180–86, 203–7; Brubaker, *Vision*, 199–205, 237–43, 412–15.

[77] Kolias, *Choerosphactès*, 80–81; above, p. 346.

[78] Nicholas Mysticus, 40–41; Oikonomides, *Listes de préséance*, 162–9, 180–81, 202–11.

[79] John the Exarch, *Hexaemeron*, ed. Aitzetmüller, VI, 3–6; I. Božilov, 'Preslav et Constantinople: dépendence et indépendence culturelles', *The 17th International Byzantine Congress. Major Papers. (Washington, DC)* (New York, 1986), 435–6; Georgiev, 'Zlatnata ts'rkva', 14–18; Shepard, 'Bulgaria', 572–3.

[80] Kolias, *Choerosphactès*, 78–9.

[81] Ibid., 76–81.

spectacular miracles of healing. Apparently soon after his accession, Symeon saw to the translation of two more martyrs' relics to the church. Further miracles ensued and they were 'everywhere proclaimed'.[82] It may not be fortuitous that the relics of St Lazarus were brought from Cyprus to Constantinople in (probably) 901, being received there with popular acclaim (above, p. 345). Leo's staging of this translation could well have been inspired by the *coups de théâtre* that Symeon and his father had pulled off near the Byzantino-Bulgarian borderland a few years before.

Sharing a common stock of religious culture, charged with political rivalries, may in the main account for resemblances between the courts of Symeon and Leo. But it could well be that they acted and interacted within a wider field of political culture, encompassing Alfred's Wessex as well as the Carolingian ruling houses. Comparable notions of the worth to kings of book-learning and theological understanding may be found in Carolingian courts, pre-eminently – but not exclusively – that of the father of Alfred's stepmother, Charles the Bald. Charles was interested enough in the accurate rendering of statements on theology to ask John Scotus to *re*-translate the writings of Pseudo-Dionysius into Latin while Hincmar of Rheims, whom Charles commissioned to write works on the role of kingship, noted Charles's concern for 'knowledge of every good thing'.[83] He was praised, albeit very rarely, specifically for his library and the Solomon-like wisdom to be gained from it,[84] while many encomia hailed the appreciation for the intellect shown at his court. Heiric claimed that the exercises in the liberal arts carried out there daily entitled it to the name of 'school'.[85] Charles was dealing with a higher élite whose members drew status from their active knowledge of Latin and of laws and other ancient works in Latin. His stance as expert on religious doctrine, imperial lawgiver in the mould of Theodosius,[86] and, in effect, philosopher-king, catered for their expectations while enhancing his own role as, in effect, anointed 'director of studies'. A lettered ruler could partake of divine wisdom and, even, dispense it.[87]

---

[82] *Historia Martyrii XV Martyrum, PG,* 126, cols 213–14; Obolensky, *Six Portraits,* 74–5.

[83] *Epistolae Karolini Aevi VI,* MGH Epistolae 8/1 (Berlin 1939), 53; R. McKitterick, 'Charles the Bald (823–877) and his library: the patronage of learning', *EHR,* 95 (1980), 35–6; *eadem,* 'The palace school of Charles the Bald', in M. T. Gibson and J. L. Nelson (eds), *Charles the Bald. Court and Kingdom* (1990), 326–9, 339; J. Nelson, 'Charles le Chauve et les utilisations du savoir', in *L'école carolingienne d'Auxerre de Murethach à Remi,* eds D. Iogna-Prat, C. Jeudy and G. Lobrichon (Paris, 1991), 39.

[84] *Poetae Latini aevi Carolini III,* ed. L. Traube, MGH Poetae 3 (Berlin, 1886), 243–4, 247–8; McKitterick, 'Charles', 28.

[85] *Poetae Latini aevi Carolini III,* 429; McKitterick, 'Palace school', 326; Nelson, 'Charles le Chauve', 39.

[86] J. L. Nelson, 'Translating images of authority: The Christian Roman Emperors in the Carolingian World', repr. in Nelson's *The Frankish World 750–900* (1996), 89–98.

[87] Nelson, 'Charles le Chauve', 44–7; *eadem, Charles the Bald* (1992), 168–9.

The conceits, images and ideas upon which Frankish rulers such as Charles drew were transferable, and also labile. Thus the figure of David, while a promising model of upward mobility, especially for Charles as a younger son, could also personify the humility due from the king before God's laws.[88] Like the cult of wisdom itself, such Old Testament models were grist to the internal tensions and political 'discourse' of ninth-century Francia. Far away in Constantinople Basil I had reasons of his own for fostering analogies between himself and David and parading his offspring's book-learning (above, pp. 341–2). At the same time it is quite likely that pre-eminent and would-be pre-eminent Christian rulers were aware of the style and ambiance of distant counterparts' régimes. Conscious emulation and alertness to telling imagery were in play and there are indications of 'competitive wisdom'. Heiric pictures an envious 'Greece' mourning for her philosophers who, 'enticed by learning', have abandoned her for Charles the Bald's hospitality.[89] Furthermore, 'worm-holes' could open up abruptly upon the arrival at courts of embassies replete with gifts and scholars, or simply of reports relaying ideas, images or symbols that could be put to new uses in diverse contexts.[90] The vitality and generating power of such circuits was not conditioned by the frequency or level of the contacts.[91] Thus exchanges of embassies between Charles the Bald and Byzantium are not recorded,[92] but one of Charles's means of displaying imperial status before diverse churchmen and other onlookers on the last day of the synod of Ponthion in 876 was to appear 'garbed and crowned in the Greek style', an unmistakably imperial form of costume apparently concocted by Louis the Pious.[93] Out of the public gaze, Charles commissioned and had personal use of a small prayerbook that is said to share many traits with a Byzantine lectionary made for Basil I, each being written entirely in golden script. An illumination occupying two folios of Charles's prayerbook shows him crowned, kneeling in a form of proskynesis before Christ on the Cross: images of rulers simultaneously majestic and in service had resonance on the Bosporos.[94]

---

[88] R. Deshman, 'The exalted servant: the ruler theology of the prayerbook of Charles the Bald', *Viator*, 11 (1980), 404–13; Nelson, *Charles the Bald*, 15, 85; H. L. Kessler, 'A lay abbot as patron: Count Vivian and the first Bible of Charles the Bald', *Settimane di Studio del Centro Italiano di Studi sull'Alto Medioevo*, 39 (1992), 661–73.

[89] *Poetae Latini aevi Carolini III*, 429.

[90] M. McCormick, 'Diplomacy and the Carolingian encounter with Byzantium down to the accession of Charles the Bald', in B. McGinn and W. Otten (eds), *Eriugena: East and West* (Notre Dame, 1994), 28–30; D. Nerlich, *Diplomatische Gesandtschaften zwischen Ost- und Westkaisern 756–1002* (Bern, 1999), 116–19.

[91] M. McCormick, 'Byzantium and the early medieval west: problems and opportunities', in G. Arnaldi and G. Cavallo (eds), *Europa Medievale e Mondo Bizantino. Contatti effettivi e possibilità di studi comparati*, Nuovi studi storici 40 (Rome, 1997), 2–3, 8–10.

[92] Nerlich, *Gesandtschaften*, 48.

[93] *AB*, 205; Deshman, 'Prayerbook', 395.

[94] Deshman, 'Prayerbook', 385–90, 394–9, and fig. 1; W. Koehler and F. Mütherich, *Die karolingischen Miniaturen, V, Die Hofschule Karls des Kahlen* (Berlin, 1982), 10, 38–9, 75–7, 80,

The portrayal of Charles performing proskynesis probably marks a current flowing westwards from Byzantium, but it would be more apt to conceive of a pool of political culture, at once wide and deep, whose ripples and undercurrents swirled in many directions. There are hints that various concepts and techniques passed from west to east during the ninth century at one level or another, prompting emulation, adaptations or reactions. It has plausibly been suggested that Photius drew on the papacy's stance for his formulation of the interrelationship between emperor and patriarch in the *Eisagoge*, a law manual compiled around 880. His ambition to expand the Constantinopolitan patriarch's scope at the emperor's expense may well have gained sustenance from papal claims to overarching hegemony.[95] Such claims were all too familiar from Photius's disputes with successive popes, though Roman bishops and other senior officials were routine enough visitors to Constantinople for their places at imperial banquets to be provided for.[96] It has also been suggested that Pope Nicholas I's excoriation of Byzantines' judicial procedures and ridicule of their ignorance of Latin may have jolted the establishment into clarifying Byzantine Greek texts of Roman law, eventually producing manuals and a new codification.[97] This and similar broadsides discharging formidable historical and theological scholarship against Byzantine assumptions of world order[98] could have spurred on the study of more general knowledge and effective argumentation in imperial circles.

At a technological level, know-how seems to have been imported from the Carolingian west, notably the manufacture of *cloisonné* enamels. This intricate technique was costly and in the east it is likely to have first found admirers and adapters at the imperial court.[99] An early example of Byzantine-made enamel work is a votive crown of Leo VI: one of its medallions shows Leo sporting *loros* and crown.[100] One should not, however, ascribe all such borrowings and adaptations to 'official' exchanges between eastern and western rulers. There were also networks of foreign notables and grandees and their sons whom the eastern emperors made a point of welcoming to court, maintaining some there indefi-

---

82, Tafeln V,1; J. Wollasch, 'Kaiser und Könige als Brüder der Mönche', *Deutsches Archiv*, 40 (1984), 15–16.

[95] Dagron, *Empereur*, 236–41.

[96] Philotheus, *Kleterologion*, 136–7, 160–63.

[97] M. T. Fögen, 'Reanimation of Roman Law in the ninth century: remarks on reasons and results', in L. Brubaker (ed.), *Byzantium in the Ninth Century: Dead or Alive?* (1998), 11–22.

[98] For example, Louis II's letter to Basil I, probably drafted by Anastasius Bibliothecarius: MGH Epp. VII (Berlin, 1928), 386–94.

[99] D. Buckton, 'Byzantine enamel and the West', in *Byzantium and the West*, ed. J. Howard-Johnston (Amsterdam, 1988), 235–44; McCormick, 'Byzantium and the early medieval west', 4–5, 10–11.

[100] D. Buckton, '"Chinese whispers": the premature birth of the typical Byzantine enamel', in C. Moss and K. Kiefer (eds), *Byzantine East, Latin West. Art-Historical Studies in Honor of Kurt Weitzmann* (Princeton, 1995), 591–2 and fig. 1.

nitely.[101] Attendance fostered an appetite for the banquets, greed for the arte-facts and an awareness of ultimate Christian majesty. Franks figured among the stipendiary 'men of the emperor' to be invited to a Christmas banquet and judging by their specified fellow-guests – Khazars, Muslims and Central Asian Turks – they were deemed to belong to powers of substance.[102] Through indi-viduals such as these, as well as the more formal medium of embassies, the Byzantine establishment had word of the images and preoccupations in vogue among the more forward Frankish élites, the other new 'Davids' and 'Solomons'. Such toings and froings and the gift-giving and comparisons accompanying them served to generate a kind of magnetic field in which bodies of disparate mass and composition interacted with one another. In that sense, the cult and the pursuit of wisdom proclaimed assiduously and more or less simultaneously by Alfred, Symeon and Leo were not sheer coincidence. They all belonged, as members active and passive, to a wider field whose most vigorous impulses probably emanated from the Carolingian courts, above all Charles the Bald's.[103]

One vignette may illustrate the workings of this field, suggesting that they were activated by a miscellany of individual initiatives and exchanges, besides grand embassies and ideological confrontations. King Alfred is said to have re-sponded to a request for alms from the patriarch of Jerusalem.[104] He seems to have sent with his alms a number of enquiries and some, at least, of Patriarch Elias's answers survive in a tenth-century 'leechbook'. This work devotes a section to ailments for which petroleum and 'the white stone' were prescribed, concluding it with the statement: 'All this *Dominus* Helias, patriarch at Jerusalem ordered one to say to King Alfred'.[105] Alfred's questions on the subject presumably stemmed from a mixture of intellectual curiosity and practical needs to do with his own physical infirmities: one of Elias's recommendations was that 'petroleum is good to drink simple for inward tenderness'.[106] At the same time, possession of this recondite yet useful information and evident willingness to disseminate it did no harm to Alfred's reputation as the learned instructor of his people. Such a reputa-tion was being burnished in Alfred's lifetime by Asser, who himself saw fit to mention the 'letters and gifts sent to him by the patriarch Elias'.[107] The route of

---

[101] J. Shepard, 'Byzantine diplomacy, A.D. 800–1204: means and ends', in J. Shepard and S. Franklin (eds), *Byzantine Diplomacy* (1992), 59–64.

[102] Philotheus, *Kleterologion*, 176–7.

[103] Alfred's responsiveness to Charles's example was noted by Nelson, 'Charles le Chauve', 42–3.

[104] *ASC, s.a.* 883, trans. Whitelock, 50; J. Harris, 'Wars and rumours of wars: England and the Byzantine world in the eighth and ninth centuries', *Mediterranean Historical Review*, 14 (1999), 38–9.

[105] *Leechdoms, Wortcunning and Starcraft of Early England. A Collection of Documents*, ed. O. T. Cockayne, II (1865), 288–9; Harris, 'Wars', 39–40.

[106] *Leechdoms*, ed. Cockayne, II, 288–9.

[107] Asser, 77; Harris, 'Wars', 37. On Asser and Alfred's reputation see the contributions of S. Keynes, M. Lapidge and D. Howlett to this volume (Chapters 10, 2 and 3).

Alfred's emissaries in the earlier 880s could well have run from Rome through Byzantine territories and the possibility that they visited the emperor's palace in Constantinople cannot be excluded. At any rate journeys to Jerusalem such as that of Sigehelm and Athelstan may help to show how the cult of wisdom became widespread and so well tended, a recognized attribute of Christian rulership. It would be vain to seek a single source for the phenomenon. The dynamics bespeak rather a kind of mutual incitement – part consensual, part competitive – that pulsed between courts from Byzantium to the downs of Wessex.

ALFRED AS ICON

Chapter 21

Alfredism: the use and abuse of King Alfred's reputation in later centuries

Barbara Yorke

The 1100th anniversary of the death of King Alfred is also an appropriate occasion on which to commemorate the centenary of the international millenary celebrations which culminated in the unveiling in Winchester of Hamo Thornycroft's massive statue of the king which has become an essential part of the iconography of Alfred. Due to uncertainty about the exact date of Alfred's death, the millenary was celebrated in 1901 instead of 1899.[1] The proceedings included a 'Meeting of Learned Societies' from all over the English-speaking world which was held in Winchester on 18–19 September and the delegates took part in the procession which preceded the unveiling of the statue on 20 September (Fig. 41).[2] The delegates included such notables as the Rev. Charles Plummer and Professor Napier, who represented the University of Oxford, but neither of them was able to contribute anything of their expertise. The delegates were there for their symbolic value rather than for a display of learning. It is one of the aims of this paper to explain why the 'Meeting', and other factors surrounding the celebration of Alfred in 1901, were so different from the more muted, academic commemorations of 1999 that have resulted in this volume. It will not be possible within the space available to review at length the scholarly, and not so scholarly, retrieval of Alfred's life and reputation, and it is unnecessary to do so as they have been covered in exemplary detail in a paper by Simon Keynes.[3] But it is necessary to outline briefly some of the main developments, looking particularly at the reasons why Alfred was taken up at different periods in the past, before concentrating on his apogee in the nineteenth century. In recent years the study of Anglo-Saxonism, a branch of Medievalism of which Alfredism may be said to be a twig,[4] has become

---

[1] W. H. Stevenson, 'The date of King Alfred's death', *EHR*, 13 (1898), 71–7 established the correct date, but it was not accepted by everyone immediately; see B. A. E. Yorke, *The Millenary Celebrations of King Alfred in Winchester, 1901*, Hampshire Papers, 17 (1999), 3.

[2] For a list of delegates and details of the proceedings, see A. Bowker, *The King Alfred Millenary. A Record of the Proceedings of the National Commemoration* (1902), 47–9.

[3] S. Keynes, 'The cult of King Alfred the Great', *ASE*, 28 (1999), 225–356; I am very grateful to Professor Keynes for providing me with texts of his article in advance of publication and for discussing topics of mutual interest.

[4] The credit for the formulation 'Alfredism' goes to John McGavin of the English Department at the University of Southampton.

a serious study in its own right,[5] and as Alan Frantzen has reminded us, 'the reception of an early culture by a late one is not only a study of scholarly discovery but also a study of self-discovery and the invention of self-image'.[6]

Alfred and Asser between them constructed a carefully composed portrait of ideal kingship which was to result in Alfred being seen, in the words of Edward Freeman, as the 'most perfect character in history',[7] but only after a gap of many centuries. Alfred's military and political successes were matched, if not surpassed, by his immediate successors, and, although Æthelweard gave him an enthusiastic notice,[8] Alfred did not tower over succeeding kings in the way his role model Charlemagne did among the Franks. It was Alfred's son Edward whose name was favoured by subsequent rulers, and after the murder of Alfred, son of Æthelred Unraed in 1036, there were no more Prince Alfreds until George III resurrected the name for his ninth and youngest son in 1780 (d. 1782). Alfred attracted little interest at the courts of his post-conquest successors. Although Asser's Alfred may have been conceived as something of a secular saint,[9] King Alfred was never culted and so not available for the post of saintly Anglo-Saxon royal supporter, in spite of the attempts by King Henry VI to have him recognized in Rome.[10] It was Edmund of the East Angles and Edward the Confessor, the preferred royal saints, whose names were given to members of the later royal houses.[11] Nor were Alfred's exploits against the Vikings sufficiently impressive to allow him to become the military hero of the new régimes. After the successful advocacy of Geoffrey of Monmouth, that post went to King Arthur, and successive dynasties were reluctant to abandon this glamorous ancestor for the good, but inescapably duller, Saxon king.

Although unable to attract patrons at the highest level, Alfred, of course, had enthusiastic advocates among churchmen and scholars. Before 1066 Alfred had appeared in legends associated with St Cuthbert[12] and St Neot,[13] famously

---

[5] See, in particular, C. T. Berkhout and M. McGatch (eds), *Anglo-Saxon Scholarship: The First Three Centuries* (Boston, 1982); C. A. Simmons, *Reversing the Conquest. History and Myth in Nineteenth-Century British Literature* (New Brunswick, 1990); A. J. Frantzen, *Desire for Origins. New Language, Old English, and Teaching the Tradition* (New York, 1990); A. J. Frantzen and J. D. Niles (eds), *Anglo-Saxonism and the Construction of Social Identity* (Florida, 1997).

[6] Frantzen, *Desire for Origins*, 124.

[7] E. A. Freeman, *The History of the Norman Conquest of England* (6 vols, 1867–79), I, 51–5.

[8] Æthelweard, 50.

[9] J. L. Nelson, 'Monks, secular men and masculinity, c. 900', in *Masculinity in Medieval Europe*, ed. D. M. Hadley (1999), 121–42.

[10] R. A. Griffiths, *The Reign of King Henry VI* (1981), 242.

[11] For instance, Edmund and Edward appear as the saintly supporters of Richard II on the Wilton Diptych; D. Gordon, *Making and Meaning. The Wilton Diptych* (1993), 53–5.

[12] L. Simpson, 'The King Alfred/St Cuthbert episode in the *Historia de Sancto Cuthberto*: its significance for mid-tenth century English history', in *St Cuthbert, His Cult and His Community to AD 1200*, eds G. Bonner, D. W. Rollason and C. Stancliffe (1989), 397–411.

[13] Keynes and Lapidge, *Alfred*, 197–202; T. Johnson-South, 'Competition for King Alfred's aura in the last century of Anglo-Saxon England', *Albion*, 23 (1991), 613–26.

burning the cakes for the first time in legends associated with the latter. Anglo-Norman chroniclers appreciated the greater documentation surviving for Alfred's reign, and added details that were to be important for his later reputation.[14] William of Malmesbury supplied the story of Alfred disguising himself as a minstrel in order to visit Guthrum's camp, and also credited him with the institution of hundreds and tithings.[15] Gaimar believed him to be the originator of the *Anglo-Saxon Chronicle* and saw his reign as the turning-point in the history of a united England.[16] Post-conquest compilations of Anglo-Saxon law made sure that knowledge of Alfred's lawmaking was not forgotten.[17] But it was Alfred's interest in education that provides the first major example of his reputation being hijacked to support a later cause when he was chosen as the founder of University College and the University of Oxford – though that soon became 'refounder' when, in order to counter upstart claims that Bede's reference to Grantchester proved the greater antiquity of Cambridge, Alfred was said to have relocated a much earlier foundation of ancient philosophers at 'Greeklade' (Cricklade).[18]

Alfred attracted more patronage at the Reformation, when as a ruler with an interest in religion and the promotion of English, and free of the stigma of being an idolatrous saint, his reign became part of the evidence for a pre-lapsarian, pre-Conquest English Church, apparently free of the yoke of Rome and with some other remarkable similarities to Elizabethan Protestantism.[19] Asser's *Life of Alfred* became more readily available thanks to an edition (with added cakes) sponsored by Archbishop Parker. But probably more important for spreading Alfred's reputation was his favourable presentation in what is popularly known as *Foxe's Book of Martyrs*.[20] The Protestant promotion of Alfred consisted not so much of adding to what was known about him as in taking certain things away. Alfred's cultivation of links with Rome was not emphasized, and many miraculous accretions were edited out of his sojourn at Athelney. But Alfred still did not attract support in the highest circles. The Tudors were reluctant to abandon Arthur, in spite of the newly raised doubts about the

---

[14] Keynes, 'Cult of Alfred', 229–35.

[15] *William of Malmesbury: Gesta Regum Anglorum I*, eds R. A. B. Mynors, R. M. Thomson and M. Winterbottom (1998), 182–4; 188–90.

[16] J. Gillingham, 'Gaimar, the Prose *Brut* and the making of English History', in *L'Histoire et Les Nouveaux Publics Dans l'Europe Médiévale (XIII–XV Siècles)*, ed. J.-P. Genet (Paris, 1997), 167–76.

[17] P. Wormald, *The Making of English Law: King Alfred to the Twelfth Century, I: Legislation and its Limits* (1999), 163–263.

[18] J. Parker, *The Early History of Oxford 727–1100*, Oxford Historical Society 3 (1885), 24–62.

[19] E. Adams, *Old English Scholarship in England from 1566–1800*, Yale Studies in English 55 (New Haven, 1917), 16–36; R. Page, 'The sixteenth-century reception of Alfred the Great's letter to his bishops', *Anglia,* 110 (1992), 36–64.

[20] The first edition, J. Foxe, *Acts and Monuments of these Latter and Perilous Days* (1560) was subsequently expanded; see D. Loades (ed.), *John Foxe and the English Reformation* (1997).

authenticity of legends surrounding him,[21] and attempts to interest the Stuarts came to nothing. Robert Powell's attempt to draw parallels between the life and character of Alfred and that of Charles I did rather strain credulity, particularly when he urged the latter to imitate the Saxon king in being governed by the country's laws.[22] The trouble was that the Anglo-Saxons generally were keeping rather louche company at this time as ancient Germanic freedoms, apparently including representation for all freemen in a Saxon parliament, were being avidly cited by opponents of the monarchy.[23] Alfred was not greatly implicated in such claims, but his law-code was one of the sources ransacked for evidence; even before the end of the Middle Ages Alfred had been celebrated as the hanger of corrupt judges,[24] and in the seventeenth century he was believed to have established trial by jury.[25]

The prospect of Alfred acquiring influential patrons improved with the advent of the Hanoverians, who could be claimed to be of Saxon stock, though the propagandic potential was not realized immediately in this period, when few people were aware that English was a Germanic language, or recognized the distinction between British and Anglo-Saxon origins, in spite of the work of scholars like Richard Verstegan.[26] The opportunity for acquiring more detailed knowledge of the king was provided by the publication of John Spelman's 'Life of King Alfred' which had been unpublished at the time of his death in 1643, in the royalist camp at Oxford, but was published in Latin by Obadiah Walker in 1678, and in English by Thomas Hearne in 1709.[27] Spelman's promotion of Alfred as 'the First Founder of the English Monarchy' was taken up in the influential *Histoire d'Angleterre* of Paul de Rapin-Thoyras, which was published in English translation in parts between 1726 and 1731, and as a two-folio volume in 1732–33.[28] Rapin's work was therefore topical when the circle which grew up around Frederick, Prince of Wales, in the 1730s and 1740s was looking to place itself in historical perspective. Frederick was in opposition to his father, George II, and the Whigs and disaffected Tories who rallied round him were united by opposition to

---

[21] M. McKisack, *Medieval History in the Tudor Age* (1971).

[22] R. Powell, *The Life of Alfred or Alured* (1634); reissued, with introduction by Francis Wilson (1996); for other relevant sources see Keynes, 'Cult of Alfred', 246–60.

[23] C. Hill, 'The Norman Yoke', in *idem, Puritanism and Revolution. Studies in Interpretation of the English Revolution in the Seventeenth Century* (1958), 50–122.

[24] *The Mirror of Justices*, ed. W. J. Whittacker, Selden Society, 7 (1895), 166–71; Hill, 'Norman Yoke', 58–9.

[25] Wormald, *Making of English Law*, 4–9.

[26] R. Verstegan, *A Restitution of Decayed Intelligence: In Antiquities Concerning the Most Noble and Renowned English Nation* (Antwerp, 1605) – the work was dedicated to James I; S. Piggott, *Ruins in a Landscape. Essays in Antiquarianism* (1976), 55–76; S. Glass, 'The Saxonists' influence on seventeenth-century literature', in *Anglo-Saxon Scholarship*, eds Berkhout and McGatch, 91–105.

[27] Keynes, 'Cult of Alfred', 254–6, 263–9.

[28] P. de Rapin Thoyras, *The History of England* (2nd edn, 2 vols, 1732–3); for details of editions see Keynes, 'Cult of Alfred', 272–4.

the prime minister, Robert Walpole.[29] They called themselves 'the Patriots'; men who protected the good of the country by defending parliamentary freedoms, which were, of course, of Saxon or 'Gothic' origin,[30] and by opposing what they saw as the corruption of Walpole's régime and his bungling of the war with Spain through failure to support the navy adequately. Alfred emerged as the earliest ruler who could be evoked – for protecting basic Anglo-Saxon freedoms, for success-fully defeating a foreign enemy and for founding the navy – as 'a patriot king',[31] and Frederick was the 'patriot prince', his natural successor. The idea was given visual form in the pleasure grounds at Stowe (Buckinghamshire), the home of Lord Cobham, one of the leaders of the patriot opposition.[32] In the 'Temple of British Worthies', completed in 1734–35 by William Kent, the bust of Alfred (Fig. 39) was placed next to the bust of an earlier prince of Wales, the Black Prince, whose excellent qualities had been inherited, of course, by Frederick, who when he became king would take Alfred as his role model rather than his own despicable father. Many poems and other works dedicated to Prince Frederick took up an Alfredian theme as well. Among the most notable was Thomas Arne's masque *Alfred*, which was first performed in 1740 before Prince Frederick at Cliveden.[33] The main text was provided by James Thomson and David Mallett, two writers who had already enjoyed the prince's patronage, but also featured an ode by Bolingbroke, another of the leaders of the patriot opposition who had defined their political philosophy in *The Idea of a Patriot King* (1738). The masque is chiefly remembered today for its concluding anthem *Rule Britannia*, which emphasized Alfred's role in preserving the country's basic freedoms ('Britons never shall be slaves') through his naval victories ('Britannia rules the waves'). Decidedly less notable was Sir Richard Blackmore's *Alfred: an Epick Poem in Twelve Books* (1723), dedicated to the Prince of Wales, which enlivened the accepted accounts of Alfred's reign with descriptions of his hitherto unrecorded extensive travels and adventures in Europe and Africa.[34]

'Poor Fred' died in 1751,[35] leaving his son George to eventually inherit the throne and many of the 'patriotic' attributes which had surrounded his

---

[29] C. Gerrard, *The Patriot Opposition to Walpole. Politics, Poetry and National Myth 1725–1742* (1994).

[30] S. Kliger, *The Goths in England. A Study in Seventeenth and Eighteenth Century Thought* (Cambridge, MA, 1952).

[31] The term was often applied to him after this time; see, for instance, A. Bicknell, *The Patriot King: or Alfred and Elvida, An Historical Tragedy* (1788).

[32] G. B. Clarke (ed.), *Descriptions of Lord Cobham's Garden at Stowe (1700–1750)*, Buck-inghamshire Record Society, 26 (1990); J. M. Robinson, *Temples of Delight. Stowe Landscape Gardens* (1990); The National Trust, *Stowe Landscape Gardens* (1997).

[33] *Alfred. A Masque Written by David Mallett and James Thomson. Set to Music by Thomas Augustine Arne*, ed. A. Scott, Musica Britannica, 47 (1981) – several different versions exist. A CD with extracts was issued by *BBC Music Magazine* June 1997, with discussion 7–10.

[34] L. W. Miles, *King Alfred in Literature* (Baltimore, 1902), 52–7.

[35] Anonymous epitaph: 'Here lies Poor Fred, who was alive and is dead'.

Fig. 39   Bust of King Alfred from The Temple of British Worthies, Stowe
Landscape Gardens (photo: author)

father, except that, particularly in the face of the wars with France, they became associated with a new loyalty and affection for the Crown, so that 'patriotism' came to take on the meaning with which we are familiar today.[36] Alfred was part of that patriotic, throne-supporting package. In this new context King Alfred plays and musical entertainments flourished well into the nineteenth century.[37] Some well-known performers were attracted to the character of Alfred, and he was played by Garrick and Macready. There was even an Alfred ballet, featuring the clown Grimaldi, and a politically incorrect pantomime of 1850, 'Harlequin Alfred the Great, or the Magic Banjo and the Mystic Raven', where Alfred and two associates arrived at the Danish camp as 'Ethiopian serenaders', with black masks and 'woolly skull caps'; Alfred played his magic banjo (a skit on the magic banner which featured in other plays) and the other two were on concertina and bones.[38] But many of the plays were extremely unsuccessful, and some were not even performed, for Alfred's reign, as presented in the survivng sources, was rather devoid of dramatic incident and not even the addition of star-crossed lovers,[39] or gruesome pagan ceremonies in the Viking camp, could solve the problem.

Alfred also attracted much celebration in verse, perhaps more than any other English historical character, but nearly all of it was dire and well down to the standards set by Richard Blackmore. First-rate writers such as Milton considered the topic of Alfred only to reject it,[40] whereas less-skilled artisans, like Henry Pye, one of the less well-known poets laureate,[41] and Joseph Cottle, who aspired to write in the style of his friends Southey and Coleridge, but unfortunately without their skills,[42] were attracted like moths to the proverbial flame. Alfred was also the subject of an early novel of sentiment by Anne Fuller,[43] loyally dedicated to the future George IV.

The growing literary and historical interest in Alfred,[44] from the latter part of the eighteenth century, was matched by his celebration in the new genre of history painting, in which scenes from the country's own history were now deemed worthy of being placed alongside moral exemplars from the Bible and

---

[36] L. Colley, 'The apotheosis of George III', *Past and Present*, 102 (1984), 94–129; *idem*, *Britons. Forging the Nation 1707–1837* (1992).

[37] See *passim* Miles, *Alfred in Literature*; E. G. Stanley, 'The glorification of Alfred, king of Wessex', *Poetica*, 12 (1981), 103–33; Simmons, *Reversing the Conquest*, 25–41.

[38] Miles, *Alfred in Literature*, 85–6.

[39] For instance, the two pairs of lovers – Corin and Emma, and Edith and Damon – that helped flesh out Thomas Arne's masque.

[40] Glass, 'The Saxonists', 95–6.

[41] Henry James Pye, *Alfred. An Epic Poem in Six Books* (1801).

[42] Joseph Cottle, *Alfred. An Epic Poem in Twenty-Four Books* (1801).

[43] A. Fuller, *The Son of Ethelwolf: An Historical Tale* (1789); Stanley, 'Glorification of Alfred', 120–24.

[44] Important historical studies include David Hume, *History of England* (1762) and Sharon Turner, *History of the Anglo-Saxons* (4 vols, 1799–1805).

classical past.[45] The increasing availability of prints and illustrated histories would have made a pictorial image of Alfred available to a greater number of people. Alfredian topics were depicted by the main practitioners, such as David Wilkie, Francis Wheatley and Benjamin West, with 'Alfred in the neatherd's cottage' proving a particular favourite, followed by Alfred's role in founding the English constitution which eventually ensured him a prominent place in the decorations for the new Houses of Parliament in the 1840s.[46] Alfred was not only in the theatre and on the walls; he was in the landscape. Knowledge of Lord Cobham's pleasure grounds at Stowe was widely disseminated in polite society through the printed accounts, including several poetic effusions, of those who had visited them.[47] The idea of placing historic heroes in an idealized landscape was taken up by others, and an Alfredian theme was particularly likely to be favoured in areas where there was an actual association with the king. Lord Bathhurst may initially have been influenced by the patriot cause in renaming his gothick 'King Arthur's Castle' in Oakley Wood in his park near Cirencester as 'Alfred's Hall', but he also believed that it was on the site of Iley Wood, where Alfred had stayed on the eve of the battle of Edington.[48] A rather more ambitious monument was the 160-foot, triangular King Alfred's Tower on Kingsettle Hill on the Stourhead estate, which Henry Flitcroft designed for Henry Hoare, and on which work was completed in 1772. The tower stands in the middle of Selwood, where three shires meet, and was believed to be the site of Ecgbert's stone where, as its inscription records, Alfred, 'the founder of the English monarchy and liberty', met his troops before Edington.[49] But the location of Alfred in the real landscape did not just involve the raising of commemorative monuments; he also came to be associated with existing antiquities. In 1738 Francis Wise, probably best known in academic circles for his edition of Asser's *Life of Alfred*, published in 1722,[50] hoped to improve his prospects of being appointed first librarian of the Radcliffe in Oxford by publishing, as a pamphlet, *A Letter to Dr Mead Concerning Some Antiquities in Berkshire*. In it he argued that the White Horse of Uffington had been carved on the orders of Alfred to

---

[45] R. Strong, *And When Did You Last see Your Father? The Victorian Painter and British History* (1978); Keynes, 'Cult of Alfred', 290–319.

[46] T. S. R. Boase, 'The decoration of the new palace of Westminster, 1841–1863', *Journal of the Warburg and Courtauld Institute*, 17 (1954), 319–58; Strong, *And When Did You Last See Your Father?*, 114–18.

[47] Clarke (ed.), *Lord Cobham's Garden at Stowe*.

[48] J. Lees-Milne, *Earls of Creation. Five Great Patrons of Eighteenth-Century Art* (1986), 23–8; Keynes, 'Cult of Alfred', 279–80.

[49] K. Woodbridge, *Landscape and Antiquity: Aspects of English Culture at Stourhead 1718 to 1838* (1970), 51–70; J. Darke, *A Monument Guide to England and Wales. A National Portrait in Bronze and Stone* (1991), 85.

[50] S. Gibson, 'Francis Wise, B.D.', *Oxoniensia*, 1 (1936), 173–95; S. Piggott, 'Antiquarian studies', in *The History of the University of Oxford, V: The Eighteenth Century*, eds L. S. Sutherland and L. G. Mitchell (1986), 757–78, at 765–68.

commemorate the battle of Ashdown with which a number of other nearby archaeological sites could also be linked. Dr Mead was an antiquary with associations with the patriot group around Prince Frederick,[51] and Wise no doubt hoped to win some influential friends through him. The White Horse was interpreted as Alfred's banner, and parallels were drawn with the white horse on the arms of the House of Brunswick. What Wise got by way of a reply was a ferocious, anonymous attack, now thought to have been written by William Asplin, a rival for the post and vicar of Banbury, in which Wise's references to an earlier legend linking the White Horse with St George were interpreted as covert support for Bonnie Prince Charlie, the chevalier de St George.[52] More to the point, Asplin pointed out that the best artistic parallels for the White Horse came from Iron Age coinage.[53] There seems to have been no tradition of Alfred being linked with the White Horse monuments before Wise's reconstruction, but such is the power of the written word that within a few years aged inhabitants were passing information on to passing antiquarians as if it were hallowed oral tradition, and further monuments in the general vicinity also came to be associated with King Alfred, such as the Blowing Stone, a sarsen deposited as a glacial erratic, with which he is said to have summoned his troops.[54] Wise's work was to inspire some of the main Alfredian celebrations of the nineteenth century when it was areas with 'a sense of place', that is with some tangible link with actual events in his reign, that embraced his cause the most enthusiastically.[55]

One of these events was the celebration in Wantage of the thousandth anniversary of Alfred's birth in 1849, but the lack of influential support for the occasion reveals that Alfred, in spite of being sufficiently advanced in the national consciousness to be the butt of pantomime jokes, still had some way to go before becoming a national icon. The idea of celebrating the millenary of Alfred's birth was promoted by the brothers J. L. and C. Brereton, proprietors of

---

[51] Gerrard, *Patriot Opposition*, 54–6.

[52] *The Impertinence and Imposture of Modern Antiquaries Displayed, or a refutation of the Rev. Mr Wise's letter to Dr Mead concerning the White Horse and other Antiquities in Berkshire* (1739). In response came a pamphlet by Richard North, *An Answer to a Scandalous Libel* (1741) and from Francis Wise, *Further Observations upon the White Horse and other Antiquities* (1742).

[53] The most recent work by scientific sampling suggests that the White Horse may have been cut in the late Bronze Age, that is *c.* 1400–1600 BC; D. Miles and S. Palmer, 'White Horse Hill', *Current Archaeology*, 142 (1995), 372–8.

[54] L. V. Grinsell, *White Horse Hill* (1939); D. Woolner, 'New light on the White Horse', *Folklore*, 78 (1967), 90–111.

[55] In addition to events at Wantage and Winchester to be discussed below, one should also note the Athelney/Wedmore area of Somerset as an area where Alfred was particularly remembered. Representatives from this area were prominent at the Wantage events commemorating Alfred's birth in 1849, organized a major celebration for the aniversary of the treaty of Wedmore in 1878 and had their own celebrations for the millenary of his death in 1901. See 'An account of the celebration of the thousandth anniversary of the Peace of Wedmore signed by Alfred and Guthrum in 878', *Wells Journal*, 15 (1878), 2–22, and 'Alfred the Great's millenary. Visit to Alfred's country', *Somerset Archaeology and Natural History Society*, 47 (1901), 67–81.

a short-lived journal called *The Anglo-Saxon*, and one of their most prolific and
enthusiastic contributors, Martin Tupper,[56] the author of a very successful, but
now completely forgotten, poetical collection called *Proverbial Philosophy* (1838).
Several national newspapers took up the call, and Tupper wrote letters to everyone of importance from the royal house downwards,[57] but in Tupper's own
inimitable words:

> Forth flew our burning words, – and *burnt* they got!
> With one consent the Great responded not.[58]

The mayor of London refused to allow the Guildhall to be used for a banquet, on
the grounds of cholera in the city, but planning went ahead for celebrations in
Wantage on 25 October.[59] A few of the local gentry were persuaded to support
the event, including John Hughes, the father of Thomas Hughes, and the Rev.
Giles, vicar of Bampton, whose edition of the *Complete Works of King Alfred the
Great* was one of the results of the celebration.[60] Between 8000 and 10,000
people were attracted for parades, speeches, the traditional ox-roast and games,
but among those 'of the better sort' who attended there were complaints about
lack of historical content, abysmal planning and no guidance on such key points
as whether the ladies should remove their bonnets to dine.[61]

The failure of the Wantage millenary and of the Breretons' periodical to
attract support from the establishment or the educated classes is all the more
surprising because many of the things they stood for had become common
currency fifty years later, when the millenary of Alfred's death was celebrated in
Winchester. Tupper's plans were in advance of their time, for the celebrations of
Alfred's birth were the first commemoration of this type for a dead ruler or
political figure in England; earlier 'jubilees' had been for men of the arts,
Shakespeare (1769) and Handel (1784), and a living king (George III) (1809).
One of the things which changed between 1849 and 1901 was increasing enthusiasm for marking the anniversaries of 'Great Men', a movement which had
begun in France following the French Revolution and was enthusiastically taken
up in Germany as well.[62] However, the basic stability and continuity of the
English constitution made it unnecessary for a cult of Alfred to be promoted by

---

[56] D. Hudson, *Martin Tupper: His Rise and Fall* (1949).

[57] Preserved in his scrapbook at Research and Reference Center, University Library of
Illinois at Urbana-Champaign, x828/T8391, Album 14; see Keynes, 'Cult of Alfred', 343, n. 571.

[58] 'The Alfred Jubilee', *The Anglo-Saxon* 1, part 4 (1849), 5–20, at 16.

[59] Tupper asserted that Alfred had been born at about the same time of year that he had died.

[60] *The Jubilee Edition of the Complete Works of King Alfred the Great*, ed. J. A. Giles, 2 vols
(1851). Giles's enthusiasm for the Wantage celebrations is partly to be explained by the publication
of his *Life and Times of Alfred the Great* (1848).

[61] For accounts see *The Anglo-Saxon* (n. 58); *Reading Mercury*, 27 October 1849; 'Specta-
tor', *The Alfred Jubilee Commemorated at Wantage, Berks, Thursday October 25 1849. In Two
Parts: Part I, As It Was, Part II, As It Ought to Have Been* (1849).

[62] R. Quinault, 'The cult of the centenary, 1789–1914', *Historical Research*, 71 (1998), 303–23.

English political leaders in the mid-nineteenth century in the way that Vercingetorix was in France or Arminius in Germany.[63] Victoria and Albert may have had themselves depicted as Anglo-Saxons by William Theed,[64] but do not seem otherwise to have consciously promoted their links with an Anglo-Saxon past;[65] rather it seems to have been others concerned with Anglo-Saxon events and publications who wanted to benefit their enterprises by royal patronage who drew attention to the continuity of descent from Alfred 'her illustrious forefather' to Victoria.[66] Nevertheless by the end of the century a general consciousness of the supposed Anglo-Saxon origins of the English character which had made Britain so successful had been established and formed part of the backdrop to the millenary celebrations of Alfred's death.

The idea that Anglo-Saxon origins were an essential component of English identity was nurtured through a new emphasis on the Germanic roots of the Anglo-Saxons in which the belief that the English parliamentary system had its origins in an ancient Teutonic world, and the concept of the Norman Yoke, was married with a new scholarly understanding of Anglo-Saxon as a Germanic language.[67] Such ideas were promoted by Kemble in *The Saxons in England*, dedicated to Queen Victoria.[68] They were popularized by J. R. Green,[69] and, above all, by Edward Freeman.[70] Freeman's encomium on Alfred as 'the most perfect character in History', against whom other candidates for the position (St Louis of France, Washington, William the Silent, Charlemagne and Edward I) were all found wanting,[71] was frequently cited.[72] Admiration for all things Germanic, especially in Liberal circles, meant that the Anglo-Saxons received added lustre when German writers looked with envy at the security of the English constitution and monarchy with its Anglo-Saxon roots. Reinhold Pauli conceived his biography of the king in response to the disturbances of 1848 in

---

[63] S. Smiles, *The Image of Antiquity. Ancient Britain and the Romantic Imagination* (Yale, 1994), 26–45; M. Dietler, 'A tale of three sites: the monumentalization of Celtic oppida and the politics of collective memory and identity', *World Archaeology*, 30 (1998), 72–89.

[64] On the suggestion of their daughter Vicky after her marriage to the German Crown Prince: E. Darby and N. Smith, *The Cult of the Prince Consort* (1983), 7–15.

[65] *Remaking Queen Victoria*, eds M. Homans and A. Munich, Cambridge Studies in Nineteenth-Century Literature and Culture, 10 (1997).

[66] Dedication of Giles, *Jubilee Edition*; see also discussion of Kemble and Lord Wantage below.

[67] J. W. Burrow, *A Liberal Descent. Victorian Historians and the English Past* (1981); Simmons, *Reversing the Conquest*, 175–202.

[68] J. M. Kemble, *The Saxons in England* (2 vols, 1849).

[69] J. R. Green, *History of the English People* (4 vols, 1877–80); *idem*, *The Making of England* (1881).

[70] Freeman, *Norman Conquest*; Burrow, *Liberal Descent*, 155–28.

[71] Freeman, *Norman Conquest*, I, 51–5. A somewhat similar passage in which Alfred also emerged 'as the most perfect character in history' had appeared in *The Anglo-Saxon* 1, part 4 (1849), 5–6, and it is possible Freeman borrowed the idea from there.

[72] Bowker, *King Alfred Millenary*, *passim*.

order to demonstrate to fellow Germans the heritage to which they should be heir,[73] while Thomas Hughes felt Napoleon III might benefit from contemplation of Alfred's interpretation of the role of king.[74] Patriotic pride could, of course, shade into 'a racial Anglo-Saxonism', all the more distasteful today because we know where such ideas of racial superiority would lead in the twentieth century.[75] Such ideas were widespread in western Europe and America in the nineteenth century, and were believed to have been scientifically proven by the work of men like Darwin and Huxley.[76]

Alfred became one of the best-known Anglo-Saxons as he was almost the only one for whom a full-length biography could be written – as a surprisingly large number of authors demonstrated.[77] The man who had once been a mirror for princes became an exemplar for Victorian schoolchildren.[78] Popular medievalism, thanks to the work of Sir Walter Scott and subsequent historical novelists, made it easier for people to relate to the medieval past,[79] and the careful researches into artefacts and costume, which once again Scott had encouraged, enabled it to be more readily visualized.[80] The popularity of tableaux and pageants at the end of the nineteenth century provided opportunities for a new intimacy with the past.[81] However, in the process it was the similarities between the ninth and the nineteenth centuries, rather than the contrasts, which came to be emphasized. Sir Walter Besant, in a lecture in Winchester, found he had no difficulty in applying Tennyson's verses on Prince Albert in *Idylls of the King* to Alfred.[82] In addition to being the father of the constitution, navy and army, Alfred was found to have anticipated various nineteenth-century advances. The Rev. C. S. Taylor complained that Alfred was being turned 'into a kind of

---

[73] R. Pauli, *König Aelfred und seine Stelle in der Geschichte Englands* (Berlin, 1851); *R. Pauli, the Life of King Alfred*, ed. T. Wright (1852); B. Thorpe, *The Life of Alfred the Great Translated from the German* (1878).

[74] T. Hughes, *Alfred the Great* (1891), 1–14.

[75] R. Horsman, *Race and Manifest Destiny. The Origins of American Racial Anglo-Saxonism* (Cambridge, MA, 1981); for Freeman's racialist views see Simmons, *Reversing the Conquest*, 195–7.

[76] S. Anderson, *Race and Rapprochement. Anglo-Saxonism and Anglo-American Relations, 1895–1904* (East Brunswick, NJ, 1981), 27–40.

[77] A useful chronological bibliography is provided in D. Sturdy, *Alfred the Great* (1995), 259–62.

[78] See, for instance, Charles Dickens, *A Child's History of England* (1851–53).

[79] K. L. Morris, *The Image of the Middle Ages in Romantic and Victorian Literature* (1984); R. Chapman, *The Sense of the Past in Victorian Literature* (1986).

[80] Strong, *And When Did You Last See Your Father?*, 29–75, 114–18.

[81] R. Withington, *English Pageantry: An Historical Outline* (2 vols, Cambridge, MA, 1918–20); see also *Romsey Millenary Celebration 907–1907* (1907) and *Winchester National Pageant* (1908). For tableaux and the 1901 millenary, see Bowker, *Alfred Millenary*, 100–101 and plates. A list of Alfredian tableaux for performance in Hampshire schools was also produced: Hampshire Record Office W/C2/6/18g.

[82] 'Who reverenced his conscience as his king;/ whose glory was redressing human wrong'; W. Besant, *King Alfred the Great* (1898), 38; Bowker, *Alfred Millenary*, 8.

ninth-century incarnation of a combined School Board and County Council'.[83] Warwick Draper in his popular biography had indeed written that Alfred 'by his invention of the shires anticipated the principles of the County Council legislation of ten centuries later',[84] while Arthur Conan Doyle believed that Alfred 'was an educationalist on a scale to which we have hardly yet attained. His standard was that every boy and girl in the whole of the nation should be able to read and write'.[85] Thomas Hughes's chapter titles included 'The King's Board of Works' and 'The King's War Office and Admiralty', and he felt that spiritual decay and love of gain were similar problems in both Alfred's day and his, for 'when that state comes, men who love their country will welcome Danish invasions, civil wars, potato diseases, cotton famines, Fenian agitations, whatever calamity may be needed to awake the higher life again, and bid the nation arise and live'.[86] Hughes was a Christian Socialist, and although Alfred was most popular with Liberals and progressives, he could be made meaningful to everyone across the political spectrum from Chartists to Conservatives. Alfred had never quite thrown off the Anglo-Saxons' radical past,[87] and, although that aspect of his *post mortem* career was muted in the nineteenth century, he did surface in Chartist songs, and was cited in support of the campaign for an eight-hour working day which Asser's account of the way the king had divided his day was believed to support.[88] In another part of the political spectrum, Disraeli sought to turn the Conservative Party into the political force which would marry the two nations of Norman (aristocracy) and Saxon (the people) and be the true protector of all that was best of the medieval past.[89] Robert Loyd-Lindsay, Conservative MP for Berkshire and later Lord Wantage, was the perfect embodiment of the Young England movement: he established model villages for his tenants,[90] and extended his patronage to King Alfred by commissioning his statue from Count Gleichen (a relative of Prince Albert) and arranging for it to be unveiled by the Prince of Wales, to whom he had been an equerry (Fig. 40).[91] Loyd-Lindsay seems to have been one of many Victorians who felt a personal

---

[83] Cited in C. Plummer, *The Life and Times of Alfred the Great, being the Ford Lectures for 1901* (1902), 6.

[84] W. H. Draper, *Alfred the Great* (1901), 12.

[85] Bowker, *Alfred Millenary*, 21.

[86] Hughes, *Alfred the Great*, 130–31.

[87] Alfred had been cited by late eighteenth-century radicals such as Catherine Macaulay and Henry Yorke, and was called in to support American Independence: Hill, 'Norman Yoke', 94–109; B. Melman, 'Claiming the nation's past: the invention of an Anglo-Saxon tradition', *Journal of Contemporary History*, 26 (1991), 575–95.

[88] Asser, cc. 103–4; Hill, 'Norman Yoke', 109–22.

[89] B. Disraeli, *Sybil, or The Two Nations* (1845); Morris, *Image of the Middle Ages*, 103–31.

[90] Lord Wantage, 'A few theories carried into practice', *Economic Review*, January 1893, 23–37; M. Havinden, *Estate Villages: a Study of the Berkshire Villages of Ardington and Lockinge* (1966).

[91] *Illustrated London News* and *North Wilts Herald*, 21.7.1877; N. Hammond, *Rural Life in the Vale of the White Horse 1780–1914* (1974), 139–45.

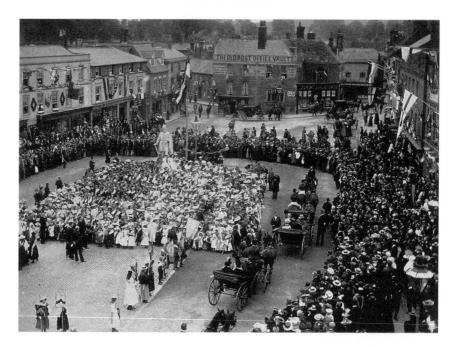

Fig. 40   The arrival of the Prince and Princess of Wales to unveil Count
Gleichen's statue of King Alfred in the Market Place, Wantage 1877
(photo: Vale & Downland Museum Trust)

identification with Alfred and the values for which he was believed to stand.
Like Alfred, Lindsay was a notable soldier who had been awarded the VC during
the Crimean War and became active in public life and charitable works, especially for the Red Cross, in spite of severe ill-health, another legacy of the war.[92]
Alfred's illnesses, which one recent historian has seen as an implausible element
of Asser's *Life*,[93] was one of the things which made him real to the Victorian
world, where many did have to live with constant ill-health.[94] To Thomas Hughes,
Alfred's experiences as a mature student could be an inspiration for others. In
his novel *The Scouring of the White Horse* (1892), a London clerk holidays in
White Horse country and, after visiting the sites associated with King Alfred and
meeting an antiquary who describes his life, is inspired to take evening classes
at a Working Men's College (where Hughes himself taught). Alfred's brand of

[92] Lady Wantage, *Lord Wantage, VC, KCB: A Memoir by his Wife* (1907); Vale and Downland
Museum and Visitor Centre, *Robert Loyd-Lindsay, Lord Wantage of Lockinge* (1994).

[93] Asser, cc. 25 and 91; Smyth, *Alfred*, 199–216.

[94] 'Endurance of severe pain ... calls for finer courage than the carnage of the battlefield'; S.
C. Budd, 'King Alfred and Winchester', *Church Bells and Illustrated Church News*, 20 September
1901.

practical piety, where he tried to let Christian morality infuse his working life, also appealed greatly to his Victorian audience, even if he could emerge as both 'a Broad-Churchman of agnostic proclivities',[95] 'a nineteenth-century radical with a touch of the Nonconformist conscience',[96] and the blessed Alfred for Anglo-Catholics.[97] There were calls for Alfred to be recognized as England's patron saint.[98] Of course, Alfred and the Anglo-Saxons were not to everybody's taste. Charles Kingsley felt that the Anglo-Saxons were effete and feminine and needed interbreeding with the truly masculine Vikings,[99] while Carlyle thought 'the gluttonous race of Jutes and Angles ... lumbering about in pot-bellied equanimity' had been in need of a good kicking from the Normans.[100] The chivalric Middle Ages and the Elizabethan Age were always to have a greater appeal when it came to romancing the past.[101]

By the end of the nineteenth century, Alfred could mean many different things to different people, but was valued by them all for apparently demonstrating that the principles or institutions with which they were concerned were deeply embedded in the English past and basic to the English character. Many of the varying strands came together at the millenary celebrations for the king's death in 1901, an event which has a number of possible interpretations depending upon the direction from which it is viewed.[102] The impetus for the celebration came from Frederic Harrison, Vice-president of the Royal Historical Society and a leading spokesman of the English Positivist movement.[103] The founder of Positivism, Auguste Comte, played a significant role in encouraging the nineteenth-century cult of the hero when he drew up his *Calendar of Great Men* to replace calendars of the saints following the French Revolution.[104] Alfred had a prominent role in the section on 'Feudal Civilization' and was regarded 'as the purest and greatest type of those who sought to defend and improve their

---

[95] Plummer, *Alfred the Great*, 6, commenting on Bishop Browne of Bristol, 'Alfred as religious man and an educationalist', in *Alfred the Great. Chapters on his Life and Times*, ed. A. Bowker (1899), 69–114.

[96] Plummer, *Alfred the Great*, 6, on D. MacFadyen, *Alfred the West Saxon King of the English* (1901).

[97] R. C. Jackson, *Alfred the Great of Blessed Memory* (1901).

[98] C. W. Stubbs, *King Alfred. Patron Saint of England* (1901); C. L. Engström, *The Millenary of Alfred the Great. Warrior and Saint, Scholar and King* (1901); and see Jackson, above, n. 97.

[99] Morris, *Image of the Middle Ages*, 82–6.

[100] T. Carlyle, *History of Frederick the Great* (1858–65), IV, 3; Burrow, *Liberal Descent*, 143, 252–4.

[101] M. Girouard, *The Return to Camelot. Chivalry and the English Gentleman* (1981); Chapman, *Sense of the Past*. 'Mrs Castle's Album' (Vale and Downland Museum 84.88.12) depicts Lord and Lady Wantage's Elizabethan Revels at Lockinge in 1885 in which Wayland the Smith appeared to conjure up the spirit of Alfred the Great.

[102] Compare E. Hammerton and D. Cannadine, 'Conflict and consensus on a ceremonial occasion. The Diamond Jubilee in Cambridge in 1897', *The Historical Journal*, 24 (1981), 111–46.

[103] M. S. Vogeler, *Frederic Harrison. The Vocations of a Positivist* (1984).

[104] Quinault, 'Cult of the centenary', 306–7.

people'.[105] Matters were very different from those in 1849, when Tupper had tried in vain to get establishment support for the millenary of Alfred's birth. From 1885 onwards there had been a spate of historical commemorations (Domesday Book 1886; The Armada 1888; Gibbon 1894; Cromwell 1899) in which Harrison was often involved alongside prominent members of the Liberal Party.[106] Lord Rosebery, who unveiled the Alfred statue in Winchester, had resigned as prime minister in 1895 after a row in the Commons over the statue of Cromwell he had commissioned for the Houses of Parliament from Hamo Thornycroft, the sculptor of the Winchester Alfred.[107] The Whig celebration of British Worthies, in which Alfred had his place, had never entirely disappeared.[108] In contrast, although there were some exceptions like Lord Wantage, the Conservatives tended to favour a generalized 'Merrie England' to concentration on specific events and individuals.[109] The 1901 millenary also needs to be viewed in the aftermath of the major celebrations surrounding Queen Victoria's Diamond Jubilee in 1897.[110] Sir Walter Besant, another who played a crucial role in getting the Alfred celebrations under way, spoke of how the Diamond Jubilee had brought home to him the necessity of teaching 'the people the meaning of what we saw set forth in that procession – the meaning of our Empire; not only what it is, but how it came – through whose creation, by whose foundation'.[111] The National Committee which was formed in 1898 declared in its prospectus that 1901 was to be 'a National Commemoration of the king to whom this Empire owes so much'. The Boer War provided added point to the commemoration and the opportunity for a display of jingoism in which contingents from all the armed forces participated, and medals were presented to men of the Imperial Yeomanry and the Hampshire Volunteers.[112] But the apparent show of consensus for Britain's imperial role during the millenary was not the whole story. The Boer War adversely affected the event, and it was acknowledged that it was a major reason why only about a quarter of the £35,000 the National Committee had hoped to achieve was raised, so that plans for a Museum of Early History had to be abandoned. There were more important calls on people's purses, but support for the war was far from uncomplicated, and some used the opportunity

---

105 F. Harrison, *The New Calendar of Great Men. Biographies of the 558 Worthies of All Ages and Nations in the Positivist Calendar of Auguste Comte* (1892), preface and 268–70.

106 Quinault, 'Cult of the centenary', 314–22.

107 E. Manning, *Marble and Bronze. The Art and Life of Hamo Thornycroft* (1982), 129 and 138. Thornycroft's statue of Gladstone in The Strand was another important Liberal commission. His wife Agatha was a Positivist and his daughters, including his biographer Elfrida, attended the progressive King Alfred's School in Hampstead.

108 See Harrison's use of the term 'Worthy' in his edition of Comte's calendar (n. 105).

109 Chapman, *Sense of the Past*, 33–58.

110 D. Judd, *Empire. The British Imperial Experience from 1765 to the Present* (1996), 130–53.

111 Bowker, *Alfred Millenary*, 8–9; Besant, *Alfred the Great*, 39.

112 Bowker, *Alfred Millenary*, 113.

of praising Alfred to criticize the conduct of the war. Charles Stubbs, dean of Ely, for instance, believed that Alfred was not only in advance of his own time in his conduct of war, but in advance of the present day, when war was not waged for defence of the country and according to Christian principles, but because of 'insolence of pride ... passion of vengeance ... lust of gold'.[113]

The Boer War also helps to explain the presence of so many American delegates at the Meeting of Learned Societies, whose representatives were otherwise drawn from the British empire. Jefferson had ensured that Alfred was one of the founding father's of American democracy, but the period 1895–1904 was a time in which the doctrine of Anglo-Saxonism was a dominant historical concept which actively influenced American political policies in favour of close ties with England, with which a significant subsection of the population could claim a common ethnic origin.[114] British political leaders, including Lord Rosebery, the most prominent of the Liberal Imperialists, were naturally keen to encourage the continuation of this entente in the context of the Boer War. The political background helps explain support at the highest level, both from British politicians and from the American ambassador, for celebrations in Winchester, and the presence of the academics whose studies actively demonstrated the common roots of American and British culture (see Figs 41 and 42).[115] American support was financially important for the millenary, as a significant portion of the £5000 needed to pay for the statue seems to have been raised there. There were also millenary celebrations in America in October, culminating in a millenary banquet at Delmonico's in New York.[116]

The millenary needs to be placed in its local as well as its national and international contexts. Among the most active members of the National Committee was its Secretary, Alfred Bowker, mayor of Winchester in 1897/8 (when he was twenty-seven) and in 1900/1. When the first suggestions had been made for the commemoration of Alfred, Bowker had moved decisively to secure the event for the city, and his drive and enthusiasm played a large part in ensuring it went ahead.[117] The corporation of Winchester was dominated by Liberals, and the growth of city and council government was actively supported by that party – Rosebery had been the first Chairman of London County Council, and Frederic

---

[113] Stubbs, *King Alfred. Patron*; the statements critical of the conduct of the war were omitted from Bowker's account of the sermon: *Alfred Millenary*, 33–7. Engström, *The Millenary of Alfred the Great* contrasted Alfred's successful prosecution of the war against the Vikings with the lack of success of the British army against the Boers (whom he thought shared many of the military characteristics of the Vikings).

[114] Anderson, *Race and Rapprochement, passim*; R. Fleming, 'Picturesque history and the medieval in nineteenth-century America', *The American Historical Review,* 100 (1995), 1061–94.

[115] Had he not died in July 1901 one of the key American Anglo-Saxonist historians, John Fiske, would have played a prominent role in the millenary celebrations: *The Letters of John Fiske*, ed. E. F. Fiske (New York, 1940), 688–90, 699–703.

[116] Bowker, *Alfred Millenary*, 154–65.

[117] Yorke, *Millenary Celebrations.*

Fig. 41   The academic delegates in the procession for the unveiling of the
Alfred statue in Winchester in 1901 (photo: Bowker, op. cit. in note 2,
between pp. 104–5)

Harrison, and a number of other promoters of the millenary, also served on the
LCC. Civic government was a democratic cause to which the traditional rhetoric
of the party, which included the Anglo-Saxons, could be adapted.[118] During his
first mayoralty Bowker had used the millenary of the death of Beornwulf, reeve
of Winchester, to celebrate one thousand years of civic government in Winchester with the issue of a commemorative medal.[119] The millenary of Alfred provided
further opportunities to strengthen the position of the mayor and corporation in
Winchester, a final domestication and recruitment to the bourgeoisie of the
once-radical Anglo-Saxons. As had often been the case, under the guise of
support for Alfred was a campaign for the greater good of the people. Bowker
raised local funds in order to acquire one of the sites in the city associated with
Alfred which could be preserved as an antiquity, but also used for public recreation. He at first hoped to buy the ruins of the medieval Wolvesey Palace, but this
was blocked by Conservative members of the House of Laymen. Instead, he
acquired the site of Hyde Abbey, including some adjacent land which today
contains the city's recreation centre.[120]

---

118 O. Anderson, 'The political uses of history in mid nineteenth-century England', *Past and
Present*, 36 (1967), 87–105.

119 L. Brown, *British Historical Medals 1837–1901* (1987), 459.

120 Yorke, *Millenary Celebrations*, 9.

Fig. 42   Crowds witness the unveiling of Hamo Thornycroft's statue of King
Alfred in the Broadway, Winchester 1901 (photo: Bowker, op. cit. in
note 2, between pp. 108–9)

That is not quite the end of Alfred's reinvention. The Anglo-Saxons and
Alfred remained popular until the First World War; the last of the English Alfred
statues was raised at Pewsey in 1913, where Alfred was 'once a chief landowner
in this vale' to commemorate the coronation of George V (1911) 'who grandly
follows in great King Alfred's footsteps'.[121] But any Germanic connections
became suspect after 1914, and subsequent Nazi misuse of the early medieval
past to support a Germanic racial identity discredited the type of racial Anglo-
Saxonism with which Alfred had sometimes been associated. When Alfred
University in New York erected a statue to King Alfred in 1990 the students saw
only a 'dead, white male' who could not adequately represent their multicultural
backgrounds.[122] Scholars of the Anglo-Saxons today pride themselves on being
removed from any political associations. Alfred's popular role has been reduced
to modest promotions in Winchester and Wessex, and the occasional punning
headlines in newspapers when a Saxon reference is needed. This may be to the
good, but as the saying goes, 'use it or lose it'. Recent debate over A-level
syllabuses in the UK has revealed that many see the Anglo-Saxons as irrelevant
to the present day and that the date of 1066 is no longer known to every

---

[121] Darke, *Monument Guide*, 90.

[122] K. F. Morrison, 'On the Statue', in *The Past and Future of Medieval Studies*, ed. J. van
Engen (Notre Dame, 1994), 273–99; Abels, *Alfred*, 6–7.

schoolchild; soon even jokes about burnt cakes may be greeted with in-comprehension. No one wants a return to the past distortions of Alfred to serve current preoccupations or to the racist associations of Anglo-Saxonism, but it is surely in the interests of all Anglo-Saxonists to recapture something of that shared identity in an Anglo-Saxon past that brought thousands on to the streets of Winchester to celebrate the millenary of Alfred's death just one hundred years ago.

Index